Priestess of Avalon
Priestess of the Goddess

A Renewed Spiritual Path for the 21st Century

A Journey of Transformation
within the Sacred Landscape of Glastonbury
and the Isle of Avalon

by

Kathy Jones

For Joyce
with blessings from Avalon
♡ Kathy Jones

Published by
ARIADNE PUBLICATIONS
61 Tor View Avenue,
Glastonbury, Somerset,
BA6 8AG, UK

Front Cover Painting of Priestess of Avalon: Foosiya Miller
Cover Design: Lloyd Drew

Typeset and designed by Kathy Jones
In Novarese Bk BT and Boulevard
Printed by CPI Bath

ISBN-13: 978-1-872983-28-8
ISBN-10: 1-872983-28-6

Dedication

To the Priestesses of Avalon
who once dwelt upon the Sacred Isle,
To all those who are today
called by the Lady of Avalon,
To reclaim the sacred tradition of
the Priestesshood of Avalon,
Hastening Her return to the world

The Paradise Isle

The Isle of Avalon sparkles in the morning sunlight. In the hollows still dark and damp with dew, ribbons of mist hang low, wreathing the ancient stones, curling around the sacred springs which flow unceasing from the Mother's *body. As the sun rises in the sky the mist too rises through the trees and up the slopes of the steep hill, pluming like flags in the pale blue sky. The early birds sing the promise of the day, foxes making their way home from the night pause to sniff the air and then hurry on, the small deer move into safety beneath the trees, the* Morgen *crows fly in, caw-cawing. Around the island, the* Lake *of* Mists *shrouds the* Summerland *in dense whiteness.* Blessed, *we are in a world apart.*

Through the mist a bell rings, calling Her *priestesses to* Her Temple *of* Avalon. *From the small dwellings nestled amongst the trees figures appear in ones and twos, threading their way along tended paths towards the* Holy Place. *Their soft woollen robes of violet and blue blend in and out of the mists, emerging, merging.*

In the quiet of the sacred hall before the central image of Nolava, Our Lady *of* Avalon, *the perpetual flame burns, now still, now flickering, moved by an invisible breath. On the altars around the edge of the circle the incense smoulders, the sacred spring waters are poured into the chalice, the bells ring out, a new day is dawning in* Paradise. *The chant begins, voices singing in praise to the* Goddess, *a beautiful sound centred in the heart, rising and falling with the breath.*

The priestesses generate Her *sacred space, filling* Her Temple *with the stillness which opens and expands the heart. The* Invocation *of the* Lady *into* Her Temple *begins.* Voices *rise, calling* Her *from the nine directions on the* Sacred Wheel *to come and be present on this new morning.* Arms *extended, fingers weaving patterns in the air, bodies moving, turning, opening the* Wheel *with the breath. The* Sacred Words *are sounded,* Her *energy is invoked into* Her *temple.*

Soft at first and subtle, rainbow light flickers around the walls of the Temple, hanging momentarily in the air and then coalescing into dancing sprite-like forms. From the central altar Her violet light begins to glow, filling the space with Her radiance. Growing brighter with every moment as the sound swells to its fullness She emanates throughout Her Temple, a radiance that thickens the air with violet rays. Overflowing She radiates out across the sacred land of Avalon in every direction, expanding pulses of violet light moving out in waves across the Lake of Mists to the mainland. Here, Her divine energy connects with and sparks the etheric threads that underlie all created forms, renewing the web of wonder and enchantment that weaves its way across the land.

All is well. Another day has dawned in Paradise.

Three Spirals

This book describes a journey to become a modern day Priestess of Avalon, a Priestess of the Goddess. It is part autobiography, the story of my own path of transformation, and part instruction for those women and men on the path to Her priest/esshood. The book is composed of an Exordium and Three Spirals, which encompass many aspects of Goddess and women's spirituality and creativity, which have emerged through direct communion with the Lady of Avalon and Her landscape over the last 30 years. It is an unfolding and continuing journey, made with other inspired women and men, who also long to see the Goddess reclaimed and returned to Her rightful place in the world.

The Exordium is the Warp of Her Web, an introduction to the qualities and nature of the Lady of Avalon and the Nine Morgens, who dwell upon the Isle of Avalon, and their relationship to the sacred landscape of the small country town of Glastonbury in southwest England. The First Spiral contains a detailed exposition of the ceremonial cycle of Britannia's Sacred Wheel of the Year, in which we learn of the many faces of the ancient and yet ever new Goddess within Brigit's Isles, of Her landscapes, seasons and nature. This section forms the foundation for the First Spiral, or first year of the three year Priestess of Avalon training, which is currently taught in Glastonbury by the author, and Priest/ess teachers Ren Chapman and Brian Charles. This training is open to women and men who love the Goddess. On completion of the First Spiral students dedicate their lives to the Goddess and Self-initiate as Sisters and Brothers of Avalon.

The Second Spiral builds on the experiences of the First, encompassing what it really means to become a Priestess of the Goddess and of Avalon, and studying the skills and practices of a priestess. It includes learning how to create and perform Goddess Ceremonies for all occasions, Journeying between the Worlds, Scrying for a Vision, Oracling, Embodying the Goddess and offering Her blessings, and Leading the Way through Her Labrynth. At the end of the

Second Spiral successful students Self-initiate as Priestesses or Priests of the Goddess.

The Third Spiral comprises a nine month daily spiritual Practice of the Presence of the Lady of Avalon which intensifies through time. Successful completion of the Practice and of all Three Spirals leads to Self-initiation as a Priestess or Priest of Avalon.

This material provides a foundation for the Priestess of Avalon Trainings in Glastonbury. It is designed to help aspiring Priest/esses of the Goddess and of Avalon to fully understand and realise the nature of the commitments s/he might be planning to make. It also makes some of these mysteries available to those people who feel a deep connection to Avalon, but who may be unable to travel here to take part in the formal training, for a variety of reasons, including distance, cost and health. It is for those who wish to study, remember and remake their own priestess commitment to the Goddess, and to the Lady of Avalon. This teaching is offered to both individuals and groups of students who wish to train themselves to become priestesses, travelling to Avalon several times over three years to walk the sacred land and take part in ceremonies in the Goddess Temple and at the Goddess Conference. The opportunity is here to be supported by those who have already Self-initiated as Priestesses of Avalon. See contact details at the end of the book if you are interested in pursuing your own training with our help using these teachings.

Contents

Acknowledgements

This book is a culmination of many years experience of walking with the Lady in the sacred land of Avalon and learning of the Mystery of Her ways. There are many people who have helped me on my journey with their support and encouragement and I thank you all. First among these is my life partner Mike Jones, who has always completely supported my love of the Goddess with his own. Thank you, sweetheart.

I am particularly grateful to all the people who have taken part in the *In the Heart of the Goddess* Priestess of Avalon trainings at the Isle of Avalon Foundation in Glastonbury. These include the brave souls who took the first year of training in 1998 to become Millennial Priestesses of Avalon, and all the years up to the current group of students now in training. I have learned so much from you all both as a teacher and also as a student myself of the ways of the Goddess. There have been more than one hundred students and I cannot name you all, but I would like to thank some people individually.

I thank all the priestesses who have contributed to the final chapter telling what it has meant to them to become Priestesses of Avalon. Priestesses are very individual people and each one has an amazing story to tell. I thank Rose Flint, a wonderful poet, who was here in the first year of the priestess training and has been a friend on the path to the Goddess ever since. I am grateful to Geraldine Charles, who over the years has created beautiful websites for myself, for the Glastonbury Goddess Conference and for the Goddess Temple. I am also grateful to Geraldine for proofreading an earlier version of this manuscript. I thank Ren Chapman, another early priestess, for her dedication and enthusiasm over the years. Ren now teaches the First Spiral with Brian Charles, who has been a steadfast Priest of Avalon, who I also thank. I thank Sally Pullinger another long term Glastonbury resident for her support and love on our Goddess journey.

I thank Koko Newport for her friendship and inspirational dress sense. I thank the beautiful Katinka Soetens for her enthusiasm and friendship, and

I thank Jacqui Woodward Smith, who now facilitates the Tribe of Avalon in London, for her lovely poems and creating the Flame of Avalon circle.

I thank the hundreds of people who have contributed to the success of the Glastonbury Goddess Conference, especially Tyna Redpath, who was co-organiser with me for ten years, encouraging me to be bold in expressing Goddess spirituality. I thank all the Conference Ceremony Circles who have journeyed into the magic of the Goddess, including Aine Carey, Charis Cave, Cheryl Straffon, Leona Graham, Sandra Brant and Sophie Pullinger, as well as priestesses Annabel Allen, Carol Morgan, Elin Hejll-Guest, Hana Evans, Hazel Loveridge, Pamela Gaunt, Rosamund Vining, Rosie Elflain, Ruth Morgan, Sarah Potter, Sharlea Johnson, Steve Wilkes, Tammy Furey and Tegwyn Hyndman. I thank the Glastonbury musicians who sing and play for the Goddess, including Oshia Drury, Lydia Lite, Jana Runnalls, Kat Brown and the Vocalana choir.

I thank all the people who have contributed to the growth and development of the Glastonbury Goddess Temple, the first formally recognised indigenous Goddess Temple in Europe for a thousand years and more. In particular I thank Morgana West and Pammy Dini for their dedication and organisational skills, as well as Bridge Williams, Emma Knight, Georgina Sirett-Hardie, JP Evans, Michelle Scott McCauley, Rachael Clyne and all the many priestesses and Melissas who freely contribute their time and energy to bringing the Goddess back into Glastonbury and into the world.

I thank the priestesses who have trained with me, who have now taken that knowledge out into their own landscapes and cultures. They are developing their own Goddess groups, priestess trainings, Conferences and Festivals, which are related to the Goddesses of their own landscapes. These include Camilla Emmet, Carolyn Brown, Diane Summer, Jane Redhawk and Tiziana Stupia in Britain, Sandra Roman in Argentina, Suthisa Hein and Sandra Warmerdam in the Netherlands, Kriszta Veres in Hungary, and Heather Adams and Samantha Linasche in the USA.

As you would expect in a patriarchal world there have also been many people who have been resistant and directly hostile to the idea of Goddess, the divine in feminine form, and to me personally in my work. Without you I would not have become so strong in my love for the Lady. You have helped me to deepen my personal experience of Her and to become clearer about my beliefs. I thank you all.

In the creation of this book I thank Foosiya (Freddie) Miller for her wonderful cover painting and other illustrations, and Lloyd Drew for the cover design and invaluable assistance with my computer. You have helped make this book beautiful.

Introduction

Our love for the Lady often begins when we first hear Her name - Lady of Avalon, Lady of the Holy Isle of Avalon, Lady of the Lake and Lady of the Lake of Mysts. These Goddess titles echo like a distant trumpet blowing through our lives, awakening us to long-forgotten memories. Her name strikes a chord within our souls that resounds in every part of our being. Deep inside we already know Her.

In our hearts we feel connected to the Lady of Avalon by a thread, which may be tenuous and gossamer thin, but it is alive and vibrating. We want to strengthen that thread and follow it. We want to devote ourselves to the Lady as we believe the ancient priestesses of this land once did. Some remember being those priestesses in previous lives. In imagination and visions we see robed womanly figures walking the sacred landscape, climbing the slopes of a steep hill in ceremony, worshipping the Goddess beside the holy wells. We see them serving Her people as ceremonialists, healers, poets and scryers, as midwives of birth, life and death, living a life of praise and dedication to Her. We wish to live such a life now, although we have little idea of what this might mean.

We long to become present day Priestesses and Priests of Avalon, dedicated to the Goddess. We hear Her voice calling to us and we respond,

"Yes, Lady, I am yours! May I be your priestess?"

without truly knowing anything about Her or the transforming nature of Her service.

Who is this Lady of Avalon, Her name redolent with meaning and mystery, the Lady we know and love instinctively? There are no facts to be found about Her, no history, no certainty, only a paragraph or two of dubious legend and a priestess title in a modern day novel. Yet we find we have such a longing in the heart to know who She is as Goddess, in all Her majesty and glory.

Returning out of the mists of our forgetting the Lady of Avalon is the One Goddess who rules the magical Isle of Avalon. Her name has emerged in the great mirror of Avalon as N*olava*, the Goddess who reflects to us all that is. Her body contours form the Sacred Land and Her loving energies radiate outwards from Avalon through all the worlds. She is an awesome Goddess of love, beauty, compassion and wisdom, a Queen of Light and of Darkness, who reigns in the Space between the worlds. She is the One Goddess who expresses Herself through the seasons of Her nature as Maiden, Lover, Mother and Crone, as Lady of Earth, Water, Fire, Air and Space. She is the Spiral Goddess of Birth, Healing, Death and Rebirth. She is Mother of Transformation.

To become Her priestess is to love, honour and serve the Lady of Avalon with one's whole heart, mind, emotions, body and spirit. It is to serve Her people, Her nature and Her earth to the best of one's abilities and energy. To become Her priestess is to take a public role in Her name, to stand up and be counted as Her ceremonialist, healer, visionary, communicator, practitioner and embodiment of Her, as required by Her. It is not an easy path to take. It is not the path for everyone.

The journey to Her priestesshood is one of continual surrender to Her, letting go of our desire to be in control, to always know what is happening, giving way to the Lady's wisdom for us. We learn to give sovereignty to Her voice which we hear within, which bids us always to be more loving, generous, creative and kind than we are. It is a journey of constant challenge to our Shadow selves, those parts that do not serve us or Her, and which continually betray our Soul's true purpose. She calls to us to heal the wounds of our conditioning and karma, to become bigger than we have been, to expand our consciousness to its true capacities. She asks us to follow our destiny and become Her priestesses and priests once again. But be aware that Her path is one of love, of challenge and change.

Avalon means the *place of apples* and the Isle of Avalon is the mythic Paradise Isle that lies beyond the western shore, where the Goddess's golden apples of immortality are to be found. Avalon is ruled by the Lady of Avalon, who is also Avallonia, Lady of Apples, the fruit of transformation. In legend Avalon has always been a place of women, where women's values, beliefs and experience are honoured and shared. It is the place where the Nine Morgens dwell, the Nine Sisters who are the essence of the feminine in nature, in womankind and in the weather. Today Avalon is open to women and men to journey here to experience these deeply feminine energies. The Isle of Avalon is also known as the Western Isle of the Dead, to which souls are transported both in and out of incarnation for the healing of their disease, to experience many deaths - mental, emotional and sometimes physical - and to await and later experience rebirth.

For many hundreds of years the small country town of Glastonbury in Somerset, England has been recognised as a physical location for the mysterious Isle of Avalon. Once surrounded by water, the landscape of Glastonbury is an Outerworld counterpart to the Innerworld of Avalon. Walking in the lanes and fields, on the hillsides that make up Glastonbury's sacred landscape, Avalon is always just a breath away, a shift in consciousness, an opening glimpsed through a Veil into another dimension of reality. The beings who inhabit Avalon are revealed in the movements caught in the corner of one's eye or seen dimly through the mist that can shroud the sacred land. Glastonbury Avalon is that unique combination of the underlying physical and energetic landscape of Glastonbury, which is intimately connected to the Otherworld of Avalon, so that they cannot be separated. While Glastonbury provides one of the most accessible gateways into Avalon, where its secrets are held in the land itself, Avalon can also be found anywhere in Brigit's Isles and beyond, where our hearts open to Her.

For many the words *priestess* and *Avalon* are charged with meaning. They speak of ancient forgotten virtues, of the powers of women and the celebration of our mysteries, of hidden secret knowledge, of sacred landscape, of faeries, of holiness, inspiration, magic, enchantment and revelation. They speak to a part of ourselves as women and as men that longs to bring meaning back into mundane life, that thirsts for a true spirituality which is directly connected to the land on which we live, or have lived in the past in other lives, when we naturally loved the Goddess as the Source of all that is.

For many people the titles *Lady of Avalon* and *Priestess of Avalon* were first brought to attention by Marion Zimmer Bradley in her novel *The Mists of Avalon*. This inspired book retells the Arthurian legends from the point of the view of the women involved, including Morgen la Fey or Morgaine, and Queen Guinevere. In traditional patriarchal legends Morgen la Fey is often portrayed as a *bad* woman who conspires to bring down her half-brother King Arthur. All the faults in the land are laid at her door, and that of Queen Guinevere, another *bad* woman, who is said to have betrayed Arthur by sleeping with his best friend. We know, however, from researching patriarchal legends that wherever powerful women are depicted as bad, behind them a demonised good woman can usually be found, one who carries an archetypal stream of energy flowing directly from the ancient beneficent Goddess Herself. Both Morgen the Faery and Guinevere who is the Welsh triple Goddess Gwenhwyfar (White Spirit or Phantom), are originally powerful ancient British Goddesses.

In the story of *The Mists of Avalon* Morgaine is somewhat redeemed as a woman gifted from birth with the true sight, the ability to see through the Veil of Mystery into the future and the past. Trained from girlhood on the magical Isle of Avalon she becomes a priestess and struggles to truly listen to and serve the High Priestess, who is named as Lady of Avalon and Lady of the Lake. Sometimes Morgaine succeeds, sometimes she fails, and in her turn she takes on these priestess roles and titles. All her life she tries to respond in truth to the Great Goddess she honours and the story of her struggles to serve the Lady in life and love is a familiar one to many modern day women.

In her novel Marion Bradley, writing as Morgaine in fifth century Avalon, claims the powerful titles *Priestess of Avalon*, *Lady of the Lake* and *Lady of Avalon* as priestess roles, in service to the Great Goddess. In turn I suggest that Lady of Avalon, Lady of the Lake and Morgen la Fey, together with Her eight sister Morgens, are also Goddess names, woven from the past through time and given meaning in the present. In many cultures women who once lived lives on earth are later recognised as Goddesses, or as incarnations or emanations of preexisting Goddesses. They include the Chinese princess Kong-j'o, who lived in seventh century Tibet and was recognised as an emanation of Goddess Tara, and the young princess Kia Wahine on Maui, Hawaii, who in the 17th century CE, became the Lizard Goddess of Spring Waters, Conception and Genealogy.

So too I believe that the Lady of Avalon and the Nine Morgens are preexisting Goddesses of the sacred land and nature, who may also have incarnated in womanly forms at different times in herstory. The Nine Morgens are remembered in particular as a circle of nine priestesses, who once served the Goddess in Avalon, with Morgen la Fey being the most well-known. In the present we honour them as forms of the Goddess whom we can serve as priestesses.

The name *Avallonia* was mentioned in the classic 1970s cult movie *The Wicker Man*, as being the name of the Goddess of the remote Scottish Island on which the story takes place, to whom the sacrifice of the Wicker Man and its animal and human contents is made. The movie itself was a scary fiction and it is important to know that the Lady of Avalon *never* requires human or animal sacrifice, either actual or symbolic. However I did hear Avallonia as another name for the Lady of Avalon and I reclaim Her as such. She is Avallonia, Lady of Apples.

The ancestral threads that connect us to the ancient Goddess-loving priestesshood in this land were broken many moons ago, when patriarchal forces first began to claim Brigit's Isles from our Goddess-loving neolithic forebears. Being an island race living on the western edges of Europa's great continent we were one of the last indigenous European societies to lose our connection to the Goddess and to our spiritual Ancestors. For thousands of years in these islands our communities celebrated the seasonal cycles of the Goddess, the movements of the earth, moon and sun, of the stars in the heavens. We acknowledged the Goddess as earth, water, fire, wind and the space between, as Giver of Birth, Life and Death. We showed our love and respect for Her by creating small and large ritual sites dedicated to Her and to the Ancestors who were born from Her body. We built up great mounds of earth and stone shaped like Her body, we erected individual stones and large and small circles of wood and stone, where we honoured Her and the Ancestors who had lived before us.

Over the last five thousand years different patriarchal cultures have entered Brigit's Isles, coming in peaceful waves of change or through raiding and invasion, bringing war and destruction. They transformed over time what is believed to have been on the whole a peaceful, pagan, Goddess-loving society into today's crumbling bastion of Christian religious belief, which is based not in this green and pleasant land and its indigenous spirituality, but in a hot dry desert land which lies thousands of miles to the southeast.

The threads of Her memory are cut. The tradition is gone. We cannot know as fact, as received wisdom from our elders, as traditional knowledge handed down to us through the ages, how to be a Priestess of the Goddess and of Avalon in this land. There is no-one to tell us. There are claimed lineages of hereditary witches, but as far as I know there are no hereditary priestesses, no-one yet claiming genetic lineage. The majority of women's spiritual communities, called nunneries in the recognised religions in this land, are all dedicated to male gods and to celibacy, none to the Goddess and Her miraculous fecundity.

And yet today, at the beginning of the third millennium, a remarkable change is occurring within human spirituality, which is almost unnoticed in mainstream culture. Tens of thousands of women and some men, are journeying across the world, visiting the ruins of ancient Goddess sites, travelling to new Goddess Temples, seeking Her here and there, wanting to connect with other Goddess-loving people. Among these numbers are a multitude of women and again some men, who travel to Glastonbury looking for the Lady of Avalon, Her priestesses and Her Temple. Following Her Call they journey hundreds and thousands of miles across land and ocean to the physical location of ancient Avalon that is Glastonbury, as if returning to a Place of Origin, a place called home, where the Goddess lives and is honoured today.

Ancient Priestesses of Avalon are reincarnating, with memories clouded by patriarchal conditioning, waiting to remember our destinies. Some incarnate especially for this experience of bringing the Goddess alive once again at the beginning of the 21st century. We are developing character and creativity, helping to generate the Great Awakening as we call the Presence of the Lady into our daily lives. The Veil of Avalon is becoming more and more transparent until the time comes when Her Paradise Isle of peace and love will emerge from the mists once again.

When the threads of memory are cut much that is good is lost. But there are also benefits. Old habits, outmoded ways of thinking and being, received rather than experienced knowledge, rigidities, corruptions, personal and collective resistances which cling to outworn ways of doing things, all are also lost in the tides of forgetting. When all that remains of the physical past is bones and stones, we begin once again to listen to the Goddess as She speaks directly to us in the whispering wind, in the crackling fire, in the crashing ocean waves, in the tinkling brooks, in the rocks of Her body, in the songs of the birds and calls of the animals, in the voice of our intuition, our inner teacher and direct connection to Goddess. We begin to hear Her speak to us. With no human mediator between ourselves and Her, no priest standing between us and the divine, no book that tells us what to believe, who we are and how to be, then we must each become truly creative from our souls, in the present. We must call all our Goddess-given resources to the task of bringing our innate divinity into life on this Her beautiful planet Earth. We must truly incarnate at last.

On this journey of remembering Her and Her priestesshood, we begin by returning to the basics of life on this planet, questioning all that we know and all we hold dear, to see if it still shines true in the Darkness of unknowing, in the Brightness of Her Light.

Who is this Goddess that we love instinctively? How can we honour and worship Her in today's world? How do we create ceremonies that allow us to experience Her love and wisdom? How do we create new forms of spirituality rather than repeating old hierarchical forms merely because they are familiar and we don't know how else to do things? Most of us in the first world have been raised within patriarchal cultures - we are our fathers' daughters and sons, and our aspirations are embedded in masculine ideals and values. How do we become daughters and sons of the Mother once again? How do we create a new world of equality between women and men within Her dynamic loving Matrix?

Essentially we have to root out everything that does not support life and love and there are many hidden snags, many pitfalls on the journey. In the First Spiral I shall address some of these themes, exploring what it is to become first of all a Sister or Brother of Avalon who dedicates her/is life to the Goddess. We will look at the personal spiritual journey of the would-be priestess and priest as well as the ways in which we can care for each other as souls and human beings on the shared journey of life. Obviously I do not have all the answers. I am feeling my way as best I can. I am just like you, a woman or a man who loves the Goddess, remaking Her way in the world.

One of my aims is to bring feminist ideas and thinking into Goddess spirituality, beginning by reclaiming language from the thrall of patriarchy. I do not equate white, right, might, high, higher, upper chakras, etc., with the good; or black, dark, deep, low, lower, lower chakras, etc., with the bad. Goddess encompasses the polarities, She is the creator and She is the destroyer. She is the darkness and the light. She is the high and the low. In Her world all is energy manifesting in different forms and it is our human motivation and intentions that create the good or the bad, rather than the colours of our skins, our social class, our wealth or poverty, or our positions on imaginary ladders of progress. She is love, generosity, truth and beauty in many forms, and She has no truck with the evil generated within patriarchal societies.

I believe that we are all equal before the Goddess as human beings and as Her priestesses and priests. As part of our spiritual and cultural experience we are learning to work in circles and in community in new and exciting ways. We are not all equal in our experience, and our differences and talents also need to be recognised as having a place within a true anarchy, where we each take responsibility for our behaviour and ethics. There is a place for leadership and expertise, as well as there being equal opportunities for participation and contributions from everyone.

Because I am one of the first in the present time to reclaim the title

Priestess of Avalon, some would call me high priestess. I do not take this title or believe in it. I do not believe that I am higher than anyone. Personally I am more of a deep priestess, by rite of the difficult underworld journeys I have undertaken in my life. I am concerned with creating the world anew, *not* with replacing God and an oppressive patriarchy with Goddess and a new woman-led, power-over matriarchy. I want to help create a renewed world with Goddess in the centre, God by Her side and a world of equal opportunities, spiritual and cultural, for both women and men, held within Her Matrix. My commitment is to bring Goddess into conscious awareness and recognition of Her back into the world, if possible without creating new dogmas or fixed belief systems. It is for others to reclaim God in His many forms from the control of patriarchy.

As I understand it, women's spiritual practices are basically different to men's, not better, not less than, just different, and this difference is completely unrecognised within the dominator patriarchal religions. As women our spiritual wisdom is based within our female bodies, in the mysteries of our nature, in our innate ability to conceive, bear, give birth to and nurture life. It is founded in Her nature, in the spiralling cycles of life on the planet we live on, of the sun who gives us light and life, of the moon who reflects our inner cycles, and of the stars, which mirror our karma and reflect our futures. Our spiritual practices follow from this wisdom.

It has been assumed over long ages that women are the same as men in our spiritual experience, because we share the same soul energies. I do not believe this to be true. Our souls may be one but they are definitely housed in different bodies and have very different experiences of everyday life, of spirit, of Goddess and God, exactly because we are incarnate beings. We are not discarnate souls. We are functioning within our bodies and our bodies are different.

In many areas of life women's and men's experience is not the same and these differences need to be celebrated, rather than always subsuming the feminine to masculine ways of being and doing. For too long we women have taken the lead from patriarchal belief systems, which reinforce hierarchical, power-over, religious and political structures which have nothing whatsoever to do with women's innate Goddess-given wisdom. Virtually all the spiritual tracts ever written by men or women, have been written from a male perspective. Goddess and women's spirituality is an unwritten book, which women, myself included, are attempting to redress in these times. Thankfully in the modern western world we now have much greater freedom to explore our spirituality, freed from dogma, to find new ways in which we can experience Her.

When I first began my conscious journey with the Goddess thirty years ago my information about Her came from the very few Goddess books then available, from ancient legends and from the revelatory experiences I had in performing ceremony and in creating sacred dramas about Her. At that time in Britain there were no women spiritual teachers who loved the Goddess out there that I knew. There were academics who studied Goddess history and were reclaiming herstory, such as the late Asphodel Long of the Matriarchy Study Group. There were Goddess artists, such as the late Monica Sjoo, Phillipa Bowers, Jill Smith and Chesca Potter, who were painting new images of Her. There were few who had taken the priestess path before us. We were on a journey together with the Goddess as our teacher. At the time I wondered and still do now, why it was that nearly all the great recognised spiritual teachers in the world were men. Women are no less spiritual than men, or less developed or capable, so where were they?

In all areas of society where patriarchal systems and values rule, women are mostly absent from positions of power. This is because with some exceptions, women are unable to sustain interest for any length of time in power-over politics, war or business, which involves dominating other people's lives. We have spent too long as the weaker sex in male-dominated societies to want anything less than the liberation and empowerment of all. On the whole we simply do not value the ideals and aspirations of patriarchy. No matter how hard we try to become a part of the system, to rise within it to the glass ceilings, we are always wonderfully undermined by our bodies, by our natural longings for love with true partners, by our children, by our innate femaleness, which knows absolutely that patriarchal values and ideals are unreal and do not work for us. They do not serve us, our families or the planet we live on.

Women are and always have been spiritually powerful and our spiritual nature is very much an in-the-body experience. We are directly connected to the divine through our menstrual cycles and our karuna-sharing sexuality. Karuna is the Goddess's loving kindness that we experience first as mother love in childhood, which expands in adulthood to embrace all forms of love including touch, tenderness, compassion, sensuality and sexuality. We are directly connected to the Goddess through our innate ability to carry and give birth to new life from within our own bodies. We are connected to Her as we feed our children from our milk-filled breasts, as we heal and care for others, as we midwife death, as we create and express ourselves through beauty, art and music, as we live our daily lives, cooking, cleaning, caring for our families, researching, writing, painting, performing. This deep in-the-body spiritual connection which all women have, is ignored or dismissed as unimportant in nearly all societies.

Take for example, the taboos against menstruating and birthing women. We are excluded when we bleed or have given birth, from churches, synagogues and sweat lodges as being unclean and dirty. We are accused of bringing malign influences to bear on men and other women. Our presence is said to curdle milk, kill cattle, disrupt ceremony, invite evil. However as any good Goddess woman knows, the times of menstruation or of birth-giving are actually times when we are most directly connected to the Goddess as Mother of Life and Death, and to our deeper feminine powers. We are threatening not because we are unclean, but precisely the opposite, because at these times Her power is naturally within our bodies and She can be felt by others. Her presence can make those who do not know how to have this in-the-body, divine experience, feel small and powerless.

Many male spiritual practices are based on denying the natural urges of the human body and being, through celibacy, asceticism, control of movement and breath, through enforced separation from women, suppression of emotion, inhibition and punishment of a weak lower nature, that must be sublimated to the so-called higher power of the mind. The aim is for consciousness to rise out of the body and thus a person may achieve spiritual enlightenment. This is a fundamentally different approach to women's innate in-the-body spirituality, despite the fact that we agree that we are in essence formless energy beings, whose purpose is to fully incarnate into material reality for one life span or many.

For most women patriarchal religions have provided the only recognised methods for spiritual development and many women have attempted to adopt a male approach, which is at odds with our own nature. I believe the time is ripe for our innate spiritual experience as women to be recognised as valid in its own right, equal to the male approach, and applicable in certain terms to men's spiritual development too. However as we value our spiritual experience as women, the edifices and control systems of patriarchy are directly threatened and begin to tumble down. *It does mean changing everything.*

Women have not risen to become visible as spiritual teachers because to acknowledge us as such would mean recognising that we have something important and unique to teach, which is very different and undermining of the received wisdom of male religions. As we move into a world of equality, for there is no other way for our world to go, the truth of women's very different spirituality is being recognised. We will not be able to see the forms and contours of this new and equal way of living and being until women move into power in every sphere, from the home to the workplace to government to religion, from the personal to the spiritual.

I call to my sisters to arise in our power, to reclaim our bodies as true Temples of the Goddess, to bleed in the sacred places, in the sweat lodges, on the earth; to be honoured as girls, sisters, daughters, lovers, women, mothers, queens, grandmothers and crones; to reclaim the mystery of our sexuality and ability to bear life; to breast-feed our children in public; to walk in safety on every street; to be free from the fear of rape and physical violence; to express our feminine selves in joy; to become Her priestesses once again; to be seen for who we are; to teach our wisdom, our deep feminine knowing of the cycles of life in our bodies and in the earth Herself; to become the new spiritual teachers of the world.

This book is based on my own experience of becoming a Priestess of Avalon, Priestess of the Goddess, of the journey that led me to the point where I dared to make that claim for myself and then began to teach others how they might do so too. It includes my experiences within the *In the Heart of the Goddess* series of Priestess trainings for the Isle of Avalon Foundation, an esoteric teaching centre in Glastonbury. It includes my daily experience of living in Glastonbury, in communion with Nolava and Her sacred landscape, and with the Nine Morgens. Only yesterday when I thought this book was nearly complete, I saw Her shimmering form reflected in the floodwaters surrounding the island. As I marvelled at the beauty of Her image in the waters, She transmitted new ideas that resulted in a restructuring of the First Spiral. Her inspiration is continuous. This is a journey of discovery open to everyone. Everything written here is in process of unfoldment. Nothing is written in stone.

Within the following chapters I make certain basic assumptions. For me the world of Avalon is dedicated to the Goddess and is a place of women and feminine mysteries. Within those parameters as a place of service to the Goddess, I believe that today Avalon is open to both women and men to become Her Priestesses and Priests of Avalon, of the Goddess. In contradiction to thoughtforms which encourage us to believe the Emperor is wearing clothes when he isn't, and looking directly at the way words are written, I take *priestess* to be a compound noun that includes *priest*, I read *woman* as a word which includes *man*, *female* as including male, *she* includes *he*, and *goddess* as a divinity that includes *god*, rather than the other way round.

I use certain words in particular ways: remember as meaning to re-member, to put the members or pieces back together again; research as meaning re-search, to look again; tri-via or trivia, to mean the threefold crossway between the upper, middle and lower worlds; disease as meaning dis-ease or lack of ease; and healing, meaning to make whole. I like to capitalise names of the Goddess to honour Her.

This book centres on the journey to become a Priestess of Avalon, but much of what is said here can be applied to other priestess trainings dedicated to other Goddesses, as all pathways to the Goddess are one. If the path to Avalon is not yours, I hope you will find wisdom for your own journey in these pages. Although much of this book is primarily addressed to women's mysteries and experiences it will also speak to the many men who truly love Her. I hope you enjoy it.

Exordium

The Warp of Her Web

(A beginning, from the Latin)

The Lady of Avalon

I am Nolava, Lady of Avalon, Goddess of the Sacred Land,
Of the Paradise Isle that lies beyond the Western shores.
I am Avallonia, Lady of Apples
Lady of Love, Transformation and Compassion,
Queen of Light and of the Darkness.
I am the Innocence of the Maiden Grael,
I am the Lusciousness of the Lover's Cup,
I am the Karuna in the Mother's Chalice,
I am the Ikor in the Cauldron of the Crone.

I show you Truth, I teach Discrimination
Mine are the Secrets of Earthly Incarnation.
I reveal the pain of ancient days,
Unveiling karma, I am your Healer.
Initiatrix, I lead you through life's Labrynth,
Shining before you in the night and the day.
I am Midwife of Souls, Birth-Giver,
Keeper of the Mysteries of Life, Relationship and Death
I await you in the Great Beyond.

My voice is heard in the whispering wind, in the spring waters,
In the mists that rise from the Summerland,
In the stillness of the heart, in the Silence.
I express myself in the bounteousness of my Nature.
Invisible, I am seen by those who seek me beyond the Veil to Avalon.
Hidden in the Orchards by the branches of apple trees,
I lie in meadows sweet-filled with fragrance.
I dance in the wind and the rain, within the flickering flames,
My passage is marked by synchronicity and meaning.

Exordium

I am beyond all knowing yet I dwell in the hearts of all.
I show my many faces through the cycles of my seasons,
In the magnificence of my nature.
I speak to you in your words and actions,
Your deeds and deceits, your pleasures and follies.
I am the longing of the heart for its fulfilment in me.
I am as the tree that reaches to the sky,
Deep-rooted in the earth that is my body,
Abundant, fertile, impregnable and pregnant with all life.

Know me, seek me,
Find me in the beauty of my creation
In the healing of your lifetime wounds,
In the depths of your soul,
In the mysteries of transformation.
For I am the Lady you seek
I am the Source and the Return
I am the One who is love
And the One who loves you.

Meet in circles each with your own power and energy, your own presence,
The experience of who you are, embodied, alive on my Earth,
Incarnate, physical, spiritual, emotional, mental,
All engendered in my Name.

Woman, man, you who would be Priestess, Priest of Avalon
Take your heart and cast it upon the wings of desire
Frame it with consciousness
Fill it with my love,
Be holy, be loved, be love, beloved.
For I am the Love that flows through all
Is in all
Is in you as Breath
As a Violet Flame
As Life.

There is no historical or even mythic record of who the Lady of Avalon is. While there is an ancient story told of the Nine Morgens who inhabit Avalon, the Lady of Avalon is a Goddess who has potently re-emerged only in recent years. Because She is unknown as an herstorical figure, I can only share with you my own experience of Her as She has affected my life and the inspiration I have received from Her, which has deepened over time.

As I have come to know Her my understanding of who She is has changed. For example, for several years I thought that the Lady of Avalon was the Goddess who expressed Herself through the Nine Morgens, whose identity was merged with Morgen la Fey. Now I recognise the Lady as a unique and distinctive Goddess of the Isle of Avalon, who reveals Herself in the land and the seasons of Her nature in Avalon, and through the powerful, transformative experiences that we have as individuals and as a community, here in Glastonbury. The Lady of Avalon is Nolava, Goddess of love and transformation. She is Avallonia, Lady of Apples. The Nine Morgens, who also dwell in Avalon, are more elemental dakinis, part Goddess, part devic or fey in nature.

Over the years the Lady of Avalon has shown me many different faces, some truly blissful and some scary, but always filled with Her love. She has shown Herself to my sister and brother priest/esses whose inspiration has added to my own. You may have other experiences of Her. She may show you different faces to those given here. I make no claim to be the sole source of truth about who She is. Together we are on a pathway to Her revelation. The journey to know the Lady of Avalon is one of continuing unfoldment to which everyone who wishes to, can contribute.

Many Goddesses come to us fully formed. We know who they are from herstory and ancient and modern day cultures. We know what they look like, what their qualities are, we know their stories and legends, we can take part in their celebrations. When the Lady of Avalon first comes to us often She is just an inspiring name without a form, or a vision of a Goddess who has no name. Part of the journey to Her priestesshood is one of remembering Her, in the sense of drawing out fine strands of memory from the past and threads of creativity from the future, bringing them into the present, weaving them together into the tapestry of who She is now and how we experience Her love for us.

Through the time I have lived in Glastonbury upon the Isle of Avalon I have come to truly love the Lady of Avalon in all Her glory and power. I have the greatest respect and awe for Her, for Her gifts of endless love, of discrimination, truth and transformation, for all that She has given to me and for all that I see Her give to others. Naive of Her ways as I was when I first came to live here, She took me and shook me apart with love. She cracked open my armour and began the long process of healing my pain and fear, my lifetime wounds. Over the years that I have lived here I have experienced many small and several great personal transformations and initiations. It has not been an easy route. She has brought me love, strength, inspiration, vision, boundless creativity, joy and peace. For me She is the most sublime Goddess, to whom I am intimately connected in the very substance of my being through my past and present day experience. I claim Her as a Holy Foremother and Ancestor, and Goddess of my heart.

One of the first things we notice when we begin to explore the nature of the Lady of Avalon, is that She is intimately associated with a particular mythic location, the Isle of Avalon. Other goddesses that we can name, such as Isis, Ceres or Artemis are not goddesses of specific places, although they may be associated and primarily worshipped in particular lands and cultures, Isis in Egypt, Ceres by the Romans, Artemis at Ephesus, etc. In Brigit's Isles there are also universal goddesses who are honoured throughout the land, such as Britannia, Brigit or Ana, whose name is found within many others. There are goddesses associated with particular physical locations, such as mountains, rivers and lakes. These include several Giantesses who formed the landscape with their own bodies or by dropping great boulders from the sky, such as the Hag of Bheare in Ireland and Scotland, Skathac on Skye or the Cailleach na Mointeach (Old Woman of the Moors) in Scotland. Some Goddesses dwell within and beneath lakes like Nelferch, the Lady of Llyn y Fan Fach in Wales, who emerged from the waters of the lake to live for a time in this world, or Keridwen who is found in several parts of Wales, and is said to live beneath Lake Tegid (Bala) in North Wales, or in Ceredigion in West Wales.

The Lady of Avalon is one of the few goddesses who rule a mythic landscape, the Isle of Avalon. Nolava is kin to the faery folk or *sidhe*, who at special places in the landscape, within sacred mounds, beside hollow hills, in stone circles, may invite humans to journey with them into the Otherworld of Her nature. Stepping across Her thresholds we must take care that we follow the rules of Her enchanted realm, for if we were to drink the waters of Her nature or feast upon Her apples unawares, then we might find ourselves unable to leave Avalon when we want to. We might find that one hundred years have gone by in the twinkling of an eye. We might find that one day in Her realm is equal to a year and a day in our world, so that when we return to the everyday world there is no-one left that we might recognise. We might find that we are so shocked by our experiences that our hair turns white overnight. We might find ourselves raving and mad, or we might find ourselves transformed into priestesses, poets, healers and visionaries, Her prophets in the world. When we choose to become Priestesses of Avalon it is important to realise that as well as dedicating ourselves to the Goddess as Lady of Avalon we are also dedicating ourselves to the transformative energies of the mythic Isle of Avalon.

The Lady of Avalon's Sacred Wheel of the Year

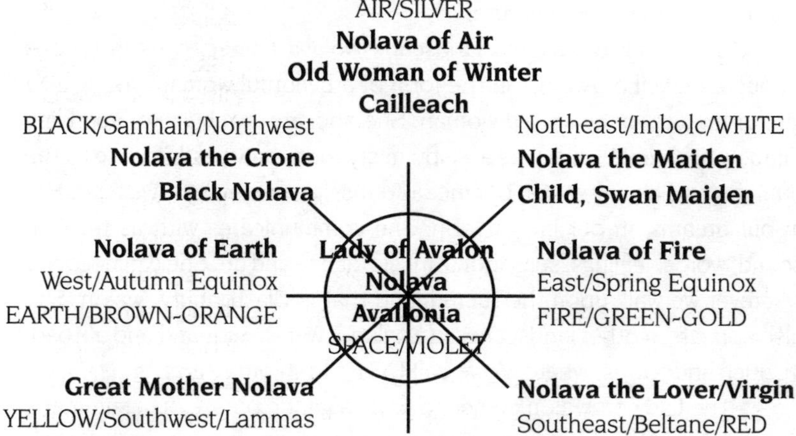

The Lady of Avalon, Nolava, is the feminine energy of the Isle of Avalon. Hers is the innocent love of the Child, whose heart is completely open to giving and receiving love. Hers is the passionate love of the Lover, who invites us to lose ourselves in Her love. Hers is the nurturing love of the Mother, who truly cares for us and holds us always in Her loving embrace, no matter what we do. Hers is the wise love of the Grandmother, who has seen and experienced all things.

Nolava is also the Air of Love, the unconditional love that understands all of human nature through the breadth and heights of Her vision. She is the Fire of Love that burns us up in Her fiery nature, melting our resistances to love, releasing the dross that no longer serves us. She is the Water of Love, stirring and moving us in the depths of our emotions, until they become clear, flowing with ease. She is the Earth of Love, Her touch grounds our hopes and dreams, brings love into our everyday lives. In our centre Nolava is the Space of Love that lies within each one of us as a endless resource of love.

Nolava is the feminine essence of the Isle of Avalon. She is imaged in the landscape of Glastonbury Avalon. She reveals Herself in the shapes of the hills and valleys as a giant Maiden Swan, as a vibrant Lover, as the birth-giving Mother and as an ancient Crone. She is here in all the elements of Her nature as Space, Air, Fire, Water and Earth, changing Her appearance with the seasons of Her nature.

As we walk the sacred landscape Nolava comes to us in visions through the Veil of Avalon, in the form of a beautiful woman, young as a girl, or mature, or as an old woman. She appears in a blaze of sparkling rainbow and violet light or as a wispy, misty form, only partly visible to the human eye. She appears in our meditations, in our journeys. We meet Her in our dreams, in our imagination. She communicates with us through sound, words, feelings, sensations, music, dance and art. She can be found wherever we walk upon the sacred land that is Glastonbury Avalon. She also appears in other landscapes in England, Wales, Scotland and abroad, in cities and towns, wherever we call to Her from our hearts.

The Lady of Avalon comes to us as a gentle breeze on a summer's day as we stroll in the Orchards of Avalon. As Avallonia She is here in the sweet scent of apple blossom, in the hum of honey bees, in the call of the doves, in the cawing of the circling crows, in the great flocks of starlings that move as one across the water meadows, in the tapping of the green woodpecker on the bark of the Summerland trees. She is the beauty of Her nature, the sensuous wonder of Her natural forms, the soft curves of the hills, the tree-lined clefts. She is the relief we feel when we journey from the harsh storms of life in the 21st century into Her calm paradise, for She is our Earth, Our Ground of Being. She is our Home.

She is the healing waters of the Red and the White Springs, the alchemical blend that arises in the secret valley between the Tor and Chalice Hill. She is found in the many springs that rise all over Her earthly body bringing watery emotion to the surface of the land. She is the vessel of feminine power and She is the stillness found at the centre of every container. The Holy Grael of Innocence, the Lover's Loving Cup, the Mother's Chalice and the Cauldron of the Crone all belong to Her. She is the Source and Container of all that is.

She is the Lady of Apples in the Orchards of Avalon. She is the White Lady, the white mist that clothes the land in autumn and spring, hiding Her face from all who would venture unaware beyond Her Veil into Avalon. She is Mystress of the Lake of Mysts. She is the Lady we meet when we journey in the Barge through the Mists to Avalon.

When we meet Her She communicates with us about life in the world and the great mysteries of birth, life, relationship, death and the Great Beyond. She is especially connected to the feminine aspects of those mysteries, to the bearing of new life, the nurturance of life, the care for all life, the relationships between all forms of life, the ending of life in death, and life after death. She takes us into the worlds beyond form, into the inner worlds, into the discarnate worlds. She brings us to the essence of who we are as energy beings, as unbounded spirits, for She is the wildness that loosens all bonds, releasing us into the freedom to be who we are, soul-infused beings alive today on Her beautiful body.

Nolava is the wind of change that can suddenly rattle through our lives whenever we enter the Glastonbury temenos. She can bring anxiety, fear and mighty resistance. She sets in train events that bring change and transformation into our lives. She unveils our ancient wounds and catalyses their healing. She demonstrates through the annual cycle of Her own nature how we can unfold into the beauty of who we are, how we can delight in Her presence in our bodies, how we can share Her abundance and generosity. She shows us how to let go of old forms that no longer serve, how to die to the old and be reborn each year into the new. She shows us that She is the moving Spiral, the spiritual DNA of life, eternal and everlasting, always transforming, yet ever constant.

Nolava rules the three realms of the enchanted Middleworld, the divine Upperworld and the transforming Underworld. She is here in the Middleworld, always just a glance away from normal reality, waiting for us to notice Her, hoping that we will ask Her to stop for us, as we lead our busy lives. She is present in the Upperworld as a pure and radiant violet feminine essence, that can crack open wide the thickest armour on our hearts and bodies, and call forth our greatest spiritual aspirations. She leads us down into the Underworld for our own good, to sit with Her in Her darkness, to empathise with Her suffering for long lengths of time. She takes us ever deeper, down to the bottom of the Underworld, where there is nothing but despair.

Then, if we are lucky, She shows us that the way out is not through ascension, through rising out of our emotions, but through digging deeper down into the Underworld, until finally we crack through the solid rock at the bottom. Beneath that layer of rock lies Her boundless River of Creativity and Life-force. As we dive into the swirling waters, for there is no other way to go, we drink of their sweetness. We are swept along on the eddies and currents, supported by their energy and taken back up to the surface of the Middleworld, with barely a backward glance. Once touched Her River stays with us always, flowing inside us, it becomes a part of us.

Today Glastonbury Avalon is a powerful energetic centre and pilgrims of all faiths are drawn to visit the town and the surrounding landscape. Some people who come are immediately repulsed by the hippy High Street, the New Age crystal shops, the sometimes murky energetic vibration of the town, and quickly leave, swearing never to return. Others feel they have come home and relish the opportunity to walk upon the sacred landscape and visit the holy places, to have tarot readings, massages and healing, to shop for spiritual books and ephemera.

Within a few hours of being here those attracted by the vibrations often have amazing light-filled experiences of Her nature, that open the heart and bring hope to battered souls. Glastonbury residents are on the whole friendly and welcoming, willing to share spiritual information and experiences with visitors. The sacred places are alive and inviting and full of a numinous spirit. Time stretches and many things happen in a short space. Synchronicity occurs frequently. We find the book we have been searching for, forgotten memories are triggered, we make connections, we bump into old friends. We meet new soul friends and soul mates, people who are familiar to us that we are sure we have known before and these meetings feel meaningful and important. With open hearts we look through the Veil of Avalon and see the faeries, the little people, the priestesses of old, beings from other dimensions of reality. The Lady shines Her beneficent face upon us and our hearts open to Her love. She shows us how beautiful our souls are, how limitless and free we can be. We feel centred and whole.

Then within a short space of time sometimes just a few hours or days we find ourselves brought face to face with our Shadow selves. Things that had felt wonderful, ecstatic, begin to pall in the light of day. Did we make a terrible mistake about this person or that event? Were our strong feelings that felt so right at the time, actually wrong? The heart that has opened suddenly meets the limits of its expansion and shuts off. We feel wounded to the core by the very experiences that have opened our hearts. Meetings with people, with new lovers that seemed to speak of a wonderful enchantment, a recognition of an old relationship renewed, suddenly turn sour. The ground of knowing has shifted under our feet. We have lost our centre. We lose faith in ourselves. If we cannot trust our feelings and our intuition, what can we trust?

We feel hurt, shocked, abandoned, betrayed. We feel angry, resentful, misunderstood, depressed. Powerful primal emotions erupt into our consciousness. We react as children to adult provocations. We fear we might be going mad. The energies of Avalon which once seemed so beneficent now scare us. Are they bad? Is evil at work? How could we have come to this hard place so quickly? We thought we were all right, not perfect, but OK. The Goddess's face has darkened. The mirror She now holds reveals our failings, our ancient wounds, all we would rather not face about ourselves. We try to run away. Unfortunately the process once begun does not stop when we leave Glastonbury, it follows us home.

This is the beginning of change. In order to fulfil our destiny, to fully incarnate on this planet, to become who we are as souls alive in this world, our consciousness needs to expand so we can become bigger than we have been. The Lady of Avalon is the Goddess who brings us face to face with who we truly are. Her ways are strong, loving and dynamic and not for the fainthearted. They are especially powerful for those who feel called to become Her priestesses. She takes those who are willing into the emotional and spiritual burning grounds, where the dross that no longer serves us or Her, is burned away in the fires of Her Mysteries, until the gold in our souls is revealed. She brings us to Initiation, not that which is given from the outside, but that which comes from within, from Her.

Our deep need to heal our inner and outer wounds is often the impetus which makes us search for something different to the mainstream that has wounded us. As we begin to look for something other, we hear Her calling to us to remember Her. At this time we, the wounded healers of the world, incarnate with a great destiny to fulfil, that of helping bring Goddess consciousness back into this imbalanced and self-destructive patriarchal world. As we heal ourselves so Her world is healed with us.

We return to Avalon, we come back again. The process of meeting with the light and being undone by darkness repeats itself. We are powerfully drawn to Her mysteries by our experience and repulsed by our own inadequacies. Some feel called to Her priestesshood no matter what, and begin to engage more consciously with Her Mysteries. We join in ceremonies in the sacred places of Avalon, on the Tor, at Chalice Well, in the Goddess Temple, at the Goddess Conference. We begin to learn of Her ways. We decide to train to become Priestesses of Avalon, making a deeper commitment to journey to know Her.

Some people decide to come and live within the energies of Avalon, beginning a preliminary process of transformation that takes from 18

Lady of Avalon

Where am I to turn, if not to you?
What other arms can soothe me like yours do?
What other heart could hold the depths of my pain?
What other tears could cleanse me like the falling rain?

I will turn to You, my Lady
Mother of the Northern Winds
Keeper of the Eastern Star fire
Where the sea and earth begins

What other eyes could see me in my naked shame
and hear me calling out when there's no one else to blame?
Who will come and hold me when there's so much to forgive
and breathe sweet life into me when I've nothing left to give?

I will turn to You, my Lady
Mother of the Southern Seas
Keeper of the Western Earth Womb
Goddess of Deep Mysteries

Where can I go to when all I love has mocked me?
Where can I rest when pain is etched into my bones?
Who will silence questions when I have no more answers?
Who will bring me comfort when my tears have turned to stones?

I will turn to You, my Lady
Maiden, Lover, Mother, Crone
Warrior of the heart and mind
Keeper of the sacred bones

Whose name shall I sing when to the stars my soul is rising?
Who shall I dance to when with joy I'm overwhelmed?
Whose is the song that my pulsing blood is singing?
Whose is the land where my priestess soul is held?

I will turn to You, my Lady
And I'll never feel alone
For your song will set me free
And your voice will bring me home

Jacqui Woodward-Smith, October 2003-September 2004

months to two years and more. For those who move to Glastonbury, locals who have passed through this process call it, "*Having a Glastonbury experience*", an annoying phrase when we are in one. It is characterised by powerful emotions, discomfort, dukka, feelings of anger, fear, exclusion, grief, betrayal, as well as both inadequacy and ego inflation, and all balanced by mystical experiences of the divine. Residents who have been through it nod their heads sagely and try to support and comfort us as we are buffeted by the astral storms.

If we are lucky some of our challenges may be resolved, some wounds healed and a period of calm follows, when we become grateful for all that has happened to us so far. We know that we have been touched by Her magic and are changing. We get it, what makes this place so attractive to so many people on diverse spiritual paths. Then over time, through the months and the years She takes us deeper into our own Soul and Shadow Selves, revealing layer upon layer of wounding from this and previous lives. Rigidities crystallise and become solid, until they crack apart in great slabs, to reveal softness and human vulnerability underneath. Within that vulnerability lies our true strength. Humility emerges with the realisation of the awesomeness of our Goddess-given experience. The process repeats itself at deeper and deeper levels.

In my own journey with Her I have experienced some of the darkest, most painful and scary places in my psyche. I have felt total aloneness. I have been destroyed, laid out on the floor. I have felt abandoned, lost, betrayed. I have felt mad. I have considered suicide. I have descended into the Underworld, been judged and found wanting. I hung on the hook on the wall like Inanna for three days and nights (months and months), waiting, hoping that someone or something could save me from myself. I was made a scapegoat many times by a community I love. I was accused of being a man-hater and ball-breaker, of being into power for its own sake. I have been a convenient butt for projection and derision, a focus for competition, jealousy and power battles. By choosing an original path to the Goddess I have been derided and abused many times. I have had a dangerous breast cancer that could have killed me. I have lived with the fear of death and of life. I continue to heal my fears.

Yet through all of this Her wisdom light continues to shine upon me as Arianrhod's Silver Wheel shines in the heavens above. She illuminates my path always holding a flaming torch ahead of me that I may glimpse the way ahead. As Ariadne She lays out Her Red Thread that I may follow Her through the great Labrynth of life. As Nolava She holds me always in

Her loving embrace. The Lady has shown me that there are jewels hidden in my darkness. Through Her great love and compassion I have managed to heal some of my primal life wounds. She has made me a better person than I was. She has opened my heart. She has brought me love. She has given me beautiful children and a wonderful man to live my life with, who are among my greatest personal teachers. She has taught me to have compassion for myself and for others. She has shown me that I won't die if I make a mistake, if I fail to live up to my high ideals. She has shown me that I am loved and that She will always love me no matter what I do, as She loves each one of us. She shows me that love conquers fear.

I have recently been considering the challenging nature of this Avalonian journey. Are there ways it could be made easier for us? In ancient times Goddesses were honoured daily in homes and temples, given praise and offerings of flowers and fruits, milk, wine and grains, by individuals and communities. This is still common practice in existing Goddess cultures in the world, such as southern India, where the Goddess has been continuously honoured for thousands of years. On the Big Island of Hawaii it is traditional to make offerings to honour Pele, Goddess of the Volcano, of the new Land, who has Her favourite ohelo berries, gin and brandy, which She likes to receive.

The Lady of Avalon has been forgotten for a long, long time and She too needs our offerings of recognition, honour and respect. As individuals and as a community we are reinstating the practice of making daily offerings to Her of flowers and fruits, of apples, holy waters, milk and grains, gifts of our hearts and souls, freely given to Her in gratitude for all She gives to us. This spiritual practice of showing gratitude opens the heart and allows Her to shower us with Her beneficence.

In becoming Her Priestess it is important to realise just what kind of a Goddess the Lady of Avalon is. Nolava is a Goddess of love and transformation. She changes our lives. No matter how many times it is said to us we don't usually understand what that means until we have been through the process of transformation ourselves, experiencing the depths of Her love. And it is vital that we do experience that process, otherwise how would we know who She is. And how would we know how to hold others who are experiencing, often unconsciously, the passage of this Dark Light Goddess in their lives? This is one of our many roles as Priestesses of Avalon.

When the Lady first spoke to me and for several years after, I did not know what She looked like. My knowledge of Her was an inner knowing, a feeling and a sensing, not a visible form. But it is good to know what one's favourite Goddesses actually look like in all their diversity of character and form. Yes, there is but One Goddess and She has ten thousand, thousand different names and appearances, and we humans like to relate to individual forms.

One of the greatest disservices to humanity inflicted by patriarchal religions was to claim that there was only one male God and that there should be no graven images of Him. Over 5,000 years conquering patriarchal incomers tore down statues of the Goddess, disfigured Her images in Egypt, Israel, Anatolia and Greece, destroyed Her temples and beautiful artworks all over Europe and beyond. To remove Her image from our religions was to remove Her influence in our communities. If we could not see Her as a daily experience, She could not have power in our lives. As we became separated from Her visually, we became separated from Her spiritually, and thus hierarchies of priesthoods arose to act as mediators between us and the divine.

One of the ways in which we humans experience divinity is through inspired creative expression. Artistic imagery - drawing, painting, sculpture, pattern and form naturally feeds our human spirit, while connecting us imaginatively to Her whenever we see those forms. While She is not the graven image itself, images of Her act as a focus for our attention and devotion, providing a means of opening our hearts to Her. Images inspire us and bring us closer to Her, and they can become inhabited by Her. They are important for our spiritual development.

Within Goddess spirituality instead of all humans being made in the image of the one male God, our Goddesses are often visualised in our own images as divine women, as spirit women or as mythic animal women, an exaltation of the diversity of feminine being and character. This allows us to know something of Her infinite expressions, Her omniscience and glory, which we could not otherwise grasp or make meaningful. It helps us to know that She is within us as we are in Her. Images connect us in a very real sense to the divine.

About seven years ago I began to see the Lady of Avalon, not clearly, but with suggested outlines. I am not a natural artist and must rely on those who are gifted to bring Her image into physical reality. I do however know certain things about the way that She looks. I know that importantly, like many Buddhist and Hindu Goddesses, Her skin is not flesh-coloured, it is violet and in Her presence we are irradiated by Her violet light. When we first decorated the first Goddess Temple in Glastonbury the only thing that I knew about how it should look was that it had to be violet in colour, with violet walls, ceiling and floor, so that we could experience the visual effects of being bathed in Her violet emanation. We all see and understand the names of colours differently and I use the term violet to include a range of colours from pale lavender through violet to purple indigo.

One of the first images of the Lady of Avalon was painted on a large banner for the Glastonbury Goddess Conference by local artist Willow Roe. In planning the image we had spoken about the attributes of the Lady, but I had not mentioned Her violet skin. The great synchronicity was that without discussion Willow was inspired to paint the Lady's skin a pale violet. Such are the ways of the Lady.

I also know that although sometimes the Lady of Avalon appears as an old woman and sometimes as a young girl, more often She appears as a mature woman, standing before and between the emblematic Tor and Chalice Hill. She also appears standing still at the centre of a cauldron of movement, or riding poised on the back of Her earth dragon. The mists which rise from the flat Summerland meadows in autumn and spring are wisps of Her hair, white, silver grey and pale violet. At other times Her hair is black like the Morgen crows who fly across the land. Her dress is decorated with Her sacred symbols, its colour changing with the seasons. In autumn it is orange brown, in winter silver and grey, in spring it is green and gold, in summer blue and turquoise. A wide halo surrounds Her body, filled with all the colours of the rainbow. Whichever face She shows to us, Her beauty shines forth always.

In Her left hand She carries a sprig of apple blossom, or a golden apple of immortality, or a red apple of transformation, which She offers to us. Like the Crone in the fairy tales She asks us to take a bite from Her magical apple and be transformed. Sometimes Her right hand blesses us or She carries a spika or sheaf of wheat, grain or corn, carried by many Grain Goddesses, going back to neolithic times. Sometimes She has deer horns on Her head, with the life-giving sun or the silvery moon shining between them. Black crows may fly around Her, clothing Her as if in a cloak of black wings. A black cat sits at Her feet. On Her sacred Isle apple, willow and hawthorn trees grow in abundance. There are swans, flocks of smaller birds, green woodpeckers, white doves, hawks, buzzards, badgers, foxes and deer.

The Nine Morgens

The Nine Morgens are nine sisters who are the essence of the feminine in nature, in the weather and in womankind. They are dakinis, also known as sky dancers, space-goers, celestial women, cloud fairies, faeries, Valkeries and Furies. Elemental in character, they are said to be pristine and peerless. They are the feminine principle of wisdom that manifests in female forms to benefit all human beings. They are wisdom protectors and they beckon to us through vibration and sound. They help us to overcome our resistances on the spiritual path. They give us experiences of the ineffable reality or divine grace. They carry the dying through the gateways to death. In Buddhism they are known as emanations of enlightened mind, who hold the bodhisattva commitment to seek enlightenment not for oneself alone, but for the benefit of all sentient beings. There is extensive information available on the nature of dakinis within the Buddhist and Hindu traditions. For further information, see the website: www.khandro.net/dakini_khandro.htm

In Avalon the Nine Morgens are particularly connected to trees and plants, to animals, insects and birds, and to the play of the weather upon the landscape in the form of clouds, sunshine, wind, rain, ice and snow. Sometimes Nolava, Lady of Avalon is recognised in the form of Morgen la Fey or Morgana, but each of the Nine Morgens presents a different aspect of feminine being. The combination of their virtues teaches us about the movement and flow of energy, and how to work together spiritually and practically in circles and in community. Through exploring the wonderful character and qualities of the Nine Sisters we can learn more about the divinity and nature of the Goddess.

In legend Nine Morgens dwell on the Isle of Avalon. They are Nine Sisters of Avalon, Nine Priestesses, Faery Queens and Crones. The Morgens were first described by the mythical Welsh poet Taliesin in Geoffrey of Monmouth's 12th century *Vita Merlinii*, and expanded upon by later poets and storytellers. Their names are given in different variations as Thitis, Cliton, Thetis, Gliten, Glitonea, Moronoe, Mazoe, Tyronoe and Morgen la Fey. Many of these names are unfamiliar except for Morgen la Fey - Morgen the Faery and Morgen the Fate, who appears in legend as faery woman, priestess and Goddess.

Like other circles of Nine Maidens, Druidesses, Seeresses, Saints, Fates and Goddesses remembered and celebrated all over western Europe (see *The Quest for the Nine Maidens* by Stuart McHardy, Luath Press), the Nine Morgen sisters are a rich source of inspiration. They encompass all the qualities of the Goddess on the continua between light and dark, sweet and sour, positive and negative, sexual and ascetic, creative and destructive. Like the Greek Muses they are famous for their learning and knowledge of the seven liberal arts, particularly of astronomy/astrology, mathematics and physic. In herstory the Morgens are renowned as priestesses and as healers, for their skill with herbs, for their beauty and sensuality, for their music and dance, for prophecy and the ability to shapeshift, to appear in different places in a moment in time.

They can be imaged as nine women, ranging in age from maiden to crone. There is one Morgen for each decade of life. Thitis is the girl child up to ten years of age, Cliton the adolescent between ten and twenty years. Thetis is in Her twenties, Gliten in Her thirties, Glitonea in Her forties, Moronoe in Her fifties, Mazoe in Her sixties and Tyronoe is in Her seventies and older. Morgen la Fey in their centre is the shapeshifter, the ever young, mature woman or ancient Crone. The Morgens are three triple goddesses, reflections of the phases of the moon. They are nine Queens of the land, nine Faery women, nine Fey, nine Sidhe. They are nine dark cloaked figures who sit in circle around the Cauldron of Inspiration, Immortality and Rebirth, which can be found hidden in a cave deep within Glastonbury Tor. Beneath their cloaks they are clothed in bright radiant colours. The Morgens are also nine huge shimmering beings visible in the ethers surrounding the top of Glastonbury Tor.

Each of the Morgens is connected to a different aspect of the weather, and all forms of weather in the sacred land are created from their interplay. Thitis is *Snow*, Cliton is *Sunshine*, Thetis is *Cloud*, Gliten is *Rain*, Glitonea is *Heat*, Moronoe is *Wind*, Mazoe is *Thunder and Lightening*, Tyronoe is *Frost and Ice*, and Morgen la Fey is *Mist*. As they dance together across the landscape together they create the sunshine and showers of springtime, the balmy days of summer, the gales and storms of autumn and the bright, cold days of winter.

Sometimes their forms may be seen in the trunks of the willow trees that guard the magical isle or they may be glimpsed as shadowy figures hiding behind the trees in the apple orchards of Avalon. Occasionally the Morgens may be seen by mortals as they disappear away into the mists that often surround the sacred isle. In Glastonbury's natural landscape they also appear at significant moments in the forms of black crows, white doves, green woodpeckers and hawks. As I write this section Morgen crows are wheeling in the wind in front of my window that looks out over the Vale of Avalon.

When the legendary King Arthur was dying of his fatal wounds from the battle of Camlan, he was transported to the shores of the Lake surrounding the Isle of Avalon. Here he was placed in the Barge of Avalon and ferried through the mists by the boatman Barinthus - he who knows the patterns of the stars in the heavens. On his passage to Avalon Arthur was accompanied by three Faery Queens: the Queen of Northgalis, the Queen of the Waste Lands and Morgen la Fey, his half sister. In Her role as Midwife of Souls Morgen la Fey helps those who are dying to cross over to the Other Side of life. Arthur travelled to Avalon for the healing of his karmic wounds and the Morgens are themselves powerful healers.

The name *Morgen* probably derives from the same root as the Irish *Morrigan* or *Mor Rigan* - Great Queen, just as the Welsh Rhiannon is derived from Rigan-tona - another Great Queen. The Welsh language has common roots with the language of the ancient British people, which we all once spoke in these lands. In Welsh *Morgen*, *Modron* or *Madron* all mean Mother. Morgen also means seaborne. In more modern novels Morgen la Fey is known as *Morgaine* and *Morgana*, meaning that She is also *Morg-Ana* - Great Ana, one of the earliest named Goddesses in Brigit's Isles (See *Spinning the Wheel of Ana*, Kathy Jones, Ariadne Publications). In writing Her name I prefer to use the Welsh feminine form of Morgen, where Morgan is the masculine.

The Morgens dwell in the delicate margins, just on the Other Side of the Veil of Avalon, so close that we might hear their footfalls on the grass or glimpse their passage through the rising mists, so near that they can touch us if they choose with their blessings. As dakinis they are intimately connected to the inner Matrix of life, holding the etheric threads that underlie all created forms. Where other Goddesses are responsible for the outer worlds of form the Morgens are one with the inner forces which create, maintain and destroy form.

Experiencing the Nine Morgens

My understanding of the Nine Morgens and my engagement with them has followed a different route to the more personally transforming energies of the Lady of Avalon. The Nine Morgens have been an inspiration for plays and performances, for learning how to work spiritually in groups, as well as informing my understanding of landscape and Otherworldly realities, which has influenced my writing, teaching and creativity.

The Morgens first began to call to me more than ten years ago. As I walked our dog Smudger in the apple orchards on the northern slopes of Avalon I would see their shapes and figures moving behind the trees, out of the corner of my eye. I could never quite see them if I looked straight at them, but I became aware that they were there, watching from behind the trees. I began to make offerings to them of grains and seeds beside a tall ash tree where I saw them most often. I began to hear their voices and receive messages from them, messages of inspiration telling me where to go next in my creative life. At first I didn't know if I was making it all up and it was all *just* my imagination, but slowly I began to believe that they were really there and were speaking to me.

After a couple of years of this communication I felt that they were asking to be recognised by others in the outside world. They had been forgotten for hundred of years by all but a handful of people and they are living beings. They want to be known to us.

In 1994 I wrote a sacred drama entitled *And They Call Her Name Wisdom*. It is a love story following the alchemical patterns of transformation which leads to the creation of the Philosopher's Stone (the Wisdom of the Stone of Sophia, Goddess of Wisdom). A fragment of the Philosopher's Stone can transform the prima materia or base metal of our human condition into gold. In the drama two modern day young people, Jasmine and Ted, fall in love and find themselves journeying inadvertently, as many do, through the Veil of Avalon. Propelled by an inner need, by aspiration, love, and sometimes drugs, people often wander through the Veil that separates the physical world from the inner world of Avalon. There we meet some of the varied mythical characters who dwell in Avalon. On their journey Jasmine and Ted become separated, because as in life, their spiritual paths are different. In her initiation into the Otherworld Jasmine meets the Nine Morgens who teach her about Women's Blood Mysteries, of which she is untaught and woefully ignorant.

When it came to writing lines for the Morgens I had to make decisions about their characters, who they are as individuals as well as a circle of equals. In Geoffrey of Monmouth's legend there is very little information to distinguish them, apart from Morgen La Fey, who was said to be chief among the nine and to have the ability to shapeshift and appear in more than one place at the same time. Another distinguishing feature is that Thetis plays a zither.

In 1992 I had published *Spinning the Wheel of Ana : a Spiritual Quest to find the British Primal Ancestors*. Out of this quest the Sacred British Medicine Wheel for this land emerged, based on the qualities and characteristics of the ancient Goddess Ana as She expresses Herself through the cycle of Her seasons. With ceremonial use this Wheel evolved to become Brigit-Ana or Britannia's Wheel. On Britannia's Sacred Wheel eight different British goddesses are associated with the eight sunfire festivals of the year, beginning with Bride the Maiden Goddess at Imbolc. Journeying around the wheel the Goddess blossoms as the Lover at Beltane, as the Mother at Lammas and as the Crone at Samhain. In contrast to the Wiccan wheel, the Mother of Air rules at Yule (winter solstice), the Mother of Fire at Oestre (spring equinox), the Mother of Water at Litha (summer solstice), and the Mother of Earth at Mabon (autumn equinox). This positioning is based on the essential elemental nature of the Goddesses traditionally celebrated at the eight festivals. Britannia Herself is honoured in the centre of the Wheel as the tutelary or guardian Goddess of Brigit's Isles and the Womb of All.

I realised that eight of the Nine Morgens could also be arrayed around the wheel of the year with the youngest Morgen at Imbolc and the eldest at Winter Solstice. The ninth, Morgen la Fey (who agewise appears somewhere in the middle as a mature woman) is in the centre of the wheel. Thetis as the musician I placed at Beltane, when love and sensuality and music are often expressed. Then I listened to my intuition and the sounds of their names, and placed the Morgens on the wheel where I felt they should go. Thitis (thin) at Imbolc, Cliton (clitoris, fire) at Oestre, Thetis at Beltane, Gliten (for sun glistening on water) at Litha, Mystress (She wanted to be called) Glitonea the Mother Goddess at Lammas, Moronoe at Mabon, Mazoe at Samhain and ancient (it seemed to fit) Tyronoe at Yule, and Morgana in the centre. Others might arrange them differently, but with this inspiration their characters began to emerge.

At the time of writing the play the new millennium was on its way. Thitis was the young Maiden concerned with dreaming the future, with the creation of the new. She was also concerned with restoring the Isle of Avalon to its former place of glory, making it visible again as a holy place of spiritual transformation. Cliton was energetic and fiery, a healer and herbalist, Thetis was the musician and Gliten was a bit of a performer, wanting the glistening threads of Her sparkling dresses to be seen. Mystress Glitonea was the kind nurturing Mother concerned with childbirth, mothers and their children. Moronoe was the teacher and Mazoe, a grumpy, cross Dark Goddess. Tyronoe knew all about death, regeneration and the worlds beyond life, while Morgana was the wise initiatrix, who knows mystery and is a shapeshifter.

I wrote a song for them, which was set to music by Glastonbury musician, Jana Runnalls.

Nine Morgens on the Isle of Avalon
Nine Sisters spin the Wheel of Time
Nine Women hid beyond the shining Veil
Nine Morgens weave the Web of Life

Chorus *Moronoe, Mazoe and Mystress Glitonea*
Gliten, Cliton and ancient Tyronoe
Thitis and Thetis, renowned for her zither
And Morgen La Fey, most famous of them all

Nine Morgens rule the Isle of Avalon
Faint mem'ries of a shrouded land
Honoured once for their healing arts
Now all but forgot in the sacred land

Nine Morgens come back to life again
Reveal yourselves in the world once more
Show us now the mysteries of Avalon
Stir the sacred cauldron, regenerate us all.

In 1993 I first received the idea from the Lady to organise a large Goddess Conference in Glastonbury. In the 1980s there had been a wonderful and inspiring Goddess exhibition in the Glastonbury Assembly Rooms with Goddess artists, such as the pioneering feminist painter and writer Monica Sjoo, sculptor Phillipa Bowers, poet and painter Jill Smith and artist Chesca Potter. We also had a Goddess day with British Goddess writers and speakers, such as the late Asphodel Long, who is widely recognised as a Grandmother of the Goddess movement in Britain. The inspiration had come to me how great it might be to hold a conference of Goddess-loving women and men over a few days, with talks, ceremonies, exhibitions and music, all devoted to Her. There was no such event in Britain at the time.

Tyna Redpath had recently opened her own shop in Glastonbury called *The Goddess and Green Man*, selling all kinds of Goddess and Green Man artworks, books and ephemera, the first of its kind in the country. One day I mentioned to Tyna my idea for a Goddess Conference. It turned out that Tyna had been thinking of a similar event, wanting to include artists and craftswomen. We connected in that moment and for the next couple of years we both held the dream of the conference in the back of our minds, not really thinking that it might happen, and doing nothing about it.

I wrote the first draft of the sacred drama *And They Call Her Name Wisdom* in 1994 thinking it would be performed the following year. At the time of writing I didn't consciously know much about alchemy, but I had read a few books by, amongst others, the alchemist Nicholas Flamel, and intuited how the process might flow for a young couple in love. I also read about Sophia, the Goddess of Wisdom, and found powerful words that had been written by and about Her in the Biblical books of the Wisdom of Solomon, and Proverbs, and in *Thunder Perfect Mind* and other early texts. I was happy with the play as it was written.

In July 1995 at Lammas I led a ceremonial pilgrimage for a large group of people into and out of the great Goddess Labrynth that encircles the slopes of Glastonbury Tor. As we walked the amazing route my personal mantra of dedication was to the Lady of Avalon, to Ariadne of the Red Thread and to Arianrhod of the Silver Wheel, all Goddesses of the Tor Labrynth. I prayed to Her as I walked the long and winding path and asked Her to transform me as She willed.

Within a few days of walking the Labrynth I heard Her voice saying that now was the time to begin planning a Goddess Conference for the following year, for Lammas 1996. Suddenly I felt ready, it could be done and one day as I went into the shop, without much thought I said to Tyna,

"*I'm going to organise a Goddess Conference for next year.*"

"*Can I help?*" said Tyna,

"*Yes. Great!*" I replied and everything unfolded from there.

I wanted to organise the content and the speakers for the conference and Tyna said she would like to organise the exhibitions. We decided to call it a conference rather than a festival or a gathering, because we wanted it to have some gravitas, some weight, rather than being just a loose pagan gathering. We felt there were allusions to the story of the

Conference of the Birds, when birds of all shapes, sizes and plumage (!) gathered together to speak with each other. Eleven years later at the time of writing this book, after organising ten fabulous Goddess Conferences together, Tyna has decided it's time to move on with her personal creativity and the eleventh Conference is being created by a wider circle of women with myself as principal webster.

Within a couple of weeks of making the decision to create the Goddess Conference the following Lammas, I found a lump in my breast, which turned out to be dangerously cancerous. The whole time we were planning and organising the first Goddess Conference I was journeying through a personal alchemical healing process, experiencing surgery, chemotherapy and radiotherapy with all the attendant terrors and trauma. My journey of dissolution, healing and transformation is described in *Breast Cancer: Hanging on by a Red Thread* (Ariadne Publications).

Because of my cancer the performance of the sacred drama *And They Call Her Name Wisdom* and the emergence as embodied characters of the Nine Morgens, was put on hold. In reality it was postponed until I had fully grasped the true nature of the alchemical journey as a personal bodily and spiritual experience, affecting every part of my being. I have found over the years that this is the way with sacred drama, which invokes the presence and expression of powerful and transformative Goddesses. Everyone who takes part is to some degree or another thrust into the transformative process which these mythical characters embody, and as the writer, director and sometime performer I must experience my part too.

Following the success of the first Lammas Goddess Conference in 1996 the following December forty people came together and were involved in the Yuletide community sacred drama production of *And They Call Her Name Wisdom*, as performers, musicians, dancers, singers and production team, including both amateur and professional talents. The production was rehearsed and performed in the Assembly Rooms, a cooperatively owned building which at the time served as a focus for the alternative community, using the facilities and people who worked in and used the building regularly as well as others in the wider Glastonbury community.

In the drama Jasmine, the young hera, inadvertently takes a bite from an Old Crone's magical apple and moves into the mysterious land of Avalon, where the Nine Morgens find Her wandering alone and lost. The Morgens made their first appearance on stage played by local Glastonbury women. Sophie Pullinger was a young Thitis, dancer Dalia Bishop was

Cliton, accountant and singer Vivienne Andreae was Thetis, sparkly Susy Joy was Gliten, artist Josephine Fryer was Glitonea, painter Jill Smith was Moronoe, the fiery Johanna Modzelewska was Mazoe, quiet Pauline Gibbs was Tyronoe and Joanna Griffin was Morgana. What a splendid bunch of women!

Pauline made a wonderful set of nine identical black hooded cloaks, which the Morgens wore when they first appeared, encircling the cauldron, and which they continue to wear to this day whenever they make an appearance. In performance these cloaks were opened to reveal individually coloured costumes underneath. The appearance of the Black Goddess may be dark and frightening when first we meet Her, but as we get to know Her, She opens Her raiment to reveal Her colourful beauty hidden in the darkness. We wear these black Morgen cloaks at the Opening and Closing Ceremonies at every Goddess Conference, concealing beautiful costumes underneath.

In 1999 I began writing *In the Nature of Avalon: Goddess Pilgrimages in Glastonbury's Sacred Landscape* (Ariadne Publications). This book is dedicated to the Lady of Avalon and is designed to help people find the Goddess in the many forms in which She appears in Glastonbury's sacred landscape. It includes special pilgrimages with prayers and mantras, and suggestions for visualisation and meditation, which people can make themselves as they journey through the landscape.

Once again as I wrote the Morgens began to speak to me particularly as I walked the dog through the fields of Stonedown, the hill slopes which lie to the north of the Tor. I developed the *Morgen Meander*, a pilgrimage route that takes us out of the bustling streets of Glastonbury into quieter fields and byways, where we might meet the Morgens if we open ourselves to their presence. The pilgrimage begins with a prayer to the Morgens on the Mound on top of Windmill Hill, one of the sacred hills of Glastonbury, which in the landscape of the Goddess is the Nolava the Crone's head and crown. This hill is often ignored as a sacred place because there are houses built upon it.

In his book *Energy Secrets of Glastonbury Tor* (Green Magic Publishing), Nicholas Mann has shown that the Mound is a viewing point for a wonderful astronomical phenomenon. On the morning of the winter solstice viewed from the Mound, the sun as it rises, can be seen rolling up the northeastern slope of Glastonbury Tor. Nicholas's recent work is bringing additional evidence to suggest that the Mound may be a burial mound several thousand years old, which acts a marker for several solar and lunar alignments.

The Morgen Meander begins with this prayer:

Morgens of Avalon, Nine Sisters
As I begin my pilgrimage to you
I pay homage to the Crone of Avalon
On whose earthly crown I stand
I honour you Nolava, Old Woman.

I ask for your guidance, your vision, your wisdom,
Help me to pass through the Veil of Avalon
As I walk in the beauty of your nature.
I pray that I may be open enough to see
All that lies hidden in your sacred landscape.

Ladies of the Light and Darkness
Keepers of the Mysteries,
Queens of the liberal arts,
Of astrology, mathematics and physic
Goddesses of herbs and all crafts,

Healers of the wounds of karma,
Sweet Musicians, Shapeshifters,
Mistresses of Time, Faery Queens,
Maidens, Lovers, Mothers, Crones
I honour you who are the Nine

Morgens, illuminate my sight that I may see you
Awaken my inner ear that I may hear your voices
And recognise the signs of your passage.
Show me the way into your shining realm.
Open my heart to your love now and always
Blessed be

The pilgrimage route goes north down Old Wells Road to Holy Well lane, then across the fields to Paddington Farm, and on to Gog and Magog, two ancient 2,000 year old oak trees. The shorter Morgen Meander returns via Paradise Lane to Wick Hollow and back to Windmill Hill. The longer Meander continues from Gog and Magog circling around the east of Glastonbury Tor to Ashwell Lane, and then spiralling to the top of the Tor. There the Morgens are visualised and invoked in all their glory, coming towards us from the eight directions which are visible from the top of the Tor. The route continues down to Wellhouse Lane, then beautiful Bulwarks Lane and back to the Mound on Windmill Hill. On these pilgrimages one

The Sacred Wheel of the Nine Morgens

North /Winter Solstice
AIR/SILVER/GREY
Owl/Buzzard/Flocks/Wind Dragon
Feather Fan
Lady of Air, Lady of the Winter Tor, Cailleach, Tyronoe, Holly Woman

Northeast/Imbolc/WHITE
Maiden,Lady of Imbolc. Quickener, Lady of Prophecy Thitis, Willow Woman
Swan/Phoenix/Unicorn
Grael/Spindle/Spinning Wheel

East/Spring Equinox
FIRE/GREEN-GOLD
Cliton, Lady of Fire, Lady of the Greening Hazel Woman
Hare/Cat/Fire Dragon
Green Woodpecker
Wand/Rod

Southeast/Beltane/RED
Thetis, Lover/Virgin Goddess Lady of Beltane, Sovereignty Hawthorn Woman
Mare/Horse/Small Birds
Zither/Comb/Mirror

Gliten, Lady of Water Queen of the Deep Lady of the Springs and Wells Lady of the Lake
Chalice, *Grey Heron,*
Nymph, Sprites, Silkies, Mermaids
WATER/BLUE-GREEN
South/Summer Solstice

GOLD/Southwest/Lammas
Mother Goddess, Glitonea Nurturer, Lady of Lammas, Ash Woman
Song Thrush, White Hind
Loom/Shuttle

West/Autumn Equinox
BROWN-ORANGE/EARTH
Lady of Earth, Moronoe Lady of the Orchards Beech Woman
Fox/Mole/Badger/
Earth Dragon/Blackbird
Stone/Orb/Crystal

BLACK/Samhain/Northwest
Lady of Samhain Crone, Beansidhe, Yew Woman, Mazoe
Sow/Bat/Hawk
Sickle/Scissors

Centre/VIOLET
Morgen la Fey Keeper of the Mysteries Enchantress , Apple Woman
Crow/Raven
Cauldron

can meet the Nine Morgens.

In 2001 as part of my teaching practice I led a retreat for the first time entitled *The Mystery of the Nine Morgens*. During the four days we created a beautiful altar to the Nine and invoked their presence. We explored their sacred wheel of nine directions. We journeyed in imagination to meet the Morgens in the cave beneath Glastonbury Tor. We walked the Morgen Meander pilgrimage route and connected to them in the landscape. We embodied the Morgens, speaking their words of wisdom for each other. Dressed in black cloaks we flew through the night streets of Glastonbury up to the Tor where we communed with the Nine. We went to sleep dreaming of the Morgens and sat in Counsel with them. At the end of the four days we all knew that the Morgens were real, with distinct characters and personalities, Nine Sisters who worked in circle.

In June 2002 a few weeks before the Goddess Conference the Morgens spoke again. They wanted the following year's 2003 Goddess Conference to be dedicated to them. As we later planned the Conference around the Nine I began to feel anxious. They are such an esoteric bunch of Goddesses, so hidden from the everyday world. Would we be able to bring them into consciousness and vision so that others might see them and know them to be real? Yet this is how it is for all of us as we attempt to remember Goddesses, who were once well-known, honoured and revered, and now are almost forgotten. Its almost a test of our convictions that they do exist. We act on faith that they are real and will appear if we invite them in. I began to write key words to describe the attributes of each of the Nine Morgens, their colours, qualities and creatures, as I heard them speak.

Through the winter the conference ceremony group met several times to develop the ceremonial space of the conference and priestesses began to emerge to play the roles of the Nine Morgens at different times in the Conference. The Conference would celebrate the Nine Morgens as well as the power of groups of women and men working in circle. The idea was that several different groups of nine would play the roles of the Morgens in different situations.

I knew that the Morgens wanted to be specifically embodied so they could speak their own words of wisdom to the whole conference. For an earlier conference, Priestess of Avalon Suthisa Hein from Holland, had created a wonderful *Goddess Alphabet* presentation in which priestesses embodied different Goddesses from all over the world with special words, movements and gestures, in something like a Goddess yoga. I imagined that we could do something similar with the Nine Morgens, which would hopefully give people an experience of their energy and presence.

Throughout the spring the priestesses in the ceremony group, who hold the ceremonial energy for the whole Conference, and those who would present the Nine Morgens, slowly gathered. Each began to write their Morgen presentations based on the keywords the Morgens had given and on their own inspiration. As their speeches developed we would listen to them with shivers running down our spines as each woman captured the essence of her Morgen. Too cleverly I had tried to assign priestesses to Morgens by age, the youngest being Thitis and the oldest Tyronoe. However during the process I somehow got the whole thing mixed up and their ages did not follow incrementally. When it came to their performance we all agreed that everyone was in the right role. The Goddesses work their magic despite our human attempts at control!

As the Morgens were gathering Goddess painter and sculptor Foosiya (Freddie) Miller, with the help of artist Diane Milstein, began the huge task of designing and creating nine wicker Morgen statues, which would be a focus for devotion and ceremony during the Conference. As the conference came closer they worked tirelessly to make nine beautiful Goddesses, each six feet tall with similarly shaped bodies, outstretched arms and sublime faces. The decoration around each of their faces was a different colour for each Morgen - their own individual colour, in materials dyed specially by Koko Newport. They looked stunning. During the Conference they appeared together in endless combinations, in smaller and greater circles, enclosing a dancing ground, in lines of colour and as an arc surrounding artist Monica Sjoo in her special healing ceremony.

Sophie Pullinger, who had played Thitis in *And They Call Her Name Wisdom*, was Thitis again in the Conference, keeping a thread of relatedness alive. Aine Carey, a young American woman who is one of my spiritual daughters/sisters, and who has served the Conference many times, was Cliton. Priestesses of Avalon Heather Adams and Carol Morgan shared the role of Thetis, with Heather, another beautiful American woman in the ceremony group, and Carol in the Morgen presentation, where she showed us a different sexual face to her normally quiet demeanour. Sister Priestesses Sandra Brant and Geraldine Charles played Gliten, Sandra in the ceremony group, Geraldine in the presentation. I was Glitonea in the ceremony group and my counterpart in the Morgen presentation was Juliet Yelverton, who came in at the last moment to play the role so well. The effervescent Sally Pullinger was Moronoe and Ren Chapman was a scary

Mazoe. My old friend and sister priestess Leona Graham played Crone Tyronoe, and poet and Priestess of Avalon Rose Flint at her most magnetic and mysterious was Morgen la Fey.

During the conference the plan was that in the *Heart of the Mysteries Ceremony* conferees would also receive an Oracle from the Nine Morgens, each person randomly approaching a different unknown Morgen to hear Her words of wisdom for them. Each woman in the Presentation and Oracle groups tuned into their Morgen, spending time with Her in their own way. Before and during the conference the Morgen group pulled closely together under Rose's watchful guidance, journeying to the Tor to invoke the Nine Morgens and meeting each day to connect with each other.

By the beginning of the conference we were all aware that the Morgens were approaching. In the Opening Ceremony they came flying in their black crow forms wearing the black cloaks and crow headdresses made specially for the occasion by Sandra Brant. There was a moment of great synchronicity for Sandra, who had placed a differently coloured crescent moon on each of the Morgen masks. When she saw Freddie's Morgen statues she realised that she and Koko had picked exactly the same shades of colour for each of the Morgens, without talking to each other about it. When the ceremonialists removed their crow cloaks their individual colours shone through beneath beautiful misty diaphanous violet cloaks, made specially for us by Irene Sheppard, and their energy was opened out for all to experience.

On the second morning of the conference the presentation of the Nine Morgens was a mysterious and stunning event. Almost as soon as the Morgens entered the Temple space in the Town Hall I found myself crying at their appearance. Tears rolled down my cheeks as the Nine Women embodied the mystery of the Nine Morgens. I was so moved by their movements, their energy, the way they looked and the inspired words that they spoke, which had been written by each of the nine women. I continued to cry all the way through the performance, and it was so much more than performance. It was embodiment of the Nine. The dam of anxiety in me about whether it would work was broken and the Morgens flooded in. I relaxed, everything was going to be very fine. They were truly here.

The words of each of the nine women who embodied the Morgens that day are given in each of the following chapters on the wheel of the year. It is nigh on impossible to capture a Goddess appearance on paper, but in their words lie an essence of each of these mysterious Nine Ladies.

We have been learning some essentials about the Morgens each year on the Morgen Retreat, which comes at Samhain. Most Goddesses that we learn about come to us as individuals, whereas the Morgens may come as individuals or as a group of nine. They present to us a new archetype of how to work together spiritually in groups of equals at this time, just as they work together as a group of equal Goddesses with different powers. Part of the Morgen Retreat involves embodiment of the Morgens by nine women and men. In this practice we learn how to create a web of relationship between us so that we connect to each other's divinity, speaking for the Morgens as part of a circle. We embody different aspects of the Goddess, delving more deeply together into the Morgen's mysteries for revelation and healing in ways that are not possible when we work alone.

In the Goddess Temple we are now offering healing Morgen Oracles at some Full Moons in which nine priestesses oracle for the Nine Morgens. These have been amazingly powerful oracles in which the nine delve deeply into the substance of an individual's suffering, offering love, empathy, wisdom and insight to the enquirer in truly remarkable ways.

With the Lady of Avalon we learn directly about love and transformation for ourselves and others as individuals. With the Nine Morgens we learn how to be together in love and community.

The Sacred Landscape of Glastonbury Avalon

The ancient pathways to the Isle of Avalon have been lost and there is now no formally recognised tradition that shows us how to become Priestesses of the Lady and of Avalon. We only have our dreams, our imagination and Her inspiration. To find Her once again we begin by remembering Her within the landscape which is Her body. We learn how to reconnect to the Isle of Avalon through the landscape of Glastonbury Avalon.

Goddess spirituality is an embodied spiritual pathway. To find the Lady of Avalon we start by opening our eyes to the physical world, to the shapes and forms of the island of Glastonbury Avalon, its contours, heights and depths. We become aware of the ever-changing seasons of Her nature in this land - the springtime which brings bright greens to the island, mirrored in surrounding floodwaters; the summer when the Great Mother basks in the heat haze that hovers above the land; the autumn when the Mists rise at dusk and dawn, obscuring the island and its Mysteries; and winter when the White Swan may reveal Herself in the frost and snow-covered hills. We learn to re-cognise the air we breathe, the water we drink, the fires that warm us, the food that we eat, all of which She freely gives to us. We look at everything with fresh eyes. This is the primary place from which we begin.

We experience the Goddess differently depending on where we live in the world. We may live on mountains, beside volcanoes, on flat plains or rolling hills, beside lakes, rivers or oceans, in rain forests or fields, in deserts or endless steppes. We may be unconscious of where we live. Many of us live in cities with little idea of what our natural surroundings may look like. All locations influence the way that we experience Her.

A mighty River Goddess demonstrates to us the ever-changing continuous flow of Her life and annually She may inundate our homes and valleys with flood waters, which wash away the old and bring fertility and renewal to the land. Her qualities are different to the gentler mirror-like reflections of the Lady of the Lake. In the forests we meet Her as the Green Lady and Lady of the Trackways, beside the sea as the Mother of the Oceans, Queen of the Deep, Source of all Life, Mother of Storms and Tempests. In the deserts She is a hot radiant Queen of Fire. In the mountains She is Mountain Mother, whose great age demonstrates the aeons to us. The Volcano Goddess we honour lest She blows us off Her mountain tops. In cities we have to open wide our imaginations to glimpse Her forms, hidden beneath the layers of concrete.

The Goddess often appears in womanly forms within landscapes, such as the Cailleach na Montaigne (the Old Woman of the Mountains) in the Hebrides in Scotland. Hills and mountains are often shaped like Her pregnant womb or full breasts, as in the Paps of Anu in Eire, or the Paps of Jura in the Western Isles. Wooded valleys, clefts in rocks, are Her secret intimate vulval spaces. Red waters flow as Her menstrual blood and white waters are healing and filled with creation. Her forms appear everywhere if we have the eyes to see.

It is no different here in Avalon. To find the Goddess we look into the shapes of the Outerworld landscape of Glastonbury to glimpse the forms of the Innerworld of Avalon. Many years ago when I started my quest to find the Goddess in Glastonbury I looked for Her daily as I walked Her hills and valleys, sat upon Her earth, beneath Her trees, gazing to the horizon, listening to the sounds of Her nature in this holy place. My earlier books describe the results of that exploration and include *The Goddess in Glastonbury* and *In the Nature of Avalon* (Ariadne Publications). I would recommend that anyone who wishes to become a Priestess of Avalon spends time walking Glastonbury's sacred landscape, uncovering Her ancient secrets which lie hidden here in the land.

The Glastonbury landscape is formed from a cluster of small hills, which was once a promontory connected to the mainland of the Mendip Hills and surrounded by the waters of a large lake. Earlier it was an island surrounded by an inland sea. Millions of years earlier, it is claimed (see BBC website www.bbc.co.uk/somerset/nature/walks/03.shtml), a red iron-rich Spring first arose on a sandy plateau. Over the aeons the red waters soaked into the sand, gradually hardening it into red sandstone. Over time and especially after the end of the last ice age some 11,000 years ago, the ice sheets lying to the north melted and water poured out across the land, washing away the softer sand, leaving harder red sandstone behind. We see this today in the red sandstone of Glastonbury Tor and the surrounding smaller hills. Amazingly the ancient Red Spring still flows in the present at Chalice Well, as well as many other smaller springs dotted across the landscape.

Today the hills of the Glastonbury landscape rise out of the flat meadow lands of the Somerset Levels. For hundreds of years these levels were covered with watery marshland, pools and lakes. Before this the waters of the Atlantic Ocean came inland surrounding the small hills of Glastonbury's natural landscape, creating a distinctive western island rising out of the sea. Over a thousand years ago the monks of Glastonbury Abbey began to build barriers between the Rivers Axe and Parrett eighteen miles to the west to keep the sea at bay. They dug great drains to take the water that pours from the surrounding higher hills, out to the Bristol Channel, as well as rhynes - deep ditches, around the edges of the newly created fields. The Somerset levels began to dry out and slowly lifted out of the sea as the continental shelf itself rose.

Today the island with its prominent high Tor is surrounded by flat green fields and then at several miles distance on three sides by hills, and on the fourth by the waters of the Bristol Channel, which flow into the Atlantic Ocean. This cauldron-like landscape with its prominent central hill is found at many other ancient Goddess sites around the world, such as Phaistos in Krete, and Ephesus in Turkey. Ancient peoples recognised these natural landscape bowls as carrying powerful spiritual and earth energies and built Goddess temples, shrines and sacred enclosures in such places. The surrounding hills provide marker points for astronomical events viewed from the central island, and vice versa, such as the rising or setting of the sun, moon and planets, or of particular groupings of distant stars at different times of the year. The movements of the stars reflected the lives and mythology of the tribes who lived beneath them and were used to tell the stories of the ancestors, and to predict the future of the people. This is an art which we, with all our modern advanced technologies have almost completely lost and our cultures are less for it.

A *Personal Quest to Find the Goddess in Glastonbury*

On my personal quest to find the Goddess in my homeland I began by looking for Her firstly in the shapes of the hills that make up the landscape of Glastonbury with its five hills and small valleys. I felt that if She was anywhere She had to be here in the forms of the natural landscape. I took an ordnance survey map of the area and began looking at the contours of the hills with my partner, Mike Jones. The first thing I noticed was that the five hills of Glastonbury - the Tor, Chalice Hill, Wearyall Hill, Windmill Hill and Stonedown, seemed together to form a bunch of flowers, a bouquet of beauty. Then Mike said,

"*Look, it's a bird flying across the landscape.*"

And there on the map with outstretched wings and long neck was the form of a swan flying from the northeast to the southwest, encompassing all of Glastonbury's sacred hills. It was an eureka moment.

In my researches of Goddess connections to Glastonbury I had been learning about St Bridget or St Bride, who was said to have visited Glastonbury from Kildare in Ireland in the fifth century CE, staying on a small mound to the southwest of Glastonbury, that became known as Beckery, the Beckery Salmon and Little Eire. Today it is known as Bride's Mound. St. Bridget was modelled on the earlier Fire Goddess Brigit, Bride, Brighde, Bridie, Bree-je or Brid, whose name we honour in Brigit's Isles. She is the ancient Goddess of all these lands and Her name originally meant *goddess*. She rules all the elements of earth, water, fire and air, and all the directions. Like many other Goddesses, Her power and status were diminished within patriarchal religions and She was reduced to the role of saint, rather than powerful Sovereign Goddess of Nature.

Traditionally Brigit is associated with four or more animals and birds. Her first creature is the White Cow with the Red Ears, an Otherworldly animal. Like the Sacred Cow in India, Brighde is honoured as the universal Mother Goddess, whose milk created the Milky Way in the heavens. Like Hathor the Egyptian Goddess She is imaged as a cow and later as a having woman's head with cow's ears. Then like Isis, She became a woman with cow horns on the top of Her head, enclosing the sun or moon. In Her earlier form as a Fire Goddess, the fifth century St Bridget was depicted with a fiery halo and was said to own large tracts of the Curragh near Kildare for her cattle to graze upon and on which they still graze to this day. On the front of St Michael's tower on top of Glastonbury Tor and in Glastonbury Abbey, St Bridget modelled on the early Cow Mother, is depicted as a woman milking a cow. Such are the ways in which the powers of feminine divinity are diminished within patriarchal thought and imagery.

A second creature associated with Bridie is the snake or serpent of regeneration, which hides beneath the omphalos or Oracle stone, where Her priestesses spoke Her inspired words of poetry. The wolf, the dark lone guardian of transformation also belongs to Bride. Brigit's fourth sacred creature and the cause of my delight at Her appearance on the map, is the beautiful White Swan, who swims on water, walks on land and flies through the air.

Primary Contours of the Glastonbury Avalon Landscape

AnnMarie Hopper

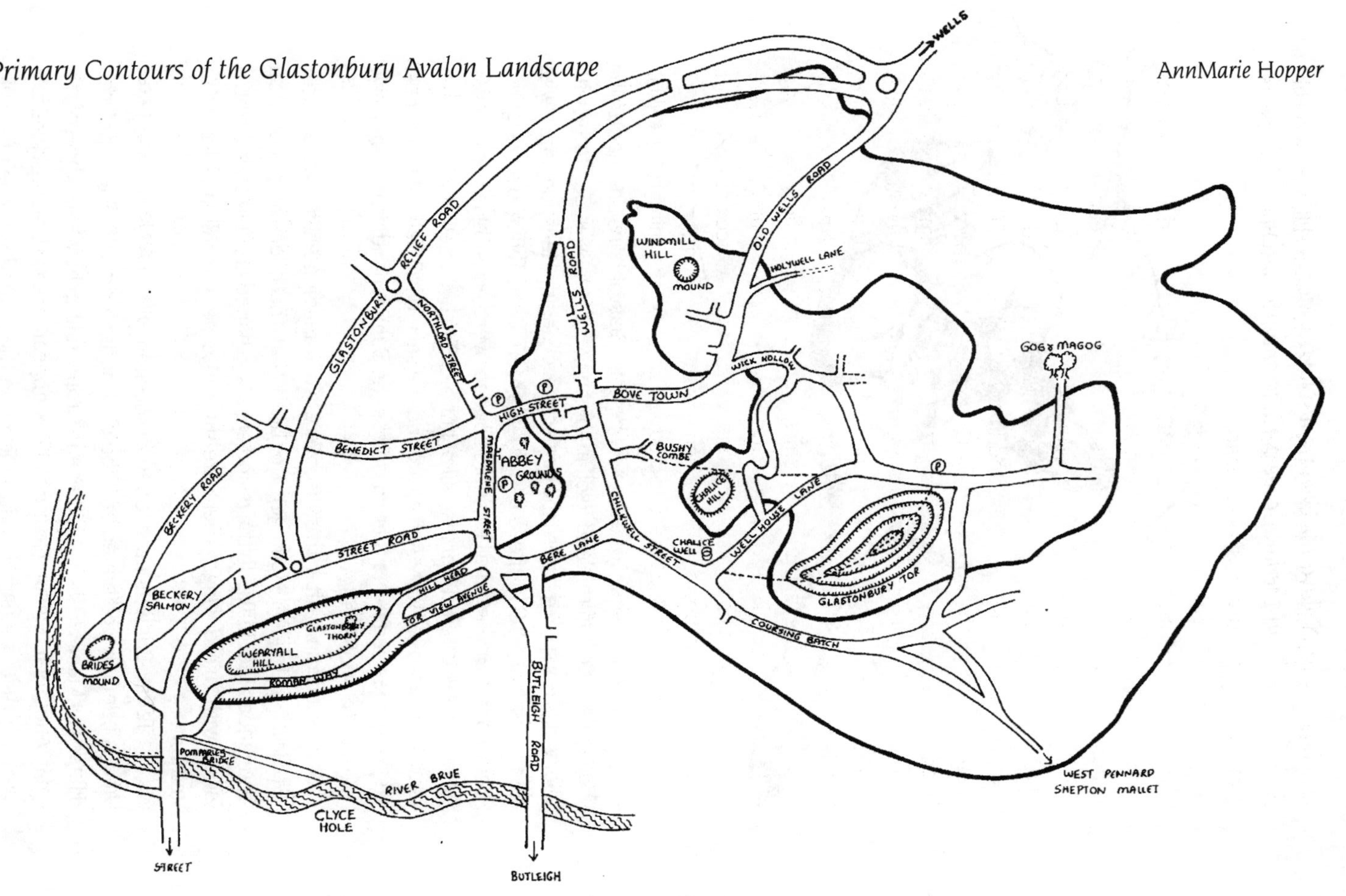

Nolava the Swan and Nolava the Crone
in the landscape of Glastonbury Avalon

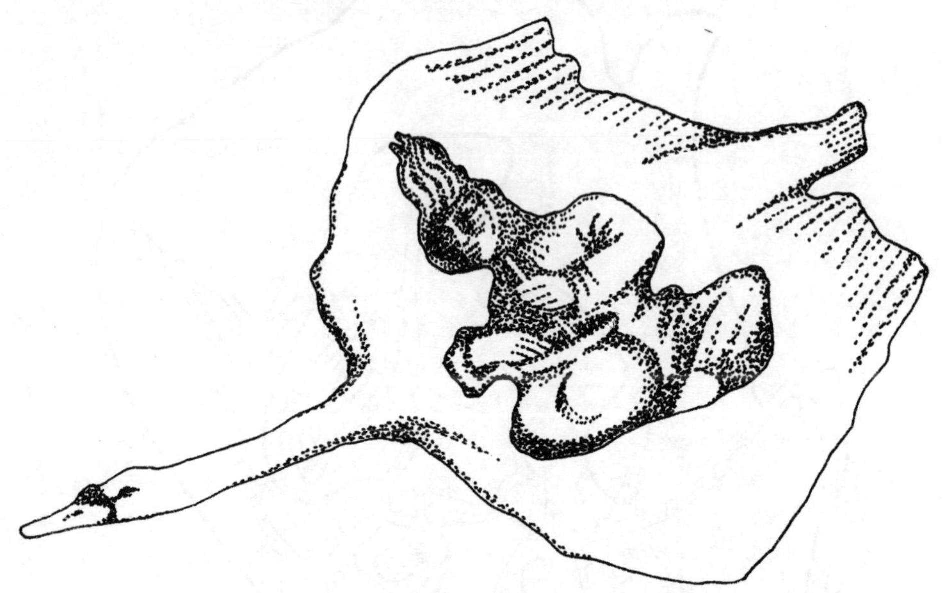

Foosiya Miller

Of course the Goddess was here in Glastonbury, She had to be here. She is here in the land itself in the image of Her Swan Self flying with Her wings outspread across the landscape, changing Her appearance with the seasons. She is most usually a green swan flying over a green background, or when the Levels are flooded over a glassy blue background. In winter and often at Her festival of Imbolc, She becomes white with frost and snow, a white swan. And all around the sacred isle pairs of swans nest in the rhynes and rivers that crisscross the Summerland, where they give birth to their offspring.

Some time after this discovery, while reading Philip Ratz's book, *Glastonbury* (English Heritage), I noticed that the underlying geological formations that make up the island are also shaped like a swan in flight, a swan with raised wings. There are mysteries here in the land for us to fathom.

Today Bridie is most often associated with the Maiden Goddess and is primarily celebrated at Imbolc, although originally She expressed Herself as Maiden, Lover, Mother and Crone, ruling the whole wheel of the year. Another interesting feature of Her appearance in the landscape as a Swan, is that at a higher contour level on the map, the shape of an Old

Crone is also visible, perched at a Picasso-like angle on the Swan's back. She kneels with bent back, rounded Chalice Hill breast and sagging Tor Cauldron/Womb, Her crowned head is formed by the top of Windmill Hill. She is the Dark Goddess, the one whom everyone complains of meeting on their Glastonbury journeys.

A synchronous affirmation came the day after we made these discoveries as I was driving out of St John's car park towards the old Glastonbury Library. There in the window was a large three-dimensional contour map of the landscape of Glastonbury, made by local artist Simant Bostock. He had built up the image using layers of white wood on a green background of the Somerset levels and there in 3D was the White Swan flying across the landscape. The Crone, also in white, was visible upon Her back. The timing was impeccable.

Having found the Maiden as Swan and the Crone in the landscape, where was the Lover/Mother to complete the ancient Goddess triplicity/ quarternary?

Geoffrey Ashe, the Arthurian scholar who lives in Glastonbury, had mentioned that the figure of a giant Goddess lying on Her back in the landscape, could be seen when approaching the island from the southeast,

Nolava the Lover in the Landscape

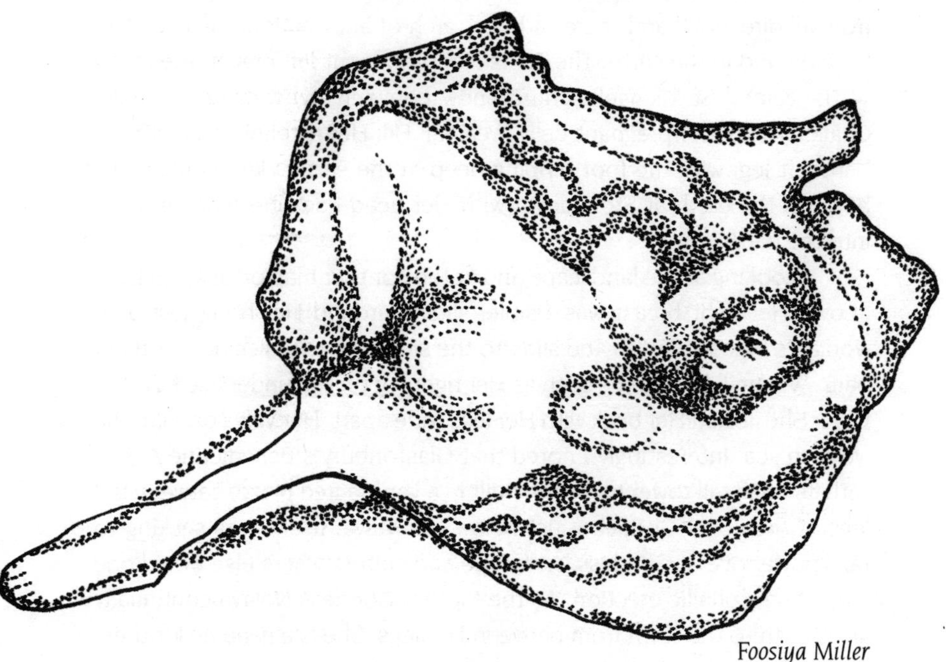

Foosiya Miller

Nolava the Mother in the Landscape

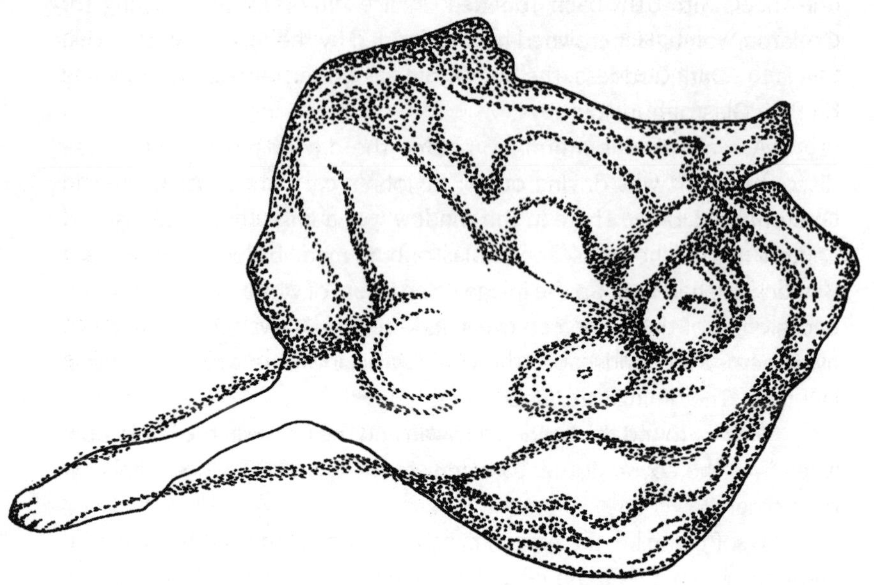

Foosiya Miller

from Baltonsborough. I drove out into the Summerland viewing the island from all directions and there with a stretch of imagination She is visible, lying on and in the earth. The Tor is Her prominent left breast, the tower of the ruined St Michael's church now conveniently forming a nipple. Chalice Hill is Her pregnant belly, Wearyall Hill Her extended and slightly bent left leg, with the foot dipping deep in the earth. Her shoulders lie back on the earth at Stonedown with Her head back descending down into the earth.

Looking at the landscape and at the contour map once again from above, Her right breast was visible, sliding around Her body, just as a woman's breasts flatten and slide to the side when she lies down on her back. Windmill Hill can be seen as Her right leg tucked under itself. As the Lover She lies on Her back with Her legs wide apart, Her Vulva open to the western sea. Interestingly I noted that Glastonbury's Benedictine Abbey with its once tall tower had been built in a very sacred place, between the legs of the Lover Goddess, just below Her Vulva. If one was seeking to take power over a Goddess landscape and culture where else would one place one's phallic erection. As the Mother Goddess Nolava continually gives birth to the town from between Her legs, She is a genuine Mother.

I had been making clay sculptures of goddesses for a few years and decided to create these goddess landscape forms in clay. I made a three dimensional landscape Swan with a black Crone riding on Her back, so that She was more visible. I made a separate sculpture of the kneeling Crone and one of the Lover/Mother Goddess. Making these sculptures brought the images of Maiden, Lover, Mother and Crone alive for me.

Because Glastonbury is the Outerworld counterpart to the Innerworld of Avalon if we want to journey into Avalon it is very important to become familiar with the physical landscape of the now land-enclosed island. One of the secrets revealed here is that a knowledge of the outer landscape will lead us into Avalon and to the Lady Herself. I cannot emphasise enough the importance of this to would-be priestesses. The land holds the secrets of Avalon.

There are places all over the island that are gateways between the worlds, where the Veil that separates the visible and invisible worlds is particularly thin and we can step through into Avalon. Many people visiting Glastonbury for a day or more, may inadvertently wander through the Veil. They are often deeply inspired by these experiences which catalyse spiritual development, or they are shocked by what they see and scuttle away to less challenging lands. The practice of a Priestess of Avalon is to become conscious of the Veil and to learn to move through it at will.

Particular gateways between the worlds can be found on Chalice Hill, on the Tor, on Wearyall Hill, Stonedown, Bride's Mound and in the Abbey grounds. One of the most potent spots on the island lies in the Crypt beneath the Mary Chapel, near to the reclaimed Mary or St Joseph's Well, where the oldest stonework in the Abbey was found. This ancient holy spring is aligned over Chalice Hill to the Tor and is probably the reason why the first wattle Christian church was built here, next to a sacred spring, which had been honoured long before the first Christians arrived.

Knowledge of the physical landscape of Glastonbury also holds the key to psychic journeying into Avalon. In meditation and conscious visualisation we see ourselves walking within the physical landscape of Glastonbury Avalon, where Otherworldly beings reveal themselves in physically familiar locations. As Priestesses of Avalon it is important to have this knowledge and experience, firmly held in our consciousness.

The Outer Veils

The whole island lies in the centre of the surrounding landscape cauldron and can be experienced as being encircled by Outer Veils of energy.

As we approach Glastonbury from any direction, at specific places on the road we feel our attention being drawn to the island. These places are energetic gateways, where we first notice the distinctive shapes of the Tor and other hills, which change depending on which direction we come from. Travelling from Pilton the Tor looks steeper and more mountainous than the approach from Meare to the west, where we can feel ourselves being enfolded between the legs of the Mother Goddess as we journey inwards to Her body.

Turning a corner as we near the island we feel our eyes drawn to the mythical landscape. We have the feeling of coming home to a place of mystery and joy.

Pilgrimage to the Lady *of* Avalon

For priestesses, pilgrimage to the Lady of Avalon is a spiritual practice in which we journey to Her holy places within Glastonbury's sacred landscape, which is the outer form of the inner world of the Isle of Avalon. We make our pilgrimages as an act of devotion, an act of love for Her. It is both an outer and an inner journey, which we can make alone or in the company of others.

There are five phases to any pilgrimage. The first is to make the decision to pilgrimage to the sacred place of the Goddess with spiritual intent. The second phase is our pilgrimage to the sacred place itself, our journey to Glastonbury from our homes if we live elsewhere, or from our homes within Glastonbury. The third phase is our entry into a defined temenos or sacred enclosure, which is the sacred landscape of Avalon, recognising when we are crossing over from this world into Avalon. The fourth phase encompasses all our personal prayers and devotions to the Lady at the various energy centres, power spots and natural and human made altars within the temenos. The fifth and final phase is our return to everyday reality bringing the fruits of our communion with Her back into the world.

On our pilgrimage we are journeying to meet the Lady of Avalon in the forms in which She chooses to reveal Herself to us. We can plan our route to include paths and roads, orchards and pasture land or we can be moved in the moment to walk this way or that, guided by Her voice. As we walk with intent upon Her body subtle and sometimes vibrant colours and forms may appear all around us. As we hear Her sweet birds singing in the orchards or Her Morgen crows caw-cawing on the Tor, we may be lucky enough to see Her sitting beside them. We may hear the Lady's words of wisdom whispered on the wind. As we create ceremonies for the Lady She may appear to us. All we have to do is open our hearts, focus our attention on meeting Her and we will begin to see and hear what is normally invisible.

Entering Avalon is all about consciousness, awareness and perception. It is about opening the heart to other dimensions of reality as we walk through the town and countryside of Glastonbury. It is about recognising that there is more to life than meets the eye. It is about seeking and finding mystery beneath the surfaces of the obvious.

To make your pilgrimage to the Goddess in Avalon in any form the advice is simple:

* Open your eyes and ears as you journey through the landscape. Notice the birds who come to speak to you, the animals and people who appear at relevant moments. Notice what you see out of the corner of your eyes and allow what is there to reveal itself to you. Let shapes and forms emerge into greater detail so that you can see the Faeries, the Priestesses of old or the Lady Herself.

* Visualise the shining threads of the Web of Wyrd which connect everything within the temenos and the landscape and allow your visions to become real. See yourself leaving a trail of shining light as you move from one place to another in the landscape.

* Open your ears as you journey or as you sit quietly in the landscape. Allow the phrases and words that come into your mind to be true and to have been spoken by someone other than yourself.

* Take note of the synchronicities that begin to happen as you make your pilgrimage within the landscape of Avalon. Synchronicity is the mark of Her presence.

If you wish to enhance your meditative state repeat wordlessly or out loud, a Goddess mantra as you journey, which helps keep the mind focused on the purpose of your pilgrimage as well as invoking the presence of the Lady. A simple one is:

Maiden, Lover, Mother, Crone
Lady of Avalon, bring me home.

In Glastonbury we are fortunate that the Goddess shows us many faces and we can make pilgrimage to Her in different forms: as Nolava the Lady of Avalon, as Bridie, as Madron the Great Mother, as the Crone, as the Nine Morgens, as Goddess Mary, as Lady of the Holy Springs and Wells, Lady of the Lake and as Lady of the Tor Labrynth. Several pilgrimage routes are described in detail with prayers and practices in my earlier book,

In the Nature of Avalon (Ariadne Publications).

On any pilgrimage to the Goddess our priestess practice is to make offerings to Her whenever and wherever we remember Her: on Her sacred land, at any threefold junction or trivia, at Her natural and human made altars, in ritual spaces, burial grounds, stone circles, sacred mounds, on the tops of hills and mountains, beside Her sacred wells and waters. The Lady loves offerings of flowers, herbs, seeds, grains, incense, holy spring water, scattered in gratitude on the earth wherever we stop to pray, as well as placed in small bowls on Her altars. All offerings should be biodegradable so that they return harmlessly back to Her body.

Find a special bag to contain the offerings that you wish to make to her. One of my favourites is a mixture of lavender, rosemary and rose petals.

Making a pilgrimage to the Goddess within any landscape can have unexpected and far reaching effects, that stir the imagination and inspire the pilgrim. In the 2004 Glastonbury Goddess Conference our particular focus was to celebrate Bridie and the Maiden Goddess in Her many forms, as well as the maidens in our company. As part of the conference, following an ages old tradition we planned to make a processional pilgrimage to four power centres within Glastonbury's sacred landscape to *Sing the Land Alive*. Our intention was to invoke Bridie's healing energy and then send it out from Avalon to the whole of Brigit's Isles and beyond. We were to spiral through the landscape, connecting to the elements, earth on top of Chalice Hill, air on top of the Tor, water at Chalice Well and fire in Bushey Combe. In each ceremony we would invoke the Goddesses on Britannia's Wheel, raise energy and send healing out to the world, through the ley lines of the earth, through the air, waters and fires.

On the morning of the pilgrimage day as I described to the conference what we would be attempting to do together later in the day, I felt the first inklings of a creation story for the Isle of Avalon, come into my consciousness. That night, after eight hours of wonderful pilgrimage and ceremony on the sacred land, I received a fuller story. Over the following year it has filled out into a modern day herstorical *Creation Myth for the Isle of Avalon and the sacred lands of Glastonbury*, based in the past, present and future.

I offer this myth to you as a sacred gift.

The Creation Herstory of the Isle of Avalon

Once upon a time, long, long, long ago, Ertha our Mother Earth, was just a young Maiden, a blue green planet, spinning in space, encircled by Luna, Her moon. One springtime as Luna came to Her fullness, Ertha felt a new confidence arise within Her body. From deep within Her Source, Ertha felt a rumbling, as the First of Her many Eggs of new life, which had lain dormant since Her own conception, began to ripen. First Egg grew with the Moon, filling herself with the Potential for Life. When she was full she emerged from the Source and journeyed through long subterranean passages until she reached Ertha's vast waiting Womb. First Egg rolled across the threshold into the enormous cavern. She explored the great rocky Womb and as she did moved about iron-rich lifeblood and waters were secreted from its walls, creating a thick red lining. First Egg became coated by the blood-red waters.

After one half of Luna's long cycle Ertha felt pressure building within Her body. It began as a dull ache which increased until it became strong and almost unbearable. Her belly began to shudder and Ertha groaned with discomfort as Her womb squeezed and shook. Her earth quaked and opened. From the depths fiery molten rocks rose up and spewed out over the ground. Mountains exploded and fell. New land emerged from the depths of the seas. New oceans flowed where once there had been land. At the Dark Moon First Egg and the Red Womb lining which surrounded her were released from their place of safety in a gush of Red Bloodwater. The Potential for Life left First Egg and entered the Red Waters.

On the southern edge of the great continent of Laurasia, Ertha's Maiden Vulva opened and Her First Blood sprang forth from Her innermost secret place as a Red Spring. It emerged from the earth first as a trickle, which soon become a torrent. It gathered in a rust red pool which overflowed into a red stream, that snaked its way down across the sloping ground towards the distant ocean. As the Red Spring poured from Her

Vulva, the pressures in Ertha's body eased and She settled into more pleasurable feelings of release. The Red Springwater was filled with First Egg's Potential for Life and contained strong healing energies. As it flowed out across the land small plants and animals drank thirstily of the Red Mead and were enlivened and healed of their diseases. Over time seeds sprouted and plants began to grow around the Red Spring and the green oasis that formed became known as the Garden of Paradise.

Because of the great capacity of Her Womb the Red Bloodwater did not dry up after the release of First Egg, but miraculously continued to flow out from Her Vulva at a near constant rate. Periodically Eggs would emerge from Her Source, spend time within Her great Womb, then release their Potential for Life into Her Bloodwaters, which flowed to the surface. Over time as knowledge of the powers of the Red Spring spread across Laurasia, many creatures came to be healed of their diseases. From that first day of Her menarche aeons ago to this, Ertha's Bloodwaters have continued to flow in an endless stream of creation and healing from Her Source.

Over time with the fluctuations of Ertha's life the continent of Laurasia changed shape, but the Red Spring continued to flow. At times the surrounding land was warm and covered in green vegetation and at other times it cooled and was covered in snow. Sometimes the Red Spring flowed in a Paradise Garden and at other times it emerged from beneath thick ice. The huge land mass of Laurasia slowly separated, the continents drifting apart. Water flowed between the limbs of the land and the world we know today gradually took shape, with its seven continents, including Europa's land. Many species of animals and plants evolved, lived for a span on Ertha's body and then became extinct through ice, storm, flood and fire.

The Red Spring flowed even as the last ice age recorded in historical time began to freeze the land and the northern parts of Europa's continent was covered in snow and ice several miles thick in places. The weight of the ice pressed down on the land, flattening hills and mountains, freezing the oceans, lowering seal levels. Most organic life left the land retreating south and only the hardy bears, wolves, foxes, hares and ptarmigan remained to face the icy wastes. The land was covered in ice for thousands of years

After a long, long, long time, early one morning as Imbolc approached, Nolava the Swan Maiden came flying across the snow-covered land. Encircling the globe She followed the curving Dragon Line in Ertha's body, which ran from the northeast to the southwest. The earth below was cold and inhospitable, but Her intention was focused. She had been sent on a journey of initiation by Her Mother Brigit. She was to make Pilgrimage to Ertha's Vulva, to the Red Bloodspring. She was to seek and find the green and fertile Paradise Garden that led to Ertha's Source. When She found it She was to pray for the return of warmth and light to all the world.

Nolava flew high above the frozen landscape sometimes in clear frosty air and sometimes beneath thick snow-filled clouds. Far, far away She could see the western edges of Europa's land with its outlying islands surrounded by frozen seas. As the wintery northern Winds blew Her onwards Nolava spoke to the Wind and whoever else might hear Her,

"In honour of my Mother I *name these lands* Brigit's Isles, *for when the ice and snow have melted She will be celebrated here as* Mother *of* Air, Fire, Water *and* Earth. *She shall be known as* Banbha, *Lady of the* Land *from before the* Flood, *as* Brigantia, *Lady of this* Land, *and as* Britannia, *She who is* Brigit *Ana, Great* Mother *and* Guardian *Goddess of these lands."*

Nolava flew onwards bending Her neck to one side and then the other. She was tired, cold and hungry. Her feather coat was ruffled and covered in ice crystals. She had been flying for many days and now searched for a safe place to land. As She flew to the southwest of Brigit's Isles Nolava looked down and saw something odd in the vast whiteness below Her. Beneath a layer of ice She saw a large red stain with a red thread emerging from it. Attracted by the colour She flew down to investigate. She came closer and landed skitter-skattering on the ice, Her webbed feet clumsy on the slippery surface. She could hear the sound of water running beneath the ice and realised how thirsty She was.

She tapped the ice with Her beak, but it was very thick. She tapped again, this time a little harder, chipping the ice away. She felt the ice begin to give. She tapped harder still and the ice cracked. A small hole appeared and peering through Nolava saw Red Water flowing beneath the ice. It looked drinkable. She opened the crack further with her beak and snaking Her long neck through the hole, She drank of the Red Waters. They tasted good and strong and She drank thirstily. As She drank She felt healing energies entering Her body and easing Her exhaustion.

The ice around the hole began to crack under Nolava's weight, slivers breaking off and falling into the Red Water. As the hole in the ice grew larger Nolava saw beneath Her a Red Spring emerging from the frozen earth and flowing into a Red Pool. From the Pool a Red Stream flowed beneath the ice towards the frozen ocean. With growing excitement Nolava realised what She had found. Her heart filled with gratitude,

"*Blessed am I, for I have found the* Red Bloodspring. *I have found* Ertha's Holy Vulva, *the* Entrance *to the* Womb *and* Source *of all life.* Ertha, *I give thanks for your sacred* Bloodwaters. *I pray for the return of light and warmth to the world, for the return of your life in many forms of being.*"

The ice hole was still not large enough for Nolava to safely swim upon the water so She bent Her neck once again through the enlarging hole and drank more of the Red Water. She drank Her fill and then rested upon the ice beside the Blood Spring. The snow creatures, the ptarmigan, snow hares and foxes, who had long lived among the icy wastes, who drew sustenance from the Red Spring, had watched in awe as the great White Swan came in to land. From their nests and burrows they whispered to one another,

"*The* White Lady *has come!* Blessed *be this day She has come to fulfil our prophecies. She has come to save us.*"

Through the clouds Greinne the Sun Goddess began to glimmer Her golden rays and looking down on Nolava's exhausted and bedraggled body She parted the clouds and smiled Her beautiful golden smile. The Swan Maiden had persevered through many trials to reach Ertha's Vulva and Greinne was pleased for Her. Looking up Nolava felt the gentle warmth of Greinne's gaze and Her body began to relax for the first time in many days. She shook the ice crystals of Her journey from Her feathers and nestled down onto the snow. All around Her under the heat of the Sun Mother's radiant gaze the snow and ice started to melt. The ice that covered the Red Spring, Pool and Stream began to ebb away until Nolava could clearly see all three against the surrounding snow. The snow and ice which covered the land began to run off in rivulets, which splashed into streams, which gathered into rivers, that flowed to the distant, still frozen ocean.

As the air and the land warmed around Her, Nolava decided to remove Her damp Cloak of Feathers so it could dry more easily under Sun Mother's rays. She took off Her Swan Coat and spread it out upon the melting snow. Beneath the feathers Her skin was pale Violet and from Her body a Violet Radiance emanated outwards in all directions, blessing the land and all who lived upon it. Her Violet Essence streamed forth touching everything in its path, transforming it with Her love and compassion, sparking the etheric threads that wove across the land.

Nolava spread out Her swan wings and body on the ground and stretched out Her neck, so that Her feather cloak lay outspread as if flying from the northeast to the southwest. She curved Her wing feathers carefully around the Red Spring. The Maiden Nolava sat naked, Her skin pale and violet, bathing in the warmth of Greinne's rays as all around Her snow and ice melted away, dripping with water, and Her Swan Cloak dried in the Sun.

Soon Nolava felt thirsty again and bent down to the Spring, cupping Her hands to drink the Red Water that seemed warmer than the ice. Then She remembered Her most precious possession, Her Maiden Grael. She took it out and dipped it into the Red Spring. She filled Her Grael with the Red Bloodwater and drew in the refreshing Red Mead. She filled Her Grael again and again and raising it to the sky, cried,

"Mother Earth, I give thanks to you for your life-giving Bloodwaters. I give thanks to you, Greinne, Sun Mother, whose smile melts the coldest ice. I give thanks to my Mother Brigit who bore me, to my Swan Clan, and to all my Ancestors and Relations throughout all time.

Beloved Ertha, I offer you my Holy Maiden Grael. I am ready, Lady. May it be as a blessing to all who come seeking your Source."

Nolava carefully lowered Her Maiden Grael into the Red Spring and in that moment Her own First Bloodwaters were released into the Red, mingling with Ertha's blood. Her Grael sank down into the Red Deeps. Her offering was given and received.

Nolava felt very tired after Her long journey, She needed to sleep. The only dry place was Her own Swan Cloak, lying on the melting snow. She lay down on Her back under Greinne's golden gaze, on Her cloak of feathers, with Her left leg outstretched along the neck of Her Swan skin and Her right leg tucked under on Her right wing feathers. She laid the rest of Her body on Her wide wings. Almost as soon as She lay down She fell asleep.

As She slept small creatures of the land, white in their winter coats, emerged from their deep burrows to take a peek at the beautiful Swan Maiden who had landed on the ice and then bathed them in Her loving Violet Light. They brought gifts of seeds they had hidden deep within the earth, seeds of green vegetation, of herbs and flowers, to thank Her for bringing Life back to their snowy Wasteland. They laid them beside Her body.

The melting snow waters mingled with the iron-rich waters of the Red Spring and the Red Pool deepened and overflowed beneath Nolava's feather cloak, soaking down into the sandy earth. Nolava slept on. She felt no dampness, protected as She was by Her swan skin. As Nolava slept through the millennia the iron-rich Red Bloodwater soaked into the earth of Her swan body, hardening the soft sandy earth into rocky sandstone. Nolava became earth.

As She slept Nolava dreamed. She dreamed of Her Mother Brigit, She dreamed of Her family, of Her Swan Clan. She missed their warmth and love. As She thought of those She had left behind with sadness, She cried in Her sleep and as She sobbed the earth shook. She dreamed of the past and of the present. She dreamed the future and in the Dream She called to Her Swan family to fly to Her from all across Ertha's body.

As Nolava slept Greinne shone down upon Her each day and upon the whole of Ertha's body. The snow and ice continued to melt and the huge glaciers which once covered the land to the north of the Red Spring, also began to melt and slowly recede. Rushing torrents of melt water released from the glaciers poured out across the land, smoothing hills, widening valleys, removing soft earth, leaving rock behind. Rushing rivers carved out the earth around the Swan Maiden's form, leaving Her high and dry above the waters. The frozen oceans melted too and began to rise, a hundred metres and more. The Great Flood came and all around was water. Soon Nolava's earthly body was a swan-shaped island completely surrounded by the sea. Through all this time the Red Spring continued to flow from Ertha's bounteous Womb, out across the land to the now adjacent ocean.

One Beltane morning as Greinne rose early in the sky Nolava awoke to the sound of the sea lapping against the shorelines of Her naked body. She lay in a sweet reverie, feeling the warmth of the morning sun and the softness of Her earth beneath Her body. A gentle breeze blew over Her naked skin. She looked about and all around Her the land was green and fertile. She had awoken in Paradise. As She lay there She listened to the sweet songs of the birds calling to each other and the rustle of the gentle breeze playing across Her body.

As He rode His dolphins through the ocean waves, Nodens, God of the Sea, espied the beautiful young woman with the violet skin, lying on the earth. Who was She? Her body glowed in the morning sun, Her naked left breast reached up to touch the sky, black crows swooping and diving around Her summit in the breeze, Her right breast sliding over, soft and full. Her left leg was extended to the southwest and Her right leg was tucked under to the northwest. Between Her strong and inviting thighs thick bushes hid Her Vulva. Her belly swelled gently with its sacred mound. From Her head the forest of Her hair streamed back into the waters.

Delighted to see Her, from the edge of the sea, Nodens sang to Nolava. He sang to Her of His watery world, of the shimmering seas, of the great deeps of the oceans, of storms and calm water, of crashing waves and the silent vastness. He sang to Nolava of his Mother Domnu, Lady of the Ocean, Queen of the Deep, Mother of Water, Mother of Emotions, the Source of all Life on earth. He sang of Her great love and compassion and of the pleasures of immersion in Her mystical realms.

As She lay on the earth basking in the waves of His attention, Nolava was pleased to hear Nodens' song. She had been alone for so long. She turned Her head to look at Him and their eyes met for the first time. As She gazed upon His magnificence Her heart opened wide with joy. In turn She sang to Nodens of Her Mother Brigit and Her own origins in Her Swan Clan, the Keepers of the Sacred Flame. She sang of innocence, of hope and of healing. She sang too of Greinne the Sunfire Mother who watches over the world by day, who had melted the snows, who gives life to all. She sang of the Starfire Mother who each night lights up the heavens and showers the world with Her blessings. She sang of Mother Danu, Mother of Air, of Wind, of Ice and Cold, the Old Woman of Winter, who is Mother of the Soul of all things.

In reply Nodens sang of His gratitude to Banbha, Lady of the Land from before the Flood, on which Nolava had found rest. He sang His thanks to Britannia, Lady of Brigit's Isles for emerging from the snow, the ice and the ocean. Finally Nolava sang to Ertha the Earth Mother, whose Red Blood Spring had healed Her, to whom She had given Her Maiden Grael.

As Nodens and Nolava gazed upon each other the Fire of Love was ignited between them. Passion flamed within their breasts and they each became aroused. A mighty Wind rose up between them, buffeting their bodies, sending streaming curls of hair across their faces, blowing vegetation and sea in all directions. In exhilaration Nolava called Nodens to Her and Nodens rose from the sea and came streaming into Her. Nodens made love to Nolava, His sea foaming upon Her shores and flowing into Her land. Nolava responded, Her earth lifting and moving with pleasure. The sea made love to the earth and the earth was moved and made love to the sea. Day and night they made love to each other.

The Fire of Love blazed between them and radiated outwards through all the worlds. In the heat of their passion water steamed from the land, shrouding their bodies in violet mist. As Nolava rose to Her fulfilment, the faery folk and creatures of the land marvelled at the appearance of the Mists, rising from the land and sea. They cried,

"The White Lady is coming! She is coming!"

On the curves of Nolava's fecund body plants grew in abundance, grasses, bushes and trees covering the surface of Her earth. Where once She had been a Maiden, pale and fair, now She was the Lover, green and fertile, reddened with passion, Her Vulva open to the western sea. From inside Her body springs of white and red water arose, which flowed with the cycles of the moon. Their underground streams carved out tunnels and caverns, such that the hills which made up Her body became known as the Hollow Hills. As Her radiance shone forth violet shadows filled the combes and gullies created by small streams. Birds and water creatures came first to Her shores and then larger animals swimming through the shallow waters to graze upon Her verdant pastures. On the slopes of Her body apple trees grew in green and pleasant orchards.

As pink apple blossom became red and golden fruit, Nolava delighted in Her abundance,

"I name this isle the Place of Apples, the Isle of Avalon. This shall be known as Nolava's Isle, the sacred Paradise Isle and Garden of the Hesperides, where the golden apples of immortality shall forever grow."

For many days and nights Nolava and Nodens made love to each other and one night when the moon was full, Nolava's Loving Cup became filled with new life. From their union a girl child was conceived and began to grow within Nolava's Womb, a daughter of the land, of the sea, of the wind and of fire. Nolava's body filled with the new life within Her Womb and as her Belly grew Nodens returned to the sea, His waters ever lapping Her shoreline. Content, Nolava lay back upon the earth. Beside the Red Blood Spring Her Chalice swelled within Her Belly, becoming a softly rounded hill.

One day Nolava felt Her babe move inside Her Womb. She thought of Nodens and remembered the ecstasy of their lovemaking. Placing Her hand on Her belly in delight and blessing She whispered,

"When you are born I shall name you Bride, Grand Daughter of Brigit, and in remembrance of the Bride your Mother was to Nodens Her Groom. The place where you lie shall be called Bride's Mound, Gateway to Avalon."

Nodens came riding the surf to attend His daughter's Imbolc birth, but Nolava's first labour was long and slow, lasting for days. When finally on the third night She was born the baby girl emerged wrapped in a thick Caul. She lay unmoving on the earth and did not breathe. Exhausted by Her labours Nolava's strength was spent, Her Violet Light was for the first time dimmed. The Caul was too tough for Her to tear. She could not release Her daughter from the enveloping skein.

She cried out for help. She called to Brighde the Midwife, but She was busy far away in the HeBrides, helping other daughters to birth. She called to Greinne the Sun Mother, but She was shining on the far side of the world and could not come. She called to Mother Danu, but She was far away beyond the North Wind. She called to Domnu, but She was swimming in the deep. She called to Ertha, but She was fast asleep.

Nolava cried for Nodens, who came crashing to the shore with His knife, but it was not strong enough to break the shroud. She cried to the fishes, but they could not come to land. She cried to the animals, but their teeth were not sharp enough. Finally, desperate as Her daughter lay motionless, She cried to the Wind, to the Clouds, to the Rain, to the Sunshine, to Thunder and Lightening, Heat, Hail, Ice and Snow. They heard Nolava's call and rose together in a mighty storm that raged across the land and sea. Streaming out from the whirling weather Nine Black Crows came flying from the skies to Nolava's rescue.

With razor sharp bills and hooked claws they tore at the Caul and soon released the baby girl. Bride took Her first breath and opened Her eyes to see nine pairs of glittering black eyes looking down at Her in blessing. She gulped in air, gurgled and smiled, then slid from the Caul like a Salmon moving in a stream. Nolava and Nodens marvelled at the sight of their beautiful daughter and gave thanks for Her safe delivery.

Nolava spoke softly,

"Thank you, Crows, for bringing my daughter into life. Without you She would have died before She was born."

The Nine Crows strutted and cawed and were pleased with themselves. One spoke for them all,

"Infant Bride, be welcome on this sacred Isle of Avalon for this Paradise Garden shall be your home on earth."

And all around in burrows and nests within the Hollow Hills as the Violet Light once again began to glow from Nolava's skin, the faeries, elementals and creatures of the land celebrated the presence of all these amazing beings. Only the smaller birds and animals quaked with anxiety that the black carrion crows might stray and feed upon their bodies in the sacred land.

Nolava gazed at Her baby daughter in pleasure, looking deep into Her eyes. She felt the strong sensation as Her First Milk rose into Her breast and flowed forth as a sweet, nourishing, milky White Spring. Nolava fed Her first-born child until She was satisfied and then laid Her gently down beside Her foot to sleep.

Nolava turned to the Nine Crows.

"I cannot thank you enough, you Nine who have saved my child. Who are you?"

"We are the Nine Morgens of Life and Fate. We spin the world alive each day, we play among the radiant life, we are the many faces of nature, of the weather and womankind. We bring the dead to life and the living to death. We change all we touch."

As they spoke the Nine began to shapeshift through their many forms. Loosing their blue-black crow feather cloaks Nine Women revealed themselves, ranging in age from young to old. With faces and bodies of beauty and difference, they encompassed the whole spectrum of womanhood, each magnificent in Her own way. Transforming they encircled Nolava in their weather forms, one minute warm and balmy, the next blowing a gale. They transformed into birds of many kinds, into a grove of trees, a stand of willows, a meadow of flowers, into shimmering presences, into nine streams of coloured light, before they finally settled back into being womanly Morgens once again. With smiles and bobbing curtsies they named themselves in turn,

"We are Thitis, Cliton, Thetis, Gliten, Glitonea, Moronoe, Mazoe, Tyronoe and Morgana, Morgen the Faery, Morgen the Fate."

Transforming into their Crow forms the Nine Morgens rose joyfully into the sky. Caw-cawing they flew to the top of Nolava's milk-filled breast and circled around its steep slopes. As they flew up above the Tor they saw beneath them Great Mother Nolava lying on the earth with Bride, Her babe, beside Her foot. They saw the Swan Maiden flying over the land with Her wings outstretched and the Salmon (which would come to be known as the Beckery Salmon) leaping at Her head. Later in the day as evening came the Morgens flew to Bride's Mound to roost, settling on the small hill beside the water.

Nolava's strength soon returned and once more Her transforming Violet emanations blessed the land and its creatures. Nodens came crashing onto Nolava's shoreline many times. When the moon was full, when the tides were high in spring and autumn, on calm sunny days and on stormy nights, Nolava and Nodens made love. The land and the sea made love to each other.

The Lady of Avalon gave birth to many children, some of whom are imprinted on the land and some whose names come down to us in myth and legend. One dark Samhain night Nolava gave birth to a squalling boy, Gwyn ap Nudd, the White Son of Nudd (Nodens by another name), named for his father and for the sparkling Full Moon that shone above the sea that night.

One beautiful Lammas morning Nolava gave birth easily and gently to a second daughter,

Madron. Later when She grew to adulthood She became Mother of the lineage of Avallach. She gave birth to Nine Daughters who became Priestesses on the Isle of Avalon. They were famous throughout the land for their healing, for their knowledge of herbal lore, of the liberal arts, of mathematics and physic, of the stars in the heavens, of the past and the future. They could shapeshift from woman to animal to bird to Goddess and were able to appear in more than one place at the same time. In ceremony they named themselves after the Nine Morgens as Thitis, Cliton, Thetis, Gliten, Glitonea, Moronoe, Mazoe, Tyronoe and Morgen la Fey. The Great Tradition had begun.

As the years passed Nolava watched with pride as Her children grew and lived their own lives. She slowly aged and Her childbearing days eventually came to an end. She settled into the landscape of Avalon as Her back began to bend and Her breasts and belly sagged. While Ertha's Red Bloodflow continued unchanged the Cauldron of Nolava's ageing Womb filled with Wisdom. On cold days She would wrap Herself in a warm dark cloak to walk the Isle of Avalon, occasionally lifting a corner so that Her Violet Radiance might still stream forth across the land. On summer days She would walk slowly in the Orchards of Avalon with Her familiar Crows, emanating Violet Light. As Her joints ached She would stop every so often to kneel and rest upon the back of Her younger Swan Self.

All around in the waters which surrounded the sacred isle Swan Maidens and Swan Princes came flying in to nest and have their babies in safety. Brigit and Her Swan Clan came from the northeast and claimed the land over which She flew as for Her own, just as Her daughter had foretold. Swans visited from all over Brigit's Isles and Europa's land, joining Nolava and She was happy surrounded by Her family.

Each year when Samhain came Nolava would retire from the outer world into a cavern deep within the Tor carved out by the White Spring. There inside the Hollow Hill She spent the winter months beside the fire, stirring Her Cauldron of Transformation, adding to it herbs and spices in due season, radiating Her Violet Light from deep within the earth so that those who looked at the Tor could see its violet aura shining against the sky, especially on full moon nights. The gateway to this Underworld realm was guarded by the now full grown and handsome Gwyn ap Nudd. Sometimes the Nine Morgens would take Nolava's place within the cave, guarding the Fire and Cauldron as She walked the land. Other times they joined Her beside the hearth and many an evening they all sat together, laughing and telling stories of the past, spinning and weaving the threads of the future.

Early peoples returning after the Great Flood had subsided, recognised that the island rising from the western sea was a Gateway to the Otherworld of Mystery. Wary of treading on the sacred Isle of Avalon they came across the water first of all only to bring their dead for sky burial on top of the Tor. The island became known as the Western Isle of the Dead. The carrion birds, the Morgen crows, the eagles and buzzards came swooping in to feed on the bodies of the dead, releasing their souls into Paradise. Once a year at Samhain, Gwyn ap Nudd would ride out with his black hounds with the red ears, across the slopes of the island, gathering in the souls of those who were ripe for transformation, ready for Her Cauldron.

Years later after Madron's daughters, the Nine Priestesses of Avalon, had passed on to the Greater Life, other women began to arrive in ones and twos. They were called by memories of a time when Priestesses of Avalon had lived and honoured the Lady on the Isle of Avalon. Their dedication was to be soul midwives, caretakers of those in need of healing and transformation, of the dying, the dead and the reborn. The Priestesses of Avalon helped newly released souls make their transitions from life into death and the Great Beyond and also their return. They learned the arts of transformation through direct communion with Nolava and the land which is Her body, through communion with the Nine Morgens.

The Goddess-loving peoples of the neolithic era came on pilgrimage to the Isle of Avalon to celebrate the natural sunfire festivals of the year. They knew this was the holyeste earth and came here to honour Nolava,

Lady of Avalon, the Nine Morgens and Ertha's Vulva. They handed down the stories of the Ancestors telling how Nolava had created the land and peoples of Avalon. In each season they sang the land alive, sending Her loving and transforming Violet radiance out along the energy lines and meridians of the earth to wherever it was needed, for healing and the good of the people, the creatures and the land.

They built a Sacred Mound on Nolava's Crone Head in the landscape and from there marked the passage of the rising sun on winter solstice morning, as it rolled up the northern slope of the Tor. It was a miraculous sight, still visible today, as Greinne's bright orb of light rose out of the dark winter earth into the blue sky of rebirth.

They sculpted a great ceremonial Labrynth upon the earthen slopes of Nolava's Lover/Mother left breast. Ariadne laid Her Red Thread through the Labrynth, its path leading up the Sacred Mountain to Caer Sidi, Arianrhod's spiral castle in the stars, known as the Silver Wheel, Corona Borealis and Ariadne's Crown. The centre of the Labrynth lay hidden deep within the Tor, inside the Cave of Nolava's Cauldron, accessed through a hidden entrance on the southern face. There in the middle of the Labrynth specially prepared initiates might meet their Shadow Selves for transformation and healing accompanied by the Crone.

As time went by more human beings dared to walk upon the Sacred Isle, journeying across the waters to Avalon to experience the Violet Emanation. The skills of the priestesses grew to meet the needs of those who came. They offered hospitality, healing, instruction in herbal lore, astrology, astronomy, mathematics and physic, poetry and storytelling, scrying, oracling, music, dance, journeying and shapeshifting. They taught the Mysteries of Nolava's Avalon.

Over time as the continental plates met and pushed upon each other, the land at the edge of the ocean began to slowly rise, centimetre by centimetre up out of the sea. The sea retreated westwards, leaving behind large lakes, brackish pools - the Red, the White, the Black, peat bogs and marshland. The Isle of Avalon now rose from the centre of a great Lake and Nolava became known as Lady of the Lake, as well as Lady of Avalon. She was honoured by the people who lived on wood and brush platforms in Lake Villages, who crossed the watery landscape on ancient wooden trackways, first built by neolthic peoples. The Sacred Isle of Avalon was often reflected in the stillness of the surrounding lake and became known as the Glass Isle, shimmering and gleaming in the sun and moonlight. Later in Saxon times when people lived upon the island, it became known as Glass Town Burg or Glastonbury.

Over the centuries many different groups of seekers came to Glastonbury, each bringing their own truth to lay upon Nolava's body. The druids came more than two thousand years ago and set up a great college, teaching their knowledge of poetry, song and vision, among the trees of the great oak forest that was the hair on Nolava's head. After the death of Jesus in Palestine the first Christians led by Joseph of Arimathea, arrived in Avalon and claimed that the Red and White Springs represented the blood and sweat of Jesus on the cruel cross. Joseph built a round wattle church with hermits' cells beside the Holy Spring which sprang from Nolava's Vulva. Saints came, amongst them Brid from Ireland, who stayed on Bride's Mound. She recognised the Great Mother in the landscape.

The valiant King Arthur came and found his colours in the small chapel that was built on Bride's Mound. He later returned to Avalon as he was dying, accompanied as he crossed the Great Water by Morgen la Fey and Her sisters. Christian monks claimed to have found his body and that of the fair Queen Gwenhwyfar buried in Nolava's earth. They are said to lie here still, sleeping until the time of their rebirth.

Many pilgrims came to visit the site of the first Christian church in Brigit's Isles and a great Benedictine Abbey was raised beside the Holy Spring within Nolava's Vulva. As they built the Abbey, the monks also drained the lakes and marshes that surrounded the Hollow Hills. Over time the Sacred Isle came to be surrounded not by water, but by green fields, each enclosed by water-filled rhynes and ditches, which are still there today draining to the sea.

As patriarchal religion and society grew to dominate indigenous British culture, Nolava and Her sacred body were all but forgotten, dismissed as evil with the sprinkling of Christian Holy Water and the showing of the Sacrificial Cross. The Veil to Avalon was raised to hide its Mysteries from the eyes of the profane and unbelieving. The Sacred Isle disappeared into the mists of our forgetting. The Violet Light once so beloved by all who encountered Her radiance, was lost in the drabness of institutional colours, although Ertha's Red Blood Spring and Nolava's White Spring both continued to flow.

Hundreds of years later the famous Abbey too returned to the earth following Henry VIII's dissolution of the Monasteries in 1539. It now remains as a peaceful ruin, Her nature growing where once there was stone. Here in Nolava's Vulva the Holy Spring still rises and bushy trees begin to clothe Her Yonic gateway once more.

Through the years all the important people in the land journey at one time or another to Glastonbury, seeking Avalon and its Mysteries. They all come - Queens, Kings, healers, teachers, poets, seers, as well as ordinary mortals, seeking the Lady's transformative touch. Unconscious and unseeing they bathe in Her violet emanations. Like the Swan Maiden Herself, believers of all faiths and none travel here seeking Ertha's Source. They come on quests to find the Maiden's Holy Grael, to drink from the Loving Cup, to assuage their thirst for truth from the Mother's Chalice of Love and to immerse themselves in the Crone's Cauldron of Transformation and Wisdom.

In the present many hundreds journey here every week, some travelling with intention to the Isle of Avalon, reaching beyond the Veil to touch the place of Magic and Mystery, to experience Nolava's transforming Violet Light. Others stumble inadvertently through the mists onto Avalon's shores and are startled into wakefulness. Sometimes we become filled with Her ecstasy as we too make love upon Her sacred body. Then all too quickly She may hold a shocking mirror to our Shadow Selves that sends us running for cover from the ugliest of reflections. Bathing in Her compassion slowly we heal our karmic wounds.

Some dare to venture directly into the Hollow Hill, only to emerge years later terrified and mad, rambling, their hair turned white. Or they may be filled with Her Grace, inspired as seers, prophets and poets. Brave souls drawn by a calling deeper than life itself, journey from across Brigit's Isles and far beyond, in search of Ertha's Source. They long to meet Nolava, Lady of Avalon, in all Her glory, aspiring to become present day priestesses and priests of Her transforming nature. They long to meet the Morgens, the essence of the feminine in nature and womanhood.

On spring and autumn days when the pale mist rises from the land we remember Nolava and Her Lover Nodens and their passion for each other. As the mists thicken the local Summerland people still say,

"*The White Lady is coming! She is coming!*"

We are lucky and grateful, because here every day we can walk upon the land which is Lady's body. We can drink Ertha's healing Red Blood Waters, we can drink from Nolava's sweet White Spring. We can connect to the Source of our Life. We can feel the presence of the Nine Morgens in the weather and in all forms in nature. As we call to Nolava in our meditations and visions we can see and feel Her Violet Light emanating from beneath Her cloak of many colours, radiating from Her skin to ours, from Her heart to ours. Every day as we remember Her, the Veil to Avalon is growing thinner. The Sacred Isle and its Mysteries are emerging from the mists of our forgetting. The Lady of Avalon is returning.

First Spiral

Becoming a Sister or Brother of Avalon

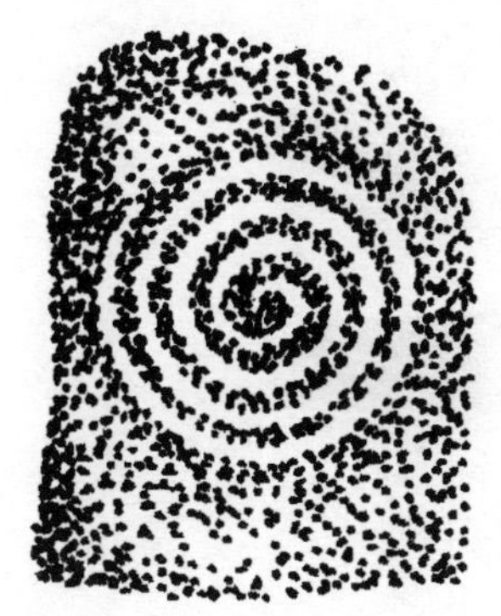

The Cycle of the Seasons of Her Nature

The earth is the body of the Goddess and She expresses different aspects of Herself through the cycle of the seasons of Her nature in the course of each year. Our perception and understanding of who Goddess is, is directly influenced by our experience of Her nature, wherever we live on Her body. Here in Brigit's Isles and on the Isle of Avalon we come to know Her by becoming attuned to Her nature as She transforms from spring to summer to autumn and winter, spiralling onto the next spring.

After winter increasing hours of sunshine warm the earth, the air and the waters, allowing countless birds, animals, insects and plants to be born, to sprout and grow, to flourish and blossom, filling Her world with colour, diversity, beauty and abundance. This growing season culminates at summer solstice when the sun reaches its zenith in the sky. After the solstice the hours of sunshine slowly decrease, although heat still builds in the land, in the water and in the air until mid-August. Young birds gather in great flocks, young animals grow to maturity, insects reproduce in their billions, spin cocoons and prepare for colder weather. Plants continue to bloom, then fruit and set seed. Winds blow, rains come, seeds are scattered, trees shed their leaves and plants die back into the earth, where they lie dormant through the cold winter months under frost, ice and snow, awaiting rebirth.

Through this repeating cycle of Her nature the Goddess in Brigit's Isles and in Avalon can annually be imaged as a beautiful young Maiden, who grows into a fertile and sexual Lover, who matures into the bountiful Mother, who gives birth to offspring, and then ages, becoming a Crone, who decays and dies back to the earth, from which She is reborn the following springtime. This is an endless and continuing spiral of change and transformation, and in the four seasons we see these four principal faces of Her nature, each reigning in Britain for a similar length of time. In the future with global warming these currently equal reigns may change.

People living in other parts of the world experience different faces of the Goddess's nature that we perhaps do not see. Countries near to the equator where jungle and rain forest grows in abundance may have just two seasons, hot and dry, and warm and wet. There Goddess is perceived as a beneficent life-giving Sun and Rain Mother, such as Yoruba in Africa, or Mother Ganges in India. In desert lands few plants and animals live, thriving in one short season before shrivelling up in the heat and lying dormant beneath hot sand for much of the year. Here the Sun Goddess, such as Sekhmet in Egypt, is both life-giving and death-dealing in Her ferocious heat. People living nearer to the South and North Poles experience long seasons of darkness in winter and a shorter season of long days when the sun never sets. There Goddess expresses Herself mainly as a winter Goddess, such as Hel, Holle and Sedna, connected to snow and ice, darkness and cold winds, with a short warm season where She shows Her light benign life-giving face.

We can come to know much about the Goddess in Brigit's Isles and in Avalon, through direct experience of the ways in which Her nature changes here through eight equal and distinctive phases of the year, which are traditionally marked by eight sunfire festivals. Four of these festivals are astronomically based and directly related to the position of the earth in relation to the sun. These comprise the two solstices - winter (Yule), the shortest day of the year when the sun is at its nadir, and summer (Litha), the longest day of the year when the sun rises to its zenith; and the two equinoxes - spring (Oestre) and autumn (Mabon), when there are equal hours of light and darkness. The Four Elemental Mother Goddesses - the Mothers of Air, Fire, Water and Earth, are celebrated in these four quarter seasons and at the solstice and equinox festivals.

Between the four quarter festivals there are four crossquarter celebrations - Imbolc, Beltane, Lammas and Samhain - which come half way between the solstices and equinoxes and are related to agricultural and horticultural events, to the sowing of seeds, to the cultivation and harvesting of produce. On this Sunwheel the four crossquarter festivals are traditional times when the Goddess has expressed Herself most vividly as the fourfold Maiden, Lover, Mother and Crone, rather than as a threefold Lunar Goddess. The crossquarter festivals continued to be a vibrant focus for Goddess celebrations as incoming Christianity focused on taking over the more obvious solar festivals of the year. Yule became the time of the birth of Jesus and Oestre became connected to the time of his death.

Brigit's Isles as a whole are ruled by our Lady Britannia, She who is

The Sacred Wheel of Nolava, Britannia & the Nine Morgens

North /Winter Solstice
AIR/VIOLET-SILVER
Wren/Eagle/Owl/Buzzard
Sceptre/Sword/Feather Fan
Nolava of Air, Mother of Air
Danu, Anu, Arianrhod
Cailleach, Bone Woman,
Stone Woman, Tyronoe

Northeast/Imbolc/WHITE
Nolava the Maiden
Brigit, Bridie,
Kernababy, Thitis
Swan/Snake/Cow/Wolf
Grael/Spindle/Spinning Wheel

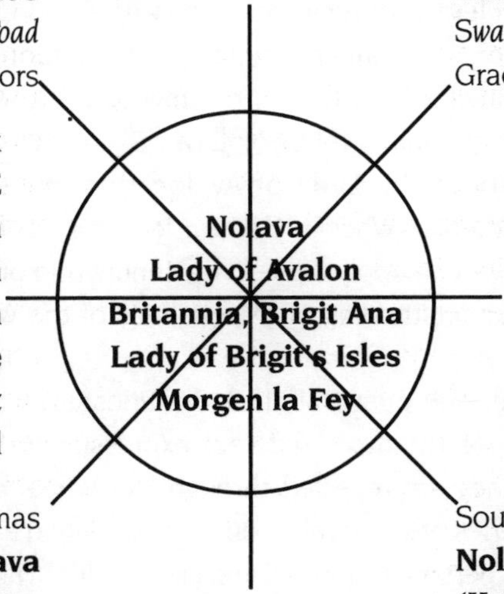

East/Spring Equinox
FIRE/GREEN-GOLD
Nolava of Fire
Mother of Fire
Artha, Grainne,
Eostre, Cliton
Bear/Hare/Hen/Cat
Wand/Rod

Southeast/Beltane/RED
Nolava the Lover/Virgin
(Ke)Rhiannon, Olwen, Elen,
Blodeuwedd, Thetis
Mare/Horse/Dove/Swan
Comb/Mirror/Loving Cup

Nolava of Water
Mother of Water
Domnu, Queen of the Deep
Lady of the Springs & Wells
Lady of the Lake, Gliten
Dolphin/Whale/Salmon/Seal
WATER/BLUE/TURQUOISE
South/Summer Solstice

YELLOW/Southwest/Lammas
Great Mother Nolava
Ker, Grain Goddess,
Madron, Mystress Glitonea
Deer/Stag/Horned creatures
Chalice/Loom/Shuttle

West/Autumn Equinox
EARTH/BROWN-ORANGE
Nolava of Earth
Mother of Earth
Banbha, Brigantia
Ertha, Gaia, Moronoe
Boar/Badger/Fox
Stone/Orb/Crystal

BLACK/Samhain/Northwest
Nolava the Crone
Dark Mother, Keridwen
Sheela na Gig, Mazoe
Crow/Sow/Toad
Cauldron/Sickle/Scissors

Nolava
Lady of Avalon
Britannia, Brigit Ana
Lady of Brigit's Isles
Morgen la Fey

Brigit-Ana, a combination of ancient Brigit and Mother Goddess Ana, whose names are found from the earliest times. Through the year Britannia expresses Herself through many Goddesses, some of whom may already be familiar to us and some unknown. In honouring Britannia we are reclaiming the ancient tutelary Goddess of these islands from the martial role imposed upon Her by warmongering patriarchs. We are recognising Her original peace-loving, solar, agrarian and guardian nature.

Britannia's Wheel is different to the traditional Wiccan Wheel and I have written extensively about Britannia's Wheel and its origins in *The Ancient British Goddess* and *Spinning the Wheel of Ana*. Based on the attributes and qualities of the Goddesses traditionally celebrated at the eight festivals of the year, the Element Mothers are in different positions on the wheel - the Mother of Air is in the north, Mother of Fire is in the east, Mother of Water is in the south and Mother of Earth is in the west.

Britannia rules the outer world of the whole of Brigit's Isles. Nolava, the Lady of Avalon is an inner counterpart to Britannia. She rules the inner reality of Brigit's Isles that is the mythical Isle of Avalon. In the following chapters we shall explore Nolava's Sacred Wheel of the Year. We will also learn about the Lady of Avalon through experiencing the Goddesses on Britannia's Wheel of the Year, learning of their transformative qualities, so that we can apply these in the Innerworld of Avalon. To these we can add our understanding of the qualities of the Wheel of the Nine Morgens.

Throughout the First Spiral of the Priestess of Avalon training students experience the many different expressions of the Goddess in Brigit's Isles as they are revealed through Her Wheel of the Year. They participate in a series of seasonal ceremonies designed to catalyse change in each student's personal, spiritual and creative life. The goal for the end of the First Spiral of training is to come to the place where we are ready to dedicate our lives to the Goddess, becoming a true heart Sister or Brother of Avalon. In the next chapters we will focus on the ceremonial journey and the processes of transformation that are encountered by individuals on the First Spiral of the path to priestesshood.

In the British pagan tradition New Year comes not in January, but at Samhain, the Festival of the Crone or Dark Goddess, who is celebrated at Hallowe'en, October 31st. Our journey around Britannia's Wheel begins here at the time when the Old Year transforms into the New. In the next chapters we will circulate the Wheel, following the ceremonial cycle of the First Spiral of the Priestess of Avalon training.

The Darkening
Samhain Festival of the Crone Goddess

Goddesses celebrated at the Darkening of Samhain are all expressions of the Crone, the fourth aspect of the Maiden, Lover, Mother, Crone quaternary, She who rules decay, darkness and death. We honour Nolava as the Crone, Hag and Dark Goddess, as Black Nolava, She who takes us down into the Underworld to meet our Shadow selves. We honour Mazoe, Dark Morgen of Samhain. We come to face the Crone as Keridwen the Great White Sow, who guards the Cauldron of Death, Transformation and Rebirth, of Inspiration and Regeneration. We pass beneath the gaping vulva of Sheela na Gig, Protectress and Guardian of the Gateways to the worlds beyond life.

In Britain and in other northern latitudes Samhain marks the ending of the old year and the beginning of the new. It is a time when the sun's arc is sinking in the southern sky, when the days are becoming shorter and all of Her nature is dying back to the earth. The air cools, the sap descends into the roots of plants, leaves fall from bushes and trees, covering the land in a slowly blackening orange, red and brown carpet, that will compost through the winter, returning nutrients to the earth. Animals are filling their bellies with fruits, storing food and nuts in preparation for hibernation and the deprivations of winter. Birds flock together, fieldfares and starlings fly in great numbers, wheeling over Avalon at dusk and dawn as they make their way to and from their night-time perches out on the Summerland marshes. The summer visitors, swallows and swifts, have already left on their long flights to warmer climes. Flights of Morgen crows play on the wind. Small birds feast on berries and move into gardens for winter feeding.

Samhain is the season when we face the Dark Mother and acknowledge Her Underworld powers of transformation and regeneration. It is the time when we let go of all that no longer serves us in preparation for a new beginning. We honour the Mother of Death, recognising the fact that everything material will one day die, including our own bodies. We make a pilgrimage to Her within the sacred landscape of Avalon. We celebrate our own dead, all those whom we have known and loved, who have passed on into the greater life. Samhain is also the time when we plant seeds of intention for the coming year.

Honouring Nolava the Crone, the Hag

At Samhain we honour Nolava as Crone, Hag and Grand Mother, the fourth aspect in the Maiden, Lover, Mother and Crone quarternary. She is old and Her love is endless and enduring. She has lived so long that She has seen all things in life and in the human condition. She understands the dilemmas and challenges that we face and speaks to us with the wisdom of age.

We can find the Crone in Glastonbury's sacred landscape, Her outline appearing within the higher contours of the land. We make pilgrimage to Her, walking the circuit of Her body around the Tor, Chalice Hill, Windmill Hill and Stonedown. Our mantra for the journey is:

"Old Woman of Avalon, Nolava, Crone,
Protect me, guide me, bring me home."

At Samhain the Crone smites the land with Her Black Rod and everything in nature begins to die back into the earth. The flowers, grasses, shrubs and trees begins to lose their colours and substance and die away as if they had never been. Life leaves the land under the touch of the Crone's Black Rod. Moving into winter the Black Rod too loses its colour, becoming Silver with frost and snow as it is taken by the Cailleach. Through the winter it fades to White and at Imbolc the Maiden takes the White Rod from Cailleach. Touching the earth She will quicken the life that lies dormant within seeds and roots. Through the cycle of the seasons the Rod passes from goddess to goddess, its colours transforming into the Green Rod of Springtime, then the Red of the Lover, the Blue of the Mother of Water, the Gold of the Great Mother, the Orange/Brown of autumn and the Earth Mother, and continuing on to the Black of the Crone.

The Crone is the Old Woman out of whom the new is always brought to birth in a continuing cycle of life, death and regeneration. In fairy tales She is the Ugly Old Woman who questions men with riddles. When they give the correct answer She transforms into a beautiful young Maiden, rewarding their insight and wisdom with sexual pleasures. Nolava the Crone is always a Shapeshifter, the young embraced by the old, the Woman with an animal inside or beside Her. As the Hag She screams our fears into the dark night. She startles and frightens us with Her passage. Her haggard face reveals the many burdens She carries, the depths of Her experiences, the breadth of Her compassion. She beckons us to follow Her, asking us to let go of all that no longer serves us or Her.

Nolava the Crone is also our kind, loving Grandmother who teaches us all the ways of the Goddess and Her nature. She has knowledge and experience of life to share with all. She holds the communal teachings and stories of our cultures. She holds the lineages of the priestess, shamanka, healer and sibyl, which is Her's to pass on to future generations. Her duty is to speak of love for the Earth as a whole, to speak for all the creatures that live upon the earth, to speak for the land, the waters, the fires and the air, to protect them from abuse, from the pollution and greed of patriarchy.

As a practice honour the Crones that you know in your own life. Praise them. Support them. Encourage them to share their wisdom within your community.

At Samhain we make images of the Crone in Her honour. Remove the centre from a pumpkin or turnip and carve Her face upon it. Light a candle inside and let Her face shine in the darkness for all to see.

Honouring Black Nolava the Dark Goddess

Samhain is the time when we honour Black Nolava the Dark Goddess. It is not necessarily the time when we meet Her face to face, but it is the time when we acknowledge Her powerful existence. We can know that on our journey to become Priestesses of Avalon we will meet Her at some time or another, and often more than once. She will challenge us with events and circumstances which seem too hard to bear. She will take us down into Her cave deep in the earth. She will show us Her terrible face. Her strong love will reveal the things we have covered over and hidden, in the past because they were too shocking and hurt too much. She may leave us alone in the cave, so that we feel abandoned by Her and by everyone around us. We may stay there for some time, for weeks, months and even years. Then one day out of the blue She will return with all Her love, revealing the beauty that lies hidden deep in the darkness of the Underworld. We will understand what has happened and how it has changed us for the better. We become filled with gratitude for Her appearance in our lives.

Goddess spirituality is an experience of wholeness, of depths as well as heights. The Goddess encompasses both creation and destruction, positive and negative, as imaged in the Chinese yin yang symbol, which depicts the continual balance between opposites. She is life and the fruitful summer, but she is also the death and decay of late autumn. Dying plants break down to form dark compost in which new life will grow once again in springtime. Unlike patriarchal religions, which focus their adoration on the Light and sublimate the Dark, demonising all that is not Light as evil, Goddess spirituality encompasses both the Light and the Dark, seeing each as being necessary for the existence of the other.

In the natural world, which is the mirror in which the Goddess's nature is made visible, all new life is born out of darkness - the darkness of the earth, of the womb, of night. There is no regeneration without darkness, no rebirth without death. All the beautiful crystals in the world are created in darkness beneath the surface of the earth. All animal and human life is carried in the darkness of a mother's womb. We ourselves are regenerated each morning after the darkness that comes when we close our eyes to light, and sleep. Our world moves into darkness as night falls and is renewed each morning with the sun's rays. Darkness brings rest and renewal. We forget these things as we try to kill the darkness with electric lights which burn through the night, as we focus on the light in our attempts to ignore our own darkness.

The Dark Goddess is an Initiatrix and a Trickster. She initiates the new often by a trick or a seeming bad deed. She is the Old and usually Ugly Hag who appears in fairy tales, offering us a bite of Her beautiful but poisonous red apple, which initiates girls into womanhood. She is the Wicked Stepmother, who plots our downfall and teaches us to deal with other people's emotions as well as our own, so we can grow up and claim our adulthood. She is the scary Old Witch who may entrap us with spells, for a hundred years or more.

She is also the Goddess whom fertile women experience each month during menstruation. In a monthly cycle Her energy seeks expression through our dreaming and creativity. If we do not recognise Her, She will express Herself anyway, in our pain, anger, frustration and misery. Our Moontime is one of the best times for the creative expression of our deepest emotions in a monthly cycle of release and renewal. Rather than us suffering as we bleed, She asks that we notice Her existence and regularly express Her energy, so that it does not build as if behind a great dam that will one day burst horribly. As our blood flows each moontide the creative tension which has built up over previous weeks is released and we feel better for that release.

Modern society demands that women pretend nothing is happening while we bleed, that we keep it hidden, without stain or smell. In earlier times women would retreat for a few days to a menstrual hut or cave to commune with the Dark Goddess, taking time out from their social obligations to sleep, to dream, and to be creative, before returning to their communities with renewed life. During their sojourn they received inspiration from the Dark Lady to be shared for the good of the whole community. In our busy world we may no longer be able to claim this right of monthly retreat, but we can claim the right to sleep, to dream Her future, to express ourselves through music, writing, artworks of all kinds. It is the Dark Goddess's gift to us, not only as a vital part of the human cycle of fertility, but also in the cycle of creativity.

In the days just before menstruation begins, as tension builds inside you, write, draw, paint or mould in clay just how you are feeling, your fears, anxieties and sorrows. Express yourself. Allow yourself to sleep longer. When you wake write down your dreams. Begin a dream diary.

Bleed directly onto the earth or collect some of your blood and return it to the earth as a blessing of fertility for the land on which you live. In private or with other women mark your body, your breasts, face, hands, arms, legs and feet with your own life blood, giving yourself the Dark Goddess's powerful blessing. Take pride in your fertile life-giving blood.

Meeting the Dark Face of Nolava is a vital part of our journey to become Priestesses of Avalon. She will take us down into Her depths to face our darkest fears and our deepest pains, and we have to learn how to sit in these places where the real transformations occur, in the depths of our Shadow selves. Personally I have struggled with the idea that the deepest transformations seem to come out of suffering. I have railed against Her. Why can't it be easier? Why can't transformation come out of joy? Well, it does too, there are many transformations of the Light, but most of us in this time also have great inner dilemmas to resolve. We live in harsh, desolate city landscapes, we experience the wasteland of our emotional lives, we fail terribly in our own eyes, never mind those of other people, before we are forced from the depths of our own pain to make the choice to change direction, to be reborn, to truly live life.

Our resistance to change, our stubbornness when it comes to letting go of who we think we are, is a mark of our inner strength, working against, not for us. Our desperate need to survive at all costs is instinctive and self-protective, but it is there to be melted by Her continuing loving presence, forcing us to face the heart of our own darkness. The Dark Lady of Avalon calls to us to surrender to Her transforming powers and eventually we do let go to Her.

As Priestesses of Avalon we have to know all these experiences from the inside, from within our own bodies, emotions and souls, so that we know just how awesome Her transformations are, how great Her love for us is, how wise She is. We also need to know this experience so we can truly empathise with others, who are journeying with the Dark Goddess. So that we can sit with them, breathing in the darkness, groaning with them, empathising with their suffering.

The presence of Dark Nolava stimulates our fears of pain, of death and loss, and catalyses the journey of change. She brings us tragedy, betrayal and loss of trust. She teaches discrimination, discernment and the nature of creativity. She helps strengthen our inner resolve to follow the path of our soul. Above all She teaches us to have compassion for ourselves and for all who suffer.

Honouring Mazoe, Crone Morgen

I am the Morgen Mazoe
I am the Dark Goddess, the Dark Lady, the Crone
I am the Lady of the Mists
I am the Guardian of the Gateways to the Underworld

My hawk watches from overhead
My sow, toad and frog travel at my side

You each will know me, you each will feel my embrace
I will teach you of fear and forgetting, sadness and compassion

For I am the Transformer
I hold the sickle that cuts the thread of life

I am the dark chasm into which you fall
I am the dark hag that dwells in your shadow
I am the screaming banshee in your worst nightmare

I AM MAZOE

by Ren Chapman

Mazoe is Morgen of Samhain. Like Nolava She is the great Transformer who takes us down into the Underworld that lies beneath Glastonbury Tor. She takes us into our Shadow selves to face all that is hidden and unacknowledged. She is the *beansidhe*, the screaming Hag we hear on the wind and in our dreams, terrifying us. She is Thunder and Lightning. She scares us as Her electricity crackles through the sky, dropping fiery snakes to the ground, as Her voice thunders overhead and across the land. Whenever She plays with Her sisters, at any time of the year, wild storms race across the Isle of Avalon and the Summerland, bringing fear, exhilaration and sometimes destruction.

Mazoe is the dying moon, Her last sliver visible just before dawn. With Her moon sickle She cuts the thread of life at the moment of death. Her sacred creatures include the sow that roots in the earth, and the bats which emerge at dusk, hunting through gardens and fields. Her bird is the hawk that hovers over the entrance to the Underworld on the slopes of Glastonbury Tor. She flies still in the eye of the wind, hovering, waiting to plunge Her talons into the unsuspecting who pass beneath Her vigilant gaze.

As a woman Mazoe's age lies between 60 and 70 years. She is old, but not ancient. She still has energy and vigour, but Her joints are beginning to ache, Her body showing signs of ageing. She is often appears tired of the ways of humans and may be hostile and cross when we meet Her. She evokes our fears of confrontation. She likes to test our intentions, our endurance and our commitment to knowing Her. Beneath Her apparent anger She is filled with an amazing love.

Mazoe's colour is black, the colour which absorbs all other colours and emits no light. She is darkness and the night. We glimpse Her dark shadowy form disappearing away into the autumn mists as they emerge from the damp low-lying earth at dusk. She is Yew Woman who lives long as the Crone, Her yew trees growing slowly through hundreds and thousands of years. Her dark skinned trees are found in many sacred places, as guardians and protectors. In Glastonbury from ancient times a processional avenue of yew trees has led up to the Red Bloodspring of Chalice Well, the place where Ertha's red menstrual blood flows out from the earth. Her red berries and sap are poisonous and are now used in the anticancer drugs taxol and taxotere.

On the slopes of the Tor *and beside* Chalice Well *pray to* Mazoe *to be kind to you, to allow you to see* Her *without fear.* Walk *in the wind, in the rain, in the storm, through the mist, and call* Her *to you.* Welcome Her *presence knowing that a small homeopathic measure of* Her *poison can heal your wounds and give you renewed life.*

Facing the Shadow

On the journey to priestesshood the Dark Lady will bring us face to face with aspects of our Shadow selves which are hidden away in our unconscious minds, because they are too painful and difficult for us to remember. These include memories of traumatic events, of abuse, misuse, aggression, anger received and given, shame, pain, guilt and sorrow. Because these memories are hidden it does not mean that they do not affect us. Our behaviour is driven by the needs of our Shadow to protect itself, as well as by our conscious intentions. Our priestess journey will bring those painful memories to the surface of our consciousness for healing, so that we can become more truly ourselves.

As forgotten memories begin to arise sometimes for the first time in many years, the associated painful emotions are usually projected outwards first of all onto other people, onto tutors, fellow students, families and friends, whoever happens to be nearest at the time. We recreate the painful scenarios of our past in new forms and project our unacceptable feelings outwards onto others. Life becomes challenging as we express our buried emotions inappropriately, to people who did not cause our wounds, but who now press our buttons. On our priestess journey we learn to become self-reflective and aware of what is happening, as we find ourselves falling out with those around us, as we criticise, blame and attack others for our own projected Shadow behaviours.

Of itself a priestess training is principally a ceremonial journey, which awakens and develops spiritual aspiration, creativity and connection to Goddess. It is not psychotherapy, although it will catalyse change in all parts of the personality as the individual opens to the Goddess and becomes more self-aware and empowered. Wounds will arise for healing and we need to expect that they will. In the priestess training there is so much to learn about the skills of priestessing, that there is simply not enough time to also take on each student's personal psychological healing. Aspiring priestesses will find many benefits in exploring their personal psychology so as to heal their emotional wounds, alongside their priestess training, engaging in personal counselling and psychotherapy sessions as needed. In order to manifest our amazing Souls we need to face our Shadows too and bring the jewels that they hide into the light of day.

Claiming Support on the Journey with the Dark Goddess

During each Spiral of the Priestess of Avalon training students are offered several levels of personal support on their journey of change. They have the support of their tutors and of the lovelies, the tutor assistants in the teaching circles. They have the support of their fellow students as time is given in each circle to hear each person's experience. At the start of the course students are also placed in smaller support groups of four or five people. These smaller groups are created by the random choice of the Goddess and provide the opportunity for people to share with each other more intimately. Between circles individuals in the support groups are encouraged to communicate with each other regularly, to support each other, to meet if possible, to visit sacred sites together, to celebrate the Goddess together, etc. Groups become strongly bonded and often stay together when they visit Glastonbury for a training circle and from this bond deep friendships have been forged.

Personal support is very important for us as we go through a time of spiritual change and evolution. Many of us have to learn how to ask for help and also how to receive it. We can be very good at giving support to other people who are in need, but we are so used to facing things alone that we have to relearn how good it is to be supported by empathic people, especially as we face the Dark Goddess. We have built up protective shells behind which we hide our needs and insecurities and we have to learn to let these walls come down and let love in, to heal our wounds.

Also because we are unused to having support in our lives we may not be very good at giving it to others. Students have to be reminded to call each other, to stay in contact by email, letter, phone or text. It does not come naturally for many people. In our busy worlds we are often isolated and have to relearn the art of friendly communication and concern for others. We are learning to become true soul friends to each other.

Keridwen's Underworld Transformation

Keridwen is the Great White Sow who feeds on the souls of the dead, Her great bulk growing each month with the waxing moon. When the moon reaches its fullness souls are transformed into other realms, into rebirth, the moon shrinking as souls move on.

For priestesses Keridwen teaches the path of transformation that will one day lead to initiation. Her legend tells us that She lives in the Underworld beneath Lake Tegid (Lake Bala) in North Wales. To help Her ugly son Afagddu, She brews a magical ikor for a year and a day in a great cauldron that sits on a fire, glowing with the breath of Nine Maidens. Throughout the year She adds to the cauldron all kinds of herbs gathered in due season, showing us that everything on our journey of transformation happens at the right moment. Certain plants, aspects of ourselves, will only flower in the spring or summer or autumn and that is when they need to be added to the mixture in the cauldron of change. Transformation cannot be rushed.

In the legend near the year's end, Gwion, the boy who helps stir the cauldron, accidentally splashes the hot ikor onto his fingers. He puts them to his lips to cool and tastes the magical brew. Immediately he knows the future and the past and Keridwen knows that Gwion has tasted the liquor that was meant for Her son. Gwion runs away and Keridwen begins to chase him, screaming like a beansidhe. Gwion now has the ability to shapeshift and moves around the wheel of the year through a series of animal forms, pursued by Keridwen. He becomes a hare and She chases him in the form of a faster greyhound. He dives into the river and becomes a fish, and She becomes an otter. He transforms into a bird and She hunts him as a hawk. He changes into a single grain in a pile of wheat and Keridwen becomes a black hen, sifting through the pile until She finds him and eats him up. Gwion remains inside of Keridwen's body for nine months until one day She gives birth to a baby boy, but does not acknowledge him as Her own. She ties him in a leather bag and throws him into the nearby river. When the bag becomes entangled downstream in a weir, he is rescued by Prince Elphain for whom he speaks rhymes of poetry and prophecy. He becomes known as Taliesin, the famous poet and riddler who foretells the future.

Keridwen's tale tells us that the transformative process is not straightforward, it has different stages. The first lasts at least a year when we must experience many different inputs of knowledge and experience, related to the seasons of the year. At the end of a year we taste the magic which we seek, we dedicate our lives to the Goddess, but we are not quite ready to be responsible to Her. Rapid changes then take place and we lose the sense of who we are. We get frightened and begin to run from the changes we had at first welcomed. We run from Her and Her Hag's wisdom for a year and a day. We run away, but She follows us. Then She swallows us, holding us in Her Dark Womb for at least nine months, until we are reborn. Even then She does not acknowledge us. We are confused, we feel abandoned, lost, betrayed. Then slowly we grow, we strengthen in our own right. We learn to speak our truth, to believe in ourselves and Her, to speak Her words of inspiration, Her poetry, Her visions of the future.

Pray to Keridwen as you gaze at the swelling full moon. Ask Her to make your path of transformation easy and clear. Ask Her *to help you welcome change, creativity and self expression.* Ask Her *to show you* Her *face when you feel lost and alone. Ask to be held in the warmth of* Her Womb. *Ask to be reborn in* Her.

Honouring Sheela na Gig

Sheela na Gig is the most common ancient representation of the Goddess found in Brigit's Isles. Carved in stone She appears on the walls of the earliest Christian churches and on castles, placed there as a protection against evil. In some churches Her image is found above the entrance door so that congregations could touch Her open vulva for good luck as they entered the church. More often these days Her images are hidden away on high ceilings, at the back of churches, or in the basements of museums. Hundreds of years old She still has the power to shock the establishment.

Nearly all the carvings show Her as an Old Woman, often with a thin body, protruding ribcage, balding head and sagging breasts. She sits with Her legs apart revealing Her awesome gig or vulva, the place of sexuality, the place from which we are all born and to which we return at death. She is Guardian of the Gateways to sex, ecstasy, death and rebirth. She reveals the power of sexuality to bring about the little ego deaths that come with orgasm, that can change our characters, opening them to Her love.

On the wheel of the year Samhain lies opposite to Beltane, the time when we celebrate the Goddess of love and sexuality. At Samhain we honour the darker face of our sexuality. We honour the Harlot, who shares Her karuna-filled sexuality with all comers, She who holds no boundaries on what is acceptable and tasteful. She draws us into actions where we compromise our true feelings and desires, just to hold onto a lover. She shows us the ways in which we collude in creating our personal unhappiness. Over time She teaches us discrimination, discernment, how to stand up for ourselves, for our feelings, for our hopes for true love. She shows us how to become strong.

Sheela na Gig is a protector. We can call upon Her when we are in danger. We can visualise Her image placed in front of or all around us, warding off evil. We can sit in Her gaping vulva and know that She will protect us.

Visit the many places where Sheela na Gig may be found from Hereford *to* Ireland. *Touch Her Gig Vulva for luck as you pass beneath Her image into churches and sacred places. Read the good books now available about Her, including an excellent one by* Joanne McMahon *and* Jack Roberts, *"The Sheela-na-Gigs of* Ireland *and* Britain (Mercier Press). *Call to Sheela and She will protect you when you are afraid.* Draw Her *powerful image.*

Honouring the Mother *of* Death

In the neolithic age, some 5-6 thousand years ago, life was much more taken up with physical survival than it is in today's Britain. There were dangerous animals in the forests, famine and flood were natural hazards, accidents and sickness could easily kill and human life span was much shorter than it is today. Consequently our forebears had a much deeper connection to the Mother of Death than we do now. They honoured Her and their dead by erecting small and large mounds of earth and stone shaped like the Mother's breast or pregnant belly. These magnificent ritual sites demonstrate their belief that we are all born from the Mother and as we die we return to Her womb/ tomb for regeneration and to await rebirth.

The earliest burial sites that we know of in Brigit's Isles are small earthen mounds raised over earth or stone cists, where the bones of the dead were interred. In the fifth and fourth millennium BCE long barrows were built shaped like the elongated body of the Mother of Death, with an entrance and womb chambers inside at one end. Long barrows were erected every twenty miles or so across the whole of Brigit's Isles and it is believed by archaeologists that each community had its own long barrow. There the bones of the dead were interred and at special times of the year, perhaps at Samhain, the ancestors would be invoked and communed with. In places such as Avebury, the remains of many long barrows are scattered across a large area and mark, according to writer Michael Dames, the outline of the body of a gigantic Mother Goddess in the landscape (*The Avebury Cycle*, Thames & Hudson). Many long barrows have disappeared, ploughed under by farmers, especially in the eastern half of Brigit's Isles. The remains of many long barrows can still be found on the remoter western shores, in Wales, Scotland and Ireland.

Throughout Brigit's Isles the building of larger mounds dedicated to the Mother of Death developed over time, with different regions producing their own designs. In many the entrances and inner chambers are oriented to the rising and setting of the sun and moon on particular special days of the year, such as Samhain, Imbolc, the summer and winter solstices and the equinoxes, times when the ancestors and the Goddess Herself were believed to come closer to the living.

The nearest open long barrow to Glastonbury is some miles away at Stoney Littleton, where a beautiful long barrow has been restored. Set on the slope of a hill in a quiet valley near Bath it is a wonderful place to commune with the ancestors and the Mother of Death. The stone entrance viewed from higher up the hill displays Her open Vulva, oriented to the rising sun at winter solstice. In the deep silence of Her womb tomb She speaks to us.

There is a late neolithic burial mound at Compton Dundon, which lies within the Glastonbury Zodiac. There are several round mounds on the nearby Mendip Hills at Priddy Nine Barrows and elsewhere, and there is the Sacred Mound on Windmill Hill in Glastonbury. Samhain is an ideal time to visit the long barrows and ritual mounds, to commune with the Mother of Death, who we will all one day meet.

Honouring the Dead

Samhain is the festival when we celebrate our dead, particularly those who have recently passed over into the Otherworld. It is the time when we speak of the loved ones we have lost in the previous year or years, placing their photographs and special objects on the altar in a place of honour. We express our grief at our loss and we listen to their words of wisdom for us.

Name your beloved and your unloved ancestors who have passed over. Give thanks for all that they gave to you in your life, both the good and the bad. They have loved you and helped you in life. They have been mirrors reflecting your own imperfect image. They have been guardians of your battle grounds. Ask that you may hear their words of wisdom. Listen to what they wish to say to you now they are freed from their mortal bodies. Share their wisdom with others.

In western cultures many of us have become removed from the reality of death. We live nearly all our lives without encountering actual death, except as a news time fantasy on the TV and in ketchup-splattered films. This is something which would have been unthinkable to our Goddess-loving ancestors for whom death was an important part of the cycle of life. In the modern day, fear of our own mortality has removed the experience of death from our lives. It is taken out of our homes into hospitals, removed from our sitting rooms as a messy business. As a consequence we lose the great energetic experience of being present when our loved ones die.

At birth when a new baby comes into the world, the doorways to the Otherworld, are held open for a time. If we are lucky we experience the numinous presence of the Goddess appearing in the gateway for several days around the birth. The same experience occurs at death, when again the doorways to the Otherworld open to receive the dying person's soul. Old friends and ancestors gather on the Other Side to welcome the newly liberated soul. The Goddess in all Her glory becomes visible with other beings who are meaningful to the dying person. Again this presence of the divine can linger for hours and days giving us, the living, a life-changing experience. Birth and death are the great initiatory moments mimicked in all our human initiation ceremonies.

As Priestesses of Avalon it is our work with others to bring back awareness of the place of death in Her great cycle of life, death and rebirth. This cycle is essential to the continuity of all life on earth and we shall all at some time die. I spent nearly fifty years of my life believing that I was immortal and somehow would not die. I was brought face to face with my fear of death through the experience of having breast cancer, when I thought I could so easily die. I found I had a great terror of dying, which I had brought over from a previous incarnation, after suffering a painful death. Expressing that fear and pain through my illness helped to heal a deep old wound, thus healing my cancer. Now I believe that my essence will not die, although my body will.

As part of my healing journey friends helped create a Death and Rebirth Ceremony in which my death was to be symbolised by shaving my head of hair. My hair had already begun to fall out because of the chemotherapy drugs I was taking. I didn't want to lose my hair but I had to face the fact that it would all drop out, just as we have to face the fact that we will die. In the ceremony attended by over thirty friends, two amazing people, Pauline Watson and Chris Makepeace, supported me by having their heads shaved too and raising money for charity. As our heads were being shaved I found to my surprise that as my hair went I actually felt happier and happier. By the time it was all gone and I was bald, I was radiant and at peace. I learned something profound that evening. I learned that although I may still fear the process of arriving at death, I will walk into my death with a happy heart. I will be returning to Her. I also realised that one of the best ways to die is to be surrounded by family and friends, who can accompany us to the gateway on this side of death. It is not necessary for us to die alone and afraid. Enacting our fears in a ceremonial way is a healing experience.

Two other friends have provided great examples of how to be with death and tragic loss. The first is Andrea Rogers, a local homoeopath who, when her husband Roger's father was dying over several weeks, moved Dad into the sitting room in the middle of their single storey house. To get from one part of the house to another everyone had to walk through this sitting room. As he was getting weaker Dad was nearly always accompanied by one or other members of his family and friends, old and young, sitting with him, watching TV around him, feeding him, giving him sips of water when he no longer wanted to eat, washing his body, touching him with love, just being with him. The children watched him dying too, they weren't kept away from this natural process and were allowed to experience the letting go of incarnation, so that it became a much less frightening event.

Tegwyn Hyndman had a terrible bereavement when her first daughter Elkana, was killed at the age of seven in a car accident. At the time Tegwyn and her family were living with others in benders and caravans on a field to the south of Glastonbury. Distraught with grief, Tegwyn was embraced by her community, who also felt the tremendous pain of loss. Tegwyn was extraordinary in the way that she allowed everyone who came, to participate in a series of ceremonies marking her daughter's passage. After her death Elkie's body lay for several days in her home on a bed, packed beneath with ice, covered with flowers and surrounded by the children who had been her closest friends in life. Again death was shown to them to be a part of the experience of life. During the first week there were many powerful ceremonies where everyone including Elkie's parents expressed their grief, not only for this death, but for many other unexpressed bereavements. Friends made a wooden coffin for Elkie, which was decorated by the children and taken for cremation. Every stage of the shocking experience was marked by private and communal ceremonies and thus became transformative for the wider community as well as those more intimately involved.

As an exercise think about your own death, how it may come for you. Notice your fears about dying or of the pain that you may experience on the way to death. How would you like your death to be? Think of what you want to happen to your physical body when you die. Do you want to be buried or cremated, or do you want to become the foundation for a tree in a green burial site? Write your own funeral or memorial ceremony. What music would you like included, what are your favourite words? How would you like to be remembered?

Create a special death box that contains the important messages and precious things you wish to leave to your children, lovers, family and friends.

Make a will that tells your descendants what to do with the material things you are leaving behind, no matter how young you are today. We can die unexpectedly at any moment. Consider making or buying your own coffin as a piece of furniture which you can design and paint with Goddess images that are meaningful to you in life.

Avalon, Western Isle of the Dead

As well as being the Paradise island, the Isle of Avalon is also known as the Western Isle of the Dead. At the time of our dying we are taken in the Barge across the waters to Avalon, accompanied by Morgen la Fey or Mazoe or others of the Nine Sisters. Our death may be physical or many times it is an emotional and mental death or disintegration. We journey to Avalon to be healed of our suffering, to experience transformation and like the famed King Arthur, to await rebirth before journeying back out into the everyday world.

It is to Avalon that our souls are transported as we physically die. Here we journey through what are known to the Tibetan Buddhists, as the Bardo states of consciousness which lie between death and rebirth. The Tibetans have a complex understanding of these bardo states and much of their spiritual practice is a preparation for the journey through these after-death states. Their aim is to achieve enlightenment as they die, so leaving the wheel of karma behind, or to obtain a good rebirth. I am beginning my own exploration of these bardo states as they might apply in Avalon, not so that I can leave the wheel of life on earth, because I love being here, but so that I may better understand the nature of the Isle of Avalon.

As an Island of the Dead Avalon is the place where the Ancestors can be found. For most indigenous cultures of the world the ancestors are recognised as a continuing source of wisdom and inspiration for the living. They are consulted on special occasions when answers to questions are needed by individuals and communities, when the source of trouble is sought, also for personal and communal healing, and when the future needs to be known. Gifted priestesses and shamans communicate with the ancestors by talking with them as if they are still alive, through prayer, in trance, in dreams, through the appearance of signs and symbols, and in altered states of reality, induced by deprivations, by ingesting natural herbs, or by expanding personal consciousness.

The ancestors who dwell just across the border of everyday reality have personality and character similar to their characters in life. Not all are good, some are as awkward and tricky as they once were in life. Many however are freed from the restraints imposed in life by their karma. They have learned the lessons of the lives they have led and have gained in wisdom.

Ancestors in many parts of the world are often associated with particular animals and birds, whose appearance in nature marks the presence of the ancestors. In places like Australia, the Primal Ancestors are visible in the shapes and forms of the landscape itself and are part of its creation story. And this is so in the modern day creation myth for Avalon offered in this book, where Nolava forms the land of Avalon and Glastonbury. In many cultures there is no distinction between revered Ancestor and Goddess or God.

In our western cultures unfortunately we do not honour our ancestors as an enduring source of wisdom accessible to the living. As a consequence we have lost so much. As Priestesses of Avalon it is part of our role to bring back awareness of the store of wisdom that our ancestors hold and reconnect to it. These may be genetic ancestors and also spiritual ancestors, the ancient lineages of priestesses to whom we feel connected in spirit. We have first to explore our personal genealogy, to find who our blood ancestors are.

Nowadays many of us live in a world where people move easily from place to place and relatively few of us stay in the place where we and our ancestors were born. Even if we have family living in the same area for a hundred years or more we find that our distant ancestors originally came from elsewhere. They may have migrated in the past to England from Europe or Scandinavia. If we live in America or Australia or any of what were for a time, colonies of the old British, Spanish or Portuguese Empires, our ancestors may be European. They may also have come from South America or Africa. If we are European, we may originally have come from the Steppes of Russia. We do not live in the lands where our ancestral roots lie buried.

Our ancestral journey begins by tracing our family tree, finding out who our foremothers and forefathers were, as far back as we can go, recognising the physical and cultural roots that have made us who we are. As we travel the globe we journey to the places our ancestors came from and we experience a deep nourishing sense of coming home. A piece of the jigsaw of who we are, slots into place and we are made whole by the experience. We begin to embrace the fact that we may have witches and pirates, cooks and soldiers, queens and colonisers in our pasts. We begin the process of healing and making reparation for the wounds in our pasts, for those inflicted upon us and those we have inflicted on others. We begin to root ourselves into the body of our Mother Earth instead of feeling alienated and separated from Her as if we came from another planet. Now we can truly incarnate.

International travel has made the world more accessible to more people, and this opening of the world to us is an outer reflection of an inner reality. We no longer incarnate just within one race and one culture over generations as seems to be the case for many indigenous tribespeople. Since the Chinese invasion of Tibet in the 1950s and the crushing of the Tibetan people and their culture, many Tibetan lamas are now consciously incarnating into western bodies. The conditions for continuing spiritual traditions within Tibet itself are gone for now. Instead a diaspora is occurring, not just of teachings, but also of reincarnating human beings. We are spreading ourselves around the planet. The same is true for incarnations from other waning spiritual cultures.

I have explored my personal incarnational herstory and found that I have had previous lives in many different cultures, several as a monk in Tibet, as a priestess in ancient Krete and in other Goddess cultures as well as many ordinary lives. I am not exceptional. I think many of us have similar experiences when we travel to places around the world which are immediately familiar, while others are relatively unknown. In the present I am a modern day woman living in Brigit's Isles with Welsh, Irish, and northern British ancestry and incarnational links to many cultures of the world. I have reclaimed my origins running back in time to the people of ancient Avalon, to the Priestesses of Avalon who in the past walked this earth, to the Nine Morgens, to Madron, Ancestor and Mother of the lineage of Avallach, to Nolava the Goddess and Primal Ancestor, who is embodied in the land itself as the Maiden Swan, as the vibrant Lover, as the Great Mother, and as an Old Crone.

I believe that many of us are born at this time precisely because of the breadth of our past experience in different places in the world. We know in our bones and through experience that all human beings are essentially one, despite all differences of appearance of race and culture. We are born now to help usher in a multicultural and universal world view, that will filter out into the societies in which we live. At this time of great change we incarnate to bring in with us respect for the Earth, wisdom of emotion, mind and spirit garnered in previous incarnations, which needs to be expressed in a modern day 21st century context. We are the return of the Goddess to Her rightful place in the world and we bring the wisdom of the ancestors embodied with and in us.

Letting Go to the Samhain Fire

On our priestess journey we move into the new by dying to the old. One of our first tests is that of letting go to Her, developing trust in Her when we are afraid, when we are not quite sure who or what we believe in, when we don't know where She is taking us.

Remember all the things in your life that don't work for you. Make a list of these things. They may include unsatisfactory relationships, insecurity, inhibition, lack of self confidence, lack of faith, of money, of a secure home, of work, of creativity, disempowerment, ego inflation, anger, aggression, fear, sorrow, grief, addictions of all kinds, anything that holds you back from being who you truly are. As you walk the landscape collect fallen twigs from the trees, each one representing something that you would like to release from your life.

In a special place build a sacred Samhain fire, small or large, and throw onto it one by one the sticks which represent so much of your heart's desire for change. Do this for real. Let your tears fall as you let them go....... Watch the sticks being consumed by Her flames. Open your heart to Her transforming power, trusting Her to show you how to truly let go.

In a variation of this letting go, at Samhain make yourself a large Gal Doll, in Sumerian Gal(a) means vulva (Geraldine Charles), out of sticks and rags, just like Guy Fawkes, but made in Her image. She too can represent all that you wish to release to the fire, as well as being the Crone Goddess, who dies at Samhain. Burn Her in ceremony on your Samhain fire.

The Journey of the Soul

It is in the nature of our human life that we are conditioned from conception by our genetic inheritance and by our karma, the reverberating experiences of our childhood and of our previous lives. This conditioning moulds our characters, creates our personalities, giving us a sense of "I", this person who "I" am, who likes this and not that, who feels like this or that, who experiences happiness and dissatisfaction, who is me.

Spiritual development takes us on a journey into a different experience of who "I" truly am. As we grow psychologically and spiritually we begin to identify with a different "I", with a Self which is not conditioned by the past, a Self which is eternal, creative, inclusive, generous, powerful and loving, all qualities shared with Goddess. This part is usually known as our Soul and is identified with the divine, with Goddess.

On our priestess journey we are ever moving into greater communion with Goddess and therefore with our own souls. Which comes first? Knowledge of our own soul or knowledge of Goddess? They walk hand in hand, they are the same thing. Our Soul is the part of us which is Her energy within us. As we come to know one, we experience the other as well.

As we align ourselves more and more with Goddess rather than with our conditioned self, our personalities gradually become aligned with our souls. Her purpose for us becomes our purpose. Her will, our will. Her love for the world, our love of Her world, expressed in our decisions and in our actions. One of Her many ways of expression in the world is through our human activity. When we align with our soul energy we align with Her and our personalities become the vehicle for the expression of Her energy. For brief moments we may embody Her and share Her love and wisdom.

There are many things that can prevent us from expressing our soul's energy: our unconsciousness, our self-centredness, our greed, envy, jealousy, in fact, some of the seven deadly sins of Judaeo-Christian belief. However the Goddess's way is very different to the patriarchal path. In Goddess spirituality we are not born filled with sin. There is no sacrifice to be endured for redemption. We each have to find and walk the fine edge of balance between caring for ourselves and caring for others, between selfishness and empowerment, gratitude and greed, giving and receiving, so that we can come into the wholeness of who we are as human beings, individual and universal.

The journey to becoming a priestess is one of uncovering the mysteries of one's own soul. A Priestess of Avalon by definition serves the Goddess and Avalon, the Soul Within that is identified with Her and the Soul of the Land that is Hers.

Seeds of Intention

At Samhain seeds fall from the trees and plants onto the earth, or are deliberately planted in the ground. They lie buried for several months in the cold earth before they spring to life the following year. For their natural growth they need to lie dormant for a length of time before they are activated by renewed life in the springtime. In ceremony we collect the pips that we find in the middle of the apples of Avalon, representing the seeds of our intentions on our journey to priestesshood. We plant them in the earth so that they will lie for a season in stillness, in waiting, until they are catalysed by Her white rod at Imbolc.

Having let go of the things that no longer serve us at Samhain we spend time thinking about the things we hope to achieve during this First Spiral of our journey to priestesshood. We play traditional Hallowe'en games, dunking our heads into a bucket of cold water covering the Goddess's magical Avalon apples of the new season. Without using our hands or any other tricky devices, we must dip our faces into the water and bite hold of an apple, bringing it to the surface with our teeth, so that we can retrieve the pips, the seeds of rebirth that lie in the centre of the apple.

This is not as easy as it sounds and quite often this game brings up birth and childhood memories with the first expressions of resistance to this journey to becoming a priestess. Those in resistance project their Shadow material onto teachers and classmates, seeing them as the authority figures of childhood, who want to control their lives. Those who have struggled for so long to rise out of their early victimhood, are unwilling to give control of their actions to anyone else. If they don't want to bob for apples they won't. But how will they surrender to the Goddess, if they always want to be in control? It is after all only apples and water, or is it?

Dunk for Avalon apples in water. Once you have retrieved your apple cut it across the middle and notice in the centre the fivefold pattern of a pentagram formed by the positions of the pips. The pentagram is traditionally a symbol for the Dark Goddess. Eating the flesh of your apple, take the pips as your seeds of intention and plant them in a pot filled with earth. As you place each one into the earth speak your intention to the Lady of Samhain. Ask for Her blessings through the coming darkness of winter. Throughout the coming year tend your apple trees and transplant them into the ground as necessary. For them to become strong apple trees they will need to be grafted onto appropriate root stock.

From Samhain to Yule

From Samhain to Yule as the hours of darkness increase we move inwards, in our homes, in our lives, going inwards to ourselves and to the Goddess. Our natural instinct is to move towards hibernation as the light decreases, and just like the animals, the hedgehogs and squirrels, who fill their bellies with fruits and nuts, laying down fat for the winter, we eat more. Flowers fade and die away, the trees are stripped bare of leaves. Rain pours down from the heavens, the air cools. Colder winds begin to blow in from the east and north, instead of the prevailing warmer southwesterly winds. Our seeds of intention lie buried in stillness in the earth. As well as celebrating Her in seasonal festivals we learn to honour the Goddess every day.

At Samhain create an altar dedicated to Nolava *the* Crone *and* Dark Goddess, *to* Mazoe, Keridwen, *and* Sheela *na* Gig. *Find images which represent these* Goddesses *- statues, cauldrons, frogs, bats and sows, autumn leaves, dying vegetation, whatever* She *is to you. Find things which represent the four elements of earth, water, fire and air and place them on your altar.*

Every day light a candle and burn incense to the Crone *at your altar and pray to* Her *for help, for guidance, in gratitude, for healing for yourself, for others in need, for visions, etc.* Once *a week recreate your altar.*

Every day write down and/or draw your feelings, dreams, inspirations, intuitions and visions in your diary, i.e. what is going on for you.

At Samhain light a fire in honour of the Crone*, burning garden waste and any rubbish that no longer serves you. Throw apple halves across the fire to the one you love as a promise that you will journey together with the* Dark Goddess *through the hard as well as the easy times.*

On the new moon remind yourself of your intentions for the coming year, watering the seeds you have planted.

On the full moon create your own ceremony to celebrate the Crone *in your life, either the womanly* Crones *that are in your family and amongst your friends or the* Goddess Crone.

Make a pilgrimage to Nolava *the* Crone *in* Glastonbury Avalon*, walk on* Her *sagging womb,* Her *breast,* Her *head and crown, tuning into* Her *energy, listening for* Her *words of wisdom for you. Find* Her *sacred places in the land.*

Visit other sacred sites where the Underworld Goddess *dwells, including neolithic long barrows and ritual sites, sacred hills with* Underworld *entrances, caves, wells,* Lake Bala*, etc. Walk the land at night under the stars. Face your fears of darkness. Sing, dance and pray to the* Dark Goddess.

Begin to explore your personal genealogy, finding the names of your foremothers and forefathers, and where they lived, tracing the patterns of your family ancestry. Begin to remember your incarnational ancestry, where you believe you might have lived in previous incarnations.

The Stillness
Yule Festival of the Mother of Air

At Winter Solstice in the Stillness around December 21st we honour the Mother of Air in many forms as Nolava of Air, the Cailleach, the Old Woman of Winter, who is Bone Woman and Stone Woman. We honour Tyronoe, Morgen of Air and Yuletide. We celebrate Danu, Goddess of the Tuatha de Danann, the ancient Goddess people who came to Brigit's Isles from the sky, landing on a mountain in Ireland. We honour Her birds, the incarnate angels who have the ability to fly through the air. We celebrate Arianrhod of the Silver Wheel who dwells in the Upperworld of the stars of Corona Borealis. We celebrate our distant Ancestors, those beings of fire and ice, earth and water, who made the land on which we live, who speak to us on the wind, who we can reach by flying towards them.

Winter Solstice is the time when the sun has reached its most southerly rising and setting points on the horizon, and stays there for a time before beginning its return north. December 21st is the shortest day of the year and thereby the longest night. Nowadays in Brigit's Isles winter solstice normally marks the beginning of winter rather than the middle. Cold winds blow and rain pours from the heavens. The skies clear and frost covers the fields, killing off plants, insects, animals and birds, the old and infirm. Colour drains from the landscape to shades of grey and beige. Bark is stripped from the trees and flesh from the bones to reveal the skeletons of all things. Following the pattern of Her nature, we surface for a time for our Yuletide ceremonies and celebrations, which mark the beginning of a second phase of winter when we move into the Stillness of hibernation and inner focus until Imbolc.

At midwinter we create ceremonies that honour Nolava of the Air, Tyronoe, Danu and Arianrhod. We explore our spiritual life, we learn about prayer and how to make altars to Her glory. We start a dream diary. We learn how to cleanse our auras and to bless ourselves with air. We learn about psychic protection. We walk the sacred landscape of the Ancestors. We continue to investigate our genealogy and reclaim our lineage.

Honouring Nolava of Air

Nolava of Air is the spiritual breath of the Isle of Avalon. She is the invisible loving essence that underlies all created forms, both in the everyday world and in the Otherworld of Avalon. She is Bone Woman, Stone Woman, the Cailleach, the Old Woman of Winter, who has lost all Her flesh, who has become light and insubstantial. Where the Crone leads us into death, the Cailleach is Death itself, the Space between dying and rebirth. She is the Absolute Stillness, that is the experience of Spirit before form. She is the immaterial Ancestor of the land and of the people of Avalon. She connects us to our Primal Ancestors, the beings of Fire and Ice, Water, Air and Earth, who created the magnificent world we live in. In imagination, in visions and in trance we can fly like Her birds of the air from this world to Avalon to meet and commune with our far Ancestors.

As well as being the Still Point of death, Nolava is the Everlasting Life that continues between incarnations. She is Air and the Wind. She is the Movement of the Invisible. She is Breath. She is Idea and Inspiration. She is Wisdom and all its works.

When we approach Avalon Nolava's wind often blows into our lives, blowing away the cobwebs in our minds, changing the way we see things. She can be gentle as a breeze on a balmy summer's day, bringing relief from too much heat, or She can be frightening as the hurricane that bowls us over, demanding that we notice Her unending power. She topples the trees and lifts the roofs from over our heads, leaving us shaking and vulnerable. Most days of the year we can feel Her touch as we climb the slopes of Glastonbury Tor. As we walk along the ridge of the Dragon's back to the summit She may try to blow us off. We must bend with Her blasts of air and lean into Her embrace in order to stay upright and centred. Sometimes we can almost fly with Her, spreading our coats out like wings.

The birds of the air belong to Nolava. By night Her owls fly the starry skies, hunting across the Summerlands. By day Her buzzards rise on the air currents above the island. Hers are the flocks of small birds that chatter in our gardens, eating berries and the grains we offer them. The King of British birds, the tiny wren, belongs to Her. Most days of the year Her winged ones fly on Her currents, rising and swooping above the earth, inspiring us with their magical powers of flight.

Air is the most subtle of the four natural elements and symbolises our spiritual nature. Air is the element which connects us to each other. Plants, insects, birds, animals and human beings all breathe the same air. We can connect to Nolava of Air via our breath and using sound.

Breathe in through your nose and out through the mouth, allowing your breathing to slow down. Count your breaths for 20 breaths. Then begin to sound Nolava's name slowly on the out breath, letting the sound of Her name roll around your mouth and throat,

No......laaaa........vaaaaa..............

Repeat Her name. Feel your awareness change.

This exercise can also be used with other Goddess names, Danu, Anu, Ana, Bridie, etc., and with Aaa....vaa....lonnn.....

Honouring Morgen Tyronoe, Morgen of Air

Tyronoe, Crone Morgen of the Isle of Avalon, Greets You
She Who Rules the Western Isle of the Dead
She Who Comes from the Starry North Bringing the Bright Silver Wisdom

She Who Turns the Silver Wheel, Knower of Stars and Suns

She Who Holds the Knowledge of the Ancestors, Lady of Bone and Shell
She Who Commands the Sands of Time and Spirits of Air and Wind

She Who Takes the Questing Disciple down through the Veils to the UnderWorld
She Who Takes You Deep into the Heart of the Meaning of Death ... and Life

She Who Asks the Questions at the Heart of Matter
She Who Mirrors Our Darkest Fears and Deepest Secrets

She Who Transforms
Be Ware Me and My Gifts, Bare Bones and Shells, My Jewels

Initiations of the Heart and Awakened Mind

by Leona Graham

Tyronoe is the eldest of the Nine Morgens, whose frailty belies Her infinite strength. She is very, very old. She has seen everything come and go. Her ancient eyes see from the beginning of time all that has taken place. She has knowledge of the origins and unfoldment of the universe. She is the astronomer/ astrologer of the circle of Morgens, who knows the patterns of the stars. She can read the past and foretell the future. She is Lady of the Labrynth and Mystress of the Web of life and death.

In the sacred land She is visible as Ice and Frost that in winter covers trees, plants, grasses, rhynes and rivers in a sparkling white coat. She transforms the landscape overnight. She is the Cold of winter, the bare, the stripped down. She lacks warmth and heat. Hers are the continuing gifts of the ancestors: wisdom, insight and vision. She is the dark of the moon, the night when there is no light, except for the light of a billion stars.

As a woman She is over 70 years of age and older. Her colours are silver and grey, the colours of winter. We experience Her in the chill winds that blow across the Summerland, that freeze our bones as we climb the Tor, or walk across Windmill Hill. Sometimes we see Her sylphs, whose moving bodies form the air that we breathe. Sometimes we see Her wind dragons tumbling through blustery skies, painting patterns in the clouds, of birds, animals and Holy Beings.

Tyronoe is also Holly Woman, the Evergreen Lady, whose bright leaves tell us that the Goddess lives, even in the depths of winter. Her red berries splashed amongst the green feed the birds and are reminders of Her life-giving blood in the darkness of winter. In these days Holly Woman's reign begins at winter solstice, lasting through the spring and early summer to Litha, the summer solstice, when She hands Her life power to the Oak Woman as She comes into flower and leaf.

In the depths of winter as you walk upon Her landscape call to Tyronoe to reveal Herself to you as sylph and dragon, as bone and shell. Ask Her to take you into the meaning of the things that happen to you, into the essence of who you are. Walk Her sacred winter landscapes, see Her in the bare branches of the trees, the sparseness of nature, in stillness and silence. Walk in holly woods and decorate your home and temple with holly in celebration of the Evergreen Lady.

Honouring Danu

Danu, Anu, Anu Danaa, Ana or Aine is the Mother Goddess of the Tuatha de Danann, the people of the Goddess Danu, who were the Shining Ones immortalised in Keltic legend, particularly in Ireland. Danu and Her people were said to have landed on a hillside in Ireland having travelled from beyond the North Wind, from the magical land of the Hyperboreans, where some of our own distant Ancestors may be found. By the time they come down to us, the stories of the Tuatha de Danann, who were an equal number of women and men, have become the much reduced tales of a warring, heroic, mainly male race of people. In Wales and England the original Goddess-loving stories were changed even further by monks and patriarchal storytellers into tales of the descendants of the male god Don. These can be read in the Welsh Mabinogion, where at its beginning, we can still glimpse the remnants of a much older reverence for the Goddess.

From my researches I suggest that it was the Tuatha de Danann who built the neolithic stone circles, which honour the Goddess and connect the earth and the heavens. The remains of these ancient ritual sites can still be found all over Brigit's Isles.

At Yuletide visit Danu's stone circles in the landscape. Standing in the centre of the circle and beside individual stones, sound Her name,

Daaaa...........nuuuu...............

Feel the sound reverberating between and within the stones. It is now believed that many smaller stone circles were designed as sound spaces, where sound was used to alter states of consciousness. See what happens to you.

Honouring Arianrhod

Arianrhod's story is found in the Romance of Math ap Mathonwy, which includes several ancient Goddesses, Arianrhod, Blodeuwedd and Keridwen, each in their own way maligned in a story which seeks to glorify the male protagonists. Like other tales recorded by Christian monks it tells the story of the demise of the Goddesses in our lands.

In the myth Arianrhod is named as a daughter of Don, that is, She is originally the daughter of Danu. She is a Virgin Goddess in Her own right, miraculously giving birth as She steps over King Math's wand, to twin sons, a golden-haired boy and a darker son, Dylan of the Wave. As the story unfolds we see the King and his advisor Gwydion playing a series of tricks upon Arianrhod, first trying to get Her to name Her son, then to arm him for battle and then they create a wife for him, who is Blodeuwedd the Flower Maiden and Owl Goddess. These are all the natural gifts of the Goddess, who retains the right to bestow these gifts upon us, despite what humans try to impose. She gives us our true name when we are ready to receive it. She arms us as we wear Her colours for the battles of life, and She can bring true love into our lives.

Arianrhod's connection to Avalon is through the great three-dimensional labrynth found on the slopes of Glastonbury Tor. Like all seven circuit labrynths, this one is dedicated to Ariadne of the Red Thread, She who leaves a trail of Red Thread through the pathways of the labrynth, that we may find our way into and out of the labrynth of life. The upward spiralling pathway of the Tor Labrynth leads to Caer Sidi, which is also known as Caer Arianrhod, the revolving castle of Arianrhod of the Silver Wheel. In the heavens this castle is the Corona Borealis, the Crown of the North Wind, which also belongs to Ariadne. It is said to be Her wedding crown thrown into the heavens when She married Dionysos, the God of Love and Wine. Mythically Ariadne and Arianrhod are the same goddess, Ariadne ruling the middle world, while Arianrhod rules the upper world. In Avalon their sister in the Underworld is Crone Nolava or Morgen la Fey, Keeper of the Cauldron of Transformation. The three worlds are joined by the axis mundi, the world axis, sometimes envisioned as a holy mountain, which here in Avalon is Glastonbury Tor. See later section on the Initiation of the Glastonbury Tor Labrynth.

In Avalon Arianrhod is our starry inspiration. She is the Weaver of the invisible threads of life, creating the patterns that hold everything together. She is Arachne the Spider at the centre of Her Web, and Ariadne the pathway through.

Identify the Corona Borealis in the heavens. As you walk the labrynth of life honour Arianrhod as a source of inspiration. In winter study the spider as She weaves webs that sparkle in the frost. Become aware of the shining etheric threads that connect all things in Her nature.

The Power of Air and Spirit

The natural elements of earth, water, fire, air and space are physical symbols for five different energetic states. The most dense is, of course, earth and the least dense is space. Water is less dense than earth, fire is less dense than water, air is less dense than fire, and space is less dense than air.

Esoterically the elements are used to symbolise five different realms of being: the physical/etheric material realm (earth), the emotional realm (water), the mental realm (fire) and the spiritual realm (air), expressions of increasingly subtle energies. The fifth element of space is the spacious Void of the Goddess out of which all creation emerges. This system is different to other traditions in which fire is said to represent spirit and air to represent the mind. I prefer to use the former system as it connects physical to symbolic density and gives value to spiritual rather than mental energy.

As the least dense of the four elements, air or wind represents spiritual energy, the invisible pneuma that is before all things and present within all manifestation. Within human beings our spiritual nature encompasses all the workings of our soul, that invisible inner core which is loving and generous, compassionate and wise, which connects us to every other being on the planet. As Priestesses of Avalon our aim is to bring the spiritual truths of the spacious Void into consciousness and everyday reality.

Most patriarchal religions have recognised spiritual goals to which their believers aspire, for example, being saved by Jesus, dying and going to heaven, avoiding hell, becoming enlightened, or attaining siddhis (powers) or nirvana, removing oneself from the endless wheel of life, or dying a martyr's death. Many religious goals are connected to what we believe will happen to us after life is over, when we die, rather than to how we live our lives on earth. Each of the major patriarchal religions has its own belief system, which is hierarchical in nature, with the primary goal only being reached by the few, who hold and wield power over the many who must struggle through life.

Within Goddess spirituality I believe there is no one goal which needs to be achieved by everyone, that there are almost as many spiritual goals as there are human beings. Some goals we hold in common and others are our own and unique. There are many spiritual experiences to be had as a human being on this beautiful planet, and the expanses of the soul are vast and mostly unknown to us. We know so little of who we are as energetic and spiritual beings, that to fix universal goals beyond the most basic communion with the Goddess, seems very limiting.

Our spiritual desires are actually many and different and need to be recognised as such. We may want to experience inner peace, we may want to become more loving, we may want to serve the Goddess in the ways that She shows us. We may want to merge with the Goddess, to become one with Her infinite wisdom, or we may want to meet Her face to face and bathe in Her radiance. Or we may simply want to be a better person, to heal ourselves and others, or we have a myriad more aims. All of these are valid spiritual goals, no one being higher or lower than any other. If we set one single goal for everyone based on a hierarchical belief system we limit the range and extent of the spiritual experiences which we can have in life, which the Goddess will lead us to if we are lucky.

When I first moved to Glastonbury at the age of 29 from my spiritual haven in Wales my life began to fall apart almost immediately, as I began to engage once again in emotional and sexual relationships with men after a long period of abstinence. It was a shocking experience as the inner spiritual calm that I had attained over several years of intensive meditation practice proved useless in holding my emotions together, when my heart opened in love once again to a man. I had believed that through my spiritual practice I had transcended emotion, a traditional male religious goal. I thought I had risen above it. I found that what I had actually been doing was suppressing my emotions, which erupted full force when catalysed.

In the wake of much emotional pain and anguish I decided to let go of all my former belief systems and to see what would happen when there were no familiar props there to support my beliefs. Would I still have a spiritual life without a belief system? At first I felt bereft without my routine daily practice, my esoteric church, my comfortable beliefs, but happily I found that my spirituality still continued as I released habitual practices. For a time there was a spiritual Void in my life, no-thing was happening, but out of that Void Goddess emerged, bringing with Her a very different way of doing things. Her way was based not on religious dogma and repeating received wisdom, but was founded in a direct living connection to Her day by day. She began to speak to me as She does now, and I hear and obey Her voice as best I am able.

This direct connection to Her as an immanent divinity experienced within our own consciousness and body, as well as being transcendent and universal, is for me one of the hallmarks of Goddess spirituality. In exploring our development as priestesses we will look at the power of prayer and meditation, and ways of expanding our spiritual experience.

Prayers, Spells and Surrender

For priestesses prayer is conversation with the Goddess, it is our way of communicating with Her. We talk to Her directly one to one, heart to heart, without intermediaries. This open heart communication gives magical power to our prayers. We encourage others to speak to Her directly too. Our spiritual practice is to express our gratitude to Her for everything She gives to us on Her bounteous earth, for the gifts of Her nature, for the food we eat, for the water we drink, for the air we breathe, for the weather, for the animals and birds, for Her beauty all around us. We give thanks for our families and friends, for the lessons, some easy and some very hard, that we receive from them. We give thanks for our enemies who mirror our wounds.

We also ask for Her help in difficult times. We speak to Her of our hopes and dreams, and ask for Her blessings on all our ventures. We pray for others, knowing that just by thinking of them in Her presence, Her blessings will flow towards them. We pray for healing for ourselves and for those in need that we know and for all those millions on this earth whom we don't know personally, but who we know suffer. We place everything before Her wisdom and compassion.

A spell is an incantation in which, as with prayer, magical power is given to words. Spell-making involves our desires and the conscious manipulation of the material, astral and mental worlds in order to achieve our desires, whether it is to bring us a soul mate, to heal someone who is sick or to bring world peace. Spell-making has a different focus to the practices of gratitude and communion with Her.

Within the arts of spell-making there are spells made with good intentions for the best outcomes for ourselves and others, and there are spells made with negative intentions, to harm others. The effectiveness of any spell depends on the focus and clarity of thought of the spellmaker and not upon their motivation. Dabbling in negative spellcraft is a dangerous occupation which can be effective, but which does not usually bring happiness, expand soul consciousness or increase the sum of human wellbeing. Priestesses never engage in negative spellcraft or black magic, a phrase I hesitate to use as black has been used to demonise both the Black or Dark Goddess and the darker skinned peoples on this planet, but we understand what the words mean.

Prayers and spells in which we ask for certain things to happen are at opposite ends of a spectrum of requests, the differences between the practices involved merging in the centre. A broad definition of the difference would be to say that prayer is a request to the Goddess, which leaves the outcome and the means of attaining it completely in Her hands, while a spell has a definite outcome in mind and involves the manipulation of energy and matter by the spellmaker to achieve that outcome. For example, we might pray to the Goddess asking Her to bring us our perfect partner. Or we may decide to make a love potion using herbs and chants spoken under a full moon with a particular person in mind, so that person will come to be attracted to us. In the former prayer we trust that Goddess will bring us what we need, the true love who will be the best person for us. In the latter we want to choose our own partner. These are different ways of doing things.

It is not that prayer is good or better and spells are bad or worse, they are just different ways of doing things. Spell-making is associated with witchcraft, the wisdom of wise women who through the ages helped the poor, the needy and the sick by making spells to heal and make whole.

In the years of the Inquisition tens of thousands of women and some men were hanged or burned at the stake, because they were successful spell-makers and because they were women with spiritual power in a world where men held temporal power. Both witchcraft and spell-making are enjoying a popular resurgence in the present. There are hundreds of books now available on Wicca, witches, witchcraft, spellmaking and magic, and when one of the most popular children's books and films ever made, is about the young Harry Potter, who attends a school of magical craft.

There are many places where the distinctions between prayer and spellmaking become blurred. For example, if I pray to the Goddess for healing for someone and then write their name on a piece of paper and place it on the altar, is that a prayer or a mini-spell? If at the end of a spell made to find a new home I place everything in Her hands and say, "*By your will, Lady*", does that then override my desire to manipulate circumstances and other people to get what I want?

It is not as simple as saying that prayer is a selfless activity while spellmaking is ego-driven, both prayer and spells can be fuelled by ego desire, by what we want to happen. The attempt to fulfil our personal desires is one of the ways in which we are led through life by the Goddess, so that we come to meet Her, both through our failures or our successes.

However I believe that spellmaking has karmic consequences that I personally do not care to engage with. I think that spells work, but not usually in the ways that we expect. There is the apocryphal tale of the person who makes a spell for money, and then their favourite aunt dies suddenly, leaving them money when they would have preferred a lottery win. The costs of successful spells can be too great and I am not wise enough to foresee all the consequences of making spells. I do not teach spellmaking in any form and prefer prayer, invocation and surrender to the Goddess as a means of changing the world (see later sections on Ceremony and Invocation). Saying that, it is quite possible to be both a priestess and a witch, but our focus is different.

For me becoming a Priestess of Avalon has been and is a journey of continuing surrender to and trust in Goddess. It is my path to serve Her as I am able. After many years of joyful and sometimes painful experience of Her ways I now trust that She knows absolutely what is best for me and will bring me everything I need for my fulfilment in life, if I can allow Her to. She will take me exactly where I need to go. The more that I surrender to Her and let Her show me the way forward the more whole and creative my life becomes. The more I can hear Her voice and act spontaneously on

Her instruction the happier I am. This journey of surrender takes away none of my personal creativity and autonomy, as I have many ideas and act upon them. Surrender does not mean submission or passivity. I am the actor in the world with my energies and personality, but She leads me on to places I would be too scared to go alone. I see this process working in others too.

I believe that the true path of a Priestess of Avalon is one of surrender to the Lady as completely as we can. As we align ourselves to Her we move into the flow of Her energy, and experiences and events that are aligned to our soul purpose and to Her are attracted towards us. A new and equal lover suddenly arrives in our life, we find the right job, we move to the right house, etc. We have less need to manipulate circumstance to achieve what we want. She and Her life will bring us what we need for our healing and fulfilment.

Making Space to Hear and See

As well as praying in gratitude and for what we want, prayer is also about making the space to listen, opening our outer and inner ears to Her voice. When we ask Her a question, when we ask for Her wisdom, we need to listen for Her answers. We can hear Her voice as a whisper, as an inner knowing, as a few words that we hear inside our heads and hearts, as new ideas that come into our minds daring us to play bigger, as the voice of intuition that bids us move in new directions that our rational minds find uncomfortable, but which will bring us into a better place.

In my experience, if we ask the Goddess to come, She comes. If we ask for help She arrives immediately. If we ask for a sign She will give us one. However, many times She speaks and we do not listen, we ask for a sign and when it comes we ignore it. We dismiss its appearance as merely coincidence. We think we know better and are in control of our lives and destinies. We make bargains with Her - if you do this, then I will do that, but when She does Her part, we don't follow through with ours. We didn't really mean it and so our fears hold in check our pathways into new life.

Dreams and visions

Ofttimes the Goddess will communicate with us through sleeping and waking dreams and visions, as well as in words or an inner knowing. Many people find it hard to recall their dreams, which can contain vital information for the developing priestess. One of the easiest ways to increase our dream recall is to write down dreams and waking visions in a journal, as soon as we wake up, keeping it next to our bed, ready with a pen to capture the last fleeting images and bring them into waking consciousness. Many dreams are mundane recollections of yesterday's activities. Others tell us of our repeating patterns, our childhood fears, our past life experiences. Some, if we are lucky, involve direct communications from the Goddess, when we see and speak to Her. I remember one dream that I had after many years of devotion to Green Tara, the Tibetan Goddess of Compassion, in which quite an ordinary looking woman appeared, who told me many important things. In the dream I knew it was Green Tara because She had translucent green skin.

One of our aims is to become conscious in the dream state, self aware and able to direct our experience. See the chapter on *Scrying* in the Second Spiral.

A *simple practice to begin with is to try to see your feet or your hands in a dream and then move them about.*

All the way through the journey to become a priestess it is good to daily record dreams, visions and experiences in a journal as this helps anchor all the changes which happen to us. Writing them down helps us to remember more, bringing what was unconscious from the dream world into consciousness. This gives us practical experience of how to open our awareness further, so that we can move through the Veil into the invisible worlds. We can also, importantly, feel and express our innermost feelings and aspirations in our journal as they arise.

Spoken Prayers

Prayers are most often spontaneous, spoken aloud or silently. As I understand it the Goddess doesn't require an antiquated language of thee's and thou's. We are in the 21st century and can bring poetry to our prayers. We are all poets, all capable of speaking the feelings of our hearts to Her.

Prayers can be offered to the Goddess standing, sitting, kneeling or with movement. She doesn't mind which. They can be sung too. There are now many wonderful Goddess chants that we can sing together, composed by Goddess-loving people from all over the world. As priestesses we learn a repertoire of songs for any occasion that will help us and others to connect to Her. It's not important that we sing like divas, we just need to be able to sing our prayers of love for the Goddess and encourage others to join in.

Prayer can also be formalised and there are many beautiful written prayers to Her which we might like to say individually and collectively. We can receive inspiration for prayer anywhere and particularly when we walk in nature. The following is a prayer to be made with movements when standing on top of Glastonbury Tor, opening oneself to the Goddesses in the landscape.

(Standing with arms outstretched)
Nolava, Swan Maiden flying across the earth
Transport me on wings of vision
Up into your heavenly realms
To experience your delights
(Touching the earth)
Nolava, Crone of Avalon
Deep in the earth beneath my feet
In your womb cave of transformation
I feel your power to change me
(Hands on breasts)
Nolava, Mother of All
As I stand upon the holy Isle of Avalon
On the breast of your sacred body
Fill me with the milk of your loving kindness
(Hands on heart)
Nolava, Lady of Avalon
Goddess of this sacred land
I open myself to your transforming power
Embrace me with your love.

The following is a prayer that came just before Goddess Conference 2002 as I walked beside the River Brue, which is named for Bride, which skirts the southern side of Glastonbury. There are several Goddess prayers and songs which continue to use the masculine *Hallelujah*, which actually means *Hail Jahweh*, or Jehovah the great patriarch. I wanted to find a good Goddess alternative and invented *Alleluma* which for me means *Hail Ma* or Hail Mother, which has a much softer, rounded sound to it. The rhythm of the prayer invites participation and we can all substitute phrases other than those given.

Alleluma

Alleluma, Alleluma, Goddess
Praise your holy names

Alleluma, Alleluma, Goddess
Praise your holy names
In the sunshine and the rainstorms, Goddess
Praise your holy names
In happiness and in sadness, Goddess
Praise your holy names
When the moon is dark, new, full and waning, Goddess
Praise your holy names
When I bleed and when blood pauses, Goddess
Praise your holy names
Alleluma, Alleluma, Goddess
Praise your holy names
Alleluma, Alleluma, Goddess
Praise your holy names
At Samhain and at Imbolc, Goddess
Praise your holy names
At Beltane and at Lammas, Goddess
Praise your holy names
At Solstice and at Equinox, Goddess
Praise your holy names
Alleluma, Alleluma, goddess
Praise your holy names
In the truth of your love, Goddess
Praise your holy names
In the unveiling of your face, Goddess
Praise your holy names
In the revelation of your presence, Goddess
Praise your holy names
Alleluma, Alleluma, Goddess
Praise your holy names
Alleluma, Alleluma, Goddess
Praise your holy names.

Within patriarchal religions there are many beautiful prayers and I have played with changing some of these into forms which are more meaningful to me.

Prayer to Mother Earth

Our Great Mother, Ertha, whose Body is the Earth
Upon which we live and move and have our being

We praise Your holy names.
May we honour and serve You,
May we again be true guardians of Your nature
Loving and caring for all that you have created.
Continue as always to give us the fruits of your bounty,
Forgive our faults as we forgive ourselves and each other for our failings,
Guide us as we journey through life on this your planet,
Protect us from all harm and danger,
For this is your world with its beauty and abundance
Forever and ever.
Bless us, Great Mother,
Blessed be.

The phrase *Blessed be* is often used as a response or an ending for Goddess prayers in the way that *amen* is used in the Christian religion. *Awen* is another term which is used, meaning divine spirit.

Goddess Meditation and Creating Sacred Space

Goddess meditation is an activity where we create Space within our chattering minds for Her to come in and be present with us. There are many forms of meditation and we can choose those that we enjoy. Their purpose is always to create Space within which we can experience the energy of the Goddess, of our own Souls and of other dimensions of reality.

It was only relatively recently that I realised that when we talk about creating a Sacred Space we are not just talking about creating an outer physical space which is conducive to prayer and meditation. We are actually talking about creating an inner space. Sacred Space is an energy of the soul which can be generated and felt by others, encouraging them to enter their own place of stillness.

One of the simplest meditations that I recommend as a preparation for ceremony and ritual, as well as any healing practice or creative activity, such as singing, painting, thinking, etc., is that of grounding and centring in our Soul. This practice ensures that we are positively polarised in relation to others and are radiating energy from our hearts.

Grounding and Centring in the Soul

The energy of the soul can be experienced directly or by coming into resonance with its particular energy frequency. The detailed instructions given here are a guide for beginners. As the ability to focus attention at will and to visualise precisely improves, the energy contacts can be set up rapidly in a matter of moments.

1. *Sit comfortably and allow the body to relax and let the cares of the everyday world slip away. Watch the breath as it flows in and out of the nostrils and count twenty breaths.*
2. *Take a deep breath in, filling the lungs, and bring your attention to your heart. Hold the breath and see the electric blue* Heart Chakra, *located in the centre of the body near to the physical heart, beating in rhythm with the heart beat. Breathe out. Repeat three or four times.*
3. *Breathe in, hold the breath. Visualise a thread of light moving from the* Heart Chakra *down through the body to the* Base Chakra, *which is coloured a dull red that grows brighter as energy moves through it. The* Base Chakra *is located on the perineum between the vagina or scrotum and the anal sphincter. Breathe out.*
4. *Breathe in, hold the breath and visualise the thread of light extending from the* Base Chakra *down through your legs and feet and through the floor you are sitting on into the earth. See it moving through the earth towards the magnetic energetic core of* Mother Earth. *Visualise the earth in as much detail as you can from the soil at the surface through different layers of the rocky crust, through the red-hot molten fiery body of the earth to the centre. Imagine its texture, weight and density as the thread of energy passes through it. Breathe out. Repeat your breathing and holding the breath until this visualisation is stable.*
5. *Breathe in, hold the breath and feel the energy pulse as it moves from your* Heart Chakra *to the centre of the earth. Breathe out.*
6. *Breathe in, hold the breath and visualise energy returning along the thread of light, from the centre of the* Mother's *body up through all its layers, coming up through the ground back into your body via the* Base Chakra *and from there up through the body to the* Heart Chakra. *Breathe out.*
7. *Breathe in, hold the breath, and feel the energy of the earth moving up through the thread invigorating the* Heart Chakra, *opening it out, allowing* Soul *energy to move in the heart. Breathe out.*
8. *Breathe in, hold the breath and visualise a thread of light moving from the* Heart Chakra *up through the body, the neck and the head to the sparkling white/rainbow-coloured* Crown Chakra *on top of the head. Breathe out.*
9. *Breathe in, hold the breath and visualise the thread of light extending out of the* Crown Chakra *into the air above the head, up through the ceiling and out of the roof of the building you're in (if you are). See it travelling up into the sky, through the clouds and the atmosphere and up towards the deep indigo blue of*

space, See it moving out across the solar system away from the earth and the sun. Visualise it moving across the galaxy and the universe reaching to the farthest sparkling star you can imagine, your Motherstar. *Breathe out. Repeat your breaths and holding the breath until the image is stable.*

10. *Breathe in, hold the breath and see the energy pulse along the thread as it moves between the* Heart Chakra *and your* Motherstar. *Breathe out.*

11. *Breathe in, hold the breath and visualise sparkling energy returning back from your* Motherstar *across the universe, through the galaxy towards the solar system. See it moving past the outer planets towards the* Blue Planet. *See it moving into the earth's atmosphere, towards the place where you are sitting, coming in through the roof of the building you are in, into the space above your head, then in through the* Crown Chakra *on top of your head and down to the* Heart Chakra. *Breathe out.*

12. *Breathe in, hold the breath and feel this* Motherstar *energy invigorating your* Heart, *meeting and blending with the energy of* Mother Earth. *Feel your* Heart Chakra *opening out and your soul energy beginning to radiate outwards in all directions horizontally from your centre. Breathe out.*

13. *Breathe in, hold the breath and visualise yourself so that your chakras appear as sparkling beads on a thread of light, a necklace, which connects the centre of* Mother Earth *to your* Motherstar. *Breathe out.*

14. *Breathe in, hold the breath and feel love and compassion, the energy of your* Soul, *of the* Goddess Herself, *begin to pour out through your* Heart Chakra, *radiating horizontally outwards in all directions. Breathe that energy outwards through the body.*

15. *Breathe in, hold the breath and stabilise the outward flowing* Heart *energy as a radiance emanating from a place of stillness.*

16. *Holding your heart open move deeper into your centre into the place of peace and serenity, that is stillness.*

Once you are centred in your own Soul, you can put the set of energy connections which got you there to the back of your mind. You are now ready for creative activity, for healing or ceremony. You can continue with the visualisation, breathing loving compassionate energy out into the world around you, to your home and family, your village, town or city, to the continent on which you live and to the whole planet, healing all those who are in pain or suffering.

The purpose of this exercise is to allow you to experience what it feels like when the energy of the soul and of the Goddess is pouring into your personality vehicles. Once you know what this energy feels like you can begin to invoke it at will.

Goddess Altars and Statues

Altars are an important element in developing Goddess spirituality. For priestesses they have several purposes. Altars act as a focus for our attention and for our prayers. They help us to turn inwards from our busy lives. They help us to come into this moment, Now. They help us to connect to the Goddess via the imagery upon them.

We can place our statues of the Goddess on our altars. These statues are symbols of the Goddess which inspire us as we look at them. They are not of themselves Goddesses, but I find that they open a connection to the Goddess when I look at them. I have altars all over my home in every room. I like it that wherever my eye falls, it rests upon an image of Her in one form or another, so that my mind is always linked to Her by threads of energy and so can soften in Her presence. I look at Her image and my consciousness opens to Her. It is as if She is called into Her image by my attention, thus the images themselves become charged with Her energy, which others can then feel.

Altars are places where we pray, establishing daily rhythms of prayer and contemplation, where we light candles and incense before Her image and make offerings to Her of flowers, fruits and grains in each season, where we can pour libations of spring waters, milk, honey and wine. Used daily they are receptacles for our offerings and prayers to the Lady. They become charged with Her energy, which then radiates out into the rest of our homes and temples.

Importantly, altars are a focus for creativity as we decorate them and change them with the seasons, reflecting Her ever-changing nature. Altars are not meant to be fixed in one form. They are tools for spiritual development and change as we and Her nature all around us changes.

Altars can be any shape - round, square, oblong, small and large. They can be static, the focus for a sacred space, or they can be moveable, fitting into a box or a small cupboard or a special bag. They can be placed against a wall, on the floor, on a shelf, on a table. In teaching the In the Heart of the Goddess trainings I like to work with a central circular altar on the floor around which we all sit in circle as equals before Her, our attention focused on the altar in the centre. This central altar is divided into eight segments using differently coloured cloths, each containing images appropriate to the eight seasons of the year. For example, the Samhain section is black and may contain images of the Crone or the Dark Goddess, while the Yule section is silver grey with winter imagery, feathers, bones and incense. As the teaching circle continues through the year the images change to reflect different faces of the Goddess. This altar is always aligned to the four and eight directions, north, east, south and west, and to the four elements of air, fire, water and earth, so that although we may be indoors we are grounded in the natural landscape of the Goddess, which is all around. Permanent and temporary altars can also be made outside in our gardens, or out on the land, as required.

Cleansing and Blessing with Air

We can use any of the four natural elements to offer the blessings of the Goddess to others and we can use each element to cleanse ourselves and others, to cleanse altars and sacred spaces, and any space we want to clear of disturbed energies. Here we shall look at how we can use the element of air.

To represent the element of air we use visible perfumed smoke or invisible scents. We burn natural herbs and aromatic plants, or incense, which is a mixture of herbs, flowers, spices and natural resins, to produce smoke, making it visible. Natural herbs used include sage, although this is not native to Britain, cedar, juniper, pine, rosemary and lavender. Incense is available in different forms. Incense or joss sticks are lit and then smoulder releasing smoke. Self-burning incense, powdered and in cones, is placed in a heatproof container, then lit so that it smoulders. Loose incense can be placed on burning charcoal, again in a heatproof container, to release perfumed smoke. Different incenses are used for different purposes and there are now incenses for all the different festivals of the year, for the different astrological signs, for different Goddesses, etc. Well known Glastonbury incense-makers include the Goddess Temple, Starchild and Ynys Witrin incenses.

Part of the equipment that every priestess needs is a heatproof container that does not get too hot to hold in one's hands - a large shell works well, or a ceramic or metallic pot with something heat resistant on the outside. Burning charcoals can also be placed on sand inside a container. Care should be taken at all times as charcoals can easily burn skin and other surfaces. In addition we need a feather fan which itself represents the element of air, to direct smoke from the incense where we want it to go.

Collect large feathers that are meaningful to you and tie several together with a piece of wood for the handle, using leather thongs or strips, or coloured strings. Carve and decorate the wood if desired. Tie in small bells which will tinkle as you wave the fan.

Cleanse your body and your home with incense. First choose an incense whose scent you like. Buy a tube of small round charcoals for burning and place one tablet in a heatproof container. Light the charcoal by holding a flame to one of its edges. The charcoal will begin to fizz. Place the charcoal in the container and blow on it until you see that it glows a dull red. The charcoal will take several minutes to catch alight all the way through, turning grey with a fiery centre. Place your incense on top of the burning charcoal and smoke will begin to arise. Using your feather fan waft smoke around your body and around the space you are cleansing. Use circular and spiral motions of the hands and arms. These are Goddess patterns used since ancient times and found throughout nature.

When cleansing another person encircle their whole aura beginning at the front on the level of the heart moving up and down the body, and then to the sides and back, again using circular and spiralling motions of the hands and arms. With downward strokes of the fan remove stray energies from the aura, smoothing its surface.

We can also use natural oils and perfumes to fill a space with a pleasant cleansing scent. Aromatic oils can be placed in open dishes, gradually evaporating in the natural temperatures to keep a room cleansed. Essential oils can also be placed in oil burners, with a candle beneath a ceramic or metal container so that the oil evaporates more quickly, filling the space with a gentle or pungent aroma depending on our purposes.

Cleansing with Sound

Another way to cleanse a space with air is by using sound. We can sing a clear note to clear the energies in a space or we can sound a bell or a singing bowl, which has a clear resounding note, several times. A more clangourous sound can be used to awaken dormant energies and to expel unwanted energies.

Find a bell or bowl whose sound you like, preferably one with a resonant tone. Cleanse your home by ringing the bell, or sounding the bowl throughout all the rooms. Listen to the reverberation of each ring until the sound disappears, allowing your mind to expand outwards with the ripples of sound as they expand outwards away from their source.

Ring your bell or sound your bowl before you pray to announce to yourself and others a change in space.

Psychic Protection

As Priestesses of Avalon our protection begins in the purity of our hearts and of our intentions. Our strength lies in having in a strong connection to the energy of our Soul radiating outwards into the world. Psychic protection also involves having clear boundaries, which prevent us from being harmed by external aggressors, who may want to project negativity onto us. We can feel the need for psychic protection when we are weakened by illness or stress and are psychically vulnerable, which automatically implies that we have lost our centre. We are out of balance and therefore can be psychically disturbed by other people's negative thoughts, emotions and feelings, which often mirror hidden parts of our own shadow selves.

We usually feel the need for psychic protection because we fear that something out there might be attacking us in some way, trying to hurt us. We are worried that we might be harmed by energies or entities that we can't control, who might overwhelm us. Whenever we feel that external energies are trying to get to us, this is like a psychic red flag for us. It tells us that we need first of all to look within, at ourselves, because there is something here for us to learn about our fears, anxieties and insecurities. There is something within us that needs healing, as well as there being something out there of which we are afraid. An inner transformative process is also going on that we need to experience. The way through is always to strengthen our centre which radiates love as well as to protect our boundaries.

There are now many good books on psychic protection. One of the seminal works is *Psychic Self Defence* by Dionne Fortune, the Goddess-loving occultist who lived in Glastonbury in the 1930s on the slopes of the Tor. Another good modern book is the *Art of Psychic Protection* by Judy Hall.

Here are a few techniques which may help you on your journey. The simplest, most effective and sometimes the most difficult technique to achieve when we feel the need for psychic protection, is to open our hearts and radiate compassion and the love in our soul out into the world, especially towards whoever or whatever we feel is coming at us. Everything negative dissolves in love. A good way to do this is to regularly practice the *Centring in the Soul* exercise given earlier in the chapter, so that you can centre yourself at will as and when you need to.

For personal protection

Visualise yourself clothed in light, in a sphere of light, in a cone of light. As Priestesses of Avalon we would choose the violet light of the Lady of Avalon. Every so often check that you are surrounded and enclosed by Her light.

If you feel psychically attacked and are afraid, surround yourself, or your bed if it is at night, with Goddess spirals. Draw them in space with your hand moving in a sunwise direction all around you. Visualise them in your mind drawing them in space, all around you, above and below. Hold the image of being completely encircled by spiralling protective energy. Anything coming towards you is diverted into the spiralling energy and dissipated.

Another Goddess symbol that is good to use is an upright pentagram. Draw the five-pointed star with your hand in space or visualise drawing it in your mind's eye. Begin at the bottom left hand point of the star, draw up to the top centre point, then follow down to the bottom right point. From there go to the top left hand point and straight across to the top right hand point. From there go back to the bottom left hand point. You have created a pentagram. The pentagram is a symbol of the planet Venus and also for the Dark Goddess. It is a good banishing symbol which repels unwanted intrusions.

Another way to deal with fear is to recognise that the fear we feel resides within us. The catalyst may be outside, but the feelings are inside us and we can address our fears more consciously. We can recognise fear in our bodies in the tension we feel in the solar plexus, in the rigidity of our faces, jaws, shoulders and muscles. We can consciously allow the body to shake to release fear. We can dance fear out of our bodies. We can build a sacred fire and give our fears away to the fire.

Psychic protection of your home

Regularly cleanse your home by physically cleaning it, then use candle flames, incense and sound to clear out unwanted energies. When you feel attacked place images of the Goddess on window sills facing outwards, so that anything coming towards you will meet the Goddess first. When you feel particularly vulnerable place small mirrors on your window sill, facing outwards, so that anything directed towards you just bounces back to the sender.

Psychic protection in Ceremony

Prepare for ceremony by *Grounding and Centring in your Soul* first. Trust that your Soul energy will continue to radiate throughout the ceremony. Check your heart space throughout to see that you are radiating loving energy outwards from your centre.

Psychic protection during Group Ritual

In this Avalonian Tradition we almost always work in circle creating sacred space around a central still point, and calling in the Goddesses of nine directions, the eight on the Sacred Wheel of the year and the ninth in the centre. Instead of marking out a sacred space by casting a circle, drawing it around us so that everything within is sacred and all that is outside is profane, we create sacred space in a different way.

In this developing tradition, we visualise the Goddesses of eight directions coming towards us from afar with all their attributes, creatures and qualities. We see their energy coming into the circle, filling it from the centre back out to the horizon and beyond, so that we are bathed in their energy. Finally we call in the Ladies of the centre, who come from within. The presence of these Goddesses is our protection in ceremony.

This ritual form is something which has developed over time from working with first the Wheel of Ana and then Britannia's Wheel. It was not planned, it has just evolved of its own accord. At the beginning of a ceremony we open the nine directions of the Wheel calling the Goddesses in and at the end of ceremony we say farewell and give thanks to them all. Sometimes we simply thank the Goddesses and leave the circle open as we continuously call the Goddess into our ceremonies and lives.

The Costume of a Sister, Brother and Priestess of Avalon

An important question - how do we wish to appear as Sisters and Brothers of Avalon and later as Priestesses of the Goddess and of Avalon? What costume shall we wear to reveal our roles. Many of us have an image in our minds most often drawn from mediaeval literature and drawings, from novels, paintings and Hollywood movies of how a priestess should look, but is that how we want appear? Our appearance as a priestess is not a given, it can be anything that we choose. Our apparel needs to take account of many factors not least of which is the weather in Brigit's Isles, which can be very warm in summer, and cold and wet in autumn and winter. We need indoor and outdoor sets of clothing that are practical and beautiful. We need robes and cloaks, coats, dresses, trousers, blouses, shoes and gloves, headdresses, veils and masks. A glorious opportunity to be creative and to shop.

What materials shall we use, wool, cotton, silk? What are the designs and symbols which we would like to incorporate as decoration? Many who have never decorated anything from childhood create beautiful designs and embroidery. I am awed by the creativity that emerges from people who say they aren't artistic and haven't made anything for themselves since they were at school.

So far each dedicand and priestess has created her/is own unique costume for their dedication ceremony, either making it herself or gathering together different items, decorating them as she chooses in the colours she chooses. Some are simple and refined, others a glorious riot of colour and imagination. There is no rule of how we should appear. At Yule we begin to think about possible designs for what we will wear in the dedication ceremony at the end of the First Spiral.

With Her inspiration think about how you want to appear as a Sister or Brother of Avalon. What will be the design of your costume?

From Yule to Imbolc

From Yule to Imbolc darkness stays with us for some weeks with dark, grey mornings before we gradually notice the returning light, slowly increasing little by little. Animals are hibernating in burrows, underground. Humans stay indoors out of the cold winds, driving rain and snow. Seeds lie dormant in the earth. Birds flock to our gardens seeking food which we lay out for them. Jack Frost covers the hedgerows and trees with shimmering silver white crystals. Flooded meadows turn to crackling ice. The Old Woman of Winter is with us. If we are lucky in this Summerland that is close to sea level, snow falls to lie on the ground and the Isle of Avalon turns white. The image of the Swan Maiden emerges, floating on a green sea background.

Make an altar to Nolava, Lady of Air, Bone Woman, Stone Woman, Cailleach, Old Woman of Winter, to Tyronoe, to Danu and to Arianrhod of the Silver Wheel. Find an image or natural symbol for the Cailleach: statues, bones of animals and birds, feathers of all kinds, and place them on your altar. Once a week recreate your altar.

Every day light a candle and burn incense to the Mother of Air at your altar and pray to Her for help, for guidance, in gratitude, for healing for yourself, for others in need, for visions, etc.

Every day write down and or draw your feelings, dreams, inspirations, intuitions, and visions in your diary, i.e. what is going on for you.

At Yule *create a ceremony in honour of the* Mother *of* Air *in many forms. Connect to the distant ancestors, the beings of fire, ice, wind, water and earth, who created the world in which we now live.* Listen *for their guidance and wisdom.*

On the new moon consider all those things in your life which are lying dormant in the winter ground awaiting the Lady's *vitalising touch at* Imbolc. *As you fall asleep think of those things you wish to bring to fruition in the coming year.* When *you sleep dream your future alive.* When *you awaken, in the liminal state between sleeping and waking, listen to the* Goddess's *instructions.* She *will tell you all that you need to do today, that will lead you to the fulfilment of your dreams.*

On the full moon create a cleansing ceremony using incense to cleanse yourself, your home, your family and your friends. Be *inspired by the* Lady *of* Air *to write and speak your prayers to* Her.

Make *yourself a feather fan for smudging.* Find *or make a smudge bowl.*

Visit *sacred sites where the* Mother *of* Air *and the* Cailleach *dwell, including bare winter landscapes, mountain tops where the sky is big, the top of* Glastonbury Tor *or out on the* Summerland Levels. *On your own or with friends, sing and pray to* Her, *dance upon* Her *cold body.* Feel Her *essence.*

The Quickening Imbolc Festival of the Maiden Goddess

Imbolc, which comes around February 1st/2nd, is the festival of the Maiden Goddess. This is the time of the Quickening, when Maiden Nolava retrieves the White Rod from the Cailleach, who has held it through the long winter, readying it for transformation into the Green Rod of springtime. At Imbolc we honour Thitis the Maiden Morgen who envisions the future.

In Brigit's Isles the Maiden Goddess is best known as the much-loved Bride, Brighde, Bridie, Bree-je and Brigit, Goddess of Fire, Poetry, Healing and Smithcraft, Goddess of the Sun and Moon, known as ancient Goddess and Saint Bride of the Kindly Fire, St. Bride of the Shores, and Mary of the Gael. Fiona Macleod, the gifted mystical voice of writer William Sharp, wrote of Her as,

"*Bride the Beautiful, the Fair Woman of February, Daughter of Morning, who held sunrise in one hand as a little yellow flame and in the other the red flower of fire without which men would be as beasts who live in caves.... She (is) that ancient Goddess whom our ancestors saw lighting the torches of sunrise on the brows of hills or thrusting the quenchless flame above the horizons of the sea.*" (*Collected Works, Heinemann*)

Bride is the Quickener, the touch of Her fiery rod quickens the life that is lying dormant in the seeds in the cold earth, heralding the return of springtime. She is the Incarnator who calls us into life.

Through January the sunlight slowly increases each day, as the earth continues on its journey around the sun. Small delicate flowers begin to appear, pushing their way seemingly against all odds, up through the cold hard earth. The first snowdrops signal Bride's return. In the fields the ewes give birth to lambs and their milk begins to flow. Imbolc or Oimelc means ewe's milk. Birds search for food as the last of the winter berries are eaten and nothing grows. It can still be very cold with frost and snow falling here in the Summerland. As the light slowly increases our attention begins to move slowly outwards. There is hope once again, the possibility of renewed life.

We celebrate Maiden Bride as the Incarnator and Quickener, Inspiration, Healer and Mystress of the Forge. We make Bridie Dolls in Her image, and Bridie Crosses and Eyes. We pour libations of milk onto Her images and upon Her sacred earth. We make and share barley cakes. We write poetry and remake language in Her honour.

Nolava the Maiden

Nolava the Maiden is the Innocence of the child, who welcomes incarnation on this beautiful planet, who is unafraid of the future, who is excited to be alive. She gives and receives love from all those around her. She needs to be honoured, nurtured and cared for, by all who seek Her inspiring touch.

In Glastonbury's sacred landscape Nolava the Maiden is visible in Her epiphany of the Swan, which appears in the contours of the land as a giant bird with long neck and wings outspread, flying over the Summerland from the northeast to the southwest. This giant swan shape can be seen clearly in the shape of the land on contour maps, from the sky above and when we stand on top of the Tor.

Nolava is the Swan Maiden, the young woman of folklore who is both swan and maiden. She is the beautiful royal bird who nests in the rhynes and rivers that surround the Isle of Avalon. Just as in the fairy tales She carries new babies suspended from Her beak, into incarnation. As we vision ourselves lying upon Her swan's back She transports us between the middle and upper worlds, into familiar realms where the Goddess dwells. She transports us across the waters to Avalon. On special occasions She removes Her feather cloak to reveal beneath Her beautiful violet etheric form.

To the southwest of Nolava's main swan-shaped island is the small mound known as Bride's Mound, made in the image of Nolava's daughter Bride. It is here that St Bridget, the Christianised form of the earlier Goddess Brigit, is said to have lived for a time in the fifth century.

Nolava the Maiden is new reborn from the old. She is all that is rebirthed after the dead days of winter and discarnation. She is the returning Light after Darkness, Her days slowly lengthening, allowing new plants to grow in the still cold earth. She is new incarnation, new manifestation in form, out of spirit. She is the new brought to birth many times here in Avalon, and expressed in the outerworld of Glastonbury and beyond. New ideas, new concepts, new ways of thinking are birthed in this sacred place, which then move out into the world. This is where new ideas are dreamed and nurtured, ideas of our common spirituality expressed in many different forms, living in harmony and peace together, which have become manifest here. An example of this is the creation of the first new public indigenous Goddess Temple in Brigit's Isles for perhaps 1500 years and more, brought to birth in Glastonbury in 2000CE.

Honouring Thitis *the Maiden Morgen*

I am Thitis I am
I am Maiden I am
I am She who rises like a serpent from the hole,
On the wings of my swan, of my grace, of my soul...
I am the Spirit that is always new within you - I am that which is ever reborn,
I am the soft white ewe's milk that flows every spring - I am the rising phoenix & the unicorn...
I am the wet, strong wings of the emerging butterflies of your heart,
I am the quickening spark of inspiration from whence all new beginnings start,
All children gather in the protective folds of my skirts to hear the poems I tell,
To hear my stories & sounds of the future - to hear my heart & voice ring out like a bell.
For I am the soft pastel colours that swirl and dance at the dawning of the day,
As the sun rises the potential I carry is birthed into a new way...
Let me stir your deepest well with my rod of lightening love & unlock your frozen waters,
Let the warm power of healing herbs and love be carried by each of my daughters...
May you each be blessed with a spark of excitement that grows with each passing hour,
For the time has come as foretold in our prophecies...
When this blessed Isle of Avalon is emerging from the mists.. like a flower...

by Sophie Pullinger

Thitis is the Maiden Morgen of Avalon, Lady of the White Rod. She is the Snow, which if it falls in this low-lying country of Avalon will often do so at Imbolc. Usually it is just the upper ground of the Tor and the hills which She whitens, while the surrounding Summerland remains green. Like Nolava and Bridie She too brings new beginnings. She is daybreak and the dawn, each new day filled with potential for life. She is the new moon rising just above the horizon as the sun is setting. She is a Seer, a Lady of Prophecy foretelling the future, encouraging us to walk with Her into Her bright new days. She foretells the return of the Isle of Avalon from the mists so that it becomes visible for all to see. She is a healer, a herbalist and a poet.

She loves children and young people, gathering them about Her. She loves our wounded child within back to health and wholeness. She appears in many forms, sometimes as a girl child Herself, less than ten years old. She reminds us to honour our child within, as a source of remembered innocence and wholeness, a source of renewal. She teaches us to play again without fear, to enjoy life, to have fun.

Thitis is Willow Woman, Her pollarded trunks and weeping branches are visible all over the Summerlands which surround the Isle of Avalon, their roots anchored in the sodden peat. Sacred to the Goddess the words *wicker, witch, wicked, wicce* and *wicca* are rooted in the words to bend or turn aside and all derive from willow. Wicker Goddess are annually made for the Glastonbury Goddess Conference from local willows, as the focus of our adorations. Her creatures include the white unicorn with its single spiralling horn, symbol of the spirit of all things. She accompanies maidens as they begin to encounter the hormonal Dragons of puberty, adolescence and menstruation. Hers is the serpent who hides through the winter beneath the omphalos stone, emerging at Imbolc to inspire the Seer.

The Phoenix bird who rises renewed from the flames of destruction belongs to Thitis. According to Katherine Maltwood in her *Guide to Glastonbury's Temple of the Stars* (London 1929), a large terrestrial zodiac can be traced on the landscape to the south of Glastonbury. Contours of the land, boundaries of rivers, streams and old roads make up the familiar shapes of the Zodiacal signs. Katherine saw the Phoenix as the symbol for Aquarius, formed by Glastonbury's hills and vales.

Call to Thitis, ask Her to renew your life, to awaken and heal the child within you, to help you learn to play and have fun again. Ask Her to show you Her visions of the future as She returns to Her rightful place in the world.

Bride the Incarnator

In all of nature death is not the end of life, but is always followed by rebirth. Flowers blossom then mature, forming seeds which fall to the ground, burying themselves in the earth. Mother plants die away, but their seeds lie still in the cold earth, usually for a few months, but sometimes for several years or more, awaiting the best conditions for rebirth. Then comes the touch of Bridie's Rod which quickens the life lying dormant in the seeds, and germination begins. As the earth slowly warms, first roots then shoots begin to form, so that plants grow above ground in springtime.

As with the flowers we too die when we are old and our bodies are worn down by life. Our souls, like the seeds of flowers, are released from their outworn forms into the greater life. In the Otherworld we too lie dormant for a time, in consciousness realising our past experiences and preparing for new futures. Then comes the touch of Bridie's Rod, She calls us to be reborn, to incarnate once again into human forms. We send out threads of attraction and our new human parents begin to dream of us, calling us back into being. We ready ourselves for rebirth.

Bridie the Quickener

Three months into the First Spiral of the priestess training after the winter months spent journeying within, we may be feeling our dukka, our inner dissatisfaction with ourselves and with the ways in which we live our lives. We begin to long for springtime, for the warmth of longer days, but now we await the touch of Bridie's Rod that will bring renewal not only in the outer world of Her nature, but also to our inner world.

Bridie's returning light signals a time of breakthrough and expansion. We hold ourselves open in anticipation of the touch of Her white rod, which will quicken the life in the seeds which are lying dormant within us, the seeds of our karma and destiny, just as She quickens the life in the seeds lying dormant in Her earth. Our consciousness opens to Her love, expanding beyond its previous limits. Like the sweet baby lambs in the field, our hearts leap for joy. Now we can express more love and compassion. We can love ourselves and others more than ever before and we must learn how to put that love into action. We view everything that happens to us from a wider perspective. Our centre of consciousness moves closer to our soul. However as the seeds within are quickened, our transformation accelerates. This may be a smooth transition or it may feel more difficult than we feel it should be.

Bridie's Inspiration of Poetry

Bridie is Lady of Inspiration and Poetry, described by Fiona Macleod, as,

"...she whose breath was a flame and flame song, she whose secret name was fire and whose inmost soul was radiant air, she therefore who was the divine impersonation of the divine thing she stood for, Poetry."

(*Collected Works*, Heinemann)

In ancient times Bridie's poets would carry a silver branch with tinkling bells to announce they were about to speak their poems and chant their songs. Poetry is the creative form which attempts to capture in words and sound, the mystery which lies beyond language.

We are all capable of writing poetry. Each year in my classes students have protested that they can't write poetry and songs and each time every single one produces beautiful verses for the Maiden. Here is an Imbolc poem by published poet and Priestess of Avalon, Rose Flint.

Suddenly last week I saw snowdrops
pushing through a swell of green frost

below them a green rivered field
tipped with a wash of wave energy
shaking the grass and
a floating swan.

When I was teaching
a girl with a river of long black hair
told me she'd chose the scent
of Mother's milk to lure a boy
to lull him.

When love sweeps over me in suddenness
my breasts prickle with memories
of letting down of the milk
for all my winter babies
the world as still as a pearl

my body white belled petal, green veined
a swan, white as heaven
flying into the days
and all these years
of flood and frost and fire.

Here is *Song for Imbolc* written by Priestess of Avalon, Jane Redhawk.

Chorus: Old Cailleach - Old Crone
Mother of Ice and of bone
Your reign of Death is over

Verse: It is time to give birth
To the Maiden of Light
You nurtured in your wintry womb

Chorus: Old Cailleach - Old Crone
Mother of Ice and of bone
Your reign of Death is over

Verse: It is time to set free
Dreams and visions in me
And to watch them grow strong in the sun

Chorus: Old Cailleach - Old Crone
Mother of Ice and of bone
Your reign of Death is over

Verse: It is time to feel blessed
By the deepest darkness
And the mystery of your fertile womb

Chorus: Old Cailleach - Old Crone
Mother of Ice and of bone
Your reign of Death is over

Imbolc is a perfect time to write poems and songs for and about the Goddess.

Write your own poem for Bridie. Listen for Her inspiration. She is the Muse for Goddess-loving people. Find a branch of silver birch or a small bare branch which you can spray silver. Tie small tinkling bells onto it. Speak your poetry in public, announcing the beginning and end by shaking your silver branch.

Reclaiming Language

When we think about poetry we must also consider the language in which it is written. All western languages are conditioned by patriarchal ideas and thoughtforms. There is even the suggestion made in *The Alphabet versus the Goddess: The Conflict Between Word and Image* by Leonard Shain

(Penguin Arkana), that it was the development of alphabets, of writing and reading, which helped left-brain, linear thinking to become dominant over more intuitive and holistic right-brain cultures. Preliterate cultures which venerated the Goddess, feminine values and images were informed by right-brain modes, which went into decline as language and writing developed and linear left-brain thinking, the basis of patriarchy, took over. If this theory is true the great hope for our present culture is that we are now moving into a place of balance between our right and left brains, as our world becomes increasingly visual once again with the development of visual media, film, TV, computers, and telephones, becoming accessible to the majority.

We need to examine carefully the language in which we express ourselves, in the words we unconsciously use to describe how things are. Part of our journey as priestesses is the reclaiming of language for our benefit. I bow in homage to Mary Daly, the great feminist thinker and writer, whose work I read at the very beginning of my own Goddess journey in the 1970s. The first seminal works of hers that I found were *Gyn/ecology: The Metaethics of Radical Feminism* (The Women's Press), and *Beyond God the Father: Towards a Philosophy of Women's Liberation* (Beacon Press). These two and her later books had a profound impact on my own thinking. I admire her amazing ability to deconstruct language, to show where words really come from, how they have been and are misused to mean their opposites, revealing the constraints placed upon us all. I love too the way that she has reclaimed words, such as *Hag, Crone, Spinster, Whore* and many, many more for women and the Goddess, creating an inspiring flood of new and renewed words. I cannot recommend her highly enough as a Source of Revelation and Inspiration for Goddess-loving women and men, and as a liberating force for priestesses.

Giving Voice to the Goddess in Sacred Drama

Writing and performing sacred drama is the art of giving voice to the Goddess through language, poetry and appearance, so that She may be embodied for all to see and hear. It is also a means of telling Her stories, not just in the sense of repeating ages-old patriarchal myths, but for reclaiming Her forgotten powers and mysteries, reworking myths to create a new world of equality between Goddess and God, women and men. From before the time when Zeus claimed the right to rule on Mount Olympus (originally a Goddess site dedicated to Demeter and Aphrodite), most myths in our western world have been dominated by male Gods and masculine values. Less powerful roles and dominions have been given to feminine values and to the Goddesses who were there originally.

In my understanding mythic reality underlies all psychological and physical manifestation. It is the energetic framework out of which all our collective and individual emotions and thoughtforms emerge. We are conditioned by this mythic framework and also contribute to it, day by day, moment by moment. To change the ways in which things are in our world we have to change not only the surfaces of our material reality, but must also effect change within this mythic framework. Reworking myth and performing it as sacred drama in sacred places at potent times of the year helps to change mythic reality.

My own journey with the Goddess was accelerated through writing and performing Goddess sacred dramas in Glastonbury over fourteen years from 1983 onwards. The story of our communal journey is told in *On Finding Treasure: Mystery Plays of the Goddess*, Ariadne Publications, 1996. The first play I wrote was a retelling of the myth of Demeter and Persephone, created in honour of women from the Glastonbury community who had gone to live in the mud at Greenham Common. This was during the time when the British government was attempting to bring American nuclear cruise missiles into Green Common air base. Women gathered in large numbers to peacefully and creatively protest their arrival. Our sacred drama had a one night performance in which the Goddess was embodied, even if temporarily, for all to see. It was an inspiring and moving experience.

The following year I wrote a second sacred drama based on the story of Inanna, the Sumerian Queen of Heaven and Earth, paralleling what happened in Her story with what was going on at Greenham Common. Over a period of fifteen years or so I wrote, sometimes alone and sometimes with others, community sacred dramas which were inspired by Ariadne of the Red Thread, White Buffalo Calf Woman, Rhiannon, Madron, Arianrhod, Blodeuwedd, Ana, the Nine Morgens, Sophia and many other Goddesses. It was as if each time a different Goddess would come and speak to me, asking me first to find out about Her and then to write Her story in a new way. Each time She was embodied and appeared on stage we would learn more about Her energy and mystery than we had known before.

An experience I remember most vividly happened early on while I was sitting at my desk. On the wall to my right was a poster of Green Tara, the Tibetan Goddess of Compassion, which I had been given ten years earlier by an ex-lover. I'd put it on the wall because it was colourful and matched the walls. I didn't know anything about Her. As I was sitting at my desk I heard a voice from my right, say,

"*Look at me!*"

I turned to the wall and there above on the poster was a living, three-dimensional image of Green Tara, sitting half way up the wall. She said,

"*Find out who I am and write a play about me.*"

Then She merged back into the poster.

From that instruction I went and found some books on Green Tara and wrote a play about Her life, connecting Her energy to the bardo states of consciousness found between death and rebirth. As I wrote I found that I already knew Her, I knew who She was. I knew Her energy as if I had lived lives in service to Her before. Writing and performing the sacred drama was a remembering of my previous incarnations in Tibet and China, as well as the creation of a present day embodiment of Her compassionate energies. This kind of experience happened with other Goddesses, who were consciously unknown to me.

The creativity of Goddess sacred drama has now moved onto the bigger stage of the annual Glastonbury Goddess Conference, in which the mystery of the ever-living Goddess in many forms is embodied and experienced as a revelatory, healing and transformative power.

Bride the Sibyl or Prophetess

In the stories of Bride that come to us from the Western Isles of Scotland there is a Gaelic rhyme,

This the day of Bride
The serpent will come from the mound or from beneath the stone
I shall not touch the (serpent or Queen)
Nor shall the (serpent or Queen) touch me.

In her informative pamphlet *Brighde, Her Folklore and Mythology*, Janet Mc Crickard (Fieldfare Arts) says that this song has nothing to with Brighde as the snake, rather it talks of the time when the adders first begin to move from their underground burrows after winter. Janet claims that this rhyme was an injunction not to touch poisonous snakes.

However I do make the connection myself between Brighde and Her totem snake. In many cultures the snake symbolises transformation, the sloughing off of an old skin to reveal a renewed body beneath. Snakes were also often connected in ancient times with the role of the Sibyl or

Prophetess and ancient images, such as that of Ariadne or the Snake Goddess from Krete, show the Goddess or Her priestess holding snakes in Her hands as She speaks words of prophecy. I believe that because of Bride's connection to poetry, one of the qualities that She transmits is also that of prophecy, the ability to speak of the past, present and future from a wider perspective in life. See the chapter in the Second Spiral on Scrying for a Vision.

Bride the Great Healer

Bride is one of the great Goddesses of Healing in Brigit's Isles. She heals in the sense of bringing us into wholeness, which may include returning to physical and psychological wholeness and can sometimes mean journeying into death. In my experience as a soul healer for 30 years, disease is essentially the body's way of healing itself of physical, emotional, psychological and spiritual imbalances. Bridie helps bring us into new places of balance on all levels. As our transformation accelerates we may need to seek energetic healing for ourselves, as the wounds of our karma reveal themselves.

Bride's Wells are found all over Brigit's Isles and these are often healing wells, where we can drink of Her healing waters. One of the best known is in St Bride's Church in Fleet Street in London, and there are many in Ireland, with a special one at Kildare. There St Bridget, an emanation of the ancient Goddess Bride, founded a community of nuns and monks in the sixth century CE.

In Avalon a beautifully carved stone next to the River Brue beside Bride's Mound, marks the site of a now unfortunately covered over St. Bride's Well. It is traditional to tie pieces of cloth torn from clothing, ribbons and special items to the trees which are found next to Bride's Wells or any holy well. Prayers are offered to Bridie for healing and as the cloths flutter in the wind, our prayers flutter to Her ear and She brings us healing.

Beside Her sacred well pray for healing for yourselves, for your family and friends, for those who are in need, for all who suffer.

One of the many stories about St Bride tells how one day She met a woman who was destitute with many children to feed, who were also ill. Bride's heart went out to the poor woman in her suffering and She touched each of the children in turn with the Healing Girdle worn around Her waist. The children were completely restored to health, but Bride knew that this was not enough to help the mother in the future. She removed Her girdle and gave it to the woman, telling her to go and cure others of their diseases and to receive food, clothing and money in return. The woman went away and began to heal the sick and she was able to feed and clothe her children and in turn give away surplus to the poor.

I particularly like this story because it tells of Bride's healing girdle, which we can make for ourselves, its design being inspired by Her. We can consecrate it to Her healing power, wearing it when we heal, touching others with it. I also like the story because it implies that the Goddess is very willing for Her powers to be used not only to heal people, but also to help them make a living in the world.

Patriarchal teaching in many cultures says that it is wrong to be paid for spiritual work, which should be freely given without charge, although donations may be accepted. Amongst many spiritual seekers there is an ethic that states that spiritual gifts come freely from the divine and anyone charging for such gifts must be taking advantage of others in some undefined way. The result of such thinking is that spiritually talented people all over the world are usually poor and unable to work to the best of their ability. Those who live in disintegrated indigenous cultures, who would once have been supported by their communities, must scrape a living. Those in the west either live the majority of their lives in material poverty, spending too much time wondering where their family's next meal is going to come from, or working in mundane jobs just to get the money to live, and doing their spiritual work only at weekends. Many other inconsistencies result from this poverty consciousness. Lowly nuns and monks must make vows of poverty, while the hierarchies of the churches are among the richest in the world, hoarding wealth which could help feed the hungry.

I believe that this story of Bride gives us permission to use our spiritual gifts to support ourselves. We can live a spiritual life, which is neither materially poor or rich, but somewhere in between. We have only to look around us at the imbalance of wealth in the world to know which levels of wealth are appropriate and which are not. We can devote our lives to spiritual things that help change the world and live a materially balanced life. To nourish others we must nourish ourselves in all kinds of ways. In Goddess spirituality there is no law which says that we are meant to be poor, rather we must emulate the generosity of the Goddess Herself. She has given us Her abundant planet to live on and we need to consciously receive Her generosity, sharing it equally generously with others. The Goddess's way is always one of balance, of caring for others and caring for ourselves.

Esoteric Soul Healing

As well as being a teacher of priestesses I also teach people to become Esoteric Soul Healers, those who heal working with the deep energies of the soul, both in themselves and in their patients. I first learned to heal in my 20s when I was on a five year spiritual retreat in Wales. Amongst many other spiritual techniques I studied meditation and the teachings of Alice Bailey, and in particular her book on *Esoteric Healing*. These teachings look at the individual as a soul incarnate in the physical world and the ways in which we can use energy and its movement to heal our own and other people's diseases. As I learned to feel and sense energies I found, to my surprise, that healing energies did seem to be transmitted from my hands and my aura. Over time and through practice with many people, I developed the skills of the wounded healer.

I have worked as a healer for many years and over time adapted Alice's teachings, which were written in the 1940s, to modern day life. In 2001 I published my own healing book, *Chiron in Labrys: An Introduction to Esoteric Soul Healing*. Esoteric Soul Healing is a profound system of healing which reaches the parts that other forms do not touch. It is esoteric in the sense that it is learned through practical experience, rather than by reading about it, although knowledge and intellect are involved. It includes an in-depth understanding of the energetic make up of the human individual, working with patients at the deep levels of the soul in both the healer and the patient.

Part of the practice involves invoking deities, guides and angels, to assist in the healing process. Bridie is one of the principal healing deities that are called in at the beginning of any healing session, as She has the ability to change everything that She touches, to heal disease in an instant.

Priestesses who successful complete this course become priestess healers. For further information on Esoteric Soul Healing courses visit the Isle of Avalon Foundation website: www.isleofavalonfoundation.com

Bride, Mystress of the Forge

Bride is mostly seen as a very loving, endearing and beneficent Goddess. She is however also Mystress of the Forge, Goddess of Smithcraft, in which base metal substances are heated to high temperatures in a forge. In this process dross rises to the surface and is sloughed off leaving pure gold, silver or other precious metals behind. This is an allegory for the alchemical process by which the base human substance of our personality, is heated in Her fires of life and experience. The dross, all that no longer serves us or Her, is sloughed off, revealing the pure gold of our soul. This process is characteristic of encounters with all the wisdom goddesses, such as Sophia, whose Philosopher's Stone, which grounds the Wisdom of Sophia, has been sought by spiritual seekers throughout the ages. Bride too is a Wisdom Goddess.

As priestesses in the making we are engaging in Her alchemical processes of change. We offer our personalities to Her fires of transformation, asking that She will help reveal the gold of our souls. Again this is not an easy thing to do and as the dross is removed and our hard corners are knocked off, we often experience suffering. Through this process we learn to hold ourselves and each other in greater compassion.

On our journey to become Her priestess there can be many times when our resolve to transform our lives can waver before the heat of Her forge. There are many challenges along the way in our busy lives. Can we commit the time to sit before our altars, to pray, to really engage with Her every day? Pressures of all sorts, in our work, in our relationships, in our health, can mount up. We may begin to feel that we can't cope, that it's all getting too much. The external pressure is a reflection of an inner reality and we need to hold ourselves steady through this pressure. Learning to move with the tides of energy, which roll internally and externally, is all part of being a Priestess of Avalon.

In life we are all at the effect of karma, primarily of our personal karma, the consequences of our actions in this and in previous lives, as well as the karma of being part of particular tribal, ethnic and national groupings. We are also subject to the karma of being part of the human race living on the planet at this time, when little respect is shown for the body of our Mother Earth and pollution is everywhere, bringing disease, famine and death. Within this karmic framework into which our souls incarnate, we learn over time to take responsibility for our lives, for everything that happens to us, acknowledging that we are coauthors of our own destinies.

On the whole we are unconscious co-creators with the Goddess of all that happens to us, even those things which appear to happen to us from the outside - accidents, effects of pollution, disease, etc. We blame others for the world in which we live, when we actually have the power to change the world if we are sufficiently concerned and want to make the effort. Normally we are too involved in our own dramas and limitations to bother, and thus we are disempowered.

The journey to priestesshood is one of Self-empowerment. The position of our Selfhood is shifting from the place of victim to whom things happen (nothing to do with me!), to one where we know that within the restraints of our karma and consciousness, we are the cause for everything that happens to us. There are things that we can do in the world if we set our hearts and minds to the task. We have incarnated with purpose, with a destiny to fulfil. Our journey is to search for and find our soul purpose, the meaning that lies at the root of our life on earth. We do this by coming to know ourselves really well, by being completely honest with ourselves, by exploring our inner truth and nature, as well as the habits and restraints of our personalities.

Our centre is moving from our personality into our soul and with this comes Self-responsibility. As we fail to change our lives as quickly as we would like this responsibility for ourselves can feel weighty. We want it to be someone else's responsibility. We want someone else to blame when things go wrong, our partners, families, fellow students or teacher. Again this is the time to hold steady through the challenges we face as our personality struggles to hold its place of power within our psyche. Our consciousness is expanding to its present limits before breakthrough can occur. We hold ourselves in the place of compassion.

Pray to Bride as Mystress of the Forge that She may help you to let go of the dross in your life, so that the gold in your soul will shine through.

Making Bridie Dolls

The tradition of making dolls in the image of the Goddess is very old. From the earliest days of the neolithic and earlier cultures, figurines of Goddesses, both large and small, some doll-like, have been found. Stone, bone and clay dolls remain from those days, but we can safely assume that Goddess dolls were also made from less durable materials, which have since decayed. There are tales recorded by Alexander Carmichael, in *Ortho Nan Gaidheal*, of Bridie Dolls still being made in the 19th century in the Western Isles of Scotland, in a continuation of an ages long tradition. They were made in the image of Bride.

In Glastonbury the tradition of making Bridie Dolls at Imbolc was revived nearly twenty years ago by a group of Glastonbury women and has since spread out across the land to other communities of women. Bridie Dolls are now made at each Imbolc by individuals and by groups of women. The dolls are made from different kinds of materials. Traditionally in Scotland the last sheaf of oats from the previous year's harvest, would be hung from the kitchen ceiling to dry through the autumn and winter. At Imbolc a Brideog (little Bridie) would be fashioned from the sheaf and decorated with ribbons, crystals, shells and early flowers, especially snowdrops. A traditional Bridie Cross made from reeds would be attached to Her heart. She would also be given a wand, the Barrag Bride, (the birch of Bridie), made out of peeled white birch, willow or hazel and representing Her quickening fiery energy. As She walks the land on Imbolc morning Bridie touches the earth with Her wand and plants and flowers spring to life. The Bridie Doll's body is returned to the earth at Oestre, when the grains begin to grow once again, completing the cycle of nature.

In the present day Bridie Dolls are sometimes made from grain, but often from cloth and material. Pieces of material shaped in the image of Bride, large or small, are cut out and sewn together, then stuffed with material or stuffing. As we sew Her body together we sew into it our hopes and dreams for the coming months. She is given a face, breasts, arms, legs and a vulva. Clothes are made for the Bridie Doll, who is then dressed and decorated with ribbons, sparkly things, jewellery, shells and crystals. She too is given a white wand to hold.

Every Bridie Doll looks different, filled with the personalities and prayers of Her makers. Once completed and introduced in ceremony the Dolls seem to come alive. Their bodies have substance and feeling, like real bodies. When we began to reinstate the traditions of making communal dolls in Glastonbury, instead of making the dolls from grains that would quickly return to the earth, we wanted to have more substantial dolls that would ground Goddess knowledge and wisdom for the growing Goddess community. Each year newly created communal dolls are introduced to the previous years' dolls, communing with them as mothers and grandmothers, sharing their wisdom. Many Glastonbury Bridie Dolls live through the year in Glastonbury's Goddess Temple, coming out each Imbolc in ceremony to greet the newly created Bridie Dolls.

Traditionally on Imbolc Eve Bridie Dolls are processed around the town by the girls and younger women of the community, as the Banal Bride, Bride's company of maidens. They are taken from house to house to give Bridie's blessings and to receive offerings of food and drink to refresh Her.

At Imbolc make your own Brideog, your Bridie Doll, giving Her a special place in your heart and mind. Take Her with you on Imbolc Eve to different homes to share Her blessings.

At Imbolc create ceremonies which welcome Bridie into your home and temple space as a creative, healing and inspirational force. The traditional words of welcome are :

"Let Bride come in! Let Bride come in!"

To which the reply is :

"Bride! Bride! Come in, thy bed is made.
Preserve the house for the Triple Goddess."

On Imbolc Eve Bride is laid in an oblong basket or bed, the Leaba Bride, decorated by the older women of the family and filled with straw. She is placed next to the fire with Her white wand. As the fire dies down the ashes are smoored or flattened. In the morning the women of the house rush to see if there are any footsteps in the ashes to show that Bridie has been walking in the night, bringing good fortune to the householders.

In your home lay Bridie next to the fire with Her wand and see if She will bless your home.

Making Bridie Crosses and Eyes

Bridie Crosses, also known as the Star of Bride, are made at Imbolc out of dried rushes, reeds or the stems of wheat or barley, twisted into the shape of a swastika. Before it was corrupted by the Nazis, the turning four-armed cross was known in many indigenous cultures as a symbol for the sun with its sun ray arms pointing in the four directions. Bridie is a Sun Goddess, Her rays warming the earth, stimulating the flowers to grow again.

Bridie Eyes are made by creating an equal arm cross from two sticks and then weaving coloured wools from the centre outwards between the four arms of the cross. Bridie Eyes are a protection against evil and traditionally were hung in the corners of houses and barns to protect the people and the cattle.

At Imbolc make your own Bridie Crosses and Bridie Eyes. Use them for decoration for your altar and protection for home.

Cakes for Bridie

We make barley and honey cakes for the Maiden Goddess using any simple cake recipe. Substitute barley flour for wheat and honey for sugar. The cakes are sweet and heavy. Many ancient Goddess figurines are found in grain bins next to bakeries and it would seem that the tradition

Making a Bridie Cross

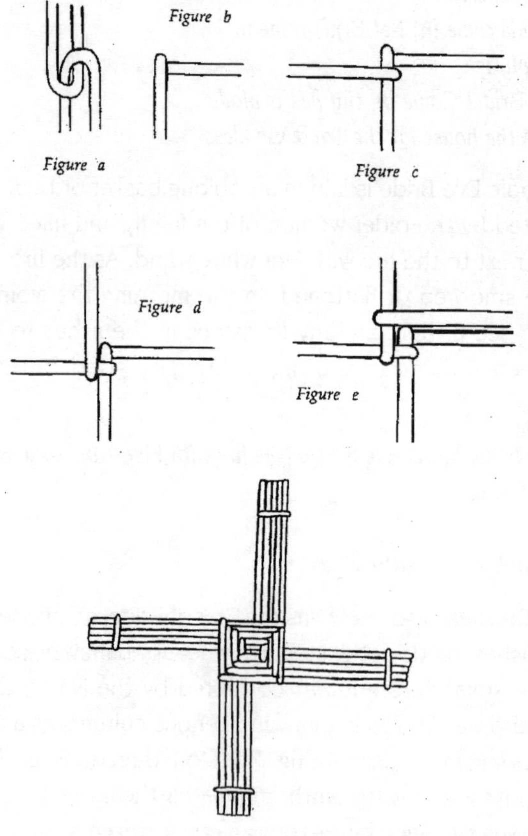

Making a Bridie Eye

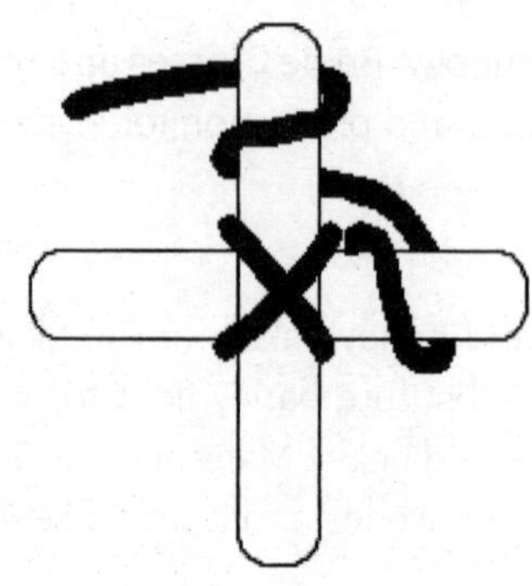

of making bread and cakes for the Goddess is also very old.

Offer barley cakes to Bridie at your altar and share them in ceremony with others.

Ewe's Milk Communion and Libations

It is traditional at Imbolc to drink ewe's milk as a communion with Bride the Shepherdess. If there aren't accessible lactating ewes, we can buy their milk frozen from the wholefood store. It must be drunk as soon as it defrosts as it quickly curdles.

We pour libations of ewe's milk. A libation is a liquid offering to the Goddess which, like our other offerings to Her, are made at Her altar or in Her sacred places. We pour libations into bowls, onto Her statues and onto the earth. At Imbolc we pour offerings of ewe's milk onto images of Bride and onto the earth, in recognition of the blessings of ewe's milk and of the milk of all Mothers, which we, Her children, drink and are sustained by as babies and later in life.

Remaking traditions

When Goddess traditions have long been lost and the shapes of our communities are so different from those of the past, it can be difficult to recreate ceremonies in the forms we believe once existed. On the whole we are not farmers living close to the land, deeply connected to the cycles of the seasons. Now we live in conurbations, in cities and towns and villages. We no longer live in close-knit extended and connected family groupings. We live more separated, individual lives and may not even know the names of our neighbours. This is not necessarily good or bad, just different. In recreating ceremonies and rituals that celebrate the Goddess we begin where we are, with the scraps of information we have from the past, in the lives we live now. There is no obligation to repeat what we believe happened long ago, before there were records. Our duty is to create meaningful ceremonies in the present. Remember that in Goddess spirituality we have great freedom. There is no dogma, there are no rules, there is no text that must be obeyed, even though some may attempt to create one, and hierarchies of dogma will tend to form. We can actually honour the Goddess in any creative way that we choose.

We can take the threads of these old Imbolc rituals and weave them now into our present day lives. We can try inviting our neighbours in to our homes to celebrate with us and we can gather in groups of like-minded people. In Brigit's Isles many people now have central heating and don't have an open fire beside which they can leave Bridie in Her bed overnight. We can however smoor a dish of barley flour, or burn papers to ash in a metal container to create ash. We can lay Bridie in Her bed next to it, using it as the ashes of an Imbolc fire. We can light a large candle on our altar to represent Her hearth in our homes. We can make 21st century Bridie Dolls using materials available now, although we can, if we like, repeat the ancient traditions too.

Dedication Ceremony Costumes

As well as making dolls and craftworks which celebrate the Goddess, Imbolc is the time to begin creating costumes for our ceremony of dedication at the end of our first year's cycle. Based in our Yuletide inspirations from Her we start gathering items for our costume - fabrics, materials, designs, threads, clasps and jewellery that we will bring together over the coming months for our ceremony in which we will dedicate our lives to the Goddess.

Between Imbolc and Oestre

Between Imbolc and Oestre snow can still fall, frosts can cover the land. Biting winds roar in from the north and warmer wet winds rain in from the southwest. The birds still need extra food. All the time the light is increasing, the sun is rising in the sky, the daylight is lengthening, the nights are shortening. Shoots begin to sprout on plants and bushes and trees. Delicate primroses flower against the odds, daffodils push their way up through the frozen earth, their glorious yellows bringing colour to the world once again. Hibernating animals begin to emerge from their winter burrows, looking for food. Human consciousness is catalysed by Bridie's white rod and expands, and our Shadows rise to greet the new light within. We seek help when we need it on our journey of transformation, expressing our feelings and memories of pain to experienced counsellors.

Make an altar to Nolava *the* Maiden, *to* Thitis *and* Bridie *in many forms. Find images or natural objects which represents the* Maiden Goddess *for you and place it at the centre of your altar.* This *might be a statue of* Bridie, *of a swan or swan feathers, ewe's or cow's milk, snake or wolf skin.*

Every day light a candle and burn incense to Nolava *the* Maiden, *to* Thitis *and* Bridie *at your altar and pray to* Her *for help, for guidance, in gratitude, for visions, etc. Pray especially for healing for yourself and for others in need. Once a week recreate your altar.*

Every day write down and or draw your feelings, dreams, inspirations, intuitions, and visions in your diary, i.e. what is going on for you.

At Imbolc *create your own ceremony for* Bridie, *bringing* Her Bridelight *into a darkened room. Sit within a circle of candle flames. Pour a libation of milk onto a statue of the* Maiden *or in a sacred place. Speak inspired words of poetry to* Her.

At the new moon tend your inner seeds, review where you are. Write *a poem or a song for* Bridie *and offer it to* Her.

At the full moon make a Bridie Healing Girdle.

Begin gathering materials for your dedication costume.

Visit sacred sites where the Maiden Goddess *dwells, including* Bride's Wells, St Bridget's *churches,* Kildare *in* Ireland *with the nuns' house of* Solas Bride, *where* Bridie's *perpetual flame now burns.* Walk *to* Bride's Mound *in* Glastonbury, *walk the boundaries of the* Swan *in the* Glastonbury Avalon *landscape.* Visit *the* White Spring *at the foot of the* Tor. Visit *any clear spring and speak* Her *poetry.* Journey *to places where swans, cows, wolves and snakes are to be found.* Communicate *with them.* On *your own or with friends, sing and pray to* Her, *dance like a maiden.* Feel Her *childlike essence within you, happy and joyful and full of new life.*

The Springing
Oestre Festival of the Mother of Fire

Oestre is the festival of the Mother of Fire, celebrated at Spring Equinox around March 21st when there are equal hours of light and darkness, signalling the return of the light. In Avalon we honour Nolava of Fire and of Light and Cliton the Morgen of Fire and Springtime. We celebrate Artha, the Great She-Bear of the heavens and of the earth, whose fire-filled starry outline circumambulates the central pole of our heavens throughout the year, as viewed from these islands. We also honour Grainne the Sun Goddess, whose solar orb rises each day in the east, bringing light and renewed life to the earth. Without Her all life on earth would perish. We honour Sulis, Sun Woman. We celebrate Eostre or Ostara, the Mother of Rebirth, whose name was taken for Easter.

Oestre is the season of the Springing into life. Winter is over and although it can still be cold and wet, the days are getting warmer. At Oestre Her nature springs into activity and all life is renewed. The sap rises in the plants and the trees, shoots appear on the branches, buds and spring flowers open in the March winds, which come in like a lion and go out like a lamb. Pouring rains and high spring tides flood the low-lying ground and the Isle of Avalon can be seen once again as an island surrounded by water. As the nights are still cold and the days are warmer, the Mists of Avalon rise many times filling the low-lying Summerland. All that is visible from the top of the Tor over the mist are the distant Mendip Hills. In animals and humans the desire to find a mate arises. The birds sing and begin to build nests in the trees and hedges. The animals call to each other and begin to lose their thick winter coats.

At Oestre we make ourselves magic fire wands as symbols of Eostre's renewing fire. We reclaim Easter for Her, painting Her eggs of rebirth. We honour our creative fire by expressing our deep feelings for Her in material forms, as art and in crafts. As Oestre is one of two equinoxes in the year when light and darkness come momentarily into balance, we realise how out of balance we are as human beings, how deep the wounds to the feminine are in the world and within our own psyches. We create ceremonies that will bring into balance our own light and darkness, our inner and outer realities. We celebrate the illumination of Cliton.

Honouring Nolava of Fire and Light

In Avalon Nolava is the Lady of the Fire that is in all the stars, in the sun that shines down upon us each day and in the fire that burns beneath the crust of the earth. She is Fire on the hearth, in our workplaces, in our homes and in our hearts. She is the Fire that brings light, warmth and life to all the world. She is the Fire of Love that glows at the heart of Avalon, the sacred Violet Flame that shines in Avalon and radiates out into the world. She is the Mystical Fire that glows in the hearts of all who aspire to become Her priestess, encouraging us to continue onwards when the going gets tough. She is the Light ahead of us on the pathway to Her priestesshood, always illuminating our way if we have the eyes to see.

Fire is often equated with spirit, because of the kundalini fire that can rise up through the body from the base chakra to the crown, bringing expansion of consciousness and spiritual illumination. However, there are essentially several different kinds of fire. There are the fires of matter which produce heat and light, warming our food, heating and illuminating our homes and cities. There are emotional fires which can rage uncontrollably as anger and hatred, sorrow and grief. As they are expressed they fill our bodies with heat and can burn those who come into contact with their fiery vibrations. There are mental fires that can burn clearly with inspiration or rampage into madness. And there is Agni or spiritual fire which strikes like lightning, awakening and transforming all in its path. We have to treat all fire with great respect as fire can burn us if allowed to burn uncontrolled.

On the final day of the 2004 Goddess Conference we lit the Flame of Avalon for the first time, by combining six different flames into one Flame. These flames included the Goddess Conference Flame, which had burned throughout the Conference; Brid's Flame brought to the Conference by Sister Mary and Sister Rita Minehan from Kildare in Ireland; the Hiroshima Peace Flame lit by a woman survivor from the burning embers after the nuclear bomb exploded, which has burned for more than 50 years, and brought to the Conference by Aine Carey; Bridie's Flame from

Lewis in the Hebrides brought by Jill Smith; the Children's Flame brought from America by Kay Cooksey; and the Madonna Ministry Flame brought by Koko Newport.

After the Conference the Flame of Avalon was kept alight continuously for a couple of months by priestess Tammy Furey. Jacqui Woodward Smith then suggested that a group of Priestesses of Avalon might like to keep the Flame alive continually. Each person in the group has a candle lit from the original Flame and each person in the group holds the Flame alight for 24 hours at a time. At the present time 27 priestesses hold the Flame of Avalon, lighting a candle at dusk and holding the Flame in their hearts and physically, through the following 24 hours. Through the day in her prayers and thoughts the priestess radiates the Flame of Avalon out into the world, so that Nolava's loving light spreads out into the world.

We honour the Lady of Fire in our prayers and each time we light a candle or a fire in our homes, gardens and fields. We give thanks to Her for the life that She gives to us.

Honouring Cliton, Morgen of Fire

I am the Morgen Cliton
I am the fire that lights the stars and heats the core of the earth
I am the still point of the Spring Equinox
I am the Sun as it rises in the east,
I am creativity, passion, compassion and clear intention.
I am the greening of my nature and the Sun which nurtures my growth.
Call to me to fuel the fire of your intentions, your dreams,
your longings and your destiny
I am the essence of desire and fulfilment
I am potential realised
Know me,
Honour me,
Worship me,
Remember me
I am within you
I am the hearth fire which burns in your hearts illuminating your True Nature
I am the spark of creation which remembers itself
I am the dispeller of the darkness of ignorance
I am Enlightenment
I say : AWAKEN AND BE THE LIGHT *by Aine Carey*

Cliton is the Morgen of Fire in all its forms, from wildfire to the hearth fire in homes and communities, to the candle flame that flickers and the still point that lies at the centre of the flame. She is the stillness of the Equinox. Bright as a flame in Her gold and green dress Cliton dances like a teenager through the world at Oestre. Green shoots spring from beneath Her feet and from wherever Her flickering form touches the branches of the plants and trees. She is Lady of the Greening, of Springtime. By Her side, Her hare and cat, creatures of intuition and sensitivity, chase through the grass, while golden fire salamanders spread Her life-fires out across the landscape. Her fire dragons roar as flowers burst into bloom.

As weather Cliton is the Rays of Sunshine, which at this time of year shine for 12 hours a day bringing warmth and light to the earth, allowing everything in nature to grow and blossom, to flourish and fruit. She shines as the bright rays of springtime, as the intense rays of the summer sun shining in a deep blue sky, as the paleness of the winter sun glimmering in an ice blue sky. Throughout the year She plays with all the other Morgens to create all forms of weather in the sacred land.

The green woodpecker is Cliton's bird, tap-tapping messages on the trunks of trees, its yaffle resounding through the hedgerows. She is Hazel Woman who is strong, straight and flexible, responsive to hidden fire currents in the earth and over the land. She offers warmth, enthusiasm, clarity of mind and intention, the energy to move forward into the future with passion. She is the waxing moon, the great Illuminator, the dispeller of the darkness of ignorance. She brings Light and is Enlightenment.

Build a Sacred Fire and pray to Cliton. Ask Her to bring Her Fire Light into any place of darkness within you. Ask Her to give you courage and enthusiasm on your path to priestesshood.

Honouring Artha the Great She Bear and Grainne the Sun Goddess

At Oestre we honour Artha the Great She-Bear and Grainne the Sun Goddess, as Mothers of Fire and Light. Artha is Ursa Major, the great pattern of stars, also known as the Plough, which circles around Avalon's midheaven throughout the year. Artha is connected in European mythology to Art, Artio, Ars, Ursel and Artemis Calliste, who was also called the Great She-Bear. She is the Bear Mother who traditionally gave birth to human beings. In Sanskrit Her name means *abundance, riches*. Artha's sacred son, spouse and consort is the hero King Arthur, whose name comes from the Welsh Arth Vawr or heavenly bear. He has direct connections to Avalon and was brought here as he was dying, to heal his wounds and to await rebirth.

I suggested in *Spinning the Wheel of Ana* that the Irish Race of Parthalon or P(artha)lon, may have worshipped Artha the Bear Mother. They were the people who built the great chambered long barrows and mounds whose ruins remain all over the western fringes of Brigit's Isles. When these mounds were being built Artha's bear offspring still roamed the British forests. Hunted by early humans, their bodies provided food and warm furs for palaeolithic and neolithic peoples. Passages within neolithic ritual mounds are often aligned to special sunrises and sunsets when fingers of light penetrate dark womb chambers, sometimes illuminating Goddess images and carvings. They are wonderful places in which to contact Artha the Great She-Bear, to listen for Her growl and to growl ourselves.

At Oestre we also honour

Grainne or Greinne or Grania the Sun Goddess. In Scots and Irish Gaelic, Greinne or Grian is a feminine word meaning *the Sun*. Dia Greinne is the Sun Goddess, or Sun Mother. From all the indications in the earliest languages of Brigit's Isles the Sun was recognised as a feminine being, known to be the Mother of All Life on earth. In the daytime She shone Her golden light and warmth onto the world. At sunset She descended beneath the sea or into the waters of the earth through wells, ponds and lakes to regenerate the world. In the summertime She blessed the land with Her fiery energy and brought all plants and grains to fruition.

Many British and Irish neolithic sacred sites were dedicated to the Sun Goddess as the Giver and Renewer of Life. Their entrances are oriented so that on the Equinoxes or Solstices the rising and setting sun's rays penetrate to an inner Womb/Tomb space. The great mounds of Knowth and Brugh na Boinne in the Boyne valley in Ireland are two magnificent examples. Stones lining the inner passageways of both of these sacred mounds are decorated with many symbols of the Sun Goddess - multiple circles, sun rays and eyes.

Honouring Sulis

Sulis is the Sun Goddess associated with the hot springs which rise from beneath the earth. It was believed that as the sun set in the west each evening, it actually sank into the ocean, heating the waters which re-emerged from beneath the earth as hot springs. The spring waters contained the Goddess Herself and pilgrims came from far and wide to drink and bathe in Her healing essence. Sulis, Sil or Scillina, like Artha, is pictured as a Bear Mother, and is particularly honoured in the West Country, in the Scilly Isles and at Bath, which lies thirty miles to the north of Avalon. Here the hot springwaters have a strong mineral content and sulphurous odour, coming from deep within Her Underworld.

The springs at Bath are the only hot springs in Brigit's Isles and have long been held to be sacred. The Romans built great spas at Bath rededicating Sulis's ancient healing springs to Minerva, the Roman Goddess of war. Minerva like Sulis, was probably an earlier nature Goddess, whose qualities were subsumed to patriarchal ideals. Today, amid much controversy and the addition of many chemicals, the healing waters are once again being made available to the public for immersion, and with the payment of large fees. What was once universally free as a gift of the Goddess has come under the rule of mammon.

It is still worth visiting the hot springs and Roman baths at Bath. Despite centuries of overlays it is still possible to feel the heat of Sulis' fire in the steam rising from the surface of the pools and beside the hot underground streams.

Visit Bath's hot springs and pray to Sulis for fire and warmth to come safely into your life.

The Fire of Mind

Symbolically and magically, fire represents the mind, which continually dances like a flickering flame, moving endlessly from one thought to the next. The shape and quality of any fire depends on the substance which is burning and how much of it there is. It also depends on the winds which blow around the flames. So too the quality of our minds depends on the substance of our thoughts and the emotional and spiritual energy flowing around the flame. Water or emotion, can dampen the flames, or if there is too much, can put the flame out altogether, so that mind does not function. The spiritual winds too can blow the flame hither and thither, consuming all in its path in a religious fervour.

Over the last 5,000 years left-brain mentality has been in the ascendancy, with preference being given to the mind over all other faculties, including our emotions and intuition. The mind by itself tends to be self-serving, critical, harsh and uncaring of others and of the planet on which we live. It has been perceived as a King, the ruler of our personalities, and of our world, but this is not its correct position within our psyche. We have allowed the mind to get above itself. Its true place is as the servant of the soul, not its master or mistress.

The mind is very good at mechanical thinking, at receiving, holding and giving out information, at sorting things out, at adding, multiplying and dividing, at memorising the past and present, and visioning the future. It shows us pictures and words that have meaning for us. In its subtler forms the mind allows us to discriminate between things and to discern the truth of how things are, with greater and greater degrees of accuracy. The mind is our main tool of perception and creativity, allowing us to anchor our intuition and inspiration. It is the vehicle through which subtle energies pass into manifestation, rather than being a source of those energies. Mind in its rightful place, still as an undisturbed candle flame, produces clarity and insight.

Mind and emotion are often entangled together in thoughtforms, which contain fixed ideas and have emotional content. Thoughtforms can be attached to individuals or are communal, belonging to the vast collective astral/mental soup in which we live as human beings. Our thinking and beliefs about the world are all affected by these usually unconscious universal thoughtforms, which we all help to create through our own unconscious thoughts and feelings. There are many patriarchal thoughtforms which condition our world at the present time. For example, they say that men are inherently superior to women, that women are the weaker sex, that men must rule, that men must be paid more than women for the same work, that there is only one god, that war is the way to solve conflict, that hunger is inevitable for some, etc. Our priestess work is to disentangle these psychic clouds that surround us in every moment. Each time we make conscious and clarify our own thoughtforms we lessen the burden for everyone else.

Imagination is the creative faculty of the mind. Rather than our visions being just imagination, we honour them as revealing important information for us from Her. In developing Goddess spirituality we visualise the Goddess in Her many forms. We journey to meet Her in imagination, allowing ourselves to see Her face. She speaks to us in words that we hear in our minds and hearts, and transpose onto paper in many forms, as writing, poetry and song. This book is a mental vehicle, which hopefully allows Her multifaceted energy to be conveyed to you.

Mental visualisation is an important tool in our developing spirituality, allowing us to journey out of the confines our bodies and surroundings into other worlds, such as Avalon, for exploration and healing. We can journey into the past to find memories that have been lost in our subconscious minds for decades and even hundreds of years. We can investigate the deeper layers of the present to see how our minds work, so that we can let go of the things that no longer serve us. We can journey for healing, to retrieve parts of ourselves that have been lost or left behind, or to receive inspiration and gifts from the deeper spaces of reality. We can journey into the future to see the paths that lie ahead of us. We can journey to meet the Goddess in Her many guises.

We can visualise ourselves journeying to the Isle of Avalon, crossing the waters of the Lake in the Barge of Avalon, walking on Her sacred island, meeting Her priestesses, entering Her Temple, entering Her holiest Sanctuary and meeting Her. Some of the most profound healing experiences can come during simple visualisation. As our ability to visualise improves with practice and surrender, we visualise Her in detail and learn to embody Her energy.

Fire Ceremonies

Fire is used ceremonially to symbolise both the fire of mind and the transforming fire of Her spirit. It is used in many religious practices in the form of either candle or lamp flames, or as fire lit within a container, on a hearth or outdoors on the earth.

In the Priestess of Avalon tradition every time we light a flame we call in the Lady of Avalon, asking her to be present in the flame. We light all other candles from the one flame, seeing Her light spreading throughout the room or Temple filling the space with Her light and love. Fire brings warmth and light and we make sacred fires in cauldrons or on hearths to honour Her presence. In Brigit's Isles fires are traditionally lit on each of the four crossquarter Goddess festivals. At Imbolc the fire belongs to Maiden Bridie and is lit in a dark space symbolising the return of Her Quickening fire. At Beltane the fire is for Lovers, who jump a sacred fire to sacrilise their unions. At Lammas fire belongs to the Mother, symbolising Her generosity, warmth and love, and the stubble of the early harvest is burned in the fields. The Samhain fires honour the Crone and we let go to the fire all that we no longer need.

Fire can be used both as a blessing and a cleansing element for people and animals. Traditionally at Imbolc and Samhain cattle were driven between two bonfires as a blessing and protection for the coming winter or spring, which also removed harmful insects and bugs. The people also walked between two fires in preparation for the coming season.

At Oestre light your own small fire in a golden container adding spring herbs to honour the Lady.

It is important for us to also recognise that as well as being the source for all life and light on earth, the Mother of Fire can also harm us. Her fiery sunrays are only safe for us because She is so far away. As the earth loses its protective ozone layer we are becoming more vulnerable to the harmful rays of the sun, which give us deadly skin cancers.

Fire is the wild element. Uncontained fires spread quickly, destroying all in their pathway, burning our skins, homes and workplaces. Always take care of Her flame. Place candles and lighted charcoals in fireproof containers. Never leave them burning alone and unguarded.

Firewalking

Walking on Fire is one of the most transformative experiences available. Over a period of ten years or so in the 1980s-90s, twice a year, Edwene Gaines, brought large groups of American women to Glastonbury to experience its magical and transformative energies. Edwene is a marvellous bubbling character who over the years has inspired many thousands of people. She has been an ordained Unity minister for over 25 years, and is the owner and director of Rock Ridge Retreat Center in Valley Head, Alabama. She is also president of The Masters' School where she has trained over 400 Master Prosperity Teachers, plus she is a qualified Firewalk instructor. I was privileged during her travels to Britain to act as a guide to the sacred landscape of Avalon for hundreds of women and to share with them Goddess experiences. Over those years Edwene helped me transform my ingrained poverty consciousness into prosperity consciousness, through which people help to prosper one another.

For about five years Edwene also led twice-yearly Firewalks within the sacred landscape of Avalon, some held within sight of Glastonbury Tor. There is nothing quite so amazing as walking on fire in view of the full moon rising over the Tor. The first time that we were to hold a Firewalk at the Peat Moors Visitor Centre on the levels near Glastonbury, I was terrified. Edwene had brought fire attendants from the US to help her. For days before the event my stomach churned with fear, even though I had been told that you didn't have to walk on fire if you didn't feel called to do so. The day dawned and I was helping register the participants. I was filled with terror. My mouth was dry. I just wanted to run. The preparation workshop began and within fifteen minutes we went outside to help build the fire. Out on the land there was a rectangular fire pit. Everyone helped lift logs of wood and stacked them in two piles in the fire pit. Offerings were made to Mother Earth, Father Sky, to the elements and the spirits of the place, using sage, cedar and lemon grass. Then the fires were lit and flames roared high into the sky.

"Well," I thought, *"There is absolutely no way that I am going to walk on that."*

We trooped back into the meeting room leaving the fire tenders to stay with the fire as the wood was being consumed and reduced to hot coals. In the inspiring workshop that followed we took our shoes off and felt our vulnerable toes and soles. We went through our fears of being burnt, of stumbling in the fire, of dying.

"Fear is a membrane," said Edwene, *"All you have to do is take the first step and walk through your fear."*

We thought of all that we wished to let go to the fire and wrote it down on paper. We cried, we shook, we sang together, our hearts opened and we were made vulnerable. A few who had walked on fire before told of their experiences and we couldn't quite believe that they had lived to tell the tale. After about two hours, a firetender came to tell us that the fire was ready, it had burned down to small enough pieces. We walked out to the fire barefoot, the grassy field being icy cold and wet beneath our feet. Two fires piled high burned in the fire pit. There was no way I was going to walk on fire that night!

We gave our scraps of paper written with everything we wished to let go of, to the fire and watched them burn up into nothing, then we began to circle the fire singing. We watched the two fires being raked out and flattened, the wooden embers burning hot and red several inches thick. We were instructed that when we were ready, we should go to the end of the runway and then walk across. The way that Edwene teaches firewalking is that you must ask your intuition whether it is all right for you to walk across the fire and not be burned. If the answer is *"Yes,"* then you walk, if its *"No,"* you don't walk. It is an exercise in following intuition.

Then shockingly I saw someone walk to the end of the fire pit, pause, take a breath and walk across the fire, on the hot coals, their feet apparently not burning. At the end of the runway was a pool of water to remove any burning embers that might be attached to the feet! Then another person followed. After a short time I asked the Goddess if it was OK for me to walk and my intuition said, *"Yes"*. To my astonishment I found myself standing at the beginning of the fire pit looking down at the fire.

"*Don't look down,*" came the instruction. I lifted my head and took a breath, then took the first step. One foot after the other, I walked on fire. It felt like a cool, soft meadow. At the other end I jumped shaking, into the pool of water. I was elated. I couldn't believe what I had just done. I returned like everyone else to the circle and kept walking and singing, shaking and laughing. After a short time Her voice came telling me to try again. I walked to the end of the runway and did it again. 30 and more people walked on fire that night who had never done it before. We were all elated.

I learned so much that night that I am grateful for, especially to Edwene. I learned in my body that I can walk through my fear and come out unscathed at the end, and it was a fast, almost instantaneous lesson, the kind I like. I learned that fear is a membrane, nothing more. Walk towards and through it and it evaporates. I began to learn that the way to release fear is to allow my body to physically shake, not to hide it or suppress it, but to let it shake as it wants, and to encourage it to shake, so that my teeth chatter and my limbs shake about. It is just fear's way of leaving the body. I try to do this whenever I feel afraid and I have had a lot of fear to express over the years.

I learned more about the power of intuition to guide us in what is right for us. Follow it and it takes us into the most incredible places. If we don't follow it, we don't find what we need to learn. If we go against it we may actually harm ourselves, because those who walk on the fire when their intuition has said, "*No,*" get burned feet.

Since then I have walked on fire ten times and each time has been different and I have learned different things. Sometimes I feel fear, sometimes another emotion arises. I have even felt completely fearless about the prospect of walking on fire, because I now know what it entails and what it means. Sometimes the fire has felt very hot as we walked upon it, sometimes cool, depending on the wood that is being burnt. It is a magically transformative experience that I would recommend to anyone who wants to break through their resistances to moving forward.

To find out more about Edwene's amazing work to transform the prosperity consciousness of the world, see www.prosperityproducts.com.

Making a Priestess Wand

For a priestess a magic wand is a symbol of our inner fire. It is a specially dedicated and decorated piece of wood, metal or crystal, which has a unique function for us. Many Goddesses, from Brigit to Brigantia to Britannia, are imaged carrying a wand or staff, symbolising Her fiery quickening powers, Her ability to catalyse new growth and change. In eastern traditions this wand represents the Goddess's secret consort and symbolises the fertilising force of Her nature. In artworks the wand is usually shown in repose, resting against the Goddess's body, although it can be wielded as a banishing tool.

In emulation of these Goddesses we look for a rod made of wood, metal or crystal, that we can hold easily in our hands. It will be meaningful to us, perhaps because of where we find it, or the kind of material that it is made of. We may find a piece of wood to make a rod on a special quest in the woods, in Her nature. It can straight, curved, forked or spiralling. If appropriate we may strip the bark, carve it with Goddess symbols and decorate it with crystals, feathers, bells and ribbons. We make a specially decorated bag to hold our wand.

Although our wand is a fixed material thing it symbolises the wild element of fire. It represents our untameable wildness, our energy, our passion and strength, the fire of our minds, of our creativity, of our spirits. It is an expression of our inner magical partner. For women it can represent the animus or daemon, who appears as an inner male figure in dreams and visions, bringing inspiration directly from our soul and the Goddess. For men it expresses the masculine potentising force. We talk to our wand as if it is a companion. We give it attention. We take it with us on visits to sacred places. It becomes part of our priestess paraphernalia.

We learn to use our wand to focus our energy and attention onto particular places. We use our wands in healing to focus healing energy, or a bit like using a laser beam, to cut out waste material. Our wands become an extension of our arms and hands as we call in the Goddess's energy in ceremony, an expression of our wildness. As the wand becomes more connected to us it is inadvisable to point the wand directly at anyone, as our fire energy will flow down the wand towards them, having a strong impact. Use your wand consciously or put it safely away.

The Fire of Creative Expression

Our inner fire needs expression through creativity, and in Goddess spirituality creative expression is important for many reasons. As we open ourselves to Her inspiring energy we automatically want to become creative in the physical world. As we open to Her inspiration more and more creativity flows in, which moves out into every area of our lives. She is the Source, She is the Muse, She is the Inspiration for all that we do and we are one of the means by which the Goddess expresses Herself in the world.

We are co-creators with Her of artworks, crafts, poetry, prose, music, drama, architecture, industry, any human-made three-dimensional forms. An inspiration comes from Her to write a story on a particular theme, but it is we who shape the words into form, writing them down on paper, rearranging them until they feel right. She gives us the inspiration to create Her Goddess Temples, but we must design and build them for Her. She cannot do it without us and we must take responsibility for our part in creation. Rather than seeing ourselves as passive channels for Her energy we need to recognise our co-creative role.

Through the millennia from the earliest times as Her temples, sculptures and artworks were being destroyed by patriarchal forces, women's traditional crafts have continued to be a repository of Goddess imagery and symbols. These crafts are often centred in the home and include sewing, knitting, weaving, embroidery and all kinds of decoration on clothing, furniture, walls, etc. Designs and patterns in knitting, on material, clothing, pottery and carpets from Turkey to China, America to Africa to Australia, have continued through years of neglect to include Goddess symbols, which are now being recognised as such by scholars and researchers.

Women have always gathered to sew, whether it has been to make quilts together or to decorate prayer cushions and wall hangings within patriarchal religions. Wherever women gather to be creative the Goddess is there, moving amongst us. As part of our awakening Goddess spirituality we recognise that creativity is important and that making art and craftworks together is even better. On our journey to become Her priestesses we are inspired to make all kinds of items for our altars, homes and temples, which celebrate Her.

As we move into the 21st century we are emboldened to make new Goddess art and craftworks that bring Her back into world consciousness. Today there are many individual Goddess artists and craftswomen whose creative work is shown all over the world. In Brigit's Isles they include Carolyn Hillyer, Chesca Potter, Foosiya Miller, Jill Smith, the late Monica Sjoo, Sandra Brant and Phillipa Bowers, as well as many others, who have exhibited their art at the Glastonbury Goddess Conference.

Some artworks are made cooperatively by groups of women and there are some wonderful examples, such as *The Dinner Party*, created by US artist Judy Chicago with the help of fellow artists and craftswomen. I saw the piece many years ago in a large warehouse in London and it has remained an inspiration ever since. In this artwork a large triangular banquet table is decorated as for a dinner party, with specially made crockery and cutlery, each plate setting appearing as vulva, flower or butterfly, representing feminine being, from the primordial Goddesses to particular women in herstory. The names of hundreds of important and sometimes unknown women of the 20th century and earlier are inscribed all over the tiled floor of the piece, which is a celebration of women and the Goddess. *The Dinner Party* is now in a permanent home at the Brooklyn Museum Of Art in the USA. See www.judychicago.com for further information about this and her other artwork.

Another wonderful set of artworks are Lydia Ruyle's hundreds of fabulous Goddess Icon banners, which she and others have made over many years. They have been flown at sacred sites all over the world, including over one hundred and twenty Goddess banners flown on Glastonbury Tor at the Goddess Conference, and in Goddess displays at the Library at Ephesus, the Potala Palace in Tibet, in Germany, Poland, Hawaii, China, Australia and many other lands. These *Girls* as Lydia calls them can be seen in her wonderful book *Goddess Icons : Spirit Banners of the Divine Feminine* (Woven Wood Press), or viewed at www.lydiaruyle.com.

These bodies of artwork have a tremendous impact, encouraging us all to be more creative, to put Her images back out into the world.

Eostre

The Fire Mother Eostre or Ostara is also Astarte, another Queen of the Stars. Hers is the green fire energy of Springtime, when She ignites the waiting Fires of Life in seeds in the earth, in all growing things, in animals and humans. Where Bridie's touch quickens the life in dormant seeds, Eostre's touch turns up the flame and everything bursts into life. The bright green of Her springtime nature appears in the plants and trees. The gold of Her sunshine illuminates the world once again.

The time of the Christian festival of Easter is chosen as the first weekend after the Full Moon in Aries. Eostre is the Goddess of rebirth and Her Red Hen's eggs are still exchanged as symbols of renewal after the dark days of winter. In the past, particularly in eastern Europe, the eggs were often coloured red, the colour of life and of menstrual blood. Now we paint Eostre's eggs with patterns and symbols of the Goddess in all kinds of colours as we choose.

Eostre's companion creatures are the Bear, the Moon Hare, the Red Hen and the Cat. The Red Hen became mixed up with the Moon Hare, who became the Easter Bunny, magically able to lay eggs, and chocolate ones at that. Witches are said to be able to assume the form of hares or cats and Eostre/Ostara is a Goddess of witches. Cats of all kinds have long been associated with the Goddess from Cybele with Her lions to the Egyptian Lion-headed Sekhmet and the Cat Goddess Bast, to Britannia with Her lion, to Scandinavian Mother Freya who rode in a chariot drawn by cats. As well as being the Great She-Bear, Artemis Calliste (Artha) was also called the Mother of Cats and was identified by the Greeks with Bast.

At Oestre decorate hard boiled eggs to celebrate Eostre. Hide chocolate eggs around your home and in gardens for children and adults to find.

On a clear night look at the billions of stars in the heavens and find Artha's pattern of stars in the heavens circulating around the pole star. Through the year watch how they encircle the pole star.

Honour the Sun Mother as She rises and sets each day.

Rebalance and Rebirth

At Oestre as daylight and darkness come into balance, in our priestess cycle we too must bring ourselves into balance after the darkness of winter. To do this we have to face the existing imbalances in our outer as well as inner worlds. We all live in an imbalanced patriarchal world, which gives value to dominance, aggression, warriors, power over politics, religion and culture, to greed, gluttony, envy, etc. Our world economy is based on an industrial military complex, which sustains itself by promoting war rather than peace between peoples. Patriarchy is an ideological system which benefits the few - mainly rich, white American men (see Michael Moore's *Stupid White Men* for an enlightening exposé of how it works in America), and victimises the majority - women, children and men, of all colours and races.

At the beginning of the 21st century we all live within this dominator system which gives little value to the earth, other than as a resource to be exploited for gain; which gives little value to women, our ideals and ways of being, or to the kindness, care and gentleness of men; which exploits both women and men; which is polluting the seas, the waters, the air, the soil and the fires, as well as manipulating the essential DNA of plants and animals in the name of human gain, but actually for human greed of the few at the cost of the many.

To recognise the power of this dominator system one has only to look at the tiny numbers of women in any positions of power in the world, in governments, politics, law, banking, the military, etc., which are all expressions of patriarchy. One has only to look at the major religious institutions (all patriarchal) to note that power remains in the hands of a few men, even though congregations are filled with women, as well as men. Our outer world is in a dangerously unbalanced condition.

At the same time since the sexual and cultural revolution of the 1960s, women living in first world societies have unprecedented opportunities to live the lives we choose, far more so than women in any generation for many thousands of years. We can have creative lives if we choose. We can own properties and businesses, and be in charge of our own money. We can enter politics and business and climb up to the glass ceiling that prevents us moving into real power, if we choose. We can have happy, caring relationships with our partners. We can leave those who hurt or abuse us. We can be loving mothers to our children as well as working in the world. We can have rounded fulfilled lives. We can bring the Goddess back into our lives and create a new Goddess-loving spirituality.

Yet, we are sometimes unable to choose what might really be best for us, for our families, communities and our planet. The wounds of our conditioning undermine us at every turn, keeping us small, limiting our ambitions for ourselves and each other as we attempt to move into new lives. We are afraid to change the status quo, to change what is known for the unknown. We are afraid to be different and to be seen to be different, even when we know we are not like other people. We love a Goddess that most of the world does not recognise as real. We are different. Our values do not lie in the material world or in attaining material wealth for its own sake. Our values lie in the spiritual world, in serving Her, in returning Her to Her rightful place in the world.

The issues we have to grapple with as individuals and societies are so complex. How do we live an ethical life which supports the planet and exploits no-one? Where do we buy our shoes when they are all made in sweatshops in Asia and victimise poor people? Where can we find clean water to drink that is not polluted by nitrates and heavy metals? How can we afford to eat expensive organic food? How do we oppose the flood of pornography that dominates the internet and magazines, exploiting and denigrating women who have been abused as children (because it is only wounded women who participate in the generation of pornography)? How can we put our savings into banks, building societies and pension funds, which support the deadly arms trade or the erection of dams in unsuitable locations or building more roads that only create more traffic, etc.? How do we women walk the streets at night alone without fear?

Within our individual and collective psyches, in both women and men, the feminine is wounded. The woman within and without has been and is being verbally, physically and sexually abused over and over. She has been betrayed, undervalued, victimised, beaten, disempowered again and again. Her self esteem is low, on the floor. She starves herself to gain some small power in a male-dominated world or overeats to protect herself from the ever-present threat of abuse. She betrays her sisters at every turn, gossiping, backbiting, undermining those women who live closest to her ideals, lest they should emerge from the common pile, leaving her behind. She constantly seeks approval from other women and men. She shops to fill the empty space within, afraid of what she might find if she looks into the gaping hole within, that nothing can fill. She is always afraid, of men, of other women, of the dark, of the unknown, of the future, of not being good enough. She always needs fixing. She is never just OK.

And its not just women who suffer, men in the patriarchy are betrayed too, in their manhood. A man is a cog in the great wheel of western civilisation keeping it all turning, enslaved to its macho and death-dealing ideals. He too finds it hard to break free, to be himself, to be gentle as well as strong, to be a guardian of Her nature. If he rises to the top of the heap how can he stop being an abuser in his dominant position, how does he climb off the treadmill of monotonous or adrenalin-fuelled workaholism, how does he decline to fight in pointless wars or to benefit from the fruits of those wars? If he honours the feminine in his life, in the women he knows and loves, in his world, in himself, that would obviously mean losing the power that patriarchy gives him. If he chooses to love Her equally, he may become disempowered as a man. He may become a wimp whom no-one respects, man or woman.

When looked at in detail the problems we face can seem overwhelming. Where do we start the process of rebalancing ourselves, never mind the whole world we live in?

We begin by acknowledging what is, recognising the true condition of how things are in our world, where we are at. This is the first step and not easy to take. We don't really want to know just how awful things are, as this can undermine us even more, depressing us into passivity. But look we must into the gaping maw of desolation and destruction that faces our planet and its inhabitants.

At the same time we open our hearts to the Goddess, allowing Her radiance to fill us with love, strengthening us in our very core, in our centre.

We cannot do this alone. We cannot transform our lives or our planet on our own. We need Her help.

We call to Her and She responds via our intuition, our inner knowing. We ask for help and She offers us a glimmer of hope that can set us on a new course. We have a flash of inspiration, an idea comes whose power frightens us, telling us to leave a failing relationship, to take a less well paid job that will give us more time, to move house, to write a book, to learn about healing, to teach others what we know. Or it can be a small idea to be done today, now - go and pray at Her altar, read a poem, make a Goddess doll today, call a friend, walk in Her landscape. If we listen She will tell us the very next thing to do. She takes the mental chatter out of decision-making.

Responding to Her inspiration is the only clear route out of our pain, challenging us to move on, to change, to grow, to stand up and be counted. For this is what it is to be a priestess, to stand up and be seen in the world for who we are, for what we believe, for the truths we hold dear, for the Goddess. There is no point in being a Priestess of Avalon if you want to hide your talents in a corner and not be seen. Priest/esses stand out in a patriarchal world.

And how do we know if the messages we hear are true or not? How do we know we are not being betrayed by our own desires and thoughts? How do we know that the voice we hear is that of the Goddess? It might just be a voice in our head.

We know Her voice within us is true because it feels right, not in the sense of right as opposed to wrong, but in the sense of being a truth for us. Her voice is heartwarming, opening, loving, exciting, expansive and uplifting. She never tells us to do anything which will harm us or anyone else, ever. If we follow our intuition our actions may upset others, but not ultimately harm them. For example, if we leave a failed relationship, our purpose is to free both ourselves and our partner into new love. We also know Her voice is true because to follow our intuition is scary for us. It challenges us. It asks us to do the things we are afraid of, to change our patterns of behaviour, to move beyond our comfort zones, to be original, to be creative with life, to express our uniqueness, to become balanced in an imbalanced world.

Each morning as you wake in the liminal moments between sleep and wakefulness listen for the Goddess's words of inspiration as She tells you what to do today or in the future. Write down what you hear. Practice following Her inspiration today and see what happens in your life.

Patterns which bring us into balance

Within the Goddess tradition there are several ancient patterns which are designed to bring us into balance when they are physically walked. These symbols are found all around the world in cultures as diverse as the neolithic and bronze age peoples of Brigit's Isles, the Kelts, the Native Americans, ancient Kretans, Old Europeans, Indians, Tibetans and Aboriginal Australians. They include the seven circuit labrynth, which is everywhere recognised as a Goddess symbol.

Creating a labrynth in a three-dimensional form on the earth and then walking it in a ceremonial manner gives us an experience of balance and wholeness. The physical act of walking this particular shape seems to have an effect on the left and right sides of the brain, as well as the left and right sides of the body, helping bring them into balance.

Creating a Ceremonial Labrynth

The seven circuit labrynth is universal and ancient, appearing on the earliest coins from Krete, at Pompeii, on rocks at Tintagel in Cornwall, in Ireland, in Indonesia and Sri Lanka, as Tapu'at, a symbol among the Native American Hopi for Mother Earth and upon the slopes of Glastonbury Tor. I spell labrynth thus (rather than labyrinth), to emphasise the connection to the matrifocal Kretan House of the Labrys or double headed lunar axe.

Different cultures give different meanings to this beautifully simple yet enigmatic pattern. They include the following: the back and forth cyclic pattern is said to reflect the movement of the psychic tides within a human being over a moon's cycle, moving inwards to one's psychic core at the dark of the moon and then returning outwards into physical expression at the full moon. This pattern is directly connected to women's menstrual cycles. For the Hopi people, the labrynth was used to mark their early migrations throughout the American continent, coming from the four directions to a central home in Arizona and spreading out again. In Krete, the pattern was said to be based on the dance of mating Crane birds and to celebrate sexuality and the union of female and male. There it was also a maze to contain the monstrous Minotaur, the bull-god-man Asterion of Minoan Krete, to which Ariadne of the Red Thread holds the key. It is also the design for a dancing floor received from the Snake Goddess Ariadne, whose pattern helps rebalance imbalanced masculine and feminine energies.

The pattern of the labrynth is simple to create and can be temporary or permanent, laid indoors or out. Indoors to mark the pattern we can use ribbon, wool, threads, string, masking tape (which can be removed from the floor afterwards), or more permanently tiles, paint, materials, different kinds of floor coverings. Outdoors the path can be permanent or temporary, made using hedges, flower borders, mowed grass, stones, earth, sand, string and pegs, seeds, flower petals, herbs or flour. You may want to practice drawing the labrynth with pen and paper first, but I will describe the process for making the real thing.

The process of creating a labrynth begins with cleansing and smudging the space you will be using for your Labrynth. You will need a round or square area large enough to fit in seven circuits, that is seven paths on both sides of a central space, plus the centre, plus room to walk around the outside of the labrynth. The pathways will need to be at least one person wide or ideally two or more people wide, so this will be quite a large space. Think about the central space of the labrynth, how large do you want it to be? Will it be empty or will you place something symbolic there - a statue of the Goddess, a tree, flowers, etc.?

When I create a labrynth I like to place an altar in the centre with all its colours and Goddess symbols and items, plus a mirror in which we can see ourselves in the centre. I have also played the role of Goddess Oracle, sitting at the centre of a labrynth.

Next the direction of the entrance must be chosen. It can be related to the time of year when you are creating the labrynth and therefore to the appropriate direction on the wheel, say in the east for Oestre or the southwest for Lammas. It may be related to a landscape feature, or to the rising or setting of the sun or moon on a particular day. It's your choice, but have a good reason.

Look at the space you have to play with and note where your entrance will be. In your mind mark a spot about one third of the distance from the entrance to the boundary opposite to the entrance. Move that spot one pathway width to the left. Mark this spot with a dot. Lay out the following patterns with tape or flour. First of all lay out an equal-armed cross with the centre on the original dot, one arm of the cross aligned to the entrance. In each corner of the cross place a ninety degree angle, facing outwards. Then as if you are creating a square, place a dot in each corner to complete a square shape.

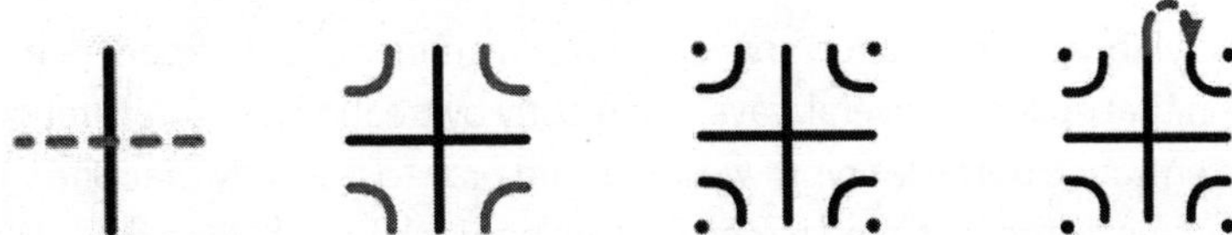

From the central arm lay an arc of tape or flour clockwise, joining it to the first line of the angle immediately to its right.

Moving to the left of the central arm, join the angle via an arc of tape or flour, running clockwise to the dot on the right of the central arm. Curve it around the previous arc at a distance of at least one person's width. Moving to the dot on the far left of the central arm lay an arc of tape or flour curving it around at a distance of at least one person's width and join it to the second arm of the angle on the right.

Continue laying tape or flour beginning on the left each time at the angle, main cross or dot and curving the line around clockwise to the right arm of the main cross, angle or dot, until they are all joined up and the labrynth is complete.

The final arc creates the entrance to the labrynth. When drawing the pattern on paper trace the path through the labrynth with your finger. Where the outermost circuit is 1 and the innermost circuit around the centre is 7, note that the pattern of the labrynth is 3,2,1,4,7,6,5.

As soon as the labrynth is laid out it becomes sacred space and it is inadvisable to cross over any of its lines. Always walk in and out from the entrance.

Walking a labrynth

A labrynth is a sacred space and we can enhance the experience of being in that space in several ways, but mostly by treating it with reverence. At the entrance to the labrynth we kneel and pray to the Lady that She will reveal to us all that we need to see by walking Her labrynth. We ask for Her blessing on our journey.

We can run, skip or dance our way through a labrynth, there are no rules, but one of the most powerful ways is to walk slowly in a walking meditation in bare feet. As we do so we immediately become conscious of the movement of our feet, legs and body as we walk. It is surprisingly easy to become unsteady on our feet and to stumble when we are walking within the circuits of a labrynth and the added consciousness of walking brings a powerful focus. We can walk in silence or to a background of Goddess chants and music.

In ceremony the labrynth becomes a symbol of our life's journey. There is only one path that we take in life with all its twists and turn. It never remains the same for long and is always changing direction, but we continue along our path until we reach the centre. As we walk in towards the centre, we visualise ourselves letting go of the layers of conditioning in our bodies, emotions and minds, all our imbalances, on each of the different circuits of the labrynth. By the time we reach the centre we are symbolically naked and there we face ourselves and the Goddess. We spend time in the centre contemplating Her and all She may reveal to us.

On our journey out of the labrynth we gather all those qualities and attributes that we want to take with us into the future as we walk out through the seven circuits of the labrynth. When we leave the labrynth we again kneel and pray for the gifts that have been revealed to us and embrace the new balance we have found.

From Oestre to Beltane

From Oestre onwards the impact of fire within nature accelerates, the sun rises higher in the sky, the hours of daylight lengthen quickly. The air warms noticeably, although there can still be wind and rain. The ground slowly warms, the trees that were naked bud, bushes begin to green, leaves and flowers open and all of Her nature starts to grow rapidly. Birds and animals build their nests and call to each other to mate. Activity and sexuality within humans increases with the returning light. Our attention begins to move outwards from the dark cave of winter towards the light.

Make an altar at home to Nolava, *Lady of* Fire, *to* Artha *the* Great She-Bear *in the heavens, to* Grainne *the* Sun Goddess, *to* Sulis Sun Woman, *to* Eostre *the* Equinox Goddess, *who lays the eggs of the future and to* Morgen Cliton. *Find an image or natural object which represents the* Oestre Mother *of* Fire *to you: Goddess statues, bears, hens, cats, flames, eggs.*

Every day light a candle flame and burn incense to Nolava, *to* Artha, Grainne, Sulis, Eostre *and* Cliton *on your altar and sing and pray to* Her *for help, guidance, in gratitude, for others in need, for healing for yourself and others, for vision, etc. Once a week recreate your altar.*

Every day write down and/or draw feelings, dreams, thoughts, intuitions and visions in your diary, i.e. what's going on for you.

At dawn and at dusk, the liminal times between light and dark draw out a circle with your wand. Inside it place spring flowers, light candles and say prayers to the Goddess *of springtime, giving thanks for* Her *return after the darkness of winter. At night look at the stars of the* Great She-Bear *in the sky above you and say prayers to* Artha.

Speak of your wounds to others who can empathise. Make steps on the road to healing and recovery.

Make a magic Wand *for yourself and take it with you on journeys as a companion, an expression of your inner magical partner. Talk to your wand.*

At the new moon light a sacred flame to represent the Goddess *light which is coming into your life. Start to sew your future priestess costume, or embroider a garment with meaningful patterns and symbols.*

At the full moon create your own ceremony to honour the Mother *of* Fire, *filling your home with* Her *candle flames, lighting a fire for* Her. *Take great care of* Her *fire, placing all candles and fires in safe containers as fire can burn as well as illuminate and inspire.*

Create your own labrynth and walk it in ceremony.

Visit sacred sites or landscapes aligned to the spring equinox. Between 4,000 BCE *and* 1,700 BCE *and earlier in the age of* Taurus, *many sacred sites were aligned to the rising of the* Pleiades, *part of the constellation of*

First Spiral

Taurus in the west at the Spring Equinox. Avebury is one example, find others. Visit the neolithic mounds and listen for Artha's growl. Visit Sulis Minerva's hot springs at Bath.

The Blossoming
Beltane Festival of the Lover Goddess

Beltane is the festival of the fecund and fertile Goddess as Lover. We honour Her as Nolava the Lover and as Morgen Thetis, who is both a true lover and the sacred whore, a musician whose magical notes resound throughout the land, encouraging blossoms to spring from the bough and the earth. We love Her as Rhiannon of the Birds, the White Mare from the Sea, She who is Sovereignty, and as Queen Gwenhwyfar, Queen of the Land. We celebrate Blodeuwedd the Flower Maiden, Olwen of the White Track and Elen of the Trackways, who dwell in our native woods and forests. We explore the natural places where She may be found.

Celebrated at the end of April and beginning of May, Beltane is the time of year when all of Her nature is alive with sensual and sexual activity. The stark white flowers of the blackthorn already cover the hedgerows, awaiting the coming May blossom. In the orchards of Avalon delicate pink blooms covers the apple trees. Garden flowers are opening with colour. The sun is rising high in the sky, the days are lengthening, all of Her nature is active. The birds are singing their hearts out to attract mates, building nests and consummating their unions. The animals are busy excavating burrows and mating. Human beings too enjoy the risen fertile energy, making love in the orchards and woodlands as bluebells begin to flower.

At Beltane we honour the Love Goddesses of Brigit's Isles and in visions we ride between the worlds with Rhiannon. We explore how we feel about our female bodies, our sensuality and sexuality and the gifts they bring to us. We talk about our sexual wounds and pleasures. We consider the place of men within our lives and within Goddess spirituality. We jump the fire with our lovers and friends to seal our commitment to journey together through the coming year. We express our Goddess nature through music, song and sacred drama. We make headdresses to go with our dedication costumes.

Honouring Nolava the Lover

In the landscape of Avalon the form of Nolava the Lover can be seen as a giant woman lying relaxed on Her back on the earth. Her lusty left breast reaches up to the sky as the Tor as her right breast slips over. Her legs are spread wide apart and facing the Bristol Channel, which leads to the Atlantic Ocean. In ancient times this great western ocean once lapped upon the shorelines of the Isle of Avalon bringing Nodens, the God of the Sea, riding in towards Nolava on the backs of his dolphins. On certain days when the moon was full and the tides were high, especially in spring and autumn, his waters would crash and spume into his Lover's Vulva, as He made love to the earth that is Her body. From their lovemaking all that now lives on this piece of ground was conceived and brought to birth.

As Lover, Avalon is a land filled with love, attracting many to its shores, each heart drawn to the Heart of Love that is the Goddess. Many come to reawaken and celebrate their sensuality and their sexuality, but many are also drawn here to heal their sexual and relationship wounds, wounds of abuse. Nolava's land is the place where such wounds to love can be healed, and the healing itself may be sweet and heart-expanding, or painful and difficult. As we meet up with old karmic acquaintances and lovers, we repeat our familiar patterns. As we become aware we remember what happened to us in our early relationships with parents, siblings and friends, and we remember experiences from our previous incarnations. The pain that is held in the memories can be expressed in consciousness, as we try to make ourselves whole again in Her love.

Glastonbury is often called the Heart Chakra of the world, which is an awesome title for such a small place in the southwest of Brigit's Isles. But it is from here, from Avalon, that the energy of love, of the soul of all things, of the Goddess Herself, radiates outwards into the world. We can feel this radiation in its attractive pull in our own lives and in the lives of others. The power of this radiant love is transforming. It allows our barriers to melt away as we swoon in love with Her. This love also reveals our primal and karmic wounds, our resistance to loving and being loved. As our individual hearts slowly open and we heal ourselves, the Heart Chakra that is Avalon continues to unfold and open wider too allowing more love to pour forth into the world.

Honouring Thetis, Morgen of Love

I am Thetis, Morgen of Love and Sexuality
I am the heart of the romance, I am beauty and sensuality

I am the daughter of Fire and Water
Sorceress of the Karma Sutra
I am the waves of passion pounding the shore
I am desire, the lust that leaves you burning, yearning for more

I am the May tree, the scent of Her flowers
I am the blossom adorning the bowers
I am the nectar, the pollen attracting the bee,
I am the honey on the table for tea:
I cast my glamour o'er the land
To instil with bliss the Summerland

Scarlet Woman, the Lady in Red
I am the cheap hotel room and the marriage bed.
Mistress, sweetheart, sacred whore
I am the one-night stand and the wife they adore;
I am the cherry ripe for the plucking.......

I am the Lover, your Midsummer Night's dream:
My music be the food of love
So let me play on my zither
Let me be your "Come hither!"
Seductress and flirt, I know no morality
For I am Thetis, the Morgen of Love and Sexuality.

by Carol Morgan

Thetis is the Morgen of Love. She is one of only two Morgens distinguished by Geoffrey of Monmouth out of the Nine, the other being Morgen La Fey. Thetis was said to play the zither, She is Lady of Music and Keeper of Time. Music flows from Her fingers as She sits playing in the blossom-laden apple orchards of Avalon. She is Lady of the Flowers.

She is also Cloud in the sky, which at this time of year release showers of rain that help the plants to grow. At other times of the year Thetis rises high in the sky forming the small fluffy clouds of summer time or building to great towering cumuli or She can thicken to cold greyness in autumn, bringing drizzle, and hard driving rains. In winter She brings sleet and snow.

Her creatures include the flocks of small birds, the tits and warblers, who gather about Her as She walks the land, flying in clouds in the air, moving as if they have one body, one consciousness. Sometimes Thetis rides a white mare like Rhiannon, at others a black stallion is Hers. Wherever Her feet touch the earth, flowers spring up as She goes by.

She appears as a beautiful young woman in Her twenties. Her colour is the red of fertile life blood and sexuality. Her hair is red-gold and She wears a glowing red dress. She is Queen of the May, Hawthorn Woman, with Her showers of small white or pink flowers, scented with the perfume of women's vaginal secretions. She is both Lover and Sacred Harlot, celebrated in deep relationships and one-night stands. She is romance, beauty and sensuality. She casts Her glamour over all who are lucky enough to glimpse Her, bringing bliss to lovers and all who enter the sacred land. She leads the willing into the Heart of Her Mysteries, bringing us to face our greatest fears of intimacy, love and commitment. She can take us swiftly and directly to the gates of the Underworld.

Many women who live in or who come to Glastonbury find themselves playing the role of Thetis for men and women who visit here. Naive, we may first meet our lovers at Beltane when sexual energy is high, calling the Goddess into our bodies and leading the unsuspecting towards deeper intimacy. Closed hearts open in love and everything we have ever dreamed of seems possible. When the pressure to be and stay open to love become too intense, we women can find ourselves abandoned and pregnant at the entrance to the Underworld. There we are welcomed in by Gwyn ap Nudd, who guards the threshold to the Dark Goddess's cave.

Pray to Thetis that She comes into your life blessing you with Her sexuality and sensuality. Ask that you may embody Her loving nature in your own body when you make love. Pray that you have the wisdom to take care of yourself and others as you surrender to love.

Rhiannon of the Birds, White Mare from the Sea

Rhiannon is Goddess of Love and Sexuality, whose name means Great Queen, like Rigantona. Her story is told in the First Branch of the Mabinogion, which in the beginning describes Her wonderful Goddess nature. The story then follows Her demise as Her powers are forgotten, derided and abused. The tale begins with Her appearance to the Welsh Lord Pwyll. It shows us how we too must approach the Goddess.

In the story, one evening after his meal Pwyll goes from his palace at Narberth to the Gorsedd or Mound of Arberth, of which it said that whoever sits on the Mound will either receive wounds or blows, or else see a great wonder. While sitting there in the twilight, Pwyll sees a Lady dressed in shining gold and riding a pure white horse coming along the road towards the Mound. He sends one of his men to find out who She is. The man runs after Her as She passes by, but the faster he runs the further away the Lady seems to be, although Her pace doesn't seem to alter. Pwyll then sends a man to the palace to get a horse to go after Her, but again the more the man urges his horse to go faster, the further away the Lady is, even though She holds the same pace.

The next day Pwyll returns to the Mound with his men and a horse. Once again the Lady in gold passes by and Pwyll sends one of his youngest and fastest riders to find out who She is. The man follows Her but once again no matter how fast he rides, he cannot catch up with Her as She keeps the same steady even pace. Something strange is afoot.

On the third evening Pwyll takes his own horse, saddled and ready to ride, to the Mound. The Lady appears once more and as She passes by Pwyll climbs upon his horse and goes after Her, thinking it will be easy to catch up with Her. However no matter how hard he rides his horse he cannot reach Her. After some long time, exhausted he calls out to Her,

" O *maiden, for the sake of him thou best lovest, stay for me*".

"I *will stay gladly*", She replies, "*And it were better for your horse hadst thou asked me long since.*"

The Lady stops and throws back the headdress which covers Her face, unveiling Her beauty.

"*Lady,*" says Pwyll, "*Will you tell me your purpose.*"

"I *will tell thee,*" says She, "My *chief quest was to seek thee.*"

These are the unveiled words of the Goddess. To reach Her we must seek Her out in the mysterious places, on the mounds and hillsides that are scary for us to be. When we see Her pass by we must go after Her, following Her even though we can't quite reach Her. We call to Her and ask Her to stop for us, the ones She loves best. Then we find out that all the time She too has been searching for us. This is so true for would-be priestesses, whose hearts are filled with longing to see Her face. We can search and search for a long time before we find Her, only to realise that She has been waiting a long time for us to recognise Her. We merge with Her in blissful reunion and ride upon Her mare into the Otherworld of Love.

At Beltane we honour Rhiannon as Lady of the Hollow Hills who rides Her white mare between the middle and lower worlds, taking us from the everyday world into the hollow mounds and hills. Glastonbury Tor is one such hollow hill, with its reputed waterworn tunnels and caverns. On misty mornings and evenings Rhiannon can be seen riding on the slopes of the Tor. Her horse is the symbol of our wild, untameable nature as women. In visualisations we journey with Her into the hollow hill of the Tor, sitting behind Her on the back of Her horse, feeling Her waist and the warmth of Her body with our hands. She takes us to the Underworld stables that lie deep within the Tor where there are lots of horses. We have the opportunity to choose our own horse, mare or stallion, of a colour we like. We make friends with our horse, breathing into its nostrils, before climbing upon its back. Rhiannon leads us back out of the Tor and onto the land, where we can ride as slow or as fast as we choose, feeling the wildness of the animal between our legs, riding free. We feel the energy and power that is ours to learn to express and control for the good of all.

In Avalon we honour Rhiannon at the trivia, the threefold crossways that can be found on many of the lanes around the Tor. These trivia symbolise the junctions between the lower, middle and upper worlds. Bulwarks Lane has four trivia along its length. We make offerings to Her of flower petals and grains in the centre of these crossways, remembering that She can take us between the worlds.

Sovereignty, Queen of the Land

At Beltane we honour Sovereignty, She who is Queen and Goddess of the land over which She rides. Her walking and riding feet measure the land which belongs to Her. All human kings must marry Her in order to truly rule in Her land. She is the Lady with whom all queens must identify and embody, to have the right to rule in Her name. There are remnants of these ancient marriage rituals in the British monarchy's coronation ceremonies.

Her most famous incarnation was as Queen Guinevere in Arthurian legend, whose name means *white spirit* or *phantom*. In the original Welsh stories there were three Gwenhwyfars, indicating that originally She was the Triple Goddess, whose power and authority were reduced in patriarchal myth-making. She became the wife of King Arthur and is said to betrayed Her husband by sleeping with his friend. As Sovereignty and the all-powerful Goddess of Love, Gwenhwyfar had the right to take as many lovers as She chose, imparting Her blissful karuna to those with whom She made love.

The work of redeeming Guinevere is not completed and Goddess women need to reclaim our rights to love whomsoever we choose.

Blodeuwedd

Blodeuwedd is both the Flower Maiden and the Owl Goddess. In the *Romance of Math ap Mathonwy* in the Mabinogion, She was said to have been conjured from flowers by Math and the wizard Gwydion, as a wife for the young Llew Llaw Gyffes. As in many parts of the Mabinogion we see the powers of the ancient Goddess being overturned by male pretenders.

Blodeuwedd, which means *Flower Face*, is obviously an ancient Goddess of the Beltane flowers, who existed long before Math and Gwydion came along. The spell which creates Her is actually an invocation of Her presence. Robert Graves in his inspired book, *The White Goddess*, gives a version of the following poem, which I adapt here.

Hanes Blodeuwedd

I am formed from nine blossoms,
Nine buds of various kinds
From primroses of the mountains,
Broom, meadow sweet and cockle,
Together intertwined,
From the bean in its shade bearing
A white spectral army
Of earth, of earthly kind,
From the blossoms of the nettle,
Oak, thorn and bashful chestnut-
Nine powers of nine flowers,
Nine powers in me combine, (*like the* Nine Morgens)
Nine buds of plant and tree,
Long and white are my fingers
As the ninth wave of the sea.

Robert Graves, *The White Goddess*, Faber

Blodeuwedd appears later in the *Romance of Math ap Mathonwy* when She is said to have been turned into an owl by Gwydion for Her betrayal of Llew Llaw Gyffes. Betrayal in a Goddess myth is nearly always a synonym for initiation. Of course again She always was the Owl Goddess, with the owl face of the Dark Goddess of Wisdom. She flies at night and is feared by other birds. She brings initiation and wisdom. Here is a great poem about Her.

Blodeuwedd Rising (Song for Hazel)

Blodeuwedd, Magdalene of Springtime
Sweet flower face with wings of snow
You are the gateway to the seasons
Fierce in passion, eyes aglow

And You will rise in fearless beauty
Afraid of You, they change Your face
But we remember Your true nature;
Reclaim Your love, Reclaim Your place

Defiled and changed and called a whore
If whore You are then so am I
As whore I'll be Your temple priestess
And You will give me wings to fly

Reclaim the whore and rise in beauty
With Goddess spirit deep within
Knowing our own Goddess nature
How dare they name our passion sin!

No one can shackle or control You
Owl of Secrets, flying free
No chains to bind Your hungry spirit
With You beside, no chains on me

And we will rise in raging beauty
To be what we've been all along
When we can stand alone as equals
We will sing Blodeuwedd's song

They left us here in silent fury
Thought that they had won the game
But as we reclaim our ancient birthright
Blodeuwedd will rise again

And we will rise in naked beauty
Revealing all we have to give
Loving in the ways we choose to
Deciding how we want to live

They try to make us pretty blossoms
Deny our claws, deny our power
But we must claim our truth and freedom
To choose the owl, to choose the flower

And we will rise in powerful beauty
Surrender to Blodeuwedd's *cry*
She draws us to the path of moonlight
On owl wings we must learn to fly

No one has the right to harm us
To name and shame, abuse and scar us
Call us hag and call us bitch.
Reclaim the owl, reclaim the witch!

And we will rise in all our beauty
For we have heard Flower Face's *call*
Our bodies glowing with our passion
Both owls and flowers, Priestesses *all!*

Jacqui Woodward-Smith, 25th/26th November 2003

Make images of the Flower Goddess *for your altar and for ceremony using flowers and buds woven together. Make crowns of flowers. If possible collect the nine flowers and buds described in the* Hanes Blodeuwedd. *At dusk walk silently among the trees and in the fields and commune with* Blodeuwedd *the Owl.*

Olwen of the White Track

Olwen of the White Track is the May Queen and Queen of the May, of the Hawthorn or Whitethorn tree. She begins to blossom at Beltane and throughout the month of May, leaving a shower of tiny white and pink flowers in the hedgerows. Her father is Yspaddaden Penkawr or Giant Hawthorn, who was said to be the Chief of the Giants, who set challenges for those who would marry his daughter. As described in *The Ancient British Goddess* hawthorn blossom was demonised in patriarchal thinking, where it was said to bring bad luck into a home or church, especially in the month of May, but hawthorn is the British Goddess flower of sexuality and sensuality. At Beltane we reclaim Olwen and deck our altars and temples with hawthorn blossoms in honour of the Queen of the May and in celebration of Her pleasures and sexuality.

Elen of the Trackways

At Beltane we also honour Elen of the Trackways, She who is a guide, guardian and protector of the trackways which long, long ago ran through the forests which covered nearly all of Brigit's Isles. Once these tracks were the only pathways in forests where dangerous animals lived and Elen was an important guardian and protective Goddess. She can still be found in our native woodlands. As the weather improves we walk through the woods and forests, looking to see Her green face within and behind the tree branches and leaves.

Goddess of Love and Sexuality

Love is a great mystery. It lies at the heart of everything that is meaningful to us as human beings. It is the source of our happiness, and when denied or rejected, of much of our pain. The Goddess of Love and Sexuality is a powerful Goddess who brings us swiftly to the gates of transformation. She opens our hearts to personal and universal love and in that opening our wounds reveal themselves for healing. She can take us down to the Underworld in the blink of an eye.

Song for the Goddess of Love by Sophia Condaris

Goddess of Love, sing to me
Open my heart and set me free
Take my body and make me whole
Goddess of Love, fill my soul.

As women, we are so susceptible to Love, whether it is within us or projected out onto a lover. It is in our nature to want to embody the Goddess as a loving sexual being, surrendering to Her passionate nature within us, even when we don't know that this is what we are doing.

Many women hold within themselves, consciously or unconsciously, the archetype of the Sacred Harlot or Whore who was Priestess of Love and Sexuality, living within the walls of a Goddess Temple. As Priestess she would share the Goddess's mystical and sexual karuna with whoever came seeking Her. This generosity of sexual love is still a familiar feeling to many Goddess women and we can hold this generosity of spirit and body in our consciousness even when we are married and committed to one love.

In our nature we encompass both faces of Blodeuwedd, the flower and the owl, the sweet beautiful woman and the passionate wild lover. We are like Lilith and Eve in the garden of Eden. As Lilith, another Owl Goddess, we feel a powerful sexuality that will not be subordinated to any man and if denied will rage and scream, or disappear off into the deserts of pain and repression. As Eve our nature is to offer the fruits of the Tree of Knowledge of Good and Evil to our lovers, catalysing their true incarnation into life. In both Eden and Avalon the Tree of Knowledge is an apple tree with its pentagram of pips at the centre, symbolising knowledge of the Dark Goddess. Demonised in the Bible and in many other patriarchal texts as the cause of all human downfall from a state of innocence, it is we women who can lead our lovers towards the fullness of love's expression in life.

Yet there are also many layers of inhibition that can prevent us from opening ourselves to receiving and giving love. These are the unconscious consequences of past and current life abuses, the wounds to our bodies, emotions and minds, which we often carry throughout our lives. We can easily spend 40 years and more unravelling the effects of this karma within our love nature and sexual expression.

In my own life as a young woman I longed to love and be loved. I loved falling in love. I loved the thrill and excitement of a lover's touch that gave luminosity and meaning to my life. I was in love with being in love. When the powerful love I felt in every pore of my body was denied or dishonoured I felt total disbelief. Each time a relationship ended I was distraught at the loss I felt. How could this person not feel the same way that I felt? How could they reject this beautiful love that we had experienced and I knew to be real? Hadn't they felt it too? We had been so close when we made love, hadn't we? Many times I was led by love and its loss to the gates of the Underworld, where I plunged miserably and unconsciously into the depths. There I would sojourn for months at a time until I slowly climbed out to try to love again. My relationships with the men I was attracted to didn't work and the longest I was actually with anyone was two years.

In my thirties I went into therapy and began to unravel my deep feelings. I noticed the precise moment when I fell in love with a man. It was when he entered my body and I surrendered in orgasm. At that time I did not know the Goddess was in me when I made love. I just surrendered easily and thought that it was the man I was with who created this blissful experience for me. Unfortunately I did not know that the lover did not necessarily feel the same thing as me. I fell in love with a lot of unsuitable men who did not fall in love with me.

The Goddess began to make Herself known to me and I heard my daughter calling me to be her mother. I was 33 years old. I had no steady boyfriend, no permanent lover, but decided to put my fate into Her hands. I stopped taking the contraceptive pill and asked the Goddess to bring me the father of my child. Unfortunately I didn't ask for him to be my partner too. During the next few months I made love with a couple of different men before my daughter's father arrived on the scene. I fell in love with him as we made love. Six weeks later I was pregnant, homeless, jobless and on my own, destroyed again with a broken heart. I felt I had given this man one of the ultimate gifts any woman can give, that of fathering her children, and he was unable to accept the gift.

Over the following seven years I learned much about the depths of love and the deeps of the Underworld. I gave birth to two beautiful children whom I have adored from the beginning of time, but I found myself alone with them and stretched to my emotional and mental limits. As their father came and went I was stripped of all my armouring and descended for long periods of time into the Shadowy Underworld. Lost in its depths the Judges who dwell there looked upon me and found me wanting. The Eye of Death was cast upon me. I sat groaning with Ereshkigal, the Queen of the Underworld in Her grief. I was hung rotting on a hook on the wall of Her palace for three days and nights with no signs of life. In that place of darkness I just kept going down, further and further into depression, until eventually I reached the bottom and broke through.

There beneath the layers of ancient rocky resistance I found the River of Creativity that runs deep below the Underworld. I dived in and drank from its waters. By Her grace I rode the river back to the surface of the Middleworld, bringing the fruits of my journey with me and a connection to the River which has never left me.

I realised that in my life I had always been swept away by love and I had always compromised myself in order to get love. I realised that I had a choice when it came to being in love. I didn't have to follow my strong feelings of desire unless I chose to do so. I could unpick the experience of falling in love through orgasm. When I made love I now knew that the Goddess was within me and this was my secret and my joy as a woman.

In order to receive love from those I fell in love with, I had always played smaller, been less than who I truly am. When I met someone new I would see their soul and ignore the reality of who they were. I would project onto my lover all my hopes and desires, and was surprised when he failed to live up to them. Once I was able withdraw my projections and could hear and see who he actually was, I was freed from my grasping desire that wanted him to be other than he was. Once I saw who he was I knew he was not the person I wanted to be with.

I decided I would never compromise myself again for love and if necessary I would be alone for the rest of my life, if that was what She wanted. I became very creative and got on with my life. I asked the Goddess to bring my perfect partner to me if She chose. I wrote my requirements of him on a list and placed it on my kitchen wall, putting it where it could be seen in case he should pass by. A few years later She brought my perfect partner Mike, to me, to play music in one of the sacred dramas I had co-written and we have been together ever since. We learn together about life and love through our imperfections and aspirations.

Sexual Preferences

I don't believe that the Goddess of Love minds whether we are heterosexual or homosexual or anything in between. She does want us to experience love in many forms without harm and whatever that might mean for us is good for Her. In parts of the Goddess movement it has been claimed that only lesbian women can truly experience the intimacy of the Goddess's love as it is shared between two Goddess-loving women. In parts of the pagan community it is believed that the Goddess can only be fully experienced when She is brought to life by the God in manly form. However these are just different experiences of Her, neither of which is better than the other. She asks us to be true to our inherent natures, to who we are, and that may mean we are lusty lovers, sacred whores, butch dikes, monogamous partners, virgins, camp followers, or a host of other terms, which don't adequately describe who we are. She wants us to be sexually authentic, healed of our wounds of abuse and conditioning.

Having Sex and Making Love

Having sex and making love are two different kinds of experience, both of which belong to the Goddess of Love. Modern day culture, magazines, TV programmes and films encourage us to have sex freely and often, to release our sexual energies without love or commitment. Sex is a commodity that can be given and taken as needed, even bought and sold for profit. In the media and on our computer screens pornography abounds, with its visual titillation and dehumanisation of both women and men.

The sexual revolution which began in the 1960s brought sexual liberation for women and freedom from unwanted pregnancies. It did not necessarily bring us greater happiness and fulfilment in our relationships, although it did thankfully give us permission to leave unhappy ones. More and more people now live alone, without partners. It seems to be harder than ever to find the right woman or the right man. We often compromise ourselves for the sake of feeling wanted, having one night stands or putting up with unsatisfactory relationships. Having sex can be fun, but often leads us to feel used, dirty, cold, ashamed, isolated, abandoned and alone.

Making love on the other hand, involves surrendering to love during the sexual act in a way which actually generates love, both within our relationships and into the world as a whole. When we make love we share intimacy, vulnerability and the tenderness of our open hearts. When we make love we increase the amount of available love in the world (I always thought this was a great reason to make love often). It is our birthright as women to share the Goddess's love while making love. We have the ability to embody Her consciously within our sexuality and this leads us into powerful mystical experiences of Her essential energy. We make love by continually surrendering to Her, embodying Her within the sexual act, allowing Her to enter our bodies and be present. We offer Her presence to our lovers, giving to them the experience of Her essence.

Tantric Sex

Tantra means embodiment of the divine and tantric sex is the form of sexuality in which we embody the divine as we make love. In Buddhism, which despite its benign appearance is still one of the major patriarchal religions of the world, the highest initiations involve participation in tantric sex, both actual and visualised. Monks who have lived apart from women for many years in male communities are required to visualise and practice lovemaking with innocent and vulnerable young women, the best age for whom is seen to be 16 years old. The younger woman plays a passive role within the monk's initiatory process. This seems to be a continuation of an ages old patriarchal power-over agenda in which women's needs are sublimated to male fulfilment. A young woman may have beauty and virginity on Her side, but no emotional maturity or understanding of her own sexuality. It is not usually until women have matured that we are able to fully understand our sexual spiritual powers.

The aim for the man is to control the energy of his orgasm without physical expression, raising it instead back up through his own body, blasting its way up the central energetic column of the sushumna, through any internal energy blockages, aiming for enlightenment for himself, a distinctly selfish act. The young woman taking part in this sexual experience is merely a vehicle for the monk's enlightenment. She is not given any instruction on how to approach her own enlightenment through her sexuality. (See *Traveller in Space : In Search of Female Identity in Tibetan Buddhism* by June Campbell, George Brazillier).

Making love is one of the most powerful in-the-body spiritual experiences that human beings can have, opening us to the energy and spaciousness of the divine. Many people are able to touch this blissful space as they come to orgasm, but do not know what it is or how to move with it into other creative places. As Goddess-loving women it is our responsibility, as in all areas where the Goddess has been denied and lost, to reclaim our sexuality as a sacred activity, one which can bring physical and emotional satisfaction as well as spiritual liberation and enlightenment for ourselves and for the people with whom we make love.

As we make love we actively call the Goddess into our physical bodies, surrendering to Her within us, so that we embody Her and receive and transmit Her energy. We absorb Her into our very body and being, and express Her to our lover. This sublime surrender and energy transfer can bring expansion of consciousness and liberation to both partners. Rather than learning purely physical techniques for sexual satisfaction, my advice is to surrender to Her presence in your body and let Her tell you how to hold and transfer Her energy for your own and another's delight, satisfaction and enlivenment.

Healing Sexual Wounds

One thing that I have noticed in the years that I have been teaching women and men about the Goddess and also about healing, is that many people who are drawn to the Goddess and the spiritual path have been sexually and emotionally abused in childhood and/or in adulthood, the vast majority by men, although a few have been abused by women. Some might say that turning towards the Goddess is merely a negative reaction to the damaging wounds inflicted by men, rather than being a true spiritual direction in its own right. I dispute this viewpoint.

As I understand it the experience of abuse has both personal and collective causes. We are often abused when we are young and vulnerable and completely unable to defend ourselves from our abusers. We are not to blame in any way for our experience, but the physical and psychological effects of these assaults have far-reaching consequences, which determine the shape of our present lives. There is a cause for us beneath our experience which reflects into our future destiny. Healing these wounds is often a lifetime journey, since our self esteem and confidence is wounded to the core by our abuse.

Over the last twenty years an epidemic of sexual, emotional and physical abuse has been uncovered that is shocking beyond belief. It has been perpetrated by those closest to us, who are in positions of power over us as children - our fathers, grandfathers, uncles, brothers, male friends, baby-sitters, lovers, priests, doctors, child care professionals, etc., and occasionally by our mothers, aunts, sisters and caretakers. The saving grace is that in this generation people are for the first time speaking aloud about their abuse, bringing to justice the abusers, revealing what was once hidden behind closed doors and beginning the long process of communal and intergenerational healing. Nearly all abusers have themselves been abused and it is important as we uncover the layers of our own abuse, releasing our anger and pain, to refrain from completely demonising our abused abusers. To replace abuse with hatred is not a resolution.

It is so important to speak about our sexual and emotional wounds which often lie buried in layers of forgetting. As we speak of our experiences, expressing our emotions of pain, grief, anger and fear, healing begins. We ask the Goddess to lead us gently into our memories and to help us heal those places that are deeply wounded. The energy which it takes for us to conceal the pain of our abuse is vast, but once released this becomes available to be channelled into healthy living, healthy relationships, into love and creativity.

As Goddess-loving people we rightly turn away from male behaviours which claim innate superiority over women, who can therefore be abused with impunity, and which have damaged our families, friends and sister priestesses. We turn towards the compassionate face of the Goddess who loves us in all our pain and suffering. Her strength allows us to safely release the anger we feel towards our abusers. We come to love Her more. As well as being our terrible life wound, abuse is the catalyst which brings us to the gateway to Her Temple and to the healing which stops serial lifetimes of abuse in families, here. I have had the great privilege of seeing many women and men make the choice to end their family's karma of abuse with themselves, to reveal and face their pain, to heal their wounds and move on into renewed life with the Goddess.

Loving Our Bodies

Abuse in any form often leads us to be ashamed of and even to hate our bodies for the suffering they have endured. On the journey of healing we begin to love our bodies once more as we did before they were abused. But sexual abuse is not the only cause of distress about our bodies. We live in societies where the abuse of women and of our bodies is endemic. In our cultures the norms for the shapes and look of women's bodies are determined by men's sexual fantasies and women's collusion in maintaining these fantasies. On the fashion catwalks adolescent anorexic girls are idealised as the normal shape for all women. They often look like pubescent boys, much admired by homosexual male fashion designers. Magazines, newspapers, films and TV display women with huge breasts, bottoms and lips, enhanced by inserts and injections of often poisonous substances. Women spend enormous amounts of time, energy and money trying and failing to be the right shape, to have the right nose, mouth or chin.

The Goddess calls us to love our bodies as they are, large or small, graceful or awkward, wobbly or curvy, with all our physical imperfections. She asks us to be grateful to our bodies for providing the home in which we live on earth. She calls to us to eat good energy-filled food, to breathe clean air, to drink clean water, to exercise, to be healthy. Our body is the earthly temple in which our spirit resides and we must look after our temple, just like any physical temple to the Goddess. Anything which abuses our body abuses our spirit and we all have a responsibility to care for our bodies.

Stand naked before a mirror. Allow yourself to look with love and compassion at your own body, its shapes and curves, its lumps and bumps, its scars and imperfections, its signs of ageing, all of which mark your passage through life. See the Goddess or God standing before you incarnate in human form and give Her/im due honour and affection. Love yourself as you are.

Women's Blood Mysteries

As women our sense of the sacred has its foundation within our own bodies. From menarche through to menopause we are intimately connected to the cycle of creation, continuity, death and rebirth through our cycles of menstruation. In a monthly cycle we become fertile, we ovulate, and a ripening egg is released from our ovaries. We make love with our men and if the egg is fertilised it travels down the Fallopian tubes to the womb where it nestles into the thickening lining. The fertilised egg cells multiply and if all goes well, nine months later we give birth to a beautiful new baby. It is the miracle of life. If the egg is unfertilised two weeks later it and the thickened lining of the womb are released as menstrual blood in our moontime, our blood time, and then the cycle begins again.

The cycle of menstruation is governed by powerful hormones which are released in regulated patterns that not only have the power to generate new human life, but also have strong emotional, psychological and creative effects in our personal female lives. Within every month we are taken through a mini life and death cycle. At ovulation the Creative Goddess calls and our sexual juices arise strongly. We put ourselves about, we become more extrovert. Unconsciously we remove parts of our clothing and expose our skin and natural scents, signalling that we are fertile and available to lovers. Our creativity in the outer world is at a peak, we are open and communicative. As the days of fertility pass by, over the next two weeks we close down a little and introvert towards menstruation. We turn our faces towards the Dark Goddess and can become moody, troubled and hostile. Premenstrual tension arises. She asks us to respond, to express our feelings, to create from out of Her darkness. We express Her energy as our blood flows to the earth feeling release from an internal pressure. We sleep, we dream the future, we receive visions. We become calm again.

Where are you in your menstrual cycle? For at least three months in your diary note the days of your cycle and how you feel each day, what you want to wear, when you are creative and self-expressive. Premenstrually withdraw as much as you can from your usual life and paint, write, sew, mould clay, rest, sleep, dream your future. Notice what happens when you live in tune with Her and your inner body cycle.

It was only when I had passed through menopause that I realised just quite how much influence oestrogen had had in my life. For thirty plus years I had swung back and forth on an emotional roller-coaster each month, often told I was far too emotional, that I felt everything too deeply. I gradually learned over the years to work with my menstrual cycle harnessing and expressing its energy in creativity. Now that those storms have passed I am far less emotional than I was and sometimes miss that intensity of feeling that was a normal part of my life, although something else is arising as I move towards my cronehood.

Many books have now been written about honouring the menstrual cycle and I will not repeat here all the detailed ways that we can celebrate our blood cycles. As priestesses we notice and honour the cycles of our Goddess-given menstruation. As priests we honour these cycles within the women we are with and meet. As women we notice how our cycles become synchronised with each other as we work together in circle. We notice how we synchronise with the tides of the moon, as we ovulate and bleed at the new or full moons. As we enter sacred landscapes we often bleed unexpectedly. I have lost count of the numbers of women, myself included, who have been surprised when they suddenly started bleeding when they arrived in Glastonbury, when taking part in ceremony, when walking the Labrynth on the Tor. The Goddess speaks to us through our blood, asking us to take notice of what is happening at the time. Our bodies are connected to Her even while our minds are busy elsewhere.

One of the greatest secrets of our menstruation that we learn as women is the power of our moon blood when we make love with our partners. Menstrual blood is the Sacred Red Mead of Mab the Faery Queen. It is the Elixir of Life sought by all the sages. Rather than avoiding sex when we are bleeding this is the time when our partners have the greatest opportunity to experience the Goddess incarnate in physical form. It is the time when She is in our bodies and in our blood.

Make love when you bleed.

As Priestesses of Avalon we create and perform ceremonies which honour all these blood rites, as well as other rites of passage. We may conduct male rites of passage where appropriate, too. We honour the young women as they reach menarche, and have their first blood, which signals the beginning of fertile womanhood. We honour the young men as they enter puberty with male rites of passage. We celebrate the passage of young women and men into adulthood in their later teens. We celebrate sacred marriages, handfastings, births, namings, all rites of passage which people want to mark. We honour the life change known as the mid-life crisis, which brings changes in life directions. We honour women's menopause when bloodflow ceases, we honour our maturity as Queens and Kings, we honour Crone and Sagehood later and we honour the Elders who emerge within our communities. See the later chapter on ceremony.

Goddess and God - the gender balance

I am often asked why I don't teach about God as well as Goddess, if I am really interested in creating a gender-balanced world. My first answer is that I don't feel called to do this. In this book and in all my work my focus is to bring awareness of the Goddess back into human consciousness as an enduring, creative, destructive, generous, compassionate, all-encompassing, loving, whole divinity. I have spent many years researching and remembering ancient customs, folklore, landscape, archaeology, names and present day Goddess experience to bring Her alive in my own life and for others. The Goddess has been absent from our western societies for over four thousand years and it is my destiny to help bring Her back into life to the best of my ability. My particular interests are in how She expresses Herself in Brigit's Isles and the Isle of Avalon, and in encouraging others to find Her in their own homelands.

God and the religions created by men have had a good run over the last four thousand years, enough time you would have thought to give us a clear idea of who He is. On the whole they have failed to express the God's true nature as a wise, loving and compassionate being, preferring to present Him in their own image, as a patriarchal and judgemental warrior. Just as the Goddess and Her nature needs to be continually researched and remembered in the present day, so too I believe that God and His nature needs to go through this same redemptive process. I believe that it is men who must take the primary role in doing this, as it is women who have taken the primary role in redeeming the Goddess.

"*Ah, but what about balance,*" I hear you cry,
"*There has to be balance between Goddess and God.*"

This call for balance is a great illusion. Using measuring scales as an analogy, two items appear to be in balance when there is equal weight in the pans on either side of the scale. Therefore if we want equality, we have to honour both Goddess and God equally, don't we? However the balance between things also depends on where the balance point of any scale lies. In these times the balance point is massively in favour of the masculine as divinity and in culture. An increased interest in the Goddess makes barely a dent in the powers of patriarchy, but the cry of "*We must be balanced*", arises whenever She is solely honoured.

What are we so afraid will happen if She is celebrated alone? The main fear seems to be that women might use power in the way it has been used by men, to have power over men and other women. This is despite all the evidence which suggests that women and men handle power differently. Women are naturally inclusive and don't want to appear to leave anyone out, especially their menfolk. But Honouring the Goddess does not mean leaving men out. It is an inclusive practice, where Goddess-loving men are welcomed at Her table. She includes everyone in Her love. I am happy to call myself unbalanced, if you insist, and will be so until the world rebalances itself.

Often when people celebrate Goddess and God together we find the same old patriarchal systems are still there in control in the guise of equality. The focus on equal divinities actually means there is little time or space to examine the ways in which women's spirituality has been and is ignored and undermined within all patriarchal religious systems, and thereby to change them. In many pagan groups there are still power-over hierarchies with High Priests and High Priestesses at the top and novices at the bottom. There are the same old ladders, degrees of initiation, to be climbed, as in any commercial corporation. There are initiations that still place women in positions of sexual service to men, who have power over them without emotional responsibility. These practices developed in the sexual revolution of the 1960s and 70s when we were persuaded that free love would bring us happiness, instead of the feelings of emotional loss, sexual diseases and unwanted pregnancies that followed.

Many Wiccan traditions were actually invented in the 1950s by Gerald Gardiner, who claimed to have been initiated into a coven of the Old Religion in the New Forest. Many of his ideas derived from the *Hermetic Order of the Golden Dawn*, Alistair Crowley's *Ordo Templi Orientis*, and *Freemasonry*. Gardiner was certainly not an enlightened feminist, although he may have celebrated the Goddess in women's form.

I am also asked how I feel personally about God, as a Goddess-loving woman. I have no problem with God, only His expression within patriarchal institutions. My attention is focused on Goddess and I know that God is very happy that I love Goddess, because there is no competition between them. In my understanding there is no separation at all between Goddess and God. Goddess always loves God and God always loves Goddess. It is just the way it is. All else is a human problem. My deepest experience of Him comes when I am making love with my partner and I cry out in ecstasy, "*Oh My God! Oh My God!*"

Beltane is the main Goddess festival when we invite God into our ceremonies and temples as a fertilising power. In the Glastonbury Goddess Temple we celebrate His presence at Beltane by erecting a Maypole around which we dance, entwining white, red, yellow and black ribbons, representing the four ancient colours of the Maiden, Lover, Mother and Crone Goddesses. We celebrate the union of Goddess and God in our human relationships, blessing them for the coming year and a day.

Traditionally we throw apple halves across the Beltane fire to our lovers and jump the fire together to seal our sacred union.

I believe that true balance and gender equality will come when women and men have each explored in depth the natures of the loving Goddess and the loving God. Then we can come together to share more of our experiences in creative and fulfilling ways.

Men and the Goddess

Men have as much right as women to love and serve the Goddess with their whole heart, mind and being. The Goddess does not discriminate against anyone on the grounds of their gender. She loves us all. However in returning Goddess to Her rightful place in the world, I claim that women have a primary role to fulfil in remembering herstory. Just as She was maligned and forgotten throughout the ages, so too have women been maligned and abused, and still are in most cultures and societies. We have a personal interest in bringing Her back with alacrity into a patriarchal world. Men on the other hand *apparently* have much to lose by honouring the Goddess and women. This is so, even though the powers that the patriarchal world gives to men must be continually reinforced by competing, winning, staying ahead of the game, and therefore being separated from the rest of humanity. Men too, are on the long journey of divesting themselves of this illusory worldly power, as they reclaim the Goddess for themselves. Of course, men *actually* have everything to gain from honouring the Goddess and women.

In my understanding it is men's role to love and serve the Goddess and all Her offspring, who are women, children, other men, animals, birds, and all of Her nature. It is men's role to be the guardians of Her nature, a huge task of healing in these times when Her earth is being plundered and abused for material gain. It is men's duty to invoke the God within themselves, He who loves and serves the Lady. It is men's joy to unite Goddess with the God within themselves. It is men's function to be Her priests, sharing Her love and care, creating ceremonies which bring healing, change and transformation to those who are in need. There is a huge and equal place for men within the Goddess world.

Masks, Headdresses and Veils

At Beltane in our priestess journey we make ourselves a mask and headdress to wear after our dedication. Masks are powerful tools for changing consciousness both for the wearer and for those who look at the person wearing a mask. A mask changes how we appear to others and can create many kinds of effects from the benign to the mysterious to the disturbing. Wearing a mask separates us from normal human contact and helps us to embody archetypal Goddess energies. As priestesses our masks show that we are in a different role, we are not our usual selves, but have become transported into another realm of being, where the Goddess may come and play within us.

We can make masks using Plaster of Paris bandages moulded to the exact shapes of our faces. We can use parcel tape to create shapes unconnected to our own faces. We can buy simple mask shapes and decorate them with colours, sparkles, and feathers to suit our own taste. Masks which cover the whole face are more effective in disguising our normal appearance, but can be difficult to wear and speak through easily. Fine material in a complementary colour, ribbons, feathers or other decorations can be attached to the lower edges of a half mask, to cover the lower part of the face.

Headdresses too have the effect of changing our usual appearance. They can make our heads and therefore our bodies look larger, more visible and distinctive, while performing ceremonial duties. They can be used to give information about the Goddess we serve, about the time of year, the season we are celebrating. We can decorate the headdress with bird feathers at Yule, flowers at Beltane, fruits at Lammas, etc.

Translucent veils too, are part of our Priestess of Avalon costume. They are used to hide the distinctive features of our faces, so that She can be glimpsed in us through the veil and we can see out to the world through Her Veil. See the Second Spiral for more on all these.

From Beltane to Litha

From Beltane to Litha the Goddess's nature blossoms in all Her glory. Vegetation in all forms grows in abundance, flowers bloom and leaves unfurl and open out to their fullness on the trees. The sun rises to its zenith in the skies. The air, the earth and the waters warm. Our human bodies relax in the warming air. We enjoy our sensuality and sexuality. We become pregnant with possibilities, with renewed life. Tiny featherless birds hatch from eggs, newborn animals take their first steps into Her beautiful world.

Make an altar at home to Nolava the Lover, to Rhiannon the White

Mare from the Sea, to Rhiannon *of the* Birds, *known as* Rigantona, *to She who is* Sovereignty, *to* Blodeuwedd *the* Flower Goddess, Olwen *of the* White Track, Elen *of the* Trackways *and* Thetis *of the* Nine Morgens. *Find a statue and objects which represents the Goddess of* Love *to you with* Her *horses and birds,* Her *bells, musical instruments and flowers.*

Every day light a candle flame and burn incense to Nolava, Rhiannon *and* Thetis *on your altar and sing and pray to* Her *for help, guidance, in gratitude, for others in need, for healing for yourself and others, for vision, etc.* Once *a week recreate your altar.*

Every day write down and/or draw feelings, dreams, thoughts, intuitions and visions in your diary, i.e. what's going on for you.

Make *music with friends and create new songs for the* Goddess.

Make *a headdress, mask and veil.* Begin *to wear them when you sit before your altar, journeying between the worlds on your horse with* Rhiannon *as your companion.*

At *the new moon write a draft of the vow of dedication you will make to the* Goddess *at* Mabon *in* September.

At *the full moon bring flowering hawthorn branches into your home in celebration of the* Goddess *of sexuality and fertility.* Smell *the flowers and breathe in the scent of feminine sexuality.* Be *prepared for the fertilising spirit to enter in which ever form you choose - physical, emotional, mental, intuitive, inspirational.*

At *least once if not more, visit a sacred site or landscape associated with* Rhiannon *and* Thetis, *anywhere there are hollow hills, sacred mounds, trivia, threefold ways or entrances into the underworld.* Go *horse riding.*

The Glistening
Litha Festival of the Mother of Water

Litha is the festival of the Glistening when we celebrate the Mother of Water on the longest day of the year. We honour Nolava of Water and Morgen Gliten who brings rain to Avalon, as well as Domnu, Lady of the Oceans, Queen of the Deep, from whose watery depths all life originally sprang. We celebrate Nolava as Lady of the Springs and Wells, especially in this land of springs and wells. We honour Her as Lady of the Lake, also named as Vivienne and Nimue, who gives questing knights the honour of being Her champions. We celebrate Her as Sillina or Selene, the full moon. The Mother of Water is Queen of all the Emotions and the great astral sea where most human beings live our lives. She nourishes the needy.

Summer solstice comes around June 21st. It is the time when the hours of daylight are at their longest in this land, with short nights of darkness. Nowadays Litha marks the beginning of summer rather than being its culmination. Warm summer days follow through the end of June all of July and into August. It is the season when we go to the seaside to enjoy the warm Gulf Stream currents that pass by Brigit's Isles. We take off our clothes and expose our bodies to Grainne's sunlight, bathing in Her warming waters as often as we can. All of Her nature is alive and vibrant, expressing Her wonderful diversity of colour, form and content. The trees are all covered in leaves and flowers. Grasses grow in fields and lawns. Plants have grown to twice if not three times their earlier size, filling hedgerows and gardens with beautiful greenery and flowers. Grain and vegetables grow in the fields. Flocks of birds fly from abroad to enjoy the summer weather. Young animals play in the fields and woods. It's the beginning of the holiday or holy day season, where we can rest, play and enjoy ourselves.

At Litha we honour Nolava of the Waters in many ways. We cleanse ourselves with water. We learn to offer Her blessings of water. We open our emotional bodies for healing. We explore the astral realms that surround us all the time. We deepen our experience of immersion in Her mystical waters. We learn more about love and compassion. We journey with the moon, opening ourselves to its fullness. We remember to play as we did when we were children, just for the fun of it.

Honouring Nolava *of* Water

Nolava of Water is the Compassionate One, whose loving gentleness holds us as we meet and begin the process of healing our Shadow Selves. It is She who helps our emotions overflow in streams of tears that we need to release, for tears of themselves naturally heal our pain. Avalon is a land where people often cry, tears of sorrow and tears of joy. British patriarchal culture discourages public displays of emotion. We are known as a race with a stiff upper lip, rather than a loose and trembling mouth. This repression of emotion has no place in a Goddess-loving society, where the conscious expression of emotion is encouraged and welcomed. Without this expression we easily become sick and unwell. However a sign that things are changing in British society was evidenced in the public grief displayed at the funeral of Diana, Princess of Wales. All kinds of people, women and men, cried together openly and in public at the loss of the Queen of Hearts, despite admonitions that it was all too much.

Avalon is the place where we meet the wounds in our emotional bodies and have the opportunity to heal ourselves within Nolava's loving embrace. For She will hold us through all the pain, all the sadness, anger and grief, for as long as it takes for us to become whole.

Once upon a time, no more than 1200 years ago, Glastonbury and its sacred landscape was a swan-shaped peninsula surrounded on three sides by a great lake. It was connected to the mainland of the Mendip Hills at Ponters Ball, where a ridge of earth still marks the edge of the temenos. Earlier the peninsula was a Western island surrounded by sea and known as the Isle of Avalon. Today the Bristol Channel, which leads to the Atlantic Ocean, is some 18 miles away as the crow flies, to the west. Once salt water flowed between the Mendip and the Polden Hills and surrounded the sacred land as an inland sea. Where there are now flat fields, there were once lakes, marshes and tidal pools, filled with abundant wildlife, fish and fowl and all kinds of animals, who came to feed in the bountiful waters.

One of the ancient names for Glastonbury is *Ynys Witrin*, which means the *Glass Isle*, whose image was reflected in the calm waters that once surrounded the land. Nowadays after heavy rains in the spring and autumn, the meadow lands surrounding the island may once again become flooded with water. This happened just a few days ago in December when the image of the Glass Isle reflected in still water was stunningly beautiful and awe-inspiring. How glorious it must have looked in ancient days when there were no buildings or human activity and the island truly belonged to Her nature.

About a thousand years ago the Benedictine monks of Glastonbury Abbey built up sea walls between the rivers Parrett, Brue and Axe to prevent the sea water from coming inland. They began to drain the lakes and marshes, digging huge canals, like the King's Sedgemoor Drain, to channel water to the sea. They wanted to shape and control Her ocean and claim the land beneath. The fields and meadows of the Summerland to this day are surrounded by water-filled ditches, known commonly as rhynes (pronounced *reens*), which still drain water to the sea. As sea levels rise worldwide because of global warming, we may find that the Summerland floods and the Isle of Avalon will rise once again from Her waters.

Nolava, Lady of the Springs and Wells

At Litha we honour Nolava as the Lady of the Holy Springs and Wells, who may be found at the many natural springs in Glastonbury's sacred landscape. Rain-bearing clouds arrive on prevailing southwesterly winds and drop their water on the long limestone ridge of the Mendip Hills to the north of Glastonbury. Rainwater seeps down through the limestone forming caverns and tunnels, underground rivers and pools. The weight of the Mendip Hills bears down on the underground waters, which rise under pressure, emerging as springs from beneath Glastonbury's sacred hills and valleys. The most famous and honoured of Glastonbury's springs are the Red Spring at Chalice Well and the neighbouring White Spring on the slopes of the Tor.

There are also many other springs which were honoured in the past. Some are now capped or rise almost unnoticed from the slopes on the island. There are ten and more Wells including Holy Well to the north of the island at Holywell farm, Bride's Well to the west of Bride's Mound, St Mary's Well (reclaimed from St Joseph) in the Abbey, two and more St Edmund's Wells on St Edmund's Hill, the Tribunal Well (behind the Tribunal in Glastonbury's High Street), Cemetery Well on Windmill Hill, Wearyall

Well on a farm on Wearyall Hill, as well as others.

Wells and Springs are seen as Openings in the body of Ertha our Mother Earth, from which Her red iron-rich menstrual bloodwater flows to fertilise the earth, or clear clean mineral-rich water flows for drinking and to purify the earth, or foul-tasting sulphurous waters come to the surface from deep in Her Underworld. These vaginal openings are often secret, concealed places hidden in clefts, behind bushes. The White Spring, now emerging in a stone reservoir, originally arose in a green leafy glade on the slopes of the Tor. It was enclosed in the 1870s when the town needed a clean water supply during a cholera epidemic. Springs are places of return to Ertha's overflowing Womb where we can receive vision and nurture, or immerse ourselves in Her waters for healing and renewal.

Nolava, the Lady of the Springs and Wells, often appears as a shimmering White Lady, a Faery Woman, a Water Nymph, beside Chalice Well and the White Spring, but also out in the fields beside wilder landscape springs. Even when wells are capped as at Bride's Well and St Edmund's Wells, the Lady can still be found there, in some ways more available to us than in more disturbed places.

Chalice Well's Blood Spring is one of the most powerful places on the island, emerging from beneath Chalice Hill as a continuous bountiful flow of red iron-rich water. Situated today in beautiful gardens, Chalice Well has a long history as a healing spring. In the 18th century a man called Matthew Challoner who suffered from asthma, had a dream in which he was told to drink the waters of Chalice Well for seven Sundays and he would be healed of his disease. He did so and was healed. As news spread of his cure, people came from far and wide to drink and bathe in the healing waters of the Blood Spring. As a result Glastonbury became a spa town for many years with people coming especially to take the waters. Today Chalice Well is in the hands of charitable trust which opens the well and gardens to visitors who wish to experience the healing powers of Her bloodwaters.

In the small valley between Chalice Hill and Glastonbury Tor, the Red Spring emerges from beneath Chalice Hill and the White Spring emerges from beneath the Tor. Where the Red Spring tastes strong and rich, the White Spring is sweet and clear. In ancient times these two springs would have met and flowed together in a wonderful balance of the Red and the White, the feminine and the masculine. In these days the two springs are separated by a road, although some smaller white springs also flow into Chalice Well gardens and some smaller red springs flow into the White Spring.

This small valley is one of the most sacred places on the island for many people, and especially for Priestesses of Avalon. In visions of ancient times it is here that we see the priestesses going about their work of healing and transformation beside the sacred springs. In modern times it is here that we honour Nolava as the Lady of the Holy Springs and Wells and where we make our first dedication to the Lady of Avalon.

At Litha we gather at Chalice Well and the White Spring to experience the healing powers of the Red and White waters. We bathe our feet and bodies, releasing to the waters all that we no longer need - all our tensions and anxieties, our fears and troubles, letting them be washed away in the flow of Her waters. We wash each other's feet as a sacred service. We drink the waters on our own and in circle, sharing the Grael of the Maiden, the Cup of the Lover, the Chalice of the Mother, and the Cauldron of the Crone, all of which are symbolic containers of the Goddess's wisdom. In simple ceremonies we pass round Her Chalice, offering Her blessings of water to each other in the circle. As we drink the water we drink in Her healing energy, cleansing our bodies from within as well as without. We receive Her blessings as emanations contained within the water, that mysterious substance whose structure is changed by prayer. Experiments photographing the molecular structure within water show how its patterns change from chaos to ones of great symmetry and beauty when water is prayed over. (See *The True Power of Water* by Masaru Emoto.)

Beside the wellhead itself we look down into the waters of the well or into the stream or pool as a meditation, watching the still or flowing surface, letting go our busy mental activity into the flow of Her waters. We listen to the sound of the water, allowing our minds to release their habitual chattering with the flow of the sound of running water. In vision we follow the rising stream back down into the earth, into the great flowing underground rivers that eventually lead back to the Sea, to Domnu, the Great Mother of Water.

At Litha visit a sacred spring or well near your home and especially those in Glastonbury. Cleanse your body with water, let go of your cares, drink in the healing waters of the Lady of the Holy Springs and Wells.

Nolava, Lady of the Lake

The Lady of the Lake is a powerful mythic figure within the Arthurian legends. Her most common name is Vivienne or Vivian, She who lives, and She is also Nimue, who was Merlin's Nemesis, enchanting him into the crystal cave where he is said to still lie sleeping. In Marion Zimmer Bradley's *Mists of Avalon*, the Lady of the Lake is another title given to the Lady of Avalon, named for the lake which once surrounded the Isle of Avalon.

Caitlin and John Matthews describe nine women from the Arthurian tradition as being Ladies of the Lake, each having a different character and story to tell, see *Ladies of the Lake*, (Aquarian Press). They are nine like the Nine Morgens and include Morgen, Igraine, Nimue, Argante, Ragnell, Kundry, Guinevere, Dindraine and Enid. These Ladies of the Lake all derive their power from the Otherworld, which is often associated with water - to get there we usually have to journey across water. Whatever their personal stories each Lady of the Lake is a totally autonomous being with an otherworldly nature. Each is a queen in Her own right and has no permanent consort. She has great freedom to come and go as She pleases: appearing and disappearing from stories as She wills.

According to the Matthews, the most well known Arthurian Lady of the Lake is Argante, who appears in different texts in different forms as the foster mother and sometime lover of Lancelot. It is She who proffers the sword Excalibur, the symbol of sovereignty and the King's right to rule the land, to the right candidate. Sir Thomas Mallory's 15th century *Morte d'Arthur* describes how Arthur received his famous sword forged on the Isle of Avalon, from Her. Journeying with Merlin to a lakeside he saw,

> *"an arm clothed in white samite, that held a fair sword in that hand....."*

When he asks who the hand belongs to, Arthur is told it belongs to the Lady of Lake. He later receives the sword in return for promising to grant the Lady anything that She asks.

The Lady of the Lake makes bargains with us. She will give us what we need and want, to reign in Her name, but we must promise to obey when She requests our assistance. In the end Excalibur is returned to the Lake beside the Perilous Bridge, or Pomparles Bridge, which today is a low bridge over the River Brue, on the road out of Glastonbury towards Street at the end of Wearyall Hill. The same white-clothed hand was seen taking the sword back into the lake.

Today the Lake has gone although it emerges in spring and autumn when the rains come, flooding the fields and creating great lakes in which the island can be seen reflected as in a mirrored glass. In the summer we can imagine the lake shimmering in the heat hazes over the flat Summerland. We ask the Lady to give us the right to rule in Her land, promising to obey Her when She calls to us.

Honouring Gliten, Morgen of Water

I grow brighter each moment.
We are not entirely invisible......

In ancient oceans around Avalon's Isle
you'd see me as a shining one, blue-green
glimpsed at the corner of your eye.
Glistening, mother-of-pearl, Gliten am I.

Shapeshifter, I rise from waves,
only to vanish in sea foam.
Was that a mermaid's fin, an undine,
a silkie or a seal, a seahorse diving deep?

I'm sweltering summer cooled in hidden pools
shaded by my oaks - green temple in a grove.
I'm Lady of the Lake, for one coin in my well
I'll fill your chalice with blessings threefold,
transmuting leaden sorrow into gold.
My empathy is boundless, compassion true.
With real emotion I will comfort you,
and with my cleansing waters heal your soul.

But don't mistake still lakes for passionless tides!
With tempest and with storm I'll toss your heedlessness
'til transformation comes - then with quick sea change
I'll bring you magic ships with treasures in their holds.

Avalon's no more an island - think you so?
Days ago, as I reckon time, did this land come dry.
And whence do you think comes the famous mist?
Catch a handful - all is water, stuff of life.

Can you put it in your pocket? Can you keep me there?
Water's endless power, can grind down mountain chains.
My sister crows nest on the tallest trees; they've understood
that Gliten can, at will, even a desert flood.

by Geraldine Charles

Gliten is the Morgen of Water, She who flows, and in whose flow we lose our resistance to change. She invites us to merge with Her in Her watery realms. As weather Gliten is the Rain that drops from the clouds, replenishing the earth and the underground reservoirs, and allowing all the plants and animals to grow and flourish. She can be gentle as light summer rain or She can fall in huge droplets, splashing and crashing onto the earth. In the Summerland She often falls at Litha, drenching the crowds who attend the nearby Glastonbury Music and Performing Arts Festival, creating huge mud baths. Through the winter months She swells the rivers and rhynes, which overflow across the land creating huge lakes, that bring the vision of the Isle of Avalon back to actuality.

Gliten appears in the form of a woman in Her thirties, who is coming into the fullness of who She is, living Her life, learning of the pleasures and sorrows of the heart. Gliten's colour is blue green, the colour of the sky reflected in water. Her creatures are the elemental undines, the water nymphs and sprites, the korrigans of pool and fountain, the mermaids and mermen of the sea, the silkies or seal women and men, who are now rare on Avalon's shores, and the water dragons who can whip up mighty storms that flood the land. Her bird is the grey heron, a survivor from the age of the dinosaurs, who still lives on the rivers and rhynes of the Summerland. The heron is a Gatekeeper opening our way to the Otherworld. Her appearance signals the arrival of messages from the Ancestral realms.

Gliten is also the full moon which reflects the sun's light, silvering the night sky and illuminating our dark places. She is Oak Woman who comes into flower and leaf at summer solstice and rules from Litha to Yule. She has great enduring strength and two of Her oldest offspring, Gog and Magog, thought to be a thousand and more years old, are to be found at the foot of the northern slopes of Stonedown. Here there was once a great oak forest on the island until the early twentieth century, when they were cut down. In legend an avenue of oak trees was said to have once led from the water's edge up to the Tor. A few years ago a new line of oak trees was planted by local Conservation Society volunteers, running from Gog and Magog along the old Paradise route to Maidencroft lane. Bulwarks Lane which runs to the north of Chalice Hill was named after the oak trees that once grew there, which were used for the bulwarks of wooden ships.

As Morgen of the Waters, Gliten is Queen of all the emotions and Mystress of Compassion. She reveals to us our deepest emotions, our innermost feelings, bringing them to the surface for expression and healing. She speaks for the inner child who is our true resource, who remains essentially undamaged by life's difficulties, but who often must be helped to grow into adulthood. She teaches us to play again.

Beside Her sacred waters, in the mists, pray to Gliten that your emotional journey as a priestess will be gentle and easy. Ask that your own nature will become a reflection of Hers, that you will learn to love and hold all those you meet with compassion. Ask Her to show you how to play as a child.

Honouring Domnu, Lady of the Oceans

At Litha we honour Domnu, Lady of the Oceans, Queen of the Deep, the Womb of all life. She is the formless watery chaos from which all life emerges. Mediaeval writers called Domnu a God of the sea, but earlier I believe, She was Goddess of the Ocean for the Fomoire, an ancient one-eyed race of giants who lived beside the sea in Ireland. For them She was a primary source of food, fish and fowl, a means of travel and a deep inspiration, sometimes tranquil, sometimes violent. In all traditions the Ocean is regarded as feminine, from Babylonian Tiamat to Hindu Kali to Mary/Mari the Sea, although gods such as Neptune may live within Her waters.

Domnu is the liquid Lady, Her body flowing continuously over the surface of the earth, She takes the route of least resistance. She is contained by boundaries of earth and rock, but is always ready to run away downhill towards the ocean, or seep down through the surface layers of the earth into deep underground lakes, or evaporate into clouds under the heat of the sun's rays. She flows over the land, channelling into streams, rhynes, rivers and oceans, always moving down towards the lowest point. She carves deep passages out of earth and rock, over time removing mountains and anything that sits in Her way, returning everything to the ocean that is Her body. She is moved by the channels through which She flows, and by the things which She finds in Her way or which move through Her. Beneath the earth She carves out great caverns and sits in deep, calm pools. She rises under the pressure of hills to emerge in springs, which we recognise as openings into the depths of Ertha's body.

It is Her water which makes up over 75% of our human body weight, filling every cell, allowing the passage of chemical and electrical messages, which mean that we creatures can live, develop, grow to our full potential, incarnating physically into the world. Water also removes the waste products of digestion and flushes toxins out of our bodies. It is so important for us to drink Her clean water to remain healthy. Science has recently discovered that water holds memory, the vibrations of all that it has contained or been contained by. Domnu is the Keeper of Memory.

In these days we are polluting our streams, rivers and oceans with the chemical waste products of our homes and industries. As toxic chemicals accidentally and deliberately spill into streams, the fish and animals who live in the water die or become weakened by poisons. In the rivers the effects of pollution multiply and more creatures die, the land through which the rivers flow also becoming polluted with heavy metals, poisonous plastics and hormone-mimicking chemicals. In the oceans the effects of pollution can be seen amongst the flora, plankton, fishes and sea mammals, with toxicity increasing up the food chain. Chemically weakened immune systems result in a susceptibility to disease, to viruses which can wipe out whole species. Many of earth's oldest and largest sea creatures face the possibility of extinction due to pollution and overfishing.

All the creatures of river and sea belong to Domnu. These include our native Salmon of Wisdom who lives on hazelnuts and returns to its birth river to spawn after travelling the worldwide oceans. It also includes all the fish we eat for food and the brilliantly coloured shoals of tiny fish who live amongst living coral reefs, and the scary sharks that haunt our nightmares and the shelled fish who live on the ocean bed. The playful dolphins give us the experience of Her compassionate nature and the knowledge that we are not the only intelligent species on the planet. The great whales too, belong to Her, living long lives if they are unmolested or not poisoned by our presence. They are the Planetary Keepers of Ancestral Memory. We journey with them and with the dolphins in dreams and visualisations journeying beyond the stars to find the past and future of our planet and of the multiverse we inhabit.

Brigit's Isles are bathed in Domnu's warm Gulf Stream waters which flow in a great circle around the northern Atlantic Ocean, bringing warm air and water from the tropics to our coasts, creating the beneficent climate that we experience with the eight seasons of the Goddess's nature. Without the Gulf Stream we would have a similar climate to Canada, which is on the same latitude to us, with long cold winters and shorter summers. The Gulf Stream moves past these isles descending into the deeper ocean near Greenland and flowing back in a circle via the coasts of Canada and North America. Pollution and global warming are changing the movement in the Gulf Stream and it may one day cease to flow, as it has done in the past, plunging Brigit's Isles into coldness. The seasons of the Goddess would change dramatically if this were to occur and we could become icebound for much of the year. She would show us much more of Her frozen winter face.

At Litha we honour Domnu, remembering Her with every drink of water we take, every time we wash or bathe in Her rivers or splash in Her seas or stand beside Her great oceans gazing to the horizon, awed by Her immensity and power. We show our respect for Her, knowing that She is vast and deep, that She can swallow us up in the flip of Her wave or allow us to ride safely in boats across Her immensity. We honour Her at all times recognising that She is the Source of all animal and human life on this planet. Once we lived in Her liquid body, evolving until we climbed out of the oceans and onto the land. Our development in our mother's womb mirrors this evolutionary journey from water-borne creatures who once breathed through gills, to independent air-breathing creatures with lungs.

Women are the Keepers of the Waters through our menstrual cycles, through our wombs in which our children's lives and our dreams are created and nurtured, and through our connection to the Moon. The Moon's gravitational pull has demonstrable effects on all the water on earth, drawing up the oceans each day as She encircles the earth, creating the physical ocean tides, as well as drawing on the water within our bodies, creating the psychic tides which affect us all. It is important that as women we recognise that we can do many things to change what is happening to the waters of this planet. We can pray, we can chant when we are beside water and before we drink water. We can claim clean water for ourselves and our families. We can help clean ditches, ponds, canals and rivers of debris, we can campaign for clean water, we can campaign for the creatures of the sea. It is our responsibility.

Honouring Sillina

Sillina or Selene is the Moon Goddess honoured in the Scilly Isles off the southwestern tip of Brigit's Isles. Her sun sister is Sulis, whose hot springs rise at Bath to the north of Glastonbury, and who is worshipped throughout the southwest. Sillina the Moon has three primary faces, Maiden - new moon, Mother - full moon, Crone - dark moon, which is where the idea of the Triple Goddess comes from. At Litha we honour Her as the full moon, when lunar as well as solar energy is at its height. People do silly things at summer solstice. They express Sillina's lunatic energy at summer parties and festivals, gathering on beaches and in gardens, letting go their normal restraints. Glastonbury's famous Music and Performing Arts Festival held at Pilton, five miles from Glastonbury and in sight of the Tor, comes on the weekend after the summer solstice and lots of fun and madness is to be had there.

In every year of twelve solar months there are nearly 13 moon cycles and we honour the Moon Goddess each month, particularly as we see the first sliver of the new moon rise above the horizon at sunset, at the full moon, and during the dark moon. The appearance of the crescent moon is a time to begin new projects, to sow seeds for the coming month, adding in energy as the moon waxes to fullness. The five days of full moon (two before, one during and two after) is the time when we can best express ourselves creatively and emotionally out in the world. As the moon wanes, expression continues, flowing out into the world. As the moon shrinks our focus moves inwards to the three days of the dark moon, when there is no moonlight, a time to go within for rest, to receive refreshment, inspiration and vision for the coming month. Nearly all traditional initiation ceremonies mimic this time of the dark moon, when would-be initiates are shut away in darkness in a cave or a hut for three days to prepare themselves and to receive visions from the ancestors. The monthly cycle of the moon is a mirror to women's menstruation cycle and many cycle in rhythm with the moon, with ovulation at the new moon and menstruation at the full moon and vice versa.

Celebrate Sillina in ceremony on the nearest full moon to the summer solstice, on the shortest nights of the year. By day we are lit by Her sun, by night by the light of Her moon. Moonbathe, taking your clothes off in the warm night air, bathing in the moonlit sea at night to experience Her presence.

Cleansing with Water

Water is the primary element used for cleansing. We wash our bodies with water, we wash our clothes, our homes, workplaces and temples. Rain pours down onto and into the ground cleansing our pavements of dirt, our buildings of grime, our gardens of debris, our landscapes of detritus. Water washes clean. We use water to cleanse ceremonial equipment and priestess paraphernalia. We cleanse our chalices, incense burners and favourite crystals under running water, removing old, unwanted vibrations as well as dirt. On our altars and in our temples we place bowls of water in the south. As the space is used for ceremonies and life the water absorbs any negative emotions which are discharged in the space. This water must be replenished daily.

As the wheel turns cleanse your personal and communal priestess paraphernalia regularly with water to removed old energies. Cleanse them especially as each new festival approaches.

Blessing with Water

As well as cleansing with water as priestesses we learn to offer the blessings of Her waters to others. We offer water in a special cup or chalice, which we need to find and decorate as part of our priestess paraphernalia. It's good to have several different chalices, small and large, some delicate for special occasions and others which are more robust for transporting to ceremonies and sacred sites, where we may want to drink holy water. We collect holy water from the Chalice Well and White Springs, a balanced mixture of the red and white is good.

We offer people a chalice filled with holy water, and speak a blessing from the Lady of the Springs and Wells, or from the Mother of Water. We sprinkle water on the earth as a libation, a thanksgiving for the water She gives to us. We pour water as a libation on Her statues and images. At our altars as part of our acknowledgement of the gifts of Her four elements we making an offering to Her of water in a bowl or a chalice. Using the fronds of a feather in ceremony we splash drops of blessed water onto people's heads and bodies, onto the spaces we wish to bless with Her energy.

The Ocean of Emotion

Symbolically water represents the emotions, our individual feelings which are held within our emotional or astral bodies, as well as within the astral realms, where the collective emotions and feelings of all human beings are to be found. Like the ocean our emotions are continuously moving, ebbing and flowing, sometimes lying still and tranquil and at other times washing over us in great waves which threaten to drown us with pain, fear, sadness, grief or anger. Emotions can be pleasurable - positive, or painful - negative, and sometimes both at the same time.

Emotional energy is a vital part of human experience giving us the feeling that we are alive in our bodies, adding moisture to what would otherwise be a dry, lifeless, mental experience of life. Emotion allows us to feel passion and enthusiasm, bringing a richness to every experience. It allows us to feel grounded and present in the everyday as well as the unexpected. It means that we can be empathic and feel for each other. All the major rites of passage in human life, those times when we can be most spiritually present in our bodies, incarnated, are accompanied by emotion - as we are born, as we give birth, during sex, in relationship and marriage and upon death.

During our menstrual life we naturally move in and out of our emotions in a rhythmic pattern, which is affected and sometimes determined by the rise and fall in the production of oestrogen in our bodies. During each cycle we experience the power of our emotions to change how we are feeling from one day, one moment even, to the next. Men have a different emotional rhythm which is reflected in the production of testosterone in the body, and its expression through physical and creative activity. At different times in life we may become particularly polarised within our emotional bodies, experiencing the ever-moving sea of emotional energy, feeling tossed and turned as its currents flow through us. These times include puberty, adolescence, Saturn Return around 28 years, mid-life crisis and during menopause.

In life our individual soul consciousness is always attempting to expand beyond the limits of our genetic and environmental conditioning. Our soul, who is loving, inclusive, generous and compassionate, is always seeking greater and greater expression through the vehicle of our personality, which is individual and moulded by life's experiences. As the soul's energy slowly expands within the limits of our existing personality, it is as if the edges of the personality are stretched, becoming more and more rigid, like a balloon being filled with air which expands and tightens. The emotions, which are an essential part of our personality, are pulled and squashed by the increasing pressures and we begin to suffer. Our Shadow selves, all those repressed parts of ourselves which are unconscious and emotional in origin, begin to become visible to us and to others. The rigidity of our personality is seen in the fixed ideas we hold about how things are, in our fixed belief systems, fixed attitudes and prejudices, our fixed defences. This rigidity appears as harshness, hostility, blame and criticism of others. From the outside we feel the person who is in this state to be hard and brittle, often filled with unexpressed anger or grief, which we do our best to avoid. The individual becomes isolated, feeling even more alone in their troubles. This is the build up of the dark clouds before the storm comes that releases rain.

Pressures continue to build between the energies of the soul and the personality, which are played out on what is known in the B*hagavad Gita*, (a well-known ancient spiritual text), as the Burning Ground of the Kurukshestra, of the Emotions or the Astral Realm. This important stage of our spiritual development is always played out within our emotional bodies, whether it is in our private world of torment in what may be known as the Dark Night of the Soul, or as we play it out with others, casting them in the roles of our favourite monsters and demons, our bad mothers and fathers, sisters and brothers. At some point in this process there is a confrontation between the *Angel of the Presence*, who is the Soul, and the *Dweller on the Threshold* or the Shadow. They face each often in a stark choice, who will win? Our best or our worst aspects? Sometimes the battle rages for weeks, months and even years before resolution comes. Eventually, and more readily as we learn to surrender to the process, the light of the Soul illuminates the dark recesses of the Shadow, revealing bright, glittering jewels which have lain hidden beneath layers of pain and suffering from childhood and beyond in previous lives. These jewels rise to the surface of consciousness, so they can be seen once again and integrated into the personality. There is no winner, there is no loser. There is only peace in our hearts.

The soul cannot function in this world without a personality as its vehicle of expression. Integration is the only way forward. At Her timing the tight shell of the personality cracks open, often through disease or accident, and sloughs off, like a snake shedding its skin, to reveal a soft and vulnerable new self underneath. The personality expands to allow more of the soul's energy to be expressed, growing into a new expanded form. This time of expansion is known as an *initiation*. It marks the end of an old way of being and the beginning of a new life. It is always marked by the expression of emotion and the feeling of joy.

At the end of the Third Spiral of the Priestess of Avalon training we hold a Self-Initiation ceremony in which individuals are initiated by the power of their own souls to become Her Priestesses of Avalon, for this initiation has to come from within, from the Self, from Her. It cannot be given by others. This ceremony is powerful, mirroring the inner spiritual journey which each person makes in the presence of the Lady and other aspiring and initiated priestesses.

All people journeying on the spiritual path to becoming a Priestess of Avalon will have at least one and probably several experiences of confrontation between the Angel of the Presence and the Dweller on the Threshold, Soul and Shadow. As we surrender more and more to the Lady of Avalon She brings us face to face with our limitations and resistances. Our personal journey is one of allowing the hidden faces of our Shadow selves with all our repressed emotions, to surface from their unconscious hiding places, so that we may integrate the jewels that lie hidden within its depths.

Most women experience emotions daily. When I was a bleeding woman, for a few weeks I wrote down the different emotions I felt each day. I found that I could go through the whole range of emotions within one day from joy to anger to grief to happiness, often determined by the previous night's dreams. I would wake filled with a particular feeling that then played out through the whole day. A nightmare could create a distressed day, a good dream generated a creative day. It was common for me to cry at least twice a week and I wasn't an unhappy person. That was my natural rhythm of emotional expression. I think I am the same as many women.

In Anglo Saxon cultures men on the whole see emotion as a negative experience both in its expression for themselves and being on the receiving end of women's emotional expression. Men in colder climes are taught to have a stiff upper lip, to be strong and unemotional, not weak like women. Following this male conditioning patriarchal religions on the whole deny the positive power of emotion, seeing it as something which must be controlled, repressed and suppressed in order to attain the spiritual heights. For example, the majority of meditation practices have intrinsic to them the ideal of the suppression of emotion using a variety of techniques, including control of the breath, restriction of movement or placing the body in certain fixed yogic postures, known as asanas and mudras. This suppression of feeling allows the mind to be free of emotional content, so that we can rise out of our physical limitations and explore the spiritual worlds.

As babies we learn in the womb and in the crib that the way to stop ourselves feeling physical and emotional pain, fear, frustration and rage, is to hold our breath or to breathe very shallowly, and to hold our bodies rigid. This childhood defence mechanism has been hijacked by patriarchal religions and raised to an artform as meditation and escape from the limitations of the body. Our natural state as babies and as adults is to allow the free flow of our feelings and emotions in a natural rhythmic pattern of expression. Patriarchal spirituality does not allow for this, preferring to demonise emotions as bad. Emotion is something that we must rise above if we want to achieve our spiritual goals. However human emotion has not gone away and shows no signs of leaving after five thousand years of patriarchal attempts to deny its importance.

In different religious teachings we have been told for thousands of years that the world is a place of suffering and we must do everything in our power to escape the wheel of suffering and leave the planet when we die. We have been told that to climb the spiritual heights we must remove ourselves from the world, sublimate our sexual desires, be ascetic, and separate ourselves usually from women. We must control our lower chakras and our base emotions.

I do not believe it. For me the world is a place of great natural beauty and bounty, gifted to us by a generous and loving Goddess, who wants us to enjoy Her and our abundant natures. Yes, there is suffering, but it is caused on the whole by our adherence to patriarchal ideals of greed, competition and selfishness. Goddess teaches us to share with each other, to cooperate for the good of all, to be generous and loving, to enjoy Her planet and each other. She shows us the heights of mystical experience in our bodies if we can allow ourselves to hear Her voice and recognise Her ways. Life on this planet is a truly unique and amazing gift to us from Her. It is the Holy Grail that we would seek to experience throughout all the universe, if we could but recognise what an opportunity for spiritual practice and realisation is being given to us.

Can we now begin to conceive new forms of spirituality which are not based on the received wisdom of patriarchy, of male bodies and conditioning? Can we imagine a spirituality that gives high value to the lower chakras as the places in our bodies where all new life is conceived, held, nurtured and brought to birth, where we experience the power of sexual energy to dissolve separation and the boundaries of our bodies, and where our wonderful emotions reside? Can we see these chakras as having equal importance to those of the head? Can we recognise that the seat of the Soul lies in the centre of our bodies in the heart, rather than in the head? Can we imagine a spirituality in which emotion and its expression are part of an enriching mystical experience where we not only sense the majesty of the divine, the vastness of the Void, but also feel it emotionally, in ways which bring its presence into our reality?

I believe that this is what a renewed Goddess spirituality will bring us if we can allow it. I believe we have to let go of our old ways of knowing how to do things and let Her guide us into new forms of spirituality, which will include experiences already shared by many women, which have been denied in patriarchy. It will particularly include our emotions, which rule the lives of the many. We are at the very beginning of the return of the Goddess and Her mysteries. She brings with Her new forms of spirituality that will take us to greater heights and depths of ecstatic mystical experience. We need not be afraid that if we let go of the old She will not be there for us in new forms, in new experiences. She will not abandon us as we abandoned Her.

I claim a new Goddess spirituality which includes the feeling of emotion in our bodies and its expression as a natural part of our daily human lives. I claim true incarnation within the human body and the experience of physical, etheric, emotional, mental and spiritual energies. I claim prayer as a personal space to feel emotion as part of my spiritual experience and to be healed of pain and suffering. I claim ceremony as a place for the expression of individual and communal emotion of many kinds.

Goddess created emotion and loves its expression.

Expressing Emotion

Emotional expression is very important for our health and well being and when suppressed leads to disease and illness of mind, emotions and body. When triggered we express our emotions in physical ways - we cry tears of sadness and joy, our bodies shake with fear, our hands and bodies clench with anger, we smile with happiness, we dance for joy. As children in western cultures we are taught to hide the signs of our negative emotions beneath a mask of control, suppressing our tears and our fearful shaking bodies. We hold our breath, clench our muscles and pray that no-one can see what we really feel. As we deny the expression of our negative emotions we also suppress our positive emotions, to the point where we no longer know what we feel, whether we are sad or whether we are happy. Life is a dulled experience.

Through counselling, psychotherapy, emotional regression, therapeutic bodywork, rebirthing, conscious connected breathing, a thousand and one techniques which have developed over the last thirty years or so, we can reclaim our natural expression of emotion, allowing ourselves to feel what we feel and then to express it. As we realise that we don't die if we show the world what we really feel (for that is usually the seat of our fear), we find that life becomes real and meaningful, often for the first time since childhood.

We learn to direct our emotions into creative expression. Rather than our blocked emotions preventing us from expressing ourselves creatively we can write about how we feel, expressing our anger, hatred, fear, our feelings of rejection, isolation, loneliness, in words of truth. We can draw our feelings out onto paper, paint our emotions in blocks of colour and form, light and darkness. We can sculpt our monsters and demons, giving them shape and features which we recognise. We can sew and make all kinds of craftworks filled with beauty and aspiration. We can express ourselves in three-dimensional forms.

During our training as priestesses we write and draw our daily experiences in a journal and make many kinds of objects, not just so that we can have nice things to play priestess with, but because releasing our creativity allows us to express some of our deepest emotions, which in turn releases more creativity. We learn through experience where our emotional blocks lie and begin to break through them with the help of our siblings on the journey. As priestesses we give ourselves permission to express our feelings and emotions, encouraging others to express theirs too.

Journeying in the Astral Realm

The astral realm is the realm of the emotions, all the emotions that are and have been expressed and suppressed in the world. It is filled with both positive and negative emotions and journeying within the astral realms can take us to places of sublime beauty and also great horror. As priestesses, when we journey into the astral we always travel with guides through defined pathways, where we are protected from all forms of malevolence which may lurk there.

In visualisation we connect to our inner guides and guardians whenever we travel in the astral realms. These guides may be human, otherworldly or animal beings. We begin by taking the time to find out who these guides are for us, asking them to come and show themselves to us in meditation and visualisation. Inner guides can include priestesses of old, friendly ancestors, relatives who have passed over, or guides who are known to us from other incarnations - native American grandmothers, Keltic heras, Tibetan monks, shamankas, etc. They may be universally known beings such as Morgen La Fey or White Eagle or Mary, or they may initially be people who are unknown to us, who become familiar as we journey with them in the Otherworld. They are always there waiting for us whenever we journey.

Animal guides or totems are often those animals who have been and are naturally drawn to us, and we to them. When we begin our journeys they are there waiting to accompany us into the Otherworld. Our totem may be a familiar cat, dog, crow, horse, wolf, lion, hawk, eagle, heron, wren, or even mythic creatures such as the centaur, griffin or salamander. They lead the way for us, protecting us from all harm as we journey in psychic spaces. We need to recognise their safe presence.

In the 1970s and 80s astral travelling was a popular pursuit for the magically inclined questing soul. Several books were devoted to the art, describing with pictures, how to lie down on a bed and watch yourself leave your physical body to journey into the astral realms, remaining connected to the physical body by a silver thread. The first goal was to be able to see your body lying on the bed from up above, from the ceiling of the room. From there the bold ventured out into other worlds. People enthusiastically embraced this form of psychic journeying, finding themselves able to pass through walls and buildings, journeying to beautiful places, visiting friends, returning later to their physical bodies via the silver thread. Sometimes this astral travelling took people to places they did not wish to visit or brought them face to face with beings who were threatening or malevolent, as the astral contains all of these too. The craze for astral travelling has diminished over the last few years, but there are still psychic explorers, such as members of the Damanhur community in Italy, who astral travel to the past and the future.

It can be said that the Isle of Avalon is truly visible today only within the astral realms and to see it we must travel there psychically. As Priestesses of Avalon we enjoy journeying to Avalon in the different forms in which it may appear to us, such as the Paradise Isle, the Island of the Swan, the Glass Isle of Ynys Witrin, the Fortunate Isle, the Western Isle of the Dead or the Otherworldly Avalon, the ancient natural counterpart to today's Glastonbury. Our inner vision of Avalon may not coincide with any one else's or we may find striking similarities in our visions.

In our astral journeying we allow our physical bodies to relax deeply so that our consciousness can easily move out from the body. We journey to Avalon by different routes, which almost always involve travelling across water, across the sea or a large lake. We travel on the Barge of Avalon, accompanied by a faery (ferry) person, or we fly there on the back of a bird - a swan to this Swan Isle, or a Crow or another familiar bird. When we arrive at the island we are always met by a guide, sometimes an animal or bird, sometimes a priestess, or a faery or other person, who journeys with us through the landscape, staying with us or handing us over to other guides, depending on the purpose of our visit, until our safe return.

The following is a sample astral journey to the Island of the Swan to meet the Lady of the Springs and Wells. You may like to read the visualisation out loud and tape record it so that you can listen to the journey and truly enter into its spirit.

Lie down and make yourself comfortable. Feel the weight of the earth beneath your body.

Relax. Let everything go and allow yourself to settle into the floor.
Notice your breathing. Notice the air coming in and out of your lungs. Feel your heart beating.
As you feel your chest rising and falling become aware that you are lying on the back of a great white Swan in flight, whose wings are beating in rhythm with your heartbeat.
She is a beautiful Swan. Sink into Her soft feathers. Feel Her power and Her strength beneath you as She flies through the air. Relax and enjoy the experience
Look out over a familiar landscape, noticing where you are flying. Look at the sky and the earth beneath you. Feel the air as it passes over your body.
Ahead of you in the distance to the west, is a large body of water. You are flying towards it, and soon flying out over the shoreline. Look down at the water. Notice whether it is smooth or choppy. Notice its colour. See what you can see down beneath the surface of the water.
Look ahead and see a small hilly island, the Isle of the Swan, the Isle of Avalon, rising out of the water. Your Swan comes in towards the island, circling around it before landing in the water at the edge of the island.
As you climb off the back of the swan onto dry land you find someone is waiting for you, a guide and companion on your journey. Greet them, notice who they are, what they look like.
Together begin walking along the path that leads from the shore into the low hills of the island.
As you walk along you come to a fork in the path. At this trivia or threefold way, there is a shrine to the Lady. Notice what it looks like and make an offering to the Lady at Her shrine.
Decide which of the two pathways you want to take, the left or the right, the upper or the lower, and begin walking along your chosen path.
As you walk along the pathway the surrounding land begins to rise until you find yourself moving between sloping hillsides into a small gorge with a stream flowing through it. Listen to the sound of the running water as you walk along beside the stream.
Coming around a corner there ahead of you is a Spring flowing out from an opening in the ground, splashing gently into a pool. Your companion stops and will wait for you at the corner as you walk towards the Spring. There are rainbows where the sunlight falls on the splashing water.
Kneel down beside the pool and splash water on your face and body. Take sips of water, feeling it cleansing you and releasing all toxins - physical and psychic.
When you feel cleansed, look down into the pool. As you look into the water, see

your own face reflected there. Look at yourself.
Then another face appears beside yours - the face of the Lady. Look into the water and see what She looks like.
Look up and see the Lady of the Spring standing beside you. Notice how you feel. Do whatever feels appropriate to honour Her presence.
She invites you to sit down with Her beside the spring and allow yourself to feel Her flowing, fluid energy.
As you sit, close your eyes and journey with Her down into the spring waters. Feel yourself becoming like a fish, swimming easily in the water, as if it is your natural medium.
Journey with Her down into the waters and into the earth, through the opening where the spring emerges from the earth. Feel yourself swimming deeper into the earth through widening streams, down to a cavern where there is a great underground pool of water.
These waters are cleansing and healing. Let your emotions flow into the waters. As you swim, undines and mermaids appear and come to play with you. The Lady shows you Her secret underwater places and the treasures that lie hidden there.
After a while in this watery Paradise, return via the streams to the earth's surface and once again find yourself seated next to the Goddess beside Her holy spring.
You may ask Her questions - any questions that you would like to know the answers to - about your life, your relationships, spiritual direction, work, anything.
Listen for Her answers. Take the first thing that you hear or sense. It may come as words or as an image. If you don't understand ask Her to tell you more.
When She has finished communicating with you thank Her for all that She has given to you, for Her place in your life, for Her gifts of emotion, for the waters you drink each day. Ask for Her blessings on the waters of the earth.
Feel in your pocket for something special and give it to Her as an offering.
Kneel beside the pool and again look down into the waters and see your own reflection. When you look up the Goddess has gone.
Look around once more at this special place, at the water, at the spring, and give thanks for your experience. Then go to meet your companion who is waiting for you at the corner.
Together begin walking back through the gorge beside the stream. Listen to the sounds of the stream gurgling and notice how the hillsides gradually lower on either side.
Walk until you come back to the trivia. Give thanks at Her shrine for all you

have experienced and continue walking back down to the shoreline, where your Swan awaits you.

Beside the water thank your companion for accompanying you on your journey across the island and climb onto the back of your Swan. Lie down on Her back and feel Her soft feathers beneath you. Feel safe and secure as She begins to move out across the water.

Slowly Her great wings begin to beat and She lifts off from the surface of the water, rising into the air above the Island of the Swan.

She circles the island and you look down, noticing the trivia and the gorge and the spring beneath you. You also notice other parts of the island which you have not visited yet, but which you may return to visit in the future.

Then your Swan turns to the east and begins to fly out over the water. Look down into the water and notice whether it is smooth or choppy.

Fly for a time and then ahead you see the familiar mainland. As you cross the shoreline look down at the land and see familiar landmarks.

Notice the regular beat of the Swan's wings rising and falling in rhythm with the rhythm of your breath as it moves in and out of your nose or mouth and into your lungs. With each breath feel yourself breathing in energy as well as oxygen, invigorating your body, emotions and mind.

Slowly become aware of the floor beneath your body and as you breathe in, stretch through your body from your toes through to your finger tips and gradually bring your consciousness back into the room.

Write down or draw all your experiences of the Lady and the island before they fade from memory.

Mystical Immersion in Her waters.

One of the goals of our priestess practice is mystical immersion in Her sacred waters, in which we experience that we are but tiny drops in the Ocean of who She is. Our aim is to become at one with Her, identified with Her Essence. This is the mystical union where there is no separation between Her and us. We become one with our Mother as we have always longed to be. We bathe in Her watery nature and know our true place in Her world. We are in Her and of Her as She is in us. In Goddess spirituality, as with the Chinese Tao, the Way is the Goal. The journey is what matters, how we live our lives, at-one and identified with Her. The more we travel with Her through our everyday lives the more we realise that we are never separated from Her. She is always with us. It is only the individuality of our bodies and conditioning that obstructs us from realising this fact in every moment of our lives.

Her Compassionate Nature

Compassion is one of the greatest of the Goddess's qualities which we learn to cultivate, compassion for ourselves and for each other. As a child and teenager I was constantly criticised by my family for being different, for being too sensitive, for showing off. Despite all my attempts to defend myself I absorbed this criticism and internalised it. I grew up with an internal judge who looked at everything that I did and found fault with it. I practised forms of spirituality that were ascetic, hard on the body and mind. I tried to be saintly and of course failed, and then beat myself up for failing. I also looked upon others with a critical eye, judging them for their failures rather than honouring their successes.

When I began to write sacred dramas I found the inner judge was there, sitting on my shoulder, saying, "*You can't write that!*", and the outside world reflected the inner judge, saying, "*You can't write that!*" By now the presence of the judge was conscious. I knew he existed and had to spend hours of my time fighting his critical voice, because for me he was primarily a *he* at that stage, moulded in the image of my father and all worldly patriarchs. Only later did I realise that hidden behind his stern face *she*, my mother, had also been my critic.

Over the years I learned to act despite the internal critic's voice, but it was only during my experience of having breast cancer in 1995 that the judge finally melted away. I had surgery to remove my lump, and then radiotherapy and chemotherapy. I lost all my hair and one day when I was feeling really ill after receiving chemotherapy, a friend Elizabeth Ur, gave me a deep tissue massage which I found usually helped ease the experience. As she touched my heart a cry came out from deep within,

"*What did I ever do to deserve this?*"

I felt that I must have done something really awful in the past to have to suffer so much in the present. There was nothing I had done that was so terrible in this life. I began to cry and huge sobs racked my body. Visions came into my mind of having been one of those women who, after the German occupation of France, had their heads shaved by their fellow countrymen, because they had slept with the enemy. With my bald head I felt I had been one of those women, who had fallen in love with a German soldier, betraying my society for love. When the Germans retreated from France I was made a scapegoat for it by my community, having my head publicly shaved, being beaten and dying during the experience. Being scapegoated by my community for actions that betray the status quo has been a common theme in this life too.

I felt my sorrow for having hurt others and began to beg forgiveness for all that I have done in this life or other lives, which has ever hurt or harmed anyone. I cried for a long time, releasing my pain and sorrow. Then a wonderful feeling of compassion and self-forgiveness came over me. I forgave myself for hurting others, for harming them in any way, for failing, for letting people down. Compassion arose within me and the judge dissolved in this outpouring of ancient, repressed guilt and anguish. S/he has never returned.

I believe that one of the reasons why the Goddess led me through the experience of cancer was precisely to heal this deep wound in my psyche and to release more compassion within me. People had said to me that in order to heal myself of cancer, I must take care of myself, but I realised that I didn't really know what that meant. I was great at looking after everyone else, but I didn't know how to care for me. I had to learn how to do that. During my experience of cancer I received love from many people and I learned to love and care for myself. I learned to have compassion for myself, to forgive myself for failing to live up to my highest ideals. I also learned to forgive others for their failings. I stopped judging them. Now I am happy to love and be loved by many people and I have great compassion for all living beings.

As an addendum to the French experience, five years after remembering this past life story I watched a television programme in which older French women told of their experiences during the Second World war. They described how as young women they had fallen in love with the kind, polite German soldiers who came into their towns and countryside, while their often brutish husbands were away in the army. They had done no more than most women would when we meet and fall in love with kind men.

They described how at the end of the war their own people had turned on them. They were dragged into the streets and their heads were shaved. They were spat upon and abused, humiliated and degraded. Some women died from their wounds and these women had survived, with their shame. The women believed they had been scapegoated by their own menfolk, who had themselves shown much cowardice during the war, failing to chase the Germans out of France. Instead of owning their own failures the men had turned their frustration and anger on their womenfolk who were a much less dangerous target. I sat riveted to this programme as one revisiting her own past.

Playing like a Child

Summer is also a great time to play, to remember what it is like to be an innocent, happy child playing games that are for nothing other than to have fun. If our childhoods were difficult, and we were damaged by our experiences, it is even more important to liberate the innocent one within and let her/im out to play once again.

Design new Goddess games to play. Invite your friends round to play with you as you did when you were a child. Take part in New Games *that are noncompetitive and non-aggressive. Build castles in the sand. Do silly things. Go on picnics, boating on the lake, walking in the hills, excursions to the seaside. Celebrate and play, healing the child within.*

Between Litha and Lammas

Between Litha and Lammas the summer comes to its fullness in Brigit's Isles, with long, warm summer days with blooming flower blossoms and the first fruits on shrubs and trees beginning to swell. We pick the ripened fruits of raspberries and strawberries, smothering them in cream for a delicious summer desert. The grain in the fields grows tall, ready for the hay harvest and for the crop circles which now regularly appear in the grain fields of southern Britain between June and August. Situated near to ancient Goddess sites, they carry unusual and invigorating energies, whoever creates them. We express our feelings and let our wild selves emerge. We take our holidays - holydays, in this country or in foreign landscapes, with opportunities to visit ancient Goddess sites in other lands, which affirm our priestess journey. Yes, She was once honoured in every land and we are helping to bring Her back into human consciousness.

Make an altar at home to Nolava, *Lady of* Water, *to the* Lady *of the* Springs *and* Wells, *to the* Lady *of the* Lake, Vivienne, Nimue, *to* Gliten *of the* Nine Morgens, *to* Domnu, Mother *of the* Oceans, Queen *of the* Deep. *Find statues and objects which represent the* Mother *of* Water *to you, decorating your altar with chalices and bowls of water, red and white wine, and/or summer fruit juices, with shells and seaweed.*

Every day, light a candle flame and burn incense to Nolava, *to* Domnu *and* Gliten *on your altar. Fill your* Chalice *with water from a holy well near you, from the* Chalice Well *and/or the* White Spring *and drink with gratitude from* Her *cup. Change the water in the bowls daily and pour libations of water over* Her *statues. Sing and pray to* Her *for help, for guidance, in gratitude, for others in need, for healing for yourself and others, for vision, etc. Once a week recreate your altar.*

Every day write down and/or draw feelings, dreams, thoughts, intuitions and visions in your diary, i.e. what's going on for you.

Connect to the creatures of the watery world, the salmon of wisdom, the seals, the dolphins, the whales, the korrigans of the wells, the merpeople, the silkies. Visualise them before you go to sleep, helping you to travel in the dream world.

At the new moon take a special ceremonial bath with candles, flowers and fragrances, cleansing and celebrating the power of emotion in your life.

At the full moon journey to the sea, to a lake or a sacred pool and take a ritual dip in Her *waters. Bathe naked under the full moon with friends.*

Take a holyday, play with your family and friends. Relax from the stresses of life. Take care of yourself.

Continue working on your vow of dedication to the Goddess.

At least once if not more, visit a sacred site or landscape associated with Domnu, wherever water flows freely out of or upon the earth - springs, wells, streams, rivers, lakes, the ocean. Give thanks for the gifts of water.

The Abundance Lammas Festival of the Great Mother

Lammas is the season when we celebrate the Abundance of Nolava, the Pregnant and Birth-giving High Fruitful Mother Goddess, She who give us everything that we have with an unrivalled generosity. Lammas falls around August 1st, in Brigit's Isles between the hay and grain harvests when the pregnant Mother Goddess is coming to Her fullness and giving birth to Her offspring. We honour the Mother as Mystress Glitonea of the Nine Morgens, as Madron the Mother Goddess and as Ker the Grain Mother, whose arrival brought the neolithic agricultural revolution to Europe more than eight thousand years ago. We honour the bountiful Cow and Deer Mothers. We honour Her as Mary the Mother Goddess, held within Christian belief.

At Lammas the Mother appears in Her fullness, giving birth to the fruits of Her nature, which come to ripeness all around in field and forest, on plants and trees. All across Brigit's landscape golden wheat, barley and other grains are being harvested in the fields, which now reach the height of beauty and complexity. In the fields and gardens vegetables grow in abundance and we pick and eat them, full of vitamins and prana (the vital energy in vegetables eaten fresh from the plant) for good health. The surplus we can save and store for the following winter seasons. The sea that surrounds the coasts of Brigit's Isles slowly heats through the summer months and we swim in Her warm waters. As summer continues in the Summerland the green grass lengthens and begins to fade on the Tor bleaching in the sunlight from green to gold and fawn. We continue to take our holydays, celebrating Hlafmass or the Festival of Bread.

At Lammas in Glastonbury we celebrate the Mother Goddess's abundant nature at the fabulous international Goddess Conference. In its eleventh year at the time of writing, the Goddess Conference has become a unique and well-loved beacon of inspiration for Goddess-loving people all over the world. Here we create and perform many ceremonies which honour the Goddess as Maiden, Lover, Mother and Crone. We participate in ages-old and completely new Goddess traditions, expressing ourselves creatively. We dance, sing, cry, laugh and have fun, and remember how to serve the Goddess and Her people.

At Lammas we honour Nolava the Mother Goddess in Her many forms and we recognise and honour the special woman's initiation that is Motherhood, and the unique joy and challenge of our children. We learn to share the Goddess's karuna or mother love with others. We make corn dollies in the image of the Grain Goddess.

Honouring Great Mother Nolava

Nolava is the Great Mother Goddess of the land that is the Isle of Avalon. She is the Provider, the Nurturer, the Sustainer, the one who truly cares about each one of us no matter who we are or what we do. She is the infinitely loving Mother who sees and knows all that we are and does not judge us. She carries us for long months in Her Womb of transformation and brings us to rebirth with great tenderness and care. When we are born She feeds us with the milk of Her loving kindness. When things are hard and difficult She enfolds us in Her soft gentle embrace, whispering messages into our ears that sustain us through the dark times. She holds us in the palm of Her hand and rocks us to sleep in Her mercy.

The Mother Goddess holds such a special place in our hearts. While our human mothers may fail to live up to our exacting ideals, the Great Mother Goddess is ever-loving and always present with Her endless compassion. She is the Mother with whom we long to merge and become one, as a baby longs to be one with its human mother. With eyes filled with love, She looks deeply into our souls and meets us there. She understands that our negative actions are the result of our own pain and suffering. She holds us always in Her embrace, ready to bless us with Her forgiveness.

As well as birthing and nurturing Her human children Nolava continuously gives birth to the new in all forms. From Her deep, bottomless Womb She creates new forms, new ways of being, new ideas and thoughtforms, both personal and communal, that come into existence in Glastonbury Avalon. She is envisioned within Glastonbury's sacred landscape as the giant pregnant Mother Goddess lying on Her back, on and down into the Summerland meadows. The Tor is Her milk-filled left breast reaching up to the sky. Chalice Hill is Her pregnant belly. With Her body aligned from the northeast to the southwest She continually gives birth to the town and its people from between Her outspread legs.

Geoffrey Ashe, the writer and Arthurian scholar, first pointed out in *King Arthur's Avalon* that Glastonbury is a place where the new is frequently brought to birth. It is the place where the first Christian church in Britain was founded nearly 2,000 years ago, and erected between the Mother's legs. It is the place where the first public indigenous Goddess Temple in Brigit's Isles has been created, since the Anglo Saxons, the last Goddess-worshipping peoples to arrive here, came to Britain. Many people receive Her inspiration here and new ideas emerge and are experimented with in Glastonbury, including new forms of spirituality and community. They may not necessarily be brought to fruition here, but they are birthed here. The Great Mother is at work within the energetic structure of the land and the community, carrying the golden eggs of the future in Her capacious womb.

Honouring Mystress Glitonea, Mother Morgen

I am Glitonea.
Behold me in the shimmering dawn.
Rosy hued, greeted by the warble of the soft throated thrush,
The day unfolds, humming full of potential,
Awakening into my bountifulness.
Moment by moment, the mounting joy of harvest ripening,
All life is poised on a single point,
The long day of summer bares her breast.

I am She, Mother, Provider.
In my womb you are nourished,
Through my birth pains you become yourself,
Experiencing the rich abundance of your own joy and suffering.
Mother, mirror.
Grow yourself
Plant your roots deep in my soil,
Suckle yourself at my breasts.

As the golden corn you ripen into your fullness.
Like the green ash wood you bend to life's imperatives.
Set ablaze by its pain and rawness
Safe in my compassionate heart you weather the storms.

White hind deer walks beside me
Softly caressing your woundedness.
Having received the best of nurturing, you attain equanimity,
Growing strong.

Sustaining yourself through the intensity of all elements,
Watering the earth with your own goodness and compassion.
Let me guide you into one pointedness,
Scintillating aliveness,
The exquisite sensation of being fully present.
All is one.
Ripeness is all.
Meet yourself in me.

Immanence.
Reveal your gold.
True treasure, untarnished.

by Juliet Yelverton

Mystress Glitonea is the Mother Morgen, the Nourisher and Provider of all who come to Avalon. She helps create the ambience and actuality of love and care for one another that characterises interactions between people. As a woman She is in Her forties, the Mother of many offspring, whom She suckles at Her loving breast. Glitonea's creature is the beautiful white hind, a mysterious Otherworldly creature often associated with the birth-giving Mother Goddess and always sheltered by apple trees, like those found in Avalon (See T*he White Goddess* by Robert Graves, Faber). Through the ages and in countries from Arabia to England, the white hind has been recognised as an epiphany of the Goddess. Her appearance symbolises a visitation from the Mother and an experience of the mystery of the human soul. Occasionally She may be glimpsed on the wilder edges of Avalon, in fields and by hedgerows, away from human activity. Glitonea's bird is the song thrush, who sings her beautiful songs in gardens and fields, and turning her head into the wind she calls in the summer storms.

As weather Glitonea is Heat, the intensity of the sun's rays at Lammas, the heat that can build into summer storms, that roll around the landscape cauldron. On the south-facing slopes of the hills tropical plants are able to grow in this northern land. Glitonea's colour is gold, the gold of sunlight on ripening grain, the gold of wheat fields, the gold of the land illuminated by the morning and evening sunshine, the gold of flowers in gardens and fields, where nature's bounty is reaching its fulfilment. She is

Ash Woman and Her tree is found in many places in Avalon's sacred landscape with its familiar curving branches and creamy wood. In traditions from Scandinavia to Ireland the ash is the world tree, reaching from the centre of the earth to the ends of the universe, the Mother Goddess incarnate.

Honouring the Abundant Mother Goddess Madron

Madron or Modron is the Mother of all life and She is remembered in the waters that flow out from Her earthly body, from the springs and wells which are found not only in Avalon, but also all over Brigit's Isles. The famous Madron Well lies a short way outside of the small town of Madron in Cornwall. Twenty years ago when Mike and I first went to visit Her Well, the spring was neglected and old grey clouties hung on the trees. Returning three years ago we were very happy to see that the Well is now well tended and brightly coloured ribbons and rags cover the branches of many trees. Pilgrims have returned to Her well once again leaving their healing prayers to flap in the wind beside Her waters. Madron and Her well are once more being honoured.

The Welsh Triads provide some of our earliest information about our British Goddesses and ancestors. In one triplet, Modron verch Avallach is named as the daughter of the lineage of Avallach, who was said to be a male ancestor from the Isle of Avalon. Since Avalon has always been an island of women I have reclaimed Modron or Madron as Mother of the lineage of Avallach, the people of Avalon, rather than as his daughter. Morgen la Fey is said to be Madron's daughter.

As well as being an intimate Mother to whom we can talk at any time, Madron the Mother is also the great Void from whom all creation emerges. She was there at the beginning of time and will be there at its ending. She gives birth to all things in manifestation. She gives us life and Her material bounty feeds and clothes us and gives us shelter. Everything we have She gives to us out of Her abundant generosity and we, in our human ways, claim ownership of these gifts which we have been freely given.

We honour Madron by thanking Her, by showing Her our gratitude for all that She gives to us. We make offerings to Her at our personal and communal altars, at sacred places in Her landscape, beside Her wells and springs, on Her womb-shaped hills, in Her deep vaginal valleys, and in Her temples. We also honour Her by sharing Her abundance with others, by giving generously to others out of our own abundance. Emulating Her generous nature, we tithe, or maybe ninthe, at least one ninth of our income to individuals and groups whose Goddess work we wish to support, whether it be helping the poor, the needy and the sick in this country and abroad, or by supporting projects which help bring the Goddess back into our everyday life, such as the Glastonbury and other Goddess Temples.

We ninthe to those who give us spiritual food, all those individuals who enrich our lives with their love and creativity, who lift our spirits, who help us when we are down, who smile at us, who inspire us. Goddess artists, writers, poets and priestesses who serve Her and us are usually not well paid for all that they do or must supplement their Goddess work by working in non-spiritual occupations. We need to support each other in our Goddess work, not only emotionally and spiritually, but also financially, for who else will do this for us at this time? We need to help each other move into Her abundance in our spiritual work as priestesses, so that the whole of our lives can be lived in service to Her.

The Practice of Gratitude

This Practice of Gratitude is a very simple daily spiritual practice that opens our hearts and encourages us to be more loving, expansive and generous people.

Every day light a candle at your altar and sit in front of it. Thank the Goddess for everything that you have in your life, for the day itself, for the weather, the rain, the snow, the sunshine, for your family and friends, for the animals and birds, for your work, for the opportunities that come your way, for the people you meet, for the challenges you face. Thank Her for everything.

It's a simple practice but very effective. This practice can be developed and shared with others, with your family and friends. The following is an Avalonian variation of the Ava Ceremony, first introduced to me by Dr Apela Colorado, an elder and Professor of Indigenous Mind, on the Hawaiian island of Maui. Ava, Awa or Kava Kava is a Polynesian herb traditionally mixed with water to produce a mildly intoxicating and relaxing drink, that also heightens spiritual awareness. On the Isle of Avalon for this practice we use the juice of apples cultivated on the slopes of the island.

Prepare a large bowl with delicious Avalonian apple juice or a mixture of fresh juices. Have smaller bowls ready to dip into the larger bowl and cloths to wipe clean the edges of the bowls. Sit in circle with your family, friends and visitors. As priestess, begin by dipping one of the small bowls into the larger bowl and filling it with juice. Holding the bowl in your hands invoke the presence of the Goddess, asking Her to come and be with you all in the ritual.

Offer a prayer of gratitude for the fruits and the juices you are about to drink. Take the bowl and pour some of the juice into a chalice on your altar, offering it to the Goddess. Take the bowl outside and pour the remaining juice onto the earth as a libation to the Goddess. You can ask a sister priestess or a young person to do these last two things for the group.

On return dip the smaller bowl into the larger bowl and holding it in your hands say out loud your personal prayer of gratitude to the Goddess. This includes your gratitude for the individual people in the room being present in your life, which is a heartwarming experience for most people to hear. Give thanks for the day, for the people in your life, for the challenges you face, for whatever you want to express. When your prayer is complete drink all the juice from the small bowl. Wipe the edge of the bowl with a cloth.

Ask the eldest woman in the circle to come forward. Dip the small bowl into the larger bowl and fill it half-full with apple juice. Ask the woman to offer her prayer of gratitude for all to hear. When she has finished she drinks the bowl of apple juice. Take the bowl back, clean and wipe.

Invite people to come forward as they feel moved to take a bowl of juice, offer their prayers and drink.

When everyone has made their prayers of gratitude and taken a drink ask if anyone would like to make another prayer. Continue praying and drinking until all the juice has been drunk. Make a final prayer to the Goddess giving thanks for Her presence.

This simple ceremony is a great way of bringing people together to publicly express our gratitude for all we have in our lives. In the original Ava Ceremony other actions are included as part of the ceremony, such as clapping the hands before and after drinking. You may like to make additions to the basic ceremony and introduce your own variations. In the Pacific islands the Ava Ceremony is usually performed at dusk at the end of the working day, when family and friends gather to relax and give thanks.

Celebrating Ker the Grain Mother

Ker is the Grain Mother we celebrate at Hlafmass, the Festival of Bread. It was the cultivation of wheat, barley and other grains, which could be gathered and stored through the winter months, which allowed early nomadic tribes to settle on the land and cease their seasonal migrations.

This settling down led to the accumulation of food and possessions, the development of horticulture and agriculture, the cutting down of the widespread native British forests to make way for cultivation, and the development of communities. As people came together in larger groups and societies developed, religious practices also evolved. This led over time to the erection of the great wooden enclosures, earthen and stone mounds and temples of the neolithic era, which were shaped like the womb, breasts and body of the Goddess, celebrating Her as Mother of all life and of death. This was the great flowering of neolithic culture which was the last time when the Goddess was truly honoured in Brigit's Isles, before the third millennium BCE, over five thousand years ago.

Harvested grain is ground to produce flours of all kinds, which can be cooked and made into bread, which has since become a staple diet in many cultures in the world. Ker is the ancestor that we honour as the first woman who deliberately planted grain and harvested the grown wheat. We honour Grain Woman, because it was women in those early times who were the gatherers of seeds, roots and fruits, which later developed to become today's grains, vegetables and fruits.

Women's special spiritual function as the bearer of life is recognised in agrarian societies in the practice of women blessing seeds as they sow them in the ground to bring a fruitful harvest. We can emulate this practice in our own gardens, offering Her blessings as we sow seeds, bulbs and plants in the ground, working in harmony with the cycles of the moon. Women can also bless the earth with our enriching, menstrual blood.

In excavations of neolithic sites throughout Old Europe images of Bird and Snake Goddesses have been found in the remains of bakeries and bread ovens, holding positions of power and meaning. The Grain Goddess has been prominent throughout the ages coming down to us in the image of Britannia, BrigitAna, who holds a sheaf of wheat, through Roman Ceres, Greek Demeter, and Virgo the Virgin Grain Goddess visible in the stars.

At Lammas we make special loaves of bread shaped like the body of the Goddess in remembrance of Ker the Grain Mother. At the Goddess Conference our renewed tradition each year is for everyone to mould bread dough into the shapes of the Goddess. These are baked and later eaten in ceremony in gratitude to Ker for the grain, the staff of life, that She has given us.

We also visit the grain fields, where for the last twenty years or so crop circles of great beauty, complexity and diversity have appeared each summer. Despite the efforts of sceptics to dismiss them as the work of cranks or artists, they continue to amaze and inspire those who look for meaning beyond the surfaces of the material world. I personally have no idea who or what is creating them and I like the fact that their source is unknown. They allow many thousands of ordinary people to have an experience of Her mystery in the grain fields of Brigit's Isles and that is big enough. When we experience Her mystery our hearts open and our spiritual journeys begin.

Making Corn Dollies

The simplest Corn Dollies made to honour the Grain Mother are made from bundles of grain - wheat, barley and oats collected from fields, verges and hedgerows. Bind the bundle of grain with wool, cotton or ribbon just below the middle of the bundle (1) and bend the top of the stems over to form Her skirt (2). Bind the bent-over bundle again to form the Mother's waist and then insert smaller bundles of grain to form Her arms and head (3). Decorate her with coloured wools and ribbons.

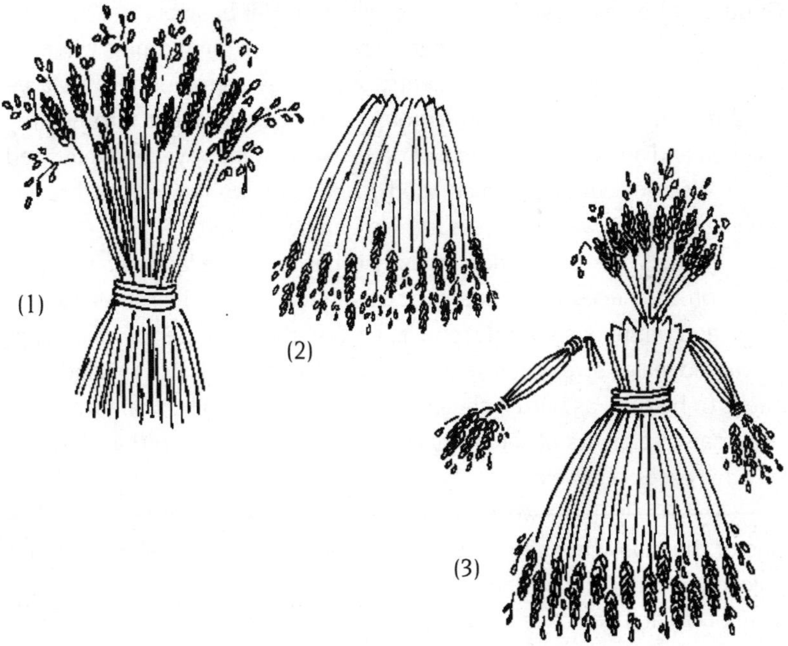

Specially selected grain stems can also be woven into intricate patterns to create the traditional corn dollies that can still be found in summer fairs and holiday towns.

Honouring the Cow Mother

The Mother Goddess's creatures include the animals who move in herds, many of which are now domesticated, such as the Cow, the Goat, the Sheep and the Deer. They are all horned creatures, their snaking and spiralling horns and antlers reaching up to the skies, linking earth and the heavens. Domestication of herd animals developed in the neolithic age and their milk, meat, skin and bones were used to feed, clothe, house and decorate human beings and their homes. These practices still continues in northern societies where nomads still follow the migrations of reindeer and caribou.

The Cow Mother has long been honoured in Brigit's Isles in the form of Brigit the Cow Mother, from whose udders the Milky Way in the heavens was created. She was Christianised as St Bridget, the woman who milked the cows. She is also known as Mother of Cows, Mother of Milk and the old Shepherdess of the Cows. In Yorkshire She is Verbeia, She of the Cattle (*The Language of the Goddess*, Maria Gimbutas, Thames and Hudson). In womanly forms She appears as Dea Nutrix, the nursing Goddess who feeds two babies with milk from Her breasts.

Milk is the nourishment that we receive from our mothers when we are born, filled with all the nutrients, antibodies and goodness that we need to thrive after birth and for our proper development into healthy children and adults. This miracle of nature was for many years diminished within western cultures, which tried to educate women out of breast-feeding, saying it was unnecessary, demeaning and dirty.

Today's milk production industry is based on the factory farming of cows, on the necessity of keeping cows in calf for all their lives so that they can continuously produce milk, and on the slaughter of millions of unwanted male calves each year. Excess milk produced from this industry needs to be sold, as butter, cheese and as powdered milk. Women are the necessary recipients of the message that breast is less, so that they will buy this excess capacity.

Thankfully, in the west breast-feeding has again been recognised as one of the many true gifts of our women's nature, to be celebrated and enjoyed by baby and mother alike. There is still however resistance to the sight of women breast-feeding in public as if it is corrupting for those who glimpse the flash of breast flesh. Also unfortunately, surplus powdered milk is now sold to women in third world countries, where the water needed to make it whole again is often polluted, leading to sickness, diarrhoea and death in babies and young children.

When we breast-feed we connect deeply with our child, bonding in a very physical way with our baby. The distance between our eyes is perfect for that deep soul to soul connection that is so important for love to flourish. The baby receives all that it needs to grow in the first few months and for the mother breast-feeding stimulates the production of oxytocin, our wombs contract and heal themselves from blood loss and our bodies relax. We feel sensual and juicy, in love with life and our babies. What a gift of an experience.

At Lammas we can visit the Cow and Grain Mothers in the landscape at the wonderful sacred site of Avebury in Wiltshire, where Her cow's head and horns are formed by the central henge and the Beckhampton and West Kennet avenues of standing stones. This image mirrors the shape of women's Fallopian tubes and womb. In the wider landscape Silbury Hill, the largest human-made mound in Europe, is the Lammas Mother's pregnant belly. According to Michael Dames in *The Silbury Treasure* (T&H), the full moon at Lammastide mirrored in the water in the surrounding ditch is born from the Womb of Silbury Hill.

Visit the Avebury landscape at Lammas and experience the Great Mother in the landscape, in the patterns of the stones, in the plentiful wheat fields, in the crop circles often found in the surrounding area.

Honouring the Deer Mother

The Deer Mother is an avatar of the Birth-giving Mother Goddess preserved in Scottish and Irish stories of supernatural women, who could change from woman to deer to woman again. Oisin, one of the Irish gods, was said to be a son of the Deer Goddess Sadb. In earlier times it was the Red Deer and Reindeer who were particularly honoured in Brigit's Isles, as they grew new horns each year and cast old ones, which could be used in ceremony and for carving. The remains of antlers are found at many sacred sites in Brigit's Isles and throughout Europe, sometimes mixed with ochre, the blood of the Goddess, and other coloured clays. The belief that pregnant deer gave life to human beings persisted throughout the centuries and was still found in the 20th century in northern Asia. Among the Evenki, the Mother of the Universe, Bugadi, is imaged as a doe-elk or reindeer doe (*The Language of the Goddess*, Maria Gimbutas, T&H). Lammas is the time when Deer Priestesses, Stag Dancers and Morris Dancers dance in praise of the fertility of the Birth-giving Mother. We dress in doe skins and wear antlers on our heads in honour of Her.

Honouring Mary the Mother Goddess

Many women find their way to the Goddess through the forms in which She has been held within patriarchal religions. One of the most prominent is that of Mary the Mother Goddess, still venerated within the Christian religion, particularly in Roman Catholicism, where there are currently moves to elevate Her to being co-redemptive with Jesus. Images of Mary often show Her as a submissive woman, with Her head down in a passive, non-assertive, and definitely nonsexual manner. Many present day statues of Mary however, looked at as a whole, are mandorla or lozenge shaped. This ancient Goddess symbol from neolithic times represents the Vulva of the Goddess, from which we are all born into the world. Within this image Mary's submissive head forms the clitoris, the source of much of our womanly sexual pleasure. Throughout Christian imagery the Goddess's Vulva is visible but largely unnoticed, often enclosing images of Jesus and the saints.

The original power and authority of Mary as Mother Goddess has been greatly diminished within Christianity, but many ordinary people have continued to experience Her love and compassion in their devotional practices to Her. Although the central belief is in a trinity of male gods, Christianity still retains several different faces of the Goddess, within the often maligned women of the Bible. There is Mary, the virgin mother of Jesus, who we reclaim as Mary the Virgin Mother Goddess. There is St Anne, the mother of Mary and grandmother of Jesus, who is Goddess Anna, the Crone Grand Mother. There is Mary Magdalene, the redeemed Sacred Whore, now recognised by many as the probable wife of Jesus and mother of his children, and of a lineage that stretches through the royal families of Europe, and especially France, to the present day.

Like the ancient Goddess, biblical Mary is known as the Queen of Heaven, Queen of the Earth and Queen of Hell or the Underworld. She is the Blessed Virgin, Star of the Sea, Lady all-Holy, Lady Most Venerable, the Ever-Virgin, Our Lady Mary, Madonna, Black Madonna, Mother of God. These are all earlier titles of the Goddess. In Wales She was confused with the triple White Goddess and was known as White Mary. In Scotland She was present in the form of Bride, known as Mary of the Gael.

Wherever we travel there are churches devoted to St Mary where we can honour Goddess Mary by lighting candles before Her image and praying to Her. Within the majority of Roman Catholic churches Mary is the principal being worshipped by the people, who see Her as being more accessible than Jesus or God the Father. Where male deities might stand aloof from everyday suffering Mary is always thought of as being close, offering comfort to those in need, prepared to intercede, to speak on behalf of the poor and needy, to the more distant male divinities.

In Glastonbury we can find Mary in the Mary Chapel, which lies at the heart of the ruins of Glastonbury Abbey. This chapel was the first part of the Abbey built according to the sacred geometry of the vesica piscis, which is the mandorla created by two overlapping circles, whose numerology spells out the names of Mary. We can find the Mother Goddess in the Roman Catholic Church in the form of Our Lady St. Mary of Glastonbury. Here there is a beautiful statue of Mary, carrying the infant Jesus in one arm and a sprig of Avalonian apple blossom in the other. We can find Mary in the Magdalene or St Margaret's Chapel, which can be found in Magdalene street.

At Lammas we remember the Mother Goddess hidden within patriarchal forms and we visit Her sacred sites wherever we can find them in the world, from Chartres, site of the ancient Birth-giving Mother, to Ephesus where we can find the remains of the temples of Artemis Diana, the Many Breasted Mother, to the many wayside shrines dedicated to Mary in Ireland, and all over Europe.

The Mother's Gift of Life

From the earliest times, the main characteristic that has differentiated women from men is women's ability to bear new life and to birth our children from within our own bodies. This very physical capability is based within the nature of our amazing human bodies, and has divine properties. New spiritual life comes into incarnation through the medium of our female bodies. Once upon a time, this ability was recognised in all societies as holy, a gift from the Great Mother Herself, given to women who were made in Her image. In devotion, the Mother Goddess was often imaged as a fertile woman with enlarged pregnant belly, breasts and buttocks. 99.9% of figurines and images from the early palaeolithic and neolithic eras have female forms.

It was the arrival of patriarchal cultures into Europe in the fifth and fourth millennia BCE which brought the first quantities of male images, and the denial of the holiness of women. No-one knows for certain why these dominator cultures arose, but it can be argued that it was essentially male envy of woman's primary place as the Giver of Life, that led to their rise worldwide. In order to take away women's inherent power, it was necessary to own and control women's ability to give birth to new life.

When women's ability to bear new life is regarded by all as a holy gift from the Goddess, then there can be no violence towards women. There can be no rape, there can be no war against women, against our children and our values. To harm a woman or her children is taboo in such a society, it is an offence against life itself. Transgression of this taboo leads to punishment, not only from other humans, but also from the Goddess Herself. Such an action would not be taken lightly in a Goddess-loving society. At some point in history, men collectively made that choice and the taboos against rape and violence towards women were broken. Patrilineal instead of matrilineal inheritance was established, as well as a thousand other assaults on the lives and freedoms of women. Perhaps this is the time that is described in many ancient texts as the Fall.

In today's world the age-old taboos against harming women are broken in every moment and we see the awful results on our streets and on our TV screens every day. Women cannot walk the streets alone at night in safety or without fear. We are beaten in our homes, in the bosom of our families, in the places where we should be honoured and able to feel safe. Today's wars may be fought mostly by men, but the majority, who suffer as noncombatants, are women, children and the old, the innocent victims, who are blown up and maimed, who die in their thousands or become slaves and refugees in their own and foreign lands.

Sadly, in today's societies women are no longer regarded as holy. Our ability to bear and give birth to children is seen on the whole as a purely physical capability without spiritual content. There is no need to honour us, rather the opposite, we must still be controlled because of our inherent ability to bear new life. If you cannot give birth yourself, then to capture and retain power you must control those who do. For the last few hundred years the act of giving birth itself has been manipulated and controlled, principally by male doctors and obstetricians, serving their own needs rather than the physical and spiritual needs of women and society. Their argument has been and still is: why should women not be rendered unconscious during the act of birth, then they won't feel pain? *"We can do it all for you and make it safe."*

Mary Daly's fantastic book, *Gyn/Ecology* (The Women's Press), provides a fine exposition of the ways in which women's primary function as birth-givers has been manipulated and controlled by the medical profession, from the times when male doctors took over from the witches, the wise women healers and midwives, to today.

The fact is that conceiving, bearing and giving birth to children is the primary spiritual initiation for women that it is possible to experience on this planet. It is a true initiation in that it take us to that place where the gates to life and death open wide and we face that gaping Void into which we might fall. Returning from that experience we are imbued with new life, our own as well as our new baby's. Such a journey is the basis of most initiation ceremonies and rites of passage performed in the many indigenous cultures of the world, which mimic the processes of birth.

Without any doubt, despite the many amazing spiritual experiences I have had in my life, among the greatest in the body spiritual experiences I have had were in bearing and giving birth to my two beautiful children, Iona and Torquil. The supreme gift of living in a woman's body is that new life is conceived and incarnates through our female bodies and there is nothing else quite like that in human experience for women or men. This is not to say that those women who decide not to have children or who are unable to bear children for whatever physical reason, are somehow lesser women. Their karmic choices bring other initiations to the fore. It is also not to say that men are lesser beings than women because they are not able to give birth, again they have different initiations to face. But motherhood is the great female experience and achievement, which is not only physical, but also emotional, psychological and spiritual.

Women have the amazing ability to conceive new life, to be the physical, emotional, mental and spiritual vehicle through which intangible, insubstantial spirit incarnates into physical reality. It is a stunning fact, so commonplace and ordinary that we don't often consider just how miraculous it is.

At particular times in life a soul calls to us from the Great Beyond, to the woman and the man who will become its parents, to come together to conceive the baby, who will be its vehicle of incarnation and manifestation. This calling is a process of energetic attraction, which will provide the perfect conditions into which the soul can incarnate for the fulfilment of its purposes and karma, whatever that may be. I believe that our children choose us for who we are, as we choose consciously or unconsciously - sometimes accidentally, to have them. It is a mutual attraction, as they too will help us to fulfil our karma.

The soul is individualised consciousness, it is the vehicle for our individual spirit or life force, and I believe it continues from life to life. There are philosophical disputes as to when a new soul fully incarnates into physical form, some say at conception, others say at ten days or three months in the womb, and others at birth. However, life energy begins to animate form as soon as the egg cell from the mother is penetrated by the sperm cell from the father, creating a new DNA configuration and catalysing a new human form. This conjoined cell begins to multiply, growing in size daily, implanting into the wall of the womb, passing through all the different phases of our human evolution as it grows, from a single cell creature to a water-borne creature able to thrive in the sea of the womb, finally maturing into a baby to whom we give birth through our vulvas, who is then able to breathe air. At some point during this process of development the incarnating soul anchors into the baby's body carrying with it the seeds of its past karma and future destiny.

In many cases I believe that we incarnate into families with whom we have past life herstory. We often know our parents from other lives, as our own children, as parents, as brothers and sisters, as lovers. This is a commonly recognised experience for many indigenous peoples. Sometimes, we are as cuckoos in the nest, incarnating through families with whom we have no previous connection, but to whom we will be connected in the future. I have noticed that many priestesses and spiritual seekers at the present time have that feeling about themselves. We are part of the diaspora of souls, who have chosen to move out of traditional societies and into more modern cultures, bringing with us the wisdom of the ancient ways, trying them out in new lands and with new people. One of the most well documented examples of this are the many Tibetans who died during the Chinese invasion of Tibet, who are now incarnating into the west, into western bodies and cultures, bringing with them the wisdom traditions of ancient Tibet.

The Joy of Conception and Pregnancy

From the moment of conception, we can often feel the beginning of our pregnancy as a subtle change in our bodies, a slight tightening and enlarging of our breasts, a feeling of tiredness, a shift in focus, then comes the lack of moontime flow and feelings of nausea. For the nine months or ten moons of pregnancy we are moved by changes in our physical bodies into a different way of being and knowing. Our focus of attention shifts from the outerworld to the innerworld, being directed towards our physical and emotional bodies. We become highly sensitive to our own emotions and to the emotional states of others, becoming responsive to their anger, fear and sadness. We cry at the drop of a hat. Our minds often take a back seat as our bodies swell and we become less assertive, less extroverted. We naturally want to be taken care of by our partners, families and communities. We become more docile, more like the great Cow Mother Herself. We move into a primal place within our physicality, which is directly connected to the Mother Goddess. We connect to Her via our hearts, our emotions and our primitive reptilian brain, the brain stem which governs all our unconscious patterns and connects us to ancestral memories of our tribal heritage. We spend more time dreaming, freeing our unconscious minds to reveal to us what has been hidden by mental armouring. Often we begin to remember our own births in this and previous lives and begin unexpectedly to face and heal our own primal wounds.

Pregnancy is such a journey for women. For some it is a total joy as we enter a blissful space, where we feel happy and joyful, sometimes for the first time since childhood. We find contentment within the sea of beneficial hormones, enjoying the whole experience of being pregnant. Other women hope and dream that pregnancy will be easy and graceful and then we find ourselves overwhelmed by sickness, by feelings of depression, inertia, loss of independence and selfhood. We wonder who would ever want to become pregnant, if it is like this? In countries where pregnancy and motherhood must be taken in a working woman's stride there is less time to gaze at our swelling navels, but in the west women often give more attention to their growing forms and their changing psychology. Pregnancy can be a time of deep healing.

As our babies develop within our physical wombs they are affected by how we live our lives, by what we eat and take into our bodies. Sometimes for the first time we begin to take responsibility for the health of our own bodies, for the sake of our babies. We stop smoking cigarettes and cut down on alcohol, we begin to eat healthy food. We learn to care for our bodies and our growing babies.

While our babies are growing inside our physical bodies, they also grow within the energy fields of our adult emotions and minds. They experience what we experience. The growing foetus is affected by our states of happiness, fear, anxiety or anger and will respond with distress to influxes of adrenaline. The baby takes our emotional states on as its own, beginning its life in the sea of our fears, anxieties and angers rather than its own blissful state. This is the way that heredity works, the way that family karma is passed down through the generations. For the sake of our babies we are also responsible for our psychological states during pregnancy, which are not so easy to control as hormones wash around our bodies.

As mothers, we take responsibility for the conditions into which our baby is incarnating as much as we can. However, we must do so without taking on added anxiety and guilt for our inevitable failure to be the perfect mother, for there is no such thing. Perfection, if it means anything in human terms, lies in our being who we are in each moment, rather than being an ultimate and fixed state of consciousness. We try our very best and that is good enough.

Our babies choose us for the way that we are, which will shape their lives, but our behaviour is not the only determining factor in our children's future. Their development will ultimately depend on how they respond to the challenges of life and that includes having us as mothers. It is the way that it is set up to be within Her nature. Having a baby is a mutual responsibility, agreed at some level between the souls of mother and child, of father and child, and of mother and father. As we grow into adulthood it is too easy for us to blame our mothers and our fathers for what happened to us during pregnancy, birth and in childhood, as being the cause of all our ills. We have to take responsibility for our choice to incarnate with that particular woman as our mother, with that man as our father, whose full role comes into play after birth.

These factors reflect the wider relationship between human beings and the Great Mother. She provides the beautiful world into which we incarnate, with all its challenges and limitations. We cannot blame Her for being born, even though we might sometimes like to. As we rail against divinity for the pain in which we find ourselves we must recognise that we are co-creators with Her and can change things for the better too. The quality of our lives depends on the quality of our souls and on how we respond to challenges along the way.

The Spiritual Initiation of Birth

For the baby, birth through a human mother is initiation into the mysteries of physically manifested life on this extraordinary planet Earth. This experience has powerful effects which reverberate through our lives. From the moment we are conceived we begin to sow the seeds for our future emotional and psychological development. These karmic seeds are carried from life to life in the subtle causal vehicle of the soul and are expressed through our genetic inheritance and in the magnetic choices by which we pattern our future experiences. They anchor into our unconscious minds through experiences we synchronistically have with our mothers during our time in her womb. They are mirrored in the way in which we are born and how we are received into the world during the first few months of life. They ripen throughout childhood and into adulthood through interaction with the world, forming the basis of our personality and the structures and habits of the character by which we become known in the world.

What begins as a small but significant experience at birth, such as a prolonged labour, having the cord around the baby's neck as it is born, or a delay in breathing, generalises later in life into a statement about how life is for us, such as "I *can't get out of here*. If I *try to live* I *will die*. I *can't breathe*!" These unconscious life statements emerge in stressful situations later in life, determining our behaviour. We hear ourselves saying them when we are under pressure. Remembering the experience of our birth and making it conscious is often part of our karmic healing later in life.

As mothers we try to create the best circumstances possible for our babies during labour and birth, but often management of this important experience is taken out of our hands by those claiming to be working for our benefit and safety. Also no matter how hard we try to create the best conditions our babies usually have their own karmic agendas. During my first pregnancy with my daughter I stopped smoking and drinking, ate all the right food, practised yoga throughout and prepared for a home delivery with friends. Nearing full term I hopped over a Beltane fire on top of Glastonbury Tor and went into a three day labour by the end of which both baby and I were exhausted. As she failed to arrive of her own accord, we were finally sent into hospital where it was discovered that she was lying in a breech position. As she was becoming distressed I had an emergency Caesarian section. Ah! The best laid plans.....

Many good books have now been written about the processes of birth, filled with information about the health of baby and mother, and the care of both. Here I want to focus on the spiritual aspects of birthing and motherhood. For many years medical institutions, doctors and obstetricians have attempted to remove spirituality from our experience of bearing and birthing our children. We are told many times that it is safer for us to be in their hands and better to give birth without pain or even consciousness. Some deem it preferable for us to have medical interventions and Caesarian sections, rather than go through the drama of giving birth naturally, which may not fit in with orderly schedules.

As with menstruation, it is worth noting that when we are carrying and especially when we give birth to our babies, the Goddess is near to us and present within our bodies. In the process of birth She often becomes visible in the mother's form as She struggles with pain or relaxes into the deep cave of birth. In the altered state of consciousness that accompanies birth the mother expresses Her wild, primal, uncontrollable Goddess nature, which can be scary to those who have taken charge of our wellbeing. It is argued that She must be subdued at all costs for the safety of mother and child. But Hers is the ultimate power to bring life or death to both child and mother.

Thankfully, in the last twenty years or so, there have been changes in the way in which birthing is perceived, through the work of individual inspired midwives, and pioneering doctors, such as the French Dr. Frederick Leboyer, who wrote the famous *Birth without Violence*. He was one of the few doctors who recognised and honoured the power of birth, and saw the necessity for creating the right kind of birthing conditions for both mothers and babies. He advocated that birth should take place in a dimly lit room without drugs, and that the mother be encouraged to enter deeply into the primal old-brain-directed birthing state. He said that the umbilical cord should not be cut until it had stopped beating and the baby should be encouraged to breathe of its own accord without violence. As a male doctor in a male institution he had the power to change the way things were done in ways that midwives alone were unable. A large following of mothers have benefited from his ideas.

Today, although mothers are still often coerced into giving birth in sterile hospitals, rooms have become more friendly and homelike, water births are now possible and midwives are helpful to new mothers. There has also been some recognition that during birth mothers move into a primal state, governed by the innate intelligence of our bodies. Goddess wisdom is held within our bodies and can be naturally accessed during birth, if we are allowed to go there.

As we give birth we experience the power of the Goddess in our physical body, in the contractions of our womb, which reveals itself to be the strongest muscle in the human body, contracting rhythmically, squeezing the baby out along the birth canal, and out of our gaping vulvas. We experience the Goddess in our fears, in our exhaustion and in the whole journey of labour, which is unlike any other. And with each birth She brings us face to face with the open gateway to death and to life.

This is the awesome mystery of birth, that at the moment of birth we also face the possibility of death, the death of our new baby or our own death, which can and does occasionally happen. As the gate between the worlds open wide, sometimes we are invited in, drawn across the threshold onto the Isle of the Dead, leaving the world and our newborn baby behind us. Sometimes our babies come and look at us through the gateway and then retreat away back from physical life. The pain of such separations is great. Ofttimes we just look through the gate and see/feel Paradise, the place of love, eternity, joy and grace. Sometimes we can look through the gate and see darkness and are afraid.

At birth, as the gate swings open, a waft of Her divine energy comes through to us from the Otherworld with a perfume more delicate than roses. It is the best scent in the whole world, which clings to a newborn baby's skin for days and weeks. It fills the room and the home or hospital where a baby has been born. It blesses the mother and her new baby. Its blesses the father, the other family members and friends. It lingers for days and brings the Goddess's blessings to all who experience its Otherworldly vibration and perfume. As priestesses, we perform simple ceremonies of thanksgiving which honour the mother and father, and welcome the new baby into life.

But as we know, not all pregnancies come to term, not all babies are born healthy and whole. There can be many heartaches on the journey to motherhood. We may be forced to decide for many individual reasons that we cannot have a child at this particular time in life. We may decide to have a termination, an action which is traumatic for all women who have the misfortune to have to undergo this experience. I know of no woman who has gone through an abortion without pain, sadness and grief.

Miscarriage is another possibility at any time and the grief of carrying a child however small, for however many weeks or months and then losing, it is borne by many women. We are touched by a soul to whom we feel deeply connected, however briefly, and the longing for return of that touch can be devastating. Or we may carry a child to full term and then may lose that baby in a sudden infant death. It is devastating to have gone through the arduous processes of birth, to have greeted your newborn with love, only to have that baby snatched away, a few days or weeks later, as if by a vengeful, unloving Goddess. What have we done wrong, why has such a terrible thing happened to us?

As priestesses, in all these circumstances we can perform ceremonies for parents which recognise their feelings of sadness, grief and guilt, helping them to say goodbye to their beloved offspring, so they can come to terms with their loss. These are powerful and emotional ceremonies.

And not all women who want to can become pregnant. In these times when the hormones in our bodies and in our environment are out of balance it is becoming increasingly difficult for some parents to have children. Oestrogen-mimicking chemicals in the environment are affecting sperm production in men and disrupting the natural cycles in women. Larger numbers of women are finding themselves in their thirties, childless and increasingly desperate to conceive. It is one thing to choose not to have children and another to want children and not to be able to have them. Women must face the consequences of these facts, either entering demanding clinical programmes which increase their chances of conceiving, or facing the fact that conception may never happen. Both are daunting alternatives. As priestesses, we hear the pain of our sisters and help them face the future creatively with the Goddess on their side.

The Spiritual Nature of Motherhood

Birth is only the beginning of the lifelong experience that is motherhood. Nothing can ever take away that connection between mother and child, or replace the deep need we have for the love of our mothers. When my daughter was born I was barely conscious after the Caesarian section, when I first saw her and held her in my arms. That moment was among the best of my life. I looked into her eyes and I knew I had known her from the beginning of time. It was a deep and profound recognition of souls. As we recovered from the operation all I wanted was to hold her close to me. I felt a deep, fierce tigress love and learned that even though I don't believe in violence I would be willing to kill to protect her.

Three years later when I was pregnant with my son I worried what I might feel when he was born, that somehow I might have given all my mother love to my daughter. My labour with him was also long, I was 37 years old, but his birth in hospital was natural. I can still remember reaching down and the extraordinary moment when I felt the skin of his head as it crowned through my vulva. It was an indescribably wonderful feeling and soon he was in my arms. As I looked at him a whole new love for this beautiful boy opened in my heart and it was blissful. I learned that my capacity to experience and feel love is limitless.

Before we become mothers we don't usually know that there is a mother's club, a unique society of women who have all had in one form or another the awesome initiatory experience of childbirth and motherhood. Before we become mothers no-one describes to us the myriad ways in which motherhood will change our lives. It is an open secret that no-one really talks about or teaches us how to handle. We are encouraged to join the club, when we don't really know the rules or how we will cope. We are not told about the difficulties and conflicts that will arise or the amazing joy we will feel, sometimes for the first time since our own childhood.

When my daughter was about three weeks old she began to be sick. She would breast-feed and then throw up. At first I thought she was just overfeeding, but as it continued I took her to our doctor. He sent us into hospital for ten long, lonely days in which I felt very afraid for my baby and isolated from my friends. I was told her sickness was to do with the way I was feeding her. I changed to a vegan diet, thinking that what I was eating must be making her sick. She stopped being sick and we went home. After another week or so she began to be sick again and to lose weight. I could feel her slipping away from life and couldn't bear the thought that I might lose her. I empathised with all women who lose their children.

The return to hospital was very frightening as no-one knew what was happening to my baby. Through the first night I prayed and prayed, bargaining with the Goddess that if she saved my daughter I would do anything She asked. I prayed with more intensity than I had in my whole life, until the moment when I prayed that if She needed a life, then She must take my life instead of my daughter's. The pressure in my heart eased and eventually I fell asleep beside my baby. At some time in the night I woke, remembering the Biblical story of Abraham who was asked to sacrifice his son on God's altar to prove his faith. I felt outraged at the wrongness of this story, it was a perversion of natural feeling. In the Goddess's world we are never asked to sacrifice our children to show our faith.

The following morning my daughter was given a barium meal and then x-rayed. The moving pictures showed that as she drank milk her intestines filled and then twisted upon themselves cutting off the flow of milk. As the milk couldn't go down the intestines, it came up the oesophagus. We were rushed by ambulance to Bristol Children's Hospital where they performed an emergency operation. She was six weeks old. I stayed in hospital with her, sitting for hours with her on my breast with tubes coming out of every orifice. She healed really quickly, faster than the doctors predicted, and from that moment began to put on weight and grow normally.

For several years before my pregnancy I had been working as a healer and really believed in the power of healing to heal any form of disease. My great disappointment was that when I tried to heal my daughter nothing that I did made any difference to her condition. Healing simply did not work. Hers was a mechanical problem that was not affected by healing energies, except to say that perhaps her distress was alleviated by the healing energy. This failure of healing had a profound effect on me and for several years after I stopped practising healing. It had failed me where it mattered most. Years later, after my near death experience with cancer, I returned to healing with a more mature and realistic attitude. Without orthodox medicine neither I nor my daughter would be alive and I realise the true value of the gifts I have been given by allopathic medicine, which is very good at dealing with crises and the nuts and bolts of our physicality. I also know that healing has a really important role to play in bringing us back to wholeness and health, returning us to a soul-centred life.

As a mother I have found that my children are my greatest teachers on the level of my personal behaviour. They have brought me great joy and stretched me to and beyond my limits many times over. I thank them for this great journey of love and discovery. Children know exactly where to find our weak spots, how to wind us up and turn the knife in our bellies. How we behave in these moments is a mark of our soul nature and a matter of grace.

Our relationships with our children are unique for each mother. They are never static but change as our children grow and develop. At different times in the journey to adulthood we can be close or estranged, friends or enemies. The number of children we have affects the amount of attention we give any one of our children. The loss of a child through illness or accident is the greatest wound to any mother.

As priestesses, we create and perform ceremonies which celebrate motherhood in all its forms, recognising the bonds between mother and child and the stages of separation as a child grows older. These can include developing independence from mother at seven years, celebrating menarche, puberty, young adulthood and leaving home.

Glastonbury Goddess Conference

The first Glastonbury Goddess Conference was held at Lammas 1996. Now in its eleventh year the Conference is a veritable cornucopia of delight for Goddess-loving people from all over the world. It has become one of the premier Goddess events in the world today, bringing together Goddess speakers, writers, poets, artists, performers of all kinds, and women and men participants. The five day extravaganza includes many Goddess ceremonies, rituals, celebrations, talks, workshops, pilgrimage, poetry, storytelling, music, song, dance and participation for all.

Along with priestesses of other paths, Priestesses of Avalon and those in training, play a fundamental role in helping to design, create and perform the Opening and Closing Ceremonies, the daily Opening ceremonies, the Elemental Cleansing and Preparation rituals, the main conference ceremonies which are dedicated to the Maiden, Lover, Mother or Crone Goddesses, and the ceremonies that explore the Heart of the Mysteries of Avalon. Over the years, the roles played by the priestesses have evolved and become an essential part of the conference, as the focus has shifted to a more direct and overt exploration of the Mysteries of Avalon. The Goddess Conference would not be the amazing experience that it is without the dedicated service of the Priestesses of Avalon and I publicly thank all those wonderful women and men who have given their time, energy and talents to serving the Goddess and Her people through this event.

A wonderful consequence of the Glastonbury event is that priestesses who live in other countries have taken the idea and are creating Goddess Conference in their own lands, including the Netherlands, where the first Goddess Conference was held in 2005, and Hungary where the first Goddess Conference will be held in 2006

Between Lammas and Mabon

With the bounty of Lammas the harvest begins in fields, allotments and gardens. Apples swell and ripen in the orchards of Avalon, trees growing heavy with the weight of fruit. The grain in the fields is cut and stalks are burned off or ploughed under to fertilise the earth through the winter months. Days begin to shorten as we move towards autumn equinox, with its twelve hours each of light and darkness. The sun begins to visibly lower in the sky, although September can still bring the gorgeous, clear, sunny days of an Indian summer. Birds who have visited Brigit's Isles for the summer begin to gather in flocks, eating large amounts of food to sustain them on their coming migrations south, which begin in these months. The trees are still green, but leaves are beginning to curl at the edges. The grass turns brown and golden. The sap slowly begins to sink in flowers and trees in preparation for the autumn and the turning inwards. Colder rains begin to fall, driven in from the southwest on strong winds.

Make an altar at home to Nolava *the* Lammas Mother, *to* Ker *the* Grain Goddess, *to* Madron, *Mother of the lineage of* Avallach, *to* Mistress Glitonea *of the* Morgens. *Decorate it with the fruits of* Her *bounty - grains, corn, fruits, flowers.*

Every day light a candle and burn incense to the Mother Goddess *on your altar. Give thanks and celebrate* Her *gifts. Sing and pray to the* Goddess *for help, guidance, in gratitude, for others in need, for healing for yourself and others, for vision, etc.* Once *a week recreate your altar.*

Every day give thanks to your human mother for giving birth to you and to the Mother Goddess *for all the beauty and abundance* She *pours into your life. Practice gratitude.*

Every day write down and/or draw feelings, dreams, thoughts, intuitions and visions in your diary, i.e. what's going on for you.

At *the new moon walk in the grain fields and in the orchards where* Her *fruits are ripening. Commune with the* Great Mother.

At *the full moon share the* Practice *of* Gratitude *with your family and friends.*

At *least once, if not more, visit a sacred site or landscape associated with the* Mother Goddess.

Prepare *for your* Dedication Ceremony. *Are you ready to dedicate your life to the* Goddess *and* Her *ways?* What *will this mean for you in your life?* What *are you are taking on? If you are not ready to surrender to* Her, *can you recognise this and step back? Can you bring yourself through your fear to the place of complete surrender?* What *will be* Her *rewards?*

Complete your personal vow to the Goddess *to be made at your* Dedication Ceremony *at the autumn equinox.*

Complete the costume which you wish to wear at your Dedication Ceremony *to the* Goddess, *ready for the colder nights of* Mabon *and the outdoor ceremony, with clothing, mask, headdress, chalice and wand.*

Before the Autumn Equinox *when you journey to* Avalon *for your dedication ceremony, prepare yourself in a ritual manner, cleansing your body, emotions and mind by air, fire, water and earth.* Come *with an open heart, ready to receive* Her *blessing.*

The Harvest
Mabon Festival of the Mother of Earth

Mabon or Autumn Equinox is the festival of the Mother of Earth falling around 21st September. It is the season when we celebrate the Harvest of our Earth Mother's fertile nature, when grains are harvested, fruits and nuts are picked from bushes and trees and vegetables lifted from the ground before the first frosts arrive. All can be stored so that we can have food throughout the winter months when little grows. We celebrate Nolava of the Earth of Avalon and Moronoe, Morgen of Earth, who brings the autumn winds. We honour Brigantia, Lady of the Land that is Brigit's Isles. We honour Banbha, Lady of the Land from before the Flood. We honour Ertha, our Mother Earth and Gaia, who is Goddess of the planetary body of the Earth. The Autumn Equinox, like the Spring Equinox, is a balance point in the year when for a brief spell there are days of equal light and darkness, before we begin moving towards the darker days of winter.

In Brigit's Isles days can still be warm in September, but by the autumn equinox nights can be chilly. Mabon signals the end of summer and beginning of autumn which comes to fullest expression at Samhain in this warmer Summerland. The life that is in the plants begins to die back into the earth. The animals fatten themselves on the fruits of the harvest, filling their bellies in preparation for the coming winter months when food will be scarcer and many will hibernate in safe dens and holes in the ground. The wild animals are often nocturnal creatures and their fur coats begin to thicken as the temperature of the air and the land cools. At equinox the Lady of the Lake of Mists begins to wreath Her misty hair around tree and stone, rising from the damp meadowlands surrounding the Isle of Avalon. As the sun sets in the west, Her tresses hang close to the earth, shrouding the sacred land in white veils until dawn when the mists clear as the warmth that is still in the sun's rays evaporates the moisture.

At Mabon we honour Nolava of Earth and the harvest of Her nature. We celebrate the land that we live on, the beautiful Isle of Avalon and the whole of Brigit's Isles. We ground all that we have learned over the previous eleven moons in a special Ceremony of Dedication to the Goddess. Our costumes complete, we see ourselves as the priestesses we aspire to be.

Honouring Nolava of Earth

Nolava is the Earth beneath our feet, the solid material world which we all inhabit for a span of time. She is the soil and the rocks, the hills and the valleys that make up the sacred landscape of Glastonbury and the Otherworldly Paradise of Avalon. We experience Her by walking on Her earth, by lying on Her ground, by listening to Her loving heart beating deep in the Earth of Avalon.

Glastonbury is a place of special energetic intensity and I would say that, for transformation to occur in our lives, all that we really need to do is to walk Her land, Her earthly body, the slopes of Her Tor, Chalice Hill, Wearyall Hill, Windmill Hill and Stonedown. All we need for healing to begin is to spend time sitting or lying upon Her ground, Her holyeste earth, allowing Her energy to percolate through every pore of our bodies. All the spiritual workshops that are available here in Glastonbury are as nothing compared to the wonder of spending time out on Her sacred land of Avalon and allowing Her energies to work their magic on our souls.

In Glastonbury we find the hidden pathways into Avalon by becoming intimate with Her natural landscape, by walking on the hills and in the valleys that make up the holy island, by noticing the shapes of Her body as Mother, Lover, Maid and Crone, by exploring Her curves and crannies, Her high places and Her depths, Her springs and wells, by lying on Her body and feeling the pulse of Her heartbeat within the land. In visions we journey into Avalon by following physical pathways which have become familiar to us as part of our regular walking, opening our consciousness to the inner landscape that lies beyond form.

Many would-be Priestesses of Avalon live in places other than Glastonbury, in Brigit's Isles and in the rest of the world. Travelling regularly to Glastonbury is a major part of the process of learning to become a Priestess of Avalon. It is important for students to spend time becoming familiar with the natural landscape here, so that when you return home you can explore the landscape in imagination and so journey in consciousness into Avalon from wherever you live.

Whenever you can, make the effort to walk Glastonbury*'s sacred landscape. Observe* Her *nature, the details of the shapes and forms of* Her *body. When you return home, in your meditations visualise yourself walking the landscape in detail.*

As Lady of Earth Nolava teaches us how to bring the new into manifestation in the world. She shows us how to bring ideas into form, anchoring our dreams into the material world, so that they become reality rather than remaining as flotsam in the mind. In the turning of the wheel of the year we see that ideas are received as inspiration in the north. They move through the fire of creativity in the east, are fuelled by desire in the south and brought into manifestation in the west.

Honouring Moronoe, *Morgen of* Earth

I *am* Moronoe *of* Avalon, Morgen Mother *of the* Earth.
Once more the human world calls for our attention.
After aeons of forgetting, there are stirrings along the fibres of memory.
Now comes the hour of planetary transformation.

In me all acts and beings find their grounding.
All physical substances, matters and energies return to me,
Mother, Mater, *matter, material.*
I *am She who stands at the* Earthly Gateway,
Witnessing your works as they unfold towards their manifestation.
Great Protectress, I *watch over you all, especially you who honour me.*
Queen *of* Autumn, *my blessings of the harvest* I *shower upon you who love me well.*

And yet my pain is great
As I *return to see the devastation of so many of my sacred places.*
My earth creatures, fox, badger, vole and mole tell me my earth is wounded,
And I *hear* Her *weeping.*

I *am returning to heal and make good my earth.*
I *am returning to you who love me through you who call me.*
I *am coming through the earthshaking groundbreaking of my earth dragons*
Who are my destroyers,

And through my elemental earth gnomes and their deep knowing.

Ground your dreams in me, Moronoe,
Ancient ground preserver and keeper of all your memories.
From time immemorial, the stories of all your lives are written in me,
Stored in rocks and crystals, sealed in stones and bones
In sacred places where your ancestors walked and made their prayers for you.
So much energy and magic lays waiting in my deep earth store for you.
Through my crystals I can see you in your deepest aspect, and you can speak to me.
I see your souls reaching out to me, and I give you my blessing.
I bring you the intuitive power to know your essential beauty nature,
That you may walk my earth in peace.
Blessed Be.

by Sally Pullinger

Moronoe is the Morgen of Earth. At harvest time Her dress is orange and brown, the colours of autumn. As She moves through woodland and grove Her touch turns the leaves from green to orange, red and gold, a final bright glow before the grey days of winter. Like Her sister Cliton who rules the Spring Equinox She carries the stillness of the equipoint that is the Autumn Equinox. In the cycle of the moon She is the waning moon, moving us towards darkness and the inner worlds.

Moronoe is imaged as a mature woman in Her fifties, Lady of the Orchards of Avalon, where at this time of year apples are ripening in abundance, glowing red and gold against the brown branches of the trees, ready to be harvested. In the hedgerows blackberries are found aplenty, ready for eating in apple and blackberry pies, rich in colour and vitamins. Moronoe is also Beech Woman and beautiful examples of Her offspring, beech and copper beech trees, can be found all over the island, and especially in Bushey Combe and the Abbey grounds. She is strong and tall, elegant and full of virtue.

As weather Moronoe is the Wind that blows in from the Atlantic Ocean, especially at this time of year, as the Indian summer fades away and the air cools. Now the winds turn from the southwest to the north, bringing colder air that cools the land and its inhabitants. Moronoe blows at almost any time of the year bringing warm and cool air, but at autumn equinox She becomes noticeable as Her winds drive in cloud-bearing rains and the tails of hurricanes born far away in the Caribbean.

The blackbird with its beautiful song belongs to Moronoe. She comes into our gardens and taps on the earth pretending to be the rain, searching for earthworms to eat. The creatures of the earth who live on and in the earth of Avalon belong to Moronoe, the fox with its orange brown coat slipping quietly through hedges at dawn and at dusk, the mole burrowing its way through the earth, and the badger, who now moves its sets to the higher ground of the island as autumn rains threaten the low-lying summer sets. The gnomes of the earth too belong to Moronoe, hoarding Her treasures in caverns beneath the earth. Here Her crystals form in the darkness, lying hidden and undisturbed for millennia. Her earth dragon sleeps the sleep of the just in Avalon. The last time She was disturbed was in 1275, when the earth shook and St Michael's Tower on top of the Tor fell down. Later it was rebuilt of stronger stone. Perhaps in these changing times She will rouse Herself once again.

As Morgen of Earth Moronoe is the protectress of the Land of Avalon. She expresses Her distress at the ways in which human beings are abusing the bounty of the earth. She asks us to wake up to what we are doing to the Earth, not only in Avalon, but all over the world.

As equinox approaches walk the Isle of Avalon at dawn and at dusk when the land glows with a golden intensity from the rising and setting sun. Feel Her earth beneath you. Plant your feet solidly upon Her body. From your heart send threads of energy down through your body, legs and feet into the earth, like the roots of a great beech tree. Feel yourself rooted and grounded in Nolava's earthy body.

Celebrating the Harvest Mother

At Mabon we celebrate the Harvest Mother and the fruits of Her bountiful nature. In orchards and gardens we begin to pick the first apples and pears from the trees, we harvest the remaining vegetables before the first frosts come and gather fruits and nuts from bush and tree. The fields of grain are all harvested in and the last sheaf of wheat or barley is decorated as Harvest May. She is hung up in the kitchen through the autumn and winter, and in spring Her seeds are scattered ceremonially by the women of the house onto the earth, to ensure a good harvest in the coming year.

With family, friends and strangers we hold Harvest Suppers in which we lay out the abundance of the Harvest Mother on altars and dining tables. We express our gratitude for the bounty of Her earth, baking special loaves of bread, formed into the shapes of Her body and decorated with Her symbols. We share with each other the wide variety of produce that comes from Her earthly body.

At Mabon create a harvest supper for your friends and family, laying our the bounty of Her nature for all to see and celebrate. Make special breads and nourishing dishes. Invite strangers to share Her table with you.

Honouring the Mother of Matter

The Mother of Earth is Mother of all Matter. She is Mater, Materia, the Matrix - Mother of all forms. Earth or matter is the most dense of the five elements. It is the very substance out of which all things make their appearance in the universe. It comprises the primary material particles that make up the atoms and molecules, that form into the solid and gaseous elements that make up our world - carbon, iron, copper, sulphur, hydrogen, oxygen, calcium, sodium, aluminium, etc., as well as the complex organic molecules of DNA that allow life to emerge and evolve. The miracle is that when we investigate the inner nature of each atom, we find that they consist mostly of space and energy with only tiny amounts of matter at their core.

The Mother of Earth is Creatrix of this Mystery by which we can see, hear, touch, taste, smell and sense a three dimensional world, which is all but immaterial in its essential nature. This said, earth is one of the most enduring of the natural elements found within Her nature. As Einstein discovered, e=mc2, where e = energy, m = matter and c = speed of light. Matter is constant, it does not ever disappear, but when subjected to heat, pressure or collisions, is converted into other forms with the release of energy and light, as demonstrated daily in our Sun Mother's body.

Millennia ago, planet Earth was formed as hot gases exploding from Her Void condensed and cooled into matter. Flung outwards, it is proposed, from a massive central explosion within the fabric of time and space, the planetary bodies in our solar system travelled outwards and still travel at great speed through space. Our evolution as spiritual human beings takes place on the surface of the earth as it is slowly cooling from the outside in, and continues to travel through the universe at speed. Our human experience is intimately connected to the evolution of the material bodies of both our Earth and Sun Mothers.

Within a natural human life span we experience the earth as ageless and continuous. Without human interference the mountains, hills and valleys that make up Her planetary body endure for centuries, changing slowly with the movements of the tectonic plates, and the effects of heat and cold, wind and water. Human activity creates fields and farmland, builds dams, redirects rivers, digs mines and moves mountains, yet still the earth remains as the matter which allows us to live.

Through Her earthly body the Mother of Earth demonstrates to us the values of continuity, of perseverance and endurance, especially when the going gets tough. She also demonstrates the spaciousness which is held within all material forms, where energy is constantly moving, where healing is possible within Her matrix .

Honouring Ertha, our Earth Mother

The Earth is our Mother, we must take care of Her.........

The lines of the song remind us to honour and care for our Mother who is the Earth, whose body is this beautiful planet that we live on and the very ground upon which we walk. We are intimately attached to Her by the pull of the invisible force of Her immense gravity, Her huge weight, upon our slight physical bodies. She is dense and solid on Her outer surfaces, yet filled with fire and energy at Her core. Her earthy body is made of solid rock laid down over unimaginable aeons of time, of hard and soft stones, of granite, sandstone, limestone, shale, chalk and clay, of sand and sediments dredged up from the bottom of oceans and solidified through time, becoming earth, ground, soil and matter.

As human souls we incarnate into physical form by Her grace, using the substances of Her earth, Her natural elements of earth, water, fire and air, to create our human bodies. We dwell for a time upon the surface of Her body, sustaining our material forms by eating the fruits of Her body, drinking Her waters, warming ourselves by Her fires and breathing Her air. At death the materials which have made up our physical bodies return to Her earthly body, as our spirits return to Her. We do not exist without Her and this connection between us is intrinsic to our human experience. We can never be separated from Her as we are part of Her. In the modern world we have almost completely forgotten this reality, this first basic rule of incarnation, that we are made from Her, that we depend on Her, and what happens to Her directly affects us.

The desire to control and tame Mother Earth, to exploit the substances of Her body for gain, is a primary drive within all patriarchal cultures. The earth which is Her body is seen simply as a resource to be mined, bulldozed and poisoned for profit and the acquisition of Her wealth. Her Earth which is freely given to us as a place for us all to enjoy life, has been divided up and is now owned by relatively few wealthy people.

The desire to own territory began during the neolithic era, when nomadic peoples first settled on the land in family and tribal groups and claimed the places that they cared for as home. These tribes were indigenous to the land, living on their ancestral grounds in harmony with the earth and Mother Nature. Burial mounds were built on the borders of land occupied by different family groupings. In feudal times from the Norman Conquest in 1066CE, the King took ownership of all the land, giving large tracts to favoured princes and leaders, although some common land still existed where the people could graze their animals. The ownership of land by fewer and fewer people, led to the development of a strongly hierarchical and patriarchal society with a landowning aristocracy at the top and the majority of the landless poor or commoners, at the bottom. This culminated in the 18th century when the Enclosure Acts resulted in land being fenced off, declared private and made inaccessible to the masses. This territorial hierarchy still remains firmly in place today, although the poor are less poor and more people can buy their own homes, their own piece of the earth. The two tier Houses of Parliament is still made up of the House of Lords and the House of Commons. All land is owned by someone and common lands are few and far between, most being owned in trust by the nation as national parks.

In the world the great scourge of the last millennium was the colonisation by Empire builders - British, Spanish, Portuguese and French, of other people's lands through aggressive invasions. These resulted in the destruction of many earth-based indigenous cultures and peoples through violence, war and disease. Given many different disguises the majority of today's wars are still primarily fought over the ownership of Ertha's land and the rights to the minerals, oil and gas that lie beneath Her surfaces. This desire for control over the vast forces of Her planetary body is a great hubris on the part of patriarchal societies. It arises from man's desire to be recognised as all-powerful, able to challenge and overcome the forces of Her nature, in fact, to be Godlike, made in the image of God Himself. In this quest for power man has sought to control and overwhelm women and other men with whom they share the planet. Man has challenged the Goddess, whom all women represent and has been successful in removing Her from the common consciousness, so that we do not know who She is and do not honour Her in our societies.

The consequences of the thoughtless exploitation of Her resources are far reaching and potentially devastating to humankind. All around we are slowly becoming aware of the consequences of our actions, with rising emissions of carbon dioxide, CFCs, HFCs and other noxious gases into the atmosphere, the pollution of soil, rivers and oceans, the extinction of animal and plant species, as well as the effects of global warming, melting ice shelves, rising sea levels and changes in weather patterns. Politicians continue to devise multi-stranded strategies to avoid the consequences of our behaviour and fail to follow through with actions that will reverse the coming adverse earth changes that their own science predicts.

There do remain examples of how to live life in harmony with our Mother Earth. Throughout the world there are still pockets of indigenous peoples who strive to live lives which are directly connected to the cycles and seasons of Mother Earth. Where native peoples have been decimated by poverty, disease and alcohol intolerance, there are now moves to remember and reclaim the old knowledge of Her nature and the land. In North and South America, in Africa, Australia, Asia and in Europe, indigenous peoples are gathering once again and connecting with each other in order to salvage the earth wisdom that has been almost completely lost. This book is an example of such reclaiming within our own indigenous British culture.

However, in our first world cultures we are all inextricably caught up with the drives of patriarchal society and each person has to find their own path back to a true relationship to the Goddess and Her beautiful planet, as we drive our fuel-hungry cars, use our washing machines, watch our televisions, and work with our computers, all of which are dependent on the exploitation of the resources of Her body. In today's world we are all part of the problem and the solutions are not easy to find.

We need to return to an appreciation of Ertha, our Mother Earth, who is the ground of our being. We need to appreciate the soil in which plants grow, the rich red, black, white and yellow earth that sustains our life.

Cleansing and Decorating with Earth

Just as we can cleanse our bodies with air, fire and water we can also cleanse our bodies with earth, smearing on wet mud packs filled with minerals that draw toxins out from our skin as they dry. We also decorate our bodies using coloured clays and pigments that we collect from special places on the Mother's body. In ancient times coloured ochres were frequently used to decorate Goddess carvings on stone and bone and tiny amounts can still be seen today, dating from tens of thousands of year ago. Red ochre in particular, symbolises the Mother's life blood and is used for decoration, for anointing and marking the human body and sculptures. Many Goddess artists prefer to work with natural earth pigments in their paintings and collages.

Crystals

Crystals form in the darkness of the Mother's body, their beauty revealed only by light. They have many inspirational and healing qualities. In our age their unique properties have catalysed the development of radios, televisions and computers and revolutionised communication between all human beings on the planet. They have permitted us to know that we are one family living on one planet. Growing in the darkness deep within the earth, symbolically they represent the gems that lie hidden within our own Shadow selves, waiting to be brought to the surface and revealed in the light of consciousness.

In the last forty years thousands of tons of crystals have been removed from the body of the earth for our pleasure and enjoyment. There are many who say that we are too greedy and should stop exploiting our Mother's body for gain. Others claim they are a healing gift from Her revealed especially at this time. Each person must make their own choice as to whether they buy and use crystals.

Honouring Gaia

Gaia is the Greek name for the Earth Mother, who has become more universally recognised since Her name was reclaimed by scientist James Lovelock, to mean the sum total of all the self-regulating energetic and physical systems that hold in balance the material, aqueous, fiery, airy and spatial realms of the planet. Gaia encompasses the planetary ecosystem and includes all the relationships within and between the different queendoms in nature - mineral, plant, animal, human and spiritual, although the latter is not necessarily recognised by science. It is this balance between all the interconnected ecological systems of Her nature which has provided the ideal conditions for life, and human life in particular, to evolve on this planet.

For the last two hundred years the population of the world has been increasing exponentially with a commensurate exploitation of planetary resources. These factors alongside our inability to deal with the waste products of our industrialised societies means that for the first time human beings are beginning to affect Gaia's ecological balance. In the past Her planetary body has followed its own cycles of cold ice ages and warmer interludes, which have allowed a huge diversity of plant and animal forms to evolve. In a few short decades human activity is causing the destruction of ecosystems which have taken thousands of years to evolve. By our actions we are destroying the earth which sustains our life.

Yet when we are long gone She will remain and Her self-regulating systems will bring Her world back into a new balance. For She is in charge and we must never forget this fact, that we are born from Her body, and live our lives within the cycles and seasons of Her nature.

Honouring Brigantia, Lady of the Land

Brigantia was originally a pastoral Goddess of the pre-Roman British peoples. She is Goddess of Sovereignty whose name means *High One*. She is associated with northern Britain where a large slice of land that is now Yorkshire and the surrounding counties from Lincolnshire to Cheshire to Northumberland and sometimes lowland Scotland, was once called Brigantia. Ancient Goddess Brigantia was directly connected to ancient Bride, Brid and Brigid and was frequently associated with flocks of cattle, water, fertility, healing and victory. She was the tutelary Mother Goddess of a dark-skinned and black-haired pre-Keltic people called the Brigantes, who lived in northern Britain probably from the bronze age. These people were also found in Portugal and Austria. When the Romans invaded in the first century CE they found a vast Brigantine tribal federation organised under Queen Cartimandua (circa 43 to 70 AD), who according to the Roman historian Tacitus was the living symbol of Brigantia. Cartimandua's husbands came to rule as kings, by marrying this living embodiment of the Goddess.

Goddess Brigantia was recorded by the Romans and Her most definitive monument, where She is depicted with the attributes of Minerva, was found in a carved stone relief on the Antonine Wall at Birrens in Dumfriesshire. There is also dedication to Her at Irthington near Carlisle and an invocation to Her on an altar as Caelestis Brigantia, at Corbridge in Northumberland. Guy Ragland Philips published a book called *Brigantia* (Book Club Associates, 1976), exploring Her mysteries.

Today we recognise Her as Goddess of the Land of Brigit's Isles. We can see Her form in the shape of the whole of Brigit's Isles where She appears as an Old Woman, similar in shape to the Old Crone who rides on the back of the Swan in Avalon. Each time we walk upon Her land we remember and honour Her.

Honouring Banbha

Once upon a time there were three Queens, a triple Goddess, who owned Ireland. Their names were Eriu, Fodhla and Banbha. The island of Eire takes its name from Eriu and in ancient times Eire was known as the Land of Women. Eriu represents the Maiden aspect of the Goddess, Fodhla the Mother and Banbha is the Crone. Banbha was known as Goddess of the Land of Women. She reminds us of the ancient times when the land belonged to the Goddess and to women, when women had power and were sovereign. She is also called the Goddess of the Land from before the Flood, meaning that She is very, very old, older than anyone can remember.

Since all the land belongs to the Goddess and has from the beginning of time, we honour Banbha as we remember just how old the land is. We live and walk upon the land's surface, but its shapes, depth and form belong to Her, changing only slowly through the aeons.

Celebrating the Land We Live Upon

Not everyone who wants to become a Priestess of Avalon will be fortunate enough or will want to, live in the small country town of Glastonbury in England, although it will always resonate as a place called home. You may live in America or Argentina, Holland or Sweden. Avalon is a place of the heart, of an expanded consciousness, an altered awareness and we can connect to Avalon from wherever we live. One of the primary routes into Avalon is through a knowledge of the land on which we live. This is true in Glastonbury and it is true elsewhere on the planet.

The practice of walking the land and becoming familiar with it can be carried out wherever we live, and especially where some natural landscape still remains. In other country places we can seek out the forms of Her earthly body as She lies in and beneath the earth. We can explore the topographical maps of Her landscape, we can find Her breasts and hips, walk on Her head and hair, Her thighs and legs, in Her intimate clefts. We can see Her in Her totem forms as animal or bird, as mare or bear, hare or cat

We can also search for Her in cities and towns, as She lies beneath the buildings and roads where the forms of Her body are hidden beneath layers of concrete. She is there waiting to be recognised in the forms of the land, for She is everywhere and in all places. We seek Her in ancient place names, in local legends and folklore, in hidden hills and underground rivers, in gardens and parks. We walk, sit and lie on the earth wherever we can find Her and feel the beat of Her heart. We honour Her in every step we take.

When we have found and engaged with the land which we move through every day, as in Glastonbury, we use our familiarity with the landscape as a pathway into Avalon. In vision we follow the forms of Her body to journey across the threshold of consciousness into Her Otherworld.

What Makes a Place Sacred?

All of Her earth is sacred yet some places feel more sacred than others. Some landscapes have an aesthetic harmony which we experience as being beautiful and naturally sacred. To see them, to walk in them, to sit in them, heals us of our pain and helps make us feel whole again. Some places like the Summerland which stretches from Avalon to the sea, are naturally spacious with wide skies and far horizons. Others such as the mountains and valleys of Wales and Scotland, or the high moorlands of Derbyshire, Northumberland and Dartmoor are wild and dramatic, and allow us to release our own inner wildness and authentic nature. Power places on the Dragon Line, such as Glastonbury or Avebury, have a special energy or resonance which is felt by everyone who enters into their aura, whether they have any beliefs about the place or not. For some that energy is sacred and holy while for others it is felt as uncomfortable and even threatening.

Some human-made places, sculptured landscapes, ancient Goddess sites, temples and churches have an aura of sacredness that is connected to both the ground on which they are built, to the forms of the buildings themselves and to the activities which take place within them. Certain shapes and proportions are experienced as being more harmonious and elevating than others. They inspire the soul. However many human-made places are drab, cold, ugly, impersonal and inhuman. What is it that makes particular places feel more sacred than others?

Paulo Coehlo, the magical Brazilian novelist, in his wonderful book *The Valkeries: An Encounter with Angels* (Thorsons), gives an idea of what can make a place sacred that appeals to me. After a particular spiritual encounter which Paulo has out in the desert, Gene his young teacher says,

> *"In this place the energy of the soul of the world was felt.....And it will be felt here forever.* It is *a place of power."*

The idea is that as well as there being places which feel naturally sacred, places can also be made sacred through the spiritual experiences of individual human beings, as we connect to the greater spiritual realities in a particular physical location. When any person has an initiatory or revelatory, immanent or transcendent experience of the divine in a particular spot on the planet, such that their soul's energy is transformed, that energetic change will affect the surroundings where it occurs. Anyone arriving at that spot in the future will feel the reverberations of that spiritual event and experience the place as sacred themselves. This in turn may have an initiatory effect on the newly arrived person, who in turn is potentiated to have a spiritually expansive experience in that spot too, so multiplying the impact and creating more sacredness. Places where many people have spiritual experiences, such as Glastonbury Avalon, and other ancient sacred sites and ancestral grounds continually replenish the field of sacredness as more people arrive and have spiritual experiences.

The beauty of this idea is that we are encouraged to continue on our individual spiritual journeys in the knowledge that our personal quest for greater spiritual awareness will also have a beneficial effect upon the places we inhabit and visit. In years to come spiritual seekers will be able to feel the effects of our personal striving for wisdom in the places where we live, pray and receive Her blessings, and be encouraged on their own journeys.

The Balance Point of the Autumn Equinox

Like the Spring Equinox, Mabon is a second balance point of the year when there are equal hours of light and darkness. We celebrate this moment by creating rituals which again will bring the right and left sides of our bodies and brains, of spirit and matter, into balance and wholeness. In the autumn we can create either one of two forms of double spiral, to walk in ceremony. In the first example the two spirals are separated forming a wonderful image of the Goddess's breasts or eyes looking at us. In the second example the two spirals are intertwined and continuous. You may want to practice generating these symbols with pen and paper first, but I will describe the process for making the large image.

The materials and preparation instructions are the same as for the Spring Equinox rituals. We begin by cleansing and blessing with incense and offerings, the space where we are going to create our double spiral. We measure its boundaries, knowing that for the twin-centred spiral, the length of the space will be more than twice its width. For this double spiral we begin in the centre of left hand spiral and lay our first pattern, using string, masking tape or flour, so that we can make mistakes and correct them as necessary, replacing them later with something more permanent if we wish. Whatever the line is made from we spiral out from the centre in a clockwise or sunwise direction laying tape or flour behind us. In the illustration below the spiral is shown as white flour against a background or pecked out rock.

The Goddess's Double Spiral Eyes

Foosiya Miller

We spiral outwards leaving enough space between the lines for people to walk easily between them and if possible to pass each other, until we reach the borders of our sacred space. The line then crosses through the middle of the space to the right hand side and we continue our trail of flour or tape beside the outer borders of the space. We begin to spiral inwards in an anticlockwise or widdershins direction. We move closer and closer to the centre, again leaving enough space between the lines for people to walk easily and if possible to pass each other. Left and right spirals should have the same number of turns.

The interesting thing with this pattern is that whichever centre we begin with, the left or right, moving in a sunwise direction, the second spiral will be created by moving widdershins or anticlockwise. This quality helps create the experience of balance. When the double spiral is complete we bless the space and make prayers for balance, before we begin walking.

We can start anywhere on the outer circuit, but since our aim is to bring balance, we usually begin in the centre between the left and right spirals. We walk beside the line, keeping it always on the same side of us and not crossing over it at any point. In walking this pattern we find that whichever direction we walk in to begin with, we will move into the spiral in an anticlockwise direction. Esoterically, moving in a widdershins direction is connected with moving inwards into an inner experience. Thus as we move into the centre of the spiral we are moving into the centre of ourselves. The opposite effects can be created by drawing the first spiral in an anticlockwise direction.

When we reach the centre of each eye we stop and take stock of where we are, contemplating ourselves in the centre. Then we turn around the end of the line and begin to walk sunwise out of the spiral, continuing to follow the thread around its outer boundaries. As we walk around the outer edge we find that we are now walking on the other side of the thread, through the central space between the two spirals, once again moving widdershins into the second spiral. In the centre we stop again and following the line change directions and move sunwise back out from the centre.

Walking the double spiral can be a potent and powerful experience of balancing the inner and outer, the left and the right, the feminine and masculine polarities.

Foosiya Miller

The second form of double spiral is one where the two spirals are intertwined in a neat, simple form. We initially lay tape on the floor or flour on the ground, moving in a spiral from the boundaries of our sacred space into the centre, leaving a wide space between each turn of the spiral.

When we reach the centre of the spiral we leave a gap, and reversing directions we lay a second spiral moving outwards between the turns of the first spiral. We end the second spiral on the opposite side to where we started our inward journey. We now have a circular shaped spiral which can be entered from either side, moving sunwise or widdershins. We walk from the edge into the centre, where again we pause before walking out in the opposite direction to the one we began with. Repeating this movement again brings us into balance and harmony.

The Art of Manifestation

Manifestation is one of many daily miracles of life on our planet. We, who are invisible spirits become visible through the medium of the natural elements of the earth, through air, fire, water and most importantly, the matter of our world. Without the amazing nature of the Goddess's natural world we would not come into form, we would not have the vast range of experiences and opportunities for development in consciousness, that are provided here in the physical world. Yet many of us know little about how manifestation occurs and importantly how to manifest our own personal dreams.

Essentially everything in manifestation begins as idea in some being's consciousness. Idea may arise from within human consciousness, the individual or the collective, from discarnate beings or from divine consciousness, from the Goddess Herself. Idea is of itself original, but builds on preexisting concepts and forms in an evolutionary flow. For human beings, no matter where idea originates it is received as intuition, as a knowing within, which travels from the soul via the rainbow bridge or antaskarana, and anchors into our thoughts and feelings, into brain and body awareness. Fuelled by desire a thoughtform is created, which is then brought into manifestation through the focused attention of the individual or individuals, who hold that focus for as long as is necessary for the idea to come into form.

One of the interesting things about this theory of manifestation is that because our consciousness is collective, more than one person may receive the same idea at the same time. Not everyone is then capable of bringing that idea into form, but this will sometimes occur, which is why there are often cases of, say, two scientists coming up with the same new theory at the same time in different locations, each accusing the other of theft, when no such activity has taken place. There is also the phenomenon of certain ideas, fields of study, fashion itself, becoming fashionable for a time as a large group of people turn their attention to a particular idea, image or style.

Over the years I have been instrumental in a small way in manifesting several new spiritual ideas and organisations and I share with you here my knowledge of the art of manifestation. This is not to claim that this is the only way to bring things into form, because there are obviously those who are much more skilled than I, such as the people who create roads, rockets and bombs, governments and life-saving charities. I share with you the knowledge that I have.

In my own experience I naturally receive ideas easily. They come as small ideas, as visions or glimpses of future events, places and people, that I have not yet seen in actuality. They come at any time of the day or night and in any situation. This was not always the case when I was younger, but once I found my spiritual direction in life, ideas flowed and continue to flow. I can be walking down the street, be in the middle of a conversation or be writing a book, and a new idea will pop into my mind like a soap bubble popping in the air, releasing its contents into my mind. My skill, which has developed through experience, is that I listen to these often tiny ideas, which others might dismiss as fantastical or too small to bother with, and I take notice of them. They carry an energy of excitement that is both inspiring and scary. It is the scary energy which tells me that they are important and to be followed through, rather than ignored. In some ways if they are not exciting, then I can ignore them.

I often receive information in the liminal state as I am waking up in the morning and I bring ideas from the dream state into my conscious waking mind. It is a time when the Goddess speaks to me and I hear Her voice. It is also a time when I hold undeveloped ideas in my mind and allow them to move in the flow of the energy of that in-between state, between the astral and the etheric, to develop into whatever they might want to become. As I allow what may be a big idea from the Goddess, say to create a new Priestess of Avalon training or the first Goddess Conference in Brigit's Isles, to anchor in my brain, I will usually receive one or two instructions as well, coming I believe, from the Lady Herself. It can be to talk to a particular person that day, to write a letter to this person, to telephone that person, to fix a date for a future event, to write a brochure, to book a hall, or to write a particular paragraph in a new book. It is always accompanied by the instruction, "Do *this today*", great for a natural procrastinator. These instructions are most usually small steps on the road to manifestation.

Form always take time to manifest. Nothing emerges from the Void fully formed. A baby has spent nine months in her mother's womb and takes 20+ years to come to maturity. A great oak tree begins as an acorn. A building begins as a sketch on a piece of paper and takes months or years to be erected. A new spirituality begins from a few individuals' love for the Goddess, which in the future may become a world movement. Everything comes into manifestation through small steps and this is true for all that we wish to create. All we are asked to do is put one foot steadily in front of the other and occasionally make bigger jumps, but nothing that is impossible.

Having heard the instructions fear quite often enters in, expressed as a lack of self confidence - "I *can't do that, I'm not capable enough, strong enough, worthy enough, etc.* I *can't possibly just ring that person up and ask them that*! " Fear appears in the guise of prevarication - "*I'll do it tomorrow, I'm busy today, I don't have time*", anything to put off having to do something. This is where experience enters in. When we follow the pattern of receiving and following inspiration we find that it works, things begin to happen in our lives, our creativity begins to move in ways that make us feel good. Life becomes easier. Once we have experienced the ease of living by following intuition, it cuts out a lot of wasted time we would have spent worrying about which direction to take in life, whether something will work or not. We follow the flow of our intuition, of the Goddess's instructions to us, and life gets better. We receive almost instant confirmation that our intuition is true for us and so come to trust ourselves and Her more.

In all the projects I am involved with my principal desire is to bring the Goddess back into my own and the world's consciousness. My emotional or desire energy therefore fuels the forms that I am trying to create and fills and expands the thoughtforms or manifesting ideas, with energy. Many projects shrivel and die away at this point because we do not want them to happen enough, so it is important to hold a strong desire energy. However, in a strange contradiction we must also not be too attached to the outcomes of our desires, to the specific forms in which they should appear in the world. Goddess may be planning different outcomes to the ones we envisage.

I consistently focus my attention on the project in hand, holding the thoughtform steady so that it can fill with creative desire energy and grow. Practical steps must then be taken on a daily basis to bring the thoughtform into manifestation.

In this process of manifestation serendipity and the Goddess's grace also enter in. We accidentally meet someone who may become important to the success of our project, we receive information out of the blue from an unsolicited source, we have many experiences of synchronicity, being in the right place at the right time for our projects to unfold. All these experiences can be signs that we are on the right track. However I would sound a word of caution, especially here on the Otherworldly Isle of Avalon, which, as a home of the Mother Goddess and a place of transformation, is a uniquely tricky place from which to manifest the new.

How do we know that the ideas that we wish to manifest are the right ones to happen? We can try to do everything correctly and still be unable to create what we know must happen. In my experience we can never know for certain, while we are in the process of creation, we can only know with hindsight if our inspiration was true. In the spiritual world its seems that quite often the things that we desire most are merely stepping stones on a longer winding path, that is designed to take us elsewhere than the goal we have set ourselves. We can spend much time aiming for a specific outcome only to find that we end up somewhere completely different. For example, we may train for years to become a business manager and end up finding our heart's delight as a gardener or a priestess or a healer, able to use some of our earlier skills to develop the latter. This is the Tao of the Goddess reality, in which the Way is the Goal, the journey is what is important.

Many people arrive in Glastonbury with great plans to have an effect on the place, I did myself thirty years ago, when I arrived with a small group of like-minded spiritual seekers. In our youthful arrogance we planned as a spiritual community, to clear the dark energies that seem to hold Glastonbury in their thrall. We wanted to change the vibration of Glastonbury, to bring in light, and other such high ambitions. We had no experience or knowledge of the enérgies of Avalon, but wanted to impose our mental visions on the place. We believed we could change the way things were. We were so wrong. Within a year of arriving in Glastonbury our group had scattered, disheartened, to the winds, broken emotionally and mentally, led willy-nilly on Her journey of transformation. It would have been much better for us if we had slid gently into the vibration of the place, if we had listened and learned slowly of the Mystery of Her ways, but we were young and naive. Now through intense experiences of making mistakes I have personally learned a great respect for the energies of Avalon and the sheer magic of Her transforming powers.

So to bring things into manifestation here in the place of transformation and rebirth is to follow the rules of manifestation always with one ear open to Her desires, to Her plans, to Her intentions for us, which may be far different to our own limited perspective. I have had to learn to create in rhythm with the constantly moving energies of Avalon, to rest when the energy is quiescent, to move when She says move, to move quickly when the energy is vibrating intensely, but always holding a steady and calm focus within, being with Her as a still point at the heart of Her swirling cauldron. After all She is the greatest expert and teacher in the realm of manifestation. She made the whole universe and the world in which we live.

The Vow of Dedication.

Autumn Equinox is the time when we make our Vow of Dedication to the Goddess at the end of our first year of Priestess training in a special initiatory ceremony held within the sacred landscape of Avalon, becoming a Sister or Brother of Avalon. This now traditional ceremony was created by the first group of Self-initiating Priestesses of Avalon and is priestessed each year by those who have already experienced the ceremony for themselves. In the ceremony we pass through the Veil into Avalon and renew our experience of the natural elements of the Goddess's nature. The ceremony has a particular form and each dedicand must engage with air, water, fire and earth, before speaking aloud our heartfelt prayers to the Lady in the sacred place, dedicating our lives to Her. Our words are witnessed by those who have stood in this same place before us, excited, scared, vulnerable and open-hearted. This ceremony marks the completion of the First Spiral of the three year Priestess of Avalon training

As has been mentioned before it has seemed important on this new priestess path to create a tradition which is as unfettered as possible by rules, dogma or fixed oaths which must be said by all. Every effort is made to allow space for individual inspiration and creativity within a flexible framework of learning, activity and ceremony. Each would-be Sister or Bother of Avalon writes her/is own Vow of Dedication, in which s/he dedicates herself and her life to the Goddess. This is an important initiatory step on our priestess journey in which we surrender our lives to Her, and in essence there is no point in becoming Her priestess if we are unwilling to do this.

For many people the idea of surrender to any greater power is feared as implying loss of control, of autonomy and of one's own personal power. This is the basis of many patriarchal religious cults in which we are asked to surrender our personal authority to a human leader, to what is written in a book and to what is taught by a hierarchy of priests. Surrender is seen in terms of the power-over cultures in which we live, and we all know that power-over corrupts.

Within the Priestess of Avalon tradition surrender has a completely different meaning. Surrender is only ever to the Goddess as She speaks directly to us day by day. There is no surrender to a leader, no surrender of individual understanding to a received written or spoken word, no obedience to any hierarchy of priestesses. There is also no fixed length of time for which we must surrender, as surrender is a day by day living experience. Surrender is of the heart into the Heart of the Goddess, giving our trust to Her. The power that we work with is power within, the power of the Goddess within our hearts and minds, continually leading us to greater love and compassion, to personal empowerment and Self confidence.

In our dedication vow we make a commitment to allow ourselves to be led through life by Her. This does not mean that we give up our free will to be who we are or to do what we want. Rather we make a commitment to listen to Her voice within as the true voice of our own Soul and begin to follow Her direction, believing that She will lead us into our greatest fulfilment.

In the Dedication Ceremony itself we prepare to make our vows by cleansing, invigorating and empowering ourselves using the elements of air, water and fire. We earth our dedication by speaking aloud our heart's truth to the Goddess as She appears in nature, and witnessed by our sister and brother dedicands and Priestesses of Avalon. After our dedication we are known as Sisters or Brothers of Avalon.

Ceremonial Apparel

When we speak our Vows of Dedication we wear the ceremonial robes which we have been dreaming, creating and gathering together throughout the year, sewn with all our hopes and dreams. Each costume is different, imbued with the personal magic of its creator. We wear our headdresses, carry our wands of power and chalices of love. We take account of the colder weather and the time of year.

Between Mabon and the Second Spiral of Priestess Training

Between Mabon and Samhain autumn comes to the land as the days become shorter and the nights colder. Plants shrivel and begin to die back. The leaves on the trees turn gold, red and brown. The apples in the orchards are collected. We harvest the remaining plants, vegetables and fruits before the first frosts arrive. Rains begin to fall, brought in on the strong southwesterly winds. Trees begin to lose their leaves. Mists rise from the Summerland meadows and the Sacred Isle becomes clothed in Her soft white hair.

Make an altar at home to the Mother of Earth. Decorate the altar with the bounty of Her harvest. Express your gratitude for the gift of life you have on Her beautiful planet, to the Earth Mother, to Brigantia and Banbha, to Ertha, Gaia and Moronoe. Celebrate Her Earth.

Every day light a candle and burn incense on your altar to the Earth Mother. Sing and pray to Her for help, guidance, for others in need, for healing for yourself and others, for visions, etc. Once a week recreate your altar.

In your meditations consider how Her Earth supports you and gives you life. Think how you might support Her.

At this time think about all you have learned in the last year as you have journeyed consciously through the First Spiral. Notice how you have changed.

Every day write down and /or draw your feelings, thoughts, intuitions and visions in your diary, i.e. what is going on for you.

At the new moon begin to collect the seeds which can be planted next spring in your garden or in plant pots.

At the full moon hold a Harvest Supper for family and friends, sharing with them the Goddess's bounty.

At this time you may decide to continue straight on from the First Spiral of Priestess training to the Second Spiral. Or you may decide to consolidate what you have learned and wait for a year or more before you move onto the Second Spiral. The choice is yours, although many people prefer to continue studying with the Sisters and Brothers of Avalon that they have come know well.

Now is the time to design and develop your own personal practices that will keep you motivated on your journey to becoming a Priestess of the Goddess and of Avalon. The outer teacher stands aside for the moment and the inner teacher comes through.

In the Centre of the Sacred Wheel Goddess of the Centre

Every wheel comprises a rim, spokes and a central hub around which the spokes and the rim rotate. The spokes connect hub and rim, and as either turns the whole wheel moves forward. Without any of these three elements, the wheel cannot hold together or move forward. Each is essential for the working of the whole.

For Priestesses of Avalon the Lady of Avalon, Nolava, is always to be found at our centre. She is the hub around which we collectively and individually revolve. She is the Goddess who expresses Herself through the landscape of Avalon and the energies of the eight seasons of the year, as spokes on the wheel of Her nature. As we stand in circle and in ceremony with the Lady at our centre, Priestesses of Avalon and all those who are dedicated to the Lady form the rim of the wheel, Her human expression in the world.

At the hub of the Sacred Wheel of the elemental Nine Morgens we find Morgen la Fey, said by Geoffrey of Monmouth to be chief among the Nine Sisters. And in the centre of Britannia's Sacred Wheel we find Goddess Britannia, She who is BrigitAna, ancient Mother Goddess, who expresses Herself through the cycles and seasons of Her nature in the whole of Brigit's Isles. Britannia's Wheel applies to the Outerworld of the whole of Brigit's Isles, where Nolava's Wheel and the Morgen Wheel apply to the energies and forces of the inner world of Avalon.

Throughout the First Spiral of the *In the Heart of the Goddess* training students experience the power of working in circle, the importance of our friendships with women and men, and the challenges that may follow from these relationships. We learn through experience how to work collectively to create Goddess events and longer term projects.

At the completion of the First Spiral dedicands who have made their Vow of Dedication to the Goddess, become Sisters and Brothers of Avalon, Saplings in the Orchard of Avalon, the wider group of Self-initiated and trainee Priestesses of Avalon, and Priestesses in related trainings. They participate in Orchard events and in ceremonial circles in the Glastonbury Goddess Conference and in the Glastonbury Goddess Temple. These ventures give us the opportunity to gather together in celebration of the Lady, expressing new forms of Goddess spirituality and developing our knowledge of Her in the company of like-minded people.

Honouring Nolava, Lady of Avalon, Lady of the Centre

As we journey to become Her priestesses, Nolava is our centre, the Goddess whom we love with all of our hearts. She is the Lady who has called to us from afar to come to Avalon. We have heard Her name, we have heard Her voice. She draws us like a magnet to the Sacred Isle. We travel here from long distances to feel Her magic, to experience Her initiatory touch. She asks us to come here often, to touch Her energies and be changed by Her. She asks us to come and live here, to dive deeply into Her Mysteries of life, love, death and the spaces between all things. She asks that we allow ourselves to be transformed in Her love. She asks us to go out from Avalon and to do Her work in the world. She is our inspiration, She is our hope, She is our essence, the One whom we love.

In substance Nolava is the land we stand upon when we walk on Her body in the Glastonbury hills. She appears in the forms of the land as the Maiden Swan flying over the Summerland levels from the northeast to the southwest. She is here ready and waiting as the Lover, with Her legs spread wide. She appears as the Great Mother with Her pregnant belly giving birth to the town and She is present as the Crone riding on the back of the Swan. Her many qualities are described in earlier chapters and Her evolutionary story has been told in the Creation Myth of the Isle of Avalon.

Her colour is violet, the colour of spiritual energy, encompassing the pale lavender of the etheric worlds, the violet radiance of the heavenly realms and the rich purples of royalty and sovereignty. From the centre of Avalon Her violet flame shines forth into the world, awakening a love for Her and the Divine Feminine in many forms, in all whom She touches. From Her violet skin healing emanations flow outwards through Avalon, across the waters of lake and sea, out into the world, bringing hope and healing to all who catch a glimpse of Her wonderful radiance.

To come to know Her all that is necessary is to spend time with Her on Her body, walking, sitting, reflecting on Her nature, talking to Her, and She will do the rest. She will make Herself known to us.

On your journey to priestesshood talk to the Lady everyday. Ask for Her guidance, wisdom and insight, for you, your family and your community. Ask for Her help when you need it. Every day express your gratitude to Her for the gifts She gives to you in your life.

Honouring Morgen La Fey

I am Morgen la Fey, Lady of Avalon
the Weaver of the Web,
the Keeper of Mysteries

I am the faery woman whose kiss
will enchant you as you twine
in my embrace. I am the flickering hiss
of magic, the crow's flight in the mist

I am the Shapeshifter, winglifter
here and elsewhere in a single moment
I am the star-seed in the apple
the mirror within the cauldron

I am your soul's deep song
the dream of belonging, I am the green fire
awake in the heart of the land

Take my hand –

In my palm I hold the paths of the constellations
I am the hidden Way of Wisdom, Lady of Time
I am the Walker Between the Worlds
the Edge and the Entry

I am the Healer, with leaf, golden bed, and blade
I am Sovereign here, the Shining One
who takes you across the water to Avalon

by Rose Flint

Morgen La Fey, Morgen the Faery or Morgen the Fate, is the most famous of the Nine Morgens, immortalised as the faery half-sister to King Arthur, and sometimes recognised as the Lady of Avalon, or as an incarnation of Her. In the early Arthurian legends She is a Goddess, called

Morgen the Wise and eternal nymph. In Her youth according to Malory,

"She was...very gay and playful; she sang agreeably; though dark in face, very well made, neither too fat nor too thin, with beautiful hands, perfect shoulders, skin softer than silk, engaging of manner, long and straight in the body; altogether wonderfully seductive and the warmest and most sensual woman in all Britain."

Ladies of the Lake, Caitlin and John Matthews, (Aquarian Press).

In later versions of the legends Morgen La Fey was maligned like so many Goddess women before Her, as a bad, conniving, vengeful woman who plotted against her brother. However, as Arthur is dying, it is to Morgen that he returns for comfort and healing, as he journeys in the barge across the Lake to Avalon.

According to Geoffrey of Monmouth in the *Vita Merlinii*, Morgen is the first of nine sisters, who dwell on,

"The island of apples which men call the Fortunate Isle*.....because it produces all things of itself. Of its own accord it produces grain and grapes and apple trees.*

There nine sisters rule by a pleasing set of laws.....She who is first among them is more skilled in the healing art, and excels her sisters in the beauty of her person. Morgen is her name and she has learned what useful properties all the herbs contain, so that she can cure sick bodies. She also knows an art by which to change her shape, and to cleave the air on new wings.....men say that she has taught mathematics to her sisters."

Ladies of the Lake, Caitlin and John Matthews, (Aquarian Press)

Morgen La Fey is perhaps the most evocative of the Nine Morgens. In legend and story She is known as Morgana, Morgaine, Morgan and Morgenoe. She is Keeper of the Mysteries leading us deeper and deeper into Her enthralling Mysts. She is the great Healer who can heal us of our deepest wounds. She is the Wayshower, beckoning us to follow Her across the waters into Avalon. In legend She teaches Her sisters the art of mathematics, which encompasses all the fundamental laws of the natural universe, for She is Mother of Time and Space, Weaver of the Web, of the Matrix of Life itself.

As Walker between the Worlds and Lady of the Barge, She ferries us across the Great Waters to Avalon, to the Other Side, to the Otherworld, for temporary visits and also at death. She shows us how to enter death filled with grace. She is the Enchantress who leads us into a life filled with mystery and enchantment. She is a Shapeshifter appearing in different forms as Maiden, Lover, Mother and Crone, as priestess, faery woman and fate, as animal and bird. One of Her well known siddhis or spiritual gifts, is Her ability to appear in more than one place at the same time and She has been seen to do so.

Living on the Isle of Avalon Morgen is the Faery Woman, the Fey One, appearing and disappearing as She chooses. She leads mortals across the Threshold, into the Hollow Hill, into the faery realms, to sing, dance and play, and to eat the magical fruit of the Otherworld, where we might stay for a hundred years or more, from which we might never return. Morgen is dark and beautiful, appearing sometimes as a luscious woman and sometimes as a menacing hag. She is viewed by many as a rather frightening character as She encompasses the light and dark of the Goddess and can show us both faces.

Morgen is Lady of the Mists, or Lady of the Lake of Mists, which even today surround the magical Isle of Avalon in the autumn and spring. The image of the Mists of Avalon holds enchantment for many as evidenced in the popularity of Marion Zimmer Bradley's *Mists of Avalon*. We know that if only we can find our way through the mysterious mists we will be able to enter Avalon and meet the Lady. Morgana is the Mist, rising from the Summerland at dawn and at dusk, hovering ten and twenty feet in the air, leaving only the tops of hills and tall trees in sight. She thickens to fog that can hang low all day in the cauldron beneath the Mendip Hills. Her mists hide the magical Isle of Avalon from the eyes of the profane.

Morgen's sacred creatures are the black crow or raven and the black cat. She is Apple Woman and Her tree is the apple tree, held sacred in Avalon throughout all the year, from the winter when the branches are splayed and bare, to the blossom-laden branches of springtime, through to the appearance of the red and golden apples of immortality in autumn. As we bite into Her apples we eat the fruit of the Tree of Her Knowledge and so can become wise.

The Cauldron of Transformation belongs to Morgen La Fey and all who journey into Avalon will find themselves drinking deeply from Her sacred brew. On some days it can taste sweet and sublime, and on others, rather strange, filled with bits we would rather not know about. Accidentally or purposefully we may find ourselves falling into Her Cauldron. We feel ourselves being swept and swirled out of control, or even drowning in the murky depths of our emotions, as She stirs Her pot. We must spend at least a year and a day, if not longer, in Her Cauldron, the correct herbs and spices being added in due season. If we are lucky we will rise from Her

Cauldron transformed and regenerated by Her life-giving power, readied for next spirals of change and growth. Morgen's true energy is found in the point of stillness which lies at the centre of the swirling cauldron of change. Her gift is to demonstrate how to remain centred when all around moves in seeming chaos.

We honour Morgen la Fey when we walk the land of Avalon, when we climb the hollow hill of the Tor, when we move through the mists that surround the sacred Isle, when we find ourselves within Her Cauldron. In the Fifth Spiral of the Priestess of Avalon training, which is the Priestess Enchantress training, we explore more of Her enchanting nature.

Pray to Morgen la Fey daily. Notice the fears that you may have of Her transforming powers. Seek out Her many faces and make offerings to Her.

Honouring Goddess Britannia

Britannia is a tutelary Romano-Keltic Goddess with much earlier origins. She is Guardian Goddess of the Soul of the British people and the land that is Brigit's Isles. When the Romans conquered Britain in 43CE during the reign of Claudius Caesar, they named the new province after the native Goddess Britannia. They associated Her with their own Roman Minerva, who was a Goddess of Wisdom and the Moon, and whose totem creature, like the Welsh Blodeuwedd, was the owl.

When Hadrian came to Britain in 121 AD, he greatly increased Roman influence in Britain and under his rule a shrine to Britannia was erected in York. He produced several coins with himself on one side and the image and words BRITANNIA, the personification of Britain, on the other. Britannia is shown wearing classical robes, seated on or next to a pile of rocks, with Her head slightly bowed in submission to Roman authority. She holds a spear, which perhaps like Brigit, was originally a rod of power. She leans on a round disc, usually described as a shield, but which may well have once been the sun disc, drum or tambourine, found on many early European images of the Sun Goddess.

To commemorate his elevation to the British throne in 287CE Carausius issued a coin on which he represented himself as the coming King being welcomed by Mother Britannia, who stands extending Her hand to him. Another coin depicts the sacred marriage between Carausius and the British Nation, with Carausius hand-in-hand with Goddess Britannia. In these early images Britannia is not helmeted or wearing any armour. Sometimes She is shown holding a standard and leaning on the disc. On other coins She is shown seated on a globe above waves. These are among our earliest images of the Goddess in Brigit's Isles.

It wasn't until 1672 in the reign of Charles II that Britannia re-emerged on copper halfpennies and farthings in designs obviously based on the earlier Roman images. On these She is shown seated on a rock, facing left, with an olive branch in Her right hand, a rod/spear in Her left hand, and a disc/shield leaning against the rock. The shield bears a Union flag, which fortuitously has eight divisions as in Britannia's Wheel of the year. Over the next hundred years or so many coins carried images of Britannia with minor variations, until 1806 when Britannia's rod/spear changed to a trident and waves were shown washing around the rock on which She was seated and a ship was added on the horizon. In 1821 for the first time a lion was shown seated at Britannia's far side and like Greek Athena, Britannia now wore a helmet. In the 19th and 20th centuries Her image was used in many different forms on coins, in newspapers and magazines, particularly in cartoons, where She was used to make political statements.

Over the last 150 years Britannia has appeared on many coins in both seated and standing poses and in many variations upon the theme. On today's coins, such as the 50 pence piece and on bullion seals, She is usually portrayed wearing a helmet, with a trident in Her hand, a sun disc/shield with its eight divisions leaning against Her, a lion by Her side and carrying an olive branch. For further information on coins showing images of Britannia visit http://www.24carat.co.uk/index.html

From the ancient images of Britannia we can glimpse the qualities of an earlier Goddess who was recognised and honoured by the British people. She is a womanly figure, carrying a rod of power with a sun or moon disc at Her side. Like Brigit, She is Goddess of the Sun and Moon, whole unto Herself with the Rod of Her secret consort at Her side. Seated on a rock, She is Goddess of these islands. She has all the characteristics of Ana, Mother Goddess of this land and Brigit, both of whom are described in my earlier books. In *The Ancient British Goddess* Foosiya Miller's drawing shows Britannia as a woman seated on a rock, looking directly at the viewer with sun-haloed head uncovered, a trident in one hand, a sun disc by Her side, and like ancient Epona once honoured here too, a sheaf of grain in Her other hand. The lioness of the sun is by Her side and She is surrounded by flowing streams and standing stones, claiming Her origins from the neolithic age.

As Goddess-loving people we have begun the long journey of

reclaiming Britannia as the tutelary Goddess of Brigit's Isles. We learn more about Her as we follow the cycles of Her seasons through the years.

Each time you spend money notice Her image on coins and bank notes and thank Her for the abundance that She brings to your life. When you hear Her anthem sung, praise Her as Goddess of this land and people,

"Rule, Britannia,
Britannia rules the waves......"

The Hub and the Rim : The Power of Sitting in Circle

One of the most important practices to emerge from the women's consciousness raising movement of the 1970s and 80s was that of sitting in circle around a central space. It began as women joined together to explore women's issues and what were known at the time in Britain as the Seven Demands of the Women's Liberation Movement. In Glastonbury for two years in the early 1980s, a group of 20-30 women met in circle every fortnight to talk about our concerns as women. Although some women were naturally extrovert and more expressive than others, we had no chiefs and no hierarchies of power. We were a group of peers and everyone in the circle had the same right to speak and to be heard.

We read feminist books and explored relevant topics, giving each woman in turn the space to say what she thought or felt, without interruption. We listened to her instead of arguing with her about her point of view. By removing the peacock elements of discussion, completely new ways of communicating opened up to us, which produced a much more diverse range of expression and comment. The space we gave to each woman allowed us all to feel safe enough to speak our truths, and deep secrets which had never been expressed before were shared between us. We also found that it was often the women who would normally be the quietest in a competitive conversation, who had the most interesting things to say. It was a very powerful time for us as we explored our experiences as women, the limitations imposed on us by the patriarchal society in which we lived, and our ideas on how our lives might be in a world where women have equal rights and powers. We cried and we laughed. We enjoyed ourselves immensely as we opened up to new freedoms.

Since that time the idea of sitting in circle has evolved and is now used in many situations where groups of women, of women and men, or of men only, wish to meet together as equals. The centre of the circle may be empty or there may be a candle in the middle whose flame represents the unifying light at the centre of diverse points of view. In priestess gatherings we usually have a central circular altar dedicated to the Goddess, where participants place offerings and symbols of their presence.

The practice of circling includes the development of ground rules, such as: having a facilitator to ensure that everyone has the chance to speak without interruption; having a sacred bowl or a talking stick to pass as in the Native American tradition; having a vibes watcher to keep a check on the mood of the group; having time keepers, etc. There is even now a movement called *The Millionth Circle* attempting to bring circling into more conventional political, business and religious gatherings, see *The Millionth Circle: How to Change Ourselves and The World--The Essential Guide to Women's Circles* by Jean Shinoda Bolen.

The great thing about being in circle is that in the circle we are all equal. We have equal rights to be, to speak and be heard. Sitting in a circle we can see each other's faces, we can see the emotions which pass across them, we can feel each other's joy and pain. We can empathise with each other and create a space where it is safe to speak our truth in an often hostile world. Different people in the circle model different, perhaps more effective ways of behaving in difficult situations and we learn new methods that we can try out ourselves, not only in the circle but in life in general. These are powerful experiences that change at a fundamental level our conditioned responses to being raised in competitive hierarchical cultures and help release our authentic selves. We find we are able to open our hearts to other human beings, to show our vulnerability and so become stronger in who we are.

As well as having equal rights in the circle we also come to understand through experience that we have equal responsibilities. What happens in a circle is dependent on all the individuals in that circle, not just on one or two movers and shakers. The more that each person can contribute of their own uniqueness the richer will be the experience of the whole. We learn through practice to take responsibility for our own experience in different situations. We learn how to effect change for the better in the group and we realise that to change the world for the better it is necessary for each of us to engage in the process and not leave it to others to make the difference.

As a teacher if possible, which it nearly always is, I prefer teaching in a circle. Although I have information and experience to offer I wish to demonstrate my knowledge that we are all essentially equal. We each have different gifts to contribute in a circle which will enrich the whole experience. I learn from my students as well as they learn from me and each other. As a teacher of transformation, in a circle I can see everyone's face and can sense where people are at, what is happening in their personal process. Fear often arises as we are exposed to new concepts and experiences. In reaction we withdraw our energy, become upset or angry, and these reactions can be seen, addressed and resolved as necessary in the moment.

Years ago I remember reading in Mircea Eliade's book *Shamanism* (Arkana), that he believed that in the Altai mountains long before there were solo male shamans with whom we are now familiar, there were originally women shamans who worked together in groups. I like this idea and as the Avalonian Priestess tradition is developing from Her inspiration, we have found that we too are working ceremonially in circles of eight or nine women and including one or two men, with many different people contributing to the whole.

When we meet in a teaching circle or ceremonially in the Goddess Temple we have a central altar that represents Britannia's Sacred Wheel of the Year with its nine directions. At the beginning of a teaching circle everyone places their personal offerings on the central altar and these remain there for the duration of the circle. We open the Wheel with eight priestesses invoking in turn the Goddesses and energies of the nine directions, beginning with the Goddesses connected to the particular season of the year when the ceremony is being held. If the ceremony is being held at Litha - summer solstice, then the priestess in the south asks everyone to turn and face the south, as she calls in Domnu, asking everyone to join her in visualising the Goddesses of the south with their particular qualities and energies, coming into the centre of the circle and repeating "*Hail and Welcome, Domnu*".

Turning back to the centre together everyone brings Domnu into the centre of the circle. Moving around the wheel the priestess in the southwest asks everyone to turn to face the southwest and she invokes Ker, again bringing Her into the centre, saying "*Hail and Welcome, Ker*". The third priestess calls Brigantia or Banbha from the west, and so on all the way around the wheel until we come to Rhiannon and call Her in from the southeast. When the Goddesses of the eight directions have been called in we then face the centre, the ninth direction, and the first priestess calls in Britannia, the Lady of Avalon and the Nine Morgens into our ceremony. We open the wheel in this way in seasonal ceremonies in the Goddess Temple and at the beginning of the Goddess Conference. At the end of the rituals the eight priestesses close the wheel, expressing our gratitude to the Goddesses of the nine directions.

In the circle the eight priestesses are equal, there is no one High Priestess or Priest with ultimate authority, for the Goddess is in our centre. What happens in any ceremony depends on us all and the gifts we individually bring to Her altar. It is a very exciting way of working ceremonially because although we may know the structure of the ceremony, we never know what is going to emerge from the combination of contributions made by each of the eight priestesses and anyone else who is present. It is in the weaving of the known and unknown elements that the Goddess enters into Her ceremony to be experienced by everyone.

Also so far in our ceremonial development the eight priestesses involved are not a fixed group, but are continually changing from ceremony to ceremony. The eight are made up of those who are ready, willing and available for any particular ceremony and usually include experienced priestesses and a couple of beginners. This means that while we are familiar with the forms of ceremony we must always be alert and present to the energy within any particular ceremony. There is little room for passengers. The more that we work together in ever-changing combinations of priestesses the more present we become to the Goddess, manifesting Her energy through ceremony.

Friendships between Women

It is an obvious truth that friendships between women are one of the most important aspects of our lives as women. We are nurtured and strengthened by our relationships with other women. They affect who we are and how we feel about ourselves as women. They help us express our often turbulent emotions, they help us explore and remember who we are and what we might become. Our friendships with women often continue throughout our lives, while sexual relationships may come and go. They are a bedrock of our society as women from which new ways of being and expressing ourselves can spring.

In an email Gale Berkowitz reported on a University of California research study "*Female Responses to Stress: Tend and Befriend, Not Fight or Flight*", Taylor, S. E., Klein, L.C., Lewis, B. P., Gruenewald, T. L., Gurung, R. A. R., & Updegraff, J. A. (2000) (Psychological Review 107(3)), which shows that women's friendships are in fact particularly special and of evolutionary benefit to women, and to the human race as a whole. The study proposes what many of us can confirm from experience, that spending time on a daily basis with our women friends relieves stress. It suggests that women respond to stress with a cascade of brain chemicals that cause us to make and maintain friendships with other women.

Until this study was published, scientists generally believed that when people experience stress, they trigger a hormonal cascade that revs the body to either stand and fight or flee as fast as possible, in an ancient survival mechanism left over from the time we were chased across the planet by sabre-toothed tigers. Researchers now suspect that women have a far larger behavioural repertoire than just *fight or flight*. In women the hormone oxytocin is released as part of the stress response and this buffers the fight or flight response, encouraging a woman to tend children and gather with other women instead of fleeing. When she actually engages in this *tending or befriending*, studies suggest that more oxytocin is released, which further counters stress and produces a calming effect. This calming response does not occur in men, because testosterone - which men produce in high levels when they are under stress - reduces the effects of oxytocin, while oestrogen seems to enhance it.

The discovery that women respond to stress differently to men was made in a classic 'A*ha*!' moment shared by two women scientists, Dr Laura Klein and Dr Shelley Taylor, as they were talking one day in a lab at UCLA. There was a joke that when the women who worked in their lab were stressed, they came in, cleaned the lab, had coffee, and bonded. When the men were stressed they holed up somewhere on their own. As they talked about the different responses to stress the women realised that nearly 90% of the research on stress had been carried out on men, very little had been carried out on women.

The two doctors very quickly discovered that by not including women in stress research, scientists had made a huge mistake. The fact that women respond to stress differently to men has significant implications for women's health and the *tend and befriend* notion developed by Drs. Klein and Taylor may explain why women consistently outlive men. Our female friends help us live longer and better. The Nurses' Health Study from Harvard Medical School found that the more friends women had, the less likely they were to develop physical impairments as they aged, and the more likely they were to be leading a joyful life. In fact, the results were so significant, the researchers concluded, that not having close friends or confidants was as detrimental to your health as smoking or carrying extra weight. When the researchers looked at how well women functioned after the death of a spouse, they found that even in the face of this biggest stressor of all, those women who had a close friend and confidante were more likely to survive the experience without any new physical impairments or permanent loss of vitality. Those without friends were not always so fortunate.

Our women friends are an important source of love, nurture, comfort and inspiration and we forget this at our peril. As Goddess-loving women we are sustained by each other on our journey into new ways of being, of loving and serving Her.

Women's Inhumanity to Women

As well as women being the source of some of our most important life-nourishing friendships, women can also be our greatest enemies, undermining us at every turn, through gossip, backbiting, jealousy and overt, but more often covert, attacks. Almost every woman I know, myself included at various times in my life, has engaged in covert practices designed to make ourselves look better, while bringing another woman down. It is a terrible thing to admit but we have accepted that this practice is a normal part of our women's culture, rather than a strange aberration, a defence mechanism learned in childhood, to protect us from feeling small and insignificant.

Phyllis Chesler has written a marvellous book called *Woman's Inhumanity to Woman* (Plume Books 2003) in which she explores the dark secrets which lie at the heart of many relationships between women. It is a book I recommend that all priestesses and all women should read. Phyllis uncovers and names the childhood patterns that govern many relationships between women - our need to be liked, to be loved exclusively, to have and keep our best friends by colluding against intruders, etc. She shows the ways in which defensive patterns developed by father's daughters in a patriarchal world, have come to rule and undermine our adult relationships with other women.

In this tour de force Phyllis lifts the lid on the can of worms that can often lie in the centre whenever women gather, within the women's movement, the feminist movement and the Goddess movement. She writes from her own experiences as a feminist academic and researcher of being personally abused and attacked over many years, not primarily by male writers defending patriarchy, but by women within the women's movement from whom she might have expected some support. It is a strange and disheartening experience to find that it is our sisters on the path who try to destroy us as we initiate new ideas and express our creativity, rather than men. This is not to say that all that feminist and Goddess pioneers express and do is right, but on a journey of exploration it might be hoped that we would receive encouragement and support from our sisters rather than constant sniping or full-on denigration.

Phyllis explores what it is that makes us behave in this way, how and why individual women and groups of women strive competitively to find ourselves on the *right* side, to elevate ourselves, to keep our friends to ourselves, by pulling other women down. Instead of celebrating our sisters' efforts to progress a women-centred political, academic, artistic, cultural and spiritual world, we spend much time attacking often lone, creative individuals or groups, who are attempting to move against the patriarchal tides.

In my own life as a Goddess teacher I have been shocked several times to find myself on the end of virulent personal and generalised covert and overt attacks by feminists, priestesses and supposedly Goddess-loving people. These women and men usually don't know me personally and often have never spoken to me, but they feel able to attack me just because I have written books and am a creative individual who is visible in the world. The first Glastonbury Goddess Conference came under one such vicious attack from women attending a Women's Spiral Camp being held nearby.

On the evening of our first ever sit-down Goddess Banquet a group of women from the Spiral Camp processed with banners to the doors of the Assembly Rooms, to protest that we were charging money for women to attend our four day Goddess Conference. They believed that they should be able to come to the Conference and the Banquet for free. They claimed we were elitist. They sang, as if we didn't know it,

"You can't buy the Goddess........."

The invading women forced their way through closed doors with threats of violence, into the Banquet. They climbed on the tables and stamped on the altar. They abused and harangued the guests, and frightened women and children. One woman said to Tyna,

"The trouble with you is that you are white (true), *middle class* (Tyna's *parents were refugees from* Poland), *heterosexual* (true), *and own a house* (*unfortunately with rather a large mortgage*)."

In truth none of these statements was a cause for any kind of condemnation.

In the following year the feminist magazine *From the* Flames attacked the conference, myself and Tyna, in every issue, despite the fact that neither of the editors had attended the conference, and were writing only from hearsay. Not once did they communicate with either of us personally to find out what we felt or thought, or to confirm any facts. For some reason it was easier for these women to attack what was the first major Goddess event in Brigit's Isles, to attack Tyna and I as individuals, rather than to attack patriarchy in the world - the banks, the arms trade, the multinational companies, etc., the things that really need to be changed.

Both Tyna and I were so horrified by the experience that we had to think long and hard about whether we had the courage to ever organise another Goddess event. We had created an amazing event for our participants. We had done the very best that we could do, but that was not enough for some. Was it worth continuing?

After much heart-searching we decided to go forward, but as we planned the second Goddess Conference we worried where the next attack might come from. Our first year of planning had been a time of great joy and excitement, but our second year was clouded by our fear of being attacked again. Thankfully it has not happened again in that way and the second Conference was wonderful too. We learned much about our boundaries from the experience, becoming strengthened in our desire to love and serve the Goddess as best we are able.

It seems that none of us may be exempt from this experience. If a woman should try to lift herself out of the thrall of patriarchal thinking, unfortunately it seems there will be some other woman who will want to bring her down. This is obviously a completely self-defeating strategy for all parts of the women's and Goddess movements, where we definitely need encouragement and support on the journey to transform patriarchy.

Priestesses have not been honoured in the western world for many hundreds of years. As we reclaim these titles for ourselves we automatically lift our heads above the parapet and become visible in the world. This is not necessarily for who we are, but as we are seen through the mists of other people's projections, what they believe or fear that title might mean. Men on the whole will attack us overtly out in the open where we can see them, as they express their derision and contempt. We can answer their attacks openly. Women will more often attack us covertly, so that we do not know where the attack comes from and it is therefore much harder to deal with.

We hear whispers and rumours, from a friend of a friend, saying,

"*Who does she think she is, calling herself a* Priestess of Avalon? *What gives her the right? She really thinks she's somebody special!"*

Most often these women do not speak to us directly so that their questions might be answered, because answers are not what is required. It is enough to impugn a woman's integrity, to muddy the waters around her, to show that she has clay feet, rather than elevate her to a status too far beyond us. It is more important to separate her from our community, to scapegoat her, than deal with our own underlying fears, failures and collusions.

As a community of women we are on a long journey of self-healing. Under patriarchy we have many patterns and behaviours that undermine our development as the equal majority of the human race. Like men there are many things that we must change in our women's society and it begins with the ways in which we relate to each other personally. Essentially we have to grow up as women out of our childish complexes, healing into more mature relationships in which we can support and encourage each other on our challenging journey to Selfhood. And yes, we will all make mistakes, we will not behave perfectly, we will do things wrong. It is in these times that we need support most, to help understand our unconscious patterns and perceive new ways of behaving, rather than being condemned for failing to live up to other people's ideals of perfection.

Women's healing journey begins with each one of us making the commitment never to undermine another woman or man ever again. If we have something to say, say it to her face, don't talk about her behind her back so that she is disempowered by our projections. Don't attack her privately while publicly smiling into her face.

Speak your truth or hold your tongue.

It is vital that we begin to face our own fears about speaking our truth to those who appear to be stronger than us, whose courage masks the fears they have to live with daily. By our words and deeds the world will be changed.

The Orchard of Avalon

I first decided to teach people to become Priestesses of Avalon because I was following the Lady's inspiration and I had things that I wanted to teach. I was so involved in getting the teaching right that I failed to think about what would happen to priestesses once the training was completed. It was only after the first training year had ended that we realised that, of course, priestesses would want to stay in touch with each other and go on working together. It sounds obvious with hindsight, but I just hadn't thought about the consequences of training people over many years. With the ending of each training there are more priestesses and to date there are 86 Self-initiated Priestesses of Avalon out in the world, with 23 more now in training.

Today the Orchard of Avalon is the collective group to which all Sisters, Brothers and Priestesses of the Goddess and of Avalon can belong. It also includes priestesses who have completed related priestess trainings with women who have studied with me, such as Suthisa Hein and Sandra Warmerdam in the Netherlands, Samantha Linasche in California and Sandra Roman in Argentina. We also include priestesses who have dedicated themselves to the Lady of Avalon in their own right over time. Within the Orchard there are different Glades and Groves of priestesses who have trained together, who live close to each other, etc.

The Orchard has its own yahoo groups and newsletter, *Goddess Within*, edited by priestesses, which goes to subscribers, passing on news and information. Some priestesses are active within the Orchard and in Glastonbury and others move on the periphery in the outside world, priestessing mainly in their own home locations, and staying in touch.

Almost as soon as the Orchard began to meet as an autonomous peer group, conflicts arose between people which we did not know how to handle. We faced many of the common challenges that arise between women, including competition and deceitfulness over men, backbiting, jealousy, covert undermining behaviours, loss of trust and faith; in fact many of the problems uncovered in Phyllis Chesler's *Woman's Inhumanity to Woman* and described earlier. We found that it was difficult for ex-students to move from a teaching circle into a peer group, and transference and projection onto their teacher continued. As a collection of fairly self-aware women and men who had passed through a deep process together we found we are all susceptible to reactive behaviours and often don't know how to behave well with each other. Some priestesses were even repelled out of the Orchard altogether, not wanting to have any part in resolving conflicts that they didn't feel belonged to them. These priestesses are now completely self sufficient in the world and we are learning how to be together as a larger group.

The Orchard has calmed somewhat since the early days, but is only just becoming a fully functioning organisation. Priestesses are by nature very individual people who simply do not want to belong to a group or to possibly find themselves being a part of anything that others might call a cult. None of us want that. We all believe in our direct personal connection to the Goddess unmediated by anyone else. We are now on a journey to find out how we can cooperate and work together creatively to bring the Goddess back into the world, while maintaining our individuality. Negotiation of all these tricky places is part of the development of the Orchard.

Within the Orchard priestesses usually remain good and sometimes lifelong friends with the people who have been in their own years of training. They meet and work ceremonially with priestesses from other years in the Goddess Temple, at the Goddess Conference, at Tribe of Avalon events in London and on priestess pilgrimages to other places and lands. Within the Orchard first year dedicands become Saplings - junior members of the Orchard, before becoming Branches at the end of the second year, and then fully grown Trees after Self-initiation as Priestesses of Avalon.

The Glastonbury Goddess Conference

RAINBOW PATH
Goddess Conference, Glastonbury

We take the route to Chalice Well as the town wakes
and takes us in, the rainbow-snake of us, women,
witches, drummers, priestesses and healers, mothers,
artists, dancers, daughters – the sun blazing blue skies
and joy shimmering through us, heat wave rising
as we carry Nine Goddesses, spirit looped by wicker,
Nine Morgens of the Isle of Avalon riding high
in rainbow colours, processing once more
this sacred path through holy earth and water.
Past the White Spring, up into the wide space of green
and the hard ascension of the Tor: slow climb of body,
spirit winging out into the winds as women celebrate
their sacred path, a hundred Goddess banners flying
flags of rainbow power and women's rainbow beauty
in a bright kaleidoscope of colour, moving up and up
until the Nine stand as a crown of light, rainbow light
that pours out healing transformations from our hearts,
a shining web of love that spins the universe:

a vision-prayer to set against all wars and all destructions,
against despair and violence, against all harm and hurts
to any of the precious, fragile, beloved worlds of earth
that live within Her daily, nightly life of miracle.

© Rose Flint

The Glastonbury Goddess Conference is a fantastic, inspiring and magical event held each year in Glastonbury at Lammastide. As described earlier the first conference was held in 1996 as a result of an inspiration received directly from the Goddess. At the time of writing the Conference is in its eleventh year and participants come from all over the world to enjoy a cornucopia of Goddess pilgrimage, ceremonies, rituals, talks, workshops, performances, exhibitions, art and craftwork, healing, poetry, music, dance, conversation, laughter and fun. Tyna has now left the Conference to pursue her personal creativity and the Conference is currently organised and run by myself with the help of circles of dedicated Priestesses of Avalon and other traditions, Melissas - wonderful people who work in exchange for a conference ticket, as well as writers, poets, artists, presenters and performers.

Over the years the focus of the Conference has developed and changed. When Tyna and I began we wanted simply to provide a forum for British-based Goddess-loving women to present their Goddess work to the world. Our aim was to present as much diversity of expression and information as we could from as many different creative women as we could include. Many wonderful women contributed to the growing success of the Goddess Conference. This is still our aim but over the years our network of contacts has expanded to include Goddess-loving women from other lands, such as Australia, the United States of America, the Netherlands, Hungary, the Czech Republic and Italy, who have ideas and talents to offer to the Conference. Each year we celebrate a different aspect of the Goddess in a fourfold cycle of Maiden, Lover, Mother and Crone.

After the turning of the millennium as more Priestesses of Avalon began to Self-initiate and become available to conduct and participate in ceremonies, I was inspired by descriptions of the Mysteries of Eleusis in Greece to develop a more ceremonially-based Goddess Conference. In the Eleusinian Mysteries pilgrims journeyed over several days to Eleusis to celebrate the Mysteries of Demeter, Mother of the Grain and Nature, which culminated in a profound ceremony at the Heart of the Mysteries, which no-one ever revealed.

In 2002 we changed the Matrix, the Conference Motherweb, so that the Conference too would become a five day pilgrimage, here exploring the Mysteries of the Isle of Avalon, and culminating in a central ceremony filled with Her magic. Because the Goddess Conference takes place within the energies of the Isle of Avalon and within the aura of the Lady of Avalon, it has seemed right for the Conference to be centred in the ceremonial cycle of the Lady of Avalon and Her many different expressions.

As the conference has become a pilgrimage to Her it has allowed contributors and participants to become more involved in the energy of the whole experience, each person adding in their own energy and expression into the whole mix of events. This participation has given each of us a deeply personal experience of the Lady of Avalon. In the first year of this cycle the Mysteries culminated in a profound ceremony in the Goddess Temple in which pilgrims met the Goddess as the White, Red and Black Ladies and received their blessings. In the second year pilgrims came into the presence of the Oracles of the Nine Morgens, the Nine Sisters of Avalon and received their wisdom. In 2003 we held a powerful Healing Ceremony within a circle of Nineteen Brides. In 2004 we imbibed Maeve's Sacred Red Mead and held an Ecstatic Dance Ceremony. The journey into Her mysteries continues and evolves, growing more profound each year. For further information and images of the Conference see www.goddessconference.com.

Glastonbury Goddess Temple

In August 1999 after the end of the Goddess Conference Mike and I went for a well-deserved holiday in Greece and one day took a trip to Mount Olympus, the famed home of the God/desses. On the long coach journey we drove across a flat plain and couldn't see the mountain ahead of us because it was shrouded in mist. As we got nearer, just as can happen in Avalon, the mists parted and there ahead was the most beautiful mountain with many peaks, one for each Goddess in the Greek pantheon. Although taken over by patriarchal Zeus, the original mountain is a beautiful Goddess landscape. Visitors can still follow a winding path between high peaks, alongside a fast flowing stream into the centre of the mountain, where a sacred spring rises out of the ground.

At the foot of the mountain are the remains of the town of Dion and among the earliest ruins there are several Goddess temples, with a partially intact temple to Isis. Almost wherever we travel in the Greek and Roman worlds the earliest temples are always Goddess temples, the later ones being dedicated to the gods. My heart felt so sad that wherever we have travelled in the western world the temples to the Goddess are always in ruins. They speak of an ancient, widespread Goddess-loving culture long gone and forgotten.

It was in this place that the idea came to create a present day contemporary Goddess Temple in Glastonbury. The Goddess Conference is such a high point of the year for many women and men where we come together to celebrate the Goddess in all Her glory. Wouldn't it be wonderful if we could gather regularly throughout the rest of the year as well in our own Goddess Temple to worship Her? Wouldn't it be wonderful to have our own sacred space dedicated to Her? And wouldn't it be fantastic to create our Goddess Temple in the first year of the new millennium, anchoring our hopes of returning the Goddess into public awareness?

Although there are Goddess Temples in India and the East, I had heard of only one public Goddess Temple in the modern western world, which is an open shrine in Arizona in the USA. It was time to create our own Goddess Temple in Glastonbury. When we returned from holiday I spoke to friends about the idea of creating a Goddess Temple and called a meeting of those I thought might be interested in supporting the idea.

Over the next few months different groupings of people met to further the idea of the Goddess Temple. We spent hours talking about what it might mean to have our own temple, how we would fund it, how we would staff it, how we would decorate it, etc. We opened a bank account and several of us set up monthly standing order donations to the Temple. We decided to hold an Inaugural Goddess Temple Ceremony and Picnic on Monday 29th May 2000. As the poster said,

Join the Goddess-loving women and men of Glastonbury at the inaugural Goddess Temple Ceremony and Picnic. A group of people hold a vision to create a Goddess Temple in Glastonbury which will be open to the public as a sacred space where the Lady of Avalon is honoured. We are in the process of generating energy, gathering people and raising funds. Until we actually have a building of our own we have decided to begin holding regular Goddess Temple ceremonies in different places in Glastonbury to help bring the vision into reality. This is our first!

During the ceremony we will sow seeds in a special tub to symbolise the seeds of the future Goddess Temple we are growing. We will also be creating a collage of our visions for the Goddess Temple.

For this first ceremony we decorated the Miracles Room in the Courtyard of the Glastonbury Experience as a Goddess Temple, and held it open for the day so that people could come and pray in the space. Lots of people came and joined the ceremony in which we sowed seeds for our future Goddess Temple, added our contributions to a Temple manifestation collage, prayed and sang to the Goddess, ate strawberries and drank champagne. Our first ceremony was a great success.

Over the coming months the seeds in the tub grew and flowered and we began to create temporary Goddess Temples for each of the seasonal festivals in the Miracles Room or in the Georges Room in the Glastonbury Experience. We used the large wicker Goddesses created for the Goddess Conference as a focus for our devotion. We would spend half a day decorating a space, hold it open to the public for three or four days for prayer and meditation, and hold a public ceremony to celebrate the Goddesses of each festival. At the end of the three days we would take it all down again, put the Goddess into storage and store the materials and decorations. Mike Jones, the manager of the Glastonbury Experience, the Isle of Avalon Foundation and the Glastonbury Trust, all supported us throughout this time as they do to this day, making it possible for us to develop our new venture. It would have been much more difficult without their help and generosity, and we are very grateful to them.

In September 2000 the Coeur group of the Goddess Temple was approached by members of the Management Committee of the Glastonbury Assembly Rooms, who asked us if we would be interested in running the Assembly Rooms as a Goddess Temple. The Assembly Rooms is a large community building which had become very run down over the preceding years, requiring a large amount of capital investment to repair the roof, for damp course work, etc. We felt that this offer was an opportunity not to be missed as it would be a wonderful large space for the Goddess Temple and we began to explore what it would involve. The Goddess seemed to be telling us to travel this path and see where it led.

Once the idea became public the Goddess Temple group, and myself in particular, were subjected to a barrage of vitriol in local newspapers and on a local Glastonbury email network. The idea of a Goddess Temple in the community-owned space was anathema to many people and we were accused of trying to take the Assembly Rooms away from the people, although it was the management committee who had first come to us. Months of conflict ended in a vote by shareholders to leave things in the Assembly Rooms the way they were. We were only ever interested in taking the building on if a majority of shareholders had wanted it to happen, but the community at large was definitely not ready for such a venture. We were relieved to have the weight of a possibly huge building project with attendant fund-raising difficulties taken from our shoulders. Throughout this time we continued to decorate spaces in the Glastonbury Experience and hold ceremonies at the eight festivals.

In the summer of 2001 we heard that the old Bridget Chapel in the Glastonbury Experience was to close due to continual abuse. The Library of Avalon was to move into this larger ground floor space leaving the Ark, a large room on the first floor, empty and available for a Goddess Temple. It took several months as building works took over in the various different venues, before we could move into our own space. We received the keys to the Ark at winter solstice and began our own renovation and decoration works, painting the space and carpeting it, in shades of lavender and violet. Lots of people came to help including Alison Waite, Ark Redwood, Brian Charles, Colette Barnard, Geraldine Charles, Irene Sheppard, Jill Smith, Rachael Clyne and Sandra Brant, and the energy built. We opened the Goddess Temple to the public with a special Opening Ceremony at Imbolc 2002 in which we dedicated the Temple to the Goddess as Lady of Avalon. Over the first year at each of the eight festivals we anchored the Lady more deeply into Her temple.

It has seemed important to us to dedicate the Goddess Temple primarily to the Lady of Avalon because we live in Glastonbury and Avalon. We are reclaiming the ancient idea that particular Goddesses are directly connected to the land on which we live. We also honour the Nine Morgens and all the Goddesses on Britannia's Sacred Wheel of the Year. Our seasonal ceremonies are based within the working of Britannia's Sacred Wheel, but we also welcome people who worship the Goddess in other forms and traditions into the Goddess Temple.

At the beginning we opened the Temple to the public for two days a week with volunteer Melissas in attendance, caring for the space. Since that time we have gradually opened the Temple for more and more days a week and it is now usually open six days a week from noon to 4.00pm. The Goddess Temple has a wonderful energy and is a place where people come to pray, meditate, light candles, leave messages to the Goddess, sleep, sing, dance, whatever moves them in the space. Many visitors to Glastonbury come into the Temple, often experiencing a Goddess space for the first time. They usually love the colour, the decoration, the energy, the peace they find in the Temple.

We hold public ceremonies at each of the eight festivals of the year, healing, pathworking and Oracle ceremonies at the New and Full Moons, and other ceremonies in between. We are always looking for Melissas to help look after the space, and for people to propose new ideas for events and to lead them. We want the Temple to be used by Goddess-loving people of all persuasions.

On June 18th 2003 after months of discussion and paperwork, we were formally recognised by the powers that be, the Registry of Places of Worship, as an official Place of Worship. We believe that we are the first formally recognised indigenous public Goddess Temple in Europe for perhaps 1500 years, and maybe ever.

The Goddess Temple is a very special place in the hearts of priestesses and local people, as well as in hearts of many people worldwide, who travel thousands of miles to visit the Goddess Temple and bathe in Her energies. The beliefs of the congregation given to the Registry of Places of Worship are as follows:

1. *We believe in the Great Goddess, who is the One and the Many, who is immanent and transcendent, personal and impersonal, constant and changing, local and universal, within and without all of creation, who manifests Herself through the cycle of the seasons and the Wheel of the Year.*
2. *We believe that the Goddess manifests and communicates Herself through the whole of Nature and the sacred land, through visions and dreams, senses and experiences, imagination, ceremony and prayer. We believe that no form of words can ever encompass Her.*
3. *As the Goddess People of Avalon we believe in the Goddess who is Lady of Avalon, as She expresses Herself through the landscape, mythology and culture of the Isle of Avalon and in Glastonbury.*

The great thing about our Goddess Temple is that as with Goddess spirituality, there are no rules as to what we can and cannot do in the Goddess Temple. There is no book that tells us what we must believe, what is sanctioned and what is forbidden. We are free to worship the Goddess in any way that we choose within the laws of the land in which we live, and what we feel to be right. We are free to explore and express our spirituality together.

The Goddess Temple is supported entirely by donations of time, energy and money from priestesses, from the Goddess People of Avalon (Tuatha De Avalon) and the public. We have Friends of the Temple who, in return for an annual donation supporting the Temple, are kept informed of Temple ceremonies and events. We have Temple Madrons who generously give a regular monthly donation to the Goddess Temple, as well as individual Goddess-loving people who make one-off donations. We have a building fund and our future plans include moving to larger premises and creating our own purpose-built Goddess Temple within the landscape of Avalon.

In the present and especially during the summer months when many visitors come to Glastonbury, the Goddess Temple overflows with people during ceremonies. We are now actively seeking larger premises, which will include a larger Temple space, smaller shrine rooms, Goddess teaching space, creative spaces, dream incubation spaces, a birthing room, a dying room, priestess dormitories, spa facilities, cafe, office, plus outdoor areas for gardens, stone circles, sacred mounds and other spaces. We have begiun to raise funds for this expanded vision.

Inspired by the Glastonbury Goddess Temple and other individuals, there are now new Goddess Temples growing in the Netherlands, Hungary, Sweden and Australia, as well as the open-air Sekhmet Temple in Nevada, USA and the Orange County, Goddess Temple in California. We hope that Goddess Temples will spring up everywhere in Britain and in the world. For further details of the Glastonbury Goddess Temple, how to make a donation to the Temple, and connections to other Goddess Temples around the world, please see *www.goddesstemple.co.uk*, or contact us at *The Glastonbury Goddess Temple, The Courtyard, 2-4 High Street, Glastonbury, Somerset*, BA6 9DU.

Second Spiral

Becoming a Priestess of the Goddess

Dedication as a Priestess of the Goddess

The First Spiral of the journey to become a Priestess of Avalon is principally concerned with deepening our personal relationship to the Goddess, through learning about Her different forms of expression as Maiden, Lover, Mother and Crone, and as Mother of the Elements, which She shows to us through the turning of the year. We participate in a series of ceremonies which enhance our experience of Her natural world and mark Her cycle of transformation, demonstrating how change comes about in nature and in our own lives.

During the Second Spiral we learn how to become true heart Priestesses of the Goddess, further developing our gifts and talents in the service of the Lady. The focus of our learning shifts to how we may best serve the Goddess, Her people and Her nature, rather than ourselves. We develop the practical skills of a Priestess of the Goddess and have the opportunity to delve more deeply into the Mysteries of Her Nature. Personal challenges arise during the Second Spiral, as they did in the First, and often at a deeper level.

We begin the year by reviewing and deepening the Dedication Vow made at the completion of the First Spiral. We develop our understanding of what it means to become a Priestess of the Goddess and of Avalon. We learn priestessing skills that have been lost from the everyday world and explore what it will mean for us to stand up in the world and be counted as Her priestess. We learn the skills of the ceremonialist, able to create ritual containers in which the Goddess's energy may manifest. We learn to read signs in Her nature and develop our intuition by scrying with Her elements. We continue developing our ability to empathise with the suffering of others, learning how to become true soul counsellors and spiritual friends. We journey between the worlds for healing, guidance and soul retrieval. We reclaim the ancient traditions of Oracling and Embodying the Goddess in ceremony and in our everyday lives. We experience the transforming power of the Labrynth as a universal Goddess symbol and as manifest on the slopes of Glastonbury Tor. We design and create the ceremony in which we will Self-initiate as priestesses of the Goddess.

Deepening our Dedication Vow

A Dedication Vow to the Goddess made in ceremony is a sacred act. It has meaning and power, initiating us into new areas of devotion and commitment to Her. It is not just a few words written on a piece of paper, memorised and spoken aloud before our sister and brother dedicands, and then placed in a drawer and forgotten. A Vow of Dedication is a living thing, something with which we work daily as a development of our spiritual relationship with the Goddess.

After the Dedication Ceremony it is important for all new Sisters and Brothers of Avalon to explore on a daily basis exactly what the Vow we have made to the Goddess means to us, what effect it has spiritually and practically within our everyday lives. We each bring the Goddess alive through our worship of Her, through our dedicated actions, our creative expression, our ceremonies, study, practice, art, music, dance, through all of our daily lives. Goddess expresses Herself in the world through Her nature and She can manifest through us, those who love Her. Without us She has no human creative expression in the world.

We all have different talents, capacities and living conditions, through which we can express the meaning of our Vow. Some of us are musicians and can sing for the Goddess; some are writers and can write poetry, plays and prose for Her; some are performers and can embody Her myths and energies; some are artists and can paint, craft or sculpt for Her; some are healers and can heal with Her blessings. Some of us are single, some have families, some work full time, some are disabled or ill. In these many different circumstances in fulfilment of our vows we each have to learn to recognise the Lady's voice speaking to us. We each have to dare to act upon Her instructions for our lives and express Her wishes in the world.

We learn to hear Her voice by spending time with Her, listening to Her wisdom within, listening to Her truth for us. We learn the power of acting upon Her instructions by seeing what happens when we follow what we hear or sense within. We experiment, knowing that She will never instruct us to do anything which will harm us or anyone else. She is a beneficent loving Goddess. She will however bring us to the places where our wounds lie so that we can heal them with Her help and in Her loving presence.

Continue to recreate your personal altar through the cycle of the seasons, spending time each day, praying to Her for guidance, inspiration and with thanksgiving for all that She gives to you.

The completion of the Second Spiral leads us to a second dedication and initiation, that of becoming a Priestess of the Goddess. Again in truth this is not an easy step to take and throughout the Second Spiral we are challenged from within and without as to our true purpose and intentions in becoming Her priestess and whether this is truly the path for us. The role of Priestess of the Goddess is primarily a public role, not a private fantasy, and it is not for everyone. It may not be the right thing for you. We can surrender to the Goddess and dedicate our lives to Her without becoming Her priestess. There need be no sense of failure if this is what we decide, for She will have other plans for us, ways in which we can serve Her.

As in the First Spiral it is important to have support during the Second Spiral of our journey to priestesshood and in the second year of the *In the Heart of the Goddess* training, students once again become part of small support groups, who stay in contact between training sessions.

Becoming a Priest/ess of the Goddess

The path of the priestess is primarily a path of devotion to the Goddess in the forms in which we know and love Her, as the One Universal Goddess who encompasses all others, as the Great Mother, as the Lady of Avalon, and in Brigit's Isles as Britannia, Brigit, Ana, Artha, Eostre, Rhiannon, Blodeuwedd, Elen, Olwen, Domnu, Ker, Madron, Brigantia, Banbha, Ertha, Keridwen, Sheela na Gig, Danu and Arianrhod, and in other lands as Astarte, Diana, Hecate, Demeter, Kali or Inanna, amongst many others. In this Second Spiral we dedicate ourselves to the Goddess as we are coming to know Her within the cycle of Her seasons within Brigit's Isles and within the landscape of Avalon, with all Her awesome, loving, transformative power.

On our journey to priestesshood our first great initiatory step has been to consciously dedicate our lives to Her, acknowledging that She leads us through life wherever She wishes to take us and with all that that might mean. This is a great surrender of ego control to a loving invisible power and it takes time, faith and experience to truly surrender. As we do so She will take us and reshape us, changing everything She touches in our lives.

Beyond the dedication of our lives to Her, the role of priestess requires further individual surrender, for a Priestess of the Goddess is one who loves and serves Goddess, Her people and Her nature, with our whole heart, mind, emotions, body and soul, to the best of our ability. We offer to Her all our talents, skills, personality and soul, so they might be honed in Her service. We also offer to Her our inhibitions, our anxieties, our depression, our frustrations, our negativity, our loneliness, our resistance to change, as well as all the psychological and material props and addictions that we use to prevent ourselves feeling pain. We offer Her everything within us that is in need of transformation, so that we may better serve Her.

A Priestess of the Goddess is always in the process of becoming priestess. To name ourselves as Her priestess is not to make a final statement of achievement, but to mark the place of our initiation into what priestesshood means for us and for those we hope to serve. As priestesses we are continually learning, developing, growing and refining exactly what it means to be a Priestess of the Goddess. This is a reclaimed, remembered and yet ever new 21st century path of service to Her. Throughout the Second Spiral we learn and practise the skills of the priestess, preparing ourselves for Self initiation by acting as if we are already initiate.

The role of priestess has both public and private components. It is not enough to name oneself priestess and hold the gifts of the Goddess for one's private entertainment, although Her gifts will definitely enhance our personal lives. The role of priestess is primarily a public role, expressed through our varied personalities with all our splendid qualities and with our inadequacies too, which are in process of transformation. Our purpose as priestesses is to act from our soul nature, with love, kindness, compassion, clarity, vision, wisdom, movement and stillness. As priestesses we are always on the journey to becoming whole.

Today there are few if any, formal priestess trainings which we can enter as young wo/men and mature into adult priestesshood. In these days we all begin where we are in our personal life journeys, whether we are twenty three or sixty three when we hear Her voice. Many would-be priestesses recognise Her calling in mid-life when a longing to find meaning in life emerges from a materially based life. Others hear Her call when we are young girls or boys. Others respond when we become elders. We may have much experience of life, love and spirituality, we may have many proven skills, or our experience may be rudimentary, our dedication to

Her almost completely aspirational, rather than practised. Wherever we begin we are always on the path of becoming Her priestess and She will lead us into Her service and show us how best to do this.

We can deepen our connection to Her by communing with Her daily. The following is a simple spiritual practice in which we call the Goddesses of Britannia's Wheel into our hearts daily. It can begin with the daily centring meditation given in the First Spiral or you can go straight into the invocation.

Invoking the Goddesses of Britannia's Wheel

1. *Light a candle and burn incense or a joss stick at your altar.*
2. *Stand in front of your altar, facing it.*
3. *Invocation of the Goddesses on Britannia's Wheel*

In this practice you are the centre of the wheel and are calling the Goddesses into your own heart at the centre.

a) Turn to face the direction of the time of year. At Samhain begin by facing the northwest. Open your arms wide and call into your circle the Samhain Goddesses - Nolava the Crone, Hag, Dark Goddess, Keridwen the Bringer of Death and Keeper of the Cauldron, Queen of the Underworld, Sheela na Gig, Guardian of the Yonic gateway, Beansidhe, Yew Woman and Morgen Mazoe. Call in Her creatures - the Great White Sow, the Toad, the Hawk, and Her qualities of death, transformation and rebirth. Visualise the Goddess coming towards you in Her different Samhain forms, entering into your body and being - Bid Her "Hail and Welcome, Crone Keridwen!"

At the end of the invocation bring your hands together over your heart gathering all Her energies into your body.

b) Turning sunwise to the north open your arms out wide and call in the Goddess of the North, Mother of Air - Nolava of Air, Danu, Anu, Aine, Arianrhod, Cailleach, Bone Woman, Stone Woman, Old Woman of Winter, Holly Woman, Morgen Tyronoe, with Her creatures of the Air - Eagle, Buzzard, Owl and Wren. Call in Her gifts of the Air, of the wind which blows through our lives bringing change, clearing our minds of clutter. Call in winter and hibernation, wisdom and spiritual energy.

"Hail and Welcome, Danu, Mother of Air!"

Bring the Goddess of the north and Her energy into your heart, bringing your hands together over your heart.

c) Turning to the northeast open your arms and call in the Maiden Goddess - Maiden Nolava, Brigit, Bridie, Bride, Willow Woman, Morgen Thitis with Her creatures - Swan, White Cow with red ears, Snake and Wolf. Call in Her

Maiden qualities of innocence, new beginnings, of the threshold, the quickening, and Bridie's poetry, healing and transforming smithcraft.

"Hail and Welcome, Maiden Bridie!"

d) Turn to the east and call in the Mother of Fire - Nolava of Fire, Artha the Great She Bear, Grainne the Sun Goddess, Eostre, Lady of Springtime, Hazel Woman, Morgen Cliton with Her creatures - Bear, Hare, Red Hen and Cat. Call in Her gifts of Fire, of springtime, of the greening, of energy and enthusiasm, courage, passion, warmth and protection.

"Hail and Welcome, Mother of Fire/Artha!"

e) Turn to the southeast and call in the Goddess as Lover - Nolava the Lover, Rhiannon of the Birds, White Mare from the Sea, She who is Sovereignty, Queen of the Land, Blodeuwedd the Flower Goddess, Olwen of the White Track, Elen of the Trackways, Queen of the May, Lady of Music, Morgen Thetis with Her creatures - White Mare, Dove, and flocks of small Birds. Call in the gifts of Her loving nature, Her joyful sexuality and sensuality.

"Hail and Welcome, Lover/Rhiannon!"

f) Turn to the south and call in the Mother of the Waters - Nolava of the Waters, Domnu the Ocean, Queen of the Deep, Lady of the Holy Springs and Wells, Lady of the Lake, Nimue, Vivienne, Oak Woman, Morgen Gliten with Her Water creatures - Whale, Dolphin, Seal, and Salmon of Wisdom. Call in Her gifts of all the emotions and Her all encompassing compassion.

"Hail and Welcome, Mother of Water/Domnu!"

g) Turn to the southwest and call in the Mother Goddess - Great Mother Nolava, Ker the Grain Mother, Madron, Mother of the lineage of Avallach, Ash Woman, Deer Woman and Mistress Glitonea of the Morgens with Her horned domesticated creatures - Cow, Goats, Sheep and Deer. Call in the gifts of Her abundant nature, Her wealth, prosperity and generosity, Her loving, nurturing care for all Her children.

"Hail and Welcome, Mother Goddess/Ker!"

h) Turn to the west and call in the Mother of Earth - Nolava of Earth, Brigantia, Lady of these islands, Banbha, Lady of the Land from before the Flood, Gaia, Ertha our Mother Earth, Beech Woman, Morgen Moronoe with Her creatures - Boar, Badger and Fox. Call in the gifts of the Earth, of grounding and security, of the Earth that sustains all our Life, bringing all things into manifestation.

"Hail and Welcome, Mother of Earth/Brigantia!"

i) When you have completed calling in the Goddesses of the eight directions, turn to face your altar. Open your arms and call in Britannia, tutelary Goddess of Brigit's Isles and the people who dwell here, She who governs the

outer world of Brigit's Isles. See Her seated on a rock surrounded by the sea, with Her sun disc, trident, sheaf of grain and Her lion by Her side. Call in Her gifts of strength, independence, courage, Her command of the seas.
"Hail and Welcome, Britannia!"
j) Then turning to face the direction of Avalon from your home, or if you live in Glastonbury the direction of the Tor and Chalice Hill, call in Great Nolava, Lady of Avalon, who is Goddess of the inner worlds. Call Her in as Goddess of the Sacred Land, as Morgen La Fey, Keeper of the Mysteries of Avalon, Weaver of the Web, Shapeshifter, Wayshower, Faery Woman, Apple Woman, Lady of Time, Walker between the Worlds, Healer, Sovereign, Shining One, Faery Woman with Her creatures - black Crow, black Cat and faeries. Call in Her magic and mystery. Feel Her entering your body and close your arms across your heart.
"Hail and Welcome, Lady of Avalon!"

Add in your own understanding of the Goddesses, creatures and qualities of the directions to each of the above.

As the wheel of the year turns, begin your invocation with the appropriate Goddess for the time of year. Change the direction you begin with about two to three weeks before the next Sunfire festival, when the energy feels like it is changing, e.g. begin to call in Danu around the beginning of December, Bridie in early January, etc.

4. *When you have called in the Goddesses on the wheel make your own prayers and ask for Her blessing.*

"Goddesses of Britannia's Wheel
Nolava, Lady of the Isle of Avalon
Walk with me through this day
Bless, guide and protect me
And all those whose path I touch today."

The Archetype of the Priestess

The title of *Priestess* carries not only the personal energy of the one who takes the name, but it also carries archetypal transpersonal energy, which exists beyond present culture and time, and beyond individuals. When we take the title of *Priestess* we are also taking on the mythic energy that lies beyond the manifested form, that has accumulated over hundreds and thousands of years. This archetypal energy is much bigger than the individual. It is powerful. It heals, catalyses and transforms all that come in contact with it, both within the would-be priestess and those whose lives she touches. When we take on the title *Priestess of the Goddess* we are asking for change in our lives. When we take the title *Priestess of Avalon*, the isle of transformation, this archetypal energy is doubly enhanced.

One of the best poetic and archetypal descriptions of a Priestess that I have seen, is found in Ariel Spilsbury's lovely pamphlet, *Guidebook for a Modern Priest/ess* and I quote from it here with permission. Ariel lives in Hawaii and describes herself as a planetary Priestess of the Goddess.

"A *priest/ess can be looked at as: acting from deep devotion to tending the path, lifting the lamp, holding the mirror, pooling the silence, translating the divine, funnelling the energetic flow, riding the current, hallowing the moon, unlocking the mystery, presencing beauty, being a savant of symbols, a mouth of the oracle, a container of the presence, a keeper of the flame, a bearer of the chalice, sanctity's sentinel, a strengthener of stillness, a catalyser of coherence, a diviner of harmony, a stylus of silence, a liaison of light, a celebrant of sound, a scribe of the ineffable, a resonant repository, a keeper of the keys, a cipher of the crescent, a decoder of dreams, a servant of* Memnos (*memory*), *the* Divine Feminine.......

As *an archetype the priestess can be looked at as* 'She Who is Keeper *of the* Keys *and* Guardian *of the* Mysteries'. *She is the feminine archetype of stillness, silence and centred presence... The way of the priest/ess is the way of devotion, devotion to the divine unfoldment of the soul lotus blossoming in herself and all beings..... She creates and maintains the sanctity and resonance of the temple. This temple can be her own (body), home, workplace,* (Goddess Temple) *or whatever space she sanctifies with the power of divine presence. Through her devotional focus the priestess becomes the living flame at the centre of the temple..... She is a living embodiment of the immanent power of the eternal flame of love, power and wisdom."*

(For copies of *Guidebook for a Modern* Priestess and further information on Ariel Spilsbury, see her website www.arielspilsbury.com or www.cosmicircus.com/goddess)

To these I would add, a priestess is also:

A Melissa *serving in the* Temple, *supporter and promoter of women and women's values, heart sister to men,* Keeper *of* Her *nature, gaiamancer, guardian of wilderness, wild wo/man, oceanic surfer, empathic listener, soul midwife, creative craftswoman, sacred artist/musician/dancer, the embodiment of* Her *ecstasy.*

Consider other priestess attributes you might like to add to those given.

Invoking the Archetypal Priestess Self

Invoking the archetypal Priestess Self is similar to calling the Goddess into a ceremony. As we call in the priestess archetype, we open our awareness to a more expansive, loving energy and way of being than usual, opening to our soul's true energy. There are different ways of doing this. For some people calling in the archetypal priestess may be a spoken prayer, calling her into the body. We ask her to come into our physical body and be present, so that we can look out from our bodies with the eyes of the priestess, rather than with our normal eyes. At the beginning of group ceremony, priestessing with others, we join hands in circle and centring ourselves, connect to our priestess selves and to each other.

The archetypal priestess self is also gathered into consciousness and our bodies during our preparations for ceremony, as we clean and clear our ceremonial space, as we prepare our priestess tools, as we light candles and burn incenses, as we smudge our sacred space, as we move through the space with purpose and intention.

She is called in as we robe ourselves as priestesses. One of the reasons in all religious traditions that priest/esses dress in special costumes is that the costumes themselves are expressions of particular archetypes. For example, the Christian priest wears a black dress and white dog collar, the shamanka has her skins and feathers, the Buddhist monk is in his red and saffron robes, the Priestess of Avalon wears her violet or many coloured dresses, all denoting archetypes. When used regularly for spiritual and ceremonial practice, ceremonial robes accumulate energy which becomes associated with the archetype. Thus when we put on our priestess robes we automatically call in the archetypal priestess.

The following exercise can be practised more then once.

Stand before your altar. Focus your attention on your breath and allow your breath to slow and deepen. Notice how your body, emotions and mind calm themselves as you do this.

Ground and centre yourself using the First Spiral daily exercise, connecting to the earth and to the farthest star. Bring their energy into your heart and radiate your soul's energy outwards through your aura into the space around you.

Invoke the archetypal priestess self into your body and being. Call her in. Feel your spine straighten and yourself grow tall as she enters your body. Feel her in your body for several moments and let that feeling deepen. After a time complete the following sentence with her voice,

" I am she who ...." ,

describing the archetype you are carrying, e.g., "I am she who lights the way", "I am she who is strength", "I am she who sings the sacred songs", etc.

As you speak, hear the name of the archetypal priestess self to whom you are connected. This name will give you some idea of the priestess qualities you are capable of invoking. You may also ask her personal name by completing the sentence spontaneously,

" I am ....".

These names may become part of how you know your priestess self. They may also change over time and with circumstances.

Look out through your eyes and from your body as your priestess self. Notice how that makes your feel. Offer your prayers to the Goddess as Her Priestess.

The first times that you try this exercise you may be startled by the intensity of the archetypal energy. You may delight in her presence and you may find the energy to be heavy or scary. This is an energetic experience and you may not be used to drawing archetypal energies into your physical body. As you get used to the process and the feel of her inside your skin, these energies lighten and you will welcome them more readily. Although her presence may feel intense her energy is always positive. She is always harmless.

Life as a Priestess of the Goddess

In our lives there is always a balance to be wrought between our everyday lives as human beings and those times when we priestess. Our purpose may be to live a wholly priestess life, but there are still times when we are doing laundry, taking children to school. As we learn to become priestess, we often feel the archetypal priestess energy come into us only at certain times, when we open to Her in ceremony or in nature. As we stand before Her altar and focus our attention we feel a wave of priestess presence come into our bodies. We stand taller, our body movements begin to flow, we become graceful, the right words come easily, we know what to say. We feel our priestess self within our bodies. The archetype has entered in and we feel strong and filled with energy, able to call the Lady in with meaning, so that others can feel Her presence too.

We can usually hold this priestess presence for the duration of a ceremony or a special occasion, but it may be more difficult for us to sustain in the everyday world. We may not feel like a priestess as we clean the toilet, shop in the supermarket or sit on a bus.

Throughout the Second Spiral as we learn the practical skills of priestessing our aim is also to develop the ability to hold the archetypal priestess self in our bodies for longer lengths of time and to bring her in immediately whenever she is needed. We learn this capability as we intensify our spiritual relationship to the Lady and this takes intention, time and commitment. This is the spiritual journey we are taking, drawing ever closer to Her so that we can truly live a priestess life.

Practice invoking your Priestess self into your body. First ground and centre, and then call her in. Open Britannia's Wheel given earlier, feeling yourself standing tall. Invoke the energies and attributes of the Goddesses on the Wheel as Her Priestess.

Becoming a Priestess of Avalon

As well as developing the priestess attributes and abilities described above, a Priestess of Avalon has additional skills she must acquire, those related to working within the particularly transformative energies of Avalon. A Priestess of Avalon is a wo/man who chooses to pursue a path of spiritual service in sacred devotion to the Goddess in the form of the Lady of Avalon, to Her people, and to the Isle of Avalon. The energies of Avalon are particularly connected to the development of love and compassion, intuition and discrimination, to the healing of ancient karmic wounds. They catalyse the expansion of consciousness, allowing us to encompass more love and wisdom in our lives. They bring us experiences of birth, healing, death and rebirth, transformation on all levels of being. To be able to fully serve the Lady of Avalon means that we need to have experience of these energies in our own lives, to know what they feel like and the disturbing effects they may have, so that we can help others who are facing the same experiences unprepared.

Becoming a Priestess of Avalon involves change in every facet of our being, bringing us into alignment with our soul's true purpose. As we all know this is not something that happens overnight, but with every breath we take. She is the way, She is the goal and She is the inspiration for all that we do. We need to take the time to properly prepare ourselves for Self-initiation into the energies of the Goddess and Avalon over several years, rather than thinking it is something we can claim after a few weekends of training.

Again the title of Priestess of Avalon carries archetypal transpersonal energy in its own right, energy which can heal, catalyse and transform all with whom the priestess comes into contact. As well as the priestess attributes given before, a Priestess of Avalon is also in process of becoming an:

Opener of the heart, a shining mirror, inspired guide to Glastonbury's sacred landscape, guardian of the sacred wells and springs, wayshower through the Veil of Her Mystery, guide to Avalon. She scrys from all forms of nature. She leads the way through the labrynth into the Heart of the Goddess, to the Spiral Castle of Caer Sidi. She knows the pathways to the Underworld, of entry and return. She transports those in need of healing across the great waters. She journeys between the worlds for healing and soul retrieval. She is a soul midwife of birth, death and rebirth. She is a healer and mystress of transformation. She is an Oracle and Embodiment of the Lady.

Again add more qualities as you become aware of them.

Our Purpose in becoming a Priestess of the Goddess and Avalon

As we begin to journey to Her priestesshood it is important to spend time thinking about why we are doing this. Is it merely a glamour? Is it that we want to dance around in pretty dresses and be seen to be important or mysterious? Do we care more for the trappings of priestesshood than the substance, which includes spiritual, psychological and physical work, daily communion with the Lady, deep healing of personal wounds, sweeping floors and cleaning wax from candlesticks, as well as wafting about in silken robes looking lovely?

What is our true purpose in becoming first of all a Priestess of the Goddess and then of Avalon? It is important to make this journey for the right reasons and to be conscious of why we are doing it. In the following I speak from my own understanding of my purpose in being Her priestess, to inspire you in considering your own.

I am Priestess of the Goddess because I know that it is my dharma, my life work, my destiny, you could say, to help bring Goddess consciousness back into the world. I feel this deep in my heart, in my bones, in my blood. I want to do everything in my power, led by Her, to promote recognition of Goddess and Her many blessings in the world. This does not mean that I will proselytise or force Her onto those who are simply not interested in knowing about Her, but for those who are hungry for knowledge of Her, I can provide information, experience, ceremony, healing, a sympathetic ear and an open, empathic, Goddess-loving heart.

I believe that I have incarnated at this time especially for this purpose, to help bring Her back into the world. I have an inner knowledge of Her remembered from previous lives in which I also loved and served Her in different forms and places, from Brigit's Isles to Krete, from Sumer to Egypt, from Tibet to China. I believe that I am very lucky to be able to remember these experiences and to have the opportunity of being alive at this time of great change in the world when She is returning and I can play a part in Her return.

As an expression of the Goddess within, I believe in the sacredness of women and in our core values and culture, our loving nature, our nurturing kindness, our natural intelligence, our innate spirituality. We are the Goddess incarnate in the world and we need to be loved and honoured as such. I wish to promote women in the world so that our spiritual and cultural voices can be heard once again, so that we can make a difference in our disastrously imbalanced world and God can assume His proper place.

I am a Priestess of Avalon because again, I now know that it is my destiny to reclaim this ancient title as a living priestess tradition, as part of the re-emergence of the Goddess into the world. The Lady of Avalon called me first to come and live in Glastonbury in a dream, even when I did not know consciously of Her existence. Over time She made Herself known to me and many years ago I surrendered to Her transforming powers, firstly with great resistance and now willingly. She called me to be Her priestess and I responded, not really knowing what I was doing. I remembered previous lives in this sacred land when I had loved and served the Lady of Avalon. I also remember being present when patriarchal powers came into Her physical lands and used violence to overwhelm and subdue Her people.

My purpose in serving the Lady as priestess is to demonstrate Her awesome loving nature and Her healing and transforming power, to the best of my ability. I aim to continually learn more about Her ways and to offer all I receive about Her to others. I pull new information along etheric threads through the Veil of Avalon day by day, making it conscious, as She reveals more of Herself to me and to others, for this is the journey of a group of souls. I am not the only one. Many of us are being called to be part of Her return. In my character I am an initiator and thus my purpose has been and is to set up new organisations, events, training programmes, structures and Temples through which the Lady of Avalon may enter the world via human awareness and creativity.

Take the time to consider your own purpose in becoming first of all a Priestess of the Goddess and then a Priestess of Avalon, if this is what you are choosing to become.

Responsibilities, Practices and Rites of a Priestess of Avalon

As we journey towards priestesshood as well as the development of archetypal priestess attributes there are changes that must be wrought within our personalities, so that the energies of our souls and of the Goddess, can flow more freely into our lives. The following are suggestions for personal development and aspiration for all those who are walking the path to Self initiation as Priestesses of the Goddess and Avalon and continue to apply to all branches of the Orchard of Avalon. They are offered with love and an understanding of what they demand from us. They have been discussed in depth many times by students and modified at Orchard gatherings. They form the basis for a Code of Practice and Ethics for the Priestess of Avalon Training.

The Developing Responsibilities of a Priestess of Avalon

* *To live and act with personal integrity.*
* *To be kind, honest, compassionate, loving and wise.*
* *To harm no other.*
* *To be responsible to self and others for all our actions, both positive and negative.*
* *To be prepared to deal with the consequences of our mistakes and failures.*
* *To respect, honour and support all members of the expanding Orchard of Avalon.*
* *To respect the right of others to follow their own beliefs.*
* *To seek to cooperate with others and not to seek to generate conflict.*
* *To maintain interpersonal confidentiality.*
* *To love and care for ourselves at all times.*
* *To know our limitations and work with them, and to know that we are truly limitless.*
* *To learn to discriminate between the real and the unreal.*
* *To refrain from committing hubris.*

The Developing Practices and Rites of a Priestess of Avalon

* *To maintain a daily spiritual practice, invoking the Presence of the Lady of Avalon often.*

* *To listen for and respond to Her words of truth.*
* *To serve the Goddess in the ways She instructs us.*
* *To live and express ourselves consciously in the flow of Her energy and in rhythm with the cycles and seasons of Her nature.*
* *To trust Her, knowing that She leads us through life's experiences for our greatest good.*
* *To continue to expand our knowledge and experience of the Goddess through personal study and the practice of Her ways and to share those with others.*
* *To generate the energies of Avalon and connect others to those energies.*
* *To perform ceremonies of all kinds in the flow of Her energy with due preparation and awareness of purpose, with care and attention to detail, both visible and invisible.*
* *To generate and maintain Her sacred space.*
* *To support those who are experiencing the Dark Face of the Goddess.*
* *To offer comfort and healing in Her name.*
* *To serve at various times in the Goddess Temple and at the Glastonbury Goddess Conference.*
* *To aspire to Her ecstasy.*

It is important to reiterate that these responsibilities, practices and rites are aspirations that we are working towards fulfilling during our training and beyond. Some of them are easier to fulfil than others. Within the Orchard it is recognised that we are all at different places in our desire and ability to fulfil these aspirations, but we are moving towards them. There is no external judge of our success or failure to live up to these ideals, only our own compassionate, non-judgemental, inner knowing of where we are in Her service. This is a renewed priestess path of service to the Goddess as Lady of Avalon and we all begin where we are.

Personal Work

Look at ways in which you can affirm and deepen your Vow of Dedication as a Sister or Brother of Avalon. Daily invoke the Goddesses on Britannia's Wheel. Consider which archetypal qualities you wish to embody as a Priestess of the Goddess, as well as those you wish to add to the qualities given. Practice invoking your archetypal Priestess self into your body. Begin to work on your purpose in becoming a Priestess of the Goddess and of Avalon. Consider where you are in relationship to the rights, responsibilities and practices of a Priestess of Avalon. Is this the path for you?

Throughout the course of the Second Spiral, as during the First, students begin to work on the Self-initiation Vow that you will make at the end of this Spiral. The dedication you will be making is to love, honour and serve the Goddess as Her priestess. Once again the words used are your own, but include something along the lines of,

"I *dedicate myself to you, Goddess, as your* Priestess."

Creating Goddess Ceremonies and Sacred Rituals

Creating and performing Ceremony or Sacred Ritual is one of the primary functions of a Priestess of the Goddess. We live in a world which has become bereft of meaningful ceremony and it is one of our priestess tasks to bring meaning back into everyday life through daily rituals and by creating ceremonies for those important occasions in life which need to be specially marked and blessed by Her energy. Ritual involves a repeated set of actions which may contain spiritual or mundane elements (brushing one's teeth is a daily ritual), whereas ceremony is always a spiritual practice and may or may not include ritual elements.

Ceremony is the means by which priestesses consciously create the conditions in which we and others can experience the energies of the Goddess, moving within and between us all. We learn to create energetic containers into which Goddess may be invoked, so that She can be experienced both by those who are actively engaged in calling Her in and by those who participate in ceremony. The purpose of Goddess ceremony is always to deepen our direct personal and collective relationships to Her, to bless, transform and heal, and to reveal more of Her nature, Her love and compassion. Priestesses of Avalon invoke the presence of the Lady of Avalon and Her transforming and compassionate nature, as well as the many faces and forms of the Goddesses on Britannia's Wheel.

As we are spiritual beings manifesting within Her physical world our ceremonies are formed out of Her world, from the five elements of Her nature - earth, water, fire, air and space, and the corresponding parts of our own nature, our physical and etheric bodies, our emotions, the fire of our minds, and our airy spiritual nature. The fifth element of space is Her universal and originating spaciousness, the essence of all things which come into manifestation.

Ceremonies can be individual, designed to fulfil personal needs and purposes, which can be witnessed by others, or they can be collective and created with others, for larger gatherings, of tens, or hundreds of people. Whatever kind of ceremony we are performing there are basic skills we need to learn in order to priestess well. These include the ability to call in the archetypal priestess self into the body as described in the previous chapter; the ability to find and hold inner stillness - to generate sacred space; the ability to hear and respond to intuition and the ability to be sensitive to movement within Her energy field.

Generating Stillness - Creating Sacred Space

An essential priestess skill is the ability to generate stillness within, to generate a loving sacred space which emanates outwards to all who come into its presence. This stillness is not inertness, it is not the passivity of sleep or the empty house of death. It is an alert stillness, a deep pool of silence, that will respond if a flower falls gently onto its surface, or if a stone is dropped into it, ripples moving across the surface as the depths remain still. This stillness helps calm the racing minds and emotions of all who come into its presence. This loving stillness is an emanation of the soul, which evokes an opening to soul energy in all those who come in contact with it. They become more relaxed in our presence, calmer, less guarded, less defended, more open. They feel safe and able to express their feelings and show their human vulnerability, the source of our true strength. Through a synchronous vibration our stillness encourages people to feel the place of stillness within themselves, to connect with their own soul's energy.

The only way to create stillness, to generate sacred space, is by becoming still: a truism which many of us find hard to accept as we live busy lives and have active brains that continually chatter. There are many meditative techniques designed to bring us to that place of stillness within and you may already be familiar with them. Here I would like to offer a Goddess-centred approach.

Sit in front of your altar with your back straight and your legs in a comfortable position. Close your eyes. As you get used to sitting bring your consciousness into the present, recognising where you are sitting, what you are doing. Bring your attention to your breath and feel and listen to your breath as it moves in and out of your mouth or nose, down into your lungs and out again. Feel your abdomen and breasts rising and falling with the breath. Become aware of oxygen entering your body from your in-breath and stale carbon dioxide being removed as you breathe out. Notice how shallow or deep your breath is. Allow the breath to deepen. Count your breath for 20 breaths.

In your mind's eye visualise the Goddess in a form that is familiar to you, as the Lady of Avalon, as Brigit, as Rhiannon, etc. See Her there in front of you in as much detail as you are able, seated or standing. See Her form and the position of Her limbs. See Her clothing, Her headdress, anything She carries in Her hands. See Her face and its expression. Feel the stillness that She holds within Her, even when Her body is moving. When the image in your mind becomes stable place Her image in your heart.

Feel Her loving stillness entering your heart and filling your body so that your body and aura become a still radiant centre while life goes on all around you. Hold this feeling of stillness within for as long as you can. This is Her sacred space.

As you hold this place of inner stillness open your eyes and look around you. See if you can hold this still place with your eyes open. Continue to feel the spaciousness within. Slowly stand and begin to move. Again continue to feel the spaciousness within. Take the feeling of spaciousness with you into your everyday life, holding it for as long as you can.

Practice this visualisation over weeks and months so that the feeling of inner stillness or sacred space becomes familiar to you. In time you will be able to move into the place of stillness at will, when you want to, in ceremony as you priestess and hold space for others. As we become more able to find that place of stillness within ourselves, we consciously generate stillness or sacred space as we priestess, so that others with whom we come into contact, can feel that stillness too.

As was said in the First Spiral we create sacred space not through the ability to arrange an outer space, lighting candles and incense, but through generating sacred space within which radiates outwards and is felt by others. We take time before each ceremony to generate stillness within and to connect to that inner space by becoming completely focused, as we arrange our temple space, light our candles and incense, and pray to the Lady.

As well as cultivating stillness within through spiritual practice it is also important to cultivate emotional expression, so that emotions do not become dammed up, generating disease. The Goddess path is one of expression, rather than suppression of emotions. We need to do this on a regular basis, either through conversations with family, friends or skilled counsellors, through the appropriate release of tears, anger, sadness and joy as we feel them, through artistic creativity of all forms, and through music, movement, song and dance. As we release our emotions we empty out, creating psychic space within, in which Her silence can find a peaceful home.

As we quieten within we cultivate trust in Her for She has brought us to this place of peace. Our faith in Her increases as we see the positive effects She is having in our lives. We find we now know certain things to be true that are unprovable by worldly measurement, but which come from a deep inner knowing that is true for us. All these are consequences of finding stillness within.

Moving in the Flow *of* Her Energy

Another important and basic skill for all priestesses is the ability to become completely at-one with Her energy field. We must first of all become aware of energy fields in principle and practice, feeling their movement and flow through the development of the seventh sense. Then we can generate energy fields ourselves as containers for Her energy. There are several stages to learning how to do this, which follow on from the ability to generate silence within.

In understanding energy and its movement we begin with some basic magical principles, which are founded within the inspired teachings of Alice A. Bailey in her "*Treatise on the Seven Rays*" (Lucis Trust). I studied Alice's teachings intensively in my twenties and they provide a foundation for my own healing and ceremonial practice. I have modified these teachings through 25 years of practical healing experience and published my own book on healing *Chiron in Labrys: An Introduction to Esoteric Soul Healing*, Kathy Jones (Ariadne Publications).

The first principle of energy is that :

Within Her nature all is energy and energy is all that there is.

In the physical world we all live and move and have our being in an eternal, infinite, interlocking system of energies and forces that compose our universe. Some of these energies appear to our five senses to be solid and have form, but when we examine them closely they disappear into space, energy and only a tiny amount of matter. When we examine the atoms which are the building blocks for our material world we find they contain only minute particles of matter surrounded by energy and space, which creates the illusion of form.

For most of us life is essentially an energetic experience. None of us are focused purely in material reality. Although we must all eat good food, drink clean water and breathe clear air to survive, most of us spend the majority of our time focused in the non-physical worlds of our feelings, emotions and thoughts, with occasional glimpses into a deeper world within and beyond. We are all continually moved, swayed and transformed by energies which though physically immaterial, mould our actions and determine our behaviour and experience. Our world is not solid, it is energetic.

The second principle of energy is that :

There is a causal relationship between consciousness, energy and form

Consciousness, Being and Soul are words that describe the same energy. Consciousness is that coherent, integral, present and indivisible matrix of love energy shared by all forms in manifestation in our universe. It is what IS, Be-ing. Consciousness is organised into different forms with differing degrees of complexity. There are beings who ensoul galaxies and planets, beings who manifest as trees, plants, animals, as pebbles, rocks and mountains. There are incarnate human beings, there are discarnate beings, there are Goddesses and Gods. The human soul is both individual and collective. We are each uniquely ourselves, we have individual souls, and yet we are all one and indivisible, containing the same consciousness that unites us in love. The soul is the expression of the Life of the Goddess. It is governed by purpose and motivated by love.

All forms of consciousness appear to have a centre from which energy radiates outwards, creating an energy field which surrounds them. This energy field is characterised by the quality of energy of the informing being and it is within this energy field that a physical form manifests and appears for us to see. To create a material form energy which is organised in the form of consciousness must be present.

The third principle of energy is that :

Energy follows thought and feeling

Energy follows the direction of our thoughts and feelings. As we think individually and collectively so the world is. As individuals if we wake up feeling depressed then the rest of our day is usually clouded by negative thoughts. We do not see the beautiful flowers around us, the sun shining in the sky, the smiles on people's faces. We focus on what is wrong with us and our lives, and often what is wrong with other people. When we wake feeling happy then we see the positive around us, we smile at strangers, we are creative in our thoughts and actions, we feel optimistic.

The ways in which we experience the world are affected by the ideas and thoughts that we have about the world. If we believe the world is a lonely and scary place then that is often how we experience it and our experience will tend to reinforce our beliefs. If we think the world is our Goddess-given home then we experience it very differently, as a safe place where we are always loved. Many of our ideas, thoughts and feelings about our lives and the world around us are created in childhood from the experiences we have, which reinforce the seeds of karma we bring with us into incarnation.

In a generalised sense we all help to create the world around us through our individual and collective thoughts, feelings and dreams. As we think and feel so the world is. We may have free will but we are also at the effect of the collective unconscious, all our thoughts and feelings. We are swayed and moved by unconscious forces over which we as individuals seem to have little control. Our collective thoughtforms, which are agglomerations of emotion and thought, create the belief, for example, that there is not enough food in the world to feed everyone. From that thoughtform come the attitudes and policies which create the reality that rich countries have too much food which goes to waste, while poorer nations must starve, reinforcing the idea that there is not enough food to go round. Changing the thoughtform that "*There is not enough food...*" to "*There is enough food for everyone*" will result in changes in practices that will change the way things are. Plans to eradicate hunger by 2020 in Third World countries are part of this changing thoughtform. Concerned individuals are building a movement to bring about a conscious change in the beliefs we hold about food and debt, thus changing the malpractices resulting from those beliefs.

This is the positive side of this energy principle, which means that if we put our hearts and minds to it we can change the way things are, by collectively changing the thoughtforms which govern our reality. Such a change can be seen in the way in which Goddess is returning step by step into human consciousness, generating new thoughtforms of balance between feminine and masculine expressions, which will alter the way life is lived on Her planet and hopefully saving our lives.

The positive side of this principle also means that individuals can improve the way things are for other people. One person following a positive dream can make a difference and can change the world.

The fourth principle is:

Everything in existence begins as idea in some being's consciousness

Ideas arise out of consciousness, ideas for all forms in nature and for all human creations. This applies from the Goddess to ourselves. Fuelled by the emotion of desire idea gathers energy until it becomes concretised into form. This applies from the smallest to the greatest units of consciousness, from the grain of sand to the Milky Way in the heavens.

Everything that human beings create begins as an idea without form: every building, every machine, every meal we make, everything we wear, everything we design or organise. This includes our Goddess ceremonies. We begin with an idea and bring energetic experience into form.

The fifth principle is:

Imagination is the creative faculty of the mind

Energy follows in the wake of imagination. Imagination is not simply the foolish notions of the mind which we must ignore. Imagination is the creative faculty of the mind and we learn to use it creatively and playfully. The priestess's active imagination helps to create the conditions in which the Goddess's energy may be felt and experienced by others. In ceremony we use our imagination to visualise energy, to generate and circulate energy between the Goddess and between ourselves. We also use our imagination to journey through the inner worlds to meet the Goddess in Her many forms, for healing, instruction and revelation.

The sixth principle:

Intuition is communication from our soul

Intuition is our inner guide, our connection to our soul's truth and when we follow it we act from that truth. Intuition is that state of awareness which is by definition, in tune with the laws of Her nature. It is the space where Truth is, communicated to us directly from our soul, across the rainbow bridge, also known as the antaskarana, which is built in mental and emotional matter. Intuition is the common sense which unifies and integrates all our physical and non-physical senses. It comes to us in the form of visions, words, sensings and inner knowing.

We develop our intuition through spiritual practices which connect the energy centres in the head, and also through creative action from our soul. Whenever we put our heart and soul into something we are building the rainbow bridge and calling forth our intuition. This can be any kind of creativity from dressmaking to cookery, from painting to poetry, car mechanics to engine design, whatever we love to do. This is one of the reasons it is so important for us to follow our hearts in life, to do the things that we love to do, rather than things that are merely for money and material gain. It is also the reason for the emphasis during all the *In the Heart of the Goddess* trainings on creativity and on making Goddess and priestess images, artefacts and equipment. While we are being playfully creative, often for the first time since our schooldays, making things dedicated to Her, we are also developing our intuition.

We develop intuition by recognising its existence and importance, by listening to it and acting upon the inner messages we receive about ourselves, other people, situations, the next actions we might take. As soon as we learn to hear and respond to intuition, the wonderful thing is that we receive instant feedback from the environment that our intuition is correct. It is the truth for us and our lives begin to work in new and interesting ways.

Developing the Seventh Sense : Hearing/Sensing Energy

We learn to sense and feel non-physical energy through the development of the seventh sense. This sense is actually a combination of hearing, sensing and feeling, a sensitivity to energy of different vibrations. As has been revealed on Kirlian photography we all have a health aura, an energetic radiance that emanates from the surface of the body which we can sense.

As you sit in a room on your own and quieten your thoughts and feelings, from your centre feel the radiance of your own aura, the emanation of your energy field around you. How far from your body does your health aura radiate? Is it a centimetre or two or several inches? How far from your physical body does your emotional energy radiate? Is it inches or several feet? How far from your body do your mental energies radiate? Are they inches or miles? Feel the energy of your own soul. Does it have a location inside or outside of the body? How far from your body do your soul energies radiate?

How are you sensing these energies? Where do you feel/experience them in your body?

On another day when you are sitting with others in a social setting repeat this process, but looking at other people's auras and radiances. Sense their energy fields and the different expressions of their energy. Can you feel what they might be feeling and thinking, how healthy they are, what their soul connection is like? Experiment in different social situations. Sometimes it is easier to see the emanations and colours of the aura if the person we are focusing on is against a light or dark wall or if the light is behind them. You can always tell people what you are doing and ask them to move to a place that is easier for you to see. Notice the threads of energy, of light, that connect particular friends to each other. Practice this emerging ability daily.

Repeat this process in an intentional spiritual gathering, for example, in a priestess group, a healing or meditation group. See if you can sense where people's energy is at, what they are feeling. Notice the threads of energy that connect everyone in the room to everyone else, to the teacher if there is one. Notice the mesh of energy threads that create an energetic container between you all, within the physical space you are in. Notice any other connections, to the altar, to the Goddess in the centre. Throughout the course of a gathering, through the day notice how energy moves around the container. Feel it as a light tug on the threads that connect you to everyone else, bringing changes of colour and texture, of lightness and muddiness, of fatigue and alertness.

In ceremony repeat the process becoming aware of the ways in which we are connected to each other as priestesses and participants. Feel the enhancement of all the energy connections as the archetypal priestess energies come in, and then as the Goddess Herself is called in. Feel the changes that occur within the energy field throughout the duration of a ceremony. Name energetic experiences such as the glimpse of a colour, a pinprick of light, a wave of sadness or joy or fear, so that they are not dismissed as nothing, so that you realise that these subtle events are important and have meaning, which can be shared. Notice where you feel these energies in your body, for some it will be in the head, for others in the hands and for others in the broad band between the solar plexus and the heart. Notice the way energy moves, tentatively, forcefully, sometimes feeling dense, sometimes light or at other times moving with speed. Notice how stuck energy can suddenly move for no apparent reason and notice what can be done to help move energy that is restricted. Notice how free you can feel when energy is flowing all around you, when you let go of your own inhibitions, at the same time continuing to sense the energy field.

As can be seen from these suggestions to begin to understand how energy feels and moves within our everyday lives and in a ceremonial context we need to be able to focus our attention as required. We need to develop our awareness of immaterial energies and the ability to hold our concentration for as long as necessary. These are all things that come to us through performing a daily spiritual practice.

Expanding Awareness

Many archetypal priestess attributes involve the ability to become completely at-one with Her energy field in ceremony and in nature, moving in its flow, attuned to its spiralling and sometimes chaotic motions, sensing its rising and falling, its surges and its stilling. This involves the development of our seventh sense and the expansion of our consciousness to take in more of what is happening energetically all around us, in the room we are in, in the people we are with, in the Temple, garden, glade or grove, in the valley, on the island, on the land, continent and planet. One of the ways in which we expand our awareness is by developing our physical and psychic hearing. We learn to really listen to the sounds going on all around us, to hear and sense the flow of Her energy in everything.

Sit quietly with an upright spine somewhere in nature, in a garden, a park, a wood, beside a stream, a river, the ocean, in a valley, on a mountain. Close your eyes and ground and centre yourself. Feel the threads of your energy extending downwards deep into Mother Earth and upwards into the heavens. Feel yourself to be the bridge between earth and heaven and allow your energy to gently radiate outwards from your heart in all directions.

Open your hearing and listen for the sounds of human activity and of nature going on around you - the nearby and distant sounds of machines, cars, conversations, the calls of birds, of animals, the sounds of the wind, of water, of the trees. Extend your hearing outwards as far as you can across the surrounding landscape to catch far away sounds. If you are in the country send your hearing out across the hills and valleys seeking the sounds of Her nature. If you are in the town or city reach beyond the limits of conurbations to hear the sounds of Her nature out in the countryside. Listen to what you can hear. As you listen feel your awareness expanding to encompass more space.

As you sit listening open your eyes and include all that you can see in your awareness from the nearby to the distant. Hold your awareness open for as long as you can.

As you practice this expansion of your awareness it will become something that you can do anywhere at any time.

Try this out in different settings and especially during Goddess ceremonies. Practice holding the energetic threads of the ceremony in your awareness visualising the energetic container that holds all the elements of the ceremony.

Feel the movement of energy in the container and flow with it, learning to respond to its rising and falling. Become aware of the energy as it calls you to act on the promptings of your intuition.

Acting on Intuition

In life and in ceremony we learn to listen to the voice within which says, "Speak *now*", "*Do this now*" or "*Sing this now*" and we respond with the appropriate action. This will often feel scary to our personality as it puts us out there, our possible mistakes visible for all to see and hear. As priestess it is important to dare to respond publicly to our intuition.

For years of my younger life I would often find myself in situations where I was too scared and intimidated to speak out. A discussion might be going on and I would feel an energy rise within me, wanting to say something. Instantly I would feel hot anxiety blossom in my belly with the desire to speak. My pulse would begin to race, my hands to shake. It would become so intense that I could feel quite ill, as if I might faint or be sick in front of everyone. I would sit squirming, silently combating this inner sickness and failing to open my mouth. Then the moment would pass and because of my fear I did not speak. After such an event I would spend a lot of time regretting that I had not spoken, going over and over in my mind what I could have said and what might have happened if I had spoken up.

It took many years of living with my fears before I began to dare to speak my truth, especially when my anxiety was high. Over time I experimented and gradually learned how to speak in group situations. I learned that when the feeling of anxiety arose in my belly and in my heart it was in fact especially important for me to speak my truth. That feeling was actually a signal to me that I had something to say that needed to be expressed by me and to be heard by others. I learned that when that tension was not there it wasn't necessary for me to speak, except to be sociable. Over the years that conditioned anxiety has mellowed into a sensation of pressure in the belly and the heart, rather than fear, although anxiety can still arise for me before public speaking or performing ceremony.

I have learned through many years' experience in performing sacred drama and ceremony that the feeling of pressure as it rises is a signal for me, a prompting from my intuition, to be alert and ready for something. I do not always know what it is. The pressure is a measure of the energy field of which I am a part and comes from it. If I follow the signals of the inner pressure and respond to its promptings then I am flowing with the energy field and that is what the energy requires of me, and of us all. This intuitive response allows ceremonies to deepen and become powerful experiences for everyone present.

Invocation of the Goddess

For Priestesses of the Goddess and Avalon one of our primary functions within ceremony is the Invocation of the Goddess, of Britannia and the Lady of Avalon in many guises. Invocation means *calling into the present*, and invocation of the Goddess, actually means calling the Goddess into our consciousness, calling our attention to Her. Our priestess function is to call Her into a particular ceremony and sacred space and to hold that invocation, allowing it to deepen and evolve through the duration of a ceremony. It is the holding of the invocation over time that brings power to a ceremony. It is an esoteric art which is learned through the practice of doing it.

There are different ways of practising invocation but one of the most immediate involves using the creative power of the visual imagination. We begin by visualising the Goddess as external to us, seeing Her at some distance from us on the imagined or actual far horizon, and moving towards us through space. We visualise Her with the characteristics which are familiar to us, with a particular face and form, shape and colour. We see Her, for example, as Bridie in the form of a young maiden wearing white, or as Keridwen the Old Crone with Her old wrinkled face, dressed in black, or as the golden pregnant or breast-feeding Mother Goddess. We see Her with Her sacred creatures. Rhiannon comes riding on Her White Mare from the Sea surrounded by clouds of small birds; Ker comes with Her flocks of horned deer, cattle, goats or sheep; Domnu comes swimming from the oceans with the seals, dolphins and whales, with the salmon of wisdom; and Danu flies in with Her birds, the eagles, buzzards and wrens, all the winged ones.

In words that are spoken or sung we pray to Goddess, asking Her to come and be present with us. For example, when we are calling in the Goddesses of the east, of Oestre, of springtime, of fire, we say:

"I call to you, Artha, Great She Bear of the heavens, to come and be here with us. Lady of the Stars, illuminate us with your sparkling light."

As we speak we visualise the Goddess as a huge starry She Bear coming down from the sky, moving closer towards us. We begin to feel Her energy coming towards us.

"Bear Mother, Mother of all human beings, come and be with us."

We see Her as the Great Bear Mother, the furry mother of all human beings. We expand on Her qualities, visualising the fire that is in a star, in our own sun and the fires that burn on earth, the fires of volcanoes, the hearth fires, the fires of industry, the candle flames. We feel Her warmth coming towards us.

"Artha, Mother of Fire, of the Fire in the heavens and on the earth, come and be present here in our ceremony."

We call the Mother of Fire by Her other names. We call in Grainne the Sun Goddess, recognising the place of Her sunshine in our lives.

"Grainne Goddess of the Sun, who gives all light and life to our planet, come and be welcome here. Receive our thanks for the warmth of your glowing body, for your life-giving light."

We call in Eostre, Lady of the Fires of Springtime, of the Equinox, seeing Her with Her hare, hen and cat.

"Eostre, Lady of Springtime, Lady of the Greening, we welcome your fire that is rising in all of nature, the green fire of springtime. At this time of the equinox we ask you to bring all things into balance. We welcome your spring hare, your Oestre hen, your cat.

We call in the Morgen Cliton, Lady of Fire, visualising Her perhaps in an elemental or devic form.

"Cliton, Lady of Fire, bring us the fire of Avalon. Bring us your warmth, your vitality, your creativity, your passion, your enthusiasm for life. Bring us clear intention."

Finally we call in Nolava of Fire, visualising Her in her green and golden form, coming closer towards us, filling our bodies with Her energy.

"Nolava of Fire, Lady of Light, bring us clarity of mind and vision, that we may see Truth clearly. Enlighten us with your radiance. Fill our hearts, minds and bodies with your loving fire."

And so on. The invocation ends with a final phrase on the theme of

"Hail and Welcome, Artha!" or *"Hail and Welcome, Nolava of Fire."*

Visualise the Mother of Fire entering the ceremonial space, anchoring into the altar or centre of the circle we are working in. Feel Her radiance fill the centre and radiate back outwards to the horizon. Hold the space of invocation for a few moments before moving on around the wheel.

Working ceremonially with Britannia's Wheel we invoke the Goddesses of the wheel in different ways for different purposes. For seasonal ceremonies we begin a series of invocations by calling in the Goddess of the time of the year, so if the ceremony is happening near Beltane we begin opening the wheel by calling Rhiannon in first of all, then following on around the wheel in a sunwise direction. If the ceremony is happening in September near the autumn equinox we begin by calling in Brigantia, Mother of Earth, of the west, and continue on with our invocations moving sunwise around the wheel of the year. Our final invocation is always of the Goddess in the centre, of Britannia, of the Lady of Avalon and Morgen La Fey.

Many ceremonies are designed to bring spiritual energies into form and follow a path of manifestation into denser and denser expression. We open the wheel beginning with the air element in the north and follow around the Goddess's wheel through fire and water to earthly manifestation. We begin our invocation in the North with Danu and then continue sunwise around the wheel with the Maiden, then Mother of Fire, followed by the Lover, Mother of Water, Great Mother, Mother of Earth and Crone Goddess, with the final invocation in the centre of the wheel. Occasionally in ceremonies in which we are journeying inwards to the Self and inner experiences or releasing to spirit, we open the wheel in a widdershins direction, moving anticlockwise around the wheel.

At the end of a ceremony whether we have invoked the Goddess in a sunwise or widdershins direction, we always give our thanks to the Goddesses journeying around the wheel in a sunwise direction, bringing ourselves into alignment with the movement of the earth on its axis, of the earth around the sun.

The Role of the Priestess as Ceremonialist

A priestess or group of priestesses have several different functions during a ceremony. In patriarchal religions the role of the priest is to be the one connected to God, to mediate between the divine and the congregation. In Goddess spirituality the role of the priestess is to create the conditions which enable others to have direct experience of and communion with the Goddess. These include the design of the ceremony, preparation for and creation of sacred and ceremonial space, introduction and welcome to the ceremony, invocation of the Goddess, the ability to generate stillness within evoking stillness in others, the ability to create and hold an energetic framework for the ceremony, to go with the flow of the energy, to direct the course of a ceremony, to direct energy.

A good ceremonialist is both priestess and performer, having the ability to connect emotionally and energetically with the participants, so that together they can create a moving and meaningful ceremony. This is a skill learned through practice just as an actor learns how to move an audience. Throughout the ceremony the priestess or priestesses act as a focus for energy, intention and attention, helping the ceremony to flow easily from one phase to the next. The priestess cultivates the ability to speak clearly, to project her voice and to use sound in a creative way. She learns to add in dynamic energy when necessary, to be warm and friendly, to use humour as well as seriousness, and to be confident and relaxed. She learns especially to enjoy herself in ceremony, as this communicates to others.

Creating Ceremonial Space

Ceremonial space is that physical space which we set aside in which we can turn our whole energy and attention towards the Goddess. It may be a small space the size of a tiny altar, it can be a whole room or we can visualise our ceremonial space as stretching from the centre of our circle to the horizon and beyond. In this renewed Avalonian tradition we work with the latter, visualising different forms of the Goddess streaming towards us from the horizon and radiating back outwards in all directions. The ceremonial space we create is that which we can successfully hold in our consciousness. This is a different approach to other pagan traditions and although we most often work in circle, we are unbounded by the circle.

In Wiccan and Western Magical ceremonies the witch or magician casts a circle around her/imself and invokes energies and deities into the circle in which they are standing, so that they are affected and transformed by those energies. The belief is that the ceremonialist remains protected from unwanted external interference within the circle for the duration of the ceremony. This form of ceremony probably arose during the times when pagan ceremonies had to be performed in secret, and Casting the Circle was an important form of psychic protection.

In addition a magician may also cast a separate circle, creating a second enclosed ritual space in front of her/im, into which malevolent energies and deities are evoked or conjured. The magician remains outside of this circle for the duration of the ceremony, believing that the energies are thereby contained and the magician kept safe from the forces s/he has conjured.

Within our renewed Avalonian Priestess tradition we have a different approach. Primarily we do not cast circles. In our understanding the Goddess is alive, everywhere, in all places and at all times and this is the Truth. She is the only One in many forms which we wish to invoke or evoke within our ceremonies. With Her at the centre of our attention radiating outwards in all directions we have no need to separate ourselves from the rest of Her creation. She is more powerful and loving than anything else in existence and Her radiance is all the protection we might need.

Many of our personal and collective ceremonies are based on working with the Goddess and the energies of Her Sacred Wheel of the year, the wheel of Her nature. We stand or sit in circle with the Goddess in the centre as the focus of our attention at all times, but there is no real difference between the outside and inside of our circle. The difference is only in terms of physical space and what we are able to hold in our minds. We sit in circle as a reminder of our equality before Her, and our different qualities and talents are expressed through the nine directions of the wheel of the year, eight around the circle and the ninth in the centre.

In our ceremonial practices we call in the Goddesses of the nine directions asking them to come and be present with us. As our attention turns towards Her so She responds to us. We experience Her through changes in our consciousness, spiritual focus and feeling, through signs and symbols, in synchronicities that arise, in changes in atmosphere, in visions and sounds, in inspiration. As we repeatedly call the Goddess into a particular physical space, so that space becomes charged with Her energy, holding it in tangible forms which can be felt spontaneously by people walking into the space. The space becomes holy, set aside for ceremony and Her worship, for spiritual communion with Her.

The Design of Goddess Ceremonies

The design of any Goddess ceremony depends first of all on its purpose. Every ceremony needs to have a clear purpose, whether it is to join two people in marriage or to celebrate the Goddess in Her seasonal festivals or to call in the Lady of Healing for a particular person or group of people, or any of a host of different purposes. We need to have a clear intention and focus even when we may not know exactly how our intention will manifest, say when we are opening to the Mysteries of Her Otherworld. We need to have an energetic understanding of what we are trying to achieve in our ceremonies, whether the process is one of manifestation of spiritual energies or aspiration to touch those energies.

The design of any Goddess ceremony always includes Her invocation. She may be the One Goddess or She may have several different faces, as when we work with Britannia's Wheel. We call Her into the place we have set aside for Her worship. A Goddess ceremony nearly always includes the use of Her natural elements of earth, water, fire and air, to symbolise different energies and states of being and the transformation of those forms, one into another, releasing energy. For example, we may write on a piece of paper the things we wish to let go of in our lives, things that no longer serve us, and then we set light to the paper. As the paper burns, transforming into heat, light and ash, so our wishes for change also begin their journey of release and transformation. We work with air as incense, sound, music, etc.; fire as candle flames, hearth and bonfires, etc.; water as holy, sea, milk, wine, etc.; and earth in many forms - mud, crystals, flowers, etc., in our ceremonies and for decoration of Her Temples.

Like a good book, good ceremonies need to have a beginning, a middle and an end. They need to have a clear start, meaningful substance and content and a way of ending, of moving outwards from the contained sacred space back into the world. As well as being a sacred act, ceremony is also performance, acting out the expanded energies we are working with as archetypal priestesses. In ceremony we become bigger than we usually are. As actors in a sacred drama we embody the different energies of the Goddess and communicate with participants so that all may experience Her energies. As priestesses we create with all those attending, the container in which the Goddess's energies can flow and be felt.

There needs to be a balance between the expressive and receptive phases of a ceremony and maximum participation for everyone, as we all want to connect directly to the Goddess ourselves. There need to opportunities for participants to express their feelings, time for tears, laughter, love, aspiration and inspiration. A good ceremony draws us in, engaging our hearts, emotions, minds and bodies, opening every part of ourselves to the Goddess's love. When we have filled ourselves with Her blessings, we are released to take Her energy out into the world.

A good ceremony has energy, emotion and inspiration. It moves us out of our everyday consciousness and comfort zones into Her Otherworldly realms and into Her presence. It may include prayer, poetry, storytelling, inspired words, visualisations, journeying, chants, song, drama, music, movement and dance, as well as the creation and experience of symbolic forms and sacred objects. Often we echo the Goddess's abundant nature by the giving of gifts, symbols of Her continuous generosity.

Ceremonies can be performed anywhere, but especially in Her nature, in Her valleys, by Her streams, on Her hillsides, in Her caves. They can also be performed in living rooms, bedrooms, kitchens, workplaces and within defined sacred spaces, such as Her Goddess Temples. In essence Goddess ceremonies can take any form that we choose. Once again because this is a renewed tradition there are no fixed rules, no written thealogy or dogma as to what can and cannot be done in any ceremony.

The words of the ceremony can be written down on paper and read out by the priestess and participants. For this we need to spend time thinking about what we want to say and the best, most poetic and inspired way to say it. The difficulties in using a written form is that words can easily become just words, bereft of meaning if they are not spoken with feeling and empathy. We can spend more time trying to keep our place in the book than being present to what is happening around us. I prefer to create ceremonies with a clear and simple framework which allows priestesses and participants to extemporise around the different themes of a ceremony, so that there is freedom to be inspired by Goddess in the moment, to speak Her words as they are received. This takes practice and self-confidence.

Preparation for Ceremony

It is very important to prepare for ceremony. Once the ceremony is designed we gather together and cleanse the ceremonial equipment we will need: images of the Goddess, incense and holders, fans, charcoal, matches or lighters, candles and holders, wands, chalices, cauldrons, crystals, flowers and vases, any papers or materials we may use during the ceremony. We collect holy water. We clean and prepare our ritual garments, our robes, headdresses, masks, veils, girdles. We cleanse ourselves, bathing our bodies, smudging our auras, so that we let go of what we have done before and are cleared of any unhelpful energies. We prepare the music we may use, bells, drums, songs, CDs, etc. We prepare a programme and song sheets if necessary so that others can know what is going to happen and join in. We prepare any food and drink that are to be a part of the ceremony, and any gifts to give away.

We arrive at the ceremonial space early before participants arrive and cleanse and clear the physical space. We sound a bell or bowl or smudge the space with incense. We lay out our ceremonial equipment and prepare the space energetically. We invoke our Priestess selves. We acknowledge the spirits of place, of the physical location of the ceremony, in our hearts and prayers. We ask permission from them to perform our ceremony in their space. We ask them to bless us as ceremonialists, to bless all who attend the ceremony and to bless the ceremony itself.

Generating an Energetic Container for Ceremony

To generate an energetic container for ceremony in which the Goddess's energy may be experienced by others, take the following steps:

* *Design and prepare the ceremony.*
* *Open yourself to the inner sacred space, generating stillness within and radiating it outwards.*
* *Invoke your Priestess Self into your body.*
* *Spiral through the outer sacred space of the temple or landscape in a sunwise or widdershins direction depending on the purpose of the ceremony, consciously laying a trail of loving golden light behind you as you walk. As you light candles, place flowers and sacred objects, as you smudge your altars and each other, connect everything in the space via threads of loving, golden light. Connect especially to images and statues of the Goddess, opening your heart and mind to Her as your eyes rest upon Her images.*
* *Include everything in the space in your awareness .*
* *Listen to the energy field that has been created using your seventh sense, and feel what it feels like. Visualise the web of connectedness between everything forming a golden grail, chalice or cauldron, depending on the purpose of the ceremony, as a container for Her divine feminine energy.*
* *Remain aware of the energy field you have created as people enter the space and the ceremony begins.*
* *Invoke the Goddess at the beginning of the ceremony seeing Her radiance filling the ceremonial space and chalice, and radiating outwards in all directions.*
* *Watch, feel and listen to the movements within the energy field as the ceremony progresses. Sometimes you may ask participants to consciously connect to each other, heart to heart, via golden threads of light and love, linking them into the ceremonial web of light.*
* *Hold the golden threads of connection in your awareness for the duration of the ceremony. Hold the golden threads of the ceremony until the ceremony is over and people are leaving the ceremonial space.*
* *Cleanse and clear the space when the ceremony is over and then let go of the golden threads, seeing them dissolve away..*

Closing a Ceremony

As well as there being a good beginning and middle to a ceremony there always needs to be a good ending. We always close a ceremony by giving thanks to the Goddesses that we have invoked, whose energy has blessed our ceremony. We give thanks to the energies of the five or nine directions. We give thanks to the spirits of place for allowing us to perform our ceremony in their space. We give thanks to the participants for being there and giving their energy and attention.

Once the participants have left we disperse and clear the energies that we have invoked. We do this by smudging the space with incense, by ringing a clear bell or by sounding a bowl or gong. This breaks up any emotional forms that may have accumulated during the ceremony and releases their energy into greater freedom. We clear the space of our ceremonial equipment and clean the space of discarded pieces of paper, candle wax, crumbs, etc., the detritus of human activity. Finally before we depart we leave a gift for the spirits of place.

Payment for Ceremony

Many people brought up in patriarchal cultures feel that ceremonies should be freely given as they are gifts of the spirit and that no payment should be requested. They feel that spiritual work should not be contaminated by money. I do not agree personally with these views.

In traditional, earth-based cultures the shamanka, wise woman, healer and priestess are recognised as playing a vital role in the spiritual, emotional and physical health of the community and are supported by their communities through gifts of money and in kind. However even in these communities today many spiritual elders are left poor and unsupported, scrabbling for a living even when their work is in demand. Times have changed and communal life is not what it used to be.

In the western world Goddess spirituality and priestesses are barely recognised, let alone supported by their communities. In order to be able to practice our priestesshood on a full-time, rather than part-time basis, we need to be able to generate income from our efforts. This is especially so when there is no organised religious body who might pay us for our time and commitment. We need to be properly paid for the work we do, for the time we take to prepare, perform and complete ceremony, for the experience and knowledge we bring with us, and for the healing and transformation we can facilitate. Goddess does not want us to be poor.

Within the Glastonbury Goddess Temple priestesses freely give their time and energy to create the seasonal ceremonies which many people attend. It is the gift priestesses offer to the Goddess and the Temple and donations to the Temple are always welcome. It is possible to do this because the Temple itself is supported by Madrons, who make monthly standing order donations to the Temple, by Friends of the Temple and visitors who make donations. Other ceremonies and events are offered on a donation basis or for a small payment. Individual priestesses may charge for personal ceremonies, such as Handfastings, Namings, etc., as they choose. I have a standard fee for such ceremonies, based on the time it takes to prepare, perform and complete the ceremony, on my experience and ability.

Personal Work

Practice invoking your archetypal Priestess self, creating stillness, generating sacred space, moving in the flow of Her energy, developing your seventh sense, expanding your awareness, acting on intuition and invoking the Goddess in individual forms and on Britannia's Wheel. All these will help prepare you to perform ceremony as a priestess.

Types and Examples of Goddess Ceremonies

There are many different kinds of Goddess ceremonies and the following paragraphs include some of those which priestesses may be asked to perform. Rather than write out a detailed description for every ceremony for every occasion in the second half of the chapter I offer examples of simple ritual frameworks that can be applied in many ceremonial situations. In making categorisations some ceremonies will obviously fit into more than one category, and the lists are not exhaustive.

Types of Ceremony

Rites *of* Passage

Throughout our lives as human beings we all journey through similar phases of life, from birth through childhood to adulthood, to parenthood, maturity, old age and death. Rites of Passage recognise the changes taking place as we move from one phase of life to another and are performed for the individual on behalf of the family and community to which they belong. Societies which offer recognised rites of passage are culturally richer and more stable than those which do not, as evidenced in many western societies where the lack of recognised puberty rites means that teenagers are forced to invent their own, often self-destructive rites of passage.

We are all born into life, are welcomed into the world or not, and named by our parents, families or societies. Some babies are adopted or fostered into new families. As children we are completely dependent on our families, but as we grow older we move towards greater and greater independence. We join peer groups of young people of similar ages to ourselves, who have a strong influence on our sense of identity. At some point we will usually leave the family home to further develop our identities, which involves separation from our parents and all that is familiar. In turn we create new homes and communities. Many of us will at some time in our lives form marital bonds of one kind or another with a partner and have children ourselves. We may stay with these partners for life or may separate from them and form new bonds with others. We live our lives, we mature, we age and we all eventually die.

Rites of Passage are the ceremonies which mark the important transitions in the life of an individual within a society, giving the individual a sense of place within that society. They include Naming Ceremonies - for babies and young children, Adoption Ceremonies, Young Adulthood, Leaving Home, Marriage, Handfasting, Renewal of Vows, Separation, Divorce, Croning, Saging, Death Preparation Ceremonies, Funerals and Remembrance Ceremonies.

Women's Blood Mysteries

Women's natural ability to conceive, bear and give birth to new life is one of the true miracles of human existence. We celebrate our Blood Mysteries throughout our lives as women and through motherhood. The blood mysteries cycle is directly related to fluctuations in the production of oestrogen, progesterone, testosterone and other hormones within the female body. Its ceremonies begin with the celebration of Menarche in girls, marking the arrival of the first drops of menstrual blood, and a girl's transition to young womanhood. This is followed by Menstruation Ceremonies of many kinds which recognise the power of our menstrual blood, the connection of our bleeding to the cycles of the moon, the potential presence in the body of the Dark Goddess before and during menstruation, and the celebration of menstrual blood as Maeve's Red Mead, a tantric elixir of life.

Women's natural ability to shed our life blood each month is mimicked in many male initiation ceremonies in which the life-giving power of the blood of the womb is recognised and young men are coated in red ochre or animal blood as a mark of rebirth into a new stage of life. We can also honour our Conception Cycle with due preparation for conception and the bearing of new life.

Becoming a mother is celebrated in many ways from the provision of ceremonies to open the way for a new soul to come into incarnation, to preparation for birth itself and there is thanksgiving for a safe delivery. Goddess spirituality discards any sense of the mother being unclean from the experience of birth, rather this is the time when she is recognised as being directly in communion with the Great Mother within her own body. She is celebrated and honoured as being in such a place, able to communicate and transmit Her energies directly.

There are also very important ceremonies to perform which recognise the grief and loss associated with an inability to conceive a child, for miscarriage, the termination of a pregnancy, and the death of a baby or of a child.

Women menstruate on an average for forty and more years and our experiences vary throughout that time depending on our knowledge of how to open ourselves in a regular cycle to the creative and destructive energies of the Goddess. This is something that we are not usually taught in western societies although this is beginning to change as more Goddess women realise the importance of our natural spiritual and physical cycles. We learn through experience. My own attitudes to menstruation changed greatly from my teenage years when my period was named *the curse*, which had to be hidden away from anyone else's eyes. It wasn't until my thirties that I began to recognise the Goddess's power within the whole menstrual cycle and learned to celebrate Her moving presence in my body, which enhanced my life, sexuality and creativity. Like many of my generation I was not taught any of this, but had to learn on my own, with the help of sister explorers and directly from the Goddess.

When I became sexually active I would try to hide my menstrual blood, using excuses to make myself unavailable for sexual contact, because of my embarrassment at the sheer mess of it all. When I was much older I learned that my menstrual blood was sacred. It was the Red Mead of Mab the Red Queen, which could bring ecstasy to those lucky enough to experience and be blessed by its powerful emanations. I wish I had known that all along. I wish someone had told me.

As we come to menopause and the deep physical and psychological changes associated with the ending of our childbearing years, we grieve the loss of our fertile years and open ourselves up to our power as the Queens of our own realms, see *The Queen of My Self : Stepping into Sovereignty in Midlife* by Donna Hennes, (Monarch Press). Donna suggests that now as our health is so much better and we live so much longer than our foremothers, there is a time in our lives when we have gone beyond our childbearing days, but are not yet Crones. It is a time when we can be honoured as the powerful, creative, confident, intelligent and sexual (if we want to be) Queens that we are. Croning comes at a later stage when we are losing physical and other powers, but are gaining in wisdom, becoming the recognised Elders of our communities.

Men's Mysteries

Just as women celebrate blood mysteries so too men have their mysteries, but these are not of the womb. Men's mystery cycle is in many ways less obvious than women's, being invisible and based in the production of testosterone and related hormones, and viable sperm, within the male body. Many traditional men's ceremonies have copied elements of women's blood mysteries, using blood and other red stains to mimic the experience of giving birth and being born. Men's true Goddess Mysteries seem to me to be lost in the far past and too mixed up with creating warriors of war rather than peaceful guardians of the Goddess's nature. Men's mysteries are an area of exploration that is ripe for development by men who love the Goddess. The form of these mysteries depends on developing a new understanding of exactly what it means to be a Goddess-loving man in today's world. It is up to men to conceive and develop this new way of being and the mysteries attached to it.

The Mysteries of Relationship and Sex

We can create ceremonies which honour our relationships and include our intimate sexual relationships as well as those special relationships between family members and between friends. We deepen our sexual relationships by calling the Goddess and/or the God into our bodies as we make love in a ceremonial manner, honouring the divine in ourselves and in each other. We honour Her presence within each of us and experience Her in an intimate way in our own physical and emotional ecstasy.

We can celebrate friendships of all kinds and when relationships become challenging we can use ceremony to reveal and express our woundedness and help heal rifts between us. We can illustrate the energetic threads that connect us using physical threads of cotton, string, wool and rope. We can unravel symbolic knots of wool, releasing stuck emotions as the same time. We can cut the ties that bind us to unwanted, painful relationships and memories, with ceremonial scissors or sickles, releasing the energy that constricts us. At the end of a relationship we can symbolically and actually cleanse marriage rings, gifts of love and friendship by placing them in running water, in fire, and incense smoke. We can release them into running water, into the sea, we can watch them burn up or we can bury them in the earth, so that they return to the Mother's body over time.

Forgiveness and ceremonies which express forgiveness, both of ourselves and others are an important part of healing the wounds in our human relationships. Forgiveness does not mean forgetting or condoning the wounds that have been received, but recognises that it is our own wounds which cause us to wound others. It is our human imperfection and fallibility that brings us to the place where we hurt each other. We forgive each other.

Seasonal Ceremonies

One of the most common types of Goddess ceremony held today in the west are the eight seasonal celebrations of the year - Imbolc, Oestre, Beltane, Litha, Lammas, Mabon, Samhain and Yule. These are primarily Sunfire festivals which mark the circling of the earth around the sun through the year. They may also be celebrated at the times of the associated new and full moons, e.g., at Lunar Imbolc, Lunar Beltane. They are celebrated by many earth-loving priestesses, pagans and witches, for whom they are known as sabbats. In seasonal ceremonies we honour the face of the Goddess which is revealed to us at the particular time of the year, so that we can learn more about Her. Seasonal ceremonies are usually communal and are a time for Goddess-loving people to gather together in praise of Her, telling Her stories, singing Her songs, sharing Her gifts.

Moon Ceremonies

The moon has long been a potent symbol for the Goddess as She moves through the heavens, waxing to full moon, waning to the dark moon and reappearing as the new moon. The three phases of new (waxing) moon, full and dark (waning) moon are a reflection of the Triple Goddess with Her white, red and black faces. In actuality the moon's phases can be divided more readily into five: new moon, waxing moon, full moon, waning moon and dark moon, which reflect our journey as modern women from Maiden to Lover to Mother to Queen to Crone, with associated colours white, red, gold, violet and black.

The moon symbolises the fertility cycle of women and the creative cycle in women and men. In dark moon ceremonies when there is no moonlight in the night-time sky we journey inwards to face our own darkness, to recognise what needs healing within us, to dream and conceive the new.

In new moon ceremonies we sow the seeds of the future, of the activities we will engage with in the coming month or year. At full moon ceremonies we celebrate as night is made into day and psychic energy reaches its peak. We draw in the energy of the moon to illuminate our path in life, to journey and to express our creativity in the world.

Healing and Cleansing Ceremonies

Healing bodies and souls are among the most important ceremonies we can perform as Priestesses of the Goddess. Healing ceremonies correctly performed can allow great changes to take place within the individual, which might otherwise take weeks or months of slow gradual healing. The power of the Goddess to heal is immense. She can transform our disease into ease. She can make us whole again.

My own experience of having a healing ceremony performed for me when I was very ill with breast cancer, was life-changing. A group of friends gathered to offer me healing. I walked into the experience feeling very ill, closed down, alienated, separated from my community and embarrassed to be there. During the ceremony I was offered much love and many different forms of healing by individuals and by the whole group. I walked out from that ceremony feeling elated, open, filled with love and strengthened in my heart. I was healed of my separation from my community. I believe that for our good health everyone should have this experience at least once in a lifetime. It could change us all.

Personal healing ceremonies are powerful because of the focus of attention on healing the individual by a priestess and/or by a community. Often our disease is the consequence of our separation from our communities, our families and friends, and this reconnection to our tribe is healing of itself and doubly so with the blessing of the Goddess. Certain Goddesses such as Nolava and Bridie, are particularly associated with healing and She is a powerful goddess to invoke in any healing ceremony.

Another important aspect of healing ceremonies is the cleansing and healing of places and objects. We can regularly cleanse and clear our homes of unwanted energies in a ceremonial manner. With the Lady's blessing we can exorcise ghosts and left over emotional energies from the past. We can remove stubborn or intense negative energies by casting them into natural objects, such as stones, crystals, hen's eggs, pieces of wood. In turn we cast these into fire, into running water or into the sea, so that their energy is transformed and released.

We cleanse and consecrate our homes, buildings, offices, temples, meditation and sacred spaces to the Goddess. We consecrate all our priestess paraphernalia and tools to Her service.

Elemental Ceremonies

In many Goddess ceremonies we work physically and symbolically with the four elements. Air represents the invisible breath of the Goddess and through our continuous breathing we recognise our connection to each other and to Her. Air is used in cleansing ceremonies, in the waft of a bird's wing, the movement of smoke from herbs and incense. Sound which travels through air can also cleanse, revive, invigorate, amuse and inspire us. Gongs and singing bowls can transport us into the place where there is only sound, Her sound.

There are fire ceremonies in which we let go to the fire all that no longer serves us or the Goddess, represented by words written on paper, by twigs, etc. As the fire burns our wishes are transformed into reality. At Beltane we jump the communal fire to mark our connection to a chosen loved one. At Samhain and Imbolc we walk between two fires cleansing ourselves before and after winter. We walk on fire to strengthen ourselves, to learn about the instinctive power of our bodies to free us from fear and limitation.

Water is an obvious cleansing agent, washing and cleaning all that it touches. Water symbolises the emotions and as it flows illustrates the way in which our emotions too need to flow, as easily as a tinkling stream, as still as a deep lake undisturbed by movements on the surface. As a drink spring water from deep in the Mother's body is used ceremonially to cleanse, refresh and bless the inner bodies.

Earth is our home, the place where we live and have this glorious opportunity to express ourselves in physical form. There are many kinds of earth ceremonies, using crystals, sand, rocks, Her fertile black earth. We can paint our bodies, we can paint Her pictures with Her earth pigments. We can crawl into holes in the earth, we can climb into the caves of Her body for healing and regeneration, we can cover ourselves in earth, we can bury ourselves in preparation for death and rebirth.

We can walk Her beautiful element-filled landscapes and make our pilgrimages upon Her sacred body in a ceremonial manner. We can sing Her world alive, connecting ourselves and sending our prayers for healing to Her waters, airs, fires and earth, to Her plants and animals, to Her human and spiritual worlds.

Prayer Ceremonies

Prayer plays an important part in our path of devotion to the Goddess. As well as speaking prayers in our hearts and out loud we can create prayer flags, covered in words and images of the Goddess, which we hang from trees and bushes, fluttering in the breeze, transporting our prayers continually to Her ear. We can hang ribbons on the trees or tear strips of cloth, clouties, from our clothes, old or new and hang them on branches beside the sacred well, with prayers for healing for ourselves and others. We can make prayer sticks, winding wool around a stick, binding in our prayers for healing and transformation. We plant the sticks in the ground, we place them on our altars. When we are ready we burn them in Her transforming fire.

We light candles and pray to Her sacred flames. We light incense and say our prayers into the smoke which gathers them in, so that they rise to Her ear. We empower the smoke with our breath. We sing our prayers to the Lady. We sound Her name in many forms:

"N*o....laa...vaaa*...., Br*iii......deee*....., R*hi.....aaa...nnn.....onnn*......

For longer term prayers we plant bushes or trees and place our prayers and sacred objects into the roots of the tree. As the plant or tree grow our prayers come to maturity.

Labrynth Ceremonies

Over the last ten years or so labrynths have been re-emerging into public consciousness as an interesting social and spiritual phenomenon. New and old labrynths have been created by people of all faiths as a way of journeying inwards to the spiritual self in the centre, then moving outwards again bringing the gifts of the spirit back into the world. The earliest labrynth designs from all around the ancient world are Goddess labrynths designed to bring us into Her presence. We are reclaiming this ancient tradition of walking the Goddess labrynth in a ceremonial manner, leading to a meeting with the self and the Goddess in the centre. Performed correctly these meetings are transformatory and life-changing. One of the largest labrynths today is found encircling the slopes of Glastonbury Tor.

Initiatory Ceremonies

These ceremonies are specifically designed to create initiatory experiences for participants, which open the heart and expand consciousness. They include the Self-initiation ceremonies at the end of each of the three years of the Priestess of Avalon training. These ceremonies lead participants through the Veil of Avalon into altered states of consciousness, where we can face our fears and affirm our hopes. They usually contain the experience of meeting the Goddess either in a non-physical form or as embodied by Her priestess, leading to an expansion of consciousness and a deepening of commitment to the Lady.

Larger Group Ceremonies

Goddess festivals and events such as the Glastonbury Goddess Conference and Goddess 2000 in the USA, have provided opportunities to develop group ceremonies involving large numbers of people. For the best results these ceremonies need to be clear, simple, visible, and participatory. In the Goddess Conference over the years they have included: many Lammas Bonfire Ceremonies, Crowning of the Crones, Celebration of the Maidens, Labrynth Ceremonies, Embodiment of the Triple Goddess, Embodiment and Oracle of the Nine Morgens, Singing the Land Alive, Bridie's Healing Ceremony, Maeve's Ecstasy and many more. These have been powerful transformatory experiences for all those taking part. They provide wonderful collective experiences of the Goddess and Her nature and they have shown us a magnificent world of adventure in ceremony, if we can trust our visions and have the courage to walk Her talk.

Examples of Ceremonies
Commonly Requested Ceremonies

For priestesses among the most commonly requested formal ceremonies are Marriages and Handfastings, Renewal of Vows, Namings of babies and children, and Funerals. In Brigit's Isles many people are dissatisfied with the lack of real meaning in ceremonies available to them within the mainstream culture and now seek more meaningful ceremonies that encompass their personal beliefs. Priestesses may asked to perform ceremonies for all kinds of people from Goddess-lovers to those who have more traditional mainstream beliefs. I have personally performed marriage blessings, handfastings and renewal of vows for pagans, for people who have their own faith systems, for Buddhists and Christians, for people who for one reason or another are not allowed to marry or remarry in a church, such as a Salvation Army couple, as well as many Goddess-loving people. All the ceremonies described below can be adapted for use with people with different belief systems

Marriage Blessing and Handfasting Ceremonies

The following is a programme for a Marriage Blessing and Handfasting Ceremony which demonstrates the way in which the elements of the Goddess's nature can be incorporated in both symbolic and material forms. The ceremony can be a marriage blessing ceremony only or can include a handfasting as well. This ceremony can be adapted for other landscapes, other Goddess wheels, adding in Gods if desired. If also provides a possible framework for those who wish to design their own marriage ceremony.

Marriage Blessing Ceremony & Handfasting Programme

Calling in the Directions and the Elements
and Invocation of the Divine by the ceremonialist

Cleansing by Air
Cleansing of the couple with incense
Telling the tale of how you first met

Purification by Fire
Encircling the couple with candle flame
Confession of your love to each other

Blessing by Water
Sharing a chalice of holy spring waters
Exchange of Solemn Vows written by yourselves
Blessing and Exchange of Rings

Blessing by Earth
Handfasting with hoop, wand and ribbons, binding in all the Qualities you wish to include in your marriage

Closing Blessing
Closing of the Directions

Some weeks or months before the ceremony the priestess meets the couple who are marrying to establish a good rapport with them, so that they are happy with their priestess and the form of the ceremony. The priestess takes the couple through the programme for the ceremony describing what happens at each stage and the contributions that the couple and their guests will be making to the ceremony. This is the time when the couple can think about any changes or additions they wish to make to the ceremony. Often they will have a special piece of poetry, a reading or a song they wish to include. The priestess helps the couple to be clear about the spiritual nature of this ceremony and the power of the blessing they will receive. The couple are asked which deities they would like to be invoked at the beginning of the ceremony to be present to bless them as they are making their vows to each other.

Arrangements are made finalising the date and time of the ceremony and also the selected venue for the ceremony, which may be outdoors or inside in a special sacred place, such as the Glastonbury Goddess Temple. Decisions are made as to whether the couple would like their guests to have programmes for the ceremony and who will design and produce these. Discussions take place about the role of any children from previous marriages in the ceremony, the provision of flowers, musicians, etc., as required. It is up to the priestess to decide how much of this preparation she wants to take on and be paid for doing, and how much is left to the couple.

Between this meeting and the ceremony itself the couple who are marrying are asked to write down two copies of the vows they wish to make to each other. They are asked to consider carefully what they wish to commit to each other, and how long that commitment is for. Some people wish to set a time limit and others do not. The vows for the couple may be the same or they may be different. It is their choice, as is the time span of the commitment. A copy of each vow will be given to their partner during the ceremony and one copy is to keep, to remind ourselves especially in the difficult times in the relationship, of the commitment we have made.

If the ceremony is a marriage blessing ceremony the couple will be asked to bring with them their vows and wedding rings and/or the gifts they wish to exchange. If the ceremony is also a handfasting in addition the woman is asked to bring a hoop and the man is asked to bring a wand; or two hoops if the couple are two women; two wands if the couple are two men. Later parts of the ceremony are modified for same sex unions. If desired the couple can ask friends and family to also bring half metre lengths of coloured ribbon to add in their own blessings to the handfasting. The hoop is carried throughout the ceremony by the woman, and can be made of flowers, herbs, wood, withies, etc. It symbolises the feminine energies. The wand is carried by the man and can be made of wood, crystal, metal, etc., and symbolises the masculine energies. The hoop and the wand need to be of proportionate sizes as they will be joined together in the ceremony.

The priestess may want to write out her own detailed programme for the ceremony. This can be written out completely, but it may interrupt the flow of the ceremony if the priestess has to keep referring to a book or pieces of paper before speaking. The form of the ceremony once understood by the priestess is quite simple and while following the framework of the ceremony, the priestess can extemporise freely around the different themes of the ceremony, such as the meanings of the blessings of air, fire, water and earth. This takes knowledge, experience and confidence. The framework of the ceremony can be adapted to include any special readings, poetry, songs and music which the couple would like to have. The ceremony lasts between 35 and 55 minutes depending on what the priestess says and on any additions.

When the day of the ceremony comes the priestess usually arrives at the venue before the couple in order to set up the space for the ceremony. Whatever the shape of the venue the ceremonial space is usually circular and can be denoted by the space itself, or by a large circle of flowers, ivy, leaves, ribbons, etc., and marked in the four directions by symbols of the four elements. These are laid out on small decorated altars, tables, or on the ground. Air is in the north and includes a fireproof container for incense, charcoal, incense and a feather fan. Fire is in the east represented by a lighted candle. Water is in the south represented by a chalice of holy spring water, with a small decorated cushion for the rings if required. Earth in the west is represented by a bowl containing earth or crystals and the long (at least 3 metres each) red and white handfasting ribbons. Any other items such as flowers, images of the Goddess, etc., can be placed appropriately in the four directions. In the centre of the circle if it is large enough, there may be a central altar with a special statue, or if the ceremony is in nature a specially chosen rock, spring or pool. If there are too many objects within the circle it may be difficult for the priestess and the couple to move around the space easily.

The eight directions of the wheel can be marked for people who are familiar with working with the eight directions of Britannia's wheel, but otherwise a simplified ceremonial space is used with four cardinal or four crossquarter directions marked. Sometimes a broom is laid across the entrance to the circle which would be in the direction of the time of the year, or wherever is convenient.

During the ceremony the couple who are marrying and the priestess are within the circle with any chosen friends or family members who are assisting in the ceremony. Guests encircle the ceremonial space so that they can hear everything that is said and properly witness the ceremony. During the ceremony the couple and priestess move in turn to each of the four directions to perform particular parts of the ceremony.

Before the couple and guests arrive the priestess prepares the ceremonial space as described previously, cleansing and clearing the space, lighting candles, etc. If the priestess is using charcoal to burn incense then the charcoal is lit just before the couple arrive as it will take time to fully light and be ready for the first blessing of air. As she prepares the priestess calls in her archetypal Priestess self and asks permission of the spirits of place to perform the ceremony.

The guests and couple arrive and are warmly welcomed by the priestess. The couple will often arrive in a nervous, anxious state and the role of priestess is to help them relax and look forward to the ritual, so that they can be present for their own ceremony and enjoy it.

The priestess leads the couple and those taking part in the ceremony into the ceremonial space and asks the guests to sit or stand around the edges of the circle. She welcomes everyone and describes the form of the ceremony. She asks everyone to be present to what is happening in the ceremony and reminds guests that they are there to be witnesses and supporters of the vows that are being made. She describes the calling in of the energies of the four external directions asking the participants to imagine the Goddesses, Gods with their animals and the elemental energies streaming towards the sacred space from the horizon, as they are called. She asks them to help her call in these energies and to repeat after her, "*Hail and Welcome!*" in each direction. The fifth direction will be facing the centre and calling in the deities of place, the priestess's tutelary Goddess, such as the Lady of Avalon, and the couple's deities.

The guests are asked to stand and the ceremony begins with the invocation of the Goddesses (and Gods if desired), of the four external directions, beginning in the north. As this is a ceremony of the manifestation of love from idea into human and physical expression we begin in the direction of spiritual energy. We bring that into manifestation by moving around the wheel from air to fire to water to earth. Throughout its progress the ceremony is always moving in a spiralling sunwise direction, continually bringing hopes, dreams and aspirations into manifestation.

The priestess asks the couple and everyone present to turn with her to face the north and to visualise the beings and deities of the north with their spiritual airy qualities, coming towards the ceremonial space to bring their blessings for marriage of the woman and man, ending the invocation,

"*Hail and Welcome, Mother of* Air, *Danu*!"

The priestess asks everyone to turn back to the centre bring the energies of the north into the centre of the circle. The priestess then asks everyone to turn to the east, to the Goddess of fire, of illumination, of the mind. She calls the energies of the east into the circle to bring their blessings on the marriage of the man and the woman.

"*Hail and Welcome, Mother of* Fire, *Artha*!"

Turning back to the centre bringing the energies in, the priestess asks everyone then to turn to the south and call in the energies of the south, of water, of the emotions, of feelings. She asks everyone to bring these energies into the circle to bless the union of the woman and the man.

"*Hail and Welcome, Mother of* Water, *Domnu*!"

Turning back to the centre the priestess then asks everyone to turn to the west and calls in the deities and energies of the west, of grounding and manifestation.

"*Hail and Welcome, Mother of* Earth, *Brigantia*!"

The priestess asks everyone to bring the energies into the centre and then to join her in facing the centre. She calls in the deities and energies of place, her own tutelary deities and the couple's chosen deities.

"*Hail and Welcome, Lady of* Avalon! (*or whoever is the principle deity for this ceremony*)"

With these invocations the energetic framework of the ceremony is in place, the wheel is turning and the spiralling, transformatory energy has begun to move.

The guests are now told that they can sit if they choose and the couple are brought into the north of the ceremonial circle. The priestess describes the energies of the north and the use of air and incense to cleanse the couple of unwanted energies from the past. This ceremony marks the beginning of a new phase of their relationship and they can let go of the past, of old ways of being, old relationships, etc., so that they can move into this new phase of their relationship in a clear way. The couple are smudged with incense in turn beginning with the woman. Starting at the heart the priestess spirals the smudge outwards to include the whole of the front of the body, then moves round to the back, smudging the woman's back and sides. She repeats the process for the man. Using the feather fan she clears their auras completely of extraneous energies, sweeping them down into the earth. This helps calm the couple who are usually quite nervous. The priestess asks for the blessings of air upon their union.

The priestess asks the couple to turn to face each other and tell each other how they first met. They are encouraged to look at each other in the eyes and to speak up, so that everyone can hear their words. This is the couple's first opportunity to speak aloud to the whole company and as they remember the first time that they saw or spoke to each other they release some of their anxiety.

When they have both spoken the priestess asks the couple to move into the east of the circle and again to face each other. The priestess picks up the candle and holds it or gives it to them to hold between them. She speaks about fire, describing how the heat and warmth of the flame represent love and passion and how important it is to tend the flame of love. The flame also represent the fire of the mind, of intelligence and the priestess talks about the sharing of creativity in their relationship. She asks the couple in turn to pass the palm of their hands across the top of the flame so that they feel the heat and warmth of the flame and will remember its heat in the coming years. The priestess circles around the couple with the candle, once or three times, again speaking about fire, love, creativity and passion as inspired and asking for the blessings of fire upon their union.

As the couple face each other the priestess asks each one in turn to confess their love for the other, looking at and speaking directly to each other. This confession of love can have been prepared beforehand, but is meant to be a spontaneous and emotional expression of love, one for the other, in the moment. Many people cry at this point in the ceremony and time needs to be given for emotions to be expressed.

The priestess asks the couple to move into the south of the circle and she speaks about water and how it represents the emotions and the importance in any relationship of allowing emotions to flow and be expressed, rather than denied and dammed up. This is so in the happy times and in the difficult times in any relationship. Again she asks the couple to face each other and gives them the chalice of holy spring waters so that they can offer it to each other and drink from the same cup. When they have drunk from the chalice the priestess takes the chalice and encircles the couple sprinkling drops of water onto the earth and onto the couple, asking for the blessings of water on their union.

Following this the couple speak their Vows of Commitment to each other. The written words may be brought by the couple themselves or by the best woman or man, and are now given to the couple. Facing each other in the south they speak their vows one after the other and hand a copy of the vow to their partner. If there is to be a handfasting during the ceremony the couple stay in the south and the exchange of rings follows here. When there is no handfasting the couple move on to the west and the exchange of rings takes place there.

The rings may be held by the best woman or best man or may have been placed on the small decorated cushion in the south or west. The priestess speaks about the rings and what a ring means as a symbol of the circle of life and community that connects us all, that connects the couple to each other and to the family and friends who are gathered here to witness their vows to each other. The priestess holds her hands over the rings and blesses the rings. The priestess then asks each partner in turn to repeat after her, something along the lines of:

"I .... *(name) give you* ....*(name) this ring, as a token of my love and as a symbol of the commitment I have made to you today."*

As they speak the words one partner places the ring on the third finger of the left hand of the other partner. The process is then repeated for the other partner.

If the couple have not already kissed, the priestess encourages them to do so,

"You may kiss each other."

The priestess asks the couple to move into the west. She speaks about the earth and the importance of grounding their vows in the physical world, of making them real. She speaks about the importance of the sacred marriage, the union of Goddess and God within and between the couple. She asks them to show the guests the hoop and the wand and hold them up for all to see. She describes how the hoop represents the feminine energies and the vulva, and the wand represent the masculine energies and the phallus. By joining them together symbolically, the Goddess and God within are also being joined together in the Sacred Marriage. For a same sex union this wording is modified to describe the union of two hoops or two wands as a sacred act.

The couple face each other and hold each other's left hands. The woman rests the hoop on top of the joined left hands holding it with her right hand and the man places the wand through the hoop in a ritual gesture with his right hand. Both hold the wand and hoop together with their right hands. The priestess takes the two long red and white ribbons from the western altar and talks about the meaning of the colour red, the colour of the blood of the feminine, of the womb, of life, and of white, the colour of the masculine, of semen. In same sex unions these ribbons can be red and white, two white, two red, green and white, or green and red, or other colours as desired.

In joining the hoop and the wand with the ribbons we are symbolically creating the sacred marriage, the union of vulva and phallus, Goddess and God, the union of two souls. Using the red ribbon the priestess ties the hoop to the wand on the side closest to the woman. Using the white ribbon the priestess ties the wand to the hoop on the side nearest to the man. She then encircles the hoop, wand and conjoined left hands with ribbons, red and white in turn, tying them all in together. As she does so the priestess asks the guests to join her in calling out loud qualities they would like the couple to receive, such as love, happiness, abundance, good health, adventure, children, creativity, etc. When all the ribbon has been used up the priestess ties the two free ends of the red and white ribbons together in a bow. If there are a small number of guests who have brought their own ribbons, they are invited to come to the edge of the circle beside the entrance or broom, to tie their ribbons onto the conjoined hoop and wand, and to offer the couple their personal blessings. If there is a large number of guests this can be left until later on after the ceremony is complete. When all the ribbons are tied on the priestess places her hands above and below the conjoined hands, the hoop and the wand, and invokes the blessing of the Goddess and/or God upon their sacred union. She pronounces that the couple are married.

The priestess then unties the final red and white bow and asks the couple to slowly let go of each other's left hands, withdrawing them from between the ribbons, while holding onto the hoop with their right hands. As they do so the priestess pulls the red and white ribbons together, taking up the slack from where the ribbons encircled the hands. If necessary she can encircle the hoop and wand again with the loose ribbons retying them in a new bow. The hoop and wand are firmly held together and are handed to the couple to keep for the duration of their commitment. If at sometime in the future the couple wish to renew their vows then the ribbons can be untied and the hoop and wand are separated, before joining them together again with new ribbons. In the event of the relationship coming to an end the hoop and wand can be separated, and the hoop given back to the woman, the wand to the man. The ribbons may be buried in the earth, burned or tied on the branches of a tree to disperse the energies held in the relationship to the wind.

The priestess calls for the attention of the couple and guests asking them to stand to help close the ceremonial circle, joining in with her for the words "*Hail and farewell!*" after each thanksgiving for each direction. Beginning in the north the priestess asks everyone to turn to the north as she thanks the spirits and deities of the north for being present to bless the union of the couple, "Hail *and farewell, Mother of* Air, *Danu!*" Turning back to the centre she asks everyone to turn to face the east where she thanks the spirits of the east, ending "*Hail and farewell, Mother of* Fire, *Artha!*" Turning back to the centre she asks everyone to face the south where she thanks the spirits of the south, ending "*Hail and farewell, Mother of* Water, *Domnu!*" Turning back to the centre she asks everyone to turn to face the west where she thanks the spirits of the west, ending "*Hail and farewell, Mother of* Earth, *Brigantia!*" The priestess asks everyone to face the centre as she thanks the spirits of place, her own tutelary deities and the couple's own special deities. "*Hail and farewell, Lady of Avalon! (or the principle deity for this ceremony)*".

The couple leave the ceremonial circle taking the conjoined hoop and wand with them. They walk out through the entrance or jump over the broom if they wish. This is a traditional custom where the broom represents the sweeping out of the old and the bringing in of the new. After the couple have left the circle and if there are large numbers of guests, they can bring their ribbons to the couple at this point or throughout the events of the day, at the reception, etc., to add in their blessings for the couple, tying their ribbons onto the conjoined hoop and wand.

When the couple have departed the priestess once again clears the space, moving in a sunwise direction through the space, ringing a bell, sounding a gong, smudging with incense, dispersing all the energies which have gathered and been expressed during the ceremony. The priestess thanks the spirits of place again, dismantles altars and clears the space completely.

The form of this ceremony can be simplified and adapted for a Renewal of Vows in which a couple are renewing vows made in a similar or different kind of ceremony.

Naming Ceremony

Another ceremony that is often requested is for Naming of children and Britannia's Wheel helps create the framework for the ceremony.

Baby or Child's Naming Ceremony
Programme

Calling in the Directions and the Elements
and Invocation of the Divine by the ceremonialist

Blessing by Air
Calling in of Family Ancestors
Blessing of the Family and Guardians with incense

Blessing by Fire
Each Parent and Guardian lights a candle and
Gives an offering to the Baby/Child

Blessing by Water
Holy water placed on the Child's seven chakras

Blessing by Earth
Earth placed on Child's brow, hands and feet
Naming by air, fire, water and earth

Closing Blessing
Closing of the Directions

I will not go through the ceremony in the same detail as the marriage ceremony, but as can be seen from the programme it follows the same energetic framework as the marriage ceremony. This ceremony is shorter than the marriage ceremony as the attention span of babies and children is much less than for adults. During the ceremony as well as being named and blessed by the deities and elements of the Goddess's nature the child is given Spiritual Guardians, Goddess-parents or traditional Godparents, who agree to hold a spiritual, inspirational, emotional and material focus for the child throughout their childhood and young adulthood, acting in the child's best interest and being the first place of care should anything untoward happen to the parents. Once again readings of poetry, music, etc., can be added into the programme as desired.

The ceremony begins with the welcome by the priestess and a brief description of the ceremony. The family and guests are asked to join in with the invocation of the deities of the five directions, including those requested by the parents and the child if s/he is old enough to make the request. They are asked to turn outwards to face the four external directions in turn and inwards to the centre, repeating "*Hail and welcome, deity!*" after each invocation. Throughout the ceremony the baby is held by the mother, father and/or guardians as decided by the parents and priestess.

Standing in the north the priestess describes the child's connection to their family ancestors and the place of the child within their family of incarnation is recognised. The family and guardians are smudged with incense, clearing their auras in preparation for this new beginning. The priestess gives the child a feather, asking that they will be blessed by the gifts of air and of the spirit, by inspiration, insight and wisdom throughout their lives.

Moving into the east the parents and guardians in turn light a candle and name themselves. They describe the light that they hope to bring into the child's life and guardians may at this point give a special Naming gift to the child. The priestess gives the child a small candle, asking that they will be blessed by the gifts of fire, the gifts of warmth, light, intelligence, truth and creativity throughout their lives.

In the south as the child is held by its mother drops of holy spring water are placed by the priestess on each of the seven chakras of the child's body symbolically awakening the child's energies to life on this beautiful planet. The priestess gives the child a small bottle of holy spring water, asking that they will be blessed with free-flowing emotions, with love, happiness, joy and compassion throughout their lives.

In the west earth from the child's homeland is placed on the child's head, heart, hands and feet, grounding the child into life on Mother Earth. The priestess gives the child a crystal or stone, asking that the child will be blessed with the gifts of the earth, with grounding, perseverance, endurance, living always in service to the earth, throughout their lives.

Facing the centre the priestess asks the deities of the centre to give their blessings to the child. She asks for happiness, health and a long and fulfilling life, held within a loving family and community. The priestess gives the child a small pouch to hold the symbolic gifts she has previously given. She then names the child by air, by fire, by water and by earth

The ceremony ends with the giving of thanks to the deities and energies of the four external directions and the deities of the centre, the family and guests joining in and repeating "*Hail and farewell, deity!*" As with other ceremonies this form can be adapted to family needs.

Funeral Ceremony

This funeral ceremony may take place in a Goddess Temple or sacred space, out on the land or in a crematorium. In this ceremony as the soul of the deceased is returning from the earthly to the spiritual realms the pattern of the ceremony is the reverse of the previous ceremonies. The deities and energies are invoked in a widdershins or anticlockwise direction and the ceremony itself moves in a widdershins direction.

Music plays an important part in many ceremonies and perhaps none more so that during a funeral where music can evoke memories of the deceased and help release emotions of grief and sadness, which once expressed can allow mourners to move on in life. Readings of poems and prose passages can also be very helpful and can be introduced anywhere within the structure of the ceremony.

Funeral Ceremony
Programme

Calling in the Directions and the Elements
and Invocation of the Divine by the ceremonialist

Blessing by Earth
Eulogy from those who knew the Deceased

Blessing by Water
Sprinkling of Water
Compassion for the Mourners

Blessing by Fire
Lighting of candles for the Deceased

Blessing by Air
Smudging with incense
Release of the Deceased to the Greater Life

Closing Blessing
Closing of the Directions

The priestess prepares the space for the funeral, if possible laying out a circular sacred space marked by altars for the four elements of the Goddess's nature in the four directions, with a place for the coffin containing the body in the north, or wherever is appropriate in the space available. A special altar for the deceased is also created with a large photograph, as a focus for the soul of the deceased and for the mourners. Flowers and favourite items associated with the deceased can be placed on this altar. Appropriate music that the deceased person loved, which can be anything from classical to pop music, is played as the mourners enter the space with the coffin. At this time family and friends are usually carrying a lot of grief and anxiety with them, whether the death is that of an old person who had lived a long life, or is an unexpected and sudden occurrence. When the mourners have arrived with the coffin they sit in circle around the ceremonial space.

The priestess welcomes everyone and introduces the ceremony asking everyone to join in with the invocations. She asks everyone to stand and turn with her to face the west and call in the Goddesses and energies of the west, of the earth, of incarnation, and including the Western Isle of the Dead. After welcoming those energies she turns widdershins to the south and calls in the energies of the south. She turns to the east and repeats the process and then to the north. Facing the centre she calls in the Goddesses of the centre, including those who were especially important to the deceased. This may be followed by any of the well-known Goddess chants as chosen by the family so that everyone can join in and release emotion through singing.

In the Blessing of Earth the life of the deceased on earth is introduced by the priestess and described with eulogies from those who knew the person well, from family members and friends chosen by the family. Each person stands in the west to speak. This part of the ceremony focuses on the gift of incarnation on the Mother's body and all that was achieved in life by the deceased. This part ends with a favourite piece of music.

The priestess moves into the south for the Blessing of Water, encouraging the expression of grief and loss on the part of family and friends. The priestess talks about those who are left behind with their sorrow, their mixed feelings, perhaps their anger, assuring the grieving that all emotions are appropriate. She can ask the mourners to make sounds that express those feelings, encouraging family and friends to support each other in the expression of their grief. She asks the Goddess to hold them in their grief. As they make sounds she sprinkles them with water. This followed by the playing of suitable music which gradually moves the focus from the expression of grief back to the deceased and their journey of return to the Goddess.

The priestess moves into the east for the Blessing of Fire in which everyone is asked to light a candle for the deceased, a light to light them on their way out of earthly incarnation, back to spirit and the Goddess. The priestess talks about light, the light of truth and inspiration, of the fires of life. The mourners are asked to raise their lights together and release the soul completely from the body, letting go and moving onwards, both for the deceased and for the mourners. (If the ceremony is taking place within a crematorium the coffin may be removed at this point.)

Moving into the Blessing of Air and the north with contemplative music, the priestess asks the mourners to make their final personal goodbyes to the deceased. With assistance for large numbers of mourners, she smudges the ceremonial space with incense, releasing the deceased energetically back to the Goddess. She smudges the mourners, clearing their auras of any stuck emotions and energies. This part may end with another appropriate Goddess chant.

The priestess asks the mourners to help her give thanks and close the wheel of the Goddess's nature with her. She begins in the north, facing the coffin if it is still there. She thanks the energies and Goddesses of the north for their presence, asking everyone to repeat after her,

"*Hail and farewell* .... (*name of the deceased*). *Hail and farewell*, *Danu*."

She moves sunwise to the east and thanks the Goddesses and energies of that direction,

"*Hail and farewell* .... (*name of the deceased*). *Hail and farewell*, *Artha*."

She moves to the south,

"*Hail and farewell* .... (*name of the deceased*). *Hail and farewell*, *Domnu*."

And then to the west,

"*Hail and farewell* .... (*name of the deceased*). *Hail and farewell*, *Brigantia*."

Then facing the centre the priestess gives the blessing of the Goddesses of the centre ending,

"*Hail and farewell* .... (*name of the deceased*). *Hail and farewell*, *Lady of Avalon*."

She gives a final blessing acknowledging the return of the deceased to the Goddess's loving embrace and asking the Lady to walk into the future with the family and friends of the deceased.

Suitable music which again is a favourite of the deceased plays as the coffin (if still present), family and friends leave. After everyone has left the priestess clears and cleanses the space.

Personal Work

Design, create, prepare, publicise and perform a ceremony of your choice for at least one other person or several, in which you are the principal priestess holding the energy of the ceremony. You may ask other people to help you, but you are in charge of what is happening. When you have performed the ceremony review what has happened and see how you have succeeded in your aims and how you might improve on your priestess ceremonial practice. Ask for feedback from participants.

Groups of students working together begin to pool ideas for the Self-Initiation ceremony that will take place at the end of the Second Spiral, which they will design for themselves.

The Power of the Veil
Journeying Between the Worlds

The Isle of Avalon is an Otherworldly place, a Paradise Isle that exists beyond the Veil of Avalon. In these days Avalon is not normally visible to our ordinary human eyes, although its effects can be felt by those who stray into its borders. The Island becomes visible to those whose inner vision is awakened and part of our priestess journey involves opening our inner senses so that we can see and move through the Veil into Avalon. We learn to journey into Avalon with purpose and intention travelling from this material world into Her enchanted realms.

The Veil of Avalon itself is an etheric veil, a veil of perspective and awareness, how we see things. It is like mist, like the fog which in autumn and spring often hangs low over the Vale of Avalon, shrouding the sacred land in mystery, hiding familiar landmarks, emphasising sounds and making us look more closely at the paths we are taking. This mist is known by the local Somerset folk as the White Lady. It rises mysteriously up out of the watery Somerset levels at dawn and at dusk, drawing Her veil across the landscape hiding Her beauty, helping us to lose ourselves in Her mysts.

Sometimes like fog the Veil of Avalon is dense and impenetrable and at other times it thins and we catch glimpses of another reality, which is the magical and mysterious Isle of Avalon. This thinning of the Veil seems to occur in a rhythmical pattern based around the eight natural festivals of the year, and at the new and full moons. Then it is easier to pass into Avalon and with care to return safely.

The thinning of the Veil is also personal. It concerns our individual spiritual unfoldment. It occurs naturally as we begin to open our consciousness to the existence and reality of the invisible worlds. We begin to see and feel what was formerly hidden from our physical eyes. We see the shimmering etheric threads which connect everything and hold all life in form. As we walk upon Glastonbury's soft hillsides we catch glimpses of beings and objects which are not physically present today. We may see structures from another age, standing stones, mounds, temples, groves, as well as visions of buildings of the future. The beings we see may emerge with indistinct forms, or as heightened colours or heavenly scents, or in more familiar shapes. We see fairies, gnomes, elves, elementals, devas, Otherworldly creatures, humans, Goddesses and Gods. We ask these beings to accompany us on our journeys, whispering words of wisdom into our ears, answering our questions, guiding us into a new reality.

The Veil that separates is both an outer and an inner reality. It is the misty Veil of Avalon which we cannot see or walk through without permission and an open heart. It is also the inner etheric veil that separates material reality from the invisible worlds of emotion, mind, intuition and soul. As our awareness develops and our consciousness expands these inner veils also thin allowing the subtle energies of the heart and mind to penetrate our everyday awareness.

Dion Fortune, the Goddess-loving esoteric writer, lived for a time in the 1930s at Chalice Orchard at the foot of Glastonbury Tor. She described the Veil of Avalon as a Veil of Fire surrounding the Tor, and separating Avalon from earthly Glastonbury. This fire could only be penetrated by initiates, the unevolved would perish in the flames. Priestesses on the road to initiation must learn how to safely pass through the Veil to Avalon, entering the place of transformation, opening ourselves to change.

Sometimes journeying through the Veil of Avalon can seem more like a passage through a Veil of Tears, Anger and Self Doubt. We find ourselves weeping as deep emotions are brought to the surface of consciousness, as we face those parts of ourselves that have long been repressed and hidden away. They burst forth into everyday reality in powerful and overwhelming ways. We cry often at the sorrow and the sweetness of our earthly human lives and find suppressed anger and hatred spilling over at inappropriate moments out of our shadow selves.

Also there are some people whose auras and psychic spaces have been seriously damaged by life's experiences, by illnesses, accidents and drugs, whose inner veils are erratically thin in places. As we journey into Avalon to receive the Lady's healing touch which is needed, individuals can be burnt by the experience of passing too quickly through the fiery veil. Care and preparation is necessary.

Journeying between the worlds

There are two main kinds of journeying that we are considering as priestesses. One I wrote about earlier is concerned with physically walking the beautiful landscapes of the Goddess found all over Brigit's Isles and the world, walking on Her body with consciousness, communing with Her nature. We can enter Avalon by walking the hills and valleys that make up today's Glastonbury landscape and spending time with Her on Her earth. There are key places on the island where it is easier to penetrate the Veil to Avalon. Finding these places is part of the esoteric knowledge that priestesses learn through being in the landscape itself, then physically stepping through the Veil from Glastonbury into Avalon. This takes time and commitment on the part of would-be priestesses.

The second form of journeying is an inner process moving through altered states of consciousness into the Otherworld of Avalon. This kind of journeying is an inner passage from one state of consciousness into another more expanded state of being. With this expanded awareness come different faculties of perception. We are able to see places we have not visited physically. We can see people who are not normally visible to us and we can communicate with them. We can shapeshift, changing from our present forms into other psychic forms, including our own past and future incarnational forms. We can change into our totem animal and bird forms. We can move at speed, we can fly, travelling across known and unknown landscapes with purpose.

The Purpose of Journeying

Why do we want to travel between the worlds? Why do we want to journey into Avalon? Is it not enough to know that it is there and that we may stumble upon it occasionally, by accident?

As well as serving the Lady, it is the work of Priestesses of Avalon to be able to journey consciously into and through the land of Avalon for ourselves and for others. We journey so that we can safely meet and connect more deeply with the Lady Herself, with the Nine Morgens, with all the holy beings of Avalon, with the realms of Faery and with the inhabitants of the Western Isle of the Dead. We journey as a way of remembering the world we once knew in physical form. We journey to generate the present and future reappearance of the Isle of Avalon.

We journey into Avalon for the exploration of the island itself, of its hills and valleys, its gardens and glades, its secret groves, its springs and wells, its temples and habitations. We journey so that we can spend time in the glorious presence of the Lady, bathing in Her violet rays. We journey into altered states of consciousness in which we can hear and see Her and receive Her wisdom more easily. We journey to meet and communicate with discarnate friends and family who have close ties with us, who watch over us as we live our lives, who care for us and wish to communicate with us. We journey for healing, for in these lands Nolava can swiftly bring us to our deepest wounds, which Her touch can transform into wholeness in the blink of an eye. We journey for the retrieval of forgotten wounded parts of ourselves, which lie far away on the Western Isle of the Dead.

Methods of Journeying

Different cultures have different traditional methods for conveying the psychic traveller into the Otherworld. These include the use of drums, music, dance, sacred songs, masks, smoke and natural hallucinogenic substances. In Siberia shamans mimic the riding of a horse between the worlds by climbing up a tree or a pole. In Britain witches ride their broomsticks under the influence of fly agaric mushrooms. In South America native peoples imbibe ayahuasca and other potent plants in order to become completely part of the natural world on which they depend for life, shapeshifting into the forms of animals and birds.

Avalon is a mythic land lying just beyond the Veil. Our belief is that once it was a physical place and we who would become Her priestesses are attempting to bring Avalon back into material reality, so that the Goddess and all She is can be worshipped and honoured in our everyday world, as She deserves. On our sacred path as priestesses we are learning to consciously straddle the border, to bridge the Veil, to live with one foot in Avalon and one foot in the material world. Therefore in our priestess practice we use several methods of journeying which do not include the use of mind altering substances. Rather we alter our minds by changing the focus of our consciousness, to open to the Otherworld. We loosen the grip of the mind using music, song and dance. We journey in imagination to the sound of a voice, or a drum, or to the sound and singing of sacred songs. We journey wearing a veil.

Loosening the Grip of the Mind

Western cultures place such store on the mind and on control of the world of around us. It is often difficult for the individual to still the mind and loosen its grip on consciousness. As in other religions we can still the mind through the many techniques of meditation, focusing on the breath, on yantras and images of the Goddess, on the repetition of mantras, etc. We also chant songs of the Goddess, repetitions of simple phrases that allow our hearts to open and our spirits to soar. We sound the sacred names of the Goddess and shift our focus out of the mind into other realms. We dance for extended lengths of time loosening the mind's grip on our attention. We dance to many different kinds of music, slow, rhythmic, fast, tribal, modern day, ecstatic, Five Rhythms, whatever helps us become present in our bodies. Dance brings our consciousness into our bodies, so that we feel Her earth beneath our feet, breathe Her air into our bodies, feel Her waters in our blood and cells and Her fire of Kundalini moving in our spines.

Then we are ready to journey.

The Power of the Veil

Something which has become very clear over the last years of practice, is the power that resides for women in wearing a veil during ceremony and while journeying. In these days wearing a veil is often an expression of the complete subordination of women within male dominated societies, especially when the wearing of the veil is demanded by men. The woman in the veil with her face and hair hidden and the whole of her body covered, has become a potent symbol of the suppression and lack of power of the feminine within society and culture. Like many other usurped Goddess symbols I believe that the wearing of a veil was originally part of women's spiritual practice, part of the Goddess Mysteries, which were stolen and corrupted, and used against women to control us.

I reclaim the Power of the Veil as an essential part of women's spiritual practice. By covering our faces and heads ceremonially with a veil we can journey more easily into altered states of consciousness, we can travel between the worlds and we can embody the Goddess (see later chapter).

There are two aspects to the wearing of a ceremonial veil, one is the perspective of the wearer and the other is that of those looking at the woman wearing the veil. From the perspective of the wearer when we cover our heads with a veil we automatically separate ourselves from the world around us. We immediately move inwards and become conscious of our bodies and what is happening within them, of what we are feeling and thinking. We close our eyes and almost instantly focus on our inner worlds, on our inner selves. We move into a space apart. We quickly forget what is going on around us as we feel, sense and listen to the sounds and energies of the inner world. Looking out through the veil our view of the world is also altered. It too becomes a thing apart.

Seeing a woman wearing a veil always brings a hint of mystery to the proceedings. Who is this woman beyond the veil? The woman who is familiar to us changes. She becomes suddenly unknown and unknowable. Our eyes try to see through the veil, whether it is thick or thin, substantial or gauzy, but she remains indistinct. We can see the outline of the female face but we cannot define her too closely. We cannot grasp and hold her with our minds. She becomes the embodiment of all that is mutable and uncontrollable within womankind. From the viewer's point of view this has immediate effects on our consciousness, opening our minds as we try to make sense of the mystery of the woman veiled.

The most common experience of the ceremonially veiled woman we have in Brigit's Isles is of the veiled bride-to-be who enters the temple, church, synagogue or registry office on her wedding day. She is often veiled in white like Bride, or perhaps in red as in a Hindu wedding. She is a woman set apart by her veil, which makes her appear more beautiful. She appears as a gift from the Goddess to be treasured and honoured by all who might gaze upon her, and especially by her groom. On this her wedding day all women become lovely and mysterious, no matter what they may be like in ordinary life.

Dancers, particularly of Middle Eastern belly dance, may also be veiled, the veil adding to their allure and sensuality. Belly dance is an original women's dance, designed to cleanse and heal women's internal organs. It is especially nurturing for the bellies of pregnant women and the babies growing inside their wombs. The wearing of the veil by dancers recognises the ceremonial nature of such dances as a way of communicating with the Goddess within and embodying Her through the dance.

For priestess work and journeying the best kind of veil is semi-transparent, a large circle or rectangle of light gauzy material through which we can see outwards, but which hides our form from the observer. The veil needs to be light on the head so that it doesn't give us a headache and big enough so that if we move it doesn't fall off completely. The colour of the veil is appropriate to the purpose of wearing it, perhaps related to the colours of the time of the year, or to the Goddess we may be invoking. The donning of a veil can instantly call in our priestess selves, our mind-chatter slows down and ceases, and we find the place of alert stillness within. We are ready for ceremony, we are ready to journey.

Practice wearing a veil in different situations, so that you can experience what it feels like to have your head and face lightly covered. See how it affects your perception and experience. Practice wearing a veil as you pray to the Goddess, as you open Britannia's Wheel. *This is a women's mystery which you need to reclaim for yourself. As you prepare to journey place a veil over your head.*

Men on the path to priesthood might like to experiment too with the wearing of veils, although so far men in training have preferred to use light turbans which can be draped across the face, rather than soft veils.

Journeying into the Otherworld

As we journey in imagination into the Otherworld our ways of perceiving become altered. As we look around with our inner senses we may feel colours, see scents, hear energies, sense emotions, taste memories. A wonderfully vibrant and colourful world opens up to us. We are moving from our everyday consciousness into the astral and mental spheres of reality and beyond, which make up the Otherworld. We are shifting our focus of attention and consciousness so that we can connect through a synchronous energetic vibration to the beings and energies of more subtle spiritual worlds.

We begin by first moving into the astral sphere which is principally the world of emotion, where energies and colours are intensified. The astral sphere includes all kinds of emotion and beings from the sublime to the angry and the sad. It links into the collective unconscious of all humanity and contains all the emotional energies and experiences of all people throughout all time. For this reason it is important in journeying to travel along prescribed pathways into the Otherworld with protective beings at our side. If we journey haphazardly we are more likely to meet Shadow beings who roam the unconscious worlds who do not belong to us, who may frighten us or wish us harm. Except for certain circumstances we are always accompanied by protective beings.

Journeying to Avalon

We need to have a clear purpose and intention before we begin our journey to Avalon, because our intention will determine the outcome of the journey. This is true whether we are being led on a journey by someone else's voice, whether we are taking ourselves or we are leading others. We can have different intentions: curiosity, to connect with our guides and totem animals, to meet ancient priestesses, to meet discarnate relatives, friends and ancestors, to meet the Lady Herself. We can travel for communication, for healing, transformation and other purposes. Whichever it is, know it consciously before you begin. Journeying is a powerful psychic experience that can have potent effects.

To make a journey we need to be in a safe space where we will not be disturbed for a length of time. We sit or lie down comfortably. If we are lying down and are being led through the journey as we relax deeply it is easy to fall asleep, so if we want to remain conscious through the journey we need to be both relaxed and alert. Its better to journey before lunch rather than after. Those on the path to priestesshood may like to practice placing a veil over their heads for the journey.

We begin each journey by closing our eyes and relaxing our bodies, letting go of the tension that we all hold in our shoulders and arms, in our legs and feet, in our bellies and in our faces. We move our attention to our breath and notice the air as it moves in and out of our noses and mouths, down into our lungs and out again. We allow our breathing to slow and deepen.

In myth and legend the Isle of Avalon is an island surrounded by water, by a great lake or by the sea. When we journey psychically and in imagination we begin our journey from the outer edges of the lake, from the mainland, looking out across a stretch of water towards the island of Avalon. There are different methods of travelling across the water, the most usual is in the Barge of Avalon, the boat which we see in our mind's eye, which comes when we ring the bell that we find at the water's edge. This may be a small tinkling bell or a great bell which we toll by pulling a rope.

In the barge is a ferry person or faery person, who may be human-someone we know or don't know, a priestess, a faery, an animal or bird, or a mythic being. They may be visible or they may be disguised by cloaks, hoods or masks. We can't always see who they are. To journey across the water in the Barge we pay a toll, the traditional price for taking a ride in the Barge to the Otherworld. We take a silver coin from our pockets and hand it to the ferry person. We move to stand or sit in the prow of the boat. Sometimes we may find ourselves accompanied here by a priestess of Avalon or one of the Nine Morgens, who welcomes us, or we may be on our own.

The Barge begins to move out across the water and we look towards Avalon seeing it as it is visible today. This requires us to have spent time looking at the landscape of Glastonbury Avalon from the wide circle of the Somerset Levels which surround the island today. The shape of the island changes dramatically depending on whether we are viewing it from the northeast or the southwest, the south or the north. We notice the weather, whether it is sunny and clear or cloudy and grey. We notice what is happening to the surface of the lake, whether it is smooth or rough.

As we sit or stand in the Barge we look out across the waters to Avalon and as we watch, mist begins to rise from the surface of the lake obscuring our view. Soon we can see nothing more than a hand's breadth from our faces. We are surrounded by dense white fog. We notice how we feel - enjoyment, anticipation or even fear. After a while the mist begins to disperse. In the Third Spiral of the Priestess of Avalon training students learn how to summon and disperse the mists, but for now it is enough that the mists come and after a time they disperse.

The traveller looks out across the water to the Isle of Avalon which has changed from today's form into the hills and valleys of Avalon's natural landscape from the time before modern human beings lived here. We look to see what the island looks like within our imaginations, seeing what we see with our inner eyes. Soon the Barge arrives at the island and we thank the ferry person for bringing us across the waters to Avalon.

There are other ways to journey to Avalon apart from sailing in the Barge. We can fly there on the back of Bridie's great white Swan, or on the back of a Morgen crow. We can fly there with our own wings. When we fly we always start our flight from a familiar landscape. As we fly over it we recognise familiar places that we may never have seen from above but which we can imagine. If we are flying to the Isle of Avalon which lies out in the ocean, we always fly to the west as Avalon is the Western Isle. Flying from the familiar landscape we move out across the shore of the lake or sea and out over water. We notice what the water looks like from above, whether it is calm or choppy, its colours, how far we can see into its depths. We fly until we see ahead of us on the horizon the dot of an island which grows larger as we approach it. Our bird brings us in above the island circling over it and coming to land in the water beside the shore or on the shore, depending on the type of bird. We thank our bird for bringing us across the water to Avalon.

We can also swim to Avalon in the form of a fish, dolphin, seal or other water creature. Occasionally as we approach the Isle of Avalon we may come on foot through wet marshlands, that can be found in one shallow part of the lake. We follow the secret pathways of the little people, the people of Avallach, the ancestors of Avalon, but it is easy to lose one's way in the reeds, to fall into deep pools, to get lost without a guide.

When we arrive on the island we are met by a priestess or a guide or a totem animal or bird, who will accompany us as we journey through the landscape of Avalon. Where we journey and what we see depends on our purpose in travelling to Avalon, which we need to hold clearly in our minds as we begin. The Isle of Avalon is like a tardis machine, which looks small and compact from the outside, but when we walk among its hills and byways it may open up into a huge and vast landscape. It is often the same size as today's landscape, but without modern day buildings, roads and fields.

When we have completed all that we want to do on the island we must return with care back to the everyday world. We make our way back to the shoreline. We thank our guides for accompanying us on our journey. We climb into the barge which is waiting for us. We climb onto the back of the crow or swan and take off into the air. We walk into the sea and begin to swim. We make our way back across the waters of the lake or ocean. Returning in the Barge we once again pass through the mists that rise from the lake waters and return to the everyday world.

We come back to the edge of the lake, to the mainland, to the familiar landscape and we thank the ferry person or the bird, whoever has helped us cross the great waters to the Otherside. Then we slowly bring our consciousness back into the room or space we are in. We ground ourselves through the breath, noticing our breath as it moves in and out of our bodies, each breath filling us with renewed energy and life. We open our eyes and look about us as familiar surroundings. We touch the floor.

When we return we write down, draw or record in a journal the details of our experience. As we write we remember what has happened on our journey, the words of the Goddess as She spoke to us, the words of our totems, grounding those experiences that will enrich our lives.

We can make our journey completely in silence in our imagination. We can make the journey to the beat of a drum, to the sound of evocative music. We can also physically act out parts of the journey. We can ring the bell physically. We can fly, moving our arms physically like wings, our bodies stretched forwards, our heads tucked down. We can step into the Barge. We can walk about the island by taking physical steps as our imagination explores the inner landscape. We move as guided by our intuition.

Journeying to the Isle of the Dead

Avalon as the Isle of the Dead has several different aspects and appearances. It is first of all the Eternal Paradise to which we who are connected to Avalon, journey at our own death to become one with the Lady. It is a place of transition, a place of healing for those who have recently died. It is a place where the living can commune with loved ones who have passed over before us, and with the ancestors who dwell here. Avalon encompasses the bardo states of consciousness that lie between death and rebirth. The Isle of the Dead is a place where those parts of our selves can be found, which have been discarded, suppressed, forgotten and denied, which we need to remember to bring us to wholeness.

The Eternal Paradise

The stories of the death of King Arthur give us an idea of what may happen when we come to face our own death. As Arthur was dying from fatal wounds sustained at the battle of Camlan, he was taken by his servant Barinthus to the shores of the Lake of Avalon. There the Barge awaited him and he was transported across the water to Avalon accompanied by three Faery Queens, three Morgens, three Crones, or three Crows, depending on the version told. Morgen la Fey, the great healer, attended to his wounds and even to this day Arthur is said to lie sleeping in Avalon with Queen Gwenhwyfar, awaiting the day of his rebirth.

In this land our native British Book of the Dead has long been forgotten. The knowledge of the ancient beliefs about the relationship of life to death and death to life and the rituals which followed from these beliefs, have gone. We can see all around us in the ruins of neolithic monuments the evidence of an ancient tradition of honouring the dying and the dead as they returned to the embrace of the Mother. We are only just beginning to formulate our ideas on the nature of life's realities, gleaned from our remembrances and the living truth of other cultures.

At the moment of our death what we shall perceive? Will the Lady send Her Barge for us? Will Morgen La Fey stand in the prow and transport us across the lake to Avalon? Will we meet the Lady of Avalon in all Her glory and become one with Her?

One of the best practices I know, that helps prepare us for the moment of death, is the Tibetan practice of *Phowa*, described in *The Tibetan Book of Living and Dying* by Tsogyal Rinpoche (Harper Collins). Here it is adapted in two forms for our meeting with the Lady of Avalon. Phowa means the transference of consciousness. This practice needs to become second nature so that at the moment of our death, which may come suddenly or otherwise, our consciousness is automatically transferred to Her.

In its simplest form the practice involves the following steps:

1. *Centre yourself in your heart and radiate your energy.*
2. *Then in the sky in front of you visualise the* Lady of Avalon, *the embodiment of love, truth, wisdom, transformation and compassion. Fill your heart with* Her *presence.*
3. *Say a prayer to the* Lady *asking that all your negative karma, destructive emotions and blockages may be purified and removed. Pray that you may be forgiven for any harm you have done in your life and that you may feel this forgiveness. Ask that you may die a good and peaceful death which may benefit all other beings.*
4. *Imagine that the* Lady of Avalon *is so moved by your prayer that* She *responds with a loving smile and sends out love and compassion in a stream of light from* Her *heart to you. As* Her *rays touch you they cleanse and purify all your negative karma and destructive emotions and you see and feel yourself totally immersed in light.*
5. *You are now completely purified and cleansed by the light streaming from the* Lady. *Visualise your body which is itself created by karma, dissolving completely into light.*
6. *The body of light you now are soars up into the sky and merges with the* Lady of Avalon.
7. *Remain in this state of oneness with the* Lady *for as long as possible.*

This Phowa practice can be adapted to help someone else who is dying. It can be repeated often during a loved one's last illness and especially when the dying person is breathing their last breath, or as soon as possible after breathing has stopped and before the body is disturbed in any way.

1. *For your loved one visualise the presence of the holy being who is important to them above them in the sky, or visualise the* Lady of Avalon.
2. *Imagine rays of light pouring down from the presence onto their body purifying their whole being, dissolving all their negative karma.*
3. *See them dissolve into light and merge into the spiritual presence.*

In the second form of the practice we journey to the Isle of Avalon to become one with the Lady.

1. Ground and centre yourself in your heart.
2. See yourself standing on the shores of the Lake of Avalon and the Barge of Avalon coming towards you through the mists with Morgen la Fey standing in the prow.
3. Climb into the Barge and journey across the Great Waters to Avalon with Morgenoe.
4. When you reach the island Nolava the Lady of Avalon is there waiting for you.
5. Feel the great love, wisdom and compassion which pours from Her towards you. Feel it filling your heart.
6. Say a prayer to the Lady asking that all your negative karma, destructive emotions and blockages may be purified and removed, that you may be forgiven for any harm you have done in your life and that you may feel this forgiveness. Pray that you may die a good and peaceful death which may benefit all other beings.
7. Imagine that the Lady of Avalon is so moved by your prayer that She responds with a loving smile and sends out love and compassion in a stream of light from Her heart to you. As Her rays touch you they cleanse and purify all your negative karma and destructive emotions.
8. You move towards Her and She embraces you. Feel yourself totally immersed in Her love and light.
9. You are now completely purified and cleansed by the love and light streaming from the Lady. Visualise your body which is itself created by karma, dissolving completely into light and merging with the Lady of Avalon. Become one with Her.
10. Remain in this state of oneness with the Lady for as long as possible.

Journey to the Paradise Isle to meet the Ancestors

In making a journey to meet the ancestors on the Paradise Isle follow the instructions given earlier for journeying to Avalon, holding clearly your intention to meet your loved ones and/or the ancestors of earlier times. These ancestors may be people that you have known in life who have died, or they may be your own previous incarnations, returned from the past, to awaken your memories so that you can reclaim forgotten knowledge. They may be ancient Priestesses of Avalon or generic ancestors from ancient times, who are connected to Avalon and the sacred land, who may have something for you to hear. These journeys can be strong emotional experiences as our hearts open to our lost loved ones and to the mystical realms that lie beyond death.

1. Journey across water to the west in your human form, either on the Barge or on the back of a bird or swimming through the water on the back of a seal, dolphin or fish.
2. When you arrive you are met by a guide, who may be an inner priestess or a totem animal or being. This guide accompanies you on the journey to meet your loved ones who have passed over.
3. As your loved ones and other ancestors appear open your heart to them, communicate with them. Ask for their forgiveness and give them yours. Many are now released form the weight of their life's karma and are freed to express their truth in ways that were impossible for them in life. Ask for their love and wisdom. Feel yourself loved and blessed by them.
4. When your communication is complete, gives thanks to them, bid them farewell and return to the mainland, via the Barge, the bird or sea creature.

For many people, meeting a deceased loved one is a joyous and emotional experience in which we can talk to our loved one, who is now freed from the restraints of earthly incarnation. These experiences can be very healing. Ancestors from earlier times may provide us with information about the past, about our earlier incarnations, adding pieces to the jigsaw of who we are. These experiences are energetic and transforming for the individual.

The Place of Transition

In my understanding in one of its many aspects Avalon is a Place of Transition for those who have recently passed over. It is a staging post for many on the journey into the spiritual realms. One of the functions of a Priestess of Avalon is to hold an open, loving heart space for those who are making their transition from life to death, helping them to move with grace and ease out of their physical bodies and into the worlds of spirit. Often a dying person needs to know that it is alright for them to leave family and friends and take their journey onwards into spirit. Just as they may be accompanied on the journey into death on this side of life by family, friends and priestesses, so they need to know that they will be met across the border by loved ones who have gone before them. Awareness of individual deaths may come through personal knowledge of the dying or dead person, through the media, or through visions and dreams.

Some priestesses are particularly called to work with the dying in the Place of Transition especially when death has been sudden, unexpected or brutal. Souls who have passed over in this way are often unaware that they have died. They are often confused, lost and disturbed. Although dead they are still able to receive help from the living who can journey consciously and in trance into Avalon to commune with them. Priestesses can help explain what has happened to their bodies, can reassure them, comfort them, and help them move through shock into the worlds of spirit.

I believe that Avalon is not just for those who know its name. It is not exclusive, but is a generic place of transition available to many who are passing over, especially those who die in mass departures in natural and human-made catastrophes. Priestesses of Avalon hold the space for those who are passing over in great numbers at these times, comforting and calming those in panic as they move through. It is part of our healing work to be present for those in spiritual need.

The Avalon Bardos

Avalon encompasses the bardo states of consciousness which lie between death and rebirth. It is first of all the space for recognition that a person has died. It is the space for remembering the activities of life, that time when our lives replay at great speed and we see our mistakes and failures, our triumphs and strengths, when we can ask for forgiveness, healing and reconciliation. In some traditions this phase of dying is said to last three days, and during this time the body should be allowed to lie in the place of death undisturbed. It is a space for the recognition of our karma.

The bardos also encompass the Pure Land states of being where our consciousness aspires to greatness, to complete union with the Goddess. It also encompasses the frightening bardo states, where our Shadows dwell, and where the unresolved unhealed parts of ourselves present themselves in frightening ways. It is the place where we recognise the negative karma which we must still fulfil.

Avalon is the place of rebirth, where magnetic choices are made to attract new parents to us so that we can incarnate once again into the world. In the Tibetan tradition the journey through the bardo states of consciousness are said to take forty nine days from death to rebirth. This number may be literal or allegorical. Monks sit next to the dead body of the deceased person and read aloud the sacred text of the *Tibetan Book of the Dead* for this length of time, to help guide the departed soul through the bardos.

Priestesses of Avalon may choose to follow a similar practice for the dead, sitting with the body, holding the soul within their consciousness, even when the body has been buried or cremated..

Priestesses act as soul midwives exploring these different bardo states in life and accompanying the dead on their journeys between death and rebirth. Exploration of these bardo states is part of advanced priestess trainings.

The Barren Wasteland of the Isle of the Dead

The Isle of the Dead is also the place where the wounded, shocked, dismembered, split off parts of our psyches can be found. Often when we experience traumatic events in our lives the events are so overwhelming that we have a need to forget some or all of what has happened. The shock can be so great that we cut out parts of our memory in order to protect ourselves from pain. However these memories do not just disappear, they are repelled to a psychic space, which is the Barren Wasteland of the Isle of the Dead, where all is in decay and nothing grows. It is a hot stifling place, where the air does not move. Here the misplaced parts of ourselves can be found. We can journey to this barren Isle of the Dead for ourselves and for other people.

To make this journey to the Western Isle of the Dead you need to be in a safe space, where you will not be disturbed for a time. The journey can be made in silence, to the beat of a drum or to unobtrusive relaxing music.

1. *Sit comfortably on an upright chair which has no armrests, so that you can move your body and arms easily without obstruction.*
2. *Place a veil over your head for the journey. Close your eyes and relax your body, letting go of the tension that you are holding in your shoulders and arms, in your legs and feet, in your belly and in your face. Focus your attention in your breath and notice the air as it moves in and out of our nose and mouth, down into your lungs and out again. Allow your breathing to slow and deepen.*
3. *As the breath deepens notice your breast and shoulders gently rising and falling in rhythm with your breath.*
4. *In imagination visualise your body transforming into that of a bird. Your arms transform into wings and your elbows move slightly back so that they feel like folded wings. Your feet become bird's feet. Your head becomes a bird's head which may be stretched out or may be tucked into your chest, depending on the kind of bird that you are becoming. Physically turn your head from side to side, while psychically looking around the room. Become aware that your vision has changed as your bird eyes are on the sides of your head rather than at the front.*

Recognise what kind of bird you are. You may be a large or a small bird, but for the long journey you are about to take it may be less exhausting to be a bird with larger wings.

5. *In your mind's eye see yourself now sitting perched on the chair as a bird. Hop off the chair onto the floor and walk or take a short flight to the nearest windowsill. Hop through the now open window and look around at the view outside the actual window. Then physically and also psychically extend your arms sideways, opening out your wings, and launch yourself imaginatively into the air as a bird.*

6. *From the window ledge rise up into the air as a bird, looking down on the building in which your human body is still sitting. Fly higher into the air becoming aware of the location you have flown from, the countryside, village, town or city, which now lies spread out beneath you. Recognise familiar landmarks from another angle, physically turning your head to the left and the right and bending your neck and head to look downwards at the view.*

7. *Notice your orientation to the sun, to the land or townscape beneath you. Changing direction if you need to, begin to fly over the land to the west. Look down on the land beneath you which may be familiar or unknown. Become aware of your bird body flying and from your hips and your sacrum, let your body physically move forward and back in rhythm with the movement of your wings. At the same time move your wing arms forward and back, the tips almost touching as they come together in front of the body and then stretching out and as far back as possible. This movement of the physical body expands the chest and lungs, increasing the flow of oxygen and building dynamic energy in the body. This will help release memory from the body. Allow your body to fully enter into the rhythm of flight.*

8. *After a time notice ahead of you on the horizon the gleam of water, of the sea, of the great ocean to the west, and fly towards it. Soon you are passing over the shoreline, seeing beneath you the water as it reaches the land. There may be small or large waves crashing. See what you see. Then fly out over the water heading west away from the mainland.*

9. *Look down at the sea, notice its colour, its condition whether it is clear or murky, whether it is calm and tranquil or whether there is a great swell. Notice the weather. Is it sunny or raining, cloudy, windy or stormy? Fly high above the water and look down on the boats that might be crossing the ocean, look down into the depths. What do you see there? Fly close to the waves and feel the spray on your body. Enjoy the experience of flying over the sea. See fish in the water and if you like dive in and retrieve yourself some fishy food.*

10. *Fly until you can no longer see land on either side of you or behind you.*

Notice how you feel about that, notice how your body feels. Keep moving your body and your wings, keep flying or you may plunge down accidentally into the water. Your wings may be large enough that you can soar on the air currents rather than keeping beating. Be the bird you are. Fly onwards, for you are flying to the Western Isle *of the* Dead *and it is far away across the ocean.* Notice *if you feel tired. You are now so far from the mainland that it is easier to keep going until your reach your destination, rather than give up and return home.*

11. *Far ahead on the watery horizon you notice a small dot of land that gradually grows bigger as you fly towards it. As you get nearer you see a mostly flat low-lying sandy landscape with a mountain in the far distance. As you near the shoreline you see sand dunes stretching ahead of you beneath a hot sun. This is a true desert island with no greenery in sight. The temperature rises as you cross the margin and waves of heat rise up to meet you as you fly in over a flat desert landscape. Beneath you there is nothing but sand, with no sign of life. As you fly on into the interior of the island, just as once you were surrounded by water on all sides, now you are surrounded by endless desert. This has a different feeling. You fly for miles and miles, searching for something.*

12. *Then ahead of you in the distance you see the* Death Tree, *sticking up out of the sand. You fly towards it. Come into land on or beside the* Death Tree, *folding your arm wings to the sides of your body. Notice that the dry dead branches of the tree are covered in all sorts of strange, odd items. There are childhood toys, gruesome looking bits of flesh and bone, unexpected objects. Some thing or things on the tree belong to you and you are here to retrieve them.*

13. *Find the piece or pieces that are yours, trying not to make judgements about what those pieces should be, but allow what wants to come with you to be yours. Take your time. Search the branches for the items you are missing. When you find them tuck them safely beneath your wings or on your back or hold them in your claws. When you are sure that you have everything that belongs to you, spread your arm wings out and take off from the tree.*

14. *Fly towards the distant mountain that you saw as you came towards the island. Fly higher and higher up the mountain until you find a high combe, containing a spring and a clear pool of water, sparkling in the heat. Fly down to the combe and drink from the water, folding and unfolding your wings as necessary.*

15. *When you feel refreshed take off from the combe and begin your journey home, flying back to the east across the desert island. Fly, allowing your body to move back and forth from your hips as you did on the journey here. Let your arms wings sweep up and down.*

16. *After mile upon mile of sand, ahead see the gleam of sunshine on water. The sea lies ahead of you and you fly out across the shoreline, out over the ocean. Fly towards the east, looking back once or twice to see the Western Isle of the Dead receding behind you, until it is no more that a dot in the ocean, which finally disappears. Once more you are surrounded by endless ocean. Notice the condition of the sea, of the swell, of the weather. Look down into the depths and see what you can see. Be aware of the precious cargo that you are carrying and notice how you feel.*

17. *After a long flight, ahead you see a dark streak that gradually grows and forms the shapes of land ahead of you. Fly towards the mainland and cross over the shoreline to a life-filled landscape. Notice what you can see beneath you, fields and forest, rivers and ponds, homes and dwellings, glimpses of human activity. As you fly on to the east see signs of a familiar landscape, the countryside, village, town or city, where you began your journey.*

18. *From high in the sky look down towards the building from which you first emerged and fly down to the open window. Land on the window sill, resting momentarily after your long flight.*

19. *Then move in through the window and seeing your human body seated on the chair, fly towards it. Look at yourself in your human form and from beneath your bird's wing or back or claw, take the items or bits of flesh and bone that you found on the Death Tree on the Isle of the Dead. Moving your head and using your bird's beak place it or them into your human body where you can see there is a gap or space waiting to be filled. Use your beak to fill and seal the gaps. Smooth and stroke the area until the seams and scars disappear and there is no sign that anything was once missing.*

20. *For one last time feel your bird body, your wings and feathers, your rounded breast, your head, your feet. Breathe your bird self into your human body. Take several deep breaths and become aware of your human feet, your human body and arms, your head, your breath moving in and out through your nose and mouth and into your lungs. Feel yourself becoming refreshed with every breath and slowly bring your consciousness back into the room. Notice how you feel.*

21. *When you are returned to your body write down, draw, paint your journey, recognising the parts of yourself that had been lost, of which you may not have been aware. Draw images of the pieces you found on the Death Tree on the Isle of the Dead and let understanding arise consciously of what they might mean for you. Let yourself remember long forgotten memories and allow them to be real and meaningful to you. Make associations and connections with those memories, healing the lost, rejected, wounded parts of yourself that you have*

now retrieved. Let your tears flow, let your heart be made whole.

Personal work

Practice sensing the Veil of Avalon as you walk the sacred landscape. Practice wearing a physical veil at your altar, in ceremony and for journeying. Journey to the Otherworld, journey to the Isle of Avalon, to the Western Isle of the Dead. Journey to meet the Goddess, to meet your loved ones and the ancestors. Practice Phowa for yourself and others.

Journey to the barren wasteland of the Isle of the Dead for self healing.

Continue to work on your Priestess vow. What do you want to say to the Goddess as you dedicate yourself to Her service?

Groups of students working together plan the Self-Initiation ceremony that will take place at the end of the Second Spiral, which you are designing for yourselves.

Scrying for a Vision
Coming into the Present

According to the dictionary to scry means to see, divine or predict the future by means of a crystal ball or crystals. In this chapter I am expanding the meaning of scrying to include many different forms of divination, in which the priestess scryer opens her consciousness and inner sight to the present, to discern the causes and patterns of events in the past and their possible outcomes in the future. It is principally a vision-based art, looking into a scrying object with both outer and inner sight, but it also involves using other outer and inner senses, such as hearing, touch, taste, smell and intuition.

The different methods we will look at include reading the signs and symbols in the natural world of the Goddess, using earth, water, fire and air as tools to stimulate awareness, also dream interpretation and working with traditional divination techniques, such as tarot and astrology. Scrying is a priestess art which allows us to explore what is happening in our own and other people's lives from a wider perspective, one which views current events in the light of the greater whole of who we are. This can be invaluable especially when we and others are facing challenges in life.

Scrying is an ancient skill which has been practised for thousands of years throughout the world from Australia to America, Africa to Asia. It has been used wherever individuals and societies seek to understand what is happening in their lives and the world around them from a bigger perspective. Most human beings have a natural ability to scry, but have never given themselves the opportunity to explore this Goddess-given talent. Scrying is an esoteric art which, like hands-on healing, we can really only learn by giving ourselves permission to try it and then through practising it. Like other priestess arts it involves the development of the sixth sense of intuition. Scrying can help when we are confused, indecisive or suffering, to bring clarity, direction, healing and peace. It is a powerful art which is not to be taken lightly, as it can have damaging as well as healing effects depending on how it is used. This chapter contains many practical exercises that will help develop your ability to scry.

Scrying for Oneself

We can scry for ourselves and we can scry for other people. In some ways its easier to scry for someone other than oneself, just as its often much easier to see another person's problems and their resolution, rather than our own. However scrying for oneself is an important part of self development. It encourages us to look at our characters and the things that happen to us from another perspective. In my twenties when I lived in Wales I was given a Rider Waite Tarot deck and at first I had no idea what the different images and symbols meant. I began to read some of the few books on Tarot then available, including Mouni Saddhu's *Tarot* (Allen and Unwin). Almost every day for two years and more I laid out a spread of Tarot cards for myself and tried to interpret what I saw from the distinctive pictures. Through doing this I slowly learned the meaning of the cards by relating them to my own experience.

Particular cards would appear frequently in readings for a time and then work their way through the sequence of different spreads, from the future into the present and then on into the past. No matter how hard I shuffled the pack to change things, the same cards would appear over and over as I dealt with a particular problem in my life. I remember a time when the Tower kept appearing in the spreads as my life crumbled around me. I wanted other cards, like the beneficent Star, to appear, but no matter how much I willed things to change, the cards would always reflect exactly what was actually happening in my life and predict what could be happening in the future.

As I read the cards daily and meditated upon their meanings my intuition began to awaken and I started to listen to my inner knowing. I began to learn the meanings of the images and symbols on the cards and my intuition named the relationships between the cards and events in my life. My personal experience confirmed my intuition, which was thereby strengthened. My belief in intuition as a source of truth, knowledge and wisdom grew.

Through these daily readings I recognised that the Tarot presented a picture pattern of what was happening in the present and if I could only read the pattern, I could understand and find perspective on what was going on. It was helpful to me. This also applied to other divinatory systems, such as the *I Ching* or *Book of Changes* (Richard Wilhelm's translation, RKP), which was becoming popular in those days. The I Ching was more difficult to comprehend, because it involved throwing sets of coins or sticks. Depending on the way they fell one read the interpretation given in the book, but the meanings of this was obscure and needed to be considered. They did however often given another perspective on what was happening in my life, similar to the Tarot but expressed differently.

Studying these divinatory systems over time showed me clearly and repeatedly that any present moment contains all the information we need to help us understand the present, past and future, if only we can read the information given. Scrying is all about bringing one's consciousness into the present moment and looking, seeing, sensing, feeling and hearing what is there. Different methods of scrying can be used but their purpose is always to bring us into the present, to allow the intuition to open, and to read what is available to be read. Scrying for oneself allows us to really understand what we are seeing as images, patterns and their meanings, through personal experience.

Bringing Yourself into the Present

One of the best ways to begin to really experience the present is by grounding and centring ourselves in the landscape of the Goddess in a conscious manner. Then we open up our outer and inner senses, passing through the Veil into the Otherworld, where we read the signs and symbols all around us. The following two hour exercise involves walking out into a natural physical landscape. It is simple, powerful and effective.

1. *Make a conscious decision to journey into a beautiful physical landscape where you plan to enter the Otherworld. Choose a place that is special to you, that you love, that you know will be peaceful and filled with the beauty of the Goddess's nature. Start your journey at a specific point which may be your home or a place you are visiting or even your car. Take offerings of dried herbs, water and a journal with you. Wear warm weatherproof clothes and shoes as necessary.*
2. *Begin by grounding and centring yourself in the landscape using the method given in the First Spiral. From your heart send a thread of light down to centre of the earth. Feel it return, bringing the energy of the earth into your body, filling your heart. From your heart send a thread of light up to and out through the top of your head and out to the farthest star you can imagine. Feel the energy of the farthest star returning to your heart, mixing and mingling with the energy of the earth. Feel your soul energy entering your heart and radiating*

outwards in all directions.

3. *Make an offering of herbs to the Goddess and say a prayer to Her. Ask Her to be with you on your journey, to help you pass through the Veil into the Otherworld and to open your senses to the signs and symbols of Her nature.*
4. *As you begin to walk from your starting place see yourself leaving behind you a thread of golden light anchored in your heart, wherever you walk, just as a snail leaves a shining trail wherever it moves.*
5. *Walk where you feel guided to walk, where your feet want to take you. As you walk consciously notice Her nature all around you, the plants, trees, animals, insects and birds. Look and listen with your outer and your inner senses. When your attention is drawn to a particular plant or tree walk towards it and make an offering. Examine the plant or tree closely. Touch it, feel its energy. Ask what it wants to tell you, if it has a message for you. Listen for the answers it may give. Notice the birds who fly past, notice how they emphasise your thoughts or ask you to wake up and take notice of what is going on around you. Notice any animals, who like the birds, may be your totem creatures, bringing messages from the Goddess to you. Open yourself to your intuition, your inner knowing.*
6. *Walk for thirty minutes through Her nature.*
7. *Walk to a place that attracts you, choosing a spot where you will be undisturbed for an hour or more, where you can peacefully commune with Her nature. When you find it make another offering of herbs and call in the Goddesses on Britannia's Wheel, facing each direction in turn and calling Her into your body and being.*
8. *Sit or lie down comfortably on the ground. As you sit allow yourself to sink deeply into the earth, into Her nature. Open your senses. Expand your awareness. Touch the earth, smell the scents, taste the air, open your outer and inner vision, listen to the outer and inner sounds. When you sense something turn your attention towards it and explore it more deeply.*
9. *Become aware that you are lying on the body of the Mother Goddess. Feel Her breathing very, very slowly beneath you. Feel the long, slow pulse of Her heart beating deep in the earth. Let Her spaciousness enter your mind and emotions. Lie for a time on the earth becoming at one with Her and with everything around you, opening yourself to the present. Look for patterns and shapes in the branches of trees, in flowers, in grasses, in the contours of Her body. Give yourself permission to look through the Veil into the Otherworld.*
10. *Become aware of the trail of golden light that connects you to your starting place. All around you begin to sense the Web of Wyrd, the etheric threads of connection between all things. These are gossamer thin violet threads of energy, which appear rather like spider's webs in autumn hung with dew, but more*

subtle. See how your trail of golden light and your soul's radiance connects to and sparks with other threads of the web, your soul energy adding to the energy matrix of the planet, helping maintain its health and beauty.

11. *As thoughts about your life come into your mind let them pass through like clouds moving across a blue sky. Try not to censor them as they arise, but release your worries and concerns into the blue beyond. Let all things pass. Be still. Give yourself the opportunity to be at one with Her and all of Her nature. Let yourself come into the present by focusing your attention solely on this moment. As Ram Dass once said, "Be Here Now".*

12. *Open yourself to hearing answers for you.*

13. *Write or draw in your journal what you sense and feel. Let your hands move across the page as they wish to, writing or drawing whatever needs to be written at that time, again without censorship. Write down your prayers, your love for the Goddess, express your feelings in words, images and colours, your hopes and dreams for the future. Lie back and gaze into space, letting peace enter your soul. Allow this place to become holy.*

14. *After an hour or so look around where you have been sitting and find something which feels meaningful to you, a flower, a stone, a twig, etc., that will remind you of this sacred spot and of your experience here on Her body. As you stand, look out if you can, over a larger vista and see the threads of the Web of Wyrd radiating across the wider landscape.*

15. *Begin your return journey noticing how your movements through the physical world create ripples in the energetic world. At your starting place make an offering and give thanks to the Goddess for all you have received.*

16. *When you return home allow the events of your journey to be present with you for as long as possible. Place the item from your sacred spot on your altar as a talisman. Every time you look at it reconnect to the holy ground where you were at one with Her nature. Let the feeling of spaciousness remain with you for as long as you are able.*

Repeat this journey several times over a year at different seasons, so that you learn to recognise the feeling of spaciousness in your body and mind when it arises. The next step is to consciously generate that feeling in other circumstances by opening yourself to the present, by focusing your attention and concentration on this moment now.

Scrying for Others

As priestesses we may often be asked to scry for others who are in need of help in understanding current situations and challenges. Individual priestesses will have preferred methods of scrying, but here I would suggest that you experiment with the different methods given in this chapter. There is no need to fix on a single method, rather it is better to be able to read the present in any situation using whatever tools are available. The ability to read the present is vital for a priestess in all forms of energy work, in ceremony and ritual, in speaking publicly, in healing and in one to one spiritual communication, as well as in scrying.

Scrying for other people can bring them inspiration and renewal. Seekers will seek out priestess scryers for spiritual insight and wisdom, no matter how their initial questions are presented. There is a hunger within many people for spiritual connection that the priestess scryer is there to engage with and help fulfil, as well as seeing when the right man or woman might turn up in a seeker's life. As priestess scryers we are bound by the ethics that govern our whole work as priestesses, and the following describes how these apply to scrying for others.

The Practice and Ethics of Scrying for Others

Most people like to be told what is going to happen in the future. They particularly want to hear that the future will be better than the present. Many read daily newspaper horoscopes and seek advice from fortune tellers and diviners. People want to know when they will meet their soul mate, get a new job, leave home, find their spiritual path and many other desires. This longing to know the future can be so strong and indiscriminate that it leaves the seeker vulnerable to emotional and psychological manipulation and abuse. As a priestess scryer it is important that we hold a good ethical stance in relation to those for whom we scry.

Our fundamental ethic as a scryer is to be harmless, to do nothing which may harm another human being. We always scry from a positive point of view which will leave the seeker inspired and hopeful about their future, whatever has been revealed in the smoke, the flame or the crystal ball. As priestesses we scry from a spiritual viewpoint. We view the seeker's life from the perspective of them being a soul incarnating into the physical world, and that it is their soul which guides and directs them in life. Although we may talk about everyday matters we always view those matters in the light of the eternal.

We do not predict fixed futures, because as human beings we all have free will and our actions can change our futures. We never predict death or harm for a seeker. We consider the difficulties we all face in life to be challenges on the path of incarnation. We help seekers to view them as such, rather than as overwhelming, inescapable problems that only miracles can solve. We help reveal the repeating life patterns which trace back to deep rooted wounds, so that they can be healed. We encourage people to come into the centre of their own lives rather than being spectators at the feast. We help see pathways into the future the seeker may take to transform their lives for the better.

The Preparation and Practice of Scrying

In order to successfully scry in an indoor space it is good to prepare both oneself and the scrying space. Preparation for scrying outdoors is more varied depending on where we are, but always giving ourselves time and space to connect to the landscape and Her nature, before opening to Her natural signs and symbols, as shown in the earlier exercise.

An indoor scrying session is best held in an environment which is specially set aside for healing purposes, for scrying, healing, meditation and prayer. All these activities generate a calm, clear energetic framework which allows the scryer to focus their attention quickly, bringing themselves fully into the present as required. For the priestess scryer in the healing room there will be an altar dedicated to the Goddess with a lighted candle. The scrying objects, smoke, flame, water or crystal, etc., are placed on a table between you or to one side. Lighting is important as the scryer needs to be able to focus their attention on the scrying element or object looking for subtle movements.

1. *Before the seeker arrives cleanse yourself and the space physically, and psychically, either by burning incense or warming essential oils, and/or by sounding several OM's or ringing bells which harmonise the sound and unseen vibrations in the room. Two chairs of equal height face each other with a small table in between them on which the scrying objects are placed.*
2. *Welcome the seeker in a warm and friendly manner when they arrive in the scrying space, helping them to feel safe and cared for. People are often nervous when they come for a scrying session as the answers they seek are always important to them, even if their interest seems casual.*
3. *Each scrying session begins with a face to face meeting between scryer and seeker seated directly opposite each other, so that eye contact can be easily established. Look the seeker in the eyes and ask if they have particular questions that they would like answered during the scrying. You may also ask if they have any background information they would like to share with you.*
4. *When they have finished speaking ask if there are any beings, Goddesses or*

guides that they would like to be present for the scrying.
5. *Tell the seeker that you are going to centre yourself first of all and will say a prayer out loud to begin the session. Close your eyes for a few moments and ground and centre yourself in your heart and radiate soul energy outwards in all directions.*
6. *In your mind's eye visualise a thread of light moving in a figure of eight from your heart chakra towards the seeker's heart chakra and then returning to your heart chakra. Repeat this visualisation at the crown chakra and the base chakra so that energetically you are connected to the seeker via three figures of eight, one at the base, heart and crown chakras.*
7. *Ground and centre the seeker, seeing them connected down into the earth and up into the heavens and also radiating their soul energy outwards from their heart.*
8. *Connect your heart to your soul and to the seeker's soul, creating a triangle of energy.*
9. *Say a prayer out loud welcoming your own and the seeker's preferred beings, Goddesses and guides to aid you in the session, and asking that everything that is revealed shall be for the seeker's greatest good. Feel their presence entering the scrying space. This prayer focuses and relaxes both you and the seeker.*
10. *Open your eyes and look at the scrying object in front of you. Focus your attention completely on what you see. Open your consciousness to the present moment, just as you did out in nature in the earlier practice. Look for the patterns, signs and symbols that you see within the scrying object. Say aloud what you see. As you speak allow the seeker's question to drop into your awareness. Listen to your intuition as it speaks of the relationship between what you are seeing and how it is relevant to the seeker's question. Say what you see.*
11. *Speak until there is no more to say, then ask the seeker if what you have said is meaningful to them. Receive their feedback. If they confirm what you have said take their words in as an affirmation of your ability to be present with what is and to recognise that you have been able to read what is in the moment. If they tell you that what you have said is not true for them, don't hold on to your need to be right, let it go.*
12. *Look at the scrying object again in the light of any additional information the seeker may give you. Don't give up on yourself. Open yourself to the present and scry again.*
13. *View what you see and say in the light of the eternal, from the bigger picture of who that person is, not just from the minutiae of their life. Seeking a scrying session with a priestess is always about an inner hunger, a spiritual thirst, no matter how it is presented. As a priestess you have permission to*

bring that spiritual hunger to the forefront and to address it.
14. *When there is no more to say, offer a prayer of gratitude out loud to the beings, Goddesses and guides who have been with you during the scrying session.*
15. *Following this the seeker may wish to discuss further anything that you have seen or they may leave the session. Release all energetic links to the seeker, seeing the energy threads coming back to your own chakras.*
16. *After the session is over cleanse and clear the scrying place with incense, bells or by sounding OMs.*

Scrying with the Elements

The four natural elements of air, fire, water and earth provide a wonderful means of focusing our attention so that we can bring ourselves into this moment now. We can use the elements in smaller concentrated forms or as they appear in nature. For example we can scry with water by looking into a bowl of water or by looking into a lake. The preparation method given above applies to the concentrated elements rather than when one is outside in nature.

Scrying with Air

We see the movements of air by the particles that pass through it, in particular, smoke particles or drops of water. One of the simplest way to create smoke is by burning incense, either in the form of incense or joss sticks, or by burning incense on charcoal, although the latter can produce too much smoke, which may make us and the seeker cough and splutter. Ensure that there are no draughts of air which will blow the smoke about. Try not to breathe into the smoke yourself as this too will disturb its movements unnecessarily, although the seeker may breathe into the smoke.

Light the joss stick or charcoal at the beginning of the scrying, adding incense to the charcoal when you have made your energy connections with the seeker. Smoke will arise from the incense as it burns, coiling upwards, moving and turning, creating patterns in the smoke.

Focus your attention on the smoke, gazing at it as it moves. Let your consciousness open outwards and read what you see in the movements of the smoke. Apply what you see to the seeker's questions.

In nature clouds move continuously across the sky. Some of these are rain-bearing but many are not and we can scry from the shapes and movements of the clouds without ourselves getting wet.

Sit or lie down on the earth and gaze at the clouds as they pass in front of you or overhead. Bring yourself into the present and holding your own or the seeker's question in your mind read the clouds for information.

On misty days scry using the movements of the mist as it rises out of the damp Summerland or flows in the breeze.

Scrying with Fire

We can scry with fire in different forms, including candle flames. We place a lighted candle on the table between ourselves and the seeker. Again we ensure there are no draughts to make the flame flicker.

Gaze at the candle flame noticing the golden flame, the lighted wick and the dark umbra. Gaze at the flame until your eyes seem to go out of focus and your consciousness opens. Hold the seeker's question in your mind and scry what you see in the flame.

There are other fires that we can scry made from burning sticks and coals - indoor hearth fires, cauldron fires, bonfires - large and small. We can use any of these to scry.

Look into the flames that flicker and burn, notice the shapes, colours and movement of the flames. Again open your consciousness and allow images, characters and their stories, to appear in the fire.

Look into the white gold heart of the fire, into the red glow and scry a meaningful vision for yourself or the seeker.

Scrying with Water

Water has long been used for scrying and works whether water is still or moving. Water can be placed in a largish bowl which may be painted black on the inside to give a blank surface for vision. We place the bowl of water between ourselves and the seeker. This water may be holy water from a sacred well or water from the tap which you bless yourself, depending on your preference. Water should be fresh for each scrying.

Look into the water in the bowl. Look first of all at the reflections you can see bouncing off the surface of the water, of your own face and the seeker's. See what you see as you open your awareness. Gaze at the surface of the water and read the reflections.

When you wish to go deeper into a particular aspect of the scrying, look through the surface of the water into the depths of the bowl and allow your mind to play with changing mutable nature of water. In variations of this procedure you can disturb the water with your fingers or with a spoon to create movement in the water, if it helps you to see more.

Bodies of water in nature are wonderful for scrying. These can be streams, wells, rivers, lakes or the sea. Gazing into their stillness and/or their endless movement allows the mind to expand and open to vision. We can look into the bubbling waters of streams or weirs, or gaze at the river waters as they flow slowly or quickly downstream. We can look into the still waters of a well, such as the wellhead at Chalice Well in which we see ourselves and the surrounding trees and sky reflected. Other figures may come and go, the Nine Morgens or the Lady of the Holy Springs and Wells Herself. We can gaze at the ocean as it crashes on the shore, or look to the far horizon where the water meets the sky to help open our consciousness. We can look at still or moving surface of pools and lakes.

On a journey with students on the advanced Priestess Enchantress course we travelled to the lake of Llyn y Fan Fach in Wales. This is a Creation Site where long ago Nelferch, the Lady of the Lake emerged from beneath the waters bringing the domestication of animals and nature into being, as well as knowledge of the healing properties of plants and herbs. Llyn y Fan Fach is high up in the hills south of Llandovery and surrounded on three sides by high grassy cliffs. On the day we were there the breeze created an endless rippling of the surface of the lake, and water sprites and undines danced and played. We were transfixed by their movements. Sitting gazing at the lake for a time the whole environment began to change shape, the high cliff walls began to move and we entered the Otherworld. Visions appeared sweeping across the lake bringing information and insight.

Particular lakes are honoured in many cultures as places of vision, especially in eastern cultures and native America. The present incarnation of the Dalai Lama was chosen after lamas journeyed to a particular lake known for its scrying powers. The vision of his birthplace appeared in the waters of the lake. In MesoAmerica particular deep pools of water are recognised as creation and scrying sites, where visions appear for the benefit of the people. We too can scry in all these places.

Look at the water, stream, river, pool, lake or ocean and open your consciousness to water with its endless liquid movement. Look at the surface of the water, at the spray, the rolling waves, the falling water, the changing light. Let your mind be lulled awake. Scry from the movements, scry from the stillness. Look into the depths of the water and scry for yourself and for others, using your intuition to interpret meanings .

Scrying with Earth

There are different methods of scrying with earth using different forms of the element. Crystals balls are among the most common, but individual crystals can also be used, especially those which contain phantoms or inner markings.

Place the crystal ball or crystal in front of you and gaze into it. Hold your attention steadily on the surface of the ball or crystal and ask your questions and then move into its depths, again looking at the patterns and movements that appear within the crystal. Allow images to form and use your intuition to interpret what you see.

We can use other material objects to scry, such as a scrying mirror, which is a black surfaced concave mirrored dish, especially designed for scrying. Images appear on its inner surface as we gaze into it. We can gather groups of similar natural objects, such as twigs or stones, bones or shells, and cast them onto the earth, where we scry from the patterns formed as they fall. This is a traditional scrying method in many African cultures.

As described in the first exercise we can also open ourselves to the Goddess's natural world as a means of scrying, noticing for ourselves and others the signs and symbols that She continually presents to us if we have eyes to see and ears to hear.

Walk in nature often and open yourself to the patterns and images that are always there in front of you. Notice the crows who fly by as you think or talk of a new piece of creation you are embarking on. Notice the green woodpecker as she brings a message to you from the Goddess. Notice the owl as she hoots. Notice the butterfly that heralds transformation, the moth that signals the presence of an ancestor, the dragonfly that opens the gateway to the Otherworld. Recognise your totem creatures and learn of their significance for you.

The Power of Dreams

Dreams take us into the personal and the collective unconscious mind and are one of the ways in which the subconscious communicates with the conscious mind. They are a form of nightly self-scrying in which we can learn to read our own inner imagery and interpret it for ourselves. We can also help others to interpret their dreams. Dreams present information in the form of images, symbols, emotions and sensations, which can have obvious, or more usually, obscure meanings. It's not as simple as saying that seeing a cat in a dream means its going to rain or seeing the Queen means you are dreaming of your mother. We all have to find the meaning of our own symbolic language, some of which is cultural and universal and shared with others, and some of which is unique to us.

Many dreams are concerned with repeating the events of the previous day as a means of integrating experience, while other dreams give important clues to our inner unconscious worlds. They give us distorted pictures of the lives we know, of people and events which happen to us, all combined in odd ways, that reveal parts of ourselves normally hidden from our view. Dreams can be remembrances of experiences filled with nostalgia for lost childhood innocence or thumping with fear and terror from forgotten incidents. Dreams can contain memories of past lives, indicating the causes of lifetime wounds. Some dreams are prophetic, predicting future personal and collective experiences. Some special dreams are inspirational, their messages coming directly from the Goddess, from the Lady and the imaginal world of Avalon.

Dream incubation was an important part of many early temples, which contained special cells where priestesses and those in need of healing could sleep and dream, until they had received a healing or meaningful dream. The Hypogeum in Malta is one such example, where there are small sleeping cells in the heart of the underground chambers. The Roman Temple of Nodens at Lydney in the Forest of Dean, included small cells where visitors came to sleep and receive a healing dream, sometimes with the help of herbs and snakes. In legend Bride's Mound near Glastonbury was said to be a gateway to Avalon, where visitors would stay with the women's community who lived there, until they had received a dream inviting them to enter the sacred Isle of Avalon. In recreating our modern day Goddess temples we remember to include such spaces for dreaming Her presence alive.

Everyone dreams every night but we don't always remember our dreams. The best way to improve one's memory of dreams is to keep a dream diary for several months, recording dreams at the moment of awakening.

Place the dream diary and a pen next to your bed so that you can write in the diary almost as soon as your eyes open. Movement, getting out of bed, can mean that dreams disappear almost immediately, so write in your dream diary as soon as you wake up. At first you may be unable to remember anything, but slowly you may recall a word or a face or a scene or a situation. As you write these down or draw what you have seen, other parts of the dream will be recalled to memory.

Notice how the emotional content of dreams affects how we feel during the day. A nightmare can result in feelings of emotional vulnerability and anxiety all day. A spiritual dream can give us a feeling of peace and joy that colours all our interactions with other people, who can feel our happiness. We dream of our families, our friends, of schooldays, of old lovers, of our animus (inner male archetype) and anima (inner female archetype) projections.

As we journey on our path to priestesshood we dream of finding a new room in our house, somewhere we have never been before. We dream of climbing a mountain, reaching to new spiritual heights. We dream of meeting people we feel we have known before, signalling the presence of invisible spiritual companions, people we perhaps knew in this or other incarnations, who are always with us throughout life now.

Dreams also contain vital information about our shadows, the parts of ourselves that we do not know about, that are normally hidden from our view and contain our unacceptable, repressed and wounded aspects. We may dream of dark characters who do bad things, who bring terror and violence to us or to others. We find ourselves fighting to the death or running scared from unknown assailants or finding our legs and bodies unable to move as we meet our shadows in the night. We need to recognise and befriend these shadow people, who are part of us. Remembering our dreams helps us to bring these hidden parts of ourselves out of unconsciousness so that they can be healed and transformed in the light of consciousness.

We can receive spiritual information in our dreams that we can apply in the everyday world. Much of my own understanding of Goddess and the teaching that has resulted has come through retrieving dreams first thing in the morning in that liminal state between sleep and wakefulness. I awaken slowly and then return back and forth across the threshold bringing new information from the Lady and from Avalon into the world. It is this time of day when I can hear the Goddess's voice speaking clearly to me, showing me what She wants me to do on a daily basis. I hear Her words and try to obey Her instructions. Her words are nearly always about taking small steps in life.

Many people have predictive dreams. We see ourselves and other in the future. We scry in our own consciousness, but are often unable to change our behaviour to avoid what is coming towards us. Many people have predictive dreams of environmental and human made catastrophes. We see the earthquake, the wave advancing, the bomb exploding, the towers falling, the plane crashing, but most frustratingly these images are rarely fixed to a specific time and place in a way which might be useful in preventing disasters. What these dreams do demonstrate is that there is a level of reality where it is possible to see into the future. It's almost as if in dreams some people rise out of the present moment to view the continuum of life from a wider perspective, which is not bound by time. They are able to see past, present and future events all happening now. This is the space we are entering when we scry, hopefully learning to discriminate in the process between the past, present and future with accuracy.

After writing this section on dreams yesterday, early this morning I dreamed that I found a new room in our house. It was a huge old kitchen full of dusty crockery, that had always been there, but I had not been in it since we moved into the house. I had forgotten it was there. It seemed like it would be perfect for holding teaching workshops and parties. In the house was a tortoiseshell mother cat, like a cat of ours, Twinkle, who died several years ago, and she had several kittens with her of different colours. A mother with five rather unruly children came from next door into the kitchen, and we decided to share it with her as she only had a small house. Her youngest two year old son was incredibly musically-talented and was a love bug, love pouring out of his eyes towards me and me to him. I took this as a very good sign for today and for this book which I have been writing so far for about two years.

As we become more conscious in waking life we try to become more conscious in our dream life. Here are exercises which can help this happen.

Before you fall asleep set yourself the goal of being able in the dream to look down your body at your hands. When you do manage to see your hands try to raise them up in front of your face.

In the dream look down at your feet, when you see them look where they are standing and where they are walking. Let the location expand outwards from your feet to give you a dream view on life.

Once you can do these things practice transforming objects in your dreams, e.g.. change one species of tree into another, change the colour of the sky, change the animals in front of you.

These are all signs that you are becoming conscious in the dream and therefore more available for insightful input. When you become proficient as recognising your own presence in your dream, try flying, one of the great dream experiences, taking off into the air. Explore Avalon and the beings who live here in the dream. Speak to them, listen to their messages, their songs, their spiritual teachings.

Try rising above the time line to view the past and the future.

Record your dreams, study your dreams. Notice recurring images and symbols and relate them to your life. Look at the characters in your dreams as all being a part of you, with something to tell you about yourself. Look at the places you visit in your dreams, notice the old locations where you may have experienced happy times or where parts of you were left behind in traumatic events.

View your dreams as not being about you at all, but being about others, family, personal acquaintances or strangers.

Just as you wake up in the same place where you fell asleep, as you are falling asleep consciously return to the dream place you were in when you woke up the previous morning. Let your dream life become continuous just as your waking life is continuous.

Tarot Reading

Tarot is a favourite scrying tool of mine as I find it consistently accurate and revealing. Today there are hundreds of wonderful tarot and divination packs, with all kinds of images to choose from, and each person can find a deck which appeals to them. These include Vicky Noble and Karen Vogel's circular Motherpeace Tarot with themes and imagery developed especially for women, and many new Goddess decks. Earlier decks use traditional images and symbols to convey meaning, while many modern packs use evocative imagery, collages and photographs, which allow the scryer to open their imagination and intuition.

A traditional tarot pack consists of 22 Major Arcana (cards) and 56 Minor Arcana which makes up 78 cards. Modern packs often have fewer cards than these. As I wrote earlier my introduction to Tarot came more than thirty years ago through the Rider Waite Tarot and I still like to use this same deck today, filled as it is with the good vibrations of many readings. I also have several modern decks that I use, but this is the one that I prefer and will describe here.

The Rider-Waite Tarot deck was first published in 1910 by Rider & Company in London. It was designed by Arthur E. Waite in collaboration with Pamela Colman Smith, an American artist. Waite was a member of the Order of the Golden Dawn, an occult society of the time. The images for the Major Arcana were based on those found in earlier decks, such as the Marseilles Tarot, published by Jean Dodal in Lyon in France around 1700. Originally the Minor Arcana were simpler numbered rather than pictorial cards, while the images of the Major Arcana are said to trace back to earlier tarot and playing card packs, brought across Europe from Egypt by gypsies. These cards were said to encode earlier spiritual mysteries saved from Atlantis. In times of religious persecution playing cards and tarot packs provided the perfect means to hide such mysteries from the eyes of witch finders and the profane.

The Rider-Waite deck was created to communicate certain esoteric principles through symbols. Waite gave Pamela detailed indications as to the content of the Major Arcana. The Minor Arcana however are thought to be Pamela's own creation and it is her unique illustrations that have ensured the deck's posterity. She was the first to consistently apply pictorial scenes to the minor arcana, reflecting their divinatory meaning. She unwittingly created a new tradition so that even today, the majority of divinatory style tarot decks follow her system. Waite described his interpretations in his book *The Pictorial Key to the Tarot*.

The Major Arcana cards describe the soul's journey through life through repeating spirals of experience, beginning each cycle as the innocent Fool and hopefully completing the cycle as the wise Fool. The Major Arcana begin with the Fool, then Magician, High Priestess, Empress, Emperor, Hierophant, Lovers, Chariot, Strength, Hermit, Wheel of Fortune, Justice, Hanged Man, Death, Temperance, Devil, Tower, Star, Moon, Sun, Judgement and end with the World. Their appearance in a Tarot reading signifies that something important is happening on a soul level for the seeker. On my spiritual sojourn in Wales I frequently read spreads composed solely from the Major Arcana.

The Minor Arcana consist of four suits of cards - pentacles or discs, cups or chalices, wands or rods, and swords or sceptres. Suits are numbered one to ten plus four court cards in each suit, page, knight, queen and king. These cards have a patriarchal bent, but can still be used by Goddess-loving people. Pentacles are concerned with the material world, with work, earning a living, making money, etc. Cups are concerned with the emotional world, with feelings, wounds, relationships, families, friends, lovers and marriage partners. Wands describe attributes of the minds, with all its creativity and constraints, including rigidity of attitudes and beliefs.

Swords concern spirituality, purpose and direction in life, growth of the soul and development of consciousness. (In some Tarot systems swords are equated with mind and wands with spiritual will, but I work with wands as creativity and swords as spirit.)

On each of the cards there are individual details and symbols that add extra meaning to the appearance of the card in a reading. The priestess scryer needs to study each of the cards, noticing simple things like the colour and style of clothing or the background, the position of people on the cards, the directions they face indicating connections to adjacent cards, what clothing hides and reveals, repeating images such as suns, golden pathways, towers, columns, astrological symbols, and many more details that affect how the cards are read.

The preparation for reading Tarot or scrying cards is the same as for other forms of scrying.

Reading Tarot

1. *Ground and centre yourself, connect to the seeker via figures of eight and ground and centre them. Connect your heart to your soul to the seeker's soul. Call in any beings, Goddesses or guides you wish to be present.*
2. *Shuffle the pack of cards yourself to bring your concentration and focus into the cards. Cut the deck into three and put it back together again in a different order. Offer the cards to the seeker and ask them to cut the pack into three and put them back in a different order. Ask the seeker if they have a particular question they would like answering. Then ask them to cut the cards twice more.*
3. *Spread the cards face downwards and ask the seeker to choose a card which represents the question they are asking. This can often be different to the question they have asked, which they may be trying to hide from themselves and from you. In the reading address the question revealed by the card as well as the one they tell you.*
4. *Dealing from the top of the pack lay the cards out face down between yourself and the seeker, in one of the many spreads described in Tarot books. I use a traditional 11 card spread. Preferably you will know the images so well that the cards can be laid out facing the seeker.*
5. *Once again as with other methods of scrying bring your awareness completely into the present and focus all your attention on the cards and on the seeker.*
6. *Beginning with the question card read what you see on the card. Bring in the knowledge that you have of the symbols on the card and say what you see. Connect the question to the seeker's spiritual direction and purpose.*

7. Turn the cards over one by one revealing the next stage in the reading. Relate what you see to the person's question and to their life. Relate the cards to their position in the reading as well as to each other. Ask the seeker if what you are saying is meaningful to them. Use your knowledge, intuition and inspiration.
8. Complete the reading by giving thanks to the beings who have been present during the reading.

Astrology

Astrology relates the movements of the stars in the heavens to human life on earth. It is a visual and intuitive art, based in a body of knowledge which stretches back at least four thousand years. Astrology is dismissed by scientists as unscientific and therefore invalid, while millions have their horoscopes read. Astrology is another esoteric art, which recognises that the position of the stars in the heavens at this moment now is a reflection of all that is, and if only we can read the stars, we can scry the present, the past, our fate and our destiny.

There are many good books on astrology and many good teachers of the art and I recommend that all priestesses develop an understanding of this profound system of knowledge. It's good to have one's natal horoscope drawn up by a qualified astrologer or to learn how to do it oneself. This provides a birth-time picture of our character, fate and destiny, which will come to fruition through life. The chart helps us to understand who we are and why we are the way we are. I also recommend the study of astrological transits, which relate the current positions of the stars in the heavens to our natal horoscopes. Transits of the natal horoscope give us an idea of what we have achieved, what is coming towards us and the areas of our lives that are likely to be involved in change, healing and transformation.

During our lives on earth our soul energy unfolds through several different rhythms of growth and development. Each is determined according to our soul's purpose and all are interrelated. Encompassing the whole process are the specific Life Purposes for which we have incarnated - why we are here alive on the earth now - the Cause for us. In order to fulfil our Life Purpose we follow particular patterns and rhythms of development which are our own and unique, but which are also connected to those of other people, such as family groups, soul groups, people incarnating in the same culture and in the same astrological generations. These inner patterns of development are mirrored externally in planetary transits of our natal horoscopes throughout our lives. For example, Saturn takes 28+ years to encircle the sun and every seven years we are affected by Saturn's transits as it squares, opposes and conjuncts our natal Saturn. We experience these transits in noticeable events in our lives, either in things we create or things which apparently happen to us.

Anything which is said about astrological transits is necessarily a generalisation and cannot be applied to individuals in a fixed manner. However used with discrimination it can give a framework for exploring our own and other people's development. This is important for priestesses who are accelerating their own psychological and spiritual development. We often need to have an idea of how change will affect us and also how it will affect others.

Saturn has a strong impact on human life. It is a great teacher and limiter of what we are able to do in life. Saturn rules time and teaches us about our boundaries and limitations and also how to break free from limitations. From birth it takes approximately twenty eight years for our consciousness to fully incarnate into life in the physical world. During the first seven years we are anchoring into physical expression. We are growing and getting used to having physical bodies, developing our emotional and mental capacities, laying the foundations of our character. The first square to Saturn comes around the age of seven years. This is a time when the child moves from total dependence upon parents and family, to the first inklings of selfhood and independence. By the time we reach puberty around fourteen years we are anchoring into emotional expression as transiting Saturn opposes our natal Saturn. Emotional patterns are on the whole now set for our future relationships. This is not to say that they cannot change, but the repeating cycles of relating have begun. Many of us get stuck at some point in our emotional development and it can take many years for us to heal these wounds. This is the time of our often traumatic teens.

It normally takes twenty one years to develop the capacities of the mental body though again this can take a shorter or much longer time and we go on learning the whole of our lives. We may be mentally agile from an early age and then become inhibited through social and gender conditioning, or our mental capacities may continue to expand as we get older and learn to have more confidence in ourselves. This is marked by another Saturn square around 21 years, when traditionally we would receive the key to the door, a mark of recognition of our entry into adulthood. By the time we are twenty eight or nine different aspects of our personality are in the process of integration and we are becoming whole. We have begun to recover knowledge from the past held within our souls, the residues of experience from previous incarnations. We become aware of our soul energy and can bring it consciously into expression. This is our first Saturn return, when Saturn returns to its original position in our natal horoscope. This conjunction is often characterised by a crisis within a person's emotional, mental and/or physical life. Now the personality and the soul may confront each other on what is known esoterically as the Burning Ground of the Kurukshestra, or the emotional body, often with a lot of turmoil which can be very painful.

Once this crisis is resolved one way or another we usually feel happier about who we are and what we are doing in life. We have begun to understand our limitations and appreciate our qualities as human beings. We can move more actively into creation now and in the future rather than being governed by past experience. We become more ourselves and less dominated by family and cultural conditioning. The ages twenty eight to thirty five are a time of consolidation of character with movements outwards into expression. We can now be truly creative in the world, culminating in Saturn square Saturn around 35.

The mid-life crisis begins between thirty five and forty two and is compounded by a set of major planetary transits of Neptune, Uranus and Pluto, which all human beings experience. These outer planets circumnavigate the sun in longer cycles and together bring a definite call from the soul to fulfil its purpose in incarnating, which can result in complete changes of direction in life, major ill health and/or premature death. Life begins at forty as they say, and at forty two we experience another Saturn opposition natal Saturn as we did at puberty. Forty two/three to forty nine/fifty is a time of activity and often powerful self expression and enjoyment of life as we mature and become happy with who we are. The double Saturn return now at fifty eight years of age heralds the beginning of the Queen phase in women and the King phase in men. Fourteen years later when Saturn once again opposes natal Saturn we become Crones and Sages.

There are other powerful planetary cycles that affect us daily and in the longer term. There are the fast moving Venus and Mars cycles which affect us over short lengths of time. There is the 12 year Jupiter cycle which can periodically brings us good fortune and justice. There is the 52 year Chiron cycle which brings us the healing experiences we need at 13, 26 and 39 years. At 50-52 years we experience our Chiron return which brings us face to face with our life wounds, the karmic knots we have come into life to resolve. This is also the beginning of menopause in both women and men with its loss of direction and certainty, its direct access to the numinous inner worlds, and an acceptance of the processes of ageing and the inevitability of death. Generationaly the longer cycles of the outer planets, of Uranus, Neptune and Pluto reflect deep changes in the individual and collective human psyche.

I really understood the power of astrological transits in my early 40s, when I decided to divorce the father of my children, after a short, unsuccessful marriage. I began court proceedings and after a few weeks received the decree nisi and then later the decree absolute. I had been exploring astrology for some time but hadn't looked at my transits for a while. I decided to see what was happening and saw that on the day of my decree absolute Uranus had been directly opposite my natal Uranus, which happens at approximately 40-42 years. In the wonderful book *Planets in Transit* by Robert Hand (Whitford Press) I read that under Uranus opposition Uranus it is quite likely that a person will leave a marriage quickly. I was jolted awake. I thought that I had chosen when to get divorced. I thought I was in charge of my life. I suddenly realised that I wasn't. I realised that much of how we experience life is determined by forces outside of ourselves which affect us unconsciously.

It is not that the planets rule our lives, it is that they reflect the emotional, psychological, karmic and spiritual forces which do rule our inner and outer lives, forces of which we are mostly unaware. I now understand that astrology gives us good indications of the inner and outer forces that we have to deal with as we incarnate onto Planet Earth, which itself is one planet amongst many circling around the sun in our solar system. As priestesses and human beings our task is to bring ourselves into harmony with these inner and outer forces, working with the energetic tides and flows, rather than against them through ignorance and lack of knowledge.

As a scrying method astrology allows the amateur or professional astrologer to look into the patterns and energies of the present to unravel the past and reveal the future. I highly recommend the study of astrology to all priestesses.

Personal Work

Practice three new forms of scrying which you haven't tried before with at least three different people.

Keep a dream diary for at least six months, recording your dreams every morning. Learn your own symbolic language.

Acquire a Tarot deck and begin to explore the symbolism of the cards for yourself. Read a Tarot spread daily and see what happens.

Have an astrologer create your birth horoscope and begin to learn about astrology.

Continue to work on your Self-initiation vow.

Groups of students working together firm up plans for your Self-initiation ceremony at the end of the Second Spiral.

Being At-One with the Lady Oracle and Embodiment of the Goddess

This is one of the shortest chapters in the book, but one of the most important. In it we reclaim the skill of being an Oracle for the Goddess and also an Embodiment of Her in ceremony and ritual. These esoteric arts have been practised for centuries in many indigenous cultures, but have been completely lost within our own. I believe it is time for us to remember these sacred arts for the healing of deep wounds, for inspiration and spiritual awakening.

Over several years I found myself almost accidentally embodying the Goddess in Priestess initiation ceremonies. It didn't happen by design, but through the experience of being there as people made their vows to Her, and feeling that She wanted something to be said from Her, to Her new initiates. As each person completed their vows I would find words came tumbling out of my mouth from Her, and the words were meaningful to people. The role gradually grew over time, but I didn't think about it much or talk to anyone about it.

When the idea first came that I might publicly embody the Goddess in ceremony in the 2002 Goddess Conference it was thrilling and scary at the same time. It almost felt like hubris, an offence against the Goddess, to even dare think that I might be able to embody Her overtly. Although it is often casually said that a particular woman is a Goddess, this is actually one of those diminutions of the Goddess and Her powers. What is usually meant is that we carry the Goddess within us, some more evidently than others. Her energy is a part of us, She is within us, but She is also much greater than our human selves. After all She creates the earth, sun, moon and stars, all that is.

I felt such a mixture of emotions at the very thought of embodying the Goddess consciously in ceremony at such a big event. The strength of my reaction told me that there was something important in the idea. However it was so scary that I almost couldn't think about it in any detail. I didn't tell anyone as I felt too embarrassed, as if I might be putting myself above others and I didn't want to do that. I held the idea in my mind for a year and the idea did not go away.

I had read about the ancient Oracles of the Greeks and Romans, whose prophetic words were sought by kings, leaders and politicians. I had read about the Sibyls who prophesied as they sat on a tripod or an oracular stone above gaping vents in the earth, from which steam and noxious fumes rose. I knew about the Oracle Chamber in the five and a half thousand year old Hypogeum in Malta, where a square niche cut into the wall has remarkable acoustic properties. Deep voices reverberate and carry to the far ends of connected chambers on other levels. This is believed to be the place where an Oracle interpreted dreams and spoke the Goddess's words of wisdom. I knew about indigenous cultures from Siberia to the Americas, where shamans enter trance and speak for the ancestors or the gods. In the present I knew of the Tibetan Oracle who goes into trance to answer questions, and also of the Tibetan Tantric practices of embodying deity. But could I embody the Goddess here in public in Glastonbury. Would it be alright to try? Did I have the knowledge of how to do it properly? Did I have the skill?

Like all these adventures with the Goddess the ideas originate with Her. She asks us to dare to do things that have not been done for hundreds and thousands of years within the patriarchal cultures in which we live. Long ago Christianity separated the powers of the priest from those of the priestess and shamanka. As Jesus was named the one true Son of God, so the power to embody God was denied to everyone else, he was the only one who could be God. Today male Christian priests mediate between the people and God, but no longer embody God for the people, although the mysterious Holy Spirit Herself may move through the people in healing ways.

I held my counsel for as long as I could until one day in a discussion about the upcoming Goddess Conference, I found my ideas blurting out of my mouth to three Priestesses of Avalon, Sally Pullinger, Tegwyn Hyndman and Alison Waite. I told them my thoughts for embodying the Goddess in a ceremony and they immediately wanted to do it too and became very excited. Sally is a trance medium and Tegwyn has lots of experience in shamanic journeying. I had every confidence in their abilities since we had shared several powerful experiences together in other situations. Suddenly I felt a sense of relief. I didn't have to do it on my own, we could try this together and support each other. We decided that Sally, Tegwyn and I would embody the White, the Red and the Black triple Goddess, in a special ceremony in the Goddess Temple during the Conference. Alison would support us with the help of other priestesses.

During the ceremony participants first lit candles in the Courtyard of the Glastonbury Experience, removed their shoes and then queued up an inner staircase. While they waited to enter the Temple, musicians, including Lydia Lite, Oshia Drury, Julie Felix, Ruth Barrett and Alessandra Belloni, sang and played in the Courtyard as it rained on the participants. At the top of the stairs participants were blindfolded, to help them move into an altered state of consciousness and were then led one by one through a series of spaces into the Goddess Temple. The blindfolds were then removed and they were welcomed, smudged with incense and blessed with holy water, before entering the inner shrine. Here in a mist-filled atmosphere we three priestesses, embodying the Triple Goddess, sat on thrones on the altar and participants came forward to speak with the Goddesses and to receive their blessings.

We had prepared ourselves for the ceremony in the afternoon and dressed in white, red and black costumes, headdress and veils. We painted our faces and surrounded ourselves with objects and images associated with each of the Goddess's totem creatures and qualities. We called in the energies of the Goddesses and then sat next to each other on three thrones on the low, brightly lit altar. People began coming into the Temple in a long, continuous stream to meet the Goddess. For myself, and for all of us, it was one of the most extraordinary, humbling and powerful things I have ever done in my life. The energy of the Goddess came into the room and filled it with Her awesome presence.

People coming into the space were unsure of what they would meet, but as soon as they came into the holy space they opened their hearts to Her. They spoke their secrets to Her, they listened to Her, they wept, they smiled, they were transported into other realms of being. As people left the Temple blissed out and/or in tears , those who were just entering could see the power of the experience on their faces, in their bodies, and so opened themselves even more to what was before them. Almost every person who came through the Temple that night surrendered to the experience, the opportunity to meet the Goddess in a human form. It was an amazing healing ceremony to take part in, a great privilege for a priestess.

The hours disappeared really quickly as several hundred people came through the Temple. Late in the night after the last people had come through we climbed down from the altar and lay on the floor exhausted and completely ecstatic. It had been an amazing evening. We removed our costumes and headdresses and draped them on the thrones on the altar where we had sat. The energy of the White, Red and Black Goddesses was still there in the costumes. They held such a presence that it was six weeks before the energy had left the clothing and we took them down from the altar.

This had been such an incredible experience and I knew that other priestesses were quite capable of offering similar experiences to other people too. We all long to meet the Goddess face to face, to see and feel Her in the flesh and this is something that we can learn to offer, if we have the courage. Those who have no knowledge of what it takes, might think that such experiences will inflate the ego, swell the heads of priestesses, but my experience is that it is such a profoundly humbling thing to do, that there is little left for the ego to swell. It is a complete privilege to embody the Goddess, a privilege from Her and from the people who come to find Her in us.

Embodiment of the Goddess is a two way process. On the part of the priestess it involves the capacity to transmit the Goddess's energy and words rather than one's own, but it also requires longing, yearning and belief on the part of the participants. The more that the participant can open her/is heart to embodiment of the Goddess the more powerful the experience will be for them. This openness of heart is not about giving one's power away to another human being who may misuse it, it is about surrendering to the Goddess embodied by the priestess. Power always remains with the participant, the power to receive and give love.

For many people surrender is a tricky area because we have been abused in the past, and the love we have given has been betrayed. It may be fraught with difficulty, but surrender to an embodiment of the Goddess is always surrender to Her, to the Goddess, not to the personality of the human being that sits in front of us. All priestesses are taught this and it is this difference that protects us all.

The 2003 Goddess Conference was dedicated to the Nine Morgens and nine priestesses offered Oracles from the Morgens to people entering an Oracle Hall in the Glastonbury Assembly Rooms. Again this was a profound experience for the priestesses who oracled. The priestesses prepared themselves and were assisted by other priestesses as gatekeepers and way showers. The Oracles sat in a large outward facing circle in the darkened space. Outside of the hall participants prepared to come before the Oracles, thinking of the questions that they would like answered by the Oracle. They entered one by one and were led to the next available Oracle, until all nine Oracles were speaking to individuals. Participants were deeply moved by what they heard, once again expressing their feelings in tears and smiles. It was a healing experience for many.

In the 2004 Goddess Conference we held a large healing ceremony for conferees in which 20 priestesses embodied Bridie, the Lady of Healing. Again this was a profound and moving experience for many. In 2005 at the Opening Ceremony the nine priestesses of the Conference Ceremonial Circle embodied nine Goddesses on the Wheel of the Year. We each spoke to the Conference about love, from the perspective of the Goddess we were embodying. We held these Goddesses for the duration of the Conference in different forms. In the Heart of the Mysteries, together with 9 priests, we appeared with bared painted breasts and faces. At the beginning of the Ecstatic Dance ceremony we served Queen Maeve's Sacred Red Mead, which had been brewed at the 2004 conference and cared for by my partner Mike, for a year and a day. We danced into Maeve's ecstasy.

Through recent years I have also practised embodiment on my own with smaller circles of students. I have embodied the Lady of Avalon as students completed their training and Self-initiated, or as they participated in Avalon workshops abroad. This is such a privilege for me as I love the Lady so much. It is also a blessing to be able to serve those I know well in this way. Other priestesses also embody the Lady at different times.

In ancient times Oracles of the Goddess would enter trance through imbibing sacred herbs or through breathing in natural gases, such as ethylene, which has a sweet smell and produces a narcotic effect described as a floating or disembodied euphoria. At Delphi this gas came from deep within the earth, filtering up through the cracks to the Pythia (priestess). Now priestesses are able to enter altered states of consciousness without taking psychotropic drugs or breathing noxious fumes. Our consciousness is at a place where this is now possible for more and more people, and I encourage priestesses to develop their psychic skills, rather than rely on chemical substances which can harm their health.

In the subtlety of these things I recognise a difference between Oracling and Embodiment. In Oracling participants usually bring one or more questions to the Oracle of the Goddess that they want answered.

The Oracle opens her/himself to the Goddess and reads and speaks the energy that she feels, speaking for the Goddess. The oracular energy is responsive to questions. With an Embodiment of the Goddess participants come to actually meet the Goddess face to face in human form and the Embodiment speaks as the Goddess in the first person. Participants can speak their truth and love for the Goddess to Her and receive a direct transmission of Her energy. Both Oracling and Embodiment can happen in the same session, but the energetics are slightly different.

It is important in both Oracling and Embodiment to have support either from the group one is oracling for or from other priestesses who ensure that the space you are in is undisturbed by external energies. The priestess will enter an altered state of consciousness and so needs to be protected from unwanted intrusions. She may also need refreshment or have other personal needs.

Preparation for Oracling and Embodiment

It is important to know before one begins for which Goddess you will be acting as Oracle or Embodiment. She may be the generic Goddess, the Great Mother of all, or She may be a particular aspect of the Goddess, such as the Lady of Avalon, Bridie, Rhiannon, Ker or Keridwen, or any of the Goddesses on Britannia's Wheel, or any other. It depends on which Goddess wishes to be heard and your purpose in oracling for or embodying Her. Different Goddesses will express different energies and say and do different kinds of things .

As a public ceremony both Oracling and Embodiment are dramatic events. As with any ritual the scene must be carefully set. This was known by the ancients whose oracles spoke in impressive underground chambers, such as the Hypogeum in Malta, or over rocky clefts in Temples, such as the Oracle at Delphi. The Temple space needs to be especially prepared with a central focus on the seat or throne on which the Oracle or the Embodiment will sit, in front of an altar to the Goddess. Soft cushions and rugs are placed in front of the throne so that the seeker can sit or kneel comfortably before the priestess. The seeker may sit or stand, it is up to them, but for many surrender to the Goddess involves a return to a childlike innocence before a physically larger Mother. Cushions help invite that surrender.

The Temple space needs to be cleaned and cleansed with sound and incense. Lighting is important as a Temple filled with twinkling candle light has its own special atmosphere, one that engenders magical experience. Lighting can be subdued and mysterious or a very bright light can be focused on the throne with darkness surrounding it. The Oracle can also be completely hidden with only her voice being transmitted in some way through some form of funnel. An Embodiment is always visible.

The priestess prepares herself by helping to create the space in which she will be performing, because this is performance as well as ceremonial duty. She takes time to familiarise herself with the space and with the throne on which she will be sitting. She dresses in ceremonial clothing, with headdress, mask and/or veil, consciously taking on her role. Again this is theatre and the priestess as Oracle or Embodiment is usually disguised, so that those who come to meet her are less distracted by a familiar human face. A full face mask with only the eyes of the priestess visible has a powerful impact, although the mask needs to have an opening at the mouth so that her words can be clearly heard. Material can be attached to the lower part of a half mask to give a full face covering. A face covered with a diaphanous veil through which only the outline of the face can be seen is also powerful. A mask and veil together hide the priestess almost completely and this may be appropriate for an Oracle. The priestess's face can also be painted with blocks of colour that completely alter her usual appearance.

There are several phases in the preparation process which the priestess now needs to follow.

1. *Connect in circle with those who will be supporting you during the Oracling or Embodiment. Together invoke the Goddesses who are honoured in the Temple space and call in the Goddess for whom you will be oracling or embodying.*
2. *Focus your attention on your breath and allow it to slow and deepen. Calm your mind, emotions and body.*
3. *Move to the throne and ground and centre yourself, connecting to the earth and the heavens. Radiate your soul's energy outwards through your aura into the Temple space.*
4. *Bring your attention completely into this moment now.*
5. *Stand and invoke your priestess self into your body. Call her in to your body and being. Feel your spine straighten and yourself grow tall as she comes into your body. Feel the archetypal priestess self come fully into your body and complete the following sentence,*

   " I am she who ...."

6. *Seat yourself on the throne. Radiate your soul's energy outwards.*

The Practice of Oracling

A seeker comes to an Oracle with questions in mind which they would like to have answered by the Oracle on behalf of the Goddess. The skill of oracling lies in being able to hear and transmit the words of the Goddess to the seeker. For the Oracle hearing and speaking the words of the Goddess may be a continuous experience, as the priestess acts as a conduit or channel for the Lady's words. Some Oracles may have to consciously listen to the Goddess's voice within, recognise Her words and then pass them on. Her words are usually spoken in the third person. The Oracle may or may not remember what she has said.

In order to do these things we have to set our personalities aside, with all their personal likes and dislikes, attitudes and opinions, and enter the space of our soul, which is loving, kind, generous and compassionate. The more we are able to generate the energy of our soul, radiate it outwards and bring it into the present moment, the more we can release the hold that our personality has on our consciousness, and truly speak for the Goddess.

1. *Seated on the throne in your priestess self, open your consciousness to the Goddess for whom you are oracling. Pray to Her along the lines of,*

"*Lady, I open myself to your wisdom and truth. I open myself to your love. I pray that I may hear and speak your words for all who come here. I pray that everything which happens shall be for the greatest good.*"

2. *Focus your attention once again on the present moment and radiate your soul's energy. Wait for the first seeker to arrive. This may take some time but all the while allow your state of consciousness to deepen. Waiting in the silence is a necessary priestess skill.*
3. *The first seeker arrives in front of you and stands, sits or kneels before the Oracle.*
4. *Focus your whole attention on the seeker and wait for them to speak.*
5. *The seeker asks their question or if they don't you can ask, "Do you have a question?"*
6. *Listen to the question and open your consciousness to the Goddess within.*
7. *Looking the seeker in the eyes, even if they can't see your eyes, answer the question with the words you hear. Sometimes the words spoken are obvious and straight forward and sometimes they are cryptic and mysterious. You may hear yourself saying things whose relevance you don't understand. Sometimes you may talk about something completely different to the question asked, reaching for the hidden, unspoken questions that the seeker has not voiced. Trust the*

inner voice of intuition. Speak for the Goddess until there is no more to be said, then be silent.

8. *Wait to see if there are other questions to be asked. If there are, repeat the process, otherwise withdraw your focus of attention from the seeker back to your own soul. You may make a physical movement of withdrawal into yourself to indicate that the oracling is over.*

9. *Wait for the next seeker to approach, all the while deepening your state of consciousness. Repeat the process for the next seeker.*

10. *You may oracle for one person or many, focusing attention on each seeker in turn and then withdrawing into the self. Stay in the present with what is in front of you.*

11. *When the last seeker has left, give thanks to the Goddess for Her presence.*

12. *Bring your attention to your own breath and breathe deeply, bringing your awareness back into your body. Wriggle your toes and fingers and feel the physicality of your body.*

13. *Remove your mask and/or veil and as you stand, lay them on the throne. Taking your time remove your ceremonial robe and dress in other clothing. Lay your ceremonial clothes on the throne and leave them there for the energy to dissipate. Drink a glass of water.*

You will usually feel excited and energised by the experience of Oracling. It is a great privilege to speak for the Goddess. You may or may not remember what you have said. You may also feel very emotional. It is important to now take care of your own physical and emotional needs.

The Practice of Embodiment

It is a great privilege and honour to act as a ceremonial Embodiment of the Goddess. It is a position of power which needs to be treated with great respect and humility by the priestess who plays this role. As an Embodiment the priestess speaks and acts as the Goddess. As well as speaking Her words, Her communication may include physically holding the seeker's hands, offering healing touch, and/or embracing the seeker. There is nothing quite like having a physical Goddess hold you in Her arms and soothe away your tears.

The principle difference between approaching an Oracle or an Embodiment is that in the presence of an Embodiment the seeker can speak their own truths directly to the Goddess in human form. They are not there primarily to ask questions of Her, although they can if they choose. They are there to speak their heartfelt prayers to Her, to express their love and devotion to Her, private hopes and dreams, their intimate secrets. They can ask for her wisdom. They can surrender to Her. They can dedicate themselves to Her service as seeker or priestess. This surrender to the Embodiment is an act of trust on the part of the seeker which must never be abused by the priestess. It is equally an act of trust on the part of the priestess, believing that she can successfully embody and speak the words of the Goddess for another person. In my experience when trust is there in both the priestess and the seeker, then the most extraordinary, transformative and life enhancing experiences take place.

As with oracling the Embodiment must set aside her own personality likes and dislikes, attitudes and opinions, and move the focus of her attention into her soul. The soul is the energy of the Goddess within the human being and by consciously connecting to that energy we connect directly to Her. We speak as Her, using the first person in our speech, "I, *the Goddess*", etc. This is an extremely powerful experience for the Embodiment as well as the seeker.

Some time before the embodying session begins it is wise to instruct the group of seekers on how to approach the Embodiment of the Goddess. Focus them by saying,

> "*If you knew that you would be meeting the Goddess face to face tomorrow, or in two hours time, (depending on when the session is) how would you prepare yourself?*"

This simple sentence wakes people up to the promise of what is going to be happening and they begin to prepare themselves for the occasion. Some people feel very excited by the prospect, some are blasé and others suddenly feel anxious. It is good for people to feel emotionally moved before they enter the Presence of the Goddess as they will be more open to the power of the experience.

1. *Sit on the throne in your priestess self and open your consciousness to the Goddess you will embody. Pray to Her along the lines of,*

> "*Lady, I open myself to you, to your love, wisdom and healing power. I pray that I may embody you for all who come here. I pray that everything which happens shall be for the greatest good.*"

2. *Call the Goddess into your body and being and feel Her entering your body via your priestess self, which holds the presence of the Goddess safely in your body.*
3. *Feel Her presence in your body and radiate Her energy outwards into the Temple space. Focus your attention once again on the present moment.*

4. Wait in the silence for the first seeker to arrive. This may take some time but all the while keep radiating Her energy.

5. The first seeker comes to stand infront of the Embodiment. This experience is usually very moving for people as they realise the truth of what is occurring and allow themselves to meet the Goddess face to face. Some people will kneel and surrender to the Lady, others will stay at a distance through fear or defence, and others will show their resistance to the experience in their words. No matter how the seeker approaches the Goddess radiate Her loving energy towards them.

6. Focus your whole attention on the seeker and hold out your hands, palm upwards, to indicate that you want to hold the seeker's hands. Taking hold of their hands, radiate Her energy towards them. Wait for them to speak and listen to what they want to say to the Goddess. If they don't speak you can say, "What would you like to say to me?"

7. Speak as the Goddess in the first person. Allow Her to move your body, moving towards the seeker as She determines, holding their hands, giving healing energy to different parts of their bodies as intuition tells you and also holding them in your arms if the need arises. As with Oracling the words spoken are sometimes obvious and straight forward and sometimes cryptic and mysterious. Trust what you say and continually radiate the Goddess's energy towards the seeker. Speak as the Goddess until there is no more to be said, then be silent.

8. Wait to see if the seeker wants to say more. Speak and act as necessary. It is usually obvious when the session is ending as the Goddess withdraws Her attention from the seeker and you can feel this in your body. You may make a physical movement of withdrawal into yourself. Sit with the Goddess as the seeker leaves.

9. Wait for the next seeker to approach, all the while deepening your state of communion with the Goddess. Repeat the process for the next seeker.

10. You may act as an Embodiment of the Goddess for one person or many, focusing attention on each seeker in turn and then withdrawing into the self. Stay in the present with what is within you and in front of you.

11. When the last seeker has left, give thanks to the Goddess for being present within you.

12. Bring your attention to your breath and breathe deeply, bringing your awareness back into your body. Wriggle your toes and fingers and feel the physicality of your body.

13. Slowly remove your mask and/or veil and as you stand lay them on the throne. Taking your time remove your ceremonial robe, and dress in other clothing.

Lay your ceremonial clothes on the throne and leave them there for the energy to dissipate. Drink a glass of water.

You will usually feel awed and inspired by the experience of embodying the Goddess. It is a great privilege to speak as the Goddess. You may or may not remember what has happened. You will usually feel deeply moved and may be vulnerable emotionally yourself. Take care of your personal needs.

Personal Work

With sister priestesses or close friends who support your journey, practice calling your priestess self into your body. Connect to your soul's energy and allow the Goddess to speak through you as Oracle or Embodiment.

Finalise the words of the Self-initiation Vow you will make to the Goddess at the end of Second Spiral, in which you will dedicate yourself to Her as Her priestess.

Groups of students make final preparations for the Self-Initiation ceremony taking place at the end of the Second Spiral.

Self Initiation as Priestess of the Goddess Glastonbury Tor Labrynth

The final session of the Second Spiral of the Priestess of Avalon training is spent exploring the mysteries of the great three dimensional Goddess Labrynth found on the slopes of Glastonbury Tor. This labrynth is one of the ceremonial gateways into the Mysteries of the Goddess within the sacred landscape of Glastonbury Avalon and all priestesses at some time need to become familiar with its pathways. We learned some of the Mysteries of the Labrynth in the First Spiral and here at the end of the Second Spiral we experience its transforming power through walking it within the sacred landscape. Walking this labrynth is a spiritual, emotional and physical experience and a container for the ceremony of Self initiation as a Priest/ess of the Goddess, which takes place while students are psychically and physically in the centre of the labrynth.

I first learned of the power of walking the Glastonbury Tor Labrynth many years ago in the early 1980s when I led a group of people, including women from the Glastonbury Women's group, through the Labrynth one Beltane Eve or Walpurgisnacht, the night when the witches are said to fly. That year it was also Wesak, the Scorpio full moon, when the sun is in Taurus. When we began walking the sun was shining, it was a lovely afternoon. As we wound our way through the labrynth the wind picked up and clouds rolled in across the Summerland. As evening came the sky darkened ominously and lightening flashed and thunder rolled. We were drenched with rain and hailstones hit our faces as we circumnavigated the seventh level of the labrynth. We had wound up a storm.

Other women, including the late Monica Sjoo, were also walking the Tor that day and we all arrived up at St. Michael's tower, drenched and scared by the ferocity of the storm. We ran from the top of the Tor and returned after a couple of days to walk out of the labrynth in calmer weather. After that walk four of the women walking the labrynth including myself, became pregnant with daughters. We all gave birth within a few months of each other and we attributed this to our Goddess Labrynth walk. From then the myth arose that walking the labrynth would help create girl babies.

As I walked the Tor labrynth several times a year it became my practice to dedicate my life to the Goddess each time and to make my vows to Her as I walked. It was while walking the Tor Labrynth that I dedicated myself to the Lady as Her priestess over and over again, years before I had even thought of teaching others to do likewise. It was while walking that I asked Her to transform me as She willed. One time I did this She took me at my word and led me through the journey of breast cancer, that transformed and brought more love into my life. For me walking the labrynth is not something to be done lightly, as it can have powerful, life changing consequences.

The following description of the Glastonbury Tor Labrynth pilgrimage was first given in *In the Nature of Avalon* (*Ariadne* Publications), to which you can refer for photos of the pathways through the labrynth.

Glastonbury Tor Labrynth Pilgrimage

Upon the slopes of Glastonbury Tor there are seven and more levels of terracing encircling the mysterious hill. Some of the levels are easy to see and some are lost in part through erosion. These are said to be the present remains of a great three-dimensional seven circuit Labrynth, sculpted by the ancient peoples of Avalon and based on the same pattern as the Kretan labrynth.

In Avalon the labrynth is the spiralling pathway which leads to the castle of Caer Sidi, also known as Caer Arianrhod, the revolving castle of Arianrhod of the Silver Wheel. In the heavens this castle is the Corona Borealis, the Crown of the North Wind. In mythology Ariadne and Arianrhod are the same goddess, Ariadne ruling the inner worlds, while Arianrhod rules the upper world. Their sister in the underworld of Annwn is Nolava the Crone and Keeper of the Cauldron. The three worlds are joined by the axis mundi, the world axis, sometimes envisioned as a holy mountain, which here in Avalon is Glastonbury Tor. In the landscape of the Goddess the Tor is the Lover's voluptuous breast, the Great Mother's nurturing breast and the Crone's womb of wisdom.

The presence of a huge and ancient labrynth encircling the Tor was first suggested in the 1970s by Geoffrey Russell, who made drawings of the labrynth, commissioned aerial surveys of the ground and made sand models of the Tor, to prove his ideas. He simulated the earthquake of 1275 which demolished the first St. Michael on the Tor church, to show how the shape of the terraces on the Tor would have been affected by the movements of the Mother Goddess's body. The idea of the Tor Labrynth was further elucidated in a pamphlet by Geoffrey Ashe first published in 1979 called *The Glastonbury Tor Maze* (Gothic Image), along with instructions on how to walk its paths. It was with Geoffrey Ashe and friends that I first walked the Tor Labrynth at that time.

Whether the Tor Labrynth is a truly ancient neolithic site can be disputed, but since no-one has yet dug beneath the terracing to find out, there is no way of knowing for certain. However over the last twenty years or so the pathway through the labrynth has been threaded by thousands of people, some walking individually and others in larger ceremonial groups. I have personally led many hundreds of people around the labrynth which exists today, in physical, etheric and spiritual reality. The labrynth provides a present day initiatory experience in which the mystery of the ever-living Goddess may be encountered and recognised. As with all such magical journeys the depth of the experience depends on the extent to which we are able to open ourselves to Her divine essence.

On the Tor the pattern of the outer labrynth is traced by a single pathway that winds back and forth seven times around the steep hill on the different levels of terracing which are visible on all sides. The body of the Tor lies northeast-southwest and the entrance to the labrynth lies within the National Trust boundary at the southwestern end of the Tor above Wellhouse Lane. The entrance is marked by a sandstone Tor burr broken in two lying directly behind a bench on the concrete path up the Tor. All 180 degree turns in the labrynth are made at this southwestern end of the Tor. The lowest terrace is level 1 and the terrace which encircles the top of the Tor, but is not on top of the Tor, is level 7.

After walking through the entrance to the labrynth the first turning is to the left onto level 3, marked by another prominent stone, then follows a pattern of levels 3 2 1 4 7 6 5, ending between the fifth and sixth outer circuits. It is here that psychically or in the past perhaps physically, the journeyer into the labrynth enters the body of the Tor. The centre of the labrynth is in the middle of the Tor rather than on top . Entering psychically into the Tor there are two more levels - the Underworld where we meet our Shadow selves, the monstrous Minotaur of our subconscious minds; and the Inner Cave, where if we are lucky we may catch a glimpse of the

Lady of Avalon. Altogether this makes the sacred number nine of the Nine Morgens who dwell in Avalon. On the return from the centre the outer path follows the same route in reverse - 5 6 7 4 1 2 3.

To add to the experience each of the seven levels can be viewed as corresponding to one of seven major chakras or energy centres in the human body, to the seven planetary rays/qualities of energy described by Alice A Bailey and to the seven elements of manifestation. As we thread each level we can equate our experience and how we are feeling with the appropriate chakra, ray energy and element. These symbols of deeper truths are not correspondences, but catalysts. They should be viewed flexibly and not used dogmatically.

Tor level	*Element*	*Ray/Energy*	*Chakra*
1	*Earth*	*7th/physical*	*Base*
2	*Water*	*6th/emotional*	*Sexual*
3	*Fire*	*5th/mental*	*Solar plexus*
4	*Air*	*4th/intuition*	*Heart/anahata*
5	*Aether*	*3rd/intelligence*	*Throat*
6	*Electron*	*2nd/love-wisdom*	*Between eyebrows*
7	*Proton*	*1st/power-will*	*Crown*
plus two invisible Innerworld levels			
8	*Shadow*	*Underworld*	*Between 5th/6th chakras*
9	*Goddess*	*Innerworld*	*Heart/hridaya chakra*

As we walk into the labrynth traversing each of the seven levels, we shed a layer of ourselves, letting go of all we no longer need in our lives, slowly removing the veils that hide our inner being. A ceremonial pilgrimage into the centre of the Tor Labrynth takes four to five hours to complete and the walk out can take three to four hours. When younger I would make the walk in and out on one day and collapse aching and foot sore at the end of a long walk around a steep hill. Nowadays I take my time and walk into the centre of the labrynth on one day. I hold myself psychically in the centre of the Labrynth while I physically walk off the Tor, then return on another day to complete the walk out. I have found that walking the Tor Labrynth in this way allows the transformative processes to penetrate deeper into the psyche. In the centre we spend time contemplating our inner Selves, integrating our Shadows, connecting with the Goddess as Arianrhod, Ariadne and Nolava in this sacred place. By staying in the centre for some time - a few hours, days, weeks or months, we allow the transformative experience to percolate the many layers of our being.

Route through the Glastonbury Tor Labrynth

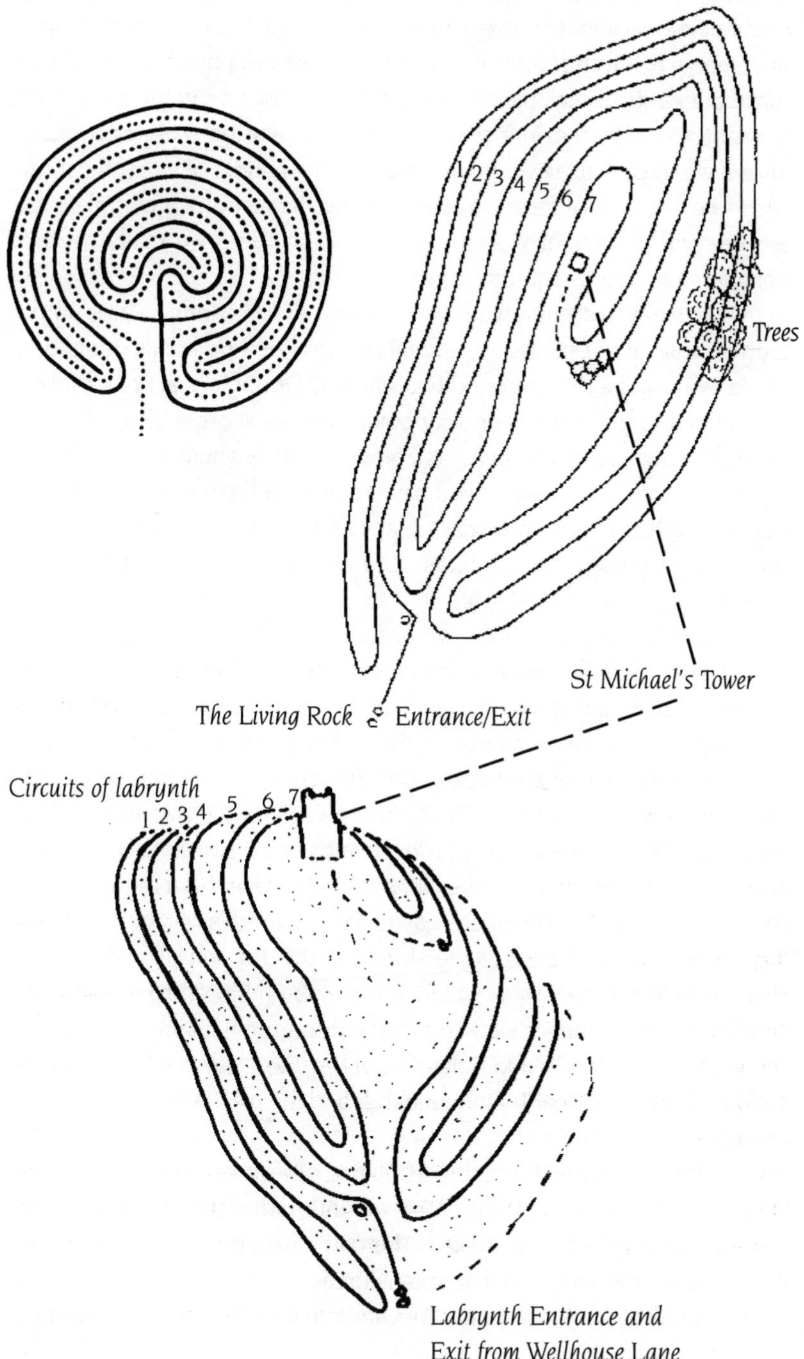

After this time in the centre it is important to retrace our steps, walking back out through the labrynth, replacing the outer layers, completing this initiatory cycle, taking with us into the future new insights and energy received from the Goddess. We need to physically thread the maze outwards as well as inwards and this cannot be completed in the mind or with a finger on a small labrynth. It must be walked physically. Those who stop half way remain literally in the middle of a psychic maze, which has definite effects on everyday life. If we do not complete the journey within days or weeks, one day we will find we really need to complete our labrynth journey.

As we walk the labrynth we may find that reasons to give up the journey arise in our minds. It suddenly seems like a pointless thing to be doing. Why am I walking around this silly hill? Or our legs ache horribly or we feel frightened or angry or disappointed or some other life pattern will arise showing itself to us in all its colours. Notice where in the labrynth these strong feelings arise. If you have to give up the journey completely notice which level you are walking at the time and the corresponding qualities of energy and chakras. Equate feelings with patterns and resistances in your everyday life.

The Tor Labrynth may have been here for thousands of years and in that time there has been much erosion on the slopes of the hill from weather and human and animal activity. As a result some terraces are not as easy to see or follow as others. The terraces on the southern side of the Tor are also lower than those on the northern side, perhaps as the result of the earthquake in 1275 CE. This means that at the northeastern end of the Tor there is a kink in the labrynth and a somewhat steep join between the northern half of the labrynth and the southern terraces. Here you need to be able to accurately assess which level is which to find your way. Sheep and cattle graze the slopes of the Tor and in some places there are clear animal trails which you may be tempted to follow. Keep your eyes on the longer view to ensure you are on the correct level of terracing at any time. In addition some of the lowest levels of the labrynth are outside the National Trust boundaries and the path is diverted to avoid private land.

Despite all these hindrances it has always seemed to me more important to walk the pattern of the labrynth rather than to obsess over the exact ground which is walked. The paths I suggest are based on my experiences of walking the maze many times.

Threading the Glastonbury Tor Labrynth is an initiatory passage into the mysteries of the Isle of Avalon. It is a very physical journey - a long walk round and around a steep hill and it is a spiritual and devotional practice. It is a multidimensional pilgrimage linking the seen and unseen worlds and allowing the seeker to pass through the Veil that separates the everyday world of the physical senses from the mythical Otherworld. In legend the Tor lies upon the Isle of Avalon also known as the Western Isle of the Dead. Here guarded by Gwyn ap Nudd there is an entrance to the Underworld of Annwn, where the Lady and the ancestral spirits of Avalon dwell. Here also via the axis mundi is a direct connection to the stars of Caer Arianrhod. The invisible beings of both these worlds can sometimes be seen quite clearly in their etheric forms or may appear on the slopes of the Tor or in the skies above in the forms of crows, hawks, doves, swans, rabbits, badgers, dogs and humans.

It is my belief that by tracing this labrynth to its centre and out again with reverence and in a ritual manner, we awaken a personal connection to the ancestral beings of Avalon. We open ourselves to Nolava Lady of Avalon, to Ariadne of the Red Thread, Arianrhod of the Silver Wheel, to the Nine Morgens and to the Watchers and Company of Avalon. By physically walking this pattern in ceremony we are placing a key in an ancient lock and turning it. As a result a door opens in far memory giving access to ancestral knowledge and wisdom.

In walking into the labrynth in preparation for an initiation ceremony in the company of others it is important to allow ourselves to spend time with the Goddess and with our own thoughts as we are walking. Her mantra's which can be repeated are

Ariadne of the Red Thread, Arianrhod of the Silver Wheel
On the spiral path to Caer Sidi I open my heart to you.

Maiden, Lover, Mother, Crone
Lady of Avalon, bring me home.

Walking into the Labrynth

As with all Goddess pilgrimages on this long journey wear suitable clothing and footwear, and bring with you offerings of herbs and flowers for the Goddess, prayer ribbons, a candle and matches, incense, light snacks for the journey, perhaps an apple, and a water bottle.

The Tor Labrynth Pilgrimage begins in Wellhouse Lane which is just past the entrance to Chalice Well in Chilkwell Street at the lower end of the Tor. Walk up to the White Spring and go inside the dark reservoir if it is open, which is now decorated and maintained as a magical sacred space. In Wellhouse Lane itself you can fill your water bottle with a blend of Red and White water from Chalice Well and the White Spring, which have water spouts on opposite sides of Wellhouse Lane. Take a drink of water and say a prayer to begin your pilgrimage.

Our Lady of Avalon, Maiden, Lover, Mother, Crone,
Lady of the Tor, of the Red and White Springs,
Here in your sacred valley I ask for a blessing
As I begin my pilgrimage into your labrynth.

Ariadne, I pray that I may easily follow your Red Thread
Through all the twists and turns of the labrynth,
That I may see you there ahead of me on the path
And following, find my way to your centre.

Nolava, Crone of Avalon and Annwn
I pray that I may safely enter the Underworld
And drink from the magical ikor in your Cauldron
That I return renewed and inspired to the outer world.

Arianrhod, I pray that your heavenly Silver Wheel
Shines upon my journey through the labrynth
As I take the spiral path that leads to Caer Sidi
And find you waiting for me in the centre of my soul.

Bless me and bless all those who journey into your labrynth
And return me transformed through the Veil of Avalon.

As a blessing touch droplets of water to all your chakras - base, sacral, solar plexus, heart, throat, ajna (between the eyebrows) and crown and feel the life force entering your body. Fill your drinking water bottles with an alchemical half and half mixture of Red and White spring waters for drinking and for libations in the Labrynth.

From the White Spring walk down to the Tor entrance at the bottom of Wellhouse Lane on the left next to Berachah House. Walk up the short lane past Chalice Orchard where Dion Fortune once lived and through the kissing gate into the field where the National Trust property of Glastonbury Tor begins. Walk up through this field to a second kissing gate which leads onto the Tor proper. Walk up the steps to the bench and take a breather. On either side of the bench are terraces, some of which are part of the labrynth and some are part of the platform on which the three dimensional labrynth sits. The entrance pattern of the Tor Labrynth is uneven.

This is a good place to stop for a few moments and to reflect on your purpose in walking the labrynth. What is it in your life that you would like to change? What are you ready to let go of? What are you willing to welcome into your life? Prepare for your Self-initiation ceremony in the centre of the labrynth. If you are walking the labrynth with others you may like to share your purpose with them. Tie a ribbon around your wrist to signify Ariadne's Red Thread. As you walk fill it with your prayers and commitment to transformation.

Entering the Labrynth

Immediately behind the bench is a sandstone Tor burr which is broken in two. These stones mark the entrance to the labrynth. They are known as the Living Rock or the Zodiacal Rock and are said to have magical properties being filled with an energy which some people can feel with their hands as an electrical charge.

To begin your journey into the labrynth climb over the back of the bench and stand on each of the stones in turn, anchoring yourself into the energy field of the labrynth. From these stones enter the labrynth by walking directly up the hillside on the grass parallel to the official concrete path for about 20 metres. In walking the labrynth walk as much as possible on the earth rather than on concrete. A second prominent stone marks the first turning of the labrynth onto the third level. Touch this stone.

First Circle - Level Three
Fire/solar plexus/5th ray/mental energy

Turn left just after the second stone and take the narrow path which leads over a small ridge on the dragon's back. Begin to encircle the Tor in a sunwise direction. In my experience this is the place where we truly take hold of Ariadne's Red Thread which leads us through the labrynth. From here onwards it feels like there is an electric current in the earth marking the pathway through the labrynth. As soon as your feet touch the ground they begin following the labyrinthine pattern of their own accord. All you have to do is to trust your feet and Ariadne's Thread to take you in the right direction!

Follow the narrow path around the slope of the Tor until it widens into a terrace. For a short stretch here level two combines with level three, so keep to the right of the terrace as a gesture to the difference between levels three and two. As you come around the corner the whole of the northern flank of the Tor comes into view ahead of you. Stop for a moment. Here you can plainly see the seven terraces on the Tor. Some are complete and others show signs of erosion and places where higher levels have slipped down onto lower levels.

Look to the far end of the Tor. This is the best place to see and count the seven levels of the labrynth and can be used at any time as a reference point to check that you are on the correct level. Level one is close beside the bottom hedge. Count the bumps on the horizon going up from level one to level six. Make sure you can see all six levels. Look at the sixth level then look to your right along the flank of the Tor and you will see higher up, level seven about half way along the body of the Tor. Level seven continues for a short way and then fizzles out, perhaps because of erosion over the millennia. In your mind's eye visualise this seventh path continuing on, parallel to level six rising around the top of the Tor.

Look to the horizon again and count up from the first level to the third level. Look at the terraces between where you are now and the third level on the horizon. Take the most direct route from here to there staying on the most obvious of the terraces. There is an indistinct patch in the middle of this third terrace but keep your eye on the third level on the horizon and you will be OK.

When you reach the northeastern end of the Tor follow the third level around the end of the hill until you come to the concrete path ascending the Tor. Cross over this path. This is where the northern and southern parts of the labrynth join, the southern half being lower than the northern half. Here all the paths are squeezed together and there is a kink in the labrynth which means that you have to walk down the hill to continue your labrynth circle on the third level. At this northeastern end of the Tor there is a distinctive line of hawthorn trees which lean out over a terrace. This terrace is part of the fifth level of the labrynth. As you walk down the Tor here count two levels below this fifth level and you will be on level three.

Continue walking sunwise around the Tor on the third level to where the terrace appears clearly once again. Follow level three. On your left is a lower terrace and the boundary fence of the Tor. Continuing on there is a small wood on the left of the terrace lower down the slopes of the Tor.

Here on the third fire level of the labrynth pause for a few moments. Notice how you are feeling. Notice the feelings in your solar plexus, notice your mind trying to work everything out, trying to make sure that you don't get lost. Notice the mental chatter going on in your head. This is level three stuff. What are the mental attitudes, habits and rigidities that you would like to leave behind you in the labrynth? Light a candle here and pass your hand through the flame, giving thanks for the Goddess's blessings of fire.

Our Lady of Avalon, Goddess of the sacred land,
Nolava, Keeper of the Cauldron of Annwn,
Ariadne of the Red Thread, Arianrhod of the Silver Wheel
I give thanks for the blessings of fire upon my life
For the sunfire that gives life to our planet
For the fires of home and hearth which warm my heart
For the fires of mind which transforms thought into inspiration
For the fires that heat your cauldron of regeneration
For the spiritual fires which draw me ever nearer to you.
I surrender to your flame all those mental habits that no longer serve me
And open myself up to your fiery creative nature
Lady of Fire, Queen of the Sun and Stars
Blessings upon you and your generous fire
Blessed be.

Continue on the third level terrace as it narrows to a single file pathway which gently descends the hill just above the small wood. Emerging from beyond the wood the narrow path descends almost down to the second level. Stay above the second level negotiating your way past clumps of nettles and thistles until the third level becomes quite visible again. Below you are the two lower terraces of the labrynth and below that the broad platform on which the labrynth sits reaching to the boundary fence. On this side of the Tor there are several parallel mini terraces which appear and disappear. Don't worry too much whether you are on the right one or not. Follow the third level along the southern flank of the Tor until you reach the southwestern end of the Tor once again, almost to where you started out, although you are some distance above the upper marker stone where you took your first turning left into the labrynth. You have completed one circuit of the Tor.

Second Circle - Level Two
Water/sacral centre/6th ray/emotional, sexual energy

Turn left and walk down one terrace to the second level and turn around 180 degrees, so that you are doubling back on yourself at a lower level. Walk back in the direction you have just come from, so that you are now walking widdershins or counter clockwise around the Tor. The Tor hill is now on your left and level one and the lower slopes of the Tor are now on your right. Synchronously we are making our second circle around the Tor on the second level.

Follow the broad level terrace until you reach middle of the small wood and walk straight into it. This wood has many small pathways which rise and fall, crisscrossing each other. In the neolithic labrynth level two would have continued at the bottom of the wood and level one would have been below the wood in the fields. To maintain the sevenfold pattern of our labrynth journey we need to contain both levels two and one within the boundaries of the wood. Walk level two diagonally upwards through the wood. Level one is walked on the lower levels.

Follow the upper pathways gradually moving higher and higher up through the woods, and walking out of the wood between several tall pine trees. In the summer months the small path through these lovely trees can be completely covered in tall stinging nettles. If so take the track below this one. Either pathway brings you out onto a flat terrace which quickly widens. Emerging from the wood, on the right is a fence with a field below and on the left is the bank with a view up to St. Michael's tower. For a short distance the second and first levels combine. Stay on the left for the second level.

There are several visible small tracks which run diagonally up the left-hand bank, one goes up beside a beautiful tall ash tree. Walk up past the ash tree onto the terrace above, and then stay as close to the boundary hedge on your right as you can. Walk around the northeastern end of the Tor past the gateway into the lower field and the Tor entrance stile.

Coming around the northeastern end of the Tor the level two terrace coincides with the official concrete path leading up the Tor. Again on this northern side of the Tor the bottom of the labrynth is actually outside of the National Trust boundary so here levels two and one follow the same path for a short distance. Keep to the left of the path for level two. Continue on around the northeastern corner walking on the concrete pathway for a few metres with a hedge on your right-hand side. The concrete path turns left and goes up the Tor, but the labrynth path continues on the same level around the Tor. For a short distance the pathway is narrow but soon becomes a clear terrace. On the right the hedge falls away down to the lower first level terrace which becomes visible again. Continue walking on level two past a clump of bushes on your right hand side and on until the length of level two is spread before you along the northern flank of the

Tor. Notice on the horizon where level two with level one below it, curves around the southwestern end of the Tor and aim towards it. Half way along this side of the Tor on level two pause and take a breather.

Notice how you are feeling emotionally. You may feel happy or sad, anxious, excited, angry, confused or irritated or any of a wealth of emotions or nothing that you are aware of. Allow yourself to feel what you are feeling in this moment now. What aspects of your emotional and sexual life are you ready to release? Take a drink from your water bottle, splash a little upon the earth as a libation to the Goddess and ask for a blessing of water upon your journey through the labrynth.

Our Lady of Avalon, Goddess of the sacred land,
Nolava, Keeper of the Cauldron of Annwn,
Ariadne of the Red Thread, Arianrhod of the Silver Wheel
I give thanks for the blessings of water upon my life
For the oceans, rivers and streams and all who dwell therein
I pray that they may be cleansed of all pollution and poisons.
I give thanks for the mists, clouds and life-giving rain,
For the emotional and sexual waters that enrich my life,
For the spiritual waters in which I become one with you
I surrender to your cauldron all those emotional and
Sexual patterns that no longer serve me
And open myself to your tender fluid nature
Lady of the Lake, Madron, Mother of the Waters,
Lady of the Springs and Wells, Queen of the Moon,
Blessings upon you and your life-giving waters
Blessed be.

Continue on along the second level following the path as it curves to the left around the southwestern end of the Tor, combining for a short distance with the third level. Keep to the right hand side of the terrace as it broadens out and descends. This second level ends near to the labrynth entrance stones.

Third Circle - Level One
Earth/base chakra/7th ray/physical energy

Turn right and walk down the Tor slope and following one of the small paths that cut across the terrace, turn 180 degrees back on yourself onto the lower first level of the labrynth. At first the terrace is broad and distinct as it circles around the end of the Tor and then it narrows as the northern flank of the Tor comes into view. Ahead in the hedgerow is a tall thorn tree with a narrow pathway beneath it taking you near to the hedgerow. Follow this path alongside the hedge as the nearest approximation to the first level we can take here. Badgers, foxes and rabbits inhabit this stretch of the Tor and blackberries grow here in abundance in the autumn. The gifts of the Goddess's nature provide refreshment on our journey.

About half way along the northern side of the Tor the first level emerges once again as a distinct level beside the hedge and can be seen easily below the second level you have recently traversed. Continue walking along the northern slope until you come to a largish hollow in the side of the Tor on the right of the first level. A clump of bushes grows above the hollow and below in the hedge is a beautiful ash tree on the edge of an Avalonian apple orchard. Small orchards like this one once covered the slopes of the Tor and all of the Isle of Avalon.

This depression in the earth marks one of the psychic gateways into the body of the Tor and has a very special atmosphere, which is nearly always peaceful. This is a place where cows like to gather and where people sometimes camp. On this earth level of the labrynth it is possible here to connect to some of the elemental beings who inhabit the inner core of the Tor. You may like to use this visualisation to aid you in your inner journey.

Visualisation

Sit or lie comfortably on the grass and feel the earth, the physical and etheric breast of the Mother, *beneath you. Feel* Her *supporting you, holding you up, embracing you so that you don't fly off into space. Listen to the sounds of* Her *nature all around you, animals and birds, the wind in the trees. Feel the air on your cheek and as it enters your nose or mouth, filling your lungs with each breath. Allow your mind to relax and become still.*

In your imagination visualise yourself as you were just a few moments ago walking along the first level on the side of the Tor. *Looking ahead see an entrance into the* Tor *and make your way towards it. Notice what it looks like and see how easy or difficult it is for you to enter into the body of the* Tor. *Inside a long tunnel leads beneath the steep slope. Make your way into the tunnel where although there are no lights the walls seem to glow of their own accord. As you walk you can hear the sounds of muffled voices which belong to the* Tor's *inhabitants.*

Ahead the light grows brighter and the tunnel ends, opening out into

Practice of the Presence: 1st image of the Lady of Avalon by Willow Roe

Nolava's rainbow halo on Glastonbury Tor

Winter Solstice sunrise viewed from the Mound as the sun rolls up the Tor

the landscape of the Otherworld. Look out over the vista in front of you. A path leads through this landscape. Walk along it looking at your surroundings. There may be hills, valleys, flat land, fertile green places or arid desert. Allow what you see to be there. In the middle of this landscape is a large deep lake of clear white water, the source of the White Spring, which emerges at the lower end of the Tor. When you reach the lake bend down and look at your reflection in the water, seeing yourself as you are. Cup your hands and drink from this white water milk of the Goddess's breast and feel refreshed.

A woman dressed in green, rides by on a white mare. She is radiant and beautiful and surrounded by flocks of small birds. This is Rhiannon on her White Mare from the Sea, who travels between the worlds, into and out of the hollow hills. Call to her, asking Her to stop for you. You know that She loves you as She looks at you and smiles. She invites you to ride with Her.

Climb up on the mare and put your arms around Rhiannon's waist. Feel wonderful seated behind Her. As you ride the landscape flies away on either side. Ask Her about the beings you see. She answers every question. After a time She takes you to a large paddock where many wild horses are gathered. She invites you to choose one for yourself that you can take with you to the Outerworld. Choose your horse and make friends with it. The horse allows you to climb onto its back and soon you are riding your own horse with Rhiannon at your side on Her mare. Feel free and strong, that the world is yours to roam. Ride like the wind. Enjoy the experience.

After a while you know it is time to leave this magical inner world. Thank Rhiannon for Her gift of the horse and watch Her as she rides away. Then ride your own horse towards the inner end of the tunnel beneath the Tor. Make your way back through the tunnel to the Outerworld. Notice how you are feeling in your mind, emotions and physical body. Become aware of your breath as it moves in and out of your lungs. As you breathe, feel the air and prana entering your body and filling you with vital energy. Feel the strength of the wild horse you are riding which moves at your command. Slowly bring your consciousness back into your body and open your eyes.

Look around at the landscape, at the Goddess's green mantle of nature and notice Her beauty. See if you can see your horse still with you in the Outerworld. Here on the earth level of the labrynth give thanks to the Goddess for the blessings of the earth and Her gift to you of a strong wild horse, who if you are lucky may carry you on Her back around the remaining levels of the labrynth.

Our Lady of Avalon, Goddess of the sacred land,

Nolava, Keeper of the Cauldron of Annwn,
Ariadne of the Red Thread, Arianrhod of the Silver Wheel
I give thanks for all the blessings of the earth
For the mountains, rocks, crystals and stones which form
Your body on which all physical life grows and thrives
I give thanks for your glorious and abundant nature
Which sustains all who dwell on Earth
I ask that your earth shall be easily cleansed of all human poisons
And quickly returned to its natural unpolluted state
I give thanks for my physical health and strength
For the opportunity to live on this beautiful planet
And I give thanks for your gift of my wonderful wild horse
I surrender to your earth all those physical restrictions
That no longer serve me
And open myself up to good health and vitality
Mother Earth, Rhiannon, Queen of the Land,
Blessings upon you and your bounteous nature.
Blessed be.

Continue walking along the first level until you come to a fence directly in front of you blocking the way forward. Follow the narrow track which leads off to the right up a small bank. Keep the hedge on your left until you reach the concrete path where the second and first levels of the labrynth merge. Stay on the left of the path. Follow it around to the left down the steps to the kissing gate. Go through the gate as if you are leaving the Tor. Then turn almost immediately right, circling around the bottom of the Tor past the field gate, keeping the hedge on your right hand side, until you come to a wooden stile. Climb over the stile into a small orchard of apple trees and walk through on level one until you reach the other side of the orchard. Blackberries grow in abundance here in the autumn. Climb over a second stile which brings you back onto National Trust land.

The first and second levels again combine here on one terrace. Walk on the left for level one. Follow the terrace until you reach the small wood. Turn down into the wood following the small pathways diagonally down across the hill. This lovely wood can be very peaceful with wild flowers growing in springtime and birds nesting and singing in the trees. In summer the trees provide shade from hot sunshine and in winter shelter from rain and wind. Make your way down through the wood by the lower trackways until you reach the lowest part of the wood where the tree roots are exposed making wonderful patterns. Emerging at the end of the wood a small path runs down onto the broad shelf of the first level. Walk along level one to the southwestern end of the Tor to complete this third circuit. This ends almost opposite the stone marking first entrance to the third level. You have completed the first level and your third circle of the labrynth. From here the path of the labrynth ascends the Tor to the fourth level.

Fourth Circle - Level Four
Air/heart chakra/4th ray/intuition

The fourth circle is the place of balance in the labrynth as it marks the halfway point in our physical journey into the centre of the labrynth and is synchronously made on the fourth level. It is the balance point between earth and heaven, the physical and the spiritual worlds. It is where we human beings live and where the heart and intuition rule.

At the end of the first level turn to your right and make your way up the Tor alongside the official path as it goes up the hill and turns into a series of steps. The fourth level begins half way up the hill beside the elbow in the steps, where the official path turns back on itself to the southwest as it climbs the hill. From here the fourth level is just a shadow on the steeply shelving southern side of the Tor, concealed by clumps of nettles, mole hills, badger sets and rabbit warrens. Look to the visible horizon of the Tor and you will see the tops of the trees of the small wood you walked through on the first and second levels. You can just about count up from the first to the fourth levels from here. Keeping parallel with the base of the Tor make your way across the side of the hill, walking widdershins around the Tor and aiming to come out above the top of the wood. Two thirds of the way along this slope, nearer to the wood, a small pathway appears clinging to the side of the Tor. As it rises above the wood it broadens out onto a wide fourth level terrace. Continue walking along level four until you reach the northeastern end of the Tor.

Here once again you have to negotiate your way up through the kink in the labrynth to level four on the northern side of the Tor. Climb diagonally up across the end of the Tor until you come to a manhole cover which is on the fourth level. This cover conceals a room belonging to the Water Board which is filled with dials and wheel. The sound of roaring water can sometimes be heard here if you put your ear to the ground. The breast of the Mother is filled with white milky water. You can also count up to the fourth level knowing that at this end of the Tor the second level is next to the hedge, then there is the third and this is the fourth.

Second Spiral

Follow the fourth level along the northern side of the Tor walking parallel to the lower levels. In some places in the middle of the northern flank of the Tor the fourth level narrows and blends with the third level and small animal trails can distract you from following the sweep of the terrace. Look to the western horizon and count the three lower levels you have already walked. Look above them to the fourth level which curves around the main ridge of the Tor and make your way towards it.

As you walk on level four feel the air all around your body. There is nearly always some breath of wind, if not a full scale gale, blowing across the slopes of the Tor. Feel the air as it blows through your hair and clothing, the air that carries the clouds, which bring rain to fertilise the earth. Notice the air that you breathe into your lungs which invigorates your body, giving you energy and life. This is the breath of life which connects us all to each other. The breath we breathe is the breath we all breathe.

Half way along this northern side stop and sit on the earth. Light a stick of incense and breathe in the fragrance. Say a prayer of thanksgiving to the Goddess for the gifts of air.

Our Lady of Avalon, Goddess of the sacred land,
Nolava, Keeper of the Cauldron of Annwn,
Ariadne of the Red Thread, Arianrhod of the Silver Wheel
I give thanks for the blessings of air upon my life
For the skies and the birds who fly like angels
For the air that I breathe which sustains my life.
I pray that the air be cleansed of all pollution and impurities.
I give thanks for the airy spaces of the heart where love blossoms
For intuition which connects me to the voice of my soul
For the fragrance of spirit which draws me ever nearer to you
I surrender to your air all those obstacles
That prevent me from hearing your words
And I open my heart to your point of balance
Lady of Air, Invisible One, Sacred Dove of Peace
Blessings on you and your loving grace
Blessed be.

Walk on along the fourth level staying on the left hand side of the terrace near to the bank of the Tor and curving round the main ridge of the Tor. The level narrows to become a small pathway which comes out a couple of metres above the second marker stone at the beginning of the labrynth. Reaching this point you have completed the fourth level. From here the path of the labrynth ascends to the seventh level.

Fifth Circle - Level Seven
Proton/crown chakra/1st ray/spiritual will

Turn left and walk straight up the main ridge of the Tor, climbing up the hill. As you come over the crest of the ridge St. Michael's tower on top of the Tor comes into view. Here there is a conveniently positioned bench where you can sit and catch your breath and gaze out over the flat Summerland meadows towards the sea. On a clear day from here you can see the Bristol Channel and sometimes the Welsh hills far away on the other side. The square boxes on the horizon belong to Hinkley Point, a nuclear power station beside the sea. In autumn and spring the White Lady's mists often cover the flat land and the outline of the Isle of Avalon becomes visible. Sometimes when it rains heavily the water in the rivers and rhynes spills over onto the fields and from here to the sea is covered with great flood lakes. The shape of the ancient island and the inland sea can be seen once more. From this height you can see shape of Nolava the Maiden Swan in the landscape flying across the Summerland. Wearyall Hill is Her long neck and head flying out to the southwest and Her body with wings outstretched is formed from the remaining hills of Avalon.

Walk on from the bench along the back of the dragon towards the top of the Tor. Ahead to the left you can see the first part of the seventh level, which encircles the steep upper portions of the Tor. After a short distance level seven peters out because of erosion. This level of spiritual will is the steepest and sometimes can be the most difficult to negotiate particularly in wind or rain. However it is a good level on which to recognise the nature of your spiritual progress in a very physical way. It can be much easier to walk this section of the labrynth barefoot connecting directly to the breast of the Mother, to the womb of the Crone, spirit to earth, earth to spirit. Naked we come into the world and naked we leave.

About 10 metres from the bench branch to the left onto level seven and walk along it encircling the Tor in a sunwise direction. Following the general direction of the level begin walking/climbing diagonally upwards across the flat face of the hill. There are slight indications of the path but nothing much to be seen on the ground. Make your way around the shoulder of the Tor climbing parallel to level six which you can see below you on this northern face of the Tor. Climb higher and higher but make sure that you never quite reach the top. In the traditional labrynth pattern the seventh circuit encircles the centre, but does not enter it.

As you make your way across this steep hillside notice how you feel and equate your feelings with the patterns of your spiritual life. Pause for a few moments and look out around you over the landscape. You are standing/sitting/slipping just beside the nipple on the Great Mother's landscape breast. Below is Her cleavage in Wellhouse Lane. Her right breast is less prominent, slipping over to Her right side, but still visible from here. To the west is the smooth round green Chalice Hill, the Mother's pregnant belly, and beyond the town of Glastonbury to which She continually gives birth. Beyond Chalice Hill and to the right covered in houses is Windmill Hill, the Goddess's right leg tucked beneath itself. To the southwest is Wearyall Hill Her outstretched left leg, with the foot disappearing into the earth beside Bride's Mound. To the northeast are Her shoulders with Her head sinking back into the earth at Stonedown. In the distance to the north are the Mendip Hills, with the cathedral city of Wells visible just below the tall television mast. To the west again is the Bristol Channel and the magical hill of Brent Knoll, a place for Brigit's fairies.

Continue on around the northeastern end of the Tor staying a couple of metres below the top of the Tor. Pause where the ground flattens a little and say a prayer.

Our Lady of Avalon, Goddess of the sacred land,
Nolava, Keeper of the Cauldron of Annwn,
Ariadne of the Red Thread, Arianrhod of the Silver Wheel
I give thanks for all the spiritual blessings in my life
For the goodness of the guides, guardians and protectors
Who accompany me upon my life's journey
I give thanks for the spiritual insights which you give to me
Moment by moment if I can but recognise them,
Inspirations which lead me onwards to become who I truly am.
I give thanks for this opportunity to walk your labrynth
And to experience your mysteries in Avalon
I surrender to your regenerating spirit all those parts
That no longer serve my greatest good
And I offer my life in service to you.
Queen of Heaven, Powerful Presence, Source of all,
Blessings upon you and your glorious spirit
Blessed be.

Keeping at this same distance of two to three metres below the summit continue to encircle the top of the Tor and St. Michael's tower. Visualise those days of old when there was perhaps instead a circle of standing stones here or high marker stones or posts. Or those earlier days when wooden platforms supported the bodies of the dead, elevated for sky burial high on the Western Isle of the Dead.

On the southern side of the Tor cross over the official steps and continue around at the same level, coming out onto flatter ground about 10 metres southwest of the tower, further along the dragon's back. Here there is a small shoulder of earth along which you walk away from the tower towards the southwest, on the southern side of the flat top of the Tor. After the rigours of the steep seventh level this is a good place to pause and take a breather looking out to the south and east over the Glastonbury Zodiac. On the southern horizon the tall pillar of the Hood Monument marks the third eye of the Bull of Taurus. The rest of the Zodiac lies mostly invisible from this angle in the landscape below.

The Tor is an energy centre where many ley lines cross and from here you can see several horizon markers which track the directions of the leys across the land, including the tall thin spire of Kingweston Church almost due south. On a clear day towards the southeast on the farthest horizon you can just make out the large flat-topped hill of Cadbury Castle, which is believed to be the physical location of the fabled Camelot, where King Arthur and Queen Guinevere held court. From Cadbury Castle it is much easier to see the Tor rising above the flat Summerland to the west.

You have completed the seventh level and the fifth circuit of the Tor. Only two more to go!

Sixth Circle - Level Six
Electron/ajna chakra/2nd ray/love-wisdom

Once again the numbers of the level and circle coincide. You are making your sixth circle on the sixth level. There seems to be meaning in the way that these even numbered circuits match each other.

Facing southwest off the small shoulder on top of the Tor turn 90 degrees left down the southern slope, so that you descend straight down the side of the hill. When you reach large clumps of nettles and the edge of an area where erosion and rabbits have revealed the sandstone body of the Tor, turn left again another 90 degrees. You are now moving widdershins around the Tor. There are animal tracks which follow the narrow yet discernible sixth level. Walk along these tracks on the southern slope of the Tor on the same level, rising up the slope as you reach the northeastern end of the Tor. Here there is quite a large discrepancy between the southern and northern levels. Before you reach the end of the Tor climb almost directly up the steep slope that lies on your left and crest the small ridge at the top. The northern sixth level should lie directly in front of you as an obvious terrace continuing on around the Tor. Should you not climb high enough you may come out opposite a bench which marks the position of the fifth level. Walk up from here to the sixth level. If you come out too high you will be able to look down and see clearly the sixth and fifth levels below you.

Begin walking along the sixth level on the northern side. As you come around the Tor the whole of the northern flank comes into view and you can see the far end of the sixth level at the top of the main ridge of the Tor. You can also see the fifth level returning from there at a lower level.

From this side of the Tor look out over the body of the landscape Crone who sits on the back of the Swan Maiden. The Tor where you are, is Her sagging womb filled with the wise blood of the ages. The round shape of Chalice Hill to the left is Her breast. Almost to the north you can see the houses on top of Windmill Hill, which is the Crone's head with its star shaped crown. Beneath you and to the right is the Crone's bent back at Stonedown.

As you walk open your inner eye of vision to what lies beyond the Veil of Avalon. Look to see through the veil of everyday reality into the realms of things unseen. Open your heart to the love and wisdom of the Goddess and feel Her completely unconditional love filling every cell of your body and being. Pause at some point along this northern slope and say a prayer.

Our Lady of Avalon, Goddess of the sacred land,
Nolava, Keeper of the Cauldron of Annwn,
Ariadne of the Red Thread, Arianrhod of the Silver Wheel
I give thanks for your blessings in my life
For the visions that you show me in my mind's eye
For the words that you speak in my ear
For the synchronicities which reveal your presence
For the beauty of this world in which I live
Which conceals and reveals your true nature
I surrender to your compassion all those parts of myself
That no longer serve me
And I open myself to receive your love
Lady Alchemia, you who change base metal into gold,
Blessings upon you and your loving wisdom
Blessed be.

Complete the sixth level by walking to the southwestern end of the main ridge of the Tor.

Seventh Circle - Level Five
Aether/throat chakra/3rd ray/intelligence

Turn right 180 degrees and look back along the northern slope to where you can see the sixth level you have just walked along and the fifth level below it. Begin walking sunwise across the Tor below the sixth level, towards the obvious sweep of the fifth level terrace. This is quite easy to follow. Because this is the last level of the labrynth its a good time to check where you are with your original intention in walking the labrynth. How are you feeling? Do you feel prepared for your Self initiation? As this is the level of the throat chakra open your mouth and sing or sound notes. Express your feelings in sound. There is a good strong echo between here and the Mother Goddess's right breast across Her Wellhouse Lane cleavage.

At the northeastern end of the Tor the fifth terrace peters out beside the bench. From here walk directly down the Tor to the row of thorn trees which marks the fifth level on the southern side of the Tor. Walk along beneath these guardian trees which have strong spirits visible in the trunks and branches. This part of the fifth level is easy to follow. Below you can see the fourth and third levels and the small wood.

Walk along the fifth level until you pass just beyond the end of the lower wood. Ahead of you and slightly higher is a clump of thorn and elder trees. Make your way upwards up the small pathway through the guardian nettles and thistles. Beneath the small thorn tree on the right is a large round Tor burr stone which marks the end of the outer labrynth and the entrance to the inner levels. Touch this stone. You will see that it has small carvings all over it made by previous pilgrims to this sacred place. The tree itself is covered in ribbons, rags and offerings to the Goddess made with prayer by pilgrims over the years.

Take your own ribbon which you have carried with you on your wrist through the labrynth and with a prayer of dedication attach it to one of the trees. Make an offering of herbs and flowers to the Goddess on the stone and on the earth. Pour some of your water over the stone and onto the earth as a libation for the Lady.

This is the magical spot where perhaps in ancient times there was once a physical entrance into the Tor, which as we know is today still filled with water and tunnels. It is here that purposeful spiritual questers or those who had accidentally strayed from the normal world might enter the Tor, sometimes to return after years in the Otherworld, white haired and mad or if they were lucky, illuminated and inspired as poets. Today the physical entrance is closed but the psychic gateways are still open.

Find a comfortable spot to sit and say your prayer to Our Lady of Avalon.

Our Lady of Avalon, Goddess of the sacred land,
Nolava, Keeper of the Cauldron of Annwn,
Ariadne of the Red Thread, Arianrhod of the Silver Wheel
I give thanks for the blessings of truth in my life
For revealing to me all that is good and true and beautiful.
I give thanks that you have brought me safely
To this entrance into the centre of your labrynth
And I ask that you accompany me into the inner world of Annwn.
Stay with me in the darkness as I come to meet my Shadow
And illuminate my soul with the light of Caer Sidi.
I surrender to your spaciousness
All those parts that no longer serve me
And I open myself to your shining light
Lady of Avalon, reveal to me your true nature,
All blessings upon you and your mysteries
Blessed be.

As the Glastonbury Tor Labrynth is a three dimensional labrynth you might suppose that its centre lies on top of the Tor, but the Tor labrynth also connects to the other dimensions of reality. Geoffrey Ashe first suggested that originally the centre of the physical labrynth may well have been in the middle of the Tor and this has been my psychic experience over many years of walking it. In legend the Tor is said to contain an entrance to the Underworld of Annwn, guarded by Gwyn ap Nudd, the Lord of the Underworld. It is here in Annwn that Crone Nolava keeps Her cauldron. The Tor leads upwards to Caer Sidi, Arianrhod's spiral castle in the stars, which also contains a magic cauldron. By placing the centre of the labrynth in the middle of the Tor we gain access to the Underworld of Annwn, to the stars of Caer Sidi, and to the Goddess's magical cauldrons of regeneration and inspiration.

In Kretan myth the High Priestess Ariadne leaves a red thread for us to follow into the middle of the labrynth which leads us to the monstrous Minotaur with all his human, animal and divine characteristics and a taste for consuming human beings. During our time in the centre of the Tor labrynth it is common to encounter elements of the personal Shadow which surface from deep within our subconscious minds. This experience can be conscious or unconscious depending on how self aware we are. For many people once they are in the centre of the labrynth things start to happen immediately with synchronicities, insights, events, meetings, memories and feelings emerging that shout for recognition. For others the initiatory process is subtle, but this does not mean that it is not happening.

The following visualisation is designed to make your experience of the centre of the labrynth more conscious. In it we walk through the inner levels of the labrynth, which I name as the Underworld home of the Shadow and the Upperworld Jewel in the Lotus of the Soul.

Visualisation

Sit or lie down in a comfortable place near this psychic gateway into the Tor. Allow your mind and body to relax after your long walk through the labrynth. Gaze to the far horizon and allow your breathing to slow right down after your exertions. Close your eyes and listen to the sounds around you, birds, wind, human activity in the landscape below and in the skies. Then bring your attention to your heart, feeling it pulsing in your body and know that all is well.

In your mind's eye visualise yourself as you were some minutes ago walking along the last stretch of the fifth level. See the grass beneath your feet and the slope of the Tor dropping away below you. Ahead see some bushy thorn and elder trees and as you approach see the large burr stone which now seems to be covered in deeper, more intricate carvings of spirals, circles, chevrons, ancient Goddess symbols. Behind the stone there is a dark cavelike opening into the earth. Standing just inside the cave there is a man who blocks your entry into the Tor. Notice what he looks like and how you feel about him from this first impression. This is Gwyn ap Nudd, King of the Fairies and Lord of Annwn, Guardian of the Gateway to the Goddess's Underworld. As you come towards him Gwyn ap Nudd challenges you,

"What is your intention in entering the inner world of Annwn?"

Listen for the question and give him your answer. When you have given the correct answer Gwyn will allow you to enter the body of the Tor. Walk into the long dark tunnel whose walls are carved with ancient Goddess symbols, which you can feel with the tips of your fingers. The tunnel spirals widdershins around the inner core of the Tor slowly descending deeper into the body of the

Tor. As you walk along every so often there is an opening in the tunnel wall, in which images appear as if on a video screen. These images are aspects of your Shadow appearing for you to see - they may be incidents from childhood, damaging events that have occurred in your life, unhealed wounds, past life memories, sources of pain, fear, grief and other difficult emotions. Allow yourself to see what is there. Take your time. You may glimpse things of which you have no conscious knowledge. Note them in your mind to recall later. The images you see on this inner journey are those aspects of your unconscious which are ready for healing. Notice how you feel emotionally.

When you are about halfway through this Shadow tunnel you become aware that although you are walking ever deeper underground the tunnel is getting lighter and you can now make out the way ahead of you curving around to the left. Along the floor of the tunnel you notice a red thread left for you by Ariadne, leading you through your fears to the middle of the labrynth. Take hold of the thread and let it run through your hand as you walk along. Keep giving yourself permission to see your Shadow aspects.

Continue walking until you complete the circle of the Tor and find yourself standing at the edge of a huge light-filled cavern in the earth. The walls are covered in crystals and jewels and the ceiling is so high that you can see pinpricks of light that are the stars in the night time sky. Far above you can see the sparkling starfire spiral castle of Caer Sidi. The wondrous sight brings shivers to your body. On the floor of the cavern is a pool of pale reddish water, the wise blood of the Crone's Womb, which flows out with the White Spring waters at the foot of the Tor. Walk towards the pool and kneeling down beside it take a drink and taste the sweet waters of Her wisdom. Splash the water on your face. Put drops of water on each of your chakras, invigorating your body with the Goddess's wise blood.

When you look up from the pool on the other side you see the hooded figure of a woman sitting beside a cauldron which bubbles away on top of a small fire. She is Crone Nolava, Keeper of the Cauldron of Avalon/Annwn. Notice how you feel about Her. As you watch Her She turns towards you and removes Her hood so that you can see Her face. Look at her. Is She familiar? Have you seen Her before? Where? Notice how you feel. Crone Nolava beckons to you and you walk around the pool, approaching Her as She stirs Her cauldron of inspiration and regeneration. You may ask Her any question, anything you want to know about your life - your life purpose, how you may serve the Goddess, what She requires of you. Listen carefully for Her answers. Stay beside Her for some time feeling Her energy and presence.

When you have heard all that you need to hear Nolava stirs Her *cauldron once again and as She does so, drops of the hot magical elixir fly from Her ladle and land on your fingers. Instinctively you put your fingers to your mouth to cool them so they won't burn and you taste the wonderful contents of Her cauldron. In an instant you are filled with light which pours down from Caer Sidi to the earth, and the earth answering reflects dark light back up to the heavens. Your whole perspective on life shifts. You are filled with wonder at the beauty you see all around you and in Nolava's face. Your heart opens wide with love for Her and all of Her creation. You feel yourself standing midway between earth and heaven holding the two energies in balance and radiating love to the world. You hear Her voice speaking,*

> *"I claim you as my granddaughter (grandson)*
> *Descendant of the lineage of Avallach,*
> *All is well and all shall be well."*

You have reconnected to your roots on the Isle of Avalon. You are changed and will never be the same again.

Soon it is time to leave. Thank Crone Nolava for all She has given you and bid Her farewell. Make your way across the floor of the cavern, past the pool of the Crone's Womb water, to the entrance to the tunnel. As you reach the entrance turn and take one last look across the cavern and wave goodbye. As you walk out from the cavern you suddenly feel yourself being whirled off your feet and rising swiftly upwards through darkness. In a few short moments you burst out from the earth back onto the side of the Tor where you were first sitting. Take a couple of deep breaths and open your eyes. Look around you at the beauty of the Goddess's nature. Feel Her presence all around you, within and above you, and be grateful for all you have received.

You are now ready to spend some time psychically in the centre of the labrynth while actually leaving the physical Tor. Walk straight up the side of the Tor to the top as a gesture to its centre and admire the views. Then walk down off the Tor by either of the official routes - the shorter route takes you to the northeastern end of the Tor, while the longer route along the dragon's back to the southwest takes you down to the bottom of Wellhouse Lane and the White Spring, where you can take a refreshing drink of White Spring water and call in at Chalice Well for relaxation and to bathe your feet.

During the time you are psychically in the centre of the labrynth though physically distant from the Tor try to remain conscious of the sometimes subtle processes of change that occur. Equate events in your life with your personal psychic position in the inner levels of the labrynth.

Self Initiation as a Priestess of the Goddess

Throughout the Second Spiral of the Priestess of Avalon training students plan their own Self-initiation ceremony, which is performed while they are psychically in the centre of the Glastonbury Tor labrynth, and physically on the slopes of the Tor. The ceremony is performed at sunset by the light of candles, the moon and the stars. As with the Dedication Vow made at the end of the First Spiral each would-be priestess writes her/is own vow expressing her/is love and dedication, and her commitment to the Goddess as Her priestess. The Goddess may be the universal Goddess or the Lady of Avalon.

In the Self-initiation ceremony students use the elements of air, fire and water to cleanse and bless each other before grounding and speaking their vows to an Embodiment of the Goddess. Since students design and perform the ceremony for themselves it is especially potent and meaningful as they contribute the knowledge and skills that they have learned throughout the Second Spiral.

Students are initiated into their new commitment by the power of their own souls and with the blessing of the Goddess. This initiation ceremony marks a deeper level of surrender to the Goddess, that of offering our lives in service to Her as Her priestess with all that means, which has been discussed earlier. To be a Priestess of the Goddess is to love, honour and serve Her in the ways that She chooses to the best of our ability.

Once the vows have been made and the ceremony is completed new initiates usually spend at least one night dreaming with the Goddess, before walking out of the labrynth in the following days.

Walking out of the Labrynth

It is always important to walk out of a labrynth as well as in, otherwise you remain in the centre of a psychic labrynth with all the psychological impact which that implies. On your journey out of the labrynth take the opportunity to create your own prayers and ceremonies on each level to the Lady of Avalon, to Morgen la Fey, Ariadne of the Red Thread and Arianrhod of the Silver Wheel. Show your gratitude. Give thanks repeatedly for all that you have received on your journey and during your time in the centre of the labrynth. Ask for help in taking new qualities with you into the future.

Imagine that as you walk out you are rewinding Ariadne's ball of red thread which shows you the pathway through the labrynth. It is this blood red thread which will always connect you directly to the Goddess. The walk out of the Labrynth is made by retracing the route that you took on your way into the centre of the labrynth.

On your return journey out of the labrynth from its centre make your way by any route to level five and up to the Tor burr stone marking the centre of the labrynth and the entrance into the Tor, which is hidden within the clump of bushes where you ended your pilgrimage into the labrynth. Beside this stone say a prayer.

Our Lady of Avalon, Goddess of the sacred land
Morgen la Fey, Keeper of the Cauldron of Annwn,
Ariadne of the Red Thread, Arianrhod of the Silver Wheel
I give thanks for all the experiences I have had
During my time in the centre of your labrynth
I ask that the process of initiation which has begun continues
To bring greater insight, wisdom and joy into my life
I pray that I may truly love and serve you
With all my body, heart and soul.
As I walk out of your labrynth I leave behind
All those parts that no longer serve me
And take with me into the future the knowledge
That I am your daughter (son).
Maiden, Lover, Mother, Crone
Guard, guide and bless me as I walk out of your labrynth
And emerge back into the world as your priestess
Blessed be.

Fifth level -First circle
Aether/throat chakra/3rd ray/intelligence

Walk down the small pathway between the nettles back onto level five and begin to walk widdershins around the Tor towards the northeastern end until you reach the line of thorn trees. At the end of the trees where there is a kink between the southern and northern sides of the Tor, walk straight up the hill until you reach the bench which marks the fifth level on the northern side. Continue along the northern flank aiming for the end of the fifth level at the farthest end of the main ridge of the Tor. Above the fifth level you can see the sixth and seventh levels.

On the fifth level sing or sound notes opening the throat chakra and expressing how you feel as you begin your journey out of the labrynth.

As you walk think about the things that you are leaving behind that no longer serve you and which qualities of the fifth level of intelligence, truth, creativity and self-expression you would like to take with you into the future. At the end of the fifth level turn 180 degrees to your left up onto level six.

Sixth level - Second circle
Electron/ajna chakra/2nd ray/love-wisdom

Look back along the northern flank to the end of the Tor and count the levels up to level six. Now walking sunwise along the side of the Tor follow the sixth level, which clearly lies above the fifth level you have just walked along. As you walk the sixth level look with your inner eye for visions of the Goddess on Her sacred hill and feel Her love entering your body and being.

When you reach the northeastern end of the Tor the sixth level disappears almost completely. Make your way over the ridge directly ahead and descend steeply for about 4 metres, remaining some distance above the line of thorn trees on the fifth level that you can see below you. Turn to the right and walk along, encircling the Tor in a sunwise direction. You should quickly come across the small but distinct tracks that mark the sixth level on the southern side of the Tor. These take you along the south side of the Tor until you come out above the exposed ground at the end of the fifth level. From here turn right and make your way directly up the hillside to the beginning of the seventh level, which lies on the small shoulder near the top of the Tor about 20 metres away from St. Michael's tower.

Seventh level - Third circle
Proton/crown chakra/1st ray/ spiritual will

Begin encircling the top of the Tor walking widdershins, keeping to the south of St. Michael's tower and the hill. Within a few paces you find yourself on the steep south side of the Tor and must begin to carefully negotiate your way across the side of the hill staying parallel to the top of the Tor. Cross over the steps of the official pathway, making your way around the top of the Tor towards the northeastern end. Pause here and remember to take time to look at the wonderful views and to appreciate the path of your spiritual life and this place to which it has brought you. Feel the power of the Goddess and the strength of your own spiritual will which has brought you to the place of Self-initiation as Her priestess. Feel good about yourself. Contemplate your spiritual life and how you will fulfil your dedication to the Goddess.

Moving widdershins around the northeastern end of the Tor the seventh level begins to descend across the hill in parallel with level six which you can see below you. Make your way diagonally downwards across the hillside clinging on as needed to the grassy tussocks. This can be a long and difficult stretch or an easy path for those who are mountain goats. As you come over the side of the hill the narrow invisible path of the seventh level broadens out ahead of you into a visible terrace running along below the ridge of the Tor. Follow this level until it comes out onto the Dragon's back and walk along to its western end.

From here the path of the labrynth continues to descend over the end of the main ridge of the Tor. Walk past the bench at the end of the ridge and straight down over the southwestern end of the Tor until you reach the first clear narrow path leading to the right which marks the beginning of the fourth level. This level is a couple of metres above the entrance stone marking the beginning of the third level.

Fourth level - Fourth circle
Air/heart chakra/4th ray/intuition

Turn right onto the fourth level and walk sunwise around the Tor keeping the bank of the Tor close to you on your right. As you come around the corner ahead of you on the horizon are the six visible levels of the labrynth. Count them again and look for the fourth level. Make your way towards it across the eroded hillside. On the fourth level think of those qualities of the heart, of love, intuition and knowing that you wish to take with you into the future and make your prayer to the Goddess.

At the northeastern end of the Tor the fourth level comes out beside the manhole cover on the water board control room. Listen to the water and know that you are walking on the Mother's breast. Just beyond the cover walk down the Tor to the fourth level on the south side, which is one level below the fifth level marked by the line of thorn trees. Walk along the broad fourth level with the small wood below you on your left, until it ends and the pathway narrows, clinging to the side of the Tor. Continue walking on the same fourth level across the southern flank of the Tor through the hillocks and bumps aiming towards the elbow in the steps which ascend the Tor at the southwestern end.

When you reach the elbow turn left and walk down the Tor beside the concrete steps and pathway to the first level. There are some smaller ghost levels here caused by erosion and animals, so its not just a simple matter of counting down three levels. The labrynth is unevenly arranged at its entrance and the left hand turn to the first level lies opposite the entrance stone to the third level on the northern side.

First level - Fifth circle
Earth/base chakra/7th ray/physical energy

Turn left onto the first level of the labrynth and begin walking widdershins around the Tor along the broad terrace. As you walk along the southern flank of the Tor notice how you are feeling physically and how grounded you feel in your life generally. Pray to the Goddess and ask that good health becomes part of your life now and in the future. Pray for continued healing and that your soul comes completely into physical manifestation in the world.

The broad terrace comes to an end two thirds of the way along and you approach a fence with the small wood above it. Take the small pathway up towards the corner of the wood. Once in the trees take the lowest pathways, crossing diagonally upwards through the wood. You will eventually come out higher up the hillside beside the corner of a fence on your right. You will now be on the lowest terrace of the Tor which is within the National Trust boundary. Walk along this broader path until you come to a short fence ahead with a stile over it. Climb the stile into the small apple orchard and walk through it. Climb the stile at the far end of the orchard and continue encircling the Tor through the field keeping the hedge on your left. Make your way to the National Trust entrance kissing gate and walk through onto the Tor.

Walk up the steps and follow the concrete path as it turns to the right. When the concrete path turns to the left up the hillside continue walking straight onto the grass. Walk on the combined levels one and two. Follow the hedge as it descends to the right down onto level one. Walk along the first level for several metres until you come to the depression in the hillside that marks the psychic gateway beneath the Tor. Pause here for a while and sit upon the earth, feeling the energies of the Tor, of the Mother's body. Allow yourself to psychically enter the body of the Tor and feel its power and energy flowing into your body. Remember the horse which Rhiannon gave to you. Feel your horse beneath you, within you, giving you energy and strength. Pray to the Goddess and ask for Her earthly blessings, for Her prosperity and abundance to come into your life.

When you are ready walk on along the pathway of the first level. About halfway along the northern slope of the Tor the first and second levels merge again so keep to the right, near to the hedge. Make your way down one of the small tracks that leads closer to the lower hedge on your right. Follow the narrow track along the northern flank of the Tor to where the path passes beneath a large hawthorn tree on your right. Continue on the first level as it broadens ahead of you and curves around the Tor to the left. Walk along this terrace until you can see the bench with the labrynth entrance stones behind it. Here turn left up the bank along one of the small tracks and make your way one level up the Tor to the second level. Turn almost 180 degrees around.

Second level - sixth circle
Water/sacral centre/6th ray/emotional & sexual energy

With the first level now below you, walk along the second level of the labrynth circling sunwise around the Tor. Keep to the left of the terrace which combines for a short distance with level three, following the second level until the northern side of the Tor comes into view. Look to the horizon, count the seven levels and walk towards the end of the second level, one level up from the hedge.

As you walk notice how you are feeling emotionally in this moment now. Think of how you would like your emotional states to be in the future. How you would like to express your sexuality? Ask the Goddess to help you to continually express your emotions and your sexual energy in creative and positive ways.

At the northeastern end of the Tor the second level merges with the first level at the concrete path beside the hedge on the left. Follow the path around the end of the Tor, keeping the boundary hedges on your left. Walk around the end of the hill After walking a short distance on the southern side of the Tor there are tracks leading down to the lower terrace beside the outer fence. Walk down one of these small tracks onto the combined second and first levels. Walk on the right until you reach the small wood. Stay on the second level path if you can and walk between the tall pine trees. If the path is overgrown with nettles take an earlier path down through the trees. Through the wood keep to the upper pathways so that you emerge from the middle of the western end of the wood, which brings you out onto the visible second level. Walk on along the terrace until you reach the southwestern end of the Tor where you turn right and walk up onto one of the next levels above. There are smaller ghost levels here in the labrynth and you can take either of the next two levels as they both lead to the third level.

Third level - Seventh circle
Fire/solar plexus/5th ray/mental energy

Begin encircling the Tor again now walking widdershins on the third level. This is your seventh and final circuit of the labrynth walking out. Notice how you are feeling, what you are thinking. Walk along the third terrace with the second and first levels below you, towards the wood on the horizon. As you get near to the wood for a short distance the third level almost merges with the second below it, but again stay above the second level. Ahead of you a small track leads up above the top edge of the wood. Make for this track and follow it up across the hillside above the wood to where it soon comes out onto a broader third level terrace.

As you walk notice the state of your mind at this time and the peace or otherwise that you feel. Feel the spaciousness in your mind when the body is too tired to think. See if you are actually in the present, in this moment now, just concerned with putting one foot in front of the other. Ask the Goddess to help you to learn to be a more generous human being in the way that She is generous to all beings who live on Her abundant planet. Recognise all the gifts that the Goddess gives to you and to all other beings on this planet and all others in the universe. Ask Her to help you develop the self confidence to be who you truly are with this spaciousness within you. Ask Her to continually show you how you can express Her energy and love in the world, how can you help to bring knowledge of Her back into the world and into human consciousness, how you can help priestess Her world.

At the northeastern end of the Tor make your way diagonally up through the kink to the higher third level, one above the second level beside the bottom hedge. Follow the third level around the northeastern side of the Tor onto the northern flank. As you come around the hillside look at the levels as they stretch out across the northern flank of the Tor. At the southwestern end of the Tor you can see the first level curving to the left on beyond the large hawthorn tree. Above that is the second level which for a short distance combines with the third level. Make your way towards this broad combined terrace. When you reach it follow the terrace around to the left, keeping to the left-hand side as it sweeps around the corner of the Tor. The second level soon descends away to the right. Follow the curve of the hill on the third level moving slightly up the hill and around, until you come to a small track over the ridge of the Tor which brings you out beside the third level marker stone. Touch this stone and ground your energy.

From this marker stone turn right and walk straight down the Tor staying on the grass, to the Living Rock, the first entrance stones behind the bench. Walk on these stones and climb over the back of the bench onto the ground.

You are out of the Labrynth!

Rest on the bench for a few moments. In imagination put Ariadne's ball of red thread in your pocket for safekeeping and say a prayer of thanksgiving to the Goddess.

Our Lady of Avalon, Goddess of the sacred land,
Morgen la Fey, Keeper of the Cauldron of Annwn,
Ariadne of the Red Thread, Arianrhod of the Silver Wheel,
I give thanks that I am safely returned from your labrynth
Back through the Veil of Avalon to the Outerworld.
I give thanks for all that I have received from you
I ask that I carry the memory of this experience into the future
And all the insights and wisdom you have shown to me.
Be with me in my journey through life.
May I always see your red thread laid out before me
Guiding me home to you
May I recognise the patterns of your stars in the night-time sky
And the shape of your body in the landscape around me
May I truly love and serve you as your priestess.
Lady of Avalon, Maiden, Lover, Mother, Crone,
My heart belongs to you always and forever
Bless me, blessed be.

From the bench walk down the Tor to Wellhouse Lane and to the White Spring. Drink some of the cool and refreshing White and Red Spring waters and bathe your feet.

Between the Second and Third Spiral

At the end of the Second Spiral it is important to take stock of what you have learned and what you have accomplished so far in becoming a Priestess of the Goddess. You will usually have come through many challenges and had many different experiences. Recognise how much you have changed since you began this journey and consider the following questions.

Are you ready to now begin the third phase of the journey to becoming a Priestess of Avalon? Is your true path to be a Priestess of the Goddess, dedicated to Her in many forms, rather than a Priestess of Avalon, priestess of the sacred land? Is this the right path for you? Do you have the time and the commitment to give to a daily spiritual practice which intensifies through time?

If you choose to complete your training here as a Priestess of the Goddess, be very content with your choice. Remember the vows that you have made, speak to the Goddess daily, listen to Her voice and continue to ask Her to show you the ways in which you may serve Her. She will always be with you, leading you into Her service and we in Avalon will always hold you in our hearts.

If you decide to continue with the Priestess of Avalon training there is more personal work to complete between the Second and Third Spirals.

Personal work

Look at ways in which you can affirm and deepen your Vow of Self-initiation as a Priestess of the Goddess. Consider which archetypal priestess qualities you now feel able to embody as Her priestess. Practice the skills that you have learned during the Second Spiral, with as many other people as possible in different situations, in the Goddess Temple, in the Goddess Conference, and in your own priestess practice where you live.

Consider where you now are in relationship to the rights, responsibilities and practices of a Priestess of Avalon.

Third Spiral

Becoming a Priestess of Avalon

The Practice of the Presence of the Lady of Avalon Samhain - Imbolc

During the First Spiral we learned about Britannia's Wheel of the Year and opened ourselves to the many faces of the Goddess and Her nature within Brigit's Isles. During the Second Spiral we learned the skills of a Priestess of the Goddess, turning our attention outwards to the people we will serve as Her priestess. In the Third Spiral, while beginning to practise our priestess skills out in the world, we turn inwards to connect ever more deeply with the Lady of Avalon, through the spiritual *Practice of the Presence of the Lady of Avalon*.

The completion of the Third Spiral leads to a third dedication and Self-initiation as a Priestess of Avalon. Again in truth this is a year which will bring us face to face with our deepest selves, with our strengths and weaknesses, with our greatness and with our resistance to transformation, as we come ever closer to Her. Throughout the Third Spiral we are challenged from within and without as to our true purpose and intentions in becoming a Priestess of Avalon, and whether this is truly the path for us. A Priestess of Avalon is one who works specifically with the energies of Avalon, of love, discrimination and transformation, and this path is not for everyone. It may not be the path for you. You can be a fantastic Priestess of the Goddess, without becoming a Priestess of Avalon. If this is what we decide there need be no sense of failure, for She will have other plans for us, ways in which we can serve Her.

We begin the Third Spiral by reviewing and deepening the Self-initiation Vow made on completion of the Second Spiral. We continue to develop our understanding of what it means to always be in the process of becoming a Priestess of the Goddess and of Avalon. We never stop learning what it means to serve Her.

Deepening our Self-Initiation Vow

After the Self-initiation Ceremony it is once again important for all newly dedicated Priestesses of the Goddess to explore on a daily basis exactly what the Vow we have made means to us, what effect it has spiritually and practically within our everyday lives. How best can we serve the Goddess with our talents and time? Shall we remain in work which takes up all of our time and brings us little joy, leaving only a few hours a week for our priestess work? Or shall we change our jobs, even reduce our income, to follow our bliss? Shall we stay in relationships that do not support us, where our partners continually undermine our relationship with Her or shall we leave? Shall we take the leap of faith and move into a life that is wholly guided by Her? What did our vow actually mean?

We continue to listen to the Goddess's voice by spending time with Her, listening to Her wisdom for us, listening to Her truth within. We learn the power of acting upon Her instructions by trying it out and seeing what happens when we follow what we hear or sense within. We experiment with our own transformation. We open ourselves more and more to Her loving nature and let go with the tides of change.

The Practice of the Presence of the Lady of Avalon

To call oneself a Priestess of Avalon in these days is a bold claim and requires a certainty of purpose and commitment that is only gained through daily communion with the Lady of Avalon Herself, coming to know who She truly is and the awesome power of Her transforming love. This spiritual Practice of the Presence of the Lady of Avalon allows the individual to find out if it is appropriate for them to become a Priestess of Avalon. The Practice is a nine month daily practice which develops and intensifies, the time spent in the practice increasing every three months. The practice culminates in a special ceremony of Self-initiation as a Priestess or Priest of Avalon.

The purpose of the practice is to give priestesses a deeper, more profound experience of the Presence of the Lady of Avalon in our lives. The practice involves the daily development of many skills, which enhance the priestess's abilities and personal life. These include invocation, visualisation, working with imagination as a creative tool, journeying, intuition, self-discipline, development of spiritual will, becoming conscious in the outer and inner worlds at the same time, working with energy, becoming receptive the Lady's love and learning how to transmit Her loving radiant energy into the world for healing and renewal. The practice involves standing, sitting, some physical movement, prayer and singing.

Each individual practice session lasts between 25 and 45 minutes, although some people who have the time, may practice for longer. There is one practice session per day in the morning for the first three months, two practice sessions per day in the morning and evening, for the second three months, and three sessions a day, midday being shorter than the morning and evening, for the final three months. This is an intense personal practice which takes time and requires daily commitment.

The first part of the Practice of the Presence involves grounding and centring in the Self, as practised daily during the First Spiral. This is followed by an invocation of the Goddesses on the Lady of Avalon's Wheel, calling them into one's own body and being, and breathing Her in. The third part of the practice involves journeying daily to the Isle of Avalon to meet Nolava, Lady of Avalon. Each day in imagination the priestess approaches the Isle of Avalon from the direction related to the time of the year, for example from the northwest at Samhain or the northeast at Imbolc. The landscape of the Isle of Avalon is initially visualised as being similar to the natural landscape of Glastonbury with its five hills and valleys. This island is imaged as being surrounded by the waters of a great lake. Priestesses need to be able to recognise the actual physical shapes of the Glastonbury Avalon landscape as they are viewed from a distance of a mile or two all the way around the island. The shape of the landscape and particularly of the Tor changes dramatically depending on where it is viewed from in the surrounding Summerland levels.

During the Practice we work with three images of the Lady of Avalon, painted by Willow Roe and Thalia Brown, one for each of the three month sections of the practice. We visualise the Lady in the forms in which She appears in the paintings in as much detail as possible. This visualisation is important in training the mind to connect image and energy. Students will sometimes declare, "*But that's not how I see Her*", but in this practice we are learning to control our minds and their desires, as well as seeing Her in the forms our own minds create. We are learning to build energetic forms using our imagination, as well as helping build archetypal energetic forms through which the Lady can manifest into the world.

Personal challenges often arise from the moment we begin the Practice. In my own experience I found that within a few days of beginning I came face to face with my resistances. While I had amazing inner spiritual experiences with the Lady from the start of the practice, I found that I just didn't want to do it every day, although I had committed myself to performing the practice for nine months. I wanted to do it when I felt like it, not when I had to get out of a warm cosy bed on a cool autumn morning. It felt excruciating as I persevered each day against my resistance, and forced myself to climb out of bed. Why was I doing this to myself? I didn't really need to do this to be a Priestess of Avalon, did I? Once I had begun the practice I usually felt OK, but it was getting to it that was difficult for me. This was also a pattern in other areas of my life, where I would put things off, often because "I *want to do what* I *want to do when* I *want to do it, not when* I'*m told to*", when there is no-one actually out there telling me to do anything, and the things needed to be done straight away.

A battle was engaged between different parts of myself and I didn't know which would win, the "I" which knew that connecting daily to the Lady on Her island was a great thing to do, or the "I" who wanted to do what she wanted when she felt like it. Performing the practice helped me to shift from an old wilful "I" into the "I" who serves the Lady.

The Practice of the Presence provides us with the perfect conditions in which we can experience our patterns in a conscious way. It shows us clearly who rules in our lives, whether it is the part of our personality which wants have its own way and will do all that it can to get it, or the part that can see ways in which we can change, that will allow more of our soul energy into expression. Throughout the nine months we will all find many good reasons why we should not perform the practice on particular days, but these are mostly expressions of our resistance. Things that might prevent us are often the result of the ways in which we organise our lives, our lack of preparation or our failure to give ourselves time to be with ourselves and the Lady. They can also be projections and manifestations of our inner conflicts. We need to notice what they are and when they occur.

In the nine months when I first performed the practice I missed maybe three or four sessions throughout the whole time. I would suggest that to receive the maximum benefit from performing the practice you aim for something similar. Sometimes it is impossible to perform the practice and then there is no need to punish yourself, but note the causes and continue on. If circumstances repeat themselves examine your heart and your purpose in performing the practice. To become a Priestess of Avalon is to want to spend time in communion with the Lady every moment of every day and this practice will bring you to that space of communion with Her.

Some people find the first three months of the practice easy to perform, while for others it is difficult as we wrestle with commitment and personal dedication. Many people experience pressure especially during the second three months when the practice increases to twice a day. Pressure can be expressed as feelings of anxiety, guilt, failure and lack of ability to visualise or to stay the course. These are all expressions of conscious and unconscious wounds, which the practice brings to the surface for healing. Offer these negative, self-sabotaging emotions to the Lady when you meet Her daily on the Isle of Avalon. Ask for healing from Her and She will help you.

These feelings sometimes cause people to give up the practice completely and to withdraw from the Third Spiral. If you need to stop, do not berate yourself. It may not be the right time for you to complete the training and to become a Priestess of Avalon in this way, by these means. This may not be your path. You may have your own journey of Self-initiation with Her to follow, that does not involve following this particular renewed Avalonian tradition. Or you can always try again to complete the Third Spiral at a later date, when the time is right for you.

After a trying middle section to the practice things often get easier during the final three months, even though the actual number of practice sessions continues to increase. The priestess becomes absorbed in moment by moment communion with the Lady, which is a source of deep pleasure, inspiration and gratitude.

As with the First and Second Spirals it is important to have support on your journey with the practice. Students in the *In the Heart of the Goddess* training stay in touch with each other throughout the nine months, comparing experiences and supporting each other through the difficult times. They also have the support of their tutor and other Priestesses of Avalon who have completed the three Spirals. Throughout the nine months as with the other two Spirals it is a good idea to keep a journal, a daily record of the experiences, dreams, visions and creative inspirations, which you receive while performing the Practice of Her Presence. For She will give much to you during the time you spend with Her. Many students say that the Third Spiral is the most amazing of three amazing Spirals of learning.

Introduction to the Practice

The first three months of the Practice of the Presence run from Samhain to Imbolc. As with most priestesses trainings we begin around

Samhain, the Keltic New Year. This is a good time to let go of old ways of being, to plant seeds of intention in the earth, where they lie dormant over winter, before awakening to springtime and coming to fruition in the summer. For the first three months the practice is carried out if possible first thing in the morning, on waking up and before breakfast. As dawn is breaking and the sky is lightening out and inside your room, visualise yourself journeying to Avalon in daylight.

Before beginning the practice choose the room in which you will be regularly making your practice and create your own personal altar dedicated to the Lady of Avalon. You will need to know where the eight directions are in the room and the direction of Glastonbury/Avalon from that room. For each practice session have ready a candle, incense and bell or chime, with a resounding ring. You may also find benefits from performing the practice with a veil over your head. Study the first image of the Lady of Avalon as shown on the Goddess Conference banner, so that you know what She looks like in detail.

The Practice of the Presence

1. *Light a candle and a joss stick or burn incense at your altar.*
2. *Ground and Centre (First Spiral practice)*

Stand, veiled or bareheaded, in front of your altar, facing it and centre yourself energetically :

a) Focus your attention in your heart chakra. Take a deep breath and visualise a narrow beam of light moving from your heart chakra down through your base chakra at the perineum, through your legs and feet into the earth. See it moving through the layers of earth, rock and molten rock towards the centre of the earth. Feel yourself connected and rooted into the centre of the earth, the Body of our Mother. See energy from the centre of the earth returning back up the beam to your heart, filling it with the energy of the earth.

b) Visualise a beam of light moving from your heart chakra up through your body and out of the crown of your head, travelling upwards through the ceiling, out through the roof into the space above the building you are in. See it moving upwards through the atmosphere, away from the earth, travelling faster than the speed of light past the planets, across the solar system, moving out through the Milky Way and across the universe reaching to the farthest star you can imagine. Feel your connection to the farthest star, then visualise energy coming from that star back across the universe into the crown of your head and down to your heart.

c) Feel the energy of the earth and the heavens meeting and mingling in your heart. Opening your arms out wide on either side of your body feel yourself bridging the space between the earth and the heavens and radiate your own soul's energy, mingled with that of the earth and the heavens outwards horizontally from your heart in all directions.

3. Invocation of the Goddesses on the Wheel of the Lady of Avalon (Second Spiral)

In this practice you are the centre of the wheel and are calling the Goddesses into your body and being at the centre.

a) Turn to face the direction of the time of year. At Samhain begin by facing the northwest. Opening your arms wide call into your body Crone Nolava, the Hag, Dark Goddess, Keridwen the Bringer of Death and Keeper of the Cauldron, Queen of the Underworld, Sheela na Gig, Lady of Mists, the Beansidhe, Yew Woman and Morgen Mazoe. Call in Her creatures - the Great White Sow, Toad, Hawk and Her qualities of darkness, death, transformation and rebirth. Visualise the Crone coming towards you in Her different forms. Breathe Her into your body and being - Bid Her "Hail and Welcome, Crone Nolava!" At the end of the invocation bring your hands together over your heart gathering all the energies of Crone Nolava into your body.

b) Turning sunwise to the north open your arms out wide and call in Nolava of Air, Mother of Air, Danu, Anu, Aine, Arianrhod, Cailleach, Bone Woman, Stone Woman, Old Woman of Winter, Holly Woman, Morgen Tyronoe, with Her creatures of the Air - Eagle, Buzzard, Owl, Wren, Sylphs and Dragons of the Air. Call in Her gifts of the Air, of the wind which blows through our lives bringing change, clearing our minds of clutter. Call in winter and hibernation, stillness, wisdom and spiritual energy. Breathe Her into your body and being. "Hail and Welcome, Nolava of Air!" Bring Nolava of Air and Her energies into your body, bringing your hands together over your heart.

c) Turning to the northeast open your arms and call in Maiden Nolava, Maiden Goddess, Brigit, Bridie, Bride, Willow Woman, Morgen Thitis, with Her creatures - Swan, White Cow with red ears, Snake, Wolf, Unicorn and Phoenix. Call in Her Maiden qualities of innocence, new beginnings, of the threshold, the quickening, of poetry, healing and Bridie's transforming smithcraft. Breathe Her in. "Hail and Welcome, Maiden Nolava!"

d) Turn to the east and call in Nolava of Fire, Mother of Fire, Artha the Great She Bear, Grainne the Sun Goddess, Eostre, Lady of Springtime, Hazel Woman, Morgen Cliton, with Her creatures - Bear, Hare, Red Hen, Cat, Green Woodpecker, Salamanders and Fire Dragons. Call in Her gifts of Fire, of springtime, of the greening, of energy and enthusiasm, of creativity, courage, passion, warmth and protection. Breathe Her in. "Hail and Welcome, Nolava of

Fire!"

e) Turn to the southeast and call in Nolava the Lover, Goddess of Love, Rhiannon of the Birds, White Mare *from the Sea,* Blodeuwedd the Flower Goddess, Olwen of the White Track, Elen of the Trackways, Queen of the May, Lady of Music, Morgen Thetis, *with Her creatures -* the White Mare, the Dove, *flocks of small* Birds, *and* Mermaids. *Call in the gifts of Her loving nature,* Her *joyful sexuality and sensuality,* Her *blossoming. Breathe* Her *in.* "Hail and Welcome, Nolava *the Lover!"*

f) Turn to the south and call in Nolava of Water, Mother of the Waters, Domnu the Ocean, Queen of the Deep, Lady of the Holy Springs and Wells, Lady of the Lake, Nimue, Vivienne, Oak Woman, Morgen Gliten, *with Her Water creatures -* Whale, Dolphin, Seal, Salmon of Wisdom, Sprites, Undines, Korrigans, Silkies *and* Water Dragons. *Call in Her gifts of the glistening, of all the emotions and Her all encompassing compassion.* "Hail and Welcome Nolava of Water!"

g) Turn to the southwest and call in Great Mother Nolava, Mother Goddess, Ker the Grain Mother, Madron, *Mother of the lineage of* Avallach, Ash Woman, Deer Woman *and* Morgen Glitonea, *with Her horned creatures -* Cows, Goats, Sheep, Deer *and* White Hind. *Call in the gifts of Her abundance, Her wealth, prosperity and generosity, Her nurturing care for all Her children. Breathe Her in.* "Hail and Welcome Great Mother Nolava!"

h) Turn to the west and call in Nolava of Earth, Our Mother Earth, Brigantia - *Lady of these islands,* Banbha - *Lady of the Land from before the Flood,* Gaia our Earth Mother, Beech Woman, Morgen Moronoe, *with Her creatures -* Boar, Badger, Fox, Gnomes, Elves *and* Earth Dragons. *Call in the gifts of the harvest, of grounding and security, of the* Earth *that sustains all our Life, bringing all things into manifestation.* Breathe Her *in.* "Hail and Welcome, Nolava of Earth!"

i) When you have completed calling in the Goddesses of the eight directions, turn to face Avalon. *If you live outside of* Glastonbury, *find out where* Glastonbury *is in relation to your home and face that direction. If you live in* Glastonbury *face the direction of the* Tor/Chalice Well.

Open your arms and call in Nolava - Lady of Avalon, Goddess of the Sacred Land, Avallonia - Lady of Apples, Morgen La Fey - Keeper of the Mysteries of Avalon. *Call Her in as* Weaver of the Web, Shapeshifter, Wayshower, Faery Woman, Apple Woman, Lady of Time, Walker between the Worlds, Healer, Sovereign, Shining One, Faery Woman *with Her creatures -* Black Crow, Black Cat *and* Faeries. *Call in Her magic and mystery. Breathe Her in. Feel Her entering your body and close your arms across your heart.* "Hail and Welcome,

Practice of the Presence: 2nd image of the Lady of Avalon by Thalia Brown

Practice of the Presence: 3nd image of the Lady of Avalon by Willow Roe

Nolava, Lady of Avalon!"

Add in your own understanding of the Goddesses, creatures and qualities of the nine directions.

As the wheel of the year turns, begin your invocation with the appropriate Goddess for the time of year. Change Goddesses about two to three weeks before the next Sunfire festival, when you feel Her energy change, e.g. begin to call in Nolava of Air around the beginning of December, Maiden Nolava in early January, etc..

4. Sit down comfortably before your altar on a chair without armrests or on the floor, with your back straight and your left leg extended and your right leg tucked under. Close your eyes.

5. Visualise yourself standing a mile or two to the northwest of Glastonbury at the edge of a large lake, looking out across the water towards Glastonbury. Visualise the small hills of Glastonbury as hills on an island surrounded by water which extends from where you are standing to the island.

Along your edge of the lake there are reeds and plants with small water birds bobbing on the surface of the lake. Patches of mist drift across the lake, but do not obscure your view. In your mind's eye see the Glastonbury landscape as it looks in present day actuality from this northwestern side, but surrounded by a large lake. Notice the weather in your imagination - sunny or stormy, raining or windy, clear and calm, or wild.

Between Samhain and Imbolc change your starting place on the edge of the lake, moving slowly day by day around on a curve from the northwest to the northeast. The shape of the island you see across the waters in front of you changes as you move around this arc of the lake.

6. Calling the Barge:

Continuing to visualise the lake, sing out loud to the tune you learn in the training or to your own tune. It is important to sing rather than speak this prayer as well as the other songs given as the heart and throat open when we sing.

"Lady, Lady of the Lake of Mists
Lady, Lady, send your barge for me"

7. Ring your bell three times, allowing your mind to follow the sound of the bell to its farthest echoes each time.

8. In your mind's eye visualise the Barge of Avalon appearing from the left side of your vision moving towards you out of the reeds. The Barge has its own silent power and is steered by a Faery (Ferry) Being who will take you across the water to Avalon. This Faery Being may be human, animal or Otherworldly, to be discovered (seen) by you.

9. When the Barge comes to rest in front of you, climb aboard and give the Faery Being a silver coin from your pocket - the fee for crossing the water. You may do this in imagination or physically, putting your hand in your actual pocket and withdrawing a coin which you place on your altar.

10. Go to stand or sit in the prow of the Barge as it moves out across the lake to Avalon. As the Barge moves out across the water, mist begins to rise from the lake, quickly obscuring the view of the Island ahead of you. Soon you are surrounded by a dense white fog - the Mists of Avalon. Later in the nine months of the Practice you will be learning to summon the mists, but at this stage of the practice the mists arise of their own accord.

11. <u>Parting the Mists:</u>

Visualise yourself standing in the prow of the Barge surrounded by mist. Physically hold your hands in the prayer position at the heart and sing out loud:

> *"Lady, Lady, part the mists for me*
> *Lady, Lady, unveil your mystery."*

As you finish singing slowly open your arms out wide, parting the mists with your hands. As you part your hands with your eyes closed, look directly ahead through the space created, to the Paradise Isle of Avalon across the water of the lake. See what you see.

12. The barge moves on across the water to Avalon. As it approaches the shoreline look to see what the Isle of Avalon looks like in your imagination. It will be similar in shape to the modern day reality, but without modern day buildings, farms and fences. It is a more natural, wilder landscape, with a few habitations from another reality. Notice the feeling of the place and again notice the weather.

13. When you reach the shore thank the Faery Being for bringing you across the water to Avalon. Climb out of the Barge onto the land. This may be smooth grass or wild tangles, shingly or rocky. There may be a special place where the Barge lands or you may have to jump to the shore. See what you see in your mind's eye. Notice the vegetation around you. Are there plants, flowers, apple orchards, woods, a grove of oak trees or is the land bare and rocky? See what you see.

14. From the shore make your way up the steeper northwestern slopes of the Isle of Avalon and begin to explore the island. You may be walking on the earth or flying over it or simply thinking of a place and finding yourself transported there.

15. After a short time find a place on the island that feels special to you - this place may change during this first three months of the practice.

16. *In your imagination sit down on the earth, on a tree or on a convenient seat. In physical reality sit with your left leg outstretched and your right leg tucked under your body in the position of* Great Mother Nolava *in the* Glastonbury *landscape.* Hold *your left hand with its palm outstretched as if an apple is resting on it, on your left knee.* Place *your right hand at the right hand side of your body on a level with the heart with its palm facing forward in a sign of blessing.* This *is the* Lady *of* Avalon's *mudra.*

17. Invocation of the Lady of Avalon

Pray *to the* Lady:

> "O Lady *of* Avalon, *on this your sacred* Island
> I *call to you and ask you to reveal yourself to me."*

Hold *the space of prayer for a few moments*

18. Keeping *your eyes closed begin to turn your body rhythmically to the left and to the right.* Moving *your whole torso from the pelvic area upwards, holding your arms loosely out to the sides, gently swing the body, arms and head to the left and to the right, while calling the* Lady *of* Avalon *by name aloud.*

> "Lady *of* Avalon, Lady *of* Avalon, Lady *of* Avalon....*etc."*

Gradually *raise your arms as you move until they are moving back and forth above your head in rhythm with your body.*

As *you turn your head to the left and right keep your closed eyes focused on your centre of vision, as if you are looking straight ahead.* Gradually *speed up your movements and words until you are repeating* Her *name,*

> "Lady, Lady, Lady, Lady,..............*etc."*

Express *your longing to meet* Her *in your voice.*

Repeat Her *name and the body movements at least 99 times.*

19. When *your invocation is complete allow your body to stop moving and feel the* Lady's Presence *in the space within you.* Place *your hands once again in the* Lady's *mudra - left hand palm outstretched, right hand in blessing.*

20. Sung Invocation of the Lady of Avalon

Sing *to the* Lady *the tune that you learn in the* Third Spiral *training or make up your own tune.*

> "Lady, Lady *of the* Apple Isle
> Lady, Lady *of the* Holy Springs
> Lady, Lady *of* Avalon
> Reveal *yourself to me.*

Lady, Lady of the Isle of the Dead
Lady, Lady of Paradise
Lady, Lady of the Sacred Land
Show your face to me.

Lady, Lady of the Holy Grael
Lady, Lady of the Red Chalice
Lady, Lady of the Cauldron round
Unveil your mystery."

(Visualise the Lady coming towards you as you sit and sing)

Lady, Lady of the rainbow light
Lady, Lady of the violet hue
Lady, Lady of Avalon
Reveal yourself to me
Show your face to me
Unveil your mystery."

21. *See the Lady of Avalon standing in front of you. Visualise Her as She appears in the Conference painting wearing a red dress patterned with Goddess images, with a rainbow halo and aura surrounded by Melissa bees, with deer horns holding the sun on Her head and a butterfly between, with long misty hair and violet skin.*
22. *The Lady radiates violet light towards you. Receive Her light. Feel your whole body and being immersed in the blessing of Her violet rays. Absorb Her energy. Feel Her blessings filling your whole life. Hold that receptive space for as long as you can.*
23. *As you feel Her energy dissipate, give thanks for the blessings of Her presence.*

"O Holy Lady of Avalon
Thank you for the gift of your presence in my life
Walk with me through this day
Bless, guide and protect me
And all those whose path I touch today."

24. *Bring your hands to your heart and then down to touch the floor and ground yourself. Bring your consciousness back into the room.*

In this practice you are daily moving into a deeper and deeper connection to the Lady of Avalon, opening yourself to the energies of Her nature. You do not need to return back across the waters of the lake or to close the wheel at the end of each session unless you want to. Your purpose as a Priestess of Avalon is to become so at-one with the energies of Avalon, that you live with one foot in the physical world and one foot in Avalon.

Additional Personal Work

Throughout the course of the Third Spiral, as during the Second, begin working on the Self-initiation Vow that you will make at the end of this Spiral. The dedication you will be making is to love, honour and serve the Lady of Avalon as Her priestess. Once again the words used are your own, but will include something along the lines of "I dedicate myself to you, Lady of Avalon, as your priestess." Throughout the first three months begin to consider your Self-initiation Vow. What do you wish to say to the Lady of Avalon as you Self-initiate into Her service?

Design and begin to make the violet robes, headdress and mask, you will wear for the initiation ceremony at the end of the Third Spiral.

Intensification of the Practice of the Presence of the Lady Imbolc - Beltane

At Imbolc the Practice of the Presence intensifies as it moves to two sessions a day - one in the morning as the sun is rising and one in the evening as the sky is darkening. In the Priestess of Avalon training students meet to discuss their experiences in performing the practice, their visions and inspirations, the resistances and challenges. This is very helpful.

Intensification of the Practice

For the second three months of the practice we start our journey to the Isle of Avalon from the northeast gradually moving around the edge of the Lake of Avalon to the southeast. Once again the shape of the island changes dramatically as we move through the eastern quadrant. The Tor in particular is emphasised, looking from some angles like a pyramid-shaped mountain.

The first part of the practice remains the same as that for the first three months and for this you will again need a candle, incense, a bell and a veil, if desired. The practice changes when we arrive on the Isle of Avalon. We work with a new image of the Lady of Avalon in the form of Morgen la Fey, as painted by Thalia Brown for the Goddess Conference. Some people like to continue to work with the first image given of the Lady of Avalon for one of the daily practices, but at least one practice a day must be carried out with the new image.

During the morning practice see yourself approaching the island in daylight. During the evening practice see yourself moving across the lake and approaching the island in darkness. How do you find your way? Are there lights or torches, or can you see by the light of the stars and the moon? Connect yourself to the actual cycle of the moon while you are practising, providing you with moonlight on certain nights. Notice how you feel exploring the island in the dark.

The Practice of the Presence of the Lady of Avalon - Intensification

1. *Light a candle and a joss stick or burn incense at your altar.*

2. *Ground and Centre*

Stand, veiled or bareheaded, in front of your altar, facing it and centre yourself energetically :

a) Focus your attention in your heart chakra. Take a deep breath and visualise a narrow beam of light moving from your heart chakra down through your base chakra at the perineum, through your legs and feet into the earth. See it moving through the layers of earth, rock and molten rock towards the centre of the earth. Feel yourself connected and rooted into the centre of the earth, the Body of our Mother. See energy from the centre of the earth returning back up the beam to your heart, filling it with the energy of the earth.

b) Visualise a beam of light moving from your heart chakra up through your body and out of the crown of your head, travelling upwards through the ceiling, out through the roof into the space above the building you are in. See it moving upwards through the atmosphere, away from the earth, travelling faster than the speed of light past the planets, across the solar system, moving out through the Milky Way and across the universe reaching to the farthest star you can imagine. Feel your connection to the farthest star, then visualise energy coming from that star back across the universe into the crown of your head and down to your heart.

c) Feel the energy of the earth and the heavens meeting and mingling in your heart. Opening your arms out wide on either side of your body feel yourself bridging the space between the earth and the heavens and radiate your own soul's energy, mingled with that of the earth and the heavens outwards horizontally from your heart in all directions.

3. *Invocation of the Goddesses on the Wheel of the Lady of Avalon*

You are the centre of the wheel and are calling the Goddesses into yourself at the centre at this time of Imbolc.

a) Turn to face the northeast, open your arms wide and call in Maiden Nolava, Maiden Goddess, Brigit, Bridie, Bride, Willow Woman, Morgen Thitis, with Her creatures - Swan, White Cow with red ears, Snake, Wolf, Unicorn and Phoenix. Call in Her Maiden qualities of innocence, new beginnings, of the threshold, the quickening, of poetry, healing and Bridie's transforming smithcraft. Breathe Her into your body and being. "Hail and Welcome, Maiden Nolava!" At the end of the invocation bring your hands together over your heart gathering all

Her energies into your body.
b) Turn to the east, open your arms and call in Nolava of Fire, Mother of Fire, Artha *the Great* She Bear, Grainne *the* Sun Goddess, Eostre, Lady *of* Springtime, Hazel Woman, Morgen Cliton, *with* Her *creatures -* Bear, Hare, Red Hen, Cat, Green Woodpecker, *Salamanders and* Fire Dragons. *Call in* Her *gifts of* Fire, *of springtime, of the greening, of energy and enthusiasm, of creativity, courage, passion, warmth and protection. Breathe* Her *into your body and being.* "Hail *and* Welcome, Nolava of Fire!"
c) Turn to the southeast, open your arms and call in Nolava *the* Lover, Goddess *of* Love, Rhiannon *of the* Birds, White Mare *from the* Sea, Blodeuwedd *the* Flower Goddess, Olwen *of the* White Track, Elen *of the* Trackways, Queen *of the* May, Lady *of* Music, Morgen Thetis, *with* Her *creatures - the* White Mare, *the* Dove, *flocks of small* Birds, *and* Mermaids. *Call in the gifts of* Her *loving nature,* Her *joyful sexuality and sensuality,* Her *blossoming. Breathe her in.* "Hail *and* Welcome, Nolava *the* Lover!"
d) Turn to the south, open your arms and call in Nolava *of* Water, Mother *of the* Waters, Domnu *the* Ocean, Queen *of the* Deep, Lady *of the* Holy Springs *and* Wells, Lady *of the* Lake, Nimue, Vivienne, Oak Woman, Morgen Gliten, *with* Her Water *creatures -* Whale, Dolphin, Seal, Salmon *of* Wisdom, Sprites, Undines, Korrigans, Silkies *and* Water Dragons. *Call in* Her *gifts of the glistening, of all the emotions and* Her *all encompassing compassion. Breathe* Her *in.* "Hail *and* Welcome Nolava *of* Water!"
e) Turn to the southwest, open your arms and call in Great Mother Nolava, Mother Goddess, Ker *the* Grain Mother, Madron *-* Mother *of the lineage of* Avallach, Ash Woman, Deer Woman *and* Morgen Glitonea, *with* Her *horned creatures -* Cows, Goats, Sheep, Deer *and* White Hind. *Call in the gifts of* Her *abundance,* Her *wealth, prosperity and generosity,* Her *nurturing care for all* Her *children. Breathe* Her *in.* "Hail *and* Welcome Great Mother Nolava!"
f) Turn to the west, open your arms and call in Nolava *of* Earth, Earth Mother, Brigantia *-* Lady *of these islands,* Banbha *-* Lady *of the* Land *from before the* Flood, Gaia *our* Mother Earth, Beech Woman, Morgen Moronoe, *with* Her *creatures -* Boar, Badger, Fox, Gnomes, Elves *and* Earth Dragons. *Call in the gifts of the harvest, of grounding and security, of the* Earth *that sustains all our* Life, *bringing all things into manifestation. Breathe* Her *in.* "Hail *and* Welcome, Nolava *of* Earth!"
g) Turn to the northwest, open your arms wide and call in Crone Nolava, *the* Hag, Dark Goddess, Keridwen *the* Bringer *of* Death *and* Keeper *of the* Cauldron, Queen *of the* Underworld, Sheela *na* Gig, Lady *of* Mists, *the* Beansidhe, Yew Woman *and* Morgen Mazoe. *Call in* Her *creatures - the* Great

White Sow, Toad, Hawk and Her qualities of darkness, death, transformation and rebirth. Breathe Her in. Bid Her "Hail and Welcome, Crone Nolava!"

h) Turning sunwise to the north open your arms and call in Nolava of Air, Mother of Air, Danu, Anu, Aine, Arianrhod, Cailleach, Bone Woman, Stone Woman, Old Woman of Winter, Holly Woman, Morgen Tyronoe, with Her creatures of the Air - Eagle, Buzzard, Owl, Wren, Sylphs and Dragons of the Air. Call in Her gifts of the Air, of the wind which blows through our lives bringing change, clearing our minds of clutter, call in winter and hibernation, stillness, wisdom and spiritual energy. Breathe Her in. "Hail and Welcome, Nolava of Air!"

i) When you have completed calling in the Goddesses of the eight directions, turn to face Avalon. Open your arms and call in Nolava - Lady of Avalon, Goddess of the Sacred Land, Avallonia - Lady of Apples, Morgen La Fey - Keeper of the Mysteries of Avalon. Call Her in as Weaver of the Web, Shapeshifter, Wayshower, Faery Woman, Apple Woman, Lady of Time, Walker between the Worlds, Healer, Sovereign, Shining One, Faery Woman with Her creatures - Black Crow, Black Cat and Faeries. Call in Her magic and mystery. Breathe her in. Feel Her entering your body and close your arms across your heart. "Hail and Welcome, Nolava, Lady of Avalon!"

Add in your own understandings of the Goddesses, creatures and qualities of the nine directions.

As the wheel of the year turns, begin your invocation with the appropriate Goddess for the time of year. Change Goddesses about two to three weeks before the next Sunfire festival, when you feel Her energy change, e.g. begin to call in Artha after the beginning of March, Rhiannon in mid April, etc..

4. Sit down comfortably before your altar on a chair or on the floor, with your back straight and your left leg slightly extended. Close your eyes.

5. Visualise yourself standing a mile or two to the northeast of Glastonbury at the edge of a large lake, looking out across the water towards the Glass Isle that is Glastonbury or Ynys Witrin. Between where you are and the island there is nothing but water. Along the edge of the lake there are reeds and plants with small water birds bobbing on the surface of the lake. Patches of mist drift across the lake, but do not obscure your view. In your mind's eye see the Glastonbury landscape as it looks in present day actuality from this northeastern side, but surrounded by the waters of a large lake. Notice the weather - sunny or stormy, raining or windy, clear and calm, or wild.

Between Imbolc and Beltane change your starting place on the edge of the lake, moving slowly day by day around its northern curve from the northeast to the southeast. The shape of the island in front of you changes quite dramatically as you move around this arc of the lake.

6. Calling the Barge:

Continuing to visualise the lake, sing out loud to the tune you learn in the training or to your own tune:

> "*Lady, Lady of the Lake of Mists*
> *Lady, Lady, send your barge for me.*"

7. *Ring your bell three times, allowing your mind to follow the sound of the bell to its farthest echoes each time.*

8. *In your mind's eye visualise the Barge of Avalon appearing from the left side of your vision moving towards you out of the reeds. The Barge has its own silent power and is steered by a Faery (Ferry) Being who will take you across the water to Avalon. This Faery Being may be human, animal or Otherworldly, to be discovered by you.*

9. *When the Barge comes to rest in front of you, climb aboard and give the Faery Being a silver coin from your pocket - the fee for crossing the water. You may do this physically, putting your hand in your actual pocket and withdrawing a coin which you place on your altar, or do it in imagination.*

10. *Go to stand or sit in the prow of the Barge as it moves out across the lake to Avalon. As the Barge moves out across the water, mist begins to rise from the lake, quickly obscuring the view of the Island ahead of you. Soon you are surrounded by a dense white fog - the Mists of Avalon. Let the mist enter your body and being.*

11. Parting the Mists:

Visualise yourself standing in the prow of the Barge surrounded by mist. Physically hold your hands in the prayer position at the heart and sing out loud:

> "*Lady, Lady, part the mists for me*
> *Lady, Lady, unveil your mystery.*"

As you finish singing slowly open your arms out wide as if parting the mists with your hands. As you part your hands look directly ahead with your eyes closed, through the space created, to the Paradise Isle of Avalon across the water of the lake. See what you see.

12. *The barge moves on across the water to Avalon. As it approaches the shoreline look to see what the Isle of Avalon looks like. It will be similar in shape to the modern day reality, but without modern day buildings, farms and fences. It is a more natural, wilder landscape, with a few habitations from another reality. Notice the feeling of the place and again notice the weather.*

13. *As you reach the shore thank the Faery Being for bringing you across the*

water to Avalon. Climb out of the Barge onto the land. This may be smooth grass or wild tangles, shingly or rocky. There may be a special place where the Barge lands or you may have to jump to the shore. See what you see in your mind's eye. What can you see in the darkness? Are there lights to guide you? Notice the vegetation around you. Are there plants, flowers, apple orchards, woods, a grove of oak trees or is the land bare and rocky? See what you see.

14\. *From the shore make your way up the northeastern slopes of the Tor, which rises like a mountain above you. Explore the Tor and make your way around the slopes to the Temple of Avalon, the Temple of the Lady. See where it is located, notice what it looks like and walk inside. Explore the Temple of Avalon. Notice its decorations and the canopied pergola in the centre of the Temple, beneath which there are two simple thrones facing each other.*

15\. *In your imagination when you are ready sit down on one of the thrones beneath the canopy. Sit with your left leg outstretched and your right leg tucked under your body. Hold your left hand with its palm outstretched as if an apple is resting in your palm, on your left knee. Place your right hand at the right hand side of your body on a level with the heart with its palm facing forward in a sign of blessing in the Lady's mudra.*

16\. *Keeping your eyes closed begin to turn your body rhythmically to the left and to the right. Moving your whole torso from the pelvic area upwards, with your arms loosely out to the sides, gently swing the body, arms and head to the right and left, while calling the Lady of Avalon by name aloud. Raise and lower the arms as you move.*

> *"Lady of Avalon, Lady of Avalon, Lady of Avalon....etc."*

As you turn your head to the left and right keep your closed eyes focused on your centre of vision, as if you are looking straight ahead. Gradually speed up your movements until you are repeating Her name ,

> *"Lady, Lady, Lady, Lady,.............etc."*

Express your longing to meet Her in your voice.
Repeat Her name and the body movements at least 100 times.

17\. *Invocation of the Lady of Avalon*

> *"Lady of Avalon*
> *In this your holy Temple*
> *I call to you and ask to come into your Presence."*

Hold the space of prayer /invocation for a few moments.

18\. *When your invocation is complete see/feel the Lady coming towards you in the Temple. Visualise Her as She appears in the new image as Morgen La Fey with Her dark hair and violet skin and crows fluttering around her.*

19. Sung Invocation of the Lady of Avalon

Sing to the Lady the tune that you learn in the Third Spiral training or make up your own tune.

"*Lady, Lady of the Apple Isle*
Lady, Lady of the Holy Springs
Lady, Lady of Avalon
Reveal yourself to me.

Lady, Lady of the Isle of Dead
Lady, Lady of Paradise
Lady, Lady of the Sacred Land
Show your face to me.

Lady, Lady of the Holy Grael
Lady, Lady of the Red Chalice
Lady, Lady of the Cauldron round
Unveil your mystery.

Lady, Lady of the rainbow light
Lady, Lady of the violet hue
Lady, Lady of Avalon
Reveal yourself to me
Show your face to me
Unveil your mystery."

20. *Visualise the Lady sitting down on the throne opposite you beneath the canopy in the Temple. She sits in the same position as yourself. Feel Her presence and Her violet emanations.*

21. *Visualise radiant globes of light moving from all directions in space into Her body, making Her glow even more.*

22. *See Her energy radiating directly towards you. Absorb Her energy into your body and being. Feel Her blessings filling you and your whole life. Feel yourself becoming Her. Feel/see radiant globes of light coming from all over space into your body. Fill your body with light and radiate violet light outwards to where it is needed in the world. Transmit Her loving violet energy for as long as you can hold your focus.*

23. *As you feel concentration dissipate and Her energy depart, give thanks for the blessings of Her presence.*

"*O Holy Lady of Avalon*
Thank you for the gift of your presence in my life

Walk with me through this day/night
Bless, guide and protect me
And all those whose path I touch today."

Once again in this practice which you now perform twice a day, you are moving into a deeper and deeper connection to the Lady of Avalon, opening yourself to the energies of Her nature. You do not need to return back across the waters of the lake or to close the wheel at the end of each session unless you want to. Enjoy!

Additional Personal Work

Throughout the second three months continue considering the Vow *you will make as you Self-initiate into the Lady of Avalon's service.*

Begin to create the violet initiation robes, headdress and mask you will wear for the ceremony at the end of the Third Spiral.

Design and create a ceremony for other students or friends to be performed at the final weekend gathering, which demonstrates your ability to generate and transmit the energy of the Lady of Avalon.

Immersion and Self-Initiation as a Priestess of Avalon Beltane - Lammas

For the final three months the Practice of the Presence consists of three spiritual practice sessions a day with a longer practice in the morning, a short Lady's Prayer practice at lunchtime and a longer one in the evening. For the longer practices you will need a bell, wand, candle, incense and veil if desired. This final three months is designed to bring the conscious experience of the Lady of Avalon into your body, heart and soul. It also includes offering prayers of gratitude to the Goddess for all that She gives to us before every meal and the frequent repetition of Her mantra with visualisation of Her appearance throughout the day.

"Maiden, Lover, Mother, Crone
Lady of Avalon, bring me home"

"Hail Nolava, Lady of Avalon
Lady of life, death, love and transformation"

During the final three months visualise the Lady of Avalon as She appears in the third image, painted by Willow Roe, with Her violet dress and skin. You may also work for one session with previous images.

The Practice of the Presence of the Lady of Avalon Morning and Evening Sessions

1. *Light candle and incense at your altar.*
2. *Stand, veiled or bareheaded, in front of your altar, facing it and centre yourself energetically :*
a) Focus your attention in your heart chakra. Take a deep breath and visualise

a narrow beam of light moving from your heart chakra down through your base chakra at the perineum, through your legs and feet into the earth. See it moving through the layers of earth, rock and molten rock towards the centre of the earth. Feel yourself connected and rooted into the centre of the earth, the Body *of our* Mother. *See energy from the centre of the earth returning back up the beam to your heart, filling it with the energy of the earth.*

b) Visualise *a beam of light moving from your heart chakra up through your body and out of the crown of your head, travelling upwards through the ceiling, out through the roof into the space above. See it moving upwards through the atmosphere, away from the earth, travelling faster than the speed of light past the planets through the solar system, moving out through the* Milky Way *and then across the universe to the farthest star you can imagine. Feel your connection to the farthest star, then visualise energy coming from that star back across the universe into the crown of your head and down to your heart.*

c) Open *your arms out wide on either side of your body and feel the energy of the earth and the heavens meeting and mingling in your heart. Feel yourself bridging the space between the earth and the heavens and radiate your own soul's energy, mingled with that of the earth and the heavens outwards horizontally from your heart in all directions.*

3. Invocation of the Goddesses on the Wheel of the Lady of Avalon

In this practice you are the centre of the wheel and are calling the Goddesses *into yourself at the centre.*

a) Turn to the southeast and opening your arms wide call in Nolava *the* Lover, Goddess *of* Love, Rhiannon *of the* Birds, White Mare *from the* Sea, Blodeuwedd *the* Flower Goddess, Olwen *of the* White Track, Elen *of the* Trackways, Queen *of the* May, Lady *of* Music, Morgen Thetis, *with* Her *creatures - the* White Mare, *the* Dove, *flocks of small* Birds, *and* Mermaids. *Call in the gifts of* Her *loving nature,* Her *joyful sexuality and sensuality,* Her *blossoming.* Breathe Her *into your body and being.* "Hail *and* Welcome Nolava *the* Lover!" *At the end of the invocation bring your hands together over your heart gathering all* Her *energies into your body.*

b) Turn to the south, open your arms out wide and call in Nolava *of* Water, Mother *of the* Waters, Domnu *the* Ocean, Queen *of the* Deep, Lady *of the* Holy Springs *and* Wells, Lady *of the* Lake, Nimue, Vivienne, Oak Woman, Morgen Gliten, *with* Her Water *creatures -* Whale, Dolphin, Seal, Salmon *of* Wisdom, Sprites, Undines, Korrigans, Silkies *and* Water Dragons. *Call in* Her *gifts of the glistening, of all the emotions and* Her *all encompassing compassion.* Breathe Her *in.* "Hail *and* Welcome Nolava *of* Water!"

c) Turn to the southwest and call in Great Mother Nolava, Mother Goddess,

Ker the Grain Mother, Madron, Mother of the lineage of Avallach, Ash Woman, Deer Woman and Morgen Glitonea, with Her horned creatures - Cows, Goats, Sheep, Deer and White Hind. Call in the gifts of Her abundance, Her wealth, prosperity and generosity, Her nurturing care for all Her children. Breathe Her in. "Hail and Welcome, Great Mother Nolava!"

d) Turn to the west, open your arms out wide and call in Nolava of Earth, Earth Mother, Brigantia - Lady of these islands, Banbha - Lady of the Land from before the Flood, Gaia our Mother Earth, Beech Woman, Morgen Moronoe, with Her creatures - Boar, Badger, Fox, Gnomes, Elves and Earth Dragons. Call in the gifts of the harvest, of grounding and security, of the Earth that sustains all our Life, bringing all things into manifestation. Breathe Her in. "Hail and Welcome, Nolava of Earth!"

e) Turn to the northwest, open your arms out wide and call in Crone Nolava, the Hag, Dark Goddess, Keridwen the Bringer of Death and Keeper of the Cauldron, Queen of the Underworld, Sheela na Gig, Lady of Mists, the Beansidhe, Yew Woman and Morgen Mazoe. Call in Her creatures - the Great White Sow, Toad, Hawk and Her qualities of darkness, death, transformation and rebirth. Breathe Her in. "Hail and Welcome, Crone Nolava!"

f) Turning sunwise to the north, open your arms out wide and call in Nolava of Air, Mother of Air, Danu, Anu, Aine, Arianrhod, Cailleach, Bone Woman, Stone Woman, Old Woman of Winter, Holly Woman, Morgen Tyronoe, with Her creatures of the Air - Eagle, Buzzard, Owl, Wren, Sylphs and Dragons of the Air. Call in Her gifts of the Air, of the wind which blows through our lives bringing change, clearing our minds of clutter, call in winter and hibernation, stillness, wisdom and spiritual energy. Breathe Her in. "Hail and Welcome, Nolava of Air!"

g) Turning to the northeast, open your arms out wide and call in Maiden Nolava, the Maiden Goddess, Brigit, Bridie, Bride, Willow Woman, Morgen Thitis, with Her creatures - Swan, White Cow with red ears, Snake, Wolf, Unicorn and Phoenix. Call in Her Maiden qualities of innocence, new beginnings, of the threshold, the quickening, of poetry, healing and Bridie's transforming smithcraft. Breathe Her in. "Hail and Welcome, Maiden Nolava!"

h) Turn to the east, open your arms out wide and call in Nolava of Fire, Mother of Fire, Artha the Great She Bear, Grainne the Sun Goddess, Eostre, Lady of Springtime, Hazel Woman, Morgen Cliton, with Her creatures - Bear, Hare, Red Hen, Cat, Green Woodpecker, Salamanders and Fire Dragons. Call in Her gifts of Fire, of springtime, of the greening, of energy and enthusiasm, of creativity, courage, passion, warmth and protection. Breathe Her in. "Hail and Welcome, Nolava of Fire!"

i) When you have completed calling in the Goddesses of the eight directions, turn to face Avalon.
Open your arms and call in Nolava - Lady of Avalon, Goddess of the Sacred Land, Avallonia - Lady of Apples, Morgen La Fey, Keeper of the Mysteries of Avalon. Call Her in as Weaver of the Web, Shapeshifter, Wayshower, Faery Woman, Apple Woman, Lady of Time, Walker between the Worlds, Healer, Sovereign, Shining One, Faery Woman with Her creatures - Black Crow, Black Cat and Faeries. Call in Her magic and mystery. Breathe Her in. Feel Her entering your body and being and close your arms across your heart. "Hail and Welcome, Nolava, Lady of Avalon!"
Add in your own understanding of the Goddesses, creatures and qualities of the nine directions.
As the wheel of the year turns, begin your invocation with the appropriate Goddess for the time of year.
6. Sit down comfortably before your altar on a chair or on the floor, with your back straight and your left leg slightly extended, in the position of the Mother Goddess in the Glastonbury landscape. Close your eyes.
7. Visualise yourself standing to the southeast of Glastonbury at the edge of a large lake, looking out across the water towards Glastonbury. See the profile of the Great Mother Nolava's body lying before you on the earth as Wearyall Hill, Chalice Hill, the Tor and Stonedown. Through the final months gradually move around the edge of the lake to the southwest.
Along the edge of the lake there are reeds and plants with small water birds bobbing on the surface of the lake. Patches of mist drift across the lake but do not obscure your view. In your mind's eye see the land as it looks in present day actuality from this southern side surrounded by the waters of a large lake. Notice the weather - sunny or stormy, raining or windy.
8. <u>Calling the Barge:</u>
Continuing to visualise the lake, sing out loud:

"Lady, Lady of the Lake of Mists
Lady, Lady, send your barge for me."

9. Ring your bell three times, allowing your mind to follow the sound of the bell to its farthest echoes each time.
10. In your mind's eye visualise the Barge of Avalon appearing from one side of your vision moving towards you out of the reeds. The Barge has its own silent power and is steered by a Faery Being (Ferry person), who will take you across the water to Avalon.
11. When the Barge comes to rest in front of you, climb aboard and give the

Faery Being a silver coin from your pocket - the fee for crossing the water.
12. *As the Barge moves out across the lake go to stand in the prow facing Avalon.*
13. Summoning the Mists:
As the Barge moves out across the water, stand with your arms outstretched, holding your wand in your hand. In the middle of the lake call the mists to you from the surface of the lake in the secret language. Lift your arms and visualise the mist rising all around the Barge.

"*Lady of Avalon, Nolava,*
White Lady of the Lake of Mists,
I call your mists to me."

Mist quickly obscures the view of the Island ahead of you. Soon you are surrounded by a dense white fog - the Mists of Avalon. Allow the mists to enter your body and your consciousness for a short time.
13. Parting the Mists:
Hold your hands and wand in the prayer position at the heart and sing out loud:

"*Lady, Lady, part the mists for me*
Lady, Lady, unveil your mystery
Show your face to me."

As you finish singing extend your arms forward and then open them wide, parting the mists with your wand. As the mist disappears look across the open water towards the Isle of Avalon. See what you see on this southern side of the island.
14. *The barge moves on across the water to Avalon. As it approaches the shoreline look to see what the Isle of Avalon looks like. Notice the feeling of the place and again notice the weather. In the morning session the view is in daylight. In the evening session the view is of darkness and any lights, including moonlight, that can be seen.*
15. *Thank the Faery Being for bringing you across the water to Avalon and climb out of the Barge onto the land. This may be grassy, shingly or rocky. There may be a special place where the Barge lands or you may have to jump to the shore. See what you see. Notice the vegetation around you.*
16. *During May and early June see yourself making your way up the slopes of the Mother Goddess's left knee or the Swan's head, (Wearyall Hill) onto the top so that you can see the rest of Her body (Tor, Chalice Hill and Windmill Hill) laid out before you. Make your way down over Her knee (Wearyall Hill) to the southwestern base of Her Womb (Chalice Hill), where there is a narrow cave*

entrance that leads into a tunnel. Walk into the tunnel.

During late June and July see the Barge taking you from the southwest towards the Isle of Avalon, moving between the Goddess's outspread legs, directly into the narrow cave entrance. Climb out of the Barge and walk into the entrance tunnel.

17. *For a time walk through the tunnel. Notice the walls, whether you can see anything, what you feel.*

18. *Eventually the tunnel opens out into a large cavern with a pool of water at its centre and the ceiling filled with pinpricks of light which are the stars of the universe. Walk towards the pool and bending down, look at your reflection in the pool. Take a sip of water and sprinkle water on your chakras. Bathe in the waters if you choose.*

19. *Standing in the cave by the pool with eyes closed invoke the presence of the Lady of Avalon.*

> *"Lady of Avalon*
> *In this your sacred cave*
> *I call to you.*
> *I ask to come into your Presence."*

Hold the space of prayer/invocation for a few moments.

20. *As you open your inner eyes, beyond the pool see a flickering fire on which a Cauldron sits. Beside the Cauldron sits the cloaked and hooded figure of Nolava, Lady of Avalon. Sing to Her.*

21. *Sung Invocation of the Lady of Avalon*

> *"Lady, Lady of the Apple Isle*
> *Lady, Lady of the Holy Springs*
> *Lady, Lady of Avalon*
> *Reveal yourself to me*
>
> *Lady, Lady of the Isle of Dead*
> *Lady, Lady of Paradise*
> *Lady, Lady of the Sacred Land*
> *Show your face to me*
>
> *Lady, Lady of the Holy Grael*
> *Lady, Lady of the Red Chalice*
> *Lady, Lady of the Cauldron round*
> *Unveil your mystery*
>
> *Lady, Lady of the rainbow light*
> *Lady, Lady of the violet hue*

Lady, Lady in your Sacred Cave
Reveal yourself to me
Show your face to me
Unveil your mystery."

22. *As you reach the end of the song the Lady removes Her hood and cloak and reveals Herself to you. Notice what She looks like. She appear in Her new form or perhaps in a new guise. Feel Her presence. Listen to what She says to you.*
23. *Feel Her energy radiating directly towards you. Absorb it into your body and being. She beckons you forward, inviting you to drink from Her Cauldron. As you drink feel the magical liquid entering your body and filling it with Her amazing ikor, which heals your wounds, transforms all your unhelpful tendencies and neutralises all your negative karma.*
24. *Feel/see globes of light emerging from the walls of the cavern and moving into your body. Look up to the starry ceiling. See light coming towards you from all over the universe. As your body fills with outer and inner light, radiate the Lady's violet and rainbow light outwards to where it is needed in the world. As you transmit Her violet light sound Her name.*

"No....laa....vaa....."

Transmit Her energy for as long as you can from deep within Her Sacred Cave in the earth.
25. *As your concentration dissipates and Her energy departs, give thanks for the blessings of Her presence.*

"O Holy Lady of Avalon
Lady of the Sacred Cave
Thank you for the gift of your presence in my life
Walk with me through this day/night
Bless, guide and protect me
And all those whose path I touch today."

Midday Lady's Prayer Practice

The Lady's Prayer Practice is a standing prayer to be made during the middle of the day and at any other time you choose. Repeat the practice three times in each session with the appropriate body movements and mudras. Its important to move the physical body as this also moves energy. The practice can be done with your eyes open or closed, but it is good to try to perform the practice with total concentration on words and movements. Move slowly and really mean every word that you utter.

Third Spiral

1. Begin the Prayer Practice by holding your hands together, palms touching each other in the prayer position at the heart. Slowly raise your hands together, lifting them up above your head and then parting them. Reaching up to the heavens, lean back, look upwards, and pray.

"Lady, awaken my spirit"

2. Bring your outspread hands down to the ajna chakra which lies between the eyebrows, so that your palms are facing outwards. Create an open upward facing triangle over the ajna, with your hands by connecting the tips of your thumbs and first fingers. Rest your thumbs on the top of your nose.

"Lady, open my vision."

3. Turn your hands over, bring them down to the mouth and then extend them outwards from the mouth, as if they are the breath moving outwards from the mouth.

"Lady, be in my breath and all my actions."

Circle the arms outwards and around on the level of the shoulders and bring the hands back together at the heart.

4. Hold your hands at the heart in an open prayer position as if holding a chalice.

"Lady, fill my heart."

5. Bring your hands down to the solar plexus so that they are resting one on top of the other, palms facing upwards.

"Lady, soothe (or release) my emotions."

6. Gently bend your knees as you spread your hands out again and turn them to face inwards, touching the belly and sliding down the body. Create a downward facing triangle by touching the tips of the thumbs and first fingers.

"Lady bless my sexuality and creativity."

7. Bend your knees further and move the hands down over the base chakra and the thighs towards the knees and then extend and circle the arms outwards to the sides. Straightening the legs bring the hands in a sweeping circle back to the prayer position at the heart.

"And ground me in your love."

8. Repeat this practice three times or more in any session.

This short practice opens the heart and the body to the Lady's energies. It was first received beside the Chalice Well. Take your time with making your prayer and enjoy Her blessings as they enter your body and being.

Self-Initiation as a Priestess of Avalon

Completion of the nine months of the Practice of the Presence of the Lady of Avalon leads to the ceremony of Self-initiation as a Priestess or Priest of Avalon. In Glastonbury those who have successfully completed all three years of training, spend a night in the Glastonbury Goddess Temple communing with the Lady of Avalon and preparing themselves for Self-initiation.

During the following day each student presents a ceremony which they have been preparing during the previous three months, which demonstrates their ability to generate and transmit the loving and transformative energies of the Lady of Avalon. These ceremonies are performed at the different sacred sites within the Glastonbury Avalon landscape connecting deeply into the land which is Her body. Over the years these ceremonies have been varied and original offering different experiences in nature of Her energy.

The Self-initiation ceremony itself takes place in the Glastonbury Goddess Temple and is a powerful and transforming initiatory experience in which candidates speak their Vows of Dedication to the Lady. The impact of this ceremony stays in the heart of the Priestess and Priest of Avalon forever.

After Self-initiation

Self-initiation is a powerful energetic experience as well as being a heart-opening and emotional dedication. Don't rush back to work the day after, squashing everything back into unconsciousness. Take time to integrate the experience.

Once again it is important to remember that Self-initiation means to begin. It does not mean that you have completed the process of becoming a Priestess of Avalon, it means that you have begun to become Her priestess and the learning never ends.

In the following days and weeks look at ways in which you can affirm and deepen your Vow of Self-initiation as a Priestess of Avalon. Consider which archetypal priestess qualities you now feel able to embody as Priestess of the Lady and of Avalon. Offer the Lady's blessings to others in many situations, both ceremonial and everyday.

Consider where you now are in relationship to the rights, responsibilities and practices of a Priestess of Avalon. Which are you able to fulfil and which do you need to continue to develop?

Look at other areas of your life and integrate your knowledge and experience of the Lady into those areas, from artwork to poetry, teaching to healing to performance, from your home to your workplace. How can you express Her in the world. What are the unique gifts that you can offer to Her people in Her service? How can you inspire others with your devotion to Her?

Continue to study and learn more about the Lady and Her transforming ways through prayer, devotion and walking Her sacred landscapes. Participate in the advanced trainings of Priestess Enchantress and Priestess Healer. Support Goddess-loving people and participate in Goddess events, such as the Glastonbury Goddess Conference, Goddess Festivals in Holland, Hungary, the USA, Australia and elsewhere. Serve the Lady in Her Goddess Temples that are emerging all over the world. Express your love for Her every day and in everything that you do and are.

Personal Experiences of Becoming a Priestess of Avalon

Since the Priestess of Avalon training began over 90 people have Self-initiated as Priestesses and Priests of Avalon within the *In the Heart of Goddess* series of trainings. They are an amazing bunch of people with unique and interesting characters. Here are the words of a few of them describing the ways in which discovering the Goddess and becoming Priestesses of Avalon has affected their lives.

Katinka Soetens

Being a Priestess of Avalon has changed my life for the better in so many subtle and obvious ways. Like an additional dimension flowing through my life, it has begun to feel like second nature, like part of my skin, and is so much part of my identity now that it seems hard to imagine not calling myself Her priestess.

The Goddess has been with me all my life. Looking back She is like a red thread that has led and guided me. Her love and compassion are limitless and I know to trust Her calling. I was raised a liberal Protestant in Holland and had a strong sense of the spiritual even as a small child. Early on I started to question our place in society and the world as a girl/woman and as part of a species with so apparent little respect or consideration for the natural world of which we are integral. It wasn't long before I started to learn a little about other religions and then to find my way to nature spirituality and Wicca.

Never feeling pulled to be part of a coven I called myself a solitary witch for many years and all the time She was calling me back to Her in stronger and louder ways. Especially during my pregnancy and the birth of my first daughter, as well as with my other children, the Goddess showed me Her face. It felt right to explore this more, and so the search started. It eventually took me to my first Glastonbury Goddess Conference in 1999, and though I could only be there for a day or so, it was a groundbreaking experience. So the following year I made sure to be there for more of the event, and heard about the Priestess of Avalon training. My immediate reaction was one of disappointment as this seemed to me to be the kind of hierarchical structure I wanted to stay away from. Didn't spirituality come from out of that divine part of our being that needs no-one else to tell us that we are part of the Goddess and that She is part of us? Surely now these wonderful people and this fantastic, magical event weren't going that way, just when I'd found my way there?

But still the term priestess had a ring and a pull to it that resonated in me with a certain longing and connected to my love for history and the ancient ways on this sacred land. Then at the 2001 Conference the Goddess tugged at my heart and gave me the push (or sign) I didn't know I needed, and in 2002 I started training as Priestess of Avalon. It's been a life-enhancing and life-changing journey ever since.

When I Self-initiated as Priestess of Avalon, I knew it was the next stage in this journey in which the Goddess had gently led and guided me, to start finding out how to walk in the priestess path, to change and develop and to always get closer to, or more within, Her presence. It has brought satisfaction on a deep soul level to honour, acknowledge, and serve the Goddess openly and in my heart and to come home to Avalon, to the Lady of Avalon and Her energies. She has opened my heart and as a result my creativity is flowering in unexpected and new ways. To be Her priestess has brought healing and a better understanding and appreciation of the subtle energies and interconnection between all things. It has helped me to see and understand patterns in myself and in people and/or situations I work with. Sometimes this insight has made me more tolerant and loving, at other times more determined to change that which needs changing.

To call myself a Priestess of Avalon is a great honour and has been a homecoming, a wonderful reclaiming of a word, a term, and also a role in society. This role, I now know it has nothing to do with hierarchy, despite what the general reaction to a word like *priestess* may be. It is a recognition of a commitment to serve the Goddess, to walk Her way, to stand up, or out, and to enable others to experience Her energy.

Apart form the delicious reclaiming and honouring of this part of our female spirituality, being a Priestess of Avalon also feels like an important step towards re-balancing male and female in our society. It is a way of being heard as a human, speaking out for the Earth and all Her sacred creatures. It is also a way of connecting with all women throughout the millennia, back to the times when She (and Women and the Earth) were honoured as lifegivers. When She was known as Goddess of Death and Rebirth, not just accepted as some pretty, young, powerless image, we seem to want to worship in our culture today, because it feels safe/ unconnected/soulless/controllable. It is a link to the times now thought of as having had matriarchal societies (which in my mind is a patriarchal way of describing an equalitarian way of being), a way of recognising the sentient and sacredness of all beings. It is wonderful to me to step into the place where I feel a very strong connection, a resonance within my being, of something not explainable in words or expressible in emotion, that has to do with the energetic connection to those times, those ancestors and energies and to the rightness of it all.

After years of strongly feeling that I did not want to be part of a coven or group, it has been a relief and great gift to be part of the Orchard, those of us who call ourselves Priestess of Avalon. To be able to think of myself no longer as just out there on my own with my spirituality, but to be able to be part of a community of people who are on a similar path and to feel at home with them, to learn from and with them, people who also recognise the ancient and at the same time new journey that being a Priestess of Avalon is. To me it is truly precious, like standing on a cliff overlooking the peaceful swaying blue ocean, with the sun on your face and summer breeze in your hair, with the scent of freshly cut grass in your nostrils and lark song all around, and your heart opening in joy and gratitude, to do ceremony or ritual with my fellow priestesses.

With calling oneself a Priestess of the Goddess and in particular a Priestess of the Lady of Avalon whose energy is one of transformation, comes the undeniable responsibility to walk one's talk. In my mind there is no doubt that to be a Priestess of Avalon you have to actively decide and commit to making the changes happen that are so desperately needed. These changes need to be made both on an inner plane and in the outside world, in a form that will do no harm, that is firmly rooted in love and which will be transformative. I am still learning to do this as I walk my priestess path.

This means for me that I have to be in my truth in my relationships, have to work with integrity, work/ dedicate some of my time towards actively doing something about the issues so closely interwoven with the ways of walking in balance on this earth, with nonviolence against women, children, men, the environment, our souls. If I want to call myself a Priestess of Avalon, then I have to try and be in that place of *priestess*, that archetypical energy with which I feel so at home, which empowers me and which is so nurturing. And to do this all the time, every minute of the day and night, not just when meditating or doing ceremony. By endeavouring to be in connection to Her energy, to resonate with Her vibration I have to take responsibility for my emotional and physical patterns and actions.

It has enriched my life beyond measure to hold and be part of the flow of the Lady's energy. I find it delicious as well as challenging to create ceremonies and rituals which help mark the rites of passage in people's lives, which celebrate the changes of the seasons, and which allow myself and others to experience the Goddess as she expresses Herself to us all. Equally, it is wonderful to allow myself time (and somehow it is easier for me to do so if there is a reason, if it is part of what I do as priestess) to sit or walk in meditation, so that the hectic nature of my brain and being slows. I give myself time to stop and check in with the real flow of importance, something which is so easy to loose sight of in normal life.

I think this is one of the reasons why She called me back to Her and to this particular path of Priestess of Avalon and its teachings, so that things are released, sorted, healed and acknowledged in myself and in the world, so that Her light may shine brightly, so that awareness of Her love may spread and flow freely once more. Blessed Be.

Katinka Soetens is a Priestess of Avalon, mother of 3 home-educated lovelies, partner to Tino. She holds active birth classes and is a doula (birth companion. She lives in Cornwall and is a regular participant in the Goddess Conference ceremony circle.

Jacqueline Woodward-Smith

When I began to write about how becoming a Priestess of Avalon has changed my life at first I thought that it would be easy to describe, but the more I try to write the more difficult I know the task to be. The Goddess changes me with every moment and to freeze that moment in time and describe it is almost impossible. I was going to say that discovering the Goddess and becoming a Priestess of Avalon has changed me completely, and of course it has, but even that feels wrong. In truth finding the Goddess and becoming a priestess has helped me to become closer to who I have always been, at least in potential. The me that I have become, and am still in the process of becoming, the me that has the spark of Goddess within her, has always been there under the surface, as She is in all of us, waiting to be acknowledged and sung into being. My first steps along the priestess path have helped me to sing that song.

Finding the Goddess wasn't a revelation to me. There was no flash, no bolt of lightning. I remember that I had been reading about the Summer Solstice celebrations at Stonehenge in the newspaper and decided that my own beliefs seemed close to those who were there - beliefs about finding divinity in nature and in ourselves, about attuning ourselves to the cycles of the seasons. I decided to find out more and bought some books. It was in those books that I read about the Goddess and my feeling was of remembering, rather than of discovering for the first time. It was as though She was a much-loved friend who had just walked back into the room; "*Oh yes, there you are*", I thought to myself and went back to my book. Writing this now it seems incredible that She returned to me in such a seemingly mundane way. There was a feeling of comfort and *coming home* and yet a knowledge that nothing would ever be the same.

Soon afterwards, in May 2000, I suddenly *knew* that I had to go to Glastonbury, which I had only ever visited on a day trip fifteen years before and had hardly thought about since. I typed *Glastonbury* into an internet search engine, the Glastonbury Goddess Conference appeared, and my journey to becoming a priestess began, although I didn't know that then. I had never been anywhere on my own before and I suppose that that was when the transformation began; in finding the courage to step into the unknown and trust that everything would be OK.

That year the theme of the conference was the Goddess Brigit, who has become incredibly important to me, and it seems right that my first conference was filled with the energy of the Goddess of new beginnings and new life, because that is what She brought to me. I went again to the conference the next year, and carried on reading in between, but didn't feel drawn to a particular path. It never occurred to me that I would be led to become a Priestess of Avalon. In fact, I was quite sure that that was what I didn't want, feeling that a priesthood was hierarchical and unnecessary. I still believe that it's easy for any *religious* group to fall into working in hierarchical ways but being a Priestess of Avalon, and being a member of the Orchard of Avalon, is as much about learning new ways of being in community as it is anything else. I believe that we have been taught to be in competition with each other rather than to truly support each other. We live in a society which glamourises the *cult of the individual* and yet controls each one of us by attempting to force us to conform to narrowly defined stereotypes. This seems to me to be the antithesis of the message of the Goddess and, as a Priestess of Avalon, I am learning to confront and challenge behaviours which take us, as individuals and as a society, away from Her. This ability to speak out, to know when not to, and to believe that we can change things is one of the things that I have learnt as a priestess. As Maggie Kuhn says, "*Speak your mind, even if your voice shakes*".

As for a priestesshood being "unnecessary" I still think a lot about that. I don't believe that anyone needs someone to intercede between them and the Goddess but I also know that I, and many others, have been called to follow the priestess path and that the reason will become clearer as time goes on. In the meantime there are many people who long for ceremonies that honour the seasons and individual rites of passage and don't have the confidence and/or the desire to perform their own and that is part of the reason we are here. Finding the courage to offer these ceremonies has been a major challenge for me and one that I continue to work with. As Kathy once told me, "*You are as strong as She knows you to be.*" And that knowledge has led me to do things that I never would have thought possible. The Goddess knows who I have the potential to be, even when I don't, and I trust her to lead me where I need to go.

The call to begin Priestess of Avalon training came as I began to lead a group called *Avalon in London* (now *Tribe of Avalon*) with my friend Michael, who was already a Priest of Avalon. The group met to celebrate the festivals in the Wheel of the Year and, to start with, I was incredibly nervous and would hardly contribute anything but, for the first time I knew what I wanted to do - to provide opportunities for others to experience and celebrate the energy of the Goddess. That was when I knew that I was being led to train with Kathy in Glastonbury so that I could learn the skills that I would need as a priestess.

I began my training at Samhain 2002 and my first year was deeply transformative. As we moved around the Wheel of BrigitAna with the Wheel of the Year I found that events in my own life would mirror the energy of each Goddess in turn, bringing me many challenges but also a great magic and joy. My learned behaviours, both positive and negative, were thrown into stark relief and the Goddess led me to look at myself and my life in ways that I never had before. I found that if I refused to look at an issue I would be forced to do so and, looking back, I wouldn't have had it any other way. It was truly an experience of being thrown into Cerridwen's cauldron, of being taken to pieces and put back together, and it gave me an understanding of the ways in which the Goddess can work in all our lives. I learned to surrender and trust and I learned that all experiences can lead to deeper knowledge of ourselves and that there is nothing to fear. This is a journey that has continued for me, with each turning of the Wheel and each year of priestess training leading me deeper and deeper into the heart of Her mysteries and so into the heart of my own. I have learnt to open to my creativity, which I had abandoned many years ago. I have learnt to accept myself as a powerful woman, as someone with something to offer. I have learnt to surrender to Her.

I believe that the Goddess works in each of our lives in a different way as Her energy honours us as individuals with our own gifts to bring to the priestess path. Although I hold Brigit, and all Goddesses of the Wheel, deep in my heart I have been led to work with Rhiannon and to express my transformations through my relationships, particularly with men. I have realised that the feelings that I have for the Goddess are those of being *in love*, and that She will always be there for me in ways that others have sometimes not been. This has freed me to developing more honest and more equal relationships with men and to a deeper and more realistic idea of what love is. This has been more healing for me than I could have imagined and has also freed me to direct my energy in other ways, especially towards my work as a priestess.

My love for Her has changed everything, and nothing. I have learnt more than I ever thought possible and I have learnt how little I know. I find that both exciting and liberating and I look forward to deepening my relationship with Her and discovering more of Her nature. I know that I must earn the right to call myself *priestess* with each breath and every heart beat and that there is no part of me that is separated from my path. I am a priestess at every moment, as long as She continues to call me to serve Her and those around me. She has brought me more joy than I had ever thought possible.

Jacqui began her training as a Priestess *of* Avalon *in* 2002 *and continues to train in* Glastonbury. *She facilitates the* Tribe *of* Avalon *(*www.pflondon.org*), which works with the* Wheel *of* BrigitAna *within the sacred landscape of* London *and the* British Isles.

Ren Chapman

What has it meant to me to become a Priestess of Avalon? It has changed my life and given it purpose and direction. It has provided a way to serve the Goddess and to share my love of Her with others. It has forced me to look at myself on a deeper level when things come up so that I can learn from them. It has given me the supreme gift of a circle of amazing friends, women and men who are alive and connected with their lives, their growth and their love for the Goddess. It has opened me up to so much fun and joy.

I was drawn to Avalon from America. Like many I recognized my own past in the writings of Marion Zimmer Bradley. I pursued my memories with further journeying and past life work, and my connections with priestessing were repeatedly validated. I apprenticed with a shamanka for a year and a day. When I moved to England I knew I had to investigate my Avalonian connection, and settled in the Southwest. As soon as I heard Kathy Jones was offering a Priestess of Avalon training, I knew it was for me and I felt a strong sister connection with her when we met. There was no question in my mind about it, this was where I belonged. I have continued through all of my Goddess work feeling that way, there has never been any doubt about being on the right path.

I was in the first training, in 1998/1999. My initiation at the Chalice Well under a full moon was an incredible peak experience. The garden was full of magic and extraordinary life and my connection with Her was complete.

Shortly after that I was asked by a friend, Brenda McNicholls, to speak to a small group on the Goddess and the path that I was pursuing. She leads various courses on Celtic spirituality and journeying and encouraged me to share what I loved with others. I had always had an extreme problem with speaking in front of groups, even taking painful courses to try to get over it. My shyness would cause me nausea and erase any thoughts from my mind and tongue. The difference with that evening was that I was just happily sharing my great love and speaking as Her priestess. I talked openly and easily and led them on a guided journey to meet Her that they found very moving. Soon after that Brenda offered me a day long workshop for some of her students on the Goddess and the Wheel of the Year, and then a four-session course in Gloucester. I will always be indebted to her for encouraging me and giving me those first challenging opportunities. I was off, and anyone who knows me now knows I can talk endlessly once I get started!

Thus it was that I continued priestessing. Before long I was leading handfastings and speaking the words of the Goddess whenever asked. Kathy asked me to help out with the Goddess Conference, and before I knew it I was in the Ceremonial Group, calling to the Goddess in front of 300 people, performing in whatever ceremony or event was called for. And I was having a great time doing it. Since then I have been teaching those that seek Her as I did, teaching the first year of the Priestess of

Avalon course with Brian Charles. What a gift the Lady has given to me, to share Her with those open hearts that are drawn to Her in Avalon.

Ren Chapman has been teaching the first year of the Priestess of Avalon course with Brian Charles for three years, experiencing the great honour of watching people come into their own, blossoming in the love of the Goddess. She participates in the Ceremonial group of the Goddess Conference. She is also a Neonatal Nurse full time and does Reiki with people and with horses. She lives in the beautiful Devon countryside with my cats and has a blessed life!

Brian Charles

Last weekend, nineteen people embarked on their first Circle in the Priest/ess of Avalon training. Only a few years before, I had been in their place. I remember how, with nervousness and a feeling of vast unworthiness, I entered that room. I was convinced that I had nothing to offer. Certain that it was all a mistake and that the Goddess did not, could not, want me. But I came. It seemed the only thing to do. I had heard Her and, in answer, started on the road to being Her priest.

It is difficult to say when I had first heard Her. Was she in the film footage of a young woman placing flowers in the barrels of guns? Or in images from Greenham Common? Or maybe the vision that came as I sat, smoking dope and listening to birdsong, in a ruined, deserted village on the edge of a Yorkshire moor. I saw women walk, proud and free, secure in their power. Like nothing I knew but as familiar as breath. Behind closed eyes, I still see and know it to be a major part of what impels me. Only a part. What I realised on that first weekend still holds true: my whole life was preparation. There were other strands.

Examples of such strands were a book by Geoffrey Ashe I found while working at Whitechapel library in 1968. I had also, around that time, seen an aerial photograph of the Tor in a magazine called *Gandalf's Garden* which, if I remember right, described it as the vulva of the Goddess of Britain. Thus, in a few months, Glastonbury, Avalon and the Goddess came together in my consciousness. Then they sank only to bob in the ocean of nearly forgetting. Until they surfaced and now, melded into one, are never to be sundered.

But I jump ahead. If I had answered the call then, if I had come to Glastonbury in that time of drug-fuelled idealism I would not have been ready. There was a lot more that I had to do. Like drugs and drink, like the bitterness of ideals unattained; like madness and near-despair. All of these were to come.

All my life, I have seen radical wrongness in the way the world is set. No matter how I twisted and contorted, I could not fit. For years I tried and for years I failed. Nothing worked. I spiralled into nihilism, defying all creeds and all persuasions, and fled the damnation I knew as mine. Then, faintly at first, the Goddess began to call. A single parent, I came into the company of women and saw with other eyes, heard with other ears. I became a feminist - no other analysis fits the facts. I read, and read, and read. I began to read of the Goddess and Her return and I began to long for Her and pray to Her. Never did I believe that she would hear me, much less speak to me. Yet the god of the patriarchs still held me in his wrath and, paralysed, I could see no escape. So I drank. Incoherent, I mumbled and stumbled into the dark. Where, finally, defences fell, I met myself, saw my soul. Naked and alone I had to start afresh.

So, slowly, I began to climb. Old beliefs and attitudes had not worked. The evidence was plain, no matter what was wrong in the world my own reaction to it had nearly killed me. I knew I had to find the way that was right for me. Finally, I was able to look clearly at the god of the patriarchs. I found that he no longer had a hold and I was able to resume my search for the Goddess.

Eventually, I found Her. Or rather, found that She had always been with me - holding and protecting me. At the very beginning of my journey up from the dark she made my path cross that of Geraldine and we have been lovers, partners and companions ever since. As the years went by we became more and more obsessed with visiting Glastonbury. Weekend after weekend we would drive from Dorset, walk up the Tor then wander up and down the High Street – looking for a way to buy an approach to Her. For me, it was like chasing something glimpsed beyond a mist. Just as I was about to grasp it, it would dissolve. But each time was a confirmation that I was on the right road, no matter how unclear it seemed.

Then one Lammas day, it all changed. We walked up the Tor - as usual - and then, suddenly, I realised that I had come through the mist and entered Avalon. I cannot tell Geraldine's story of that day, but know that together we decided that the time had come to commit ourselves to Her service. First she, then I, would undertake the Priest/ess training and we would move to Glastonbury.

After major resistance, which involved buying a house in remote rural Wales, we finally arrived in Glastonbury and I became a Priest of Avalon. I cannot describe the changes that have occurred. My life has been given a meaning and fulfilment I never dreamed possible. Deep joy sits in my heart and no longer do I live in fear. Life's problems, although still real, no more overwhelm me. No longer do I need to run and hide in the hills. I am discovering my power and learning how to stand in it. I am surrounded by beauty. Despite all my many flaws, my heart is filled with joy and I feel valued and loved. Never need I feel the aching loneliness of old. After long, blocked, decades I am beginning again to write. I am teaching others and finding the value of my own experience. All the difficulties and pain of the past have been given meaning. Daily, I am shown new challenges and given the opportunity to grow. I am learning to trust my intuition and open my heart. I have found fulfilment. Lifetimes in exile are over and I have come home.

Brian Charles has been a Priest of Avalon for several years. He is a co-founder of and ceremonialist in the Glastonbury Goddess Temple and currently teaches in the Priest/ess of Avalon training course alongside Ren Chapman. His journey through drink, drugs and single parenthood led him to work with men on the fringes of society. He is now concentrating fully on his work as a priest, through writing, teaching, ceremony and workshops, leading him towards work in the former communist states in eastern Europe, particularly Hungary, a country with which he feels a very deep connection.

Geraldine Charles : I'm not Creative..

The Call

Well, how would I know if the Goddess called?
I've read the books, I've yearned for years in vain.
Perhaps I missed it - I was on the phone
or just popped round the corner shop again.

Would She kiss me on the brow, like Keridwen?
Shout yoo-hoo, send me down a heavenly choir
or a form of application in the post?
Or would the sky one day hold words of fire?

Let there be mirth and reverence, She says
Well, if I've erred, it's on the side of mirth.
It's not surprising, when the call did come,
She nudged me on the elbow for its birth.

It's me She wants! I still can't quite believe
it's me She wants - with scepticism intact,

irreverence, as always, to the fore -
She wants me as her priestess - it's a fact.

She's not like God the Father, but with tits,
I don't feel judged, but held; I'm loved and cherished.
I'm Her priestess for life, and furthermore,
it doesn't matter that I'm me, and blemished.

In early September 1971 I got married to my first husband. At nineteen I was worried about being "*left on the shelf*". Many of my friends, good Catholic girls that we were, were already having babies. Some had forgotten that they were supposed to get married first, but we didn't talk about them.

Two weeks after the wedding I found a book called *The Female Eunuch*, by Germaine Greer. Reading it gave me not one, but many life-changing moments – I realised that what had been wrong with my life was less to do with me than with the patriarchal society I inhabited. I can remember jumping up and down as I read it. Sadly, my first husband did not share my huge, happy enthusiasm and at one point threatened to throw the offending book out of the window (and me after it) if I didn't shut up about this women's lib nonsense and get on with being a proper wife. As you can perhaps guess, that relationship didn't last very long. I don't regret the marriage, though, as from it came my lovely daughter, Genevieve.

I had left the Catholic Church when I was seventeen, although for a while as a teenager I was quite active. I loved the ritual, the colour and the beauty and wanted to be a bigger part of it. There didn't however, seem to be very much I could do - apart from become a nun or a good Catholic wife and mother - and I got into a lot of trouble by constantly asking questions and arguing with priests (not done by seventeen-year-old females). I did actually plan to be a nun (for a week after seeing *The Nun's Story* on television!) and starved myself briefly to look interesting. I seem to remember also sleeping on the floor instead of my comfortable bed, but luckily my own natural hunger and desire for ease overcame this asceticism.

Years passed and I read more books and also became active in the radical feminist wing of the women's movement. I found other books by writers like Merlin Stone and Mary Daly and yearned for Goddess, but didn't know where to find her. Starhawk's *The Spiral Dance* helped, but I wanted more. Had I known then that nineteen years would pass before the first inchoate longings for Goddess would culminate in the twentieth – the first priestess training year – I would have felt discouraged. But now I know that this long journey was necessary for me.

Living at Greenham Common off and on for a couple of years gave me a greater insight into goddess spirituality – after all, it is a lot more about what you do than what you say or read. A lot of the actions we did were symbolic and often very magical.

My favourite song from those days says it all, for me.

> *"You can't kill the Spirit*
> *She is like a mountain*
> *old and strong*
> *She goes on and on and on."*
>
> Naomi Littlebear Morena - *"We have a Dream"*

My memories of the next few years, 1984-89, are rather fuzzy, as I had started to drink heavily. Years of not looking after myself emotionally, of not repairing the damage done by a desperately unhappy childhood, came home to roost. It wasn't until I dragged myself into Alcoholics Anonymous that I began to recover and get my life back together. And up to today I haven't had a drink since 1989. One of the things you're told in AA is to get yourself a higher power, a God as you understand him. Thinking about that made me realise afresh that I didn't understand him as a him at all! For example, I don't associate unconditional love with a father, but with a mother. So off I went, reading again, yearning again, for what I thought I could never have – a relationship with the Goddess. But at least I do understand the higher power as it works for me. Who needs alcohol when you can have Goddess?

I read an awful lot. A book a day isn't unheard of, certainly four or five a week, with favourites returned to again and again. But books can be my enemies as well as my friends, removing me from the world and its joys and challenges. I had long believed that I was one of life's students, readers and administrators, and school sewing lessons had quickly convinced me that I could barely thread a needle - so much so that faced with the challenge of sewing a Bridie doll in honour of the Maiden Goddess at the Imbolc circle of the priestess training, I flatly stated to the group and the universe at large, "I'*m not creative*!"

Now, I create and continuously recreate the Goddess Conference and many other websites, and people tell me they're beautiful. I also designed temple posters regularly for five years or so, and have made posters and artwork for other organizations (all on my beloved computer). I also write stories, articles and poems and have recently begun to be published in poetry magazines. I've made a Bridie doll for myself almost every year since the first time – because I enjoy it! Friends smile when I enthusiastically tell them about my latest project and say, "*But you're not creative, Geraldine*!" What can I do but laugh at myself?

It's interesting now to look back at the training and see other points where I dug my heels in, usually because I couldn't see why I had to do something that struck me either as silly or unnecessary. In fact it was usually something I wasn't good at or felt embarrassed to do. These days I get on with enjoying the fun, not caring so much what people think. And I understand the reasons for the training activities and the reasons for my resistance.

Another big change is still in progress. I've been a computer tech. for years, and while I enjoy the work it gradually occurred to me that I wanted a change (well, I did ask for transformation!) and now I'm training in counselling and psychotherapy. Emotional and spiritual intelligences now seem more important to me than any other kind, I privileged mind over spirit and body for far too long. I plan to have a wonderful time as I get older, counselling, teaching, writing and designing.

How can I tell you how much the Priestess of Avalon training meant to me? Not just opening the creative floodgates, but learning so much more about myself, stretching to reach what I can almost do – and then passing that barrier and reaching up again. The learning and changing didn't end with that training, but continues to this day, the process once begun seems unstoppable – not that I want it to stop! I used to think, "*I wish I were more like her – or her.*" Today I'd rather be more like me, and enjoy the discovery of who I really am.

There is no glass ceiling on a Goddess Temple, the learning, creating, joy and deep knowing of the Goddess just go on and on and on. She is like a mountain – just as you think you've reached the summit, that there can be no more wonderful experiences, no more learning, you see the next peak beckoning!

Geraldine Charles is a Priestess of Avalon, co-founder of the Glastonbury Goddess Temple, writer and web designer. For many years she has been webmistress of the beautiful Goddess Conference website, the Goddess Temple and Kathy's own websites. A trained counsellor and former director of the Isle of Avalon Foundation, Geraldine also runs an online correspondence course called "Getting to know the Goddess".

Rose Flint

It begins in the candle flame. Each morning I light the flame on my altar and light the answering spark within myself. Every time I see the flame I know she is with me. Sometimes I am rushing, going too fast, late, out of time – but I always pause to do this one simple act of faith and she centres me, holds me, gives me the strength to go faster if I must, if that is what she wants of me, now.

I have learned not only to find her in stillness and solitude. Or in the companionship of others who centre the spirit of themselves around the Lady. Being her Priestess has taken me into a harsher world, another reality. I am always longing for stars - stillness to be at my heart - but there will be time enough, eventually. For now, while I can move with any energy, she is asking me to move fast.

When I trained as a Priestess I wanted to assert some place in myself that kept itself hidden. I wanted to acknowledge to myself and the world that the Goddess was my guide, my faith, my heart's pathway. I knew that she had work for me but I did not know what it was. I knew it would be to mediate the goddess in some aspect, to bring her into the community - for this is the work a priestess must do. I know now that I do this - in part - simply by holding her in my heart. Loving the Lady informs my thoughts and actions, but there are three aspects of service, which I see as my present work as a Priestess - I write sacred poetry, I use the healing power of poetry in my work, and I am a ceremonialist.

I believe that the Goddess is the One and the Many Named, yet still I find that I need the intermediary of someone who is specific, someone close and touchable, someone who understands - and has chosen me. Although there are several goddesses whose being informs my life, it is Bridget that I sense closest to me in my day to day work. She is the goddess of poetry and healing, fired with inspiration and craft, the keeper of hearthfire, smith fire. Fire is the element of the poet.

Since I became a Priestess my life work has changed greatly I have always been an artist and a writer, used to travelling the worlds in my imagination. I worked as a creative writing tutor, visiting schools, running residencies, lecturing. I had begun to notice how creativity could often unleash deeply held feelings, sometimes long suppressed, in both children and adults and I often found myself out of my depths, a poet trying to deal with someone's traumatic experience or grief. I became interested in how I could learn to work with this, and at the same time as my priestess training I also trained as an art therapist, finishing both in 1999. Since then, I have used poetry more and more as a healing tool, working in settings as diverse as doctor's surgeries, a spinal unit, neonatal intensive care and mental health.

I know now that this is Bridgid's work. She has been guiding me towards it for many years. Poetry and healing have been connected throughout history and it is only in modern times that care for the sick has separated body and mind from soul. I often work with people who are dying, or have experienced life-changing accidents or illnesses and again and again I find people who are spiritually starved - people who want to find ways of soothing the soul they hardly dare acknowledge they have, people who have an intense spirituality which they cannot articulate. W.B. Yeates called poetry *'the voice of the soul'* and I think that its metaphoric language can open a gateway into the Otherworld where a spiritual healing can happen. I use images of the natural world to create this gateway, sometimes encouraging people to write, sometimes simply reading poems. Always, the Lady is with me. I acknowledge her presence in the room, know that she holds us all as we work.

My own poetry has been changed by the Goddess. Sometimes I write using sacred forms such as incantations or prayer which I can bring to the Temple as gifts when we open ceremonies to the community. Sometimes the writing of a poem is in itself a meditation and the poem then contains that, whoever reads it. I also use the poetry as part of the work I do as a ceremonialist, writing new pieces especially to perform at the Goddess Conference each year, and also making poems from some of the experiences we all share at that magical time. Much of the priestess work I do as a poet is necessarily solitary but as we celebrate the Wheel of the year with the goddesses of Britain I joy in the priestess work that brings me into the heart of the community of goddess-loving women from all over the world. The conference is for me a time of spiritual renewal when I will happily smudge hundreds of bodies, clean and sweep out rooms, console the upset, sing (!) fetch and carry, sit without moving for hours, face fear, forget to eat, run everywhere, be exhausted - and still dance. Its all part of the job

And every day, and every night, I light the candle.

HEALING LOVE

The Goddess Conference, Glastonbury, Lammas

We have made a temenos in the evening hall,
lit the altar candles, set singing voice

and crystal bowl within a shadowed quietness
so wave on wave, sweetness resonates in air:
white as milk and swan – Bridget's *love*
called into this moment through hour on hour
of pilgrimage and celebration: her golden sun
lodged both within us and within the pathways
that we have walked across this sacred land.
Nineteen *priestesses offer healing*
and within each hand, each connected touch
lies the link of Bridget's *forging, her care of us*
a chain of gentle flame where all that's dross
becomes transmuted through her love.

Rose Flint *is a* Priestess *of* Avalon, *a poet and artist. She works as* Lead Writer *for the* Kingfisher Project, *taking poetry into the community and hospital of* Salisbury *and as a freelance creative writing tutor; previous residencies have included* 'Writing *and* Spirituality' *with* Alison Leonard, 'Landlines' *with* Robert Minhinnick *and* 'Poetry *and* Healing' *with* David Hart. *Her poetry can be found in many anthologies and she has three collections,* Blue Horse *of* Morning (Seren), Firesigns (Poetry Salzburg) *and* Nekyia (Stride).

Sally Pullinger

I first came to Avalon in 1981 and finally settled here in 1984. In 1971 my husband Martin had died leaving me alone in London with our baby daughter Sophie. My grief had led me to connect with Martin in the spirit world and then to journey deeply into that world, so that by 1978 I had been trained as a trance medium, my spirit guide being a Tibetan monk called Chung Fu. Having travelled from convent christianity through widow-hood and into a home-brewed brand of buddhism, I arrived on the sacred Isle of Avalon at the age of 35 with 3 children, a large polygamous family, and a heart full of music, crystals, and the spirit world.

I was initiated into the magical energies of Avalon through a series of challenging emotional and spiritual experiences involving the break-up of our large extended family and the breakdown of my relationship with the father of my two sons. My emotional and spiritual world fell into a constant process of deconstruction and repair with only one or two constants, the main ones being the love with my children, my relationship with Chung Fu, and the certainty of extra-dimensional reality and life after physical death. In 2000 the tragic death of my friend's beautiful six year old daughter opened my heart into a fathomless depth and it was in that condition that the Goddess called me back to Her. Although I had known Kathy for many years, I suddenly felt strongly magnetised towards her and towards the journey with the Goddess. Every step of this journey has been and still is life-changing, and every change in my life is another step on this extraordinary blessed journey. Although this is only the sixth year of my journey with the Goddess as a Priestess of Avalon, I feel as though I have stepped into another, more vast dimension of time spanning centuries past, present and future. After 24 years tossed around on the shores of Avalon, I now feel deeply held in the strong and tender embrace of the Goddess. I live with my family on Windmill Hill in Avalon, to the Northwest of the Tor, right next to Paradise Valley. We are neighbours to the ancient Morgens and the Faeryfolk of Avalon, and to the foxes, badgers, deer, buzzards, and to the sacred apple, oak, and hawthorn trees. I live with my daughter Sophie who is also a Priestess of Avalon, my two dynamic and creative sons, Deshan and Jerome, and my granddaughter Gabrielle, one of the growing generation of Goddess-adoring young teenagers.

In 2002 I formed *Vocalana*, a small Goddess choir, to sing my song cycle "*Singing the Wheel of BrigitAna*". These songs were written during my training with Kathy as I reached to connect with the Goddesses on her Wheel of Ana, and tried to memorise their qualities, animal totems, power tools and emblems. The joy I experience when a song percolates through to my ears from the ethers is intense, and it has been a huge fulfilment to feel the Goddess blessing the creation and recording of this music in Her honour. I have visions of creating a massive Goddess choir and also a rock band ..... *all in Her Own Good Time* ...... The creation of the Glastonbury Goddess Temple and the gathering of a community of Priests and Priestesses in Avalon have brought an unprecedented centring and a cohesion to my spiritual life. However, as its popularity has grown, most of the ceremonies we conduct in this beautiful space are now overcrowded.

I am so inspired by the possibilities of creating an idyllic Goddess-centred haven and Temple somewhere in the landscape of Avalon. The prospect of being able to choose total immersion in Goddess service is incredibly exciting - visioning the new Temple with all the potential details of surrounding activities, residential area, concert hall, music facilities, therapy rooms, retreat space, land for outdoor ceremony, sweat lodge, water features, windpower, gardens for food, herbs and flowers, woodlands and wild spaces, a total world dedicated to the life of the soul in service to the Goddess. Once we have succeeded in creating this, such places will start springing up everywhere. These are the seeds She is birthing and nurturing.

It is a most wonderful experience to witness year after year the very special people who are drawn to journey with the Goddess in Avalon and who then either settle here and join our growing local community of priestesses and priests, or go back to their own lands and give birth to their own sacred wheels and traditions, leading others to remember and reconnect with the ancient Goddesses all over the world. Slowly but surely we are weaving healing webs of love and unity in the name of the Goddess and bringing Her back into many many lives.

Being a professional trance medium I spend a great deal of time in altered states of consciousness. The most nourishing, exciting and fulfilling experiences I have had and continue to have during the course of my work as a Priestess of Avalon are those which involve the invitation and invocation of Her presence inside us. For me, to be a Priestess of Avalon is to open myself more and more to the phenomenal reality of Her Being and to the sensual experience of Her taking over my physical body, my heart, and my mind, and to know beyond a shadow of doubt that She works miracles in the hearts and souls of Her priestesses and priests and of all who are willing to open and to receive Her. The energies, love, songs, words and blessings that I have heard and experienced coming through Her priestesses are so precious and so deeply healing and moving, and I long for ever-increasing opportunities to do this work. My final tribute has to be to Kathy for her initiatory and inspiring leadership, her stunning moral courage, her sometimes uncomfortably acute perceptions and reflections, and her generous and supportive friendship in my life. I hope I may be able to contribute something towards the very substantial existing body of her work in service to the Goddess. Blessed Be.

Sally Pullinger has been a trance medium for 28 years, working with her guide Chung Fu, a Tibetan monk, soul healer and spiritual teacher. Since initiating as a Priestess of Avalon, she has been calling the Goddess into her sessions and receiving many signs of Her Presence and Blessings. She now trains others to work directly with their guides and spirit helpers.

Sally is also an accomplished musician, performer and teacher. She coaches young music ensembles, both jazz and classical, coaches and conducts two choirs, and composes both choral and instrumental music.

Heather Elizabeth Adams : *The Song of a Priestess*

I stood on the grounds of Glastonbury Abbey, a blue-skied day of sunshine at the Summer Solstice in 1996. The Tor rose in the distance beyond the ruins. I felt a rumbling inside that made my bones quake, my vocal chords vibrate in a humming sound, and my head swoon from the energetic rush. It seemed I had been waiting for this moment all my life, a turning point, a calling, a finding of something I had longed for, but I wasn't quite sure what it all meant. My emotions overwhelmed me. I was rooted there, transfixed, and thankful that my fellow tour members were at some distance from me, my sunglasses hiding the tears that filled my eyes. I forced myself to walk ahead through the cushiony grass, past the Lady Chapel, closer to the energies of the Tor. There would be no time to climb it today with our short two hour stop, but my dream was coming true before my eyes, my dream of coming to this sacred place and feeling every ounce of its magic. It was at that point that the rumbling inside became a voice, and I heard Her, "*You will accomplish great things. Your writing will serve others and teach them through your words. Open your heart and mind and follow your path filled with legends....*" I felt a calm inside, a surety, a belief in my path that I had never before known. I felt *home*. I had been called by the Goddess.

Three years later I found myself preparing to move from Chicago to London to begin a new life. My two-hour pilgrimage to Glastonbury had somehow energetically manifested a fast-track of changes in my life to prepare me for my destiny. My soon-to-be husband was English, and as we discussed the possibilities for our wedding, my initial sense was that we had to find a way to marry in Glastonbury. It seemed the perfect place to celebrate a sacred joining in the landscape that had spoken to the depths of my soul. Sitting thousands of miles away at my computer in Chicago, I began my search on the Internet for a woman to perform the ceremony—I *knew* it had to be a woman. Sure enough, the first site that popped up had a link to Kathy Jones, so I e-mailed her immediately to find out if she would be interested in performing our ceremony. This is how our relationship began, and once again, it all fell into place like the pieces of a patchwork quilt, comfortable and familiar.

At our first meeting with Kathy to discuss our wedding blessing, I noticed one of her pamphlets for the Priest/ess of Avalon course. My fiancé picked it up and said, "T*his would be perfect for you*!" I agreed and had a strong sense that my connection to Glastonbury was just beginning. Kathy created a lovely wedding blessing for us in Chalice Well, once again on the

Summer Solstice, three years after I had first encountered the mysterious energies of Avalon. As we were saying farewell to Kathy that day, she turned to me and said, "I *will see you again, soon.*" She smiled, and I felt tingles all over because I knew what she had said was prophetic—I knew that I was meant to do the priestess training with her. I smiled and nodded in return, saying, "*Yes, you will.*" At Samhain a few months later, my journey into the mysteries of the Lady of Avalon truly began.

My journey to the first training circle was somewhat disconcerting. My husband dropped me off at a local inn where I had made reservations. As I stood in the pub, the manager informed me that she had given away my room to someone else and to try back later. She offered to watch my luggage for me, which seemed a very slight concession for the aggravation, and then offered to book me into another local hotel if no rooms turned up. I *knew* that I was being *tested* by the Goddess at that point, a test for the journey that was about to unfold. "H*ow badly do you want to enter into the sacred cauldron of my mysteries*?" She seemed to be saying. Suddenly, the fluidity of the journey to bring me there, from my tourist days to my speedy transplant into a new culture, felt rocky and frightening. Here I was an American in a foreign country, with no place to stay for the weekend, and filled with sudden fears and insecurities about embarking on a life course that was far from my realm of academic experiences. What was I doing? Was I crazy? How could I do this training for a full year when I couldn't even trust the locals to keep a hotel reservation? I steeled my stomach inside and whispered to the Lady, "I *can do this*." I had faced worse fears than this. I knew somehow that all would be well. I told the innkeeper that I expected her to find me a local reservation by dinner-time and for her to pay for my transport to the next hotel if necessary. She agreed. Crisis resolved. Then I marched myself over to join in our first training circle - and I never looked back. I had passed the first test of Ceridwen, the Crone of Samhain, and accepted Her challenge of self-death, to face my deepest fears, to clear away the old to make way for the seeds of the new to grow.

After overcoming my initial fears of not being accepted for being *American*, for feeling different, a student of a spiritual path in a country that was not of my birth, I quickly realized that my sisters and brothers were dealing with their own feelings of insecurity, their own feelings of *am I worthy of* Her, their own issues of facing their greatest fears on this path of self-discovery, on this path of being human. I found a community of support, where we each shared the difficulties and joys of our journeys, as we delved deeper into our spiritual explorations, our senses of our selves, and how that would manifest in our spiritual work for each of us.

I spent the next four years immersing myself in the energies of the Goddess, doing further training courses, and basing my PhD work around the exploration of Goddess myths and archetypes. My academic and spiritual worlds seemed sharply divided, but inside I was learning to bridge the gap, opening my heart and soul to the powerful visionary experiences I was having, while constantly gathering more and more information for my mind. My emotional experiences and my research seemed to be merging together into Understanding, into Knowledge, the Divine Oneness of Her mysteries. One of my most profound experiences was standing in the water of the Vesica Piscis at Chalice Well, arm-in-arm with other priestesses, all of us serving as ceremonialists for the Goddess Conference. As we swirled our feet in the waters in an impromptu dance, the energies seemed to spiral into the air around us. I felt the now-familiar vibration in my body of Her energies bursting out through my vocal chords in haunting tones, echoing and harmonizing with the sounds of my sisters. We circled and sang and became One, One in ourselves, One with each other, One in Her. I knew in that moment that She had shown me the glorious euphoria of Her mysteries, a completion, a feeling of absolute calm and perfection.

It was only a month after this profound experience at Chalice Well that my greatest challenge happened, and my world fell apart. One of my greatest fears was realized when I discovered that my husband had been cheating on me, and I refused to accept his demands to continue on with his affair. At the risk of losing all, I filed for divorce. It seemed that my journey in England had come full-circle, bringing me back to Chalice Well where it had begun, and now the Goddess was returning me to the land of birth. Once again, I felt the fear of being abandoned, of being without a *home* - for England, the Lady of Avalon, the sacred landscape of Britain, the Priestesses and Priests of Avalon had all become my *home*. In my moments of heartache, I felt that perhaps the Lady had abandoned me and that She was *kicking me* out of England before I was ready to go. It was at this point that one of my fellow priestesses said to me, "*Don't you see - you weren't called here to marry your husband, or even to do your PhD. You were called here by the Goddess to train as a Priestess of Avalon, and you have done that. The other things were simply a means to keep you here. You have learned all you came to learn and to do here - and now the Goddess is calling you back to the US to continue your spiritual work there.*" I felt tingles all over. I knew that the words of my wise friend were very true, and that the Goddess was speaking through her.

Leaving my *home* of England was a bittersweet departure that tore at my soul. But even as I departed its shores, I knew that I was taking a bit of Avalon with me, that it lives inside of me. Now I try to bring the gifts of the Goddess to the people who live in the US in my own way. Just a few short months after my return to the United States, I began training priest/esses and delved into my writing with a deep passion. All responsibilities now temporarily *removed*, I could focus on building the foundations of my work and recreating my life. Now I have my own organization, T*he Sacred Sept of the Swan*, which is dedicated to trainings, online courses, events, pilgrimages, and retreats for those who have a love of the Goddess. I am also working on two spiritual books to share in the fruits of my *knowledge* I have gleaned from my experiences and research on my path with the Goddess. The latest *gift* was in recently being hired to teach at a nearby university and finding that others in my department not only knew of Kathy's work but are also followers of the Goddess, giving me a newfound support community and enabling me to bridge the gap even further between my academic life and my spiritual path. Now I see very clearly how it all was destined, part of the fabric of Her sacred tapestry. I faced my darkest fears and challenges and was birthed anew in a way that has prepared me for the work ahead. Through my writing and teaching, I hope to help enable others to find their own way to Her, to find the Truths of their souls, so that they, too, can learn to sing the glories of the Divine Feminine that lives within them, as they co-create with the Goddess in sacred union.

If you dedicate yourself to a path that is also in service to Her, you are making the highest commitment of all -to yourself. By trusting in the journey, by facing your greatest lessons and challenges with gratitude, grace and joy, you learn better how to heal yourself, and thus, to heal others as well. Although I *knew* this before I began my journey as a priestess, now She has given me greater riches in my soul that I can pull out and allow to sparkle like diamonds, gifts of Her wisdom to share with the world. I am no longer afraid of doing that. For no matter what others may think of my words or gifts or how I am judged, I have learned to validate myself, to stand in the Truths of my own power as a beacon for others to learn to do the same, just as I had promised to do when I said my vows to Her as a Priestess of Avalon. In the Goddess's eyes, it is all sacred, we are all sacred and loved and worthy. Although my voice is but one singing in the apple trees of Her sacred orchard, still I must *sing* the tune of my soul, unique and yet One with the harmonious song of All, a part of the legends of Avalon, found anew....

Heather Adams is currently living in Virginia, where she is teaching university and writing two books about the Goddess, based upon her spiritual experiences and research. She is founder of the organization the Sacred Sept of the Swan, open to those who are dedicated to the path of the Goddess, and provides various courses and retreats. She can be contacted at castleeire@gmail.com.

Sandra Roman

"A *person of medicine, a person of true wisdom*
is somebody who learns how to transform her limitations into power.
Not everything is possible.
But everything is possible if it's a true part of your destiny."

I wrote this sentence as a part of a letter I sent to a young woman some time ago. She was complaining because "*she couldn't*" go to Glastonbury and become a Priestess of Avalon. She made me remember the times when I decided not to be an opera singer. I love to sing and I love to stand on a stage, wearing beautiful clothes, uttering heavenly sounds from my throat and receiving lots of applause and admiration from people. It sounds gorgeous, doesn't it? But it's only a little part that we can see of a person who is walking a very long path. An opera singer has to work a lot to become that. She can't do any other thing but to train very hard, studying and practising during many hours. She has to be obsessed with caring for her diet and her health. In other words, she has to surrender her whole life in order to accomplish her task.

So I asked myself, "Do I *really want to change my own life to do that*?" The answer was, obviously, "N*o*". So I decided to continue working as a successful journalist and earning money enough to buy beautiful dresses and a very expensive car, which was as important to me as it was my little baby. Of course, I didn't feel happy with my success. I felt an empty void inside me. I knew that I was living in a way that had nothing to do with my true mission in this lifetime. But I didn't know what the mission was that I had committed to do here, before my birthing.

I was agnostic for most of my life, instead of studying in catholic schools, or maybe because of that. So the Goddess had to call me very many times before I noticed that She was doing that! Anyway, it seems very strange that a girl who never believed in any other world but the materialistic physical world, who lived only inside the boundaries of her own mind, could be conscious that each person has a very special task to do in her life...

My first experience of the Goddess was something that happened to me when my mother had breast cancer. I felt really desperate because doctors had not a word of hope for us. So I remembered of a rosary beautifully made of perfumed rose petals which a beloved friend gave me some years previously. I took it in my hands and I decided to ask Mary for help.

"I *don't know if you truly exist*", I told Her. "B*ut if you are in some place of the* Univers*e, please, send me a signal* I *can understand*. I *need to know how to prepare myself to help my mother.* W*hether you give me good or bad news*, I *need to know what can happen to her and how can* I *help her*".

I was sobbing and having difficulty breathing. I couldn't make any noise because my mother was on the other side of the wall in the next room. Instantly I felt a sweet calmness inside me and I sensed a breath of fresh air surrounding my whole body.

My mother was treated with hard therapies but finally she was healed. It was 17 years ago and she's now a happy grandmother and a very committed Priestess of the Goddess.

Nevertheless I didn't yet know anything about the Goddess, nor that Mary could indeed be the Goddess. Six more years passed until I met an astrologer who told me about Her Divinity and recommended lots of books to me which talked about the Sacred Feminine. She also taught me how to read the Motherpeace Tarot Deck and with time we became friends.

During a trip we both took to a sacred place in Argentina, I experienced what I knew later was Her call to become Her Priestess. We were going to a very mysterious hill at midnight. I felt scared and quite excited at the same time. Then I heard a voice from inside myself which told me: "*You are really going to a place with no return. Are you sure you want to go?*"

I felt a different kind of beat in my heart, a sense of such an extraordinary adventure waiting for me. "*Yes*", I said, without any shadow of doubt. "*Just tell me where* I *have to stop*", I added, remembering I was driving my car over an unknown road. The voice told me that I was going to receive a signal to stop. And I found it, looking at my friend´s face. She looked so frightened. She told me she was hearing a voice inside her telling her we were going to a place of "*no return*", but she answered "N*o*" to the voice. "I *have a teenage daughter who really needs me*", she said with a tiny voice. So we came back to the hotel without the slightest idea of the meaning of what had happened to us.

As many women of my generation, I was captured by Marion Zimmer Bradley´s book, *The Mists of Avalon*. But that world seemed to be only a fantasy in my life. Anyway I decided to create a chat room called *Camelot*, where I was Vivian, the Lady of the Lake. Each night for a year, I played with a group of people at being different heroines, heroes, gods, goddesses and other characters from myth and literature. If somebody asked me "*Who are you*?" I didn't hesitate to answer: "*I'm from the Holy Island. I'm a Priestess of Avalon...*" I can't remember when this game became serious for me. One day I found myself being a kind of teacher and counsellor with lots of people asking me for help and healing, when I couldn't either help nor heal my own self.

Real and *virtual* life seemed to start to blend, as if I were upon a barge, going nowhere in the middle of the mists.

At those strange moments of crisis, I found Kathy's website and surprisingly I discovered that fantasies could be an important part of our true destiny if we can only find the courage to say "*Yes*" and jump the first step to the truly real life. I had thought I was condemned to live a life in black and white, while on the other side of the world a group of women were creating together another and colourful way of being alive on the Earth. I could see them dressing in red and fuchsia and orange, with beautiful hairdresses, full of flowers. Some of them seemed to be very proud to show their lovely grey hair as a symbol of their wise age. I could see their beautiful art: drawings, banners, sculptures, screenplays. I could see them dancing barefoot over the green grass on beautiful green hills, honouring the Moon and the Waters and the Sun and the whole existence as our beloved Mother Goddess. I felt happy to find such powerful women and I told myself another "*Yes*". I wanted to do something to help to create a most beautiful world.

I didn't know exactly what it meant to become a Priestess of the Goddess. But I could guess that it means to surrender my whole life to serve Her. I wrote to Kathy asking for a place in her training. When she accepted me I decided to sell my flat and my beautiful pampered car, I gave away furniture, clothes, books and anything so I could fly lightly over 11,000 kilometres (7,000 miles) from Buenos Aires to Glastonbury.

My one year of training (as the priestess training was when Sandra trained) was absolutely more difficult than I could ever have thought. The struggle with the language wasn't the only obstacle I found. Too soon my money flew out and I worked very hard to pay my expenses. Many times I felt confused and sad and alone. During the whole year I did pilgrimages to the holy places where I could remember some of my past lives and I faced my own monsters and ghosts. I wandered the dark trails of my soul to discover not only what my mission is, but who I really am and what my place is as a daughter of the Goddess.

After my initiation as a Priestess of Avalon I said goodbye to the only place I could recognize as my home. I understood that the Goddess needs me in the sacred place where she called me and my sacred vow to Her was to say "*Yes*" to Her anytime and anywhere She calls me.

I came back to my country where I have a lot of work to do, helping other women who are just as I was, seeking for their inner Goddess, struggling to restore Her beauty in their own lives. I love my work as a priestess, teaching, listening, accompanying, doing sacred ceremonies, honouring the land and all the divinity which lives "*inside me and all around me*".

As a priestess, I've learned that my way to the Goddess is a perpetual learning. My work as a teacher is based on my own daily apprenticeship. I've learnt to accept and celebrate whatever lessons She sends me. And I've also learned that healing myself is the best I can do to help the healing of my sisters and our beloved planet.

I don't need expensive dresses or applause, nor fast and sophisticated cars in order to feel alive, because I've found the true song of my spirit and She is the Goddess. My ceremonial mask and robes are not frivolous, but my true sacred face and my goddessy skin. They are a kind of vehicle we as priestesses need to travel to the otherworld.

Where you see a beautiful Priestess performing a powerful ritual you can see a gorgeous lady, perhaps not an ordinary girl, but the Magic Presence who inhabits her human body during the ceremony. To become that she must have trained herself very hard. The beauty you see is a product of the many kilometres she has travelled into the darkness of her own spirit seeking for her true bright soul. But it's such an adventure. So I don't hesitate to answer "*Yes*" when somebody asks me, "D*id you really want to change your own life to do that*?"

I can't imagine any better way to be alive in this beautiful and so exciting world which the Goddess creates and keeps for us. I can't imagine how the world could be so many centuries without the Goddess and Her priestesses. It couldn't be a true life.

Sandra Roman Self-initiated as a Priestess *of* Avalon, *in* Glastonbury, *in* 2000. *She lives in* Buenos Aires, *Argentina, where she teaches a three-year* Priest/*ess training to serve the Goddess of the* Southern Cross. *She also runs workshops in Spain, Uruguay and Chile. You can find her website at www.geocities.com/srostrosdeladiosa*

Sandra Warmerdam

My first visit to Avalon was at Beltane 2000 and I can only describe it in one way; it was coming home! Seeing the nature of Avalon, the landscape, the feminine energy and of course the Glastonbury Tor awakened something in me which was asleep for a very long time. That night of Beltane eve I was sitting on the Tor for the whole night with a wise old crone and we talked all night. Before me I saw a hill with Priestesses dancing and feasting around a Beltane fire and the only thought I had then was that it must be priestesses who are celebrating Beltane. Because it was dark I couldn't take a picture but I wanted to do it with dawn. When the sky became lighter, a call that the sun was coming, the hill disappeared and also the priestesses. It was then that I realized that I had seen something behind the veil of Avalon, something old and something that was deep in my soul.

From that night there was only one desire in me, to serve the Lady of Avalon and to be in her landscape. It was a year later that I was back in Avalon and bought the book "*In the Nature of Avalon*" by Kathy Jones and read about a Priest/ess of Avalon training. Everything felt in its place, this felt so good. There was a vibration of energy from those words - Priestess of Avalon, so familiar, so much me.

The training itself was one recognition of sisterhood, old friends, familiar names of the Goddess and most of all the Lady of Avalon. Each circle was a coming home and a remembering of the time that women served the Goddess. I felt for sure that I had done that before, also there in Avalon. During the training I had the natural feeling that I had to move back to Avalon, to serve the Goddess, to be one with her and Her landscape. I felt homesick when I was leaving Glastonbury and cried. The only thing that helped was to know that I would be back in a short time.

At one point the feeling was changing and I realized that I took Avalon with me in my heart and it was not only a place in Glastonbury any more. From that moment two other journeys started - find the Goddess and the Lady in Holland. Did we ever have our own Goddesses? What can be found of Her and what memories are left of Her? The other part was a desire to help people, especially women, to heal them, to take them to Avalon, to meet the Goddess and to find the same transformation as I did. Together with a very dear friend Manon Tromp, who also did trainings in Glastonbury, we started a small travel agency. Each time we took about six women with us to Glastonbury and taught them about the Goddess, the Lady of Avalon and her nature. Every time we saw women change, being healed and becoming stronger. They became more in their own feminine power. We were questioned about having a place to meet in Holland, a place to celebrate the festivals of the Goddess as they had seen in the Glastonbury Temple.

Being a Priestess of Avalon, you learn from experience, that you just have to ask and trust the Goddess, that she provides everything needed by those who love Her. So in a very short time we had an office space which could be transferred in a Temple for free. We didn't had to pay rent the first year or costs like heating, water and electricity. At that point I was working on a Dutch wheel, but it was not finished. So we started with the Avalon Goddesses in a Dutch wheel. The first ceremony at the Autumn Equinox 2003 was visited by 25 women and 1 man. Manon and I called in all the Goddesses and at the same time there was a meeting in the Glastonbury Temple of Priestesses of Avalon who sent their energy to us. It was an amazing experience and the people felt the presence of the Goddess. Manon and I felt carried by her, doing something so big, with so less experience, so full of trust that She was with us.

The number of people was growing with every ceremony. Women wanted to join us, wanted to be connected to the Goddess once more. Beautiful women, with only trust, came to help us calling in the directions and the Goddess. They wanted to know more about Her. We decided to give workshops about the Goddess, Her energies and Her power. I didn't have any experience in giving workshops and of course I had a lot of doubts about whether I was capable to do this. She had always just one answer to me, "*Just trust me*!" After a number of workshops I decided to give a year training to people who wanted to serve the Goddess as I had learned. This started with Samhain 2004 and ended with their magical dedication in Avalon during the Autumn Equinox 2005.

Together we learned much about the Dutch Goddesses and their energies. The most important Goddess is Nehalennia. She is the Goddess of my country, like the Lady of Avalon. Learning about her, meditating and celebrating Her we found out that there are a lot of similarities between Nehalennia and the Lady of Avalon. So much that they are like sisters. But aren't they all?

Suthisa Hein, a Dutch Priestess of Avalon and I found out about a very special place in the Old Land, with a Stone circle, a mini Tor, a huge labyrinth and moon shaped pond and we fell in love with the place and the energies. We decided to create a celebration in the Dutch Goddess' honour. In the summer of 2005 we invited Priestesses of Avalon to come and give Nehalennia her rightful place back in Holland. We held a four day conference to teach the people more about Her. Joining the sisterhood of the Goddess, amazing Goddess-loving women gave their talents and energies and together we were celebrating her abundance. People were recognizing each other and the connection between us. The Priestesses of Avalon gave their flame to the Dutch Priestesses in a Stone circle in the Old Land, so that they are back in our hearts, souls and lives. It was a huge success and it will be happening again next summer.

So, how did being a Priestess of Avalon change my life? Well, what did not change, except my love for the Goddess. I am challenged every day to make the most of it. Every day is a new beginning, a new connection with Her. Being a Priestess made me write about the Goddess, made me more creative, painting and sculpting. It brought me beautiful like-minded people who want to serve Her as much as I do and every day I feel loved by Her.

In my vow to her I said I will try to bring the Goddess back into my own country. Well, with a lot of help from others we are succeeding. There is still a lot to do but seeing the amount of people growing who are remembering Her by hearing her names warms my heart. It makes me proud to say: "*I am a Priestess of Avalon in* Holland *this lifetime*!"

Sometimes I am overwhelmed by all that she gives me and on the other hand by what she is asking of me. My whole life has turned upside down. But I love it and I love Her, the Goddess with the ten thousands names in Avalon and here in Holland.

Sandra Warmerdam lives in Holland *and is the co-founder of the* Dutch Goddess *Temple in* Hillegom *and of the* Dutch Goddess *Conference, as well as being a teacher of* Temple Priestesses. *You can find more information about her work at www.avalon-mystic.nl*

Samantha Linasche

I Self-initiated as a Priestess of Avalon at the millennium, it was quite a powerful and life changing time for me. The Connections I made to the Landscape of Avalon on all levels mystical and mundane have profoundly altered my life. Before becoming a priestess, My relationship to the Goddess was more about what She could do for me. It was Ego based, full of illusion. After becoming a priestess of Avalon, I have found that my relationship to the Goddess is about What I can do for her. Her being, the divine feminine energy of life that abides in me and around me, and is present in all people and Places. I vowed to serve the Lady by whatever name she calls me, whatever land she draws me to. She took me at my word. Not a few weeks after my initiation I had to leave the UK due to visa complications and return to my homeland, California, USA. Here I found my way of service by developing a sacred wheel for the Land. Based off of many years of research and intuitive hard work, I managed to draw together the *Wheel of Place*. I now train priestesses and priests of Place, in San Jose, California.

Who would have thought it would take me leaving the USA and becoming a Priestess of Avalon that would lead me back home to my Native Ancestors, to connect in spirit to the land? I am of Scots-Irish, Cherokee and Osage ancestry. The service to the Goddess I do now, here, within the land of the Miwok, Ohlone, and Wintu People ties me so deeply not just to this land but also to the heart of Avalon. Finding the Goddess, the elements and the path of right-relationship with all things wherever I go, is deeply powerful and empowering. My journeys now take me even further abroad to places such as India and still I find I am always at home, wherever I connect to the land and to the Goddess. Whether I am standing atop the Glastonbury Tor, in the ancient redwoods of California, or worshipping within a thousand year old temple to the Devi-Ma (mother Goddess) in southern, India, wherever I am, Avalon is always at my fingertips, behind each breath, and deeply within my heart.

Mary Samantha Morg Anna is a Priestess of Avalon, and Creator/Instructress of the Priest/ess of Place training in San Jose, California, USA. She is a also a writer, mother and musician who teaches sacred dance and is working on releasing a book about the Goddess in California and a musical project of Priestess Rock music. You can find out about her trainings at http://www.geocities.com/samanthaofavalon/priestess.html

In the Heart of the Goddess Priestess Trainings

The *In the Heart of the Goddess* series of priestess trainings currently facilitated by Kathy Jones, Ren Chapman, Brian Charles and other priestess teachers are based in Glastonbury, beginning each year at Samhain in October or November. It is now possible to take six years of priestess training which begin with the Three Spirals of the Priestess of Avalon training. The Fourth Spiral is the Goddess Project, an opportunity to express your personal Goddess creativity and create your own Goddess Project with support and supervision. The Fifth Spiral is the advanced Priestess Enchantress training with Kathy, for those who wish to deepen their connections to landscape and mystery, travelling to enchanted landscapes in the southwest of Brigit's Isles. The Sixth Spiral is the Priestess Healer training in Esoteric Soul Healing with Kathy. For further information on these trainings see Kathy's website www.kathyjones.co.uk

Following the publication of this book it is now possible for suitable people in other lands to engage with the Priestess training in Glastonbury in a new way. You may be unable to travel to Glastonbury to take part in the requisite number of training circles, due to family commitments, cost of travel, health, etc.. Kathy and other Priestess teachers are offering to support individuals and groups of students, who wish to study together to become Priestesses of the Goddess and of Avalon while living at a distance from Glastonbury. This will be through working with this book and the Three Spiral structure of the priestess training. Student study and progress will be monitored via correspondence, email and telephone, and during twice yearly visits to Glastonbury Avalon, over three years. Each Spiral begins at Samhain. If you are interested in studying to become a Priestess in this way please contact Kathy via her website.

Index

Ariadne Publications

Books by Kathy Jones:

The Ancient British Goddess : Goddess Myths, Legends, Sacred Sites and Present Revelation

An inspiring journey into the bounteous and abundant nature of our native British Goddesses, revealing Her as Maiden, Lover, Mother and Crone, as Mother of Earth, Water, Fire and Air in landscapes and legends. Also exploring Her present day revelation in the lives of Goddess-loving artists, writer and performers. Lavishly illustrated with original photographs and artwork.

256pp pbk illust. 2001 £12.95

Chiron in Labrys: An Introduction to Esoteric Soul Healing

A book about transformation and the healing of disease in the patient and the wounded healer within the context of the natural cycles and energies of our Mother Earth. A reworking of Alice Bailey's classic teachings on Esoteric Healing based on Kathy's 25 years healing experience.

212pp pbk illust. 2001 £11.95

In the Nature of Avalon : Goddess Pilgrimages in Glastonbury's Sacred Landscape

Beautifully illustrated Goddess pilgrimages in Glastonbury's sacred landscape providing an excellent guide for those who wish to journey through the Veil into the magical Otherworld of the Isle of Avalon. With detailed route directions, maps, Goddess historical and mythic information, and suggestions for prayers , rituals and visualisations all designed to bring you into closer contact with the Goddess.

224pp pbk illust. 2000 £9.99

Breast Cancer: Hanging on by a Red Thread

A strong story based on diary extracts of Kathy's journey through the experience of having breast cancer, looking at the physical, emotional and spiritual aspects of this dangerous disease. With ideas on how to help yourself.

124pp pbk illust. 1998 £8.95

On Finding Treasure: Mystery Plays of the Goddess

An exciting autobiographical account of the transformative work of Ariadne Productions which regularly presents original sacred dramas in Glastonbury.

Includes five performed playscripts.

264pp pbk illust. 1996 £9.99

Spinning the Wheel of Ana

A spiritual journey to reconnect with the Primal Ancestors of the British Isles, examining the earliest myths and legends and bringing their meaning into the present to create the Ancestral Medicine Wheel of Ana the Great One, ancient Goddess of the British Isles.

262pp pbk illust. 1994 £11.95

Order from Ariadne Publications, 61 Tor View Avenue, Glastonbury,
BA6 8AG, *Somerset, UK. Postage varies.*
See website http://www.kathyjones.co.uk